ROUTLEDGE LIBRARY EDITIONS:
ACCOUNTING

Volume 11

BRITISH COST ACCOUNTING 1887–1952

BRITISH COST ACCOUNTING 1887–1952

Contemporary Essays from the Accounting Literature

Edited by
TREVOR BOYNS,
MALCOLM ANDERSON, AND
JOHN RICHARD EDWARDS

Routledge
Taylor & Francis Group
LONDON AND NEW YORK

First published in 1996

This edition first published in 2014
by Routledge
2 Park Square, Milton Park, Abingdon, Oxfordshire OX14 4RN

and by Routledge
711 Third Avenue, New York, NY 10017

Routledge is an imprint of the Taylor and Francis Group, an informa business

First issued in paperback 2015

British Library Cataloguing in Publication Data
A catalogue record for this book is available from the British Library

ISBN 978-0-415-53081-1 (Set)
eISBN 978-1-315-88628-2 (Set)
ISBN 978-0-415-85645-4 (hbk) (Volume 11)
ISBN 978-1-138-98794-4 (pbk) (Volume 11)
ISBN 978-1-315-88647-3 (ebk) (Volume 11)

Publisher's Note
The publisher has gone to great lengths to ensure the quality of this reprint but points out that some imperfections in the original copies may be apparent.

British Cost Accounting 1887–1952

Contemporary Essays from the Accounting Literature

Edited by
Trevor Boyns,
Malcolm Anderson,
and
John Richard Edwards

Garland Publishing, Inc.
New York and London 1996

Library of Congress Cataloging-in-Publication Data

British cost accounting 1887–1952: contemporary essays from the accounting literature/ edited by Trevor Boyns, Malcolm Anderson, and John Richard Edwards.
p. cm. — (New works in accounting history)
includes bibliographical references.
ISBN 0–8153–2240–2 (alk. paper)
1. Cost accounting—Great Britain—History. 2. Managerial accounting—Great Britain—History. I. Boyns, Trevor. II. Anderson, Malcolm. III. Edwards, J. R. IV. Series.
HF5686.C8B6765 95–37266
657'.42'0941—dc20

All volumes printed on acid-free, 250-year-life paper.
Manufactured in the United States of America.

Design by Marisel Tavarez

Contents

INTRODUCTION

Solomons' seminal article entitled "The Historical Development of Costing" (1952) is divided into two parts which, respectively, focus on developments prior to "The Costing Renaissance"—considered to start around 1870—and

> The second part of the story, which spans the three-quarters of a century down to our own day, [1952 which] is concerned, not with a rather narrow technical problem in book-keeping [seen as the focus of developments over the preceding 500 years], but with the broader issue of making the accounting records mean something, of making them flexible and capable of providing information which would be significant not for one purpose (say, the measurement of profit or loss) or two (say, in addition, the fixing of selling prices) but for any of the purposes which, in modern business, figures may be called upon to serve (1952: 2).

In the second part of his paper Solomons focuses on the accounting treatment of overhead cost in the endeavour to identify "actual" cost (1952: 20), before moving on to examine early recognition of the variation of costs with output, the developing literature on standard costing and budgetary control and the growing interest in uniform costing stimulated by the actions of trade associations beginning with the National Association of Stove Manufacturers in America in the 1880s.

Much of the material used for the purpose of Solomons' masterly exposition is drawn from the overseas literature, particularly from the United States, and there are relatively few citations dated later than the second decade of the twentieth century. It is of course well known that Solomons drew heavily on Ronald Edwards' earlier work (1937a and 1937b) when tracing developments in Britain and France before 1870 and in Britain thereafter. The lack of citations in Solomons (1952) post-1920 is consistent with Edwards' conclusion that "I do not think that in the last 30 years cost accountants have added much to the theory of their subject" (1937a: 344). However, it may also reflect too great a reliance on Edwards' work and/or a failure to investigate the full range of relevant literature, especially that contained in contemporary accounting journals.

The purpose of this anthology therefore is to provide readers with a flavor of the development of cost accounting and emerging management accounting literature from "The Costing Renaissance" down to the date of Solomons' paper. We agree with Solomons and Edwards that many of the issues which were prominent in the middle of the twentieth century and, indeed, are still pressing issues today, received important early treatments. A more balanced longitudinal coverage of the relevant material however enables readers to trace the development of new attitudes to problems which had been recognized early on, and to become aware of the fact that different issues tended to dominate the literature as time went by.

Sources

In his work, Solomons gave particular attention to the content of engineering journals such as *Engineering, The Engineer*, and *The Engineering Magazine*, especially the last named. These are important sources of illumination concerning early costing developments which would undoubtedly repay further study. Indeed, other contemporary journals, such as and *The Mechanical Engineer, The Railway Times, The Journal of Gas Lighting, Water Supply and Sanitary Improvement* and *The Electrician*, contain a great deal of material which is worthy of examination by those interested in the development of costing techniques and management information systems.

A distinct feature of this anthology, however, is that it focuses on material published in accounting journals. The relevant sources examined in the process of compiling this text include *The Accountant*, first published in 1874, *The Cost Accountant* (1921), now called *Management Accounting*, the *Incorporated Accountants Journal* (1889), today called *Accountancy*, and *The Accountant's Magazine* (1897). We have chosen to focus principally on the contents of the first two named publications partly because of limitations of space.[1] We also chose to focus on *The Accountant* and *The Cost Accountant* because their contents enable a contrast to be made between attitudes from what might be regarded as the two sides of the profession. *The Accountant* claimed to represent the interests of chartered accountants whereas *The Cost Accountant* was established by The Institute of Cost and Works Accountants (today called The Chartered Institute of Management Accountants), whose formation has been attributed, in part at least, to the failure of the elite Institute of Chartered Accountants in England and Wales to cater for accountants working in industry.

The publication of Garcke and Fells' *Factory Accounts* (1887) is often referred to as heralding the emergence of a costing literature in Britain, followed two years later by the publication of George Pepler Norton's *Textile Manufacturers' Book-keeping*[2] Garcke was of course an electrical engineer while Fells was, at the time of writing, the assistant secretary of the Anglo-American Brush Electric Light Corporation. He became a member of the Society of Incorporated Accountants and Auditors in 1902 and, in due course, a fellow of the Institute of Cost and Works Accountants. Norton, on the other hand, was a chartered accountant with the firm of Armitage, Clough and Norton, having previously been a "prize man" in the final examination of the ICAEW, June 1883. Another chartered accountant, Arthur H. Gibson had already written (1887) the first article published in *The Accountant* to give significant attention to costing matters (reproduced as item no. 1 in this anthology). Other writers, reproduced here, possessing the chartered qualification include Warwick (item no. 2), Mann (4), Plumpton (5, 6, 9), Cudworth (11), Caldicott (12), Addinsell (13), Goode (14), Urie (17), Hamilton (20), Jenkinson (21, 29), Allen (28), Cathles (31), Gill (37, 39), Lunt (44), Annan (49), Smallpeice (66), Glendinning (71), Risk (72), Morrow (73).

One might imagine that the interest of chartered accountants in costing matters reflected a focus on this area of activity by the firm for which they worked. Certainly this was the case with Norton who tells us that his knowledge of textile operations was derived from general practice and from the investigation of corporate failure (1889, Preface). In other cases it is probably a consequence of the fact that the chartered accountant had already moved over to industry and had become directly involved in costing matters on a day to day basis. Basil Smallpeice, for example, moved from Bullimore & Co. immediately on qualification, in 1930, to become accountant and assistant secretary at Hoover Ltd. He joined Doulton & Co. Ltd in 1937 where he became secretary and chief accountant responsible for costing and accountancy at the factories (*The Accountant*, 7 January 1950: 10–11).[3]

There are of course numerous contributions from cost and works accountants including articles by Fells (25, 30), Todman (34), Jenkins (38, 43), Blyth (41), Walker (50), Staniforth (52), Dunkerley (53, 65), Saunders (59), Reece (60), Roddick (64), Brown (68), Marshall (77), Kirkham (78). The chartered accountants Gill, Lunt, Annan, Allen, Glendinning, Risk and Morrow also held the cost accounting qualification. Some of the accountants in industry were in prominent management positions, e. g. Roland Dunkerley was Director and General Manager, Quilt Manufacturers Ltd.

Certified accountants represented amongst the list are Showell (16), Edwards (56), Roddick (also a cost and works accountant) and the thrice qualified Fells. There are also three chartered secretaries—Allen (28), Lunt and Roddick (triple qualification)—and three engineers Elbourne (35), Jenkins (also a cost and works accountant) and Rose (46). The series of papers by David Cowan (15) was reprinted by *The Accountant* with permission from the *Transactions of the Institution of Engineers and Shipbuilders in Scotland*. Cowan's qualification is unknown but, as he also wrote extensively in *The Mechanical Engineer*, it is likely that he was a practising engineer. The academe is represented by W. Annan who was Professor of Accounting and Business Methods at Edinburgh University, Ronald Edwards, then Assistant Lecturer in Accounting and Business Administration at the London School of Economics, and E. D. McCallum (47) who was Lecturer in Economics at Armstrong College, University of Durham.

The papers were in the main initially presented as lectures (Edwards' series of papers is a notable exception). In the early years these lectures were generally presented to chartered accountants student societies in London and the provinces; later on principally to district branches of the Institute of Cost and Works Accountants and the annual costing conferences held by the ICWA commencing 1922. There are also published a significant number of leading articles and editorials, a letter (9), two book review articles (3, 57) and individual publications by the Federal Trade Commission of Washington USA (23, "Fundamentals of a cost system for manufacturers"), and by the Council of the ICWA (55, "Costing Terminology").

Issues

A summary of the main topics covered in the papers reproduced is given in Table 1. This can be read in conjunction with the list of contents to provide a fuller idea of the way in which the literature developed as time went by.

3. He was appointed director of costs and statistics at the British Transport Commission in 1948 and became financial comptroller of the British Overseas Airways Corporation in 1950. He was the elected to the council of the ICAEW in 1948—the third non-practising member to be elected to this position.

References

Battersby, Thomas. *The perfect double entry book-keeper (abridged) and the perfect prime cost and profit demonstrator (on the departmental system), for iron and brass founders, machinists, engineers, ship-builders manufacturers &c.*, Manchester & London: John Heywood, 1878.

Edwards, R. S. "Some notes on the early literature and development of cost accounting in Britain," *The Accountant* (1937a), 7 August: 193–95; 14 August: 225–31; 21 August: 253–55; 28 August: 283–87; 4 September: 313–16, 11 September: 343–44.

Edwards, R. S. *A Survey of French Contributions to the Study of Cost Accounting during the 19th Century*, London: Gee & Co., 1937b.

Garcke, E., and Fells, J. M. *Factory Accounts*, London: Crosby Lockwood, 1887.

Norton, G. P. *Textile Manufacturers' Book-keeping for the Counting House, Mill and Warehouse . . . .*, Huddersfield: Alfred Jubb, 1889.

Solomons, D. "The historical development of costing," in D. Solomons (ed.), *Studies in Costing*. London: Sweet & Maxwell, 1952, pp. 1–52.

Acknowledgments

We are grateful to the Economic and Social Research Council for financial support for the research which has enabled the preparation of this text. The editors also wish to thank the Chartered Institute of Management Accountants and Lafferty Publications for their kind permission to reprint articles previously published in *The Cost Accountant* and in *The Accountant*.

BIRMINGHAM ACCOUNTANTS' STUDENTS' SOCIETY.

"TRADING AND PROFIT AND LOSS ACCOUNTS."

BY MR. ARTHUR H. GIBSON, F.C.A.

At the Sixth Ordinary Meeting of the Sessions held at the Colonnade Hotel, New Street.

Present:—Mr. G. C. T. Parson, F.C.A., Chairman; Mr. Howard S. Smith, F.C.A., Mr. A. H. Gibson, F.C.A., Mr. J. Findlay, A.C.A., Mr. H. J. Cross; Mr. T. S. M. Mullard, A.C.A., H. Walker, (Hon. Secty.), and 23 others.

A letter of apology for non-attendance was received from Mr. Walter N. Fisher.

Mr. Parson, in a few words, introduced the Lecturer, Mr. Gibson to the Meeting:—

Mr. Gibson delivered the following address:

The subject of my lecture this evening is not one which at any point passes over into the territory of legal training, the boundaries of which are so jealously guarded by young solicitors. I sometimes think that the model accountant, according to the ideas of some young lawyers, would be an animated Arithmometer, similar to that ingenous piece of mechanism which Mr. Howard Smith has in his private office—a being which, when placed before a column of figures, should instinctively begin to add, and there its powers should end. If it wanted to write a letter, however simple, or give a receipt for a sum of money however small, it should then, also instinctively, run at once to its legal adviser, and ask him to draft the epistle, frame the receipt, and state the value of the stamp to be affixed. Such ideas prevail, but only among very young practitioners. With solicitors of experience difficulties on this head never arise, and, in matters in which the two professions are engaged, solicitors are as glad to have the points explained by accountants who can grasp the legal questions involved, as accountants are to explain them to solicitors who have a knowledge of accounts. The fact is, every profession is entitled to and necessarily must know the law relating to its particular calling. Of what use would an architect be who was ignorant of all details of the law of party walls, lateral support, and ancient lights? Must not a mining engineer know every detail of mining law, a doctor of medical law? and so an accountant, who is required to have technical skill in all commercial matters, must have a sound knowledge of all branches of commercial law. The knowledge of the law, and the practice of the law as a profession, are however, two distinct things; and so long as we keep away, as we are bound to do, from the latter, our friends the solicitors will not complain, as they have no right to complain, about the former.

However, the subject of my lecture this evening is one which is peculiarly our own. The legal mind which has only faint glimmerings of the meaning of a balance sheet, has none of the effect and purpose of a Trading Account. This lack of knowledge extends through the whole legal body from bottom to summit. Our Courts of Law, for example, know nothing of the difference between an Income and Expenditure, or Profit and Loss Account, and a Cash Account, and when they wish to impound from a Receiver the net revenue of a going concern, they seize on the balance of the Cash Account, which of course may be more than, or less than, the net revenue, just as the Receiver likes to advance or retard his payments.

My purpose this evening is not to take you through the simple construction of a Trading or Profit and Loss Account, which would only waste your time and mine, for that forms indeed the rudiments of an accountant's training. The particular view I wish to impress upon you is, that our profession is a progressive one; that excellence in it is not attained by mere theoretical knowledge of figures, however perfect, but that the oldest accountant, as well as the youngest, has the daily opportunity of adding to his store of technical skill, and thereby not only increases his own utility, but also pushes onwards the whole profession. And I am going to illustrate this by the development, which within my own experience as an accountant going back for something over twenty years, has become apparent in relation to Trading and Profit and Loss Accounts. I do not want, for my present purpose, to enforce the distinctions which we often make between a Trading Account and a Profit and Loss Account, but I want you to look upon the two indiscriminately and collectively as the summary of the transactions of a trading concern for any period. A balance sheet shows what are the results of such transactions, a Trading or Profit and Loss Account shows, or should show, how those results have come about.

But a Trading or Profit and Loss Account, also answers another purpose of special moment to accountants. It proves the correctness, not of the balance sheet but of the mere book-keeping. A preliminary point I would insist upon, because it touches an error which in my experience young accountants are prone to, is that the Trading Account does not prove the correctness of the balance sheet. When after wading one's way through a mass of figures, sorting and arranging them in proper nominal or personal accounts, at the end, one gets a figure balance, the whole looks so symmetrical and pretty that one feels one's labours are happily concluded, and that the whole thing is right. But that is not necessarily so. Double entry book-keeping is a very useful mill which will grind out anything, but it all depends on what you put in what you will get out of it. Accounts will balance although you have put on the debit side in your ledgers assets which are not assets, and though you have left out on the credit side many things which should come in. My word of warning is then: Don't be mislead by a figure agreement between the Trading Account and balance-sheet, but, after you have got such agreement, investigate fiercely both sides of the balance-sheet to be assured that it agrees, not with the Trading Account, but with the actual facts. Your balance-sheet is the principal account: the Trading Account is purely subsidiary. The truth of the balance-sheet must be ascertained independently and the Trading Account must be made to accord with it.

Our Trading Accounts then serve two purposes, they prove the correctness of the book-keeping, and they summarise the transactions of trading concerns. Now, twenty years ago I saw many instances, and I not unfrequently see some now, of sets of accounts where the man who opened them knew nothing of the details of the business, and the man (proprietor or manager) conversant with the details of the business knew nothing about the possibilities of a Trade Account. The consequence was that the books were opened to construct a Trading Account, which proved the correctness of the book-keeping it is true, but which had no practical use whatever as a summary of the trading transactions. This point will be clearer for an illustration. Let me refer you to account No. 1.

Dr. ACCOUNT	£	s.	d.	No. 1. *Cr.*	£	s.	d.
1881.				1882.			
Dec. 31—To Stock	2570	10	0	Dec. 31—By Contracts completed and Sundry Sales	116446	11	3
„ Contracts in progress	15690	0	0	„ Stock	3760	9	4
1882.				„ Contracts in progress	16420	8	7
Dec. 31—To Purchases	65210	8	6				
„ Wages	42700	18	9				
„ Carriage	1169	2	7				
„ Engine and Machinery Expenses.	1160	8	1				
„ Rents, Taxes, and Insurance ..	1210	5	4				
„ Salaries	700	18	6				
„ Interest and Bank Charges ..	300	16	10				
„ Depreciation	676	4	8				
„ Incidental Expenses	460	2	8				
„ Balance, being profit	4777	13	3				
	£136627	9	2		£136627	9	2

This is the trading account of a builder, and is in the precise form of actual accounts which have come before us.

Now, this account except that it is a link in the chain which establishes the correctness of the book-keeping is utterly useless. It shows that during the year the builder, who has completed contracts to the amount of £116,446, and has incompleted contracts in progress, the work on which he values at £16,420; has in the same period bought goods to the value of £65,210; has paid wages to the amount of £42,700; has paid for carriage £1,169, and so on. But this information serves no practical purpose. It does not enlighten the trader whether such purchases or wages are too much, or too little. If you work out the percentages and say that his purchases come to so much and his wages to so much per cent on the work done, the statistics are still useless, for there is no standard of relation between expenditure under those heads and the work done. One contract may be of a kind requiring a large amount of wages and a small amount of materials, and in another one the proportions may be reversed. A trade account in such a form with its awful and purposeless array of figures was akin to "a tale told by an idiot full of sound and fury specifying nothing." The trader regarded it with that mingled awe and admiration which is always inspired by the incomprehensible, but if a brother trader asked him what use it was, he was likely to be non-plussed.

Now, all the while the very information which a Trading Account ought to have afforded to the trader was absolutely necessary for him, but was prepared not by, but independently of, the accountant. For the purpose of obtaining architects' certificates, and for the purpose of making out his accounts for extras, the builder was obliged to follow both the purchases and wages to their destination, and divide them over the particular contracts to which they belonged. In large building and contracting concerns a separate department—the prime cost department—was created, with which the accountant had no concern. The prime costing formed no part of the system of accounts, and was a sort of *terra incognita* to the young accountant of the past.

In a building concern where I was called upon to continue the plan which, in this particular had been adopted for many years—and *en passant* let me say that traders and their principal clerks in matters of accounts are the most stupidly conservative section of the community—I remember submitting the proved results, according to my Balance Sheet and incomprehensible Trade Account, to the partners who said to me that the results could not be right, that their prime cost accounts showed that they had made so much on this contract and so much on that, and where had the money gone to? I told them I could not make my Balance Sheet agree with their prime cost accounts, but, if they would give me time and pay my fees, I would make their prime cost accounts agree with my Balance Sheet. The difference involved amounted to several thousands, and I was instructed accordingly. My friend Mr. Whitehall, who took up the work for me, soon demonstrated the worthlessness of prime cost accounts constructed independently of the trading account, and from that time onwards the prime costing has been part of the system of accounts, and on its results the Trading Account is built.

Similarly in manufacturing and mining concerns prudent managers have found it necessary to work out elaborate stock and stores accounts and analysis of wages resulting in Cost Sheets. Such accounts are almost conditions of successful management in times of general depression, such as we have recently seen. A little time of idleness and a small amount of material wasted by each workman each day, multiply the cost of such time and material by the number of workmen in a concern, and by the number of working days in the year, and you will probably arrive at a figure of waste equal to a handsome profit on the capital of a concern. Economical consumption, through the somewhat childish characteristics of our working classes, can only be assured by such statistical and analytical methods. The manager's eye cannot always be on everybody, and what is necessary is a system which shows by results that the men are working as well and as economically when his eye is not on them, as when he is overlooking them. Such accounts in the past were constructed generally quite independently of the professional accountant. In this class of concerns also, instances have come before me where the works manager has disbelieved in the Balance Sheet, because his cost sheets showed different results. Such cost accounts are the proper work of an accountant, and to be really reliable should be made the basis of the Trading Accounts.

I will now illustrate shortly the methods I have been discussing by reference to the accounts given herewith. Let me first mention three common types of businesses, which come frequently before us, and which, in relation to their respective Trading Accounts, require distinct treatment. I will call these Constructive trades, Convertive trades, and Distributive trades.

Constructive trades are those which are concerned with what are called large constructions, *i.e.* large works not of identical character. Types of these are builders, road and railway contractors, heavy engineers, and ship-builders.

Convertive trades are those which are concerned with the continuous conversion of certain materials into products identical with each other, but essentially different from the original materials. Such as millering, producing flour from wheat; ironworks producing, pig, bar and sheet iron from ore and coal; woollen and cotton mills producing textile fabrics from raw wool, and cotton.

Distributive trades are those which are concerned with the sale of goods in the same, or nearly the same, condition as they are purchased. This includes the business of the large class of middlemen, merchants, factors, shop-keepers, &c.

The foregoing do not of course include all, or even the larger portion, of trading concerns, but only attempts a classification of some very common industries. Neither is it intended to imply that all of such trades can be distinctly marshalled under one or other of the above classes.

Many trades will partake of the characteristics of two of such classes or perhaps of all three. The classification is only intended to mark distinct types, to which particular trades may more or less approximate.

I will take as an illustration of the constructive trades the builder to whom I have already referred, and the results of whose trading are supposed to be summarised in the Trade Account No. 1 already mentioned. It is of course obvious at a glance how the accounts would be constructed to bring out those results. The Purchase Journal or Guard Book would be arranged in columns, one of which would be headed "Materials" and the others to correspond with the other several heads of expenditure. Wages and expenses, which did not pass through the Purchase Journal, would be posted direct from the Cash Book to the various nominal accounts. In this class of trades—which I have called the Constructive—the welding of the chain between the accountant work and the practical work is very easy.

Instead of jumbling up all materials in a "Materials" account it is just as easy to have a column in the Purchase Journal headed "Prime Cost Ledger," and then to post the items therefrom, as a subsidiary posting to the prime cost ledger.

Similarly the wages, instead of being all muddled together to show no result, may be just as easily distributed at once to the particular contracts to which they relate. In account No. 2. I give you the Trading Account which results from the new method.

Dr. ACCOUNT No. 2. *Cr.*

1882.	£	s.	d.	£	s.	d.
Dec. 31—To General Charges, viz.:—						
Wages not chargeable to contracts	614	5	3			
Engine and Machinery Expenses ditto	235	8	6			
Rent, Taxes, and Insurance ditto	616	1	5			
Salaries and Office Expenses ditto..	546	18	6			
Incidental Expenses ditto	348	18	11			
Interest & Bank Charges	300	16	10			
Depreciation	676	4	8			
				3338	14	1
To Balance, being net profit				4777	13	3
				£8116	7	4

1882.	£	s.	d.	£	s.	d.	£	s.	d.
Dec. 31—By Profits on Contracts, &c., viz.:—									
Windsor Hotel				650	1	6			
Criterion Theatre				1012	17	1			
Southwark Station ..				879	14	10			
Whitby Docks..				3553	1	9			
Leeds Arcade				1580	2	1			
Paddington Stables ..				741	2	8			
Sundry Jobbing Work ..				685	2	3			
				9102	2	2			
Less Losses, viz.:—									
Pontefract Barracks	621	8	9						
Beechwood Hall	340	7	3						
Eastbourne Public Offices	23	18	10						
				985	14	10			
							8116	7	4
							£8116	7	4

Now, this is something which is both intelligible and useful to the practical manager of the business. It follows the operations of his mind in the control of his trade, it shows definitely how far his estimates have been proved by results; it ensures that everything for which he has paid has found an acknowledged resting place; it follows out what has become of the gross profits which he has made; and particularly it directs his attention to the figures of wages and expenses which are not allotable to any contract, which are unproductive and must be allowed for as a percentage in making his estimates.

Let us follow this first example a little into details, and see what has been done. The purchases, amounting to £65,210 in Account No. 1, have, unless they belong to one or other of the items of General Charges in Account No. 2, been charged item by item against the several contracts appearing on the credit side of Account No. 2. No invoice has therefore been passed for payment unless the responsible foreman of the contract it referred to has acknowledged that it is a charge against the cost of the contract being executed under his supervision. On the other hand, no prime cost account is rendered incorrect because of the omission to charge to it goods used up in the execution of the contract, for every item of goods for which the trader is called upon to pay must be traced out to its ultimate consumption. The wages in Account No. 1, £42,700, are, in Account No. 2, similarly sorted away to the respective contracts, except £614, which consist of wages in the nature of general charges and allottable to specific contracts. The separation of the latter item from the productive wages is a matter of first importance to the successful management of a business of the kind we are dealing with, and such separation is never accurately done when the prime costs are not made the bases of the Trade Account. The next item in Account No. 1 is "Carriage, £1,169;" in Account No. 2, this item has disappeared; its constituents have been spread over the several contracts, in respect of which the expense was incurred. I think there is no item in the old-fashioned Trade Accounts which was treated with more stupid inconsistency than carriage. The carriage on goods bought is a part of the cost of such goods; the carriage on goods sold is a deduction from the selling price of such goods. In purchasing goods, such as timber for example, there are always two prices quoted or quotable—one the price at the shipping-port or wherever the timber may be lying, the other the price delivered at the purchaser's yard. It is a matter of arbitrary arrangement on which of these principles a builder buys; if on the former, he has to pay the carriage himself, and the amount of it increases *pro tanto* the cost of the timber. Now, in the old useless form of trade account, such as Account No. 1, it would happen that, if the trader bought a lot of timber delivered at his yard, the whole cost of it would be rightly analysed as purchases. If the following week he bought a precisely similar lot of timber at the same cost delivered, but arranged to pay the carriage himself and deduct it from the cost, the reduced price only would be entered as purchases, and the carriage would be analysed as carriage. The account of carriage once opened would also be the receptacle for carriage on goods delivered by the trader, and would result in a figure which was a meaningless jumble, having no logical relation to the other figures in the Trade Account. The carriage on goods purchased should always be analysed as part of the cost of such purchases. The carriage on goods sold, when an enhanced price is obtained in respect of delivery, should always be deducted from the selling price of the goods; when there is only one common price for the goods whenever delivered, the cost of carriage on the sales may in such case be rightly regarded as a general expense, and I have so treated it in a subsequent account I shall presently refer to. When my friend, Mr. Whitehill, was engaged in harmonising the Prime Cost Accounts and Balance Sheet to which I have referred, a principal source of error in the former was the omission to charge the contracts with carriage on the goods bought; the invoices of the goods had been handed over to the prime cost clerk, and entered by him, but with the monthly accounts delivered by the railway companies, in which purchases and deliveries were mixed up, he had not concerned himself. I do not think I need follow the remaining items in Account No. 1, as they only further illustrate what I have already said. By comparing it with Account No. 2, you will find that many amounts of salaries, rents, etc., in the first account have in the second account found resting places by being charged to the several contracts. The general charges left on Account No. 2 are legitimate general charges only, and afford reliable data on which the trader can base his calculations, when sending in his estimates. There are numerous incidental advantages in amalgamating the prime cost in such cases with the system of book-keeping. Time will not allow me to enlarge upon them, but your experience will make them sufficiently obvious to you.

The second class of trades to which I shall refer is what I have called convertive trades. In this class the systematising of the practical production accounts, so as to work in with the book-keeping, is a tax of much more complexity and difficulty than in the constructive trades; but it is in this class of trades that the labours of an accountant are most likely to lead to substantial results in economising the cost of production. In the principle of taking costs there is an essential difference between these and the constructive trades.

In the latter the cost of the particular thing constructed is followed through *ab initio*, so as to say in the end what that particular house, or road, or ship has cost. In the convertive trades, where large numbers of identical things are produced, this is impracticable. In a cloth works or a tinplate we do not earmark all the processes on a particular piece of cloth or particular box of plates and say this piece of cloth or this box of plates has cost so much.

But we say, the production of a box of plates involves twelve distinct processes; in this or that week the cost of each of those processes per box was so much, and the cost of producing a box of plates is the aggregate of the cost of those several processes.

Thus, it may be that a particular box of plates went through part of the processes one week and part another. But that is immaterial. It is the cost of the several processes which is required, not the cost of a particular box produced.

To illustrate what is possible in this class of trading concerns I am going to take an example of some complexity—the manufacture of woollen fabrics. In the case supposed please imagine that there are two staple articles produced in considerable quantities—tweed and serge—and also a number of other fabrics in smaller quantities. First let me give you a Trade Account of this business in the old form. This is Account No 3, and it is unnecessary for me to add anything to what I have already stated as to its useless character.

ACCOUNT No. 3.

Dr.		£	s.	d.	*Cr.*		£	s.	d.
1881.					1882.				
Dec. 31—	To Stock	36540	18	2	Dec. 31—	By Sales	52651	19	11
1882.						,, Abatements on Purchases	145	8	7
Dec. 31—	To Purchases	28710	1	4		,, Stock	34430	16	2
	,, Wages paid for manufacture	9175	2	4					
	,, Abatements on Sales	4966	1	1					
	,, Carriage	618	2	10					
	,, Salaries	1981	9	5					
	,, Travelling Expenses	690	5	1					
	,, Rent, Rates, Taxes, &c.	1620	4	1					
	,, Interest and Bank Charges	421	8	6					
	,, Depreciation	624	8	5					
	,, Bad Debts	416	1	8					
	,, Balance, being profit	1464	1	9					
		£87228	4	8			£87228	4	8

Now, let us shortly trace the cost of producing a piece of tweed cloth from the raw material. The complications begin with the purchase of the wool, which may be in one of three states—greasy, which is just as it is cut off the sheep's back; fleece, which has been scoured on the sheep's back before shearing; and scoured, which has been more completely scoured after shearing. It follows that the yield of yarn from fleece is greater than from greasy wools, and the yield from scoured wools is greater than from fleece.

Great judgment is, therefore, wanted in the purchase of the wools; the buyer, from inspecting the sample, has to judge the percentage of yield, and the variation is so great that one lot of wool at 9d. per pound will prove to be a very much dearer purchase than another lot at 1s. 6d. per pound.

Judgment in the purchase of the wools is, perhaps, the most important element of success in this trade. From an employer's point of view, it thus becomes of vital importance to know whether his buyer's judgment is reliable—*i.e.*, whether the actual production of yarn from the wool corresponds with the buyer's anticipations. It is, therefore, essential to the proper management of a concern that the actual yield of every lot of wool should be worked out. But, to continue, the bales of wool are first broken up, as it is called, which is separating what is suitable for warp from what is suited for shoot, and the separated wool is then scoured.

It is in this process that the great loss of weight occurs.

The next step is dying such portions as are intended for coloured yarns. Now dye wares are very expensive materials, and a careless or wasteful dyer may easily injure the Profit and Loss Account to the extent of hundreds of pounds per annum. It is, therefore, of great importance that his results, in weight dyed and consumption of dye wares, should be known from week to week. Next follow a lot of processes such as willoughing, picking, oiling etc., which lead up to spinning. Now, in spinning, although it is done mainly by machinery, there is, as in everything else, all the difference between good and bad workmen. One man will bring out a full yield in yarn and very little waste: another, with the same materials, will furnish a short yield in yarn and a disproportionate quantity of waste. To insure the best results, a record must be kept of the weight of wool issued to each man, and of the results of his work in yarn and waste.

Each man's results are thus in continual comparison with the results of other men, and with his own previous record, and good and bad workmen alike build up their own characters. The subsequent processes are—doubling the warp, warping, weaving, scouring the cloth, drying, burling, milling, and a number of other processes involved in finishing, and in one and all of these what I have said respecting dyeing and spinning applies with equal force.

In each one, if waste of material or careless work is to be prevented, production and consumption accounts from week to week must be kept. Now, I will not trouble you by sketching the character of books required to get the results; that is very simple work for an accountant If he only takes the trouble to properly investigate each process, the right form of book at once occurs to him. I will, therefore, carry you forward to the focussing of all these results in a weekly cost sheet, which you will find in Account No. 4.

ACCOUNT No. 4

WEEKLY YARN COST SHEET.

		£ s. d.	lbs.	Tweed. Weight	Tweed. Per lb. s. d.	Tweed. Amount. £ s. d.	Serge Shoot. Weight	Serge Shoot. Per lb. s. d.	Serge Shoot. Amount. £ s. d.
Yarn Produced				2200	1 6·50	169 11 8	3146	7 14	93 11 10
Per centage for loss				6	1·11	10 3 6	12	·86	11 5 5
Breaking up and Scouring—	Wages ..	3 13 8	2,100		·55	5 0 10		,,	,, ,, ,,
	Materials	1 3 0							
Deying	Wages	5 10 0	3,550		1·63	14 15 2		,,	,, ,, ,,
	Materials	18 6 5							
Spinning	Wages ..	42 1 9	6,446 ..		2·60	23 16 8		2.60	31 1 8
	Materials	27 14 8							
Doubling	Wages ..	5 8 10	2,647 = ·55		·26	2 7 8		,,	,, ,, ,,
	Materials	0 12 6							
					2 0·65	225 15 6		10 60	138 18 11

WEEKLY COST SHEET OF FINISHED PRODUCE.

	Tweed. Production. 8½ oz.	Tweed. Amount £ s. d.	Tweed. Cost p. yd. 8½ oz. s. d.	Serge Production 16 oz.	Serge Amount £ s. d.	Serge Cost p. yd. 16 oz. s. d.	Sundries. Production	Sundries. Amount £ s. d.
Yarn consumed in pieces woven	2,100	138 6 9	1 3·81	2,000	135 0 0	1 4·20		77 5 7
Warping	1,710	2 4 2	·31		,, ,, ,,	,,	422	0 11 0
Weaving	1,710	13 17 10	1·95	1,810	16 13 4	2·21	680	5 10 6
Scouring, Drying and Milling	2,615	6 10 9	·60	1,810	9 1 0	1·20	1,016	2 10 9
Burling	1,710	4 14 1	·66	1,810	1 5 8	·17	708	1 19 0
Finishing	1,710	6 19 8	·98	1,810	11 15 4	1·56	1,114	4 11 0
Engine & Machinery Expenses	2,100	8 6 3	·95	2,000	13 3 4	1·58	780	3 1 9
Pattern Weaving	2,100	2 12 6	·30		,, ,, ,,	,,	550	0 13 9
Dyeing Pieces	—	,, ,, ,,	,,	2,000	38 5 0	4·59	690	13 4 0
General Charges	2,100	32 16 3	3·75	2,000	31 5 0	3·75	1,207	20 9 4
		216 8 3	2 1·31		256 8 8	2 7·26		129 16 8

That account I think sufficiently explains itself, but, at the risk of repeating what is obvious, I will say a few words about it. Firstly, let me ask you to notice that the proportion of the weekly wages and materials other than those belonging to the two staples, tweed and serge, are all thrown together in the sundries column. These are a number of small dissimilar products, the working out of the separate cost of which would involve too great labour.

Looking now at the weekly yarn cost, we find the necessity is obvious of taking the cost of each process separately, because the several processes do not advance *pari passu*, while 2,200 lbs. of tweed yarn have been produced, the dyeing has represented a production of 3,550 lbs., and the doubling (as only about half the weight of yarn has to be doubled) is equivalent to a much larger production. In the following week these proportions might be reversed, though let me say that, in well-managed concerns, we generally find the production in each process does advance nearly *pari passu*, and one great advantage of proper cost sheets is that they enable the manager to see that the different departments are working up to each other. The second item of the Yarn Cost Sheet, "Percentage for Loss," is the ascertained loss of weight for that week in all the several processes involved in turning raw wool into yarn. Thus 2,200 lbs. of tweed yarn produced represents a consumption of raw wool 6 per cent. more than that weight, and the price of raw wool is therefore increased by the same per centage. The whole of the processes pertaining to tweed yarn do not apply in our supposed case to serge shoot. We will suppose the serge warps are bought as spun yarn, and that breaking up and doubling are not therefore required; we will also suppose that the serge goods, instead of being dyed as yarns are died after the pieces are woven; for that reason no cost is put against those items in the serge column. Turning now to the cost sheet of finished products, you will here meet with one of the principal difficulties in preparing reliable cost sheets—the reduction of all the production to common denominators. The production of tweed, for example, will include cloths of varying substance from 6¼ ozs. per yard up to 20 ozs.; choice has then to be made of a standard, which should be the cloth of which the production is greatest. In the supposed case we have assumed this to be cloth weighing 8½ ozs. per yard. Now, as far as the yarn consumed is concerned, the denominator is readily arrived at—a yard of cloth weighing 17 ozs. per yard (if such a size were made) is the equivalent of two yards weighing 8½ ozs. Coming to the next process, warping, we must calculate the cost on a different scale. A yard of 17 ozs. costs no more to warp than a yard of 8½ ozs., and so the divisor in this case must be the number of yards warped, irrespective of substance. The same principle governs the weaving. Scouring, drying, and milling introduce us to a fresh denominator altogether; these processes follow neither the principle of yarn consumed nor of warping, but the cost varies according to the substance of a cloth on a scale applicable only to the processes, and ascertained by experiment. In like manner

Dr. ACCOUNT

		Cost. *per lb.* s.	d.	Tweed. £	s.	d.	Cost. *per lb.* s.	d.	Serge. £	s.	d.	Sundries. £	s.	d.
1882. Dec. 31—To Raw Wool consumed		1	7·80	8520	7	6		8·11	6140	18	9	1560	17	1
,, Breaking-up and Scouring			·53	220	17	0		·02	12	10	0	60	18	10
,, Dyeing			1·54	640	1	8		·01	10	14	8	20	4	7
,, Spinning			2·63	1095	4	6		2·64	1954	17	2	205	0	4
,, Doubling			·25	106	4	10		,,	,,	,,	,,	10	6	4
		2	0·75	10312	15	6		10·78	8119	0	7	1857	7	2
,, Decrease in Stock				,,	,,	,,			,,	,,	,,	89	10	11
,, Yarn bought				200	18	11			3616	1	6	1600	2	7
				£10513	14	5			£11735	2	1	£3547	0	8
		per yard					*per yard*							
,, Yarn consumed in pieces woven brought down		1	3·89	9985	15	1	1	4·16	11312	2	8	3462	18	7
,, Warping			·32	206	7	8		,,	,,	,,	,,	48	17	1
,, Weaving			1·92	1241	8	2		2·19	1485	7	2	464	8	2
,, Scouring, Drying, and Milling			·61	367	1	4		1·22	591	2	8	104	7	2
,, Burling			·66	420	17	2		·18	120	8	6	70	4	3
,, Finishing			·96	601	4	1		1·52	802	2	8	85	9	6
,, Engine and Machinery Expenses			·93	579	4	11		1·60	941	2	8	146	2	7
,, Pattern Weaving			·31	185	9	7		,,	,,	,,	,,	28	17	10
,, Dyeing Pieces			,,	,,	,,	,,		4·61	3001	14	11	624	18	1
,, General Charges, viz.:—														
Packing Materials	£80 2 7													
Carriage on Sales	360 4 8													
Office Salaries & Expenses	520 6 1													
Travellers' Salaries & Expenses	1580 4 2													
General Salaries & Wages	571 4 3		3·69	2342	19	3		3·69	2639	14	7	795	8	11
Rent, Rates, Taxes, &c.	1620 4 1													
Interest and Bank Charges	420 8 6													
Depreciation	624 8 5													
	£5778 2 9													
		2	1·29	15930	7	3	2	7·17	20893	15	10	5831	12	2
,, Discounts			3·38	2160	4	8		3·13	2245	8	1	560	8	4
,, Decrease in Stocks			,,	2070	8	4		,,	,,	,,	,,	741	2	8
,, Balances, being profit on Tweed and Serge carried down			3·88	2480	8	7		1·08	771	7	2	,,	,,	,,
		2	8·55	£22641	8	10	2	11·38	£23910	11	1	£7133	3	2
,, Loss on Sundries brought down												685	0	5
,, Deficiencies in Yarn Stocks brought down, viz.:														
Tweed	£187 10 6													
Serge	320 11 1													
Sundries	84 2 1											592	3	8
,, Deficiency in Dyewares												94	8	3
,, Bad Debts												416	1	8
,, Balance, being net profit												1464	1	9
												£3251	15	9

have to be determined the principles of division for the other items of cost. Again, certain items, such as "Engine and Machinery Expenses" and "General Charges" are divisible over the three branches of the trade—viz., tweed serge, and sundries, and the relative proportions for each branch have to be determined—*i.e.*, for this purpose a yard of tweed has to be brought to a common denominator with a yard of serge. A little patience, however, enables an Accountant to overcome all these difficulties, and, as I have already stated, I have purposely chosen a cost account of special complexity to illustrate this part of my lecture.

Now, having got our cost sheets, the great thing to be done is to build our Trading Account upon them, for it is only by the Trading Account that the correctness of the cost sheet is proved. The figures of the cost sheet may be all pretty and symmetrical, but when you get out the balance sheet at the end, the owner of the mill may be astounded by results altogether different from what he has been led to expect. The mill manager will, of course, swear by his weekly costs, and unless you can put your finger on the discrepancy, the matter will remain a mystery. It is obvious that Trade Account No. 3 won't help you, but it is also obvious that you can easily frame a trade account that will. If we open a wool account, and charge it with all the wool that comes into the place, and credit it with all issued for yarn making according to the cost sheets, we shall see whether the cost sheets are right as far as wool is concerned. Following the same process with dye wares, stores, coal, yarn, etc., we shall be enabled to locate exactly where the difference between the theoretical results of the cost sheets and the actual results of the balance sheet arises. No. 5 Account is a Trading Account constructed on this principle.

No. 5. *Cr.*

	Tweed. £	s.	d.	Serge. £	s.	d.	Sundries. £	s.	d.
1882.									
Dec. 31—By Yarn consumed in pieces woven carried down	9985	15	1	11312	2	8	3462	18	7
,, Increase in Stock	340	8	10	102	8	4	,,	,,	,,
,, Balances carried down, being deficiencies in Yarn Stocks	187	10	6	320	11	1	84	2	1
	£10513	14	5	£11735	2	1	£3547	0	8
,, Sales	22641	8	10	23562	8	4	6448	2	9
,, Increase in Stock	,,	,,	,,	348	2	9	,,	,,	,,
,, Balance, being loss on Sundries carried down	,,	,,	,,	,,	,,	,,	685	0	5
	£22641	8	10	£23910	11	1	£7133	3	2
,, Profit on Tweed, brought down							2480	8	7
,, Ditto Serge ditto							771	7	2
							£3251	15	9

Let us investigate shortly the information obtained from account No. 5 which could not be obtained from account No. 3. By account No. 3 we were only enabled to tell the proprietor that all his transactions, jumbled up together, resulted in a profit of £1464. We are now able to tell him that the two staples, Tweed and Serge gave a much larger profit, but that the production of Sundry Goods resulted in a loss of £685. His attention is therefore directed specially to that branch of his business, in order to ascertain whether the bad result is due to causes preventible or non-preventible to lax control or to the general condition of trade. If the former, the remedy can be applied; if the latter, we can now also furnish him with data for determining whether or not he had better discontinue the production of Sundry Goods. This question is not finally determined by the mere fact that a loss has resulted, for we now proceed to point out to the proprietor that the loss of £685 is after charging the Sundry Goods with £795 as their share of General Charges, so that in fact, while the Sundry Goods have made no profit, they have provided £110 towards the General Charges of the concern; we then go through the constituents of the General Charges and determine if any, and if so, what reduction can be made therein, by discontinuing the trade in Sundry Goods; if thereby a reduction of more than £110 can be foreseen, there are strong *primâ facie* grounds for relinquishing that branch of the trade. But further, by account No. 5 we are in a position to inform the proprietor that his profits would have been £686 more but for deficiences not accounted for in his stocks of yarn and of dye wares, and here we find the special advantage of building up the Trade Account on the Cost Sheets. We point out that the aggregated results of the Weekly Yarn Costs show that so much yarn has been paid for as produced; the aggregated results of the Weekly Costs of finished products show that so much yarn only has been consumed in the pieces woven and that the value of the stocks ascertained by actual weighing at the end of the period was £592 less than, accordingly to the aggregated results of the Cost Sheets, they ought to have been. We thus land the practical manager in this trilemma: we say to him either you have paid the spinners for more yarn than they actually produced, or you have understated the yarn you have consumed in the woven pieces, or you have allowed the stock of yarn to be pilfered. Similarly we place the dyeman on the horns of a dilemma; either he has understated his weekly consumption of dye wares, or his dye wares are being pilfered. Thus, the points of leakage are at once detected and the proper remedy is applied.

The last class of trades to which I will refer is the Distributive trades or those concerned with the sale of goods in the same, or nearly the same, condition as that on which they are purchased, I will take a metal merchant as a type of this class. The Accountant's duty in this, as in all other cases, is to place himself in the position of the trader, and determine what form of account is best adapted to aid the proprietor's work of supervision. Here there is no question of cost sheets, but profit is built up by profitable contracts for purchase and sale of the same material. Let us suppose the case of a merchant dealing in copper, tin, and spelter. His transactions run into very large figures, and the matter of first importance for his accounts to prove is that all his stock is accounted for, so that by no chance has any lot of metal delivered by him been omitted. To carry out this a convenient form of journal can be devised, whereby all copper, tin and spelter which he buys are charged respectively to copper, tin, or spelter stock accounts. Similarly his sales are credited to the like stock accounts; and the ledger is ruled to provide for weights as well as for amounts. Then each stock account proves that all he has paid for has been sold or remains in stock, and further shows the total profit made in that particular commodity. The Trade Account then, takes the form given in account No. 6, which is so simple that no words of explanation are required.

Dr. ACCOUNT No. 6. Cr.

1882.	£	s.	d.	£	s.	d.
Dec. 31.—To GENERAL CHARGES, viz.:—						
Salaries and Office Expenses	481	7	3			
Commission	795	1	11			
Rent, Rates, and Taxes	150	9	10			
Bank Charges and Interest ..	41	8	1	1,468	7	1
To Bad Debts				65	1	4
To Balance, being net profit				1,485	10	11
				£3,018	19	4

1882.	£	s.	d.	£	s.	d.
Dec. 31.—By Profit on sale of—						
Copper	2,280	13	4			
Tin	1,380	4	1			
	3,660	17	5			
Less Loss on sale of Spelter	641	18	1	3,018	19	4
				£3,018	19	4

Here end my illustrations, but I want to refer for a few moments to the bearing of Trade Accounts, such as I have indicated, upon auditing. Twenty years ago, after the collapse of many companies in the storm of 1866, there were frequent discussions in commercial circles and in the press as to the utility of an audit. Several audited concerns failed, and it was then found out that unreliable Balance Sheets had been issued, which were certified by accountants of whose *bona-fides* and high standing there could be no question.

In concerns of the kind which I have called constructive and convertive it was found that the auditors had been compelled to take the valuations of the stocks upon trust, and, when directors had awkward results to face, or when they wished to inflate the market in order to unload their own shares, they would quietly write up the value of the stocks by £20,000 or £30,000. The question was debated very thoroughly, and some accountants accepted the position that as auditors they were not responsible for the valuation of the stock. Now, as the object of an audit is to ascertain the result of the trading, and as that result depends generally more upon the valuation of the stock than upon any other figure, one wonders what is the utility of an audit which declines responsibility for the most important figure in the accounts.

If you have a steed in a stable with six doors to it, and you only lock five of the doors, you may just as well leave all six open, because, if a thief comes, he wont waste his time battering at the five doors which are locked, but he will walk through the one which is not. Similarly if the officials of a company wish to deceive an auditor, they will not select one of the five figures which he can check, but the sixth which he cannot. But if our Trade Accounts are built upon the prime costs and cost sheets, in the manner indicated in this paper, we can most securely double-lock and bar this sixth door.

It is impossible to imagine that an accountant could be deceived as to the valuation of the stock on such a system.

The deception would have to be carried through every cost sheet from week to week. It would have to be started at the beginning of the year, before the officials could know whether they would want to deceive or not, and it would throw up the most contradictory results in the weekly cost sheets which the auditor could not fail to notice. Indeed, by such a system instead of the auditor being doubtful about the valuation of the stock there is no figure in the Balance Sheet of which he can speak with more certainty.

It is interesting to note as bearing on the subject of my lecture, that, in recent times, the Legislature appears to have become alive to the necessity of proper Trade Accounts. The references to the Accounts of trading concerns in old Acts of Parliament are all obscure, intangible, and in general terms and a literal compliance with them could be arranged so as completely to hide the information which accounts are intended to show. In certain cases, however, in which the public nature of the undertaking renders a knowledge of the inner working of the concern advisable, Parliament has now laid down the form in which the Trading Account shall be drawn up. Examples of this are the forms attached to the Railway Regulation Act, and to the last Gas Works Clauses Act, and compared with the old regulations, these mark a distinct advance in the direction of the principles advocated in this lecture.

I have thus sketched out imperfectly a development which has taken place in our profession within my recollection, and which promises a still more widely extended field for us in the future. The question will perhaps occur to you whether this is not expecting too much of Chartered Accountants—whether it does not involve that, besides being men of figures, they must also be qualified builders, engineers, ironworkers, mining engineers, woollen manufacturers, and so on. The answer is no!

The principles of costs of construction and production are always the same; the qualified accountant has only to learn to apply those principles to varying circumstances.

An architect has to acquire a complete knowledge of the science and art of construction. He has then to plan one day a brewery, then a cotton-mill, a workhouse, a gaol, or a club. He must be able to adapt his knowledge to each of these; this does not mean that he must be qualified to manage a brewery, mill, workhouse, gaol or club, but he must know the requirements of each and provide for them.

This is an exact analogy to what is required from us.

We must acquire sufficient knowledge of each kind of trade to enable us to follow the processes and pick out the vital points where continued supervision is necessary.

We must then adapt our knowledge of methods to the requirements of each particular trade and as that sentence shortly summarises all that I have said to you I will therewith conclude my lecture.

At the conclusion a general discussion ensued. The Hon. Sec., referred to the meeting as being the closing one of the Session and that although it was last on the list it was not, by a long way the least instructive, and would rank as one of the best lectures the Society had ever had. He also congratulated the members upon the increased attendance which had averaged 29 against 12 in 1885, and ventured to express the hope that in the forthcoming Sessions it would still go on increasing; but that that would only be arrived at by each member taking his individual part. He then proposed a cordial vote of thanks to Mr. Gibson for his Lecture, which was unanimously accorded.

A similar compliment to the Chairman for presiding brought the evening to a close.

SHIPBUILDERS' ACCOUNTS.

By T. H. Warwick.

(Chief Clerk with Messrs. John Routh & Co., Chartered Accountants, Leeds.)

The subject of Shipbuilders' Accounts is, in itself, a large one, and it would occupy a much longer time to consider the whole system than I feel justified in asking you to give me at once, and I therefore propose to deal only with that part of it which relates to the "Cost Accounts"; leaving until another opportunity the remaining portion bearing upon the ordinary books and accounts generally used.

In order to make the subject as interesting and instructive as possible, I invite you to accompany me to one of our large Shipyards, and there to notice the incessant din, the bustle, and confusion going on; the clattering and clanging of the hammers; the creaking of the cranes; the buzz and the whirr of the steam saws; and the heavy clack of the punching machines; and in the midst of this uproar we will endeavour to trace the meaning of it all until eventually we come to the £ s. d. of the matter as it appears in the accounts of the firm; for each "bat" of the hammer, and each punch of the machine, represents a certain amount of work done for a particular object, and the sum total of such "bats" and "punches," at last find their place on the pages of the firm's books.

I will divide my subject under two heads, viz:—

Materials.

Labour.

Dealing first with the materials, which comprises, principally, (1) Plates and Angles and other wrought iron; (2) Rivets; (3) Timber; (4) Sundry Stores (such as the smaller castings; the necessary fittings and furnishings; nails, screws, and the like); (5) Special or *Direct* Stores, such as Anchors and Cables, Donkey Boilers, Winches, Windlasses, &c.; (6) Rigging Chains and Ropes; (7) Paint, &c.

It is not necessary, for the present purpose to go into all the details connected with the ordering of the materials, and the gradual building up of the vessel. We will suppose a steamer has been finished and the total cost is required.

First, we want to know the total quantity of Plates, Angles, and other wrought iron used. This is usually given by the draughtsmen who have had the ordering of the iron, and whose duty it is, generally, to work out the total weights used in the various departments of the vessel. This is done in great detail; the draughtsmen first of all making an analysis of the weight of iron used in each compartment of the ship, such as the Frames and Floors, Shell plating, Iron Decks, Beams, Bulkheads, Hatches, Bunkers, Ballast Tanks, &c., &c., and finally putting the same into the form of a summary, (an illustration of which I give further on), showing the *total* weight of Plates, Angles, &c. When the weights have thus been arrived at, we must fix what we consider a fair price at which to charge the iron. as in many cases it is contracted for at different mills and at various prices, and it is only by a system of judicious averaging that a reasonable figure can be decided upon. After we have fixed the prices and made the calculations, we have now to consider the fact that a certain amount of waste has taken place in punching the holes in the Plates and Angles to receive the rivets; and in the shearing of the Plates, &c., but seeing that the waste thus created is not *all* a loss, but that the weight of such waste can be sold as Scrap Iron, it is obvious that only the difference between what it cost and what is realised for it should be charged to the ship, so that the estimated gross value of iron used in the ship will be charged *less* the amount realised for Scrap Iron. The amount of waste varies according to the type of vessel built, but from 10 to 15% on the net weight has been found by experience to be a fair calculation.

As the Iron Account forms the chief feature in the Cost Account, I give here an illustration of the manner in which it is finally worked up, the figures, of course, only being fictitious.

S. S. No......................IRON ACCOUNT.

	Tons. Cwts. Qrs.	Price.	£	s.	d.
Plates and Beading	600	7/-	4200	0	0
Angles and Bulbs	200	5/10/-	1100	0	0
Packing Iron	50	4/10/-	225	0	0
Smith's „	100	8/-/-	800	0	0
	950		6325	0	0
Estimated waste— TONS. Say 10%—95—costing 632 10 0 Sold at £3 5 0 per ton 308 15 0	95		323	15	0
To debit ship........ 325 15 0					
Forgings	20	10/-/-	200	0	0
Total of Iron A/c.	1065		6848	15	0
Rivets..........	150	7/-/-	1050	0	0
Gross weight of Iron..........	1215	£	7898	15	0
Less estimated waste	95				
Net weight of Iron	1120				

The Rivets Account is a comparatively easy matter to deal with, as the stock of Rivets is, as a rule, under the control of a Storekeeper, who keeps an account of all he gives out, with the number of the vessel for which they are used, and on its completion he sends his account into the office, where the price is fixed, the calculations made, and the amount transferred to the Cost Sheet as shown above.

We now come to the Timber, and it will be somewhat difficult to explain the usual working of this department.

In most Shipyards where a saw mill is running, the timber is bought in the log, which, before it can be made into boards and ready for use, has to undergo a variety of changes, a considerable amount of waste consequently taking place.

The following facts may be regarded as a fair basis of calculation to aid us in fixing a price at which to charge the timber.

(1). If there was no waste in converting log timber into boards, then 1/12th part of a cubic foot would equal 1 superficial foot, 1 inch thick.

(2). Assuming that 5/32nds of an inch is the amount of wood destroyed by a saw-cut, then the loss equals 1 superficial foot 5/32nds thick, upon each superficial foot of boards irrespective of their thickness, and the cost of this forms an addition of a constant amount to the cost per superficial foot.

(3). The cost per superficial foot of sawing forms also a constant amount per superficial foot.

(4). Beyond the waste by saw-cuts (as in 2) is that of two slabs, and the saw-cut for the first one, and loss of measurement through round edges, the taper of the log, and other defects, the amount of which can only be ascertained by experience upon each kind of timber, and is more nearly proportional to the cubic than to the superficial foot.

(5). The waste in No. 4 must be put into the form of a proportionate or percentage addition to the net product of the log, and this percentage must be added to the cubic foot price, and from this amount a list can be made proportionately for every thickness required in the schedule.

(6). To the above list then add two constant sums representing:—

(as per 2) cost of wood destroyed by sawing,
(as per 3) cost of destroying same by sawing,

and the final sum will be the required schedule list.

Example *1-in. Yellow Pine, Waney Board.*

Cost 2s. 4d. per cubic foot.

1/12th =	2⅓d.	per supl. foot 1-in. thick.
add	·4167	= 17·86% found by experience to be the required addition to net
	2·75	product (as per 4) making cost up to 2·75d. per supl. foot of 1-in. at this stage.
add	·365	pence = cost of 1 supl. foot, 5/32nds thick being the saw cut of one edge.
add	·375	pence = cost of destroying this by sawing.
	3·49	pence = Schedule cost of 1 supl. foot of 1-in. Waney Board.

From this a list can be formed for all sizes of the timber used by the joiners and carpenters. The foremen over these departments keep an account of the sizes and quantities of all wood used by them, and on the completion of the vessel their books are sent to the office; the various sized timber grouped together, and an abstract made, this is priced and calculated and the amounts transferred to their proper place on the Cost Account Sheets.

The Sundry Stores is the next item, but requires very little explanation. The storekeepers when they give out any of their stock at once enter the same into their "Ships' Stores Book" stating the number of the ship and all the other necessary particulars. These are priced, worked out in the usual way, and the amount transferred to the Cost Sheets. The *Riggers'* and the *Painters'* Stores are treated in the same way.

The Special or Direct Stores, such as Donkey Boilers, Anchors and Cables, &c., are taken *direct* from the Invoices, as these kind of goods are always bought for a specified vessel, the number of such vessel being marked upon the Invoices as they are received. In making up the Cost Account, it is only necessary to refer to the Invoice, and put down the amount on the Cost Sheets, so that no difficulty whatever is experienced in dealing with them.

There are other charges such as Coals, Carriage, Rents, Rates, Gas, Water, &c., which of course can only be treated as a proportionate charge on each ship.

I now come to the Labour, and will divide this again under two heads, viz:—

Time Work.

Piece Work.

Taking the time work first.—Each time workman on entering the shipyard to commence work is given a time board, numbered, and a corresponding number is kept by the Timekeeper in his time books, along with the name of the workman.

On finishing his day's work the workman writes up his time on this board, stating the No. of the ship he has been engaged upon; the particular part of the ship; and the number of hours occupied. This board is signed by his foreman and given to the timekeeper, who daily enters up his books from the boards, taking care to note that each bears the signature of the foreman, and that it states on which part of the ship the work has been done. The time books are then, once a week, given to the clerk whose duty it is to make the calculations, total them up and prepare a weekly abstract of the wages; separate sheets being kept for the different ships, and the totals of these sheets brought forward from week to week, so that it can be seen at a glance what amount is being paid in wages *weekly* on any particular ship, and also the *total* amount of wages paid on them up to the last pay week. On the completion of the vessel the total is transferred from the "Abstract" to the "Cost" Sheets.

The Piece work is treated in very much the same way, excepting that the foremen keep the account of work done, and the amount or rate at which it has been agreed to do it. He also renders his books weekly to the abstracting clerk who proceeds in the same way as with the time work.

But there is also other items of labour performed which cannot be charged *direct* to any particular ship; such as salaries of the officials and foremen, the wages of unskilled labourers, &c., but must form a proportionate charge in the same way as pointed out in "Materials."

The foregoing treats (though only superficially) with the manner in which the total cost of a ship is arrived at. I have endeavoured to explain the working of the different departments of a large shipyard, and to trace to their ultimate result all that appeared confusing and perplexing when we entered, and I will now finish by attempting to show how it looks when finally put into the form of a summary. The figures being again, only fictitious.

COST ACCOUNT SUMMARY, S.S. No............................

	Iron A/c.	Rivet A/c.	Timber A/c.	Sundry Stores A/c.	Direct Stores A/c.	Painters' Stores A/c.	Riggers' Stores A/c.	Sundry Charges.	Labour.	Total.
	£ s. d.	£ s. d.	£ s. d.	£ s. d.	£ s. d.	£ s. d.	£ s. d.	£ s. d.	£ s. d.	£ s. d.
Carpenters work	—	—	1500 0 0	100 0 0	—	—	—	—	300 0 0	1900 0 0
Rigging Items	—	—	200 0 0	50 0 0	—	50 0 0	150 0 0	—	100 0 0	550 0 0
Accommodation	—	—	300 0 0	150 0 0	—	100 0 0	—	—	150 0 0	700 0 0
Winch &c., Outfit:—										
Steam Winches	—	—	—	—	250 0 0	—	—	—	—	—
Donkey Boiler	—	—	—	—	75 0 0	—	—	—	—	325 0 0
Cementing	—	—	—	—	—	100 0 0	—	—	50 0 0	150 0 0
Painting	—	—	—	—	—	150 0 0	—	—	70 0 0	220 0 0
Water Ballast Items	—	—	—	250 0 0	—	—	—	—	85 0 0	335 0 0
Lloyds' Equipment Items:—										
Anchors and Cables	—	—	—	—	145 0 0	—	—	—	—	—
Windlass	—	—	—	—	85 0 0	—	—	—	—	—
Towlines and Hawsers	—	—	—	—	30 0 0	—	—	—	—	—
Steel Wire, Ropes, &c.	—	—	—	—	15 0 0	—	—	—	—	275 0 0
Boats:—										
Boats	—	—	—	—	110 0 0	—	—	—	—	—
Sundry timber and furnishings	—	—	50 0 0	15 0 0	—	10 0 0	20 0 0	—	50 0 0	255 0 0
Sundry Purchases:—										
Hand Pumps	—	—	—	—	70 0 0	—	—	—	—	—
Steering Gear	—	—	—	—	100 0 0	—	—	—	—	170 0 0
Sundry Stores:— Compasses, Flags, Cabin Stores, &c., &c.	—	—	—	150 0 0	—	—	—	—	—	150 0 0
Iron Labour	—	—	—	—	—	—	—	—	2000 0 0	—
Other direct labour	—	—	—	—	—	—	—	—	500 0 0	2500 0 0
Trial Trip Charges, &c.	—	—	—	—	—	—	—	100 0 0	—	100 0 0
Iron Account	6848 15 0	—	—	—	—	—	—	—	—	6848 15 0
Rivet Account	—	1050 0 0	—	—	—	—	—	—	—	1050 0 0
	6848 15 0	1050 0 0	2050 0 0	715 0 0	880 0 0	410 0 0	170 0 0	100 0 0	3305 0 0	15528 15 0

Of course there is an enormous amount of detail work to be accomplished before a summary is arrived at, but it would be almost impossible to explain it here. The most important thing is to have a thoroughly systematic method adopted in the counting house, giving each clerk, if necessary, charge of a particular department, the whole being supervised and passed by the chief official who is responsible to his employers for the correctness of the Cost Account.

ENGINEERING COSTS BOOK-KEEPING.

The stout volume before us on "Engineering Estimates and Accounts" (London, Crosby Lockwood & Co.) compiled by a "General Manager" aims at remedying a defect in the training of young engineers, by affording them an insight into the commercial and financial side of an engineering establishment, in which department they rarely receive any systematic instruction, or have the opportunity afforded them of acquiring the knowledge necessary to enable them to prepare a formal tender or even to give a simple quotation. With this laudable object in view the author has gone at very great length into such questions as detailed and general specifications, calculations of quantities, rough and finished dimensions, and indirect and departmental expenses, upon which he seems to have a most thorough practical knowledge, and although the technical part of these matters is somewhat beyond us, we have read with great interest the chapter bearing upon Costs' Book-keeping, which has been carefully compiled and thought out. The leading principles governing the question of cost are clearly set forth, and very exactly expressed. For instance, as to the elements constituting the cost of an article, it is said—"The cost of any piece of machinery may best be considered as made up of three elements, viz., the cost of material used for the construction of the article; the cost of labour directly expended upon it; and a sum most conveniently determined by a percentage upon the direct wages, to cover all the indirect expenses of the establishment," (generally termed 'Oncost,') and the reasons why labour should be found the most natural basis upon which to calculate these indirect expenses are well expressed. We also agree with the author that such items as management, office expenses, and interest on capital should be treated as elements of the cost of production, and that every item of expenditure, even expenditure on Capital Account, should be passed through the Cost Books to ensure the satisfactory working of any scheme of cost keeping.

In spite, however, of the very great fulness with which the numerous excellent examples of forms and books are set out, there would seem to be generally a want of cohesion among them—they do not sufficiently dovetail in with each other and form one connected series, as should be the very essence of a proper cost system.

In no place is it fully explained how the Stores Account should be credited with the items of stores which are charged to the job or customer, nor is it shown how the total debited to the Cost Ledger, the Oncost Account, and the Stores Account are made to agree in total with the items credited through the Invoice Book, so as to enable the store-keeper to see that he has all the stores on hand which he has not charged out in the Stores Ledger, for if these totals do not agree quantities of stores might be apparently used for one job which were from some accident omitted to be charged, and this would not be discovered. A most convenient way of checking the Cost and Stores Ledger is to have a "Cost Ledger total Account," and a "Store Ledger total Account" in the General Ledger.

In the Invoice Book there ought to be four columns given:—"Cost Ledger," "Stores Ledger," "On cost Account," and "General Ledger."

The form of "Order Book" given seems a useful one, and is here appended:—

Date when ordered.	Order No.	Name and Address of Customer. Description of Order.	Estimate Book folio.	Specifications or Tender Book folio.	Date when delivered, and space for any Remarks or Notes it may be desirable to record during progress of work, or for Instructions as to delivery of goods.	Folios in Sales or Day Book or No. of Delivery Docket.
188 . Jan. 6th	67	Thos. Robinson & Sons, Victoria Saw Mills, Blanktown. One Horizontal High-pressure Non-condensing Steam Engine, &c.	9/82	8/99	Forward per G.N.R. to Blanktown Station: Robinson's will cart to Mill.. .. .. See letter Jan. 24 .. .. Delivered Feb., 188 . Completed Feb. 22, 188 .	Docket Nos 672 694

As for the question of wages, a novel and excellent suggestion is made with regard to workmen's sheets. It is suggested that the men should each be provided with a block formed by a stout piece of common cardboard, with thirteen sheets of paper attached to it and to one another, by being thoroughly gummed all round their edges, except at one corner—like an ordinary sketching block in fact. Each sheet should be large enough to contain a week's record, and be ruled with columns for the order and man's number or name, the description of the job, and for each day of the week. When the sheet is filled, it is raised at the ungummed corner, and a knife slipped under, and run all round, thus detaching the sheet, and leaving a new one for a new week. The blocks would of course be collected before breakfast one morning a week, left in the costs' office, and distributed again during the forenoon, and each sheet should be signed by the foreman.

These particulars are recommended to be entered in weekly "Work Books," of which a specimen is given as follows:—

WORK BOOK.

Week ending 6th Dec., 188 .

Workman's Number.	Workman's Name and No. of Order or Customer's Name.	Description of Job.	F.	S.	M.	T.	W.	Th.	Total Hours.	Rate Wages.	£	s.	d.
	TURNING	SHOP.											
124	William Brown ..	60-inch Rope Wheel	9½	6½	9½	7	—	—	32½	—	0	19	8
	601	Brass Gland	—	—	—	2½	—	—	2½	—	0	1	6
	Armstrong	.. ..	—	—	—	—	9½	—	9½	—	0	5	7
	640 .. .. 584	Valve Gear Engine .. .. Gland Cylinder .. .. ..)	—	—	—	—	—	9	9	—	0	5	4
									53½	32/-	1	11	8
201	John Jones .. .. Walker & Co... ..	(Fitter) Out Time per signed Docket ..	—	—	—	—	—	—	54	30/-	1	10	0
		Allowance	—	—	—	—	—	—	—	—	0	6	0
											1	16	0
340	Thomas Green .. Shop	(Labourer)	—	—	—	—	—	—	46½	13/-	0	11	8

We think it will be found much more convenient to enter these particulars direct into the Wages Abstract Sheet instead of in a book, and in any case an extra column ought to be given for the totals at the end of the week.

In the specimen "Wages Abstract Sheet" given, the particulars set out in analysis columns, are the classes of work, the hours worked, and the wages earned. The sheet would be much more instructive if the percentage of Oncost on wages were given, and the abstract were ruled in the form given beneath, including columns for the total wages chargeable; for the total Oncost; for the total including wages and Oncost chargeable to the job; and for the Cost Ledger folio. We append a form which has been found to work capitally in a very large establishment. It should be ruled at the end of the Wages Pay Book.

WAGES ABSTRACT BOOK.

Week ending................

No. of Job.	Workman's Number	Labourers.	Draftsmen.	Pattern Makers. — per cent.	Turners. — per cent.	Drillers and Slotters. — per cent.	Smiths. — per cent.	Total Wages Paid.	Oncost or General Establishment Charges.	Total chargeable to Job.	Cost Ledger folio.
								(Credited to Cash.)	(Credited to Oncost.)	(Total of this column charged to "Cost Ledger Total A/c.")	

Had our author been a little more of an accountant, he would doubtless so have interwoven his system of books into a harmonious whole, that there would have been no occasion for these criticisms. However, as the book stands, we welcome it as a useful contribution from a practical man, and it undoubtedly ought to prove an invaluable aid to young engineers when they have got past the preliminary stage of performing with a sledge hammer on bolts and clenching rivets, and are beginning to have a look round them and endeavouring to acquire some inkling of the theoretical and economical part of their useful profession; and from it accountants can also glean a good deal of useful information.

Glasgow Chartered Accountants' Debating Society.

NOTES ON COST RECORDS:

A NEGLECTED BRANCH OF ACCOUNTANCY.

A Paper read before this Society by Mr. JOHN MANN, Jun., M.A., C.A.

DEFINITIONS.—ELEMENTS OF A PRODUCT.

I SHALL first define my terms:—

Prime Cost is, of course, literally *first cost*, and I shall use the phrase to mean either (1) the sum expended in purchasing a complete article, for sale in the state in which it is bought, or (2) the sums expended in raw material, *plus* the labour of converting same into a complete article. The word *cost* alone I employ to mean the total or *full cost*, being the *prime cost plus expenses*. The *difference* between the *cost* and the *selling* price of the *product* is, of course, the *trader's net profit or loss*. *Oncost* is a strange word. It seems intended to describe generally *cost added on*. But I think its real origin is in mining phraseology, where "under cost" and "oncost" are spoken of, the first to indicate "costs underground," the second "costs on surface," and as surface expenses were often equivalent to wages of superintendence and general charges, "on cost" came to have the wider meaning of all expenses not directly productive. As usually understood, it represents wages of superintendence, rent, interest, depreciation, and what are known as general charges. I prefer, however, not to use the word "oncost" at all, but to speak of *expenses*, and to divide these into *direct* and *indirect*.

Direct Expenses include those which can at once be charged to a particular contract, piece of work, or a department of a business, and would therefore include wages of foremen and superintendents, and of general hands, outlay for fuel, lighting, heating, &c.; rent, taxes, and insurance; and, if these can be separated, depreciation of special machinery used in a department. Strictly speaking, direct expenses are elements in prime cost, and in a proper system should be so treated; that is, they are *expenses of production* rather than of distribution.

Indirect Expenses may perhaps best be defined negatively, as all expenses other than direct expenses; that is, all expenses that cannot be applied to a particular contract or department. Generally they are expenses of *distribution*, of finance, of general control, and are not so closely connected with production as direct expenses are. Roughly, they include office salaries and office expenses, provision for bad debts, and for interest on capital and loans.

The division between direct and indirect expenses may not at first seem clear; it is one of the refinements of bookkeeping; and of course where there are no large contracts, and no departments of a business, it will often vanish; but, as a general rule, it will be found useful to observe the distinction. For instance, in opening or remodelling a set of books, a clear grasp of the distinction will enable a list of nominal accounts to be framed sufficiently complete to supply all the materials for ascertaining the cost of goods and the result of trading, and that without descending to the very minute, hairsplitting, analysis of expenditure which bookkeepers so detest. We all know how difficult it is to observe minute distinctions in the pressure of work, and how very often at the year's end no use is made of the results, either because the principals do not know how to use them, or, if they do know how to use them, because they consider them unreliable.

I should add that these definitions are necessarily vague and general; were I dealing with some particular trade they might be more distinct.

A product may therefore be analysed into its elements thus:—

(1) *Material.*
(2) *Labour.*
(3) *Departmental* or *Direct Expenses* (of *production*)
  Wages of Superintendence, Foremen, &c.
  Lighting, Heating, Rent, Taxes, Insurance, Depreciation and Upholding — of Plant and Buildings.
— (1) to (3): Prime Cost.

(4) *Indirect Expenses* (of *distribution*).
  Salaries of officers and directors.
  Up-keep of office or warehouse.
  Financing and distribution expenses.
  Interest.
  Bad debt reserves.

Material + Labour + Direct Expenses = Prime Cost.
Prime Cost + Indirect Expenses = Cost.
Prime Cost + Gross Profit = }
Cost + Net Profit or Loss = } Exchange Value of Product.

ADVANTAGES OF COST RECORDS.

I must now try to convince you that a thorough-going system of recording prime cost is an essential part of the bookkeeping in nearly every kind of business. The objects of such a system are broadly two-fold:—

1. *To examine and explain past results.*
2. *To form a guide for future trading.*

I have often been disappointed, and no doubt you also have been so, at the slight attention paid by a manufacturer or a trader to the details of his Profit and Loss Account prepared from his books with so much trouble.

You point out to him his total sales, his opening and closing stocks. "Yes," he knows all that already. Then you detail to him all the expenditure, carefully "branched out" and grouped under the most suitable headings. These details seem meaningless to him; they do not interest him, they are of no value to him. Apparently he looks to the resulting balance of profit or of loss and to that alone, and having made a mental note of the amount he snaps to the patent lock of his private ledger, and does not re-open it until another year's trading is complete.

You say to yourself "My labour is thrown away in ascertaining accurately all these details, in discriminating between wages and salaries, between works expenses and office expenses—a Balance Sheet or even a state of affairs is good enough for such a man." But perhaps the fault is your own. You have not succeeded in making your elaborate results interesting enough. Can you not make them more *interesting?* I think you can.

Other men, again, when you take in the result of their trading for discussion, are at once able to say "Yes, I thought it would be something like that. You remember we had a good margin on so and so, or we dropped £2,000 on so and so"; or it may be "Well, I can't understand that at all; we have had a fairly good year, yet you show a loss, how is it"? Of course, you assure him your results are right, and that they are just the logical results of the trading as recorded in the books. You go over with him all the details of his Trading and Profit and Loss Accounts; they are practically meaningless; he is still dissatisfied. How can you convince him that you are right, and that he is wrong? You may treat him to some well worn platitudes of the infallibility of double entry, but in many cases that client has a lingering feeling that your bookkeeping or auditing has been of no practical help to him in his daily work, has not cleared up the fog that he is in, and when it comes to paying your fee, it may be grudged, and perhaps the audit given up.

We can in return mentally dub our client a blockhead with no grasp of bookkeeping—that will not mend matters. But are we not in fault in refusing to give the man what he wants? He wants *not only* to know whether he has made a profit or a loss, and how much, but *why, where,* and *when* he has made it. Now, many a trader or manufacturer instinctively checks, and, if possible, reconciles his audited Profit and Loss Account with the results of a process of "prime costing" that he has been mentally carrying on during the year. If your result and his agree he is satisfied, but if not he is dissatisfied, and but too often is he dissatisfied.

You may, perhaps, succeed in overcoming or allaying his disappointment by hinting that, perhaps, he has forgotten in his rough calculations to take into account losses from bad debts and allowances for depreciation, interest on capital and loans, &c. When you do this you give him a lesson in costing, but at the same time *you* receive or should receive a lesson as to the advantages of keeping a proper record of prime cost.

I think it was a case such as that I have been describing which some years ago turned my mind to a "prime cost record" as a valuable supplement to a Trading Account. In the instance I refer to, the principal partner was dissatisfied with the Trading Account submitted. He was a very shrewd, sharp man, with a wonderful memory—one of the old school who seem to do all the necessary bookkeeping in their heads; and a system of prime cost formed an essential part of *his* mental bookkeeping. After looking over the papers, he stamped up and down, inveighed against Accountants and their finicking ways, swore that he had made much more profit, that he *knew* he had, and that the books must either be arithmetically wrong, or that the money had been made away with. In support of this he made up a note in a short time, partly from memory and partly from the books, showing the main items in his trading for the year, and his result certainly did *not* reconcile with the result of the books. This note of his was really a note of the prime cost of all his contracts and the resulting profit. What was to be done? We set the manager to verify his opening and closing stocks of material, while we hunted up and down in a forlorn way for errors in the books which we could not imagine existed. At last the manager confessed that he had found a very serious error in taking his closing stock, and this, when rectified, brought the books into agreement with the mental cost results which the principal had prepared. A bad half-hour for that manager followed, and the Auditors were not altogether absolved, although the error lay entirely outwith what is considered their province.

All this, I think, bears out my contention that in very many cases the Profit and Loss Account is of little or no value to our clients in their day-to-day work. It is little more than a lump sum of profit or loss, difficult or impossible to break up into its elements. But I hold that, when supplemented by a proper system of Cost, it becomes an infallible record of the year's work, localizing the profit and loss in the most minute way.

Without some such system it is impossible to determine what parts of a business pay best, or which department is most profitable. It can hardly be ascertained whether, indeed, one department does not actually result in a deficit which is borne by the other departments; or one class of work may for years be carried on at a serious loss at the expense of other classes of work, which accordingly appear less profitable than they really are: therefore I maintain that a Trading Account is merely a storehouse of the most valuable information, of which a Cost System is the key. The profit or loss is there, and we know it is there, but we can only guess at how it came there. Or, again, I make bold to say that a mere Trading Account is not so very far removed from the crude method of ascertaining profit which consists in making up a state of affairs and comparing it with the previous state of affairs, the difference being called profit or loss, and being merely the result of a most heterogeneous mass of figures.

Indeed, I do not think I am going too far in saying that in some trades a Profit and Loss Account *without* a Cost System in connection with it is really an *irreconciled difference in the books.* The balance of profit and loss we write off, but it may be the difference of much larger profits or losses than appears on the surface; just as we know sometimes that a trifling difference in a set of books may, when investigated, prove to be the result of differences of thousands of pounds on each side.

A Cost System possesses an equally great value in enabling *estimates* to be prepared with practically absolute certainty; in enabling *contracts* to be taken in the knowledge of the cost of similar work in the past, and so giving the contractor a confidence in entering the market which he can get in no other way. When tenders are invited for work, what does the manufacturer say? "I made a similar machine," or "I did work like this before. What did it cost me?" He should be able to turn up the cost in a few minutes, and (after adjusting his data to the state of the market, after making any necessary modifications arising from changes in the price of raw material, or in the rates of wages) he should be able to prepare and make an offer without any blind guess-work, without any reckless slumping of figures, but in the knowledge that if his offer is accepted, his anticipations will probably be realised.

A knowledge of prime cost is becoming every year more essential. The tendency to ask a price before ordering is steadily growing. You will hear *that* on every side; trifling work that was formerly simply ordered right off is now first quoted for. The competition on all sides seems to be intensifying; margins are becoming reduced; and an old, and at one time valuable, connection is of no avail unless prices are right.

Every prudent man must therefore know exactly the cost of what he sells, and he must have this knowledge promptly. He cannot wait for the result of his trading until his stock-taking comes round and his books are balanced; that is not enough. With such sudden and extreme variations in wages and in prices, it is imperative to know from week to week or from month to month what the cost is, so that when any branch of a business fails to pay, the failure to pay may at once be apparent, and steps taken to suspend work in it, or perhaps restrict it until prices rise or cost can be reduced. A prompt and systematic recording of costs is in most businesses therefore a *sine quâ non*. Of course its uses are not restricted to cases where there is a fluctuating market. It is equally applicable to cases where there are standard prices subject to little variation, for these prices should always from time to time be revised by a comparison with the actual ascertained cost.

Then, again, when there is no estimating, a proper cost record is simply invaluable in making up and pricing accounts. To some men the pricing of their accounts is, I know, a horrible nightmare, and the process is always delayed as long as possible. On the other hand, where the costing department is conducted on a proper system and up to date, the pricing of work and the addition of the profit should prove a specially attractive and satisfactory part of a principal's duty.

Not only should selling under cost be guarded against; there is the equally disastrous error of selling at prices unduly over cost. With such intense competition as now rules, no matter how good or stable a firm, unless it has some peculiar specialty, or an undoubted monopoly, it cannot afford to add too large a margin and take too great a profit. Competition will be fostered and encouraged by that very fact, and perhaps ultimately oust an old firm.

An instance of that is within my own knowledge, where for years a firm had been obtaining large, regular, contracts for a special article. The orders suddenly ceased, and when they applied to know the cause, they learned that a younger firm had taken up the contract at very considerably lower rates. It turned out that the cost system of the old firm was extremely loose; they had been charging an excessive profit —without really knowing what profit they *were* charging—the customer began to think he was paying too much, obtained quotations elsewhere, found prices very considerably lower, and was so exasperated at finding he had for years been paying too much, that he transferred his custom without giving his former suppliers an opportunity of reducing their prices.

Perhaps I have now laid before you a sufficiently strong indictment of a Profit and Loss Account unsupported by a prime cost system, and also pointed out the benefits of a prompt and thorough record of prime cost. It now falls to me to satisfy you that it is comparatively easy to introduce the cost system that I am contending for, and I therefore proceed to outline a system of Cost Books.

(To be continued.)

Glasgow Chartered Accountants' Debating Society.

NOTES ON COST RECORDS:

A NEGLECTED BRANCH OF ACCOUNTANCY.

Paper read before this Society by Mr. JOHN MANN, Jun., M.A., C.A.

(Continued from our last issue.)

OUTLINE OF SYSTEM OF COST BOOKS.

Perhaps, however, I should here explain that I am fully ware that cost systems are not infrequent, and that, for istance, in every engineering business of any size, there is special costing department, all *that* I know, but, as I shall iow you, I also know that, where a system exists, the rinciples followed are not always correct. In outlining Cost ooks I cannot do more than give the *main* outlines, for details f bookkeeping vary with the business, and this is especially ue of Cost Books. Of course, every right-minded accounint would desire to see the Cost Books so completely intervoven with the Commercial Books that they formed an itegral part of the whole. This is the ideal system, and here possible it should be adopted. It is not always ossible to adopt it at first, as it is sometimes wise to creep before we gang," and it may in various cases be riser in practice to introduce a partial or incomplete ystem rather than have none at all. I shall, meantime, lescribe in its main features what I would call the thorough r *ideal system* of Cost Books, for if you have this fully in your ninds, and see through "to the backbone" as it were, what I am contending for, you will then be able to adapt that complete system, and to modify it to suit the various cases you may meet with in actual practice.

I have noted on the black board the principal books necessary to a costing system.

ORDER BOOK.

Labour.	*Material. (Invoices)*	*(Material) Stores.*	*Expenses.*
Daily Work Sheet. [Record by each man of quantity of labour on each job.] *Checks with Daily Time Book.*	Invoices of Special Goods for orders. [Per column in Purchase book.]	Daily Stores Warrants. [Record material given out of store for each job.]	Indirect expenses and Establishment charges ascertained by percentages based on past experience and calculated upon Wages alone or Wages and Material.
Weekly or Fortnightly Work Book. [Abstracted from Work Sheets and Pay Bill, and shows value of time on each job.] *Agrees with Pay Bill.*		Weekly or Fortnightly Stores Issued. [Posted from Store Warrants and shows value of material consumed in each job.] *Checked by Double Entry applied to Store Ledger.*	

COST BOOK, showing details for each job of

(1) Labour (2) Material (3) Percentage for Expenses (4) Selling Price (5) Profit or Loss

COST SUMMARIES, to complete Double Entry of Cost Books and form connecting link to Commercial books.

To begin at the beginning, when an order is given either for a customer or for stock it is recorded in an Order Book and receives a number under which it is known. If the order involves more than one distinct part or distinct article, a separate order number, or a sub-number, is given to each part; especially where t may afterwards be of use to know the cost of such distinct part—for instance, where renewals or duplicate parts may be required. These orders are duplicated and distributed to the foremen of the various departments which may be involved in the manufacture of the goods required.

A Cost Book is opened in which each order is entered as it appears, and ample space is allotted for all details of its cost. Into this book the separate records of wages and material are posted, and when completed the percentages for direct and indirect expenses are applied. When the order is completed, the result is summarized and brought into the Cost Summary. It is through the Cost Summary that the Cost Books are welded on to the Commercial Books.

I shall now take the various elements of cost *seriatim*.

As to the Labour.—Every workman must record daily the quantity of labour (not the value) spent on each job. These daily totals agree with the Daily Time Book, and are also checked by the foremen. The means taken to obtain this record vary. Weekly Sheets, or Block Books, are sometimes used, or a sheet is detached and sent in every day—or Pass Books or slates may suffice, according to circumstances.

From the daily record a weekly or fortnightly abstract is prepared, showing the quantity of time and its value as spent on each job. The total of this abstract or "Work Book," as it may be called, agrees with the weekly or fortnightly Pay Sheet—just as the daily record will agree with the Time Book. This abstract may, if necessary, show the wages paid in the different departments on each job.

The totals in the Work Book are posted to each order in the Cost Book. As I have said, the totals of the Work Book agree with the Pay Sheet, and the totals of the wages when paid are first debited to the Wages Account in the Commercial Books. To work in the Cost system, a Ledger Account is opened called *Cost Ledger Account.* The wages paid are, when balancing the Commercial Books debited to *Cost Ledger Account*, and credited to *Wages Account*, closing the latter and leaving the amount at debit of *Cost Ledger Account*.

In the Cost Book the wages spent on the various jobs are from week to week posted to the debit of the jobs, and the periodical total of such wages (taken out either periodically or when an order is completed) is credited to a *General Ledger Account* in the same Cost Book. The balance of this *General Ledger Account* should agree with the *Cost Ledger Account* in the general Ledger, thus forming the connecting link between the Cost Books and the Commercial Books.

As to Material.—Goods bought for direct use (that is, which do not require to go through any process) are so noted in the invoices—*e g.*, parts of a machine (patented appliances not made on the premises, for example)—all these are collected in a column of the Purchase Book called say *Cost Ledger Column*. Other purchases of material are debited to *Stores Account*, or to the various *Expenses Accounts*; and of course each item is credited to the merchant supplying.

The details of items in the Cost Ledger column are posted in the Cost Books to the debit of the job for which they were specially purchased, and the totals of course credited to General Ledger Account in the Cost Ledger.

As to material given out of store, a careful record must be kept, and for this it is essential to have (what is so often forgotten) a store and an intelligent storeman. No material should be given out without production of what may be called a "store warrant," granted by the foreman requiring the material. This states the order number for which the material is wanted. These warrants are posted into a Stores Issued Sheet, showing weekly or fortnightly the value of the material consumed on each job.

These total values are debited to each job in the Cost Books, and the total carried through the General Ledger Account to the credit of "*Stores Account.*" *Stores Account* will therefore be debited with the cost of stores purchased, and credited with the cost of stores used, and the balance at any point should agree with the cost of the stores on hand. Thus a very valuable result is arrived at, apart altogether from the value of a system of Prime Cost, for it becomes possible by knowing approximately the value of stock in hand to balance the whole books at shorter intervals, say quarterly or half-yearly, instead of yearly, without going through what is so often the horrible ordeal of stocktaking.

The result of the "Stores Account" may, of course, from time to time be verified with the stock actually on hand, and any discrepancy traced out. Such discrepancies might arise from under or overcharging orders, or from depreciation or appreciation of the stores, or from their disappearance.

But an *annual* stock-taking (when the stock on hand is actually weighed and counted) would suffice. The trader would know almost exactly, say every three months, what progress he was making. I am sure that balancing at shorter intervals would be appreciated by our clients when it did not involve the nightmare of stocktaking.

STOCK OR STORE BOOKS.

Although I may be wandering from my main subject, I cannot refrain from pointing out how essential is a thorough check upon stock or stores; especially where the principal cannot always or often be on the spot. Apart from manufacturing businesses, to which, of course, a cost system mainly applies, efficient Stock or Store Books can be kept, and are a great safeguard against fraud or pilfering. In large wholesale houses, for instance, the Stock Books may be checked by *quantity*. If soft goods, the number of pieces purchased of each class of goods is debited in its column day by day, and the pieces sold, credited. Pieces cut up for samples are accounted for, and the whole balances and proves with the stock sheets. That is a proof by *quantity*. This is successfully carried out in my own experience. In one case the principal has refused to sign the stock sheets till the errors were corrected, and the desired agreement arrived at.

In retail businesses a certain amount of proof may be

obtained by a check upon *values*. The salesman is debited at the start with quantities in the inventory, but at selling prices, and debited in same way with deliveries; he is credited with the total sales; and the balance at any time should agree with the stock on hand, at selling prices. This is almost always adopted in the spirit trade. In the jewellery trade, stockkeeping can, and must, be carried to perfection. There every article of stock is recorded and numbered, when sold it is credited in the Stock Book, and thus every article can be traced, and must either be accounted for by being in stock or being in the Sales Book. This, I think, is a means of checking fraud which we, as accountants, too often ignore, and you will find it wonderful in how many cases it is possible to institute this check on pilfering. It is obvious that it forms a check not only upon disappearance of stock, but against stock being sold, invoiced, and paid for but not entered in the books. Stock may not be readily stolen, but sales, especially cash sales, may not find their way into the Sales Book, and, as you know, this is a kind of fraud that we accountants cannot profess to check or find out—unless such a Stock Book as I am advocating is kept. Not only does it detect pilfering, but, as I have said, it enables the books to be balanced and the result of the trading arrived at, at any time. From still another point is it valuable, as in the event of fire it enables a very reliable claim to be made as to the quantities and value of the material and the stock on hand. I know of cases where Stock Books, and most elaborate Stock Books, were introduced mainly for this last purpose.

Direct and indirect expenses cannot be charged to each order in such a definite way as labour and material, but are applied in per centages, arrived at and applied in a manner I shall describe later on.

The amount of such expenses having been ascertained and applied, the total cost of each complete order is ascertained and stands at the debit of each in the Cost Book. The selling price having been credited, the resulting profit on each job is brought out. The Cost Book is then summarised into the Cost Ledger or Cost Summary, showing in columns for each job: (1) labour; (2) material; (3) percentage for expenses; (4) profit; (5) selling price; the latter agreeing with the Day Book after adjusting jobbing work.

The first three (wages, material and expenses) are credited to the General Ledger Accounts for "wages," "stores" and "expenses." The fourth and fifth to the Goods Account or Trading Account, when they should practically agree with the total sales and the net profit respectively. In this way you will see that the Cost Books can easily be made to fit in most thoroughly with the Commercial Books, while leaving the Commercial Books still free to be balanced without them at any time, and the profit ascertained in the usual way. The Cost Summaries or "Cost Ledgers" are generally private books for the use of the principals, and, it will be found, are of infinitely greater value to them, and much more appreciated, than the Private Ledger which is only opened at times of balancing.

ESTIMATES.

A Cost Ledger is in constant use, and no contract is made without its being referred to. Preparation of estimates is closely allied to cost keeping; indeed, the comparison of the Estimate Book and the Cost Book is one of the most instructive processes possible. If a large estimate is in preparation involving work from all departments of a large business, special detailed estimates are obtained from each department for its own work. These are then focussed and the percentages adjusted.

I show you a page of such an Estimate Book: it is of a large Shipbuilding and Engineering work.

For
Dimensions of Vessel
Speed of ,, or I.H.P.

ENGINES.
- Type of Engines
- Cylinders, Diameter, and Stroke
- Shafting
- Propeller
- Spare Gear
- Ballast Engine and Steam Connections

BOILERS.
- Type of Boilers
- No. of Boilers
- Furnaces
- Plates
- Heating Surface
- Pressure

Time for Delivery	Estimated Cost of Engines	£
	Do. do. Boilers	
Remarks		£
	Charges	
		£

	DEPARTMENTS.	Inv. Weight	Rate.	Material.	Labour.	Total Cost.
	Hull					
A	Flitch Plates,					
	Keel and Stem,					
	Stern-post and Rudder,					
	Steel Plates,					
	Iron ,,					
	Steel Angles and Bulbs,					
	Iron ,, ,,					
	,, or Steel Bulb T,					
	,, ,, ,, Angles,					
	,, ,, Z or E,					
	,, Slips,					
	,, Rivets,					
	Steel ,,					
	Total Material.					
	Labour (framing & beaming)					
B	Smithwork Department,					
	Mechanics' ,,					
C	Shipwrights' ,,					
	Joinery ,,					
	Cabinet ,,					
	Special Cabin Fittings,					
	Hardware,					
D	Brasswork,					
	Coppersmiths,					
	Plumber and Tinsmiths,					
	Painting,					
	Cementing,					
E	Deck Machinery,					
F	Boats,					
	Spars and Rigging,					
	Anchors and Chains,					
G	Cooking Apparatus,					
	Lighting Appliances,					
	Upholstery and Bedding,					
	Nautical Instruments,					
	Signals,					
	Chandlery Stores,					
	Table Furnishings,					
H	Launch and Trial Trips,					
	Fees, Tonnage, and Classification,					
	Sundries,					
	Current Charges %					
	Special Extras,					
	..nnage Bm., tons, at / ,, Gross, tons, at } Total Cost Hull, inc. % Charges.					
	Indicated HP at ,, Machy. ,, % ,,					
	Profit					
	£					

You will see that the estimated cost of engines is calculated, then of the boilers, and the total is worked out into a price per indicated horse power. Then we have no less than 39 items in the cost of the hull, each involving separate detailed estimates, either prepared in the works or obtained from outside merchants.

A proper system of prime cost, therefore, for such a yard involves bringing out separately the cost of each of those items to enable the difference between the original estimate and the actual cost to be ascertained in each department.

It may happen that some serious error may have been made in *one* department involving perhaps an under-estimate of cost which might swallow up all the profit in the contract, or it might have involved as serious an over-estimate of cost which might, on the other hand, nearly have caused the loss of the contract.

APPLICATION OF EXPENSES TO PRIME COST TO ARRIVE AT COST.

What is the principle to be followed in distributing the expenses over the various pieces of work? Is it by a percentage upon the *total prime cost* or upon the *wages alone*, or upon the *material alone*, and in the same *ratio* or in different *ratios*? Great diversity of opinion and uncertainty prevail on this subject, and the most extraordinary differences in costing have emerged from absence of a proper principle. Of course it is obvious that in a new business the probable annual expenses must be estimated; but in an established business the Trading Accounts should afford most valuable material from which a forecast of Current Expenses may be prepared, and this data being at hand, the only question is, How are the Current Expenses to be spread over the Current Work?

I shall first mention one or two simple cases.

Take, in the first place, *distributors*, or those who merely buy and sell without adding to their wares, perhaps never seeing or handling them. The principle here adopted is a uniform addition to the buying price, on the ground that the expenses, to use a mathematical phrase, *vary directly* with the turn-over. Of course, in distributive businesses, where the stock is expensive and in but limited demand (*e.g.*, jewellery or pianos), the percentage added on is large. Still it varies pretty constantly with the prime cost of the goods, as the difficulty of selling expensive stock and the interest on its cost when lying unsold coming into play tend to justify an equal rate of loading upon the cost, say, of a simple gold stud and a diamond necklace.

The principle of charging expenses in all purely *distributive* business may, therefore, be put thus:—

The cheaper and simpler the goods the easier and quicker the sale.

The easier and quicker the sale the less trouble and expense.

Therefore, expense varies directly with the cost.

Therefore, there should be a uniform addition for expenses over the total sales.

As to *Production*, which is the province with which we have principally to deal, I may first mention a simple but rather exceptional case—that of Coal Mining. In the case of coal the colliers are paid by piecework, by the quantity sent to bank, so that the wages vary directly with the quantity or output. On every pay sheet is generally noted the average cost of "winning" the coal—so much per ton at pit head. Then the coalmaster knows accurately what the weekly or fortnightly expenses of his "oncost men," as he calls them, come to, and with his output before him, he finds his prime cost at so much per ton; with the addition of royalty (if any), also at so much per ton, and general expenses, he gets his cost price per ton. In coal, therefore, the expenses may be calculated upon *the output*, not upon *the value*. For instance, a coal salesman is generally remunerated at so much per ton sold, not so much per £ of sales. The discount to customers for cash is generally 1d. per ton, not 5% or 10% as in other trades. The daily prices are so well known and yet so variable that this is found simpler, and perhaps it is a less complicated mental calculation to make "on Change" in the midst of the higgling of the market.

I might here point out that not only in coal, but in other businesses, it would be well to ascertain at *very short intervals* what the expenses amount to, so that they may be compared from week to week or from month to month. The measure of uncertainty that always attends the use of a percentage can best be minimized by comparing the assumed percentage with the actual expenses at short intervals.

Take now an ordinary Manufacturing concern, where labour is expended upon raw material. This is altogether different either from a purely *Distributive* business or a *Mining* business. I have already analysed the expenses of such a manufacturing business and broken them up into their elements. The expenses may be, in theory at least, divided into :

(1) Expense of buying in raw material or partially manufactured material. This may be said to vary directly with the cost of the goods or raw material bought. That is to say, there is the financing, correspondence, and book-keeping, of which the principal element will be the interest upon cost while they are being manufactured. Before taking the Expenses of Manufacturing proper let us turn to the other end and take another element of a manufacturer's expenses,

(2) Expenses of Selling or Distribution. This, of course, is parallel with the expense of a business solely distributive. As with expenses of *buying* raw material, it therefore varies directly with the final cost or, as I may say, with the selling price of the completed product. This is very clear, for instance, where a commission is paid for selling.

In these two cases of the Indirect Expenses, those of buying and of selling, the manufacturer can find no difficulty in applying the Expenses. For all practical purposes they vary with the turn-over.

(3) But turning now to the Expenses of Production proper (what I called before Direct Expenses—mainly superintendence and up-keep of plant and buildings), to what do these vary in proportion?

In other words, are such direct expenses of manufacturing greater or less

(1) As the *number of men* is greater or less, or
(2) As their *wages* are higher or lower, or
(3) As *material used* is greater or less in quantity, or
(4) As *material used* is higher or lower in price.

That is, do direct expenses vary

(1) With *quantity of time* worked, or
(2) With *value of time* spent, or
(3) With *quantity of material* used up, or
(4) With *value of material* used up.

This is really one of the most essential points in our whole enquiry, and is worth minute attention. Unless in very special cases (where the cost of raw material is practically the whole cost, *e.g.*, a foundry), the direct expenses of production have little or no appreciable relation either to the quantity or value of the raw material used up; the expenses certainly do not rise and fall with the markets for the raw material. We may, therefore, dismiss these two cases (*Nos.* 3 *and* 4 *above*).

I now refer, remember, to direct expenses; *part* of the indirect expenses, as I have just pointed out, do bear a relation to the value of the material used up.

We are, therefore, reduced to the *labour* expended. Do the direct expenses in theory vary with the labour? My answer is that they do—not so much with the *value* of the labour as with the *quantity*, and my conclusion is that in theory direct expenses of production bear the closest relation to the time expended, and that, therefore, in determining prime cost such direct expenses should be distributed *rateably over the work* in proportion to the *time expended* on each job.

Consider for a moment. Take a quick, expert, efficient workman: does he require as much instruction, control and supervision as a lazy, inefficient man? does he waste material, gas, water, fuel, tools as much as the lazy, inefficient man? No, he does not. Of course, if two such men get the same rate of weekly wages for working the same time, as they so frequently do under present trade union principles, it is immaterial whether we charge our direct expenses in proportion to the time spent or to the wages paid for each job. The work of the inferior man will always be more costly, and will be so shown. Now, if we charge direct expenses upon wages, the higher the wage the greater the burden of direct expenses it bears, whereas it should really be the other way. I think it clear then that direct expenses vary most closely with the time occupied on each job, and can be best applied in proportion to the time, and not the value of such time as expressed in the wages paid. Direct expenses vary directly with the time occupied, and inversely as the wages paid. This is corroborated by the admitted fact that, within certain limits, it is really cheapest in the end to employ efficient and thoroughly competent hands.

Now this as I have said is the theoretical position, but I am afraid it is rarely, if ever, carried out in costing, probably because the records of the value of wages paid for each job are of themselves such a prominent element in, costing that they are taken as the foundation for direct expenses, rather than the time occupied, which lies behind those wages. For nearly all practical purposes, however the *direct expenses may be safely applied in proportion to the wages paid*.

This elementary principle is too often ignored in practice, and direct expenses loaded on to *both* materials and labour. One instance will make apparent the necessity of more exact methods. Take the cost of the propeller or "screw" for a large Atlantic liner. If made of steel the material costs, say, £100, but in special circumstances it is made of *phosphor bronze*, which, as perhaps you know, is not so brittle, —may be knocked into almost any shape without breaking.

The comparative cost of two such propellers would by many men be made up in the following way:—

	Bronze.	*Steel.*
Material say	£700	£100
Labour "	100	100
	800	200
Expenses say 10%	80	20
Totals	£880	£220

or a difference of £60 in the expenses, although such expenses in two actual cases would hardly differ at all. The same figures will serve to point out another argument. Suppose the price of steel suddenly rose from £100 to £700 for such a propeller, why should the shipbuilder charge £60 more for the direct expenses of manufacturing? I may add that in glaring cases such as these, the principle followed is so obviously wrong that it has to be modified, but such modification must simply result in a still more arbitrary method being adopted.

According to my ideas, the proper method of comparing the cost of a bronze and a steel propeller would be as follows. The percentages are, of course, fictitious.

	Bronze.	*Steel.*
Material	£700	£100
2 per cent. for indirect expenses	14	2
Wages	100	100
20 per cent. thereon for direct expenses	20	20
Totals	£834	£222
In other	£880	£220

Here the cost of the bronze propeller is brought out £46 less than by the cruder method. This is but an exaggerated example of what is going on from day to day in, I believe, very many manufacturing businesses in Glasgow. Very few business men I have met seem to have given much thought to arriving at the true method of costing, and if I may so put it, "bad costing is costing them more than correct costing would cost." In the building trade, especially, the various quotations sent in by competing firms are often most ludicrous. In total they may be almost the same, while in various items very large and unaccountable variations appear—all going to prove how much of the estimating is purely guess-work.

There is one special method of costing adopted in works using large tools or machines—that is, to charge a fixed rate per hour for the machine, along with the workman's time; for instance, in a forge, where a steam hammer with smith and striker may be charged, say, 3s. or 5s. per hour on each job. The other, and, perhaps, the more correct method, is practically that already explained—to ascertain the wages in the usual way, and distribute the expenses, depreciation, interest, &c., over all.

In certain cases it may be possible to ascertain the number of hours run by each machine in each job; then, having estimated the use expected of the machine during the year (it may be a special machine, used upon occasion only), the hourly cost for interest, depreciation, &c., is ascertained and charged to the job. At the year's end it would be useful to make out a small Profit and Loss Account for each machine, showing how much each has earned, and whether it has really paid to have such a machine at all.

I need only repeat that, where there are several departments of a business with varying rates of expenses, it becomes necessary to distinguish the charges for each department and apply the proper percentage for each. Bear in mind that, after all, these percentages for expenses must always be regarded as approximations. The trader, however, almost instinctively applies a corrective—for, although the rate of expenses may vary from month to month, or from year to year, owing to the fluctuation of turn-over, these fluctuations of turn-over are always present to the trader's mind when fixing his selling price in the market. If his sales have fallen off he reduces his prices to attract buying, and as long as he bears steadily in mind what his Prime Cost Books teach him, he cannot go far wrong. The manufacturer should know the cost of his wares, if not absolutely, at least as accurately as possible. It will pay him to do this. I am sure it will, and, of course, let him make it part of his auditor's duty to include the Cost Books in the audit and bring them approximately at least into reconciliation with the Profit and Loss Account. This can be done, and you will be surprised, as I have been, with the trifling additional trouble it involves when once a carefully thought-out system is applied to meet the necessities of the particular case. When the record is kept up from day to day, or from week to week, as part of the ordinary duties of the bookkeeper, or as the duty of a special costing department, the whole work proceeds smoothly and satisfactorily, and in cases where costing is in use, see that it is upon a scientific and sound basis, and the client will think more of your profession and of yourself than ever he did before.

I have now, gentlemen, given you definitions of my terms; I have set forth what I deem to be undeniable advantages of a proper costing system; I have endeavoured to give you a general outline of Cost Books, omitting necessarily all special details; and, finally, I have explained some of the principles upon which I hold that the expenses direct and indirect should be allocated upon the work done. To some of you these matters are not new, but to others I believe they will indicate fresh lines of study and work.

I shall be abundantly satisfied if I have persuaded you, as I have persuaded myself, that the introduction of a cost system is a first-class way, if not the only way, by which we accountants can make our audited accounts of more immediate use, of more practical value, indeed, of essential daily value to our clients, and by so welding the system into the ordinary books that the Commercial Books and the Cost Books (while remaining distinct and performing separate functions) yet form one harmonious whole.

I believe that we only need to point out the advantages that would flow from a more general introduction of such systems, and a remodelling of existing systems, to ensure a vastly increased sphere of usefulness for ourselves. Clients who already have a system will want a proper system, and will want it to some extent audited, clients who have *no* system, and whose business admits of a system, *will have it introduced*, will gladly *pay for its introduction* and for its subsequent *supervision*. I, therefore, look forward to the time when a proper cost system will form a part of every well conducted office, and as every well-conducted office has an *auditor* just as it has a *landlord*, so the knowledge of costing principles will form part of the equipment of every trained accountant.

Manchester Chartered Accountants Students' Society.

MANUFACTURING COSTS.

By Mr. THOMAS PLUMPTON, A.C.A.

AT a meeting of the above society, held on the 14th March, 1892, Mr. PLUMPTON delivered the following lecture:—

IN the introduction of the series of lectures which it is my intention to give to the members of this Society on the duties and possible attainments in the mastery of a thorough system of costs necessary for the guidance of a manufacturing community, I shall briefly introduce the subject to-night, the magnitude of which is so great and comprehensive that, to do justice and give a clear elucidation of detail so necessary for an intricate subject, I have found it imperative to arrange the lectures in a series, in which I will give separate papers for different trades later on.

At present I shall content myself with dwelling on:—

1.—Introduction of the subject.
2.—Necessity of costs.
3.—What are Cost Accounts.
4.—Advice to students.

INTRODUCTION OF THE SUBJECT.

It should be borne in mind that, although costs are, and have been in the past, a speciality in the way of keeping accounts, yet, with the march of events and the progress of science in general, it will form one of the leading parts of a Chartered Accountant's duties in the future. The subject is of an interesting nature, and with a varied practice will certainly develop a studious mind; and, like the problems in the books of Euclid which our students so ably master for their examinations, it will be found to explain the "why and wherefore" in their various details.

Hitherto the nature of the duties falling to the sphere of accountants has been confined to some few leading points or parts of their practice, and like the medical faculty, some of the members have entirely devoted themselves to certain branches of the profession. But with the advent of our Institute of Chartered Accountants, which I am happy to say has of recent years found appreciation with the manufacturing community, it behoves us, as members of a recognised profession, to so direct our studies that nothing in the vocabulary of figures will be beyond our comprehension or manipulation, and we must put forth our energies in every direction conducive to the interests of our clients, so that the standard mark defined by the term "Chartered Accountant" will be the test of efficiency on which a client may pin his faith that he will receive every assistance in the management of his business that can be obtained by the use of accounts. Furthermore, our members will feel that, when a client's business is placed under their supervision, a moral responsibility rests upon them to so direct the accounts as to give the acme of results attainable.

NECESSITY OF COSTS.

In a lecture I gave you a short time ago on the Practice

of Auditing, I dwelt strongly upon some of the weak points, and the object of my paper to-night is to carry further the arguments there adduced. I laid particular stress on the fact of the auditor contenting himself with tracing the liquid items of consumption and production to Profit and Loss Account, and thus terminating his research, resting content on the arithmetical accuracy of the figures; and the only tangible piece of information for his client being the amount of profit or loss during the period under supervision.

Manufacturers need more assistance than what is ordinarily contained in an audit. They require assistance in their costs; for, in these times of keen competition, where a slight deviation of prices controls and directs large contracts, it naturally follows that, to successfully control a manufacturing business, the costs of production must be correctly ascertained, and no such business can firmly maintain their prosperity without a thorough and correct system of costs.

As an instance, no firm of engineers would seek to carry on their business without some description of costs, for it is the backbone of their business. They must systematically work up cost accounts on, say, different kinds of machinery, by analysis of wages paid to workmen, and dissemination and recapitulation of the various purchases that are used or consumed in the manufacture of their productions, to be able to know whether quotations of prices are resulting in profit or loss.

Now, it is an inherent part of an engineer's business to know the cost of every kind of machine or engine or boiler that he makes, to ascertain whether he has made any profit or otherwise, and it forms a guide, and a valuable one, to him when in the future he has enquiries for a similar article. Again, if an engineer has various departments, such as a foundry, a boiler-yard, a forge, and numerous other departments generally found in a millwright's or general engineering establishment, it is necessary that his accounts should be so regulated that he may tell at the end of each year whether departments are making their manufactures at less cost than he can buy any particular branch of production in the market. Frequently it happens that they find, with the keen competition before them, that they cannot make or carry on certain departments except at a loss; hence they often choose to buy from others that may happen to be better managed or have more special advantages of production. As another example, take the case of a shipbuilder. A ship is required to be built, and estimates are obtained from various firms. These frequently vary; and it very often happens that, in judging an estimate, the standing reputation and manufacture of the firm is weighed in the balance. But just let us look into the matter, and see how it comes to pass that a shipbuilder can make out his estimate for completing a ship. Why, the secret lies in the fact that, by a system of costs and years of experience and work, he can tell the cost, not only of every ship, but of every part of a ship; he can, on reference to his cost books, tell how much it has cost from the laying down of the keel to the erecting in frames, the rivetting and plating of the sides, the building of the bulkheads, the carpentry work in laying down the decks and bulwarks, the costs of his engines and boilers, the rigging and fitting-up of the masts, the furnishing of the cabins, the painting and decorating of the ship, and its final outfit.

It may be argued that these instances that I have drawn out are the practical results which are obtainable through the medium of engineers working out their quantities. Let me dispel that illusion, for I can assure you that the most carefully drawn estimates have often been found deceptive, and nothing but absolute figures of results (more especially where labour is concerned) are reliable, and these results are only obtainable through what is called the cost office. This department has hitherto been a secret closed chamber to the professional accountant, for it has been presumed by the public that an accountant's duty is simply to furnish a financial statement; and manufacturers have considered that such work could best be accomplished by the election of men who had been trained as specialists, even so much so that whenever a vacancy has occurred in the cost office they have seldom sought assistance from the ranks of Chartered Accountants. I will certainly admit that hitherto the scope of our profession has to a great extent been debarred from such practical work, but I consider the vista opening out before us. In future it will bring a vast amount of such work to our profession. As an instance, last year my assistance was required in the formation, designing, and establishing of a thorough system of departmental costs in a large steel works not many miles from here, a firm that employs some 1,500 workmen.

I may say the results were satisfactorily worked out, and each department was charged with its own consumption and credited with its own production, showing results which afterwards proved the accuracy of the work by verification with the total profit in the Balance Sheet.

Another illustration to show you the necessity of Cost Accounts: take the case of a chemical manufacturer. It is a well-known fact that certain chemicals are made through the result of certain mixtures; all these mixtures have their relative component parts. Well-known and successful chemical manufacturers would never have obtained their successes in business without most elaborate Cost Accounts, which materially assist them in knowing how to fix prices upon the market for their manufactures.

I may tell you that a successful chemist must be a mathematician, so that he may know exactly how to mix his various ingredients, and it naturally follows that his business cannot be carried on with any success without correct and accurate accounts being kept of the chemicals used in the various processes, and he even goes to the extent of weighing every barrow-load of coal that is used in the burning of the furnace. It may seem startling when enunciating such detail as I have described, but I can assure you that when a thorough system is laid down, the accounts work as smoothly as the fine little wheels in a watch, with everything in its place, and nothing getting out of order—an occurrence which, should it happen, is soon detected by the practised eye.

Collieries also keep elaborate Cost Accounts of their workings; the expenditure of wages alone is divisible over numerous descriptions of work done, followed by materials consumed, steam power, royalties, wagons, &c., and the standing trade charges, which, on being calculated upon the tonnage of coal produced, give their respective costs, and, on comparison with previous periods, soon show when any leakage takes place and from which source the remedy is applicable.

Builders who contract to build various buildings, although in a great measure protected by the architects' bills of quantities, find it is necessary to keep the costs of the various stages of the building to prevent waste, which may turn a remunerative contract into a loss.

There are many other manufacturing trades, all absolutely requiring the keeping of correct costs of the work in progress, about which I will not further digress.

The neglect to keep a perfect system of Cost Accounts has frequently resulted in the non-success of many manufacturing concerns, and it is the most suicidal policy possible for any firm to blindly manufacture goods and sell them without knowing their cost, simply because other firms are quoting the same prices; acting on the rule-of-thumb system that because their neighbours or competitors prosper they may do likewise. There may be elements in their competitors' works which they are almost entirely ignorant of, such as more modern machinery, better skilled workmen, and the general labour-saving arrangements of the works, cheaper access for goods by water carriage, and numerous other details that may give one firm decided advantages over others. Hence each manufacturer should thoroughly grasp such leading facts as the cost of his own productions. I once had an argument propounded that the keeping of Cost Accounts would not influence or raise the market prices of manufactured goods. Certainly not; but such Accounts would teach the manufacturer where the elements of cost lay, so that he could direct his energies to cheapen any excesses and increase the margin of profit.

Surely, it must never be forgotten that goods are an equivalent to money, and, as every trader is careful to see that the indebtedness created by the purchase of same is discharged by a cash payment, he should with equal zeal follow that transformed cash payment in the shape of the goods purchased through its various ramifications until returnable again in the shape of a cash receipt from a customer. Hence I declare that the uses of materials should be as minutely followed as current coin of the realm would be; manufacturers who have monopolies never know how soon younger firms may spring up to compete with and endeavour to wrest the trade from them.

Again, where many departments are at work making separate manufactures, unless their respective costs are kept it might just be possible that some departments are being worked at a loss, but the profit-earning power of other departments on the business being massed as a whole entirely hides from view the losses aforementioned, which may travel on for years undiscovered, whereas, on true departmental costs, such an event would soon be discovered and remedied or curtailed. Frequently I have heard manufacturers allege that they buy their materials at a price, and sell their manufactures at a price, sufficient to leave a good trade margin for profit, and, calculating on this basis by the turnover, conclude that a certain gross profit has been earned; yet, when their financial year terminates and a Balance Sheet prepared, they are startled at the non-realisation of their anticipations of profits. Another great feature in the advocacy of costs is the fact that, on similar lines to the tracing of money to its final extinction, so does a perfect system of costs trace all materials until consumed or transferred into another shape; that the door for defalcations is entirely closed, for I can assure you that known instances have occurred in my experience where both materials and finished goods have disappeared from the manufacturer's premises during regular business hours, apparently in the regular mode of trading, without even being recorded in the firm's books. Such matters could not occur where a system of Cost Accounts were kept, for it would be plainly visible where the leakage occurred. Furthermore, it is essential that a manufacturer should know periodically what the costs of his productions are, without waiting until the financial year terminates, and then be informed generally of the total result of the year's trading, for verily it is then like telling him to close his stable door after his steed is gone.

Passing now to another part of the subject, viz.:-

"WHAT ARE COST ACCOUNTS?"

These accounts are practically records of goods passing through the various stages of manufacture, with their respective values being determined at each stage. There are many systems in vogue. I have frequently seen an engineer's cost of an engine or boiler, partly made up in the drawing office from quantities worked out on the drawings, partly from the firm's accounts, finishing up with approximations to cover incidentals, without any reconciliation with the year's profit in the Balance Sheet. Such a system is most dangerous and misleading, there being no safety in the results against blunders, and they are the frequent causes of the discrepancies in many tenders for the same work by different firms.

The only true and correct system of Cost Accounts is that worked out on double entry system. This may be done by the Commercial Accounts being interwoven with the Cost Accounts; but, inasmuch as in large concerns that is almost unworkable owing to the magnitude of the work, then in such cases abbreviate the Impersonal Accounts in the General Commercial Books, and open up separate Cost Ledgers to take up the threads where the Commercial Books terminate, making the Cost Accounts form a system of double entry within themselves, free and apart from the Commercial Accounts, but the total result of profit agreeing with the same figure in the Balance Sheet. The advantages of making the Commercial Books entirely separate and distinct from the Cost Books are, that the regular counting house work is not disturbed, and certain results of trading, such as total amounts of purchases, sales, wages, &c., are available as before, and the further detail is ascertainable in the Cost Accounts, in whatever line of business, added to which is the privacy thus secured.

Of course, in a comparatively small business, it would be more advantageous to amalgamate the Commercial Accounts with the Cost Accounts, keeping a Cost Ledger with the requisite accounts for departments, and posting direct both purchases, sales and direct charges, and apportioning indirect charges and trading expenses with further Analysis Books for full details. I think it may interest you to hear the leading heads of such a system as I recommend. Take first that of a workman's wages. I have in my mind a firm where I have audited, who pay nearly £1,000,000 a year as wages to workmen. Presuming that such a vast amount of money was paid in a mercantile sense, it will be manifest to you that a correct record of every payment should appear and be specifically charged to every separate individual, in order to discharge and exculpate the trader from his liabilities. In designing Cost Accounts, a manufacturer looks upon every payment to his workmen as discharging a liability, from which he naturally expects a compensating asset in the form of work in progress. Further, he so arranges his departments as to be able to check the amount of wages paid in each separate department; or, if he should be an engineer or a shipbuilder, he generally has his productions regulated in numerals, and the first progress begins with the analysis of his weekly wages. I may say that every employer of labour keeps a Wages Book, in which every man's hours worked per day are regularly recorded; so that, by keeping a proper Wages Book recording the men's time, with description of work engaged upon, the hours worked each day, with the total hours each week, at his rate per hour and the amount paid each man, by a simple process of analysis, the cost in wages of each man, and the respective work that he has been engaged on during the week, with the total cost upon each class of work, can be with ease ascertained. And, if each department has its own Wages Book, the matter is further simplified. When, however, as in the case of engineers, a system of numerals are adopted, then further detail is required to ascertain the expenditure upon each of these costs of the week in wages. Next follows the purchases. If, in the case of departments only, then each invoice of purchase should be duly marked with the particular stamp of the department, saying where the goods have gone to; but if, as previously described, order numerals or numerals of costs are adopted, then such particular purchases require further analysis so as to bring the purchase chargeable to the particular order for which it was intended.

Now, the most difficult part of Costs next comes--Internal Departmental Exchanges. I mean by that, where a manufacturer has many departments, and some of these departments are small compared to the amount of his manufactures, such as, we will say, mills and forges where the raw material is produced by its originating department, requiring machining or manipulation to bring it out in the form of a finished article. Again, take the case of a foundry, which is a department producing numerous castings; these castings in a raw state are passed on to other departments to be machined, and worked down to the requisite form required by the firm's customer.

It is found necessary to ascertain the separate costs of each department,--that is, the working cost of maintenance of the intermediate departments,--in order to arrive at the enhanced value put on the work in progress. Of course it is needless to tell you that, as the manufacture progresses in the separate stages, the work in progress becomes of enhanced value until final completion is reached.

Direct expenses, such as the management of departments by foremen, managers, &c., unless they can be specially assigned to separate departments, are divisible by a percentage upon the wages expended.

Indirect expenses, such as office management, commissions, directors' fees, auditors, rates and taxes, &c., are divisible by a percentage upon the value of the output.

Sales are, of course, divisible as credits to the various departments, as also are the stocks at the end of the financial year.

I have necessarily made my preceding sketch of Cost Accounts brief, in view of the greater detail that I intend giving when treating the subject later on in subsequent lectures, specifying different trades; and my object will be accomplished if I can awaken a sufficient interest in my hearers to study Cost Accounts, and prove the possibility of a Chartered Accountant becoming a master of Cost Accounts with a slight knowledge of the technicalities.

I fully comprehend the difficult task before me of making myself understood, bearing in mind that in early youth I had the advantage of a thorough training in a large engineering concern, manufacturing locomotive and marine engines, boilers, and every kind of machinery, where the Cost Accounts were so interwoven with the Commercial Accounts as to form an integral part of the whole on the system known as the Italian System, which until recent years was so universally adopted. Besides, I had the advantage of frequent inspections of the manufactures whilst in progress, which materially assisted my comprehension of the costs, afterwards followed by a similar experience in shipbuilding; and during my professional career I have kept the Cost Accounts of large chemical manufacturers and others. I found that once the principles were thoroughly grasped it was perfectly immaterial to what business they were applied, and no difficulty was found in reconciling the accounts to suit the respective trades.

ADVICE TO STUDENTS.

I have now explained briefly the merits of a system of Cost Accounts by which we, as Chartered Accountants, can make ourselves much more valuable to our clients than our profession has been in the past. To some of you, doubtless, the subject is not entirely new, but to others it will open up a new feature of study to the advantage of themselves and the profession generally. Clients only need the advantages explained and see the system developed, to warmly embrace the results attained; and those who have an imperfect system will gladly allow us to reconstruct and put them on a proper system with subsequent supervision, which will tend to add to the duties and emoluments of our profession by increased work for our members, which I can assure you will be very acceptable when we consider the encroachments by Government officialism in other directions. I am sure that our students will find due appreciation, when passing their examinations, of any knowledge displayed in the way of Cost Accounts, for the examiners know the value of such knowledge.

If I have convinced you, as I am convinced myself, of the necessity of the introduction of a perfect system of Cost Accounts amongst the manufacturing community, then at no distant date I may rejoice to see the profession generally actively engaged upon such work; for, assuredly, it materially adds to our practice and status by maintaining the commercial stability of our clients, and guiding them clear of those financial rocks called losses in trading which bring disaster and wreckage; and let us prove to the world that our mission is to save, restore, and maintain the prosperity of those who put their faith in us, and, as a body, we will earn that sterling test of merit for which our Institute of Chartered Accountants is so justly proud of maintaining for its members.

Manchester Chartered Accountants Students' Society.

MANUFACTURING COSTS AS APPLIED TO ENGINEERING.

By Mr. Thomas Plumpton, A.C.A.

A paper read at a meeting of this society, held 24th October, 1892.

According to the promise of detail given in my introductory lecture of the series of lectures that I intend givin to this society on Manufacturing Costs, I have adopted in this paper the trade of Engineering, and as I have previously dealt with the necessity of costs, and other preliminary matters relative thereto, I will not further dwell thereon, but at once proceed to the subject on the supposition that my audience have previously read my introduction of these subjects.

ENGINEERING.

The branches of Engineering are numerous in their variety, some firms adopting special lines, and producing specialities such as pumps, wheels and pulleys, aqua-thrusters, sprinklers, cotton machinery, and other varieties too numerous to mention, all of which claim the right to be called Engineering, but for the purpose of my paper I shall ignore all offshoots of the original standard of "Engineering," and delineate the accounts of a thoroughly equipped and substantial manufactory of engineering, where the raw materials enter the establishment, and only leave it in the form of locomotives, marine and stationary engines, boilers of all descriptions, forgings, cranes, steam hammers, machines,&c.,&c.,which practically means that I shall conduct my hearers through all the respective departments wherein the component parts are manufactured, and explain them in as simple language as possible, bearing in mind that I have to deal with technicalities which may or may not be known to my audience.

Engineers must of necessity keep correct costs of their manufactures, in fact they could not possibly carry on their business without costs. It forms a key-note to all their estimates, because, frequently they are given repeat orders, and if they found the previous order unproductive, they can then say so, and seek a better price, or economise the production. Costs are absolute facts, and facts are stubborn things to gainsay, not so with estimates, which are generally very elastic, and the most carefully drawn estimates are but approximations.

If I was addressing an audience of Engineers, the trade technical terms would require no explanation whatever, but to make my paper interesting to my hearers, I have to use phraseology that is comprehensible to the uninitiated and of easy assimilation of the subject to enlightened minds. With that object in view I have considered it necessary as a prelude to the stating of accounts to familiarise my audience with a brief recital and explanation of the respective departments.

I do not intend to give a practical essay on Engineering, but sufficient description as will be explanatory of the accounts which follow.

Now let me picture to your view such an establishment as I have previously described, employing say about 1,000 men, and having drawing offices, pattern shops, foundries, forges, smithies, machine shops, fitting and erecting shops, &c., &c., all necessary for the production of the completed articles. Let me be your guide for a few minutes, and show you around the works. We first approach a large set of gates which, on being opened, ushers us into the factory, as doubtless some of my hearers are aware: the first sensations of the noise of hammering, exhaust steam, smoke, and the busy appearance of the workmen, each man apparently occupied on his own work, apart from his neighbour, all pass in review before the visitor, and cause him to wonder how all this bustle and activity can be encompassed and accurately gauged in accounts. So much for the first blush after the first sensations are over.

I will now take you through the departments, beginning with the

DRAWING OFFICE.

We here enter a long, well-lighted office where all noise is carefully excluded, or as much so as possible, where are seated some draughtsmen busy engaged making the working drawings for separate parts of engines, boilers, or whatever is going on in the shops. This department, as you will perceive, is where all orders are issued to the various foremen of departments by the Chief Draughtsman, who alone is responsible for any inaccuracies in the drawings which may cause a block in the works. We next come to the

PATTERN SHOP.

Here we find a number of men like joiners making curious shaped articles in woodwork, perhaps we may find a large piece of framework being put together on the floor with curious knobs, &c. This would probably be a pattern for what is called a bedplate or foundation frame for an engine. Here and there we find some wooden spur wheels: in fact everything made in this department is of wood and principally for the foundries. These wood patterns are made specially from drawings supplied from the Drawing Office. Any defect here in the construction, if not detected before leaving the department, might cause a large casting in the foundries to be worthless, for all castings in iron or brass are made from patterns supplied from this department, and the foreman is responsible for any blunders: so it is necessary for him to prove that he has worked true to his drawings. We now pass on to the

CAST IRON OR METAL FOUNDRY.

On entering the foundry we find the building generally constructed like a large shed with only a roof and four walls, usually with pillars down the centre supporting travelling cranes overhead near the roof, and a cupola or melting furnace at one end where the iron is melted, and the floor is covered with dark loamy sand. Here will be found a number of workmen called "moulders" making, what would appear to the uninitiated, numerous kinds of imitations of pieces of machinery in the loamy soil of the floor, encased in iron frames called "moulding boxes," very like what a little boy endeavours to make on the sands at the seaside, but much more effectual: for all these moulds are made from wood patterns supplied from the "pattern shop," and are true and accurate to a nicety, for it is by these moulds, after they have been tempered and hardened, that the liquid iron is poured into, which makes the casting, and if we watch the moulder a few minutes we shall see what tiny steel tools of peculiar shapes he uses in following his avocation. We now turn to the lower end of the shop where the cupola or melting furnace is fixed; we see that it is in full blow, for they have been working at it for some hours, getting up a heat of molten iron. The ordinary cupola or melting furnace is generally built vertical (*i.e.*, upright), being constructed wider at the base or bottom part, and tapering into the size of a chimney at the roof, from the base to the charging platform it is generally built of firebrick to stand the heat, after which it is sometimes continued in brickwork or iron casings. Standing at the base of the cupola you will hear the buzzing noise of the blast fan driven by steam blowing a strong current of air into the cupola which causes the charges to burn (such charges after the first lighting of the cupola consists of alternate mixings of metal and coke spread in layers) until a sufficient quantity of metal is molten for the intended castings to be made that day. Now we see simultaneously with the preparations at the cupola that the moulders have been finishing their moulds and have got all their covers on called "moulding boxes" with weights or iron fasteners called dogs to keep them firm, with inlet gutters to receive the molten iron, and ready for the casting operations shortly to be commenced. All is now activity, for the overhead crane is travelling along with the empty ladle hung on its chains to the cupola to receive its quantity of molten iron, soon the bottom of the cupola is tapped and out rushes the molten stream of iron down a prepared staple into the iron ladle placed ready to receive it. After the ladle has received its quantity, the cupola is plugged and the flow of molten iron stopped: the overhead crane then lifts its burden and carries the ladle of the molten iron down to the moulds, then by a hand-wheel arrangement the ladle is gently canted, or sometimes it is arranged like the furnace with a plughole and spout at the bottom, which is gently tapped and the molten iron allowed slowly to flow into the moulds. Great care is here used to avoid accidents, for should any of the gear give way many lives might be lost by the scattering of the molten iron over and around the number of men necessarily engaged in the operations of casting.

A few hours suffice to solidify the molten iron, and soon the overhead crane is at work lifting off the covers called "moulding boxes"; and, as the casting operations generally occur in the afternoon, on the next day the now solid castings will be lifted out of their position and removed to some other part of the shop into the care of men called the "fettlers." These men with hammer and chisel will clean the castings of all sand and knock off all superfluous excrescences and make them ready to be passed to the machine shop for planing, drilling, &c., of which I will treat later on.

The principal materials used in the foundry consist of pig iron of various brands, which are so mixed in the melting, according to their respective brands, as to give the desired hardness or otherwise to the varied castings, also scrap metal, coke, lamp black, blacking, charcoal, loam sand, and numerous other details. We now pass on to the

BRASS FOUNDRY.

This department is somewhat differently arranged than the Cast Iron Foundry, for instead of seeing the vertical or upright cupola to melt the metal, we find a coke furnace sunk underground, the top of which is level with the floor, with traps or apertures for lowering conical shaped fireclay pots (called crucibles) containing the metals direct into the furnace, but so arranged that each pot will stand erect in the hot furnace until the intense heat penetrates through the pot, and so melts the metal it contains, much on the principle of boiling a kettle of water. It is interesting to watch how the men can deftly lower and hoist out of the furnace the crucible pots, with long iron plyers, without spilling the liquid metals or yet breaking the pots, which are, when withdrawn, under an intense heat, for assuredly the melting of the ingredients for brass castings requires a much greater heat than iron.

You will have noticed, when looking at the engines on board of the Isle of Man steamers, that all the parts where most friction arises are made in brasswork, such as the bushes on the bearings, &c. Well, brass is a metal that is softer than iron or steel, and will bear friction until worn away like boot leather; but let me tell you that there are many alloys of brasswork, from the cheap and common brass pipes and fittings used by plumbers to the gun metal brass used in the best engine work: the former has a large percentage of lead, and the latter consists principally of block tin, which generally costs about £100 per ton. I mention these facts to show that the skill of the brassfounder lies in making his alloys to suit the purpose intended.

With the exception of the furnace and the use of crucible pots, the work here in moulding and casting is similar to the other foundry, which I will not repeat. We will now direct our steps to the

FORGES.

As we enter the forge we hear the heavy thuds of the powerful 100-ton steam hammer, probably busy forging the propeller shaft for a pair of marine engines, or the less heavy but more frequent blows of the 20- or 30-ton hammers, the former making the ground vibrate as we walk. Near it we see men withdrawing the "heats" from the furnaces, and placing them on the anvils to receive the blows of the steam hammers, to reduce what seems a mass of pulp into shape.

On looking around we see heaps of scrap and malleable iron, that is, numbers of pieces of iron in all conceivable shapes probably some old boiler plates, clippings from the boiler yard, or from shipbuilders, and varieties of collections from dealers, but let me add that all this scrap iron must be of wrought iron, that is, iron that has been hammered, and on no account must cast iron be found amongst it; because when once iron has been made malleable it will always anneal again when heated and placed under the hammer. We see a few men busy at the scrap, taking large pieces to a shearing machine and clipping them small; further on, we see other men neatly piling the small pieces into blocks of about a cubic foot, these blocks are placed in the furnace, and when under a sufficient heat, all the small pieces run together and form a solid block called "a bloom," which, after a few blows from the steam hammer, is converted into a solid piece of iron, ready, when again heated, to be added on the forging that the men are making, so that you will readily understand that all those massive iron forgings about a pair of engines are made by numberless small pieces of iron heated up and hammered together.

The foreman of the forges is supplied with drawings or sketches by the drawing office, from which he makes the forgings. I may here say that all forgings are made somewhat larger than the articles will be when finished, because they require machining down to the desired sizes, and turned smooth, which makes that polish when seen fitted up in an engine. Having now explained the workings of the forges, we will pass to the

SMITHIES.

On entering this department we see a number of small fires or hearths, and at each one a smith—or what is commonly called a "blacksmith"—with his assistant, called his "striker," are busy at work. The smith is deftly handling with a pair of plyers or tongs small pieces of iron which he has just withdrawn hot from his firehearth, and placed upon his anvil. He is busy hammering them into various shapes. The assistant, or striker, stands near with a larger hammer (called a quarter hammer) ready to give the heavy blows when required by the smith. You will notice numbers of tools hanging on the walls within easy reach; these have all got their uses, and are fixed in strands of wood (being twigs of bushes or small trees): some of these tools are for the purpose of making the iron round or square, or twisting the iron into any fantastical shape; for malleable iron when hot is very pliable, it is only when cold that it hardens.

The smiths make all the small articles that are required about an engine or machine, such as bolts, nuts, handles, levers, crank pins, and numerous variety of things requirèd; —all made to certain sizes given in drawings or sketches—also finishes off the rough parts of forgings. We will now pass on to the

BOILER SHOP.

As we enter this department the noise of the rivetters hammering away on hollow shells of boilers is somewhat deafening, in fact, sometimes we have to speak into each other's ears. I do not know what other effect it has upon the men, but more or less they become hard of hearing. The foreman is supplied with full and complete working drawings of the boilers that he has to make, and for what they are intended; his plates are specifically ordered to certain sizes, and brands numbered with the number on the drawings. His first care is to see from his drawings that he has got all the plates requisite before commencing to construct the boiler, otherwise a block will occur with the men, and the work delayed. I may here say the drawings show exactly all seams of plates and where the bendings occur, for, as doubtless you are all aware, boilers are not made like square tanks, but round or oblong squares, and various other shapes in marine boilers to fit the ships for which they are intended. The men called "platers" take the plates in hand and first mark off all the parts where rivet holes have to be made; then the plates are taken to the punching machine and, where these marks appear, holes are punched through the plates, after which they are passed through the rolls or bending machine. Then follows the fixing together to form the boiler—here and there possibly some plates will require clippings to be taken off. Finally, the platers, after getting all the plates in position, insert screw bolts in the rivet holes so as to keep the fabric together. And if the work to this point is true to the drawings and fits well, the outer shell of the boiler is ready for the rivetters, who are another set of men quite distinct from the platers, and usually work in sets of three men and a boy, two of whom are called "rivetters," the third is called the "holder on," and the boy is called the "heater," because he works with a small portable smith's fire and heats the rivets (which, by the way, are similar to nails, but larger and thicker, and usually have good round heads) these rivets are passed by the boy red-hot in a pair of pinchers to the third man (usually inside the boiler), he in turn with his pinchers picks up the hot rivet and inserts it through the holes of the two plates which are being seamed together, and having a large hammer he places it against the head of the hot rivet that he has just inserted so that the two men on the other side may, with their smaller hammers, by numberless raps, while the rivet is still hot, gradually hammer the end of the rivet until it is flattened into a head on the outside of the boiler; and when cold the rivet tightens the two plates together, and is fixed by having two heads, one on each side, and thereby cannot work loose.

What I have explained refers to hand rivetting, and in making marine boilers for ships the work cannot be done otherwise on account of their shape, but for the ordinary egg-ended boiler, many boiler makers do this work by a "rivetting machine" driven by hydraulic power, and the boiler is first screwed together and ended up by a tower hoist in front of the rivetting machine. The hot rivet is then inserted into the holes of the plates, and the machine with one pressure does the work of the three men previously described.

After being rivetted together, and the internal flues fixed, in the case of marine boilers for ships, in lieu of the open space above the firehole to contain the water (which boils and creates steam) certain brass tubes are inserted longitudinally or length ways, so as to keep the water and steam in circulation, these are called multitubular or marine boilers.

When finally finished, the boiler is put under hydraulic pressure to test all seams and tensile strains, after which it is then ready for delivery.

Hitherto I have only spoken of boilers, but in this department there are generally quantities of girders and bridge work turned out, details of which I will pass over, and take you forward to the

COPPERSMITHS' SHOP.

It is in this department that all the copper pipes are made for connecting the boilers with the engines. These pipes are made from sheet copper by a coppersmith and his assistant, who is merely his labourer. Certain wood templates or patterns of the intended pipes required, with all their bendings and twistings so as to go around corners, are supplied to the coppersmith. He cuts from the sheets of copper a slip and makes his pipes therefrom. This is a small department, and one coppersmith will generally be able to make all the copper pipes required for an establishment like what I have pictured.

I have now taken you through all the producing departments, that is, departments from which all the component parts of engines originate; you will bear this in mind when dealing with the Cost Accounts. We will now proceed to the intermediate or finishing departments, where the products from the producing departments are passed on for final completion, such as the

MACHINE SHOP.

Here we find a large well-lighted shop, consisting of a room partly of glass and four walls. Down the centre of the shop are a row of pillars supporting rails which carry the overhead cranes that are used in lifting heavy pieces of enginework, &c. In this department are all kinds of machines used for the purpose of planing, drilling, cutting slots or grooves, in the rough castings from the foundry, and forgings from the forges, and in all respects for making the rough parts adaptable for their places when being put together to form a complete engine or machine. Now I might here digress upon the different classes of machines in operation, but neither time nor space will permit: suffice it to say that a visit would give a better impression. However, I may say that the men here engaged are called "machinists," who control their machines, and execute their work to drawings or sketches supplied by the drawing office; the men do their work with care, for if an eighth part of an inch was taken off in excess the casting or forging might be rendered useless for its purpose.

Of course, it necessarily follows that the component parts of engine work, after having been passed through the process of machining, as described, are of enhanced value thereby although of diminished weight; consequently records of the cost are kept, particulars of which will be seen in the accounts later on. We next come to the

FITTING AND ERECTING SHOP.

It is in this department that all the relative parts of engines, machines, cranes, &c., &c., are collected together, and for the first time fitted together. The results of all other departments are here shown. Blunders (if any) are now detected, for all parts of the engine or machine are required to be fitted in its place to form a complete engine or machine &c., which, when erected, is put under steam and tested to the satisfaction of any inspectors that may have been deputed to inspect the work during its progress, and if proved satisfactory, then dissected and packed and delivered. Such an establishment as I have depicted would also have a

JOINER'S SHOP,

where a few joiners would be kept to repair buildings, make tools for the respective departments, making packing cases to pack all the small parts of machinery, and numberless other small matters too numerous to mention.

Having completed our ramble around the works, I finally lead you into the stores.

STORES.

It is here that all the promiscuous consumable articles required by all the departments are deposited on first arrival after purchase; it is simply a distributing department, more like a hardwareman's shop than anything else, and forms a depot where all departments can draw upon for such articles as oils, tallow, spunyarn, files, Indiarubber goods, pressure gauges, small brasswork, and numberless other things, which on being served out are duly recorded, and the separate departments or working costs charged with the materials withdrawn.

Hitherto I have purposely refrained from looking in at the counting house or commercial office, but having exhausted our survey of the works, we will now direct our steps to the

COUNTING HOUSE, OR COMMERCIAL OFFICE.

As anticipated, we now approach the business books of the firm, and, as my mission is the Cost Office, I will content myself by stating that the firm keeps the Commercial Accounts by double entry, that is to say, there are the following books:—

Cash Book.
Day Book.
Purchase Invoice Book.
Bought and Sold Ledgers.
Nominal Ledger.
Private Ledger.

And that the Balance Sheet gives particulars of liabilities and assets in the usual way, and the Profit and Loss Account shows the relative purchases, sales, wages, expenses, and other details—all of which I have no desire to change, for the system I shall endeavour to describe in Cost Accounts will not in any way interfere with the foregoing, but form a separate and distinct set of Double Entry Accounts, avoiding the detail of information relative to Personal Accounts, but giving minute detail of costs. We will now pass on to

THE COST OFFICE.

This is now the leading point of my paper to-night, for I am about to explain to you what has been for years, and is to a fair extent now, a "secret closed chamber," where no other members of the staff are allowed to assist, not even the professional auditor of the firm or company; only the principals or managing directors are permitted access to its secrets. And very properly so, for (with such keen competition as at present in the market) were it openly known in what line or direction certain firms made their profits, they would have many imitators, and eventually old-established firms would lose their grip of the markets for their productions.

The only exception that I would allow is the firm's professional auditor, for surely he should have their confidence, especially if wisely selected from the ranks of Chartered Accountants, besides the assistance he can give in the arrangement and design of the Cost Accounts is being felt and appreciated by manufacturers.

Having now explained the importance of secrecy in the work, I will proceed to explain how the Cost Books should be designed.

COST ACCOUNTS.

The system that I advocate for a concern like the one I have depicted would be on purely double-entry lines consisting of—

1. Net Cost Ledger (Nominal Accounts and Departments).
2. " (Engines, Boilers, Cranes, Hammers and Order Numbers).
3. Journal.
4. Day Books for Departmental Issues.
5. Wages Books.
6. Abstract Books.

Although the Cost Books are arranged separate and apart from the Trading or Commercial Books, yet as the intention is at the end of each financial year to make both sets of books agree as to the profit shown on the Balance Sheet, I now refer you to Form No. 1 for particulars of my first or starting Balance Sheet, dated 31st December, 1891, which for the nonce I have called the Ouseburn Engine Works.

With the Balance Sheet before me, I at once proceed to make the opening entries in the Cost Journal, because I always advocate that the books should show the source from whence entries arise without trusting to loose papers, which may get lost.

On turning to Form No. 2, being the Cost Journal, you will see how the entries are made. The first entry is by a debit to Capital Account and Credit Mortgage Account, Sundry Creditors Account and Bills Payable Account. The second entry is by debiting Land and Buildings Account, Plant, Machinery, and Fixtures Account, Loose Tools Account, Sundry Debtors, Bills Receivable, Bank, Cash in Hand Accounts. Then follows the dissection of the various stocks, as it is the intention of opening up these Departmental Accounts, viz., Iron Foundry, Brass Foundry, Forge, Boiler Yard, Smithies, Timber, Copper Shop and Stores. Next follows the costs of work in progress under their respective numbers of the Engines, Boilers, Cranes, Hammers and Order Numbers, the whole of which is credited to Capital Account. When these entries are posted, the Capital Account Balance brought down will agree with the balance in the Balance Sheet, and the respective accounts will be opened in the Cost Ledger; see Form No. 3.

Thus far you will perceive that the Cóst Ledger begins the year with the same figures as the Commercial Books. You will notice that I have opened separate Ledger Accounts for the departments, commencing with the stock in each department to debit, in order to keep Cost Accounts of these departments. You will also notice that I have opened separate Ledger Accounts under the respective numbers of Engines, Boilers, Cranes, Hammers and Order Numbers, the explanations of which will follow later on.

On true Accountancy principles I have shown how I make my first break into the Cost Accounts; but it must be presumed that I had my instructions earlier; and, in anticipation of the 31st December, 1891, that I had my detail working books all ready; for, strictly speaking, the Balance Sheet at that date would not be ready, and to be accurate in detail and in the order of events, I would have commenced with my Detail Books for material and labour with the very first week of the year, but not to keep your minds in suspense I took the Ledger opening entries first, but in point of fact I should have begun with the first initial stages. However, I will retrace my steps.

As some of you are aware, the whole gist of Costing lies in the compilation of workmen's time and materials, and, as the clock will not wait for any man, I will begin with the records of the men's time.

All engineers find it a most convenient plan to record all orders received in what is called the "Orders Received Book," giving engines, boilers, cranes and hammers separate lots of numbers, the numbers following each order in order of date, also keeping a separate set of numbers for promiscuous orders for repairs, duplicate parts of engines and general work; see Form No. 4 from the Orders Received Book. The drawings in the Drawing Office are marked with the respective numbers, from which the various departments copy, and thus spread the numbers through the entire works.

As to the keeping of the workmen's time, every man is known by a number. Each department will take a set of numbers, say "fitting shop" will perhaps start with No. 1 to 100; the "machine shop" will start with 101 to 200, and so on all through the works. When the men start in the morning they pass singly through what is called the "time office," where large wooden boards are hung with numbers painted on, under which are brass hooks, and on these hooks are hung the metal tokens with the number stamped on it; thus each man in passing through takes his own numbered token, and when the gates are closed the "timekeeper" examines the numbers of the tokens left on the board, and records these men as absent, unless they subsequently turn up after breakfast, anyway they have lost that quarter day; the same process is repeated at half-day time, with the same result; so practically the timekeeper knows the absentees by their tokens being left on the hooks. At a period between each break of the day, the timekeeper or timekeepers go around the works, finding each man at his work, he enquires the number of the engine, boiler, crane, hammer, order numbers for repairs, or whatever he is employed at, and books it accordingly; thus daily recording, in what is called the Wages Books, the number of hours worked by each man, and the description of work that he has been engaged upon; for examples of such Wages Books see Forms Nos. 5 and 6. The Form No. 5, as you will notice, gives the value of each man's time upon each class of work each day, and by this form the daily cost for wages on the separate work in progress can be ascertained; but on Form No. 6, the daily cost is not shown, but is ascertained at the end of each week. Where a high standard of efficiency of costing wages is adopted, the Form No. 5 would be likely to suit the object, but for all general purposes I think a weekly cost of wages would suffice; therefore, I recommend No. 6 Form. This form, to be complete, requires a Summary Book. which collects all the items and draws them together in a total cost per week for each job.

I may here mention that all management expenses of each department, viz.: foreman's wages, &c., are spread over the work in progress of each department "ad valorem" on the amount of wages expended.

Also all standing salaries for general management, office salaries, draughtsmen's salaries, gatemen, watchmen, or any other fixed salaries should be spread over the entire wages weekly "ad valorem," and incorporated as net cost.

Each department should have its own Wages' Book, but in such producing departments as iron foundry, brass foundry, and coppersmiths' shop, I would suggest another form of Wages' Book (see Form 7), avoiding all detail in costing the time, because these departments will be costed within themselves, and their products will be taken at their cost price on the tonnages. To illustrate my meaning, all castings and forgings will appear in departmental issue Day Books, and their cost value will be ascertained on the tonnage; therefore the department will receive credit for productions at a fixed rate per cwt. or ton.

Now having settled the wages and the weekly pays costed in summaries, I will leave it for awhile, and as you must buy materials before having any productions, I will now turn to the purchasing of same.

Bearing in mind that the cost accounts must bring out the same total results as the balance sheet at the close of the financial year, it necessarily follows that the particulars must be eliminated from the commercial books, substituting sundry debtors and creditors in lieu of personal accounts. I will deal with one month's transactions only.

Having got the stocks all correctly entered, the assimilation takes place by first dealing with the purchases and charging them to the departments or order numbers that have absorbed them; this is effected by taking the Invoice Purchase Book and with monthly rests preparing an analysis of all goods purchased.

By the "Goods Received Book," usually kept in well-regulated establishments, each invoice is duly marked with the department or order numbers that they are intended for: thus, for instance, an invoice for pig iron will be marked "Iron Foundry," also wrought iron scrap will be marked "Forges," and boiler plates will be marked "Boiler Yard," with the number of the boiler they are intended for. With this explanation you will perceive that the analysis spoken of is compiled. (See Form 8.)

With the purchases for the first month, say January, compiled in this form the same is now journalised (see Journal, folio 4) which are posted to their respective accounts in the Cost Ledger.

Next follows the Sales from the Commercial Day Book, which simply deals with completed work and is journalised in a similar manner, debiting sundry debtors and crediting separate order numbers (see Journal, folio 5) which are posted to their respective accounts in the Cost Ledger, thus showing the contract or invoice price on the credit side of the Ledger Cost Account.

The Commercial Cash Book is next dealt with, and if arranged with columns on both sides for Bills Receivable and Payable, Personal Accounts, Discounts, Bank, I would suggest an additional column on the credit side for Wages and Salaries, after which I would certainly draw the line against any impersonal accounts appearing on either side of the Cash Book, raising all credits or debits as personal accounts through the Purchase Invoice Book or Sales Day Book (or Journal if used). With these provisions the Cost Journal entry is made, as per folio 5, by debiting Cash Account and crediting, say, Bills Receivable, Sundry Debtors (plus discount) (Bank withdrawals), and Discount Account for all receipts for the month, adopting the totals in the columns in the Cash Book at the monthly rests, and *vice versa* debiting Bills Payable, Sundry Creditors (plus discount) (Bank lodgments), Discount Account, and Wages and Salaries for all payments, and similarly adopting the totals in the columns (see Journal, folio 6). Of course, as you are all well aware, with Bank Columns in which the Bank Debit is recorded on the Debit or Receipt side of the Cash Book, and the Credit to Bank on the Credit or the payment side, it would be necessary to reverse the sides in the Journal entry, similar to the reversing of the totals of the discounts.

From the Cost Journal the postings are made to the Cost Ledger. It may appear at first sight to be somewhat unnecessary to deal with such accounts as bank, cash, discounts, &c., in the Cost Ledger, but it must be borne in mind that as we raise (on double entry system) total sums of Debit and Credit of Sundry Debtors and Creditors, to adjust and make the totals agree with the schedules of the Balance Sheet, it is imperative to deal with the cash transactions, but only in totals.

Where a Journal is used, in which both personal and impersonal accounts are found, then make a dissection of same at the usual rests, so that Sundry Debtors and Creditors and Impersonal Accounts, will receive their debits and credits in totals, similar to the postings in the Commercial Books.

After exhausting the Commercial Books of their transactions, we next turn to the departmental issue Day Books, see Forms Nos. 9 and 10, commencing with Form No. 9, the Issue Day Book for the iron foundry. You must understand that the iron foundry is a producing department, and a Cost Ledger Account is kept, wherein all consumables, in the form of pig iron, scrap cast iron, coke, loam sand, lamp black, blacking, and numerous withdrawals from the firm's store house, wages, repairs, depreciation, and a just proportion of the standing charges are regularly debited, and the total expenditure (plus any diminution or minus otherwise of stock) is divisible over the total tonnage of castings produced, thus giving the cost of iron castings per ton or cwt. for the prices in the Issue Day Book; and having worked this cost out for previous years, a basis is formed on which to charge the cost of iron castings to the respective cost order numbers of engines, boilers, cranes, hammers, and repair order numbers.

At this stage it should be borne in mind that no provision, by way of profit or interest on capital, should enter and form part of the costs of any department, for it is a fallacy to expect departments to make profit upon each other or the cost orders, and when massed as a going concern to anticipate profit on the whole, for that would represent double profits; the accounts must work true to actual costs.

By the Iron Foundry Issue Day Book you will perceive that a daily record of all castings charging the order numbers is kept, and each item carried out to value at prices ascertained as mentioned; this book has monthly rests, and a summary is made which gives the figures for the Cost Journal Entry.

Form 9 shows the Brass Foundry Issue Day Book, which is also a producing department, making brass castings, the costs of which are arrived at on a similar process to the iron foundry, which it would be unnecessary to repeat, save that the alloys for making brass castings are block tin, copper, lead, scrap brass spelter, and the other consumables similar to the other foundry.

Form 9 shows the Copper Shop Issue Day Book, another producing department, for all sheet copper is charged to this department, also all consumables, &c., similar to the foundries, and the cost per lb. for pipes ascertained, which is adopted as the basis to charge to the respective order numbers, &c.

Form 9 shows the Forge Issue Day Book, which is also a producing department, and the workmen's wages are usually fixed by piece work on the tonnages, and the men work at all times day and night, by what is called heats, that is, when the furnaces are in full blow. This department is also costed like the foundry on the tonnages, and the prices ascertained to charge for the forgings produced in order to charge to the respective order numbers.

Form 9 shows the Smithy Issue Day Book. The principal items of consumption in this department are iron and steel from which the numerous details of enginework are made. This iron and steel is usually purchased in what is called a merchantable form, in convenient sizes of bars, round and square, and when manipulated by the smithy, the material assumes various names according to the articles made. All the items are made from iron or steel bars, and, inasmuch as the workmen's time is charged direct through the Wages Books to the respective order number of engines, boilers, &c., the prices charged in the Smithies Issue Day Book simply cover the value of material plus allowance for waste and shop charges, which are ascertained by costing the department over previous years to form a basis.

The Form No. 10 shows the Timber Issue Day Book. This is a mere Stock Account, for the timber is usually purchased in convenient planks or deals, and placed in a store yard; and when withdrawals take place by the joiners or pattern-makers, a record is kept and charged to the respective order numbers (the purchase or invoice prices plus shop charges are adopted as the cost in the Issue Day Book.)

Form 10 shows the Stores Issue Day Book, which is also a Stock Account, and, as previously explained, this department is merely the repository of consumables on their arrival in large quantities, where they remain until dispensed. Amongst the departments the storekeeper keeps a daily record of his issues, affixing the values which are similar to the purchase or invoice prices, or as near thereto as possible, bearing in mind waste and leakage.

Having explained all the departmental Issue Day Books, which, by the way, we will presume contain all the monthly issues for January, 1892, the next step is to collect the summaries of same, and make the necessary entries in the Cost Journal (see folio 6 to 12 inclusive). You will perceive that order numbers of engines, boilers, &c., departmental repairs, &c., &c., are debited, and each department credited with its own issues or productions, and when posted, thus forming the credit entries for the Ledger Accounts in the Cost Ledger.

Next follows the Cost Journal entries for wages for the month. As previously recorded, the wages are compiled in weekly summaries. It will be here necessary to embrace in the Journal entry for January just as many weeks as shown to the debit of wages in the Cash Book for that month, so that Wages Account being debited through the Cash Book now requires to be credited with the same amount, and the respective departments and other numbers debited; thus Wages Account will be written off each month (see Journal folios 13 and 14) which, after being posted, carries the respective costs for wages to all the accounts for that month.

If you have followed me closely you will have discovered how the first break or opening entries are made from the Balance Sheet at Dec. 1891, followed by the elimination of the transactions from the Commercial Books, which comprise all purchases, sales, and cash transactions, after which the departmental issues are dealt with, also the wages of workmen. Thus, so far, all costs of labour and materials are recorded.

The direct charges, such as rents, rates, taxes, gas, water, repairs, depreciation, &c., where possible should be charged to the respective departments, but where there is perhaps an open yard space probably laid with rails, and a locomotive employed in drawing materials common to all departments, then a separate cost should be kept called "Yard Charges," and the cost apportioned to the departments *ad valorem*, according to the values of their productions.

In the intermediate or finishing departments, where the work in progress passes through as previously explained, the workmen's time and stores are charged direct to the order numbers, &c., and the shop charges are also charged *ad valorem* according to the wages expended on the respective order numbers and incorporated as cost.

Next follow the indirect charges, such as commissions, agencies, bad debts, discounts, management expenses, bank charges, incidental expenses, &c. These are generally divisible *ad valorem* over the sales. On their being ascertained for previous years an average percentage may be found. In any case it would be found advisable to charge these items to an account called "Trade Expenses," from which the various apportionments may be made.

Presuming that the Cost Accounts are being regularly written up monthly in the Cost Ledger in totals, we now turn to the Abstract Books (see Form No. 11), from which will be seen the detail so essential for guidance in the manufacture, for on the regular keeping of these abstracts, a manufacturer can closely watch the cost and progress of the work in the shops, and, comparing same with the estimates and contracts, he can soon discover when any miscalculation in the estimate has occurred, or he can closely watch the margin between cost and sale price, so as to economise, or otherwise give better finish to the work.

At the close of the financial year the stock is again taken into the accounts, fixed charges and expenses apportioned, and finished order numbers balanced, and results transferred to Profit and Loss Account, which if accurately carried out should agree with the Balance Sheet.

The Cost Accounts are now completed for one year, and the results form a basis for the subsequent year as to costs of productions of departments and results of the trading generally. In conclusion, I may say that the system I have propounded has many advantages in favour of its adoption. Firstly, there is secrecy by being kept apart from the Commercial Accounts; secondly, there is accuracy secured by adopting double entry; and lastly, there is a method in its workings that any member of our profession may soon master.

I have largely drawn upon the use of the Cost Journal solely for the purpose of uniformity and for focussing my several detail books, and also for the reasons that in the Journal an entry is never made without both a debit and credit being provided for, thus reducing the risk of balancing to a minimum. When any of my hearers are called upon to prepare such accounts, I strongly advise them to make a study of the work as practically carried on in the shops. It will be found interesting, and the knowledge so acquired will be of considerable assistance when dealing with the accounts.

In smaller establishments, where from 100 to 200 men are employed, then I should probably advocate the amalgamation of the Cost Accounts with the Commercial Accounts, keeping the separate Cost Ledgers in addition to the ordinary books.

The subject of my paper covers a wide field, and I have felt a difficulty in dealing with the mass of detail necessary to make my views clear; in fact, I feel that with all my endeavours I have only given a birdseye view; but I shall have accomplished my object if I have been successful in inducing our students to further investigate the systems of Costs, for assuredly it is certain to come to the front rank of Accountancy, and form a valuable adjunct to our practice in the near future, and give that status to the profession, and recognition of its merits, so justly deserved.

(To be continued.)

Manchester Chartered Accountants Students' Society.

MANUFACTURING COSTS AS APPLIED TO ENGINEERING.

(Continued from our last issue.)

MR. CARSE, in proposing a vote of thanks to Mr. PLUMPTON, said that they had heard an interesting paper dealing with accounts peculiar to the North. He should like to ask the lecturer how he arrived at the percentage of standing charges (such as management) to be apportioned to each job.

Mr. PLUMPTON replied that the producing charges were placed direct to their own accounts, and that the other expenses were spread over the year and averaged by the turnover.

Mr. GRIERSON seconded the vote of thanks, and asked how Mr. PLUMPTON would deal with interest on capital, bank interest, and bank charges; if the latter only were included in the Cost Accounts, there would be a considerable difference between concerns which had a large balance to credit at their bankers, and those whose account was overdrawn.

Mr. PLUMPTON replied that in the Costings no direct charge was made for interest on capital, and therefore that did not affect the matter. Generally speaking, 10 per cent. was charged to cover the working expenses.

Mr. COUTTS asked whether travelling expenses, discount, etc., should be charged to the separate jobs, or treated as indirect expenses.

Mr. PLUMPTON said that there were always a number of comparatively small items which it was almost impossible to charge direct, as, for instance, a steam engine employed in the works-yard, which would run about the place and do work for almost every department, and the only way to deal with such a case was to have a "Yard Charges Account" and apportion the amount to the various departments, either in proportion to the turnover or in such a manner as the peculiar circumstances of the case might call for.

The CHAIRMAN heartily supported the vote of thanks to Mr. PLUMPTON, which was carried unanimously.

FORM I.

OUSEBURN ENGINE WORKS.

BALANCE SHEET, 31st December, 1891.

LIABILITIES.	£ s d	ASSETS.	£ s d
Capital Account		Land and Buildings	
Mortgages		Plant, Machinery, and Fixtures	
Sundry Creditors		Loose Tools	
Bills Payable		Stock of Materials	
		Stock of Work in progress	
		Sundry Debtors	
		Bills Receivable	
		Bank	
		Cash in hand	

FORM II.

COST JOURNAL.

1892		Fo.	£ s d	Fo.	£ s d
Jan. 1.	CAPITAL ACCOUNT. *Dr.*				
	To Sundries				..
	Mortgage on Land, Buildings, and Machinery		..		
	Sundry Creditors		..		
	Bills Payable		..		
"	SUNDRIES. *Dr.*				
	To Capital Account				..
	Land and Buildings		..		
	Plant, Machinery, and Fixtures		..		
	Loose Tools		..		
	Sundry Debtors		..		
	Bills Receivable		..		
	Bank		..		
	Cash		..		
	Stock of Materials, viz:— £ s d				
	Iron Foundry ..				
	Brass do. ..				
	Forge ..				
	Boiler Yard ..				
	Smithies ..				
	Copper Shop ..				
	Timber ..				
	Stores ..		..		
	Stock of Work in Progress, viz:— £ s d				
	No. 101 Engine ..				
	" 102 " ..				
	" 103 " ..				
	" 104 " ..				
	" 105 " ..				
	" 301 Boiler ..				
	" 302 " ..				
	" 303 " ..				
	" 304 " ..				
	" 305 " ..				
	" 71 Crane ..				
	" 72 " ..				
	" 73 " ..				
	" 501 Hammer ..				
	" 502 " ..				
	" 503 " ..				
	" 504 " ..				
	" 505 " ..				
	" 1001 Order ..				
	" 1002 " ..				
	" 1003 " ..				
	" 1004 " ..				
	" 1005 " ..				
	" 1006 " ..				
	" 1007 " ..				
	" 1008 " ..				
	" 1009 " ..				
	Forward		..		..

1892		Fo.	£ s d	Fo.	£ s d
Jan. 31.	Brought forward		..		..
	SUNDRIES. *Dr.*				
	To Sundry Creditors for purchases during the month.				..
	Iron Foundry		..		
	Brass do		..		
	Forges		..		
	Copper Shop		..		
	Smithies		..		
	Timber		..		
	Stores		..		
	No. 101 Engine		..		
	" 102 "		..		
	" 301 Boiler		..		
	" 305 "		..		
	" 71 Crane		..		
	" 1001 Order		..		
Jan. 31.	SUNDRY DEBTORS. *Dr.*				
	To Sundries for Sales during the month.				..
	No. 101 Engine		..		
	" 102 "		..		
	" 301 Boiler		..		
	" 302 "		..		
	" 71 Crane		..		
	" 501 Hammer		..		
	" 502 "		..		
	" 1001 Order		..		
	" 1002 "		..		
Jan. 31.	CASH ACCOUNT. *Dr.*				
	To Sundries for Receipts during the month.				..
	Bills Receivable		..		
	Sundry Debtors (plus discount)		..		
	Bank (withdrawals)		..		
	Discount (received)		..		
Jan. 31.	SUNDRIES. *Dr.*				
	To Cash for payments during the month.				..
	Bills Payable		..		
	Sundry Creditors (plus discount)		..		
	Wages and Salaries		..		
	Bank (lodgments)		..		
	Discount (paid)		..		
Jan. 31.	SUNDRIES. *Dr.*				
	To Iron Foundry for Iron Castings during the month.				..
	No. 101 Engine		..		
	" 102 "		..		
	" 103 "		..		
	" 104 "		..		
	" 105 "		..		
	" 301 Boiler		..		
	" 302 "		..		
	" 303 "		..		
	" 304 "		..		
	" 305 "		..		
	" 71 Crane		..		
	" 72 "		..		
	" 73 "		..		
	" 501 Hammer		..		
	" 502 "		..		
	" 503 "		..		
	" 504 "		..		
	" 505 "		..		
	" 1001 Order		..		
	" 1002 "		..		
	" 1003 "		..		
	" 1004 "		..		
	" 1005 "		..		
	" 1006 "		..		
	" 1007 "		..		
	" 1008 "		..		
	" 1009 "		..		
	Iron Foundry Repairs		..		
	Machine Shop "		..		
	Forge Repairs		..		
	Building "		..		
	Tools Account		..		
	Railway Repairs		..		
	Forward		..		..

1892		Fo.	£ s d	Fo.	£ s d
	Brought forward ..		..		..
	SUNDRIES. *Dr.* To Brass Foundry for Brass Castings during the month				..
	No. 101 Engine		..		
	" 103 "		..		
	" 105 "		..		
	" 301 Boiler		..		
	" 71 Crane		..		
	" 501 Hammer		..		
	" 502 "		..		
	" 1001 Order		..		
	" 1002 "		..		
	" 1007 "		..		
	" 1009 "		..		
	Iron Foundry Repairs ..		..		
	Copper Shop do. ..		..		
	Buildings do. ..		..		
	Forge do. ..		..		
	Railway do. ..		..		
Jan. 31.	SUNDRIES. *Dr.* To Copper Shop for Copper Pipes during the month.				..
	No. 302 Boiler		..		
	" 303 "		..		
	" 305 "		..		
	" 501 Hammer		..		
	" 504 "		..		
	" 1001 Order		..		
	" 1005 "		..		
	" 1009 "		..		
Jan. 31.	SUNDRIES. *Dr.* To Forges for Forgings during the month.				..
	No. 101 Engine		..		
	" 102 "		..		
	" 103 "		..		
	" 104 "		..		
	" 105 "		..		
	" 501 Hammer		..		
	" 502 "		..		
	" 505 "		..		
	" 1005 Order		..		
	" 1008 "		..		
	Machine Shop Repairs ..		..		
	Tools Account		..		
Jan. 31.	SUNDRIES. *Dr.* To Smithies for Smith work during the month.				..
	No. 101 Engine		..		
	" 102 "		..		
	" 103 "		..		
	" 104 "		..		
	" 105 "		..		
	" 301 Boiler		..		
	" 303 "		..		
	" 305 "		..		
	" 501 Hammer		..		
	" 502 "		..		
	" 503 "		..		
	" 504 "		..		
	" 505 "		..		
	" 71 Crane		..		
	" 72 "		..		
	" 73 "		..		
	" 1001 Order		..		
	" 1005 "		..		
	" 1009 "		..		
	Iron Foundry Repairs ..		..		
	Brass " " ..		..		
	Copper Shop " ..		..		
	Forges " ..		..		
	Smithies " ..		..		
	Buildings " ..		..		
	Tools Account " ..		..		
	Railway " ..		..		
Jan. 31.	SUNDRIES. *Dr.* To Timber Account for Timber used during the month.				..
	No. 101 Engine		..		
	" 105 "		..		
	" 303 Boiler		..		
	" 72 Crane		..		
	" 503 Hammer		..		
	" 1005 Order		..		
	" 1008 "		..		
	" 1009 "		..		
	Foundry Repairs		..		
	Machine Shop Repairs ..		..		
	Buildings " ..		..		
	Tools Account		..		
	Forward ..		..		..

1892		Fo.	£ s d	Fo.	£ s d
	Brought forward ..		..		..
Jan. 31	SUNDRIES. *Dr.* To Stores for sundry Stores used during the month.				..
	No. 101 Engine		..		
	" 102 "		..		
	" 103 "		..		
	" 104 "		..		
	" 105 "		..		
	" 301 Boiler		..		
	" 302 "		..		
	" 303 "		..		
	" 304 "		..		
	" 305 "		..		
	" 71 Crane		..		
	" 72 "		..		
	" 73 "		..		
	" 501 Hammer		..		
	" 502 "		..		
	" 503 "		..		
	" 504 "		..		
	" 505 "		..		
	" 1001 Order		..		
	" 1002 "		..		
	" 1003 "		..		
	" 1004 "		..		
	" 1005 "		..		
	" 1006 "		..		
	" 1007 "		..		
	" 1008 "		..		
	" 1009 "		..		
	Iron Foundry		..		
	Brass "		..		
	Copper Shop		..		
	Forges		..		
	Smithies		..		
	Machine Shop Repairs ..		..		
Jan. 31.	SUNDRIES. *Dr.* To Wages Account for Wages during the month.				..
	No. 101 Engine		..		
	" 102 "		..		
	" 103 "		..		
	" 104 "		..		
	" 105 "		..		
	" 301 Boiler		..		
	" 302 "		..		
	" 303 "		..		
	" 303 "		..		
	" 304 "		..		
	" 305 "		..		
	" 71 Crane		..		
	" 72 "		..		
	" 73 "		..		
	" 501 Hammer		..		
	" 502 "		..		
	" 503 "		..		
	" 504 "		..		
	" 505 "		..		
	" 1001 Order		..		
	" 1002 "		..		
	" 1003 "		..		
	" 1004 "		..		
	" 1005 "		..		
	" 1006 "		..		
	" 1007 "		..		
	" 1008 "		..		
	" 1009 "		..		
	Iron Foundry		..		
	Brass "		..		
	Copper Shop		..		
	Forges		..		
	Smithies Repairs		..		
	Forges "		..		
	Foundry "		..		
	Brass Foundry Repairs ..		..		
	Building " ..		..		
	Copper Shop " ..		..		
	Railway " ..		..		
	Machine Shop " ..		..		
	Tools Account		..		
	Yard Charges		..		

FORM III.

NET COST LEDGER No. 1.

Nominal Accounts and Departments.

Dr. **Capital Account.** *Cr.*

Date	Particulars	J	£ s d	Date	Particulars	J	£ s d
1892 Jan. 1	To Sundries	2		1892 Jan. 1	By Sundries	2	
	Balance						
				,,	By Balance		£

Dr. **Mortgages Account.** *Cr.*

Date	Particulars	J	£ s d	Date	Particulars	J	£ s d
				1892 Jan. 1	By Capital A/c	2	

Dr. **Sundry Creditors.** *Cr.*

Date	Particulars	J	£ s d	Date	Particulars	J	£ s d
1892 Jan. 31	To Cash			1892 Jan. 1	By Creditors		

Dr. **Bills Payable.** *Cr.*

Date	Particulars	J	£ s d	Date	Particulars	J	£ s d
1892 Jan. 31	To Cash			1892 Jan. 1	By Acceptances		

Dr. **Land and Buildings.** *Cr.*

Date	Particulars	J	£ s d	Date	Particulars	J	£ s d
1892 Jan. 1	To Valuation						

Dr. **Plant, Machinery and Fixtures.** *Cr.*

Date	Particulars	J	£ s d	Date	Particulars	J	£ s d
1892 Jan. 1	To Valuation						

Dr. **Loose Tools.** *Cr.*

Date	Particulars	J	£ s d	Date	Particulars	J	£ s d
1892 Jan. 1	To Valuation						

Dr. **Sundry Debtors.** *Cr.*

Date	Particulars	J	£ s d	Date	Particulars	J	£ s d
1892 Jan. 1	To Debtors			1892 Jan. 31	By Cash		
31	,, Sales						

Dr. **Bills Receivable.** *Cr.*

Date	Particulars	J	£ s d	Date	Particulars	J	£ s d
1892 Jan. 1	To Acceptances			1892 Jan. 31	By Cash		

Dr. **Bank.** *Cr.*

Date	Particulars	J	£ s d	Date	Particulars	J	£ s d
1892 Jan. 1	To Balance			1892 Jan. 31	By Cash		
31	,, Cash						

Dr. **Cash Account.** *Cr.*

Date	Particulars	J	£ s d	Date	Particulars	J	£ s d
1892 Jan. 1	To Balance			1892 Jan. 31	By Payments		
31	,, Receipts						

Dr. **Iron Foundry.** *Cr.*

Date	Particulars	J	£ s d	Date	Particulars	J	£ s d
1892 Jan. 1	To Stock			1892 Jan. 31	By Issue		
31	,, Purchases						
,,	,, Stores						
,,	,, Wages						

Dr. **Brass Foundry.** *Cr.*

Date	Particulars	J	£ s d	Date	Particulars	J	£ s d
1892 Jan. 1	To Stock			1892 Jan. 31	By Issue		
31	,, Purchases						
,,	,, Stores						
,,	,, Wages						

Dr. **Copper Shop.** *Cr.*

Date	Particulars	J	£ s d	Date	Particulars	J	£ s d
1892 Jan. 1	To Stock			1892 Jan. 31	By Issue		
31	,, Purchases						
,,	,, Stores						
,,	,, Wages						

Dr. **Forges.** *Cr.*

Date	Particulars	J	£ s d	Date	Particulars	J	£ s d
1892 Jan. 1	To Stock			1892 Jan. 31	By Issue		
31	,, Purchases						
,,	,, Stores						
,,	,, Wages						

Dr. **Boiler Yard.** *Cr.*

Date	Particulars	J	£ s d	Date	Particulars	J	£ s d
1892 Jan. 1	To Stock						

Dr. **Smithies.** *Cr.*

Date	Particulars	J	£ s d	Date	Particulars	J	£ s d
1892 Jan. 1	To Stock			1892 Jan. 31	By Issue		
31	,, Purchases						
,,	,, Stores						

Dr. **Timber Account.** *Cr.*

Date	Particulars	J	£ s d	Date	Particulars	J	£ s d
1892 Jan. 1	To Stock			1892 Jan. 31	By Issue		
31	,, Purchases						

Dr. **Stores.** *Cr.*

Date	Particulars	J	£ s d	Date	Particulars	J	£ s d
1892 Jan. 1	To Stock			1892 Jan. 31	By Issue		
31	,, Purchases						

Dr. **Discount Account.** *Cr.*

Date	Particulars	J	£ s d	Date	Particulars	J	£ s d
1892 Jan. 31	To Cash			1892 Jan. 31	By Cash		

Wages and Salaries.

Dr.		J	£ s d	Cr.		J	£ s d
1892 Jan. 31	To Cash ..			1892 Jan. 31	By Wages ..		

Iron Foundry Repairs.

Dr.		J	£ s d	Cr.
1892 Jan. 31	To Iron Castings			
,,	,, Brass ,, ..			
,,	,, Smithwork ..			
,,	,, Timber ..			
,,	,, Wages ..			

Brass Foundry Repairs.

Dr.		J	£ s d	Cr.
1892 Jan. 31	To Smithwork ..			
,,	,, Wages ..			

Copper Shop Repairs.

Dr.		J	£ s d	Cr.
1892 Jan. 31	To Brass Castings			
,,	,, Smithwork ..			
,,	,, Wages ..			

Machine Shop Repairs.

Dr.		J	£ s d	Cr.
1892 Jan. 31	To Iron Castings			
,,	,, Forgings ..			
,,	,, Timber ..			
,,	,, Stores ..			
,,	,, Wages ..			

Forges Repairs.

Dr.		J	£ s d	Cr.
1892 Jan. 31	To Iron Castings			
,,	,, Brass ,, ..			
,,	,, Smithwork ..			
,,	,, Wages ..			

Smithies Repairs.

Dr.		J	£ s d	Cr.
1892 Jan. 31	To Smithwork ..			
,,	,, Wages ..			

Buildings Repairs.

Dr.		J	£ s d	Cr.
1892 Jan. 31	To Iron Castings			
,,	,, Brass ,, ..			
,,	,, Smithwork ..			
,,	,, Timber ..			
,,	,, Wages ..			

Railway Repairs.

Dr.		J	£ s d	Cr.
1892 Jan. 31	To Iron Castings			
,,	,, Brass ,, ..			
,,	,, Smithwork ..			
,,	,, Wages ..			

Tools Account.

Dr.		J	£ s d	Cr.
1892 Jan. 31	To Iron Castings			
,,	,, Forgings .			
,,	,, Smithwork ..			
,,	,, Timber ..			
,,	,, Wages ..			

Yard Charges.

Dr.		J	£ s d	Cr.
1892 Jan. 31	To Wages ..			

NET COST LEDGER No. 2.

Engines, Boilers, Cranes, Hammers, and Order Numbers.

No. 101 Engine.

Dr.		J	£ s d	Cr.		J	£ s d
1892 Jan. 1	To Net Cost ..			1892 Jan. 31	By Sales ..		
31	,, Purchases ..						
,,	,, Iron Castings..						
,,	,, Brass do. ..						
,,	,, Forgings ..						
,,	,, Smithwork ..						
,,	,, Timber ..						
,,	,, Stores ..						
,,	,, Wages ..						

No. 102 Engine.

Dr.		J	£ s d	Cr.		J	£ s d
1892 Jan. 1	To Net Cost ..			1892 Jan. 31	By Sales ..		
31	,, Purchases ..						
,,	,, Iron Castings						
,,	,, Forgings ..						
,,	,, Smithwork ..						
,,	,, Stores ..						
,,	,, Wages ..						

No. 103 Engine.

Dr.		J	£ s d	Cr.
1892 Jan. 1	To Net Cost ..			
31	,, Iron Castings			
,,	,, Brass ,, ..			
,,	,, Forgings ..			
,,	,, Smithwork ..			
,,	,, Stores ..			
,,	,, Wages ..			

No. 101 Engine.

Dr.		J	£ s d	Cr.
1892 Jan. 1	To Net Cost ..			
31	,, Iron Castings			
,,	,, Forgings ..			
,,	,, Smithwork ..			
,,	,, Stores ..			
,,	,, Wages ..			

No. 105 Engine.

Dr.		J	£ s d	Cr.
1892 Jan. 1	To Net Cost ..			
31	,, Iron Castings			
,,	,, Brass ,, ..			
,,	,, Forgings ..			
,,	,, Smithwork ..			
,,	,, Timber ..			
,,	,, Stores ..			
,,	,, Wages ..			

(To be continued.)

Manchester Chartered Accountants Students' Society.

MANUFACTURING COSTS AS APPLIED TO ENGINEERING.

(Concluded from our last issue.)

NET COST LEDGER No. 2, ETC. (*continued*).

Dr. No. 301 BOILER. *Cr.*

1892		J	£ s d	1892		J	£ s d
Jan. 1	To Net Cost ..			Jan. 31	By Sales ..		
31	„ Purchases ..						
„	„ Iron Castings..						
„	„ Brass „						
„	„ Smithwork ..						
„	„ Stores ..						
„	„ Wages ..						

Dr. No. 302 BOILER. *Cr.*

1892		J	£ s d	1892		J	£ s d
Jan. 1	To Net Cost ..			Jan. 31	By Sales ..		
31	„ Iron Castings						
„	„ Copper Pipes						
„	„ Stores ..						
„	„ Wages ..						

Dr. No. 303 BOILER. *Cr.*

1892		J	£ s d
Jan. 1	To Net Cost ..		
31	„ Iron Castings		
„	„ Copper Pipes		
„	„ Smithwork ..		
„	„ Timber ..		
„	„ Stores ..		
„	„ Wages ..		

Dr. No. 304 BOILER. *Cr.*

1892		J	£ s d
Jan. 1	To Net Cost ..		
31	„ Iron Castings		
„	„ Stores ..		
„	„ Wages ..		

Dr. No. 305 BOILER. *Cr.*

1892		J	£ s d
Jan. 1	To Net Cost ..		
31	„ Purchases ..		
„	„ Iron Castings		
„	„ Copper Pipes		
„	„ Smithwork ..		
„	„ Stores ..		
„	„ Wages ..		

Dr. No. 71 CRANE. *Cr.*

1892		J	£ s d	1892		J	£ s d
Jan. 1	To Net Cost ..			Jan. 31	By Sales ..		
31	„ Purchases ..						
„	„ Iron Castings						
„	„ Brass „						
„	„ Smithwork ..						
„	„ Stores ..						
„	„ Wages ..						

Dr. No. 72 CRANE. *Cr.*

1892		J	£ s d
Jan. 1	To Net Cost ..		
31	„ Iron Castings ..		
„	„ Smithwork ..		
„	„ Timber ..		
„	„ Stores ..		
„	„ Wages ..		

Dr. No. 73 CRANE. *Cr.*

1892		J	£ s d
Jan. 1	To Net Cost ..		
31	„ Iron Castings..		
„	„ Smithwork ..		
„	„ Stores ..		
„	„ Wages ..		

Dr. No. 501 HAMMER. *Cr.*

1892		J	£ s d	1892		J	£ s d
Jan. 1	To Net Cost ..			Jan. 31	By Sales ..		
31	„ Iron Castings..						
„	„ Brass „ ..						
„	„ Copper Pipes..						
„	„ Forgings ..						
„	„ Smithwork ..						
„	„ Stores ..						
„	„ Wages ..						

Dr. No. 502 HAMMER. *Cr.*

189		J	£ s d
Jan. 2			
1	To Net Cost ..		
31	„ Iron Castings..		
„	„ Brass „ ..		
„	„ Forgings ..		
„	„ Smithwork ..		
„	„ Stores ..		
„	„ Wages.. ..		

Dr. No. 503 HAMMER. *Cr.*

1892		J	£ s d
Jan. 1	To Net Cost ..		
31	„ Iron Castings..		
„	„ Smithwork ..		
„	„ Timber.. ..		
„	„ Stores		
„	„ Wages		

Dr. No. 504 HAMMER. *Cr.*

1892		J	£ s d
Jan. 1	To Net Cost ..		
31	„ Iron Castings..		
„	„ Copper Pipes..		
„	„ Smithwork ..		
„	„ Stores		
„	„ Wages		

Dr. No. 505 HAMMER. *Cr.*

1892		J	£ s d
Jan. 1	To Net Cost ..		
31	„ Iron Castings..		
„	„ Forgings ..		
„	„ Smithwork ..		
„	„ Stores		
„	„ Wages		

Dr. No. 1001 ORDER. *Cr.*

1892		J	£ s d	1892		J	£ s d
Jan. 1	To Net Cost ..			Jan. 31	By Sales		
31	„ Purchases ..						
„	„ Iron Castings..						
„	„ Brass „ ..						
„	„ Copper Pipes .						
„	„ Smithwork ..						
„	„ Stores						
„	„ Wages						

Dr. No. 1002 ORDER. *Cr.*

1892		J	£ s d	1892		J	£ s d
Jan. 1	To Net Cost ..			Jan. 31	By Sales		
31	„ Iron Castings..						
„	„ Brass „ ..						
„	„ Stores						
„	„ Wages						

Dr. No. 1003 ORDER. *Cr.*

1892		J	£ s d
Jan. 1	To Net Cost ..		
31	„ Iron Castings .		
„	„ Stores		
„	„ Wages		

Dr. No. 1004 Order. *Cr.*

		£ s d	
1892 Jan. 1	To Net Cost ..		
31	" Iron Castings..		
"	" Stores		
"	" Wages		

Dr. No. 1005 Order. *Cr.*

		£ s d	
1892 Jan. 1	To Net Cost ..		
31	" Iron Castings..		
"	" Copper Pipes..		
"	" Forgings ..		
"	" Smithwork ..		
"	" Timber.. ..		
"	" Stores		
"	" Wages		

Dr. No. 1006 Order. *Cr.*

		£ s d	
1892 Jan. 1	To Net Cost ..		
31	" Iron Castings..		
"	" Stores		
"	" Wages		

Dr. No. 1007 Order. *Cr.*

		£ s d	
1892 Jan. 1	To Net Cost ..		
31	" Iron Castings..		
"	" Brass " ..		
"	" Stores		
"	" Wages		

Dr. No. 1008 Order. *Cr.*

		£ s d	
1892 Jan. 1	To Net Cost ..		
31	" Iron Castings..		
"	" Forgings ..		
"	" Timber.. ..		
"	" Stores		
"	" Wages		

Dr. No. 1009 Order. *Cr.*

		£ s d	
1892 Jan. 1	To Net Cost ..		
31	" Iron Castings..		
"	" Brass " ..		
"	" Copper Pipes..		
"	" Smithwork ..		
"	" Timber.. ..		
"	" Stores		
"	" Wages		

FORM IV.

ORDERS RECEIVED BOOK.

Date.	Names.	Descriptions.
1891. July 21.	B. S. Co. Barrow.	No. 101 Engine. One Pair Triple Expansion Surface Condensing Engines to specification and drawings.
"	"	No. 301 Boiler. One Multitubular Boiler, double flued to work at 100 lbs. pressure, as per specification and drawings.
July 22.	J. B. York.	No. 71 Crane. One 50 ton Overhead Travelling Crane, fitted with Donkey Boiler to specification and drawings, to be erected at York.
	H. B. Manchester	No. 1001 Order. Repairs to Engine and Boiler, new Flywheel and Steam Chest Boiler Flues to be repaired.

FORM V.

TIME BOOK AND PAY BILL.—No. 85 PAY.

No.	Names.	Rate per day.	Thursday.			Friday.			Saturday.		
					s d			s d			s d
1	John Jones	4/-	1 1 1 1	101 Engine 102 " 103 " 104 "	1 0 1 0 1 0 1 0	.. .. 2 2	.. .. 101 Engine 102 "	.. .. 2 0 2 0	.. .. 1 3	.. .. 101 Engine 102 "	.. .. 1 0 3 0
2	Jos. Robinson	4/4	2 2	101 Engine 105 "	2 2 2 2	1 3	104 Engine 105 "	1 1 3 3	.. 4	.. 103 Engine	.. 4 4
3	Fred. Williams	5/-	2 2	71 Crane 72 "	2 6 2 6	1 3	71 Crane 72 "	1 3 3 9	.. 4	.. 73 Crane	.. 5 0
4	Isaac Roberts	2/6	2 2	501 Hammer 502 "	1 3 1 3	1 3	501 Hammer 502 "	7½ 1 10½	.. 4	.. 501 Hammer	.. 2 6
5	Thos. Watson	2/-	 4	.. .. .. 1,001 Order	.. .. .. 2 0	1 1 1 1	1,002 Order 1,003 " 1,004 " 1,005 "	6 6 6 6	.. .. 2 2	.. .. 1,001 Order 1,003 "	.. .. 1 0 1 0
6	John Wood	3/-	1 1 2	301 Boiler 302 " 303 "	9 9 1 6	.. 2 2	.. 302 Boiler 303 "	.. 1 6 1 6	 4	.. .. 301 Boiler	.. .. 3 0
7	Robt. Black	4/6	1 1 2	71 Crane 72 " 73 "	1 1½ 1 1½ 2 3	.. 2 2	.. 72 Crane 73 "	.. 2 3 2 3	 4	.. .. 73 Crane	.. .. 4 6

FORM VI.

TIME BOOK AND PAY BILL.—No. 85 PAY.

No.	Names.	Description.	Thurs.	Fri.	Sat.	M n.	Tues.	Wed.	Total.	Rate.	s d	£ s d
		No. 101 Engine	¼	½	¼	1	½	¼	2¾		11 0	
		" 102 "	¼	½	¾		½	¼	2¼		9 0	
		" 103 "	¼					¼	½		2 0	
		" 104 "	¼					¼	½		2 0	
1	John Jones								6	4/-		1 4 0
		No. 101 Engine	½			½	1	¼	2¼		9 9	
		" 105 "	½	¾		½			1¾		7 7	
		" 104 "		¼				½	¾		3 3	
		" 103 "			1			¼	1¼		5 5	
2	Jos. Robinson								6	4/4		1 6 0
		No. 71 Crane	½	¼		½	1	¼	2½		12 6	
		" 72 "	½	¾		½		¼	2		10 0	
		" 73 "			1			½	1½		7 6	
3	Fred. Williams.. ..								6	5/-		1 10 0
		No. 501 Hammer	½	¼	1		¼		2		5 0	
		" 502 "	½	¾				½	1¾		4 4½	
		" 503 "				½	¼	½	1¼		3 1½	
		" 504 "				½	¼		¾		1 10½	
		" 505 "					¼		¼		0 7½	
4	Isaac Roberts								6	2/6		0 15 0

FORM VII.

TIME BOOK AND PAY BILL No. 85 PAY.

FOUNDRIES AND COPPER SHOP.

No.	Names.	Rate.	Thurs.	Friday.	Sat.	Monday.	Tues.	Wed.	Total.	Rate.			
1	John Jones	4/-	1	1	1	1	1	1	6	4/-	1	4	0
2	Jos. Robinson	4/4	1	1	1	1	1	1	6	4/4	1	6	0
3	F. Williams	5/-	1	1	1	1	1	1	6	5/-	1	10	0
4	Isaac Roberts	2/6	1	1	1	1	1	1	6	2/6		15	0

FORM VIII.

PURCHASES ANALYSIS BOOK.

JANUARY, 1892.

No.	Names	Description	Total	Iron Foundry	Brass Foundry	Forges	Copper Shop	Smithies	Timber	Stores	No. 101 Engine
			£ s d	£ s d	£ s d	£ s d	£ s d	£ s d	£ s d	£ s d	£ s d
1 ..	Barrow Hematite Co.	Pig Iron ..	..	..							
2 ..	Jones Bros. ..	Merchant Iron ..	..								
3 ..	Wylie & Co. ..	Timber ..	..						..		
4 ..	Dundee Oil Co. ..	Engine Oil ..	..							..	
5 ..	Watson & Co. ..	Brass Dome ..	..							..	
6 ..	Spelter & Co. ..	Spelter ..	..		..						
7 ..	Birmingham Copper Co.. ..	Sheet Copper	..				..				

FORM IX.

IRON FOUNDRY ISSUE DAY BOOK.

JANUARY, 1892.

Date	Description	Ts. cts. qs. lbs.	Rate		
1892	*No. 101 Engine.*		per cwt.	£ s d	£ s d
Jan. 21	One Cylinder Cover	2 21	11/-	7 6	
	Steam Pipes ..	5 0 0	,,	2 15 0	
					3 2 6

BRASS FOUNDRY ISSUE DAY BOOK.

Date	Description	Ts. cts. qs. lbs.	Rate		
1892	*No. 101 Engine.*		per lb.	£ s d	£ s d
Jan. 10	Bushes for bearings	3 7	10d	3 15 10	
	Brass Taps ..	21	,,	17 6	
					4 13 4

COPPER SHOP ISSUE DAY BOOK.

Date	Description	Ts. cts qs. lbs.	Rate		
1892	*No. 101 Engine.*		per lb.	£ s d	£ s d
Jan. 24	Copper Pipes(straight)	2 4	1/2	3 10 0	
	,, ,, (bent)..	1 2	1/3	1 17 6	
					5 7 6

FORGE ISSUE DAY BOOK.

Date	Description	Ts. cts. qs. lbs.	Rate		
1892	*No. 101 Engine.*		per cwt.	£ s d	£ s d
Jan. 25	One Double thro' CrankShaft and sundry other forgings ..	4 10	22/-	99 0 0	
					99 0 0

SMITHIES ISSUE DAY BOOK.

Date	Description	Ts. cts. qs. lbs.	Rate		
1892	*No. 101 Engine.*		per cwt.	£ s d	£ s d
Jan. 22	Sundry Levers, Pins, &c. ..	2 1	18/-	2 0 6	
					2 0 6

FORM X.

TIMBER ISSUE DAY BOOK.

JANUARY 1892.

Date	Description	Ft.	Ins.	Ins.	Ins.	Ft.	Ins.	Rate		
1892						Super			£ s d	£ s d
Jan. 10	*No. 101 Engine.*									
	Am. deal for pattern of cylinder cover ..	4	0	11	1	3	8	3d	11	
	do. do. ..	20	0	,,	,,	18	4	,,	4 7	
										5 6

STORES ISSUE DAY BOOK.

JANUARY 1892.

Date	Description	Tons cwts qrs lbs	Rate		
1892				s d	s d
	No. 101 Engine.				
Jan. 10	6 Candles		½d	3	
	½ Gallon Engine Oil ..		3/6	1 9	
	1 Hand Smooth File 16"			1 4	
	Bolts and Nuts ..	21	20/-	3 9	7 1

FORM XI.

ABSTRACT—DEPARTMENTS.

FOUNDRY.

1892	WAGES			Pig Iron.	Scrap Metal	Loam, Blacking, &c.	Stores	Consumables	Tools, Brushes &c.	Bolts and Nuts	Repairs	Metal Castings	Standing Charges	M'nagement	Depreciation	Total Cost
	Moulders	Fettlers	Labourers													
	£ s d	£ s d	£ s d	£ s d	£ s d	£ s d	£ s d	£ s d	£ s d	£ s d	£ s d	£ s d	£ s d	£ s d	£ s d	£ s d
Jan. 1 Stock ..				..	..	..	..	..	..	..						..
Jan.31..	..	..	..	..		..	..	..	..	..	..	..	..	..	..	..
Less Stock 31 Dec. 1892																

Total Cost divided by weight of Castings made during the year gives the cost per ton.

ABSTRACT—No. 101 ENGINE.

1892	Wages							Iron Castings	Brass and Copper Works	Forgings	Smith Work	Timber	Pat-terns	Stores and Sundries	Total Cost
	Pattern Makers	Joiners	Machinist	Smiths	Fitters	Labour-ers	Outside Time								
Jan. 1	£ s d	£ s d	£ s d	£ s d	£ s d	£ s d	£ s d	£ s d	£ s d	£ s d	£ s d	£ s d	£ s d	£ s d	£ s d
NetCost	..	..	..	..	..	..		..	..	..	..	..	..	..	..
Jan. 31															
Feb. 28															
Mar. 31															
Apl. 30															
May 31															

(FINIS)

COST ACCOUNTS.—I.

UNTIL recently the question of Cost Accounts was one that rarely, if ever, attracted the attention of the professional accountant. It seems to have been considered that an audit should properly be confined to a verification of the financial books, and as Cost Accounts (at the time we are speaking of, at least) were almost invariably quite distinct from the books of account proper, it naturally followed that they formed no part of the usual professional audit. It seems probable that the idea that an audit should be confined to the financial books of a concern arose originally either from oversight, or from a disinclination upon the part of accountants to embark upon a line of action that necessitated a more or less intimate acquaintance with the *technique* of each different class of business whose accounts they were called upon to verify.

3 5 ★

However this may be, the practical result seems to have been that, while the financial books of manufacturing concerns were gradually raised to the very high state of practical and scientific excellence at which they now stand, the Cost Accounts —being deprived of the natural advantages of professional scrutiny—remained upon a comparatively primitive level. Designed by practical men they naturally aimed at showing the results that these practical men required of them, but they remained defective as to the means by which these results were obtained—being generally excessively cumbrous, and consequently were (not having been audited) inaccurate in detail, and not infrequently defective in principle.

The inevitable consequence of this system of "dual control" was that the results obtained by the cost books were not in accordance with the results shown by the financial books; and owing to the attitude of the profession at that time the results remained unreconciled. A more unsatisfactory condition of affairs—so far as the manufacturer himself was concerned—can hardly be imagined. He understood his cost books, and believed in the results they indicated; while even when he did not actually distrust the results produced by the auditors from his financial books, he naturally came to regard them as something mysterious and altogether beyond his comprehension, and being human he ceased to take any interest in what he was obliged to confess himself unable to understand. For some time things seem to have drifted thus, until accountants turned their attention to Cost Accounts, and so systematised them that they yielded the true results of manufacture as shown by the financial books. From that time Cost Accounts may be said to have become a "system."

Like all improvements, the formation of Cost Accounts upon a scientific system was a work of gradual growth, and as many eminent accountants have for some time past given the matter a considerable amount of attention, these accounts are now very generally in a high state of practical efficiency. It is only of quite recent years, however, that any literature available to accountant students has appeared upon the subject.

If we remember rightly, the first lecture ever delivered to a society of accountant students upon "Cost Accounts" was that by Mr. JOHN MANN, Junr., C.A., of Glasgow, who described in general terms what appeared to be a very excellent system of Cost Accounts as applied to mechanical engineers, which was, perhaps, chiefly notable for the fact that the Cost Accounts were grafted on to the general financial books by means of an Adjustment Account in the General Ledger. Mr. MANN's lecture was duly reported in our issue of August 29th 1891, and should be carefully studied by all who desire a further acquaintance with this subject.

The next contribution of any importance was a lecture by Mr. PLUMPTON, A.C.A., of Manchester, which is valuable on account of the specimen rulings with which it is copiously illustrated. The system described is, however, somewhat unwieldy. Mr. PLUMPTON's lecture was also duly reported in these columns, and will be found in our issues of November 19th and 26th, and December 3rd, 1892.

Another and more detailed contribution upon the subject of Cost Accounts is to be found in the third part of Mr. DICKSEE's "Bookkeeping for Accountant Students," in which will be found fully illustrated the financial as well as the cost accounts of a building contractor. As with the system portrayed by Mr. MANN, a simple arrangement of adjustment accounts unites the cost to the financial books, while the arrangement of the Cost Ledger Summary in a tabular form enables this account to do duty for both Cost Account Summary and Profit and Loss Account. The arrangement of each account in the Cost Ledger in tabular form also adds greatly to the clearness of these accounts while materially simplifying the keeping of the book.

In the short series of articles which we now propose giving in these columns we shall treat with a system of Cost Accounts applicable for general purposes, which is more or less suggested by a system recently described in an essay that appeared in *The Accountants' Journal*, to which was awarded the first of the prizes offered monthly by our contemporary. Before proceeding to do so, however, it seems desirable that we should give a few specimens of Cost Sheets (or Cost Book Summaries) designed to meet the requirements of various kinds of manufactures, as by this means it is hoped that the reader will more readily grasp the precise object that is aimed at in the framing of Cost Accounts.

Our first *pro formâ* Cost Sheet is one designed for the use of manufacturers of bar iron, but the same form would apply equally well, *mutatis mutandis*, for ironfounders, steel manufacturers, and smelters generally. The account is taken at frequent intervals, and it will be seen that the main object is to ascertain in detail the total cost per ton of each different manufacture. The form recommended is as follows:—

Dr.

COST OF MANUFACTURE.

Tons Cwts. Qrs. lbs.
Make 639 13 1 12

	Weight	Average price per ton	Amount	Cost per ton	Consumption of materials per ton of iron
	Ts. cts. qs. lbs.	£ s d	£ s d	£ s d	Ts. cts. qs. lbs.
To Puddled Bars	316 9 3 0	3 5 7	1,037 8 10	1 12 5·25	9 3 16
,, Scrap Iron	413 11 0 14	2 11 0	1,054 2 4	1 12 11·25	12 3 11
	730 0 3 14	—	2,091 11 2	3 5 4·50	1 2 3 9
,, Coal	564 18 0 0	7 8	214 5 5	6 8·40	17 2 18
,, Firebricks, Clay, and Sand			33 3 4	1 0·44	
,, Stores			57 8 11	1 9·55	
,, Repairs—Materials			41 15 2	1 3·67	
,, Do. Labour			22 5 10	8·36	
,, Trade Charges			32 12 8	1 0·24	
,, Rent, Rates, and Taxes			54 18 6	1 8·60	
,, Gas and Water			10 17 6	4·08	
,, Office Expenses			31 13 6	11·90	
,, Wages and Salaries			467 11 4	14 7·43	
Total Cost			£3,058 3 4	4 15 7·17	
,, Balance, being Profit (carried to Profit and Loss Account)			249 8 8	7 9·85	
			£3,307 12 0	5 3 5·02	

Cr.

	Ts. cts. qs. lbs.	£ s d	Ts. cts. qs. lbs.	£ s d	£ s d
By Bar Iron			646 14 1 21	3,593 2 9	Value per ton
Less					
Discounts and Allowances	6 1 0 9	94 10 7			
Carriage, Freight, &c.	..	165 14 3			
Commission	..	47 10 0	6 1 0 9	307 14 10	
			640 13 1 12	3,285 7 11	5 2 6·77
Deduct					
Decrease in Stock of Bar Iron.—					
Stock at 1 Jan. 1892..	19 0 0 0	104 10 0			
Do. 31 July 1892..	18 0 0 0	90 0 0	1 0 0 0	14 10 0	—
				3,270 17 11	5 2 3·22
By Mill Cinder Scale, &c. .. 145 tons 10 cwt.			..	36 14 1	—
Total make and value of same			639 13 1 12	£3,307 12 0	£5 3 5·02

The Accountant

THE ORGAN OF CHARTERED ACCOUNTANTS THROUGHOUT THE WORLD.

(**Awarded Silver Medal, Esposizione Italo-Americana, Genova 1892.**)

VOL. XX.—NEW SERIES.—No. 1026. SATURDAY, AUGUST 4, 1894.

Leading Articles.

COST ACCOUNTS.—II.

OUR next example of a Cost Sheet is one applicable to a gas company, and in reproducing it in these columns it is but fair that we should state that the form reprinted below is that appended to the lecture delivered by Mr. ALFRED LASS, F.C.A., Assoc. Inst. C.E., before the Chartered Accountants Students' Society of London on 4th December, 1888. The lecture and the *pro forma* accounts were duly reproduced in these columns at the time, and form the most valuable contribution upon the accounts of gas companies that has yet appeared in print, but the Cost Sheet, or working statement, was not then given, and we now publish it in these columns for the first time. It is as follows:

——— GAS COMPANY.

WORKING STATEMENT for the year ended ——— 18—

		Cubic Feet	
Gas made, as per Station Meter		156,288,000	
Gas sold: Private Lighting	137,963,400		
Public Lighting	10,953,450	148,916,850	or 95·28 per cent. on make.
		7,371,150	
Gas used on Works and Offices, as per Meters		2,500,000	or 1·60 do.
Gas unaccounted for		4,871,150	or 3·12 do.
			100·00

Capital employed	£76,689 0 0
do. per Ton of Coal Carbonised	5 6 0
do. per 1,000 cubic feet of Gas sold	0 10 3
Coal Carbonised. Common	14,117 Tons or 97·62 per cent.
Cannel	344 " 2·38 "
	14,461 " 100·00 "

Gas made per Ton of Coal Carbonised	10,807 cubic feet.
Gas sold per Ton of Coal Carbonised	10,298 cubic feet.
Coke made	14,460 chaldrons.
Coke made per Ton of Coal Carbonised	36 bushels.
Coke used for fuel per cent. on make	22·18
Tar made	150,180 gallons.
Tar made per Ton of Coal Carbonised	11 gallons.
Liquor made	405,594 gallons.
Liquor made per Ton of Coal Carbonised	28 gallons.
Net average price realised for Coke sold	8s. 2¾d. per chaldron.
do. do. Breeze sold	2s. 8¼d. per chaldron.
do. do. Tar sold	1½d. per gallon.
do. do. Liquor sold	34s. per 1,000 gallons.
Net proceeds of Coke and other Residuals per cent. on cost of coal	73·32

———	———		Per ton of Coal Carbonised.		Per 1,000 Cubic Feet Sold.	
	£ s d	£ s d	s d	s d	Pence	Pence
Coal		8,791 0 11	..	12 1·90	..	14·17
Less Residuals—Coke	4,633 0 4	..	6 4·89	..	7·47	
Breeze	118 6 0	..	1·96	..	0·19	
Tar	1,002 10 3	..	1 4·64	..	1·62	
Liquor	692 3 0	..	11·49	..	1·11	
Total Residuals		6,445 19 7		8 10·98		10·39
Net for Coal	..	2,345 1 4	..	3 2·92	..	3·78
Purifying	443 7 11	..	7·36	..	0·71	
Salaries of Engineers	350 0 0	..	5·81	..	0·56	
Wages and Gratuities at Works	1,436 0 11	..	1 11·83	..	2·31	
Repair of Works and Plant	3,816 7 6	..	5 3·34	..	6·15	
Salaries of Inspectors and Clerks	341 0 0	..	5·66	..	0·55	
Repair of Mains and Services	115 7 3	..	1·91	..	0·19	
Repairing and Renewing Meters	687 10 6	..	11·41	..	1·11	
Lighting and Repairing Public Lamps	558 17 10	..	9·28	..	0·90	
Rates and Taxes	738 16 3	..	1 0·26	..	1·19	
Directors' Allowances	420 0 0	..	6·97	..	0·68	
Salaries of Secretary, Accountant, and Clerks	148 5 0	..	2·46	..	0·24	
Collector's Commission	400 0 0	..	6·64	..	0·65	
Stationery and Printing	119 11 8	..	1·99	..	0·19	
General Establishment Charges	170 14 7	..	2·83	..	0·28	
Auditor	31 10 0	..	0·52	..	0·05	
Bad Debts	60 8 11	..	1·00	..	0·10	
Allowances	20 2 5	..	0·33	..	0·03	
Total Working Expenses		9,858 0 9		13 7·60		15·89
Coal and Working Expenses, less Residuals	..	12,203 2 1	..	16 10·52	..	19·67
Sale of Gas: Private Lighting	17,245 8 6					
Public Lighting	1,848 13 3					
	19,094 1 9	..	26 4·89	..	30·77	
Rental of Meters	554 6 10	..	9·20	..	0·90	
Rents	92 19 2	..	1·54	..	0·15	
		19,741 7 9		27 3·63		31·82
Profit		£7,538 5 8		10 5·11		12·15

It will be seen that the sheet is ordinarily prepared annually, when the usual accounts are taken out; but it not infrequently happens that an interim statement is desired, and this, of course, is prepared upon the same lines, except that, in such a case, many of the expenses would be estimated, and not actual, figures. The various lines of income and expenditure are, it will be noted, identical with the items stated in the statutory form of Revenue Account, but they are differently arranged, so that the net cost of coal and total working expenses may be separately shown.

A very similar form is used by water companies; but with these undertakings the most suitable bases for the decimal calculations are "per service" and "per thousand gallons of water supplied."

Accounts of a similar nature would be prepared by railway and tramway companies, the basis of the decimal calculations being "per train-mile" and "per tram-mile" respectively.

From the examples we have given it will be an easy matter for the intelligent reader to construct Cost Accounts applicable to any industry dealing in a "single line." The question of Cost Accounts as applied to heterogeneous manufactures is a matter that will next claim our attention.

COST ACCOUNTS.—III.

THE system of Cost Accounts that we are now about to describe, details the cost of manufacture in a general business, and shows the method of arriving at this result by means of a double analysis of the Wages and Stock Books. Each analysis is complete in itself: the first analysis gives :—

The cost of each department, or process ot manufacture ;

while the second analysis shows :—

The cost of the different kinds of goods under manufacture, or of work in progress.

It is recommended that the Cost Accounts be kept entirely separate from the Financial Books, so that at the periodical stock-taking the Trading Account and its Cost Account Summary may form a mutual check upon any errors that may have crept into the preparation of either or both ; but those who prefer that the two sets of accounts shall form a complete and scientifically constructed whole may really modify our system to meet this end by means of Adjustment Accounts. Although theoretically preferable this method is not recommended, however, as it increases the complications of—and so the difficulty in correctly keeping—the accounts.

Reverting to the Cost Accounts, the books required are:

(1) Wages Book.
(2) Stock Book.
(3) Cost Book.
(4) Summary of Cost Accounts.
(5) Reference Index.

Wages Book.—The most satisfactory method of recording workmen's time is to depute this work to a time-keeper who should take particulars daily in a book ruled as follows:—

Week ending 7th January 1890.

No.	Name	Department	Monday				Tuesday				Wednesday				Thursday				Friday				Saturday				Total hours	Rate	Amount
			Hrs.		Job No.	Fo.	Hrs.		Job No.	Fo.	Hrs.		Job No.	Fo.	Hrs.		Job No.	Fo.	Hrs.		Job No.	Fo.	Hrs.		Job No.	Fo.			£ s d
1 ..	John Davies ..	Castings ..	12	7 5	816 104	*10* *20*	10	3 7	104 200	*20* *10*	13	10 2 1	816 104 200	*10* *20* *10*	11	11	200	*10*	12	9 3	816 109	*10* *50*	7	7	109	*50*	65	7d.	1 17 11
2 ..	T. Mason ..	"B" Machine..	10	9 1	801 500	*70* *65*	12	8 4	500 104	*65* *20*	11	5 6	801 500	*70* *65*	9	4 5	104 801	*20* *70*	13	10 3	200 104	*10* *20*	7	7	200	*10*	62	7d.	1 16 2

When, however, the number of workmen employed is larger, and the smallness of the number of jobs on hand at any one time renders such a course practicable, it is desirable to so modify the above arrangement that *one posting* will suffice to record the number of hours spent upon any one job in each day, instead of a separate posting being necessary for each man's time as shown in the above form; but, of course, this modification is only applicable so far as the men are paid the same rate of wages.

Stock Book.—This is a most important book and is one that gives more trouble than anything else in connection with a system of Cost Accounts; but the following specimen will be found to answer well under ordinary circumstances, although in very large concerns—where one stock-keeper, cannot look after the whole stock kept—it may be found necessary to provide a separate Stock Book for each separate department.

Dr. STOCK ACCOUNT .... 189 . *Cr.*

A					B										C							D									
Date	P'ticul'rs	Quantity	Cost Price	Total											Date	P'ticul'rs	No. of Job	Quantity	Cost Price	Total	Returns										
			l s d	*l s d*		*l s d*		*l s d*		*l s d*		*l s d*		*l s d*					*l s d*	*l s d*	*l s d*		*l s d*		*l s d*		*l s d*		*l s d*		*l s d*

The stock in hand and the "incoming goods" are entered in columns marked A, and classified (quantity and cost) under the heads of their general substance, in the columns marked B. The "outgoing goods" (quantity and cost) are entered in the columns marked C, with the particulars and the department and number of the "job" for which they were used. The returns are entered in the next column. The "outgoing goods" are then classified in "D" to correspond with the entries on the other side, and posted into the Cost Book to the various accounts.

The difference between the two sides could represent the stock in hand.

Goods of various substances could be classified in one column if necessary, provided that the quantities were all expressed by the same measure.

Cost Book.—This is practically a Tabular Ledger arranged in the form of a double analysis (as before stated); Section I. showing the cost of each department or process of manufacturing, while Section II. shows the cost of the different classes or qualities of goods manufactured, or, where necessary, the cost of each separate portion of such work. The form of the book is as follows:—

Section I. Section II.

Date	Particulars	No. of Work		Hours (A)						Total	Rate	Total Wages and Stock (B)	Percentages charged (C)			Departments (D)						Cost of Goods and Work completed													Sun	dr's
														M. & Est. Exps.	Dpn. &c.																					
												l s d		l s d	l s d	l s d	l s d	l s d	l s d	l s d	l s d	l s d	l s d	l s d	l s d	l s d	l s d	l s d	l s d	l s d	l s d	l s d	l s d	l s d		l s d

COST ACCOUNTS.—IV.

COMING now to the method of keeping the form of Cost Book shown in our last issue, and dealing first with Section I. thereof: The workman's time is posted from the Wages Book in the columns marked "A," with the name, the number of the work, and the machines (departments) at which they are working. When necessary, the hours entered in these columns should be added in horizontal lines, and the totals will be priced out at the proper rates into the column marked "B."

The cost of the stock used (as per Stock Account) is also posted from the credit side of that book into the column marked "B," full details being entered in the column marked "particulars."

The proportions of Management Expenses and Depreciation and other charges to be inserted in column "C," are in the nature of percentages upon either the gross profit, or the number of hours employed. The latter is generally considered the juster basis, and is, therefore, recommended; but, in any case, the percentage must be fixed with the greatest care, for, although these figures are only estimates based upon past experience, it is of the utmost importance that they should be as reliable as it is possible for mere estimates to be.

The proper figures being inserted in the columns "B," "C^1," "C^2," the horizontal totals of these three columns are extended under the headings of the proper departments into the columns marked "D."

It now remains for us to deal with Section II., which supplies statistics as to the cost of different classes or qualities of goods manufactured; or—in trades where structural work is undertaken—the cost of each portion of such work.

For manufacturers who make their goods to put into stock awaiting sale, this section is to be used as a means of ascertaining the difference, from time to time, of the cost of making various classes of goods; while in trades, such as millwrights, where estimating for contractual work is very extensive, this section is arranged to show the cost of making each portion of a job separately; to be used as a means of reference to facilitate estimating, and to show the fluctuations in the cost of making the same portions of work, as a guide to future costing.

To enter up this section, therefore, the numbers or distinctive marks set out in the first section against each item are referred to, and the particular portions for which these numbers stand ascertained, when the items in Section I. analysis are then entered in this section (in a line), in one of the columns reserved for the cost of the respective parts of the job.

It will, therefore, be seen that this section will include the cost of all the portions necessary to complete the required structure.

The arrangement of the accounts in the Cost Book would not be the same for all trades. Where goods are manufactured and put direct into stock, awaiting sale, only one account for each class of goods manufactured is necessary, of which Section II. would be used to show the cost of the different qualities of goods in that class.

On completion of the manufacture of "one lot," the cost thereof entered up is ruled off, and the ascertained weight entered against the total.

To arrange the Cost Book for such trades as Shipbuilding, Engineering, Bleaching and Finishing, Building, &c., where business is received through contracts, an account for each "job" is necessary, with the name and full particulars stated therein.

As the contracts and orders are completed, and the Cost Accounts posted up, the columns of the two sections are added up and the accounts closed.

Cost Account Summary.—The totals of the cost of each job, as shown in the analysis (Section I.) of the Cost Book, are now transferred to the Summary, which may conveniently be ruled as follows:—

COST ACCOUNT SUMMARY FOR ENDING 189

Date	Name	Fo.	Cost	Man'ge-m't, &c. Ch'rges	Depreciation, &c.	Departments						Total Cost	Fo.	Contr'ct Price		Profit	Loss
			£ s d	£ s d	£ s d	£ s d	£ s d	£ s d	£ s d	£ s d	£ s d	£ s d		£ s d		£ s d	£ s d

A separate line is, of course, devoted to each contract, and side by side with the "Total Cost" is inserted the "contract price," the difference between the two figures thus represents either the net profit or the total loss upon each column, and is inserted in one of the last two columns accordingly. The difference between the total of the "Profit" column and the total of the "Loss" column should agree with the balance of the Profit and Loss Account for the corresponding period; but in practice—partly on account of clerical inaccuracies, and partly because the "management expenses" and "depreciation, etc.," employed in the Cost Accounts are only estimated amounts and not actual facts—there is usually a small difference. The clerical differences, unless of trifling amount, should be sought for and eliminated; while, if the percentages of management expenses and depreciation, etc., have been carefully fixed, the difference between the estimates and the actual results will not be large, and is dealt with as shown in the following:—

TRIAL BALANCE OF THE COST ACCOUNTS FOR 189 .

	£ s d	£ s d		£ s d	£ s d
Profit and Loss Account:			**Cost Accounts:**		
Sales..	5,196 14 2		Total Cost (from Summary)	..	3,876 19 4
Less Gross Profit	1,319 14 10	3,876 19 4	Percentages charged (from Summary), viz.:—		
Management and Establishment Expenses	401 2 0		Management and Establishment Expenses	406 8 2	
Depreciation	262 0 0		Depreciation and other charges ..	460 0 0	
Interest on Capital	195 0 0	858 2 0		866 8 2	
			Less (over-estimated)	8 6 2	858 2 0
		£4,735 1 4			£4,735 1 4

The analytical Totals of Section II. of the Cost Book are posted up in the *Reference Index*, the object of this book being to retain a record of the actual costs at different times of manufacturing similar articles. This, of course, is a purely statistical book, and its purpose will be readily understood after a perusal of the accompanying specimen page:—

1890.

Date	Particulars	Size	Name	Fo.	30 to 35 inches	35 to 40 inches	40 to 45 inches			
C Cylinders					£ s d	£ s d	£ s d	£ s d	£ s d	£ s d
1890 Jan. 29		30in.	A. & B. Co., Lim. ..	9	101 4 1					
Feb. 5		39in.	J. P. & Co.	21	..	143 15 0				
15		30in.	Tobin & Co. ..	53	105 8 0					
21		39in.	Leigh, B.	40	..	139 19 6				

COST ACCOUNTS.

IN a series of articles commencing on the 28th July last, we dwelt upon the advantages to be derived from a properly arranged system of Cost Accounts in every class of manufacturing business; and, in view of the scarcity of professional literature upon the subject, we went so far as to indicate the general lines upon which such a system might advantageously be based.

It would appear that our comments have aroused dire dismay and bitter wrath in the breast of one at least who has hitherto been accustomed to formulate Cost Accounts according to his own sweet will. In *The Practical Engineer* for the 26th ult. appears a somewhat hysterical and inconclusive article upon the subject of "Engineering Cost Accounts," which, strange to say, is backed by the editor of our contemporary, who gravely informs his readers that, "the writer, who has an intimate knowledge of the subject, refers to the efforts that are being made by the Institution (*sic*) of Chartered Accountants to seek legislative recognition of their right to interfere with the section of the books of a manufacturing establishment that have hitherto been regarded as quite outside their sphere and influence, viz., those devoted to the question of costs and estimates." Let us consider this remarkable statement for a moment. In the first place, if the "Institution of Chartered Accountants" already possesses the "right to interfere with . . . costs and estimates," it is not quite clear why they should now be seeking "legislative recognition" of that same. We may, perhaps, re-assure our contemporary, and also "the writer who has intimate knowledge of the subject," if we inform them that it is not claimed that the auditor of a joint-stock company has the "right to interfere with . . . costs and estimates," that no effort is being made by auditors to obtain this right by means of legislation, and that—so far as we are aware—no auditor is desirous of interfering with "estimates" in any way. So far as we are aware—and we may claim to have some little knowledge in this matter—the desire of the profession to go into the question at all is solely with a view to seeing that the Cost Accounts are prepared upon correct principles in the simplest possible manner, and that they are capable of being—and are—verified by periodical aggregation and comparison with the results produced by the Trading Account. Whatever may be said to the contrary by "writers who have an intimate knowledge of the subject," Cost Accounts that cannot be reconciled with the actual results of manufacture, as shown by the financial books, are altogether valueless and dangerously misleading. It may well be that many engineering undertakings possess adequate Cost Accounts that have never been framed by professional accountants: still the fact remains that in the majority of cases the "accounts" that have been formulated by amateur accountants are inadequate, and hence has arisen the demand—which is unquestionably increasing—for the proper systematisation of Cost Accounts upon a scientific basis.

With reference to the article in our contemporary, a few words of comment seem desirable; but, lest we should be doing an injustice to the writer, we propose to reproduce his text in full, introducing our notes and corrections as we proceed.

The professional accountants who audit our Balance Sheets and liquidate our insolvent companies have lately discovered a new source of revenue in cost accounts, and are now blazoning forth with such audacity the necessity for preparing these on a scientific basis, and by professionally scientific men, that we are tempted to ask if there were no mathematicians before the charter, nor bookkeepers before the incorporation.

Perhaps it is hardly reasonable to expect too much appropriateness from this preliminary flourish, but it may be mentioned that "mathematicians" possess no *primâ facie* qualification as framers of a system of accounts, and that "bookkeepers," as a class, have no very noted aptitude in that direction.

The Joint Stock Companies Act of 1866 contemplated a purely critical position for the auditors, but by patient continuance in well or evil doing this has become enlarged into a supreme dictatorial authority, before which must bow not merely the executive officers of the companies, but the chairman and directors also. Hitherto the cost accounts and estimates of engineering firms have been kept outside the auditor's scrutiny, but the efforts of the Institute of Chartered and Society of Incorporated Accountants will in future be directed to bringing these into the same category as the financial books, and thereby increasing the members' emoluments and control over the more technical portions of the business. It would be well, therefore, for engineers and engineers' accountants to carefully consider the effect of the new departure before it is too late to resist it.

It seems beside our present purpose to correct the writer's fantastic views as to the position of the auditor of a joint stock company, nor need we stop to enquire what is meant by "the Joint Stock Companies Act of 1866;" but it may, perhaps, be well just to mention in passing that, so far as we are aware, accountants do not contemplate checking the estimates of engineering firms. This apparent inability to distinguish between Cost Accounts and estimates is very curious: an accountant would as soon think of supervising a company's correspondence as of checking its estimates; but the Cost Accounts are records of transactions, and as such should be verified by the auditor, who is also interested in seeing that they are formulated upon proper lines.

A contemporary, which styles itself "the recognised organ of Chartered Accountants throughout the world," has been producing a series of articles on cost accounts, which contain the latest and most profound investigations of the profession into the subject, and the formation therefrom of a scientific system. But to the general and unprofessional reader the most curious point is that all this labour does not produce cost accounts at all, but merely elaborate departmental accounts. Indeed, neither the writer of the articles nor the eminent accountants whom he quotes appear to understand what engineering cost accounts really are, nor for what purposes they are required. We do not feel much surprise at this, since each distinct branch of industry has technical requirements which cannot be fully understood and appreciated without some knowledge of the industry; but the audacity of the accountants is exemplified in thus preparing useless forms of accounts, and lauding them as superior to the primitive forms which at present supply the engineer with an approximation of the information he requires.

The engineer and contractor requires the cost of each item of his contract so detailed that he can compare it with the original estimate. He does not seek to learn the cost of his foundry or smithy without any reference to the details of the work done therein. To compile from the ordinary books of record an estimate of the cost of producing a certain tonnage of pig iron in one, two, or twelve months is not a very great mathematical feat. We could find dozens of boys in any higher grade board school in London, Manchester, or Birmingham who could accomplish it, and who, indeed, perform more elaborate calculations, and arrive at more abstruse deductions every day in the year, without indulging the bantam's crowing propensities. The cost per unit of gas produced or water consumed is likewise a simple arithmetical calculation, requiring, indeed, certain data and some careful plodding, but certainly not involving any abstruse mathematical knowledge nor the application of the special science, whatever that may be, which accountancy has evolved.

The jubilant tone in which the above paragraphs are penned shows that the writer considers he has now practically settled the question. As a matter of fact, however, he has merely demonstrated his inability to comprehend the scheme we have described. We are not altogether surprised at this, for our articles presupposed some little acquaintance with accountancy upon the part of our readers; but it may be worth while to repeat a few matters mentioned in our previous articles that appear to have escaped the attention of "the writer of intimate knowledge." Thus on page 689, when describing a form of Cost Book, we expressly stated that "Section II. shows the cost of the different classes or qualities of goods manufactured, *or, where necessary, the cost of each separate portion of such work.*" Strange as it may seem, we are not unmindful of the requirements of either the engineer or the contractor; but, unlike the writer of the article in our contemporary, we have not forgotten the fact that there

51 *

are numerous other classes of manufacturers requiring Cost Accounts; while it is abundantly clear to anyone who cares to read that our scheme of accounts is a general one, requiring more or less modification before being adapted to any particular set of circumstances.

But it is in the accounts of more complicated companies that the instructor chiefly displays his ignorance. Railway and tramway companies are dismissed with the remark that similar accounts can be prepared as for gas and water companies, the basis of the decimal calculations being per train mile or per tram mile; the writer evidently being unaware that railway companies, and sometimes tram companies, build their own engines and carriages, construct stations and permanent ways, and perform other erective works, for each of which the engineer in charge requires detailed costs, and not a mere accountant's decimal arrived at over the whole line. We do not propose to discuss the forms given for the books of the more complex concerns. Any of the despised bookkeepers of our northern shipyards or large engine works will at once see that they are totally inadequate for their professed purpose, and utterly useless in any shop much larger than a country smithy. It is on the writer's sins of omission we would chiefly animadvert. He is ignorant of the fact that engineers require not merely the total cost of a contract, but also the cost in wages and materials of the individual items of it, and that with these latter details they are already supplied by their own bookkeepers. Improvements can doubtless be made in our present forms of Cost Accounts, but these improvements will certainly not be in the direction our contemporary and the lecturers he quotes advocate.

It is little use to the builder of a ship to know she costs £40,000, and to have that figure expressed in some æsthetic decimal. He requires to know the actual cost of the framing, the plating, the decks, the deck fittings, &c., each by itself, and to have these items detailed under the heads of materials and different descriptions of labour. He has based his estimate on some unscientific and rule-of-thumb conception (for engineers never take measurements, nor make calculations, we presume) of the wages which will be expended for shipwrights, platers and riveters, fitters, blacksmiths, and labourers, and the materials used by those tradesmen on the sternpost of H.M.S. Revenge, and he requires his Cost Accounts to show what has actually been so expended. No nicely balanced decimal points of the total cost of the ship will satisfy or be serviceable to him, and he will continue to keep his own accounts, and act on them, without regard to the "science" now so kindly presented to him. Nor does the writer seem to have any knowledge of the variation of establishment charges; the same percentage, based on the results of the previous year, is to be taken, whether the place be full of work or slack. The question of depreciation is not even touched upon, except as a percentage, although to every practical user of machinery it is evident that depreciation and repairs are of material importance in arriving at the cost of work, and that they vary in ratio to the varying speed of running. Even on the allocation of these precious percentages the writer has no definitely formed opinion, for he permits them to be based either on the gross profit, or number of hours employed, as the whim of the auditor may dictate. If by this he implies that it is of no consequence either way for purposes of accuracy, we quite agree with him, since both will prove delusive.

The reference to railway costs is too childish to merit serious attention. We are not aware that we suggested that a railway company should reduce the costs of its locomotive yard, &c., to decimals of a train mile, nor do we suppose the writer of the article we are quoting was so foolish as to suppose that we did.

The conclusion to the article is, perhaps, even finer than what has gone before. It reads as follows:—

And this is the latest effort of a profession which is seeking to arrogate, by legislative enactment, exclusive powers and privileges for its members, and the right alone to use the sacred appellation of accountant. Time was when the legal papers were weekly filled with complaints of accountants trespassing on the preserves of solicitors, and acting as hedge lawyers. They have made up their quarrel with the lawyers, and compensate themselves by intruding into every other branch of business, and instructing the practitioners thereof how to conduct it. But when we see such ignorance displayed in a matter of which they claim to have made a special and scientific study, it is at least permissible to doubt their infallibility, or the wisdom of granting them greater and more dictatorial powers than they now possess. It would be wiser for the engineering profession to rely on the efforts of cost engineers, and their own trained bookkeepers, for improvement in this most important branch of their accounts, and resist zealously the intrusion therein of those accountants and auditors who have no special knowledge of, nor aptitude for, the difficulties and requirements of all classes of engineering. If it is necessary, in order to satisfy the present fashion, to bedizen clerks and bookkeepers with diplomas and certificates, and all the other paraphernalia of education and examinations, our various societies could surely concoct some such scheme themselves, without ruining the practical efficiency of their assistants, or depreciating the usefulness of the statistics and returns they prepare.

From this we conclude that the class of engineer represented by our contemporary feel a marked disinclination to having their work overhauled. We should have profited ill by the lessons afforded by the past did not this suggest to us the possibility that engineers' Cost Accounts are even more in need of independent verification than we had at first supposed. Bookkeepers, and so-called accountants, who are conscious that their work is unchallengeable, do not usually shriek so loudly when any suggestion of auditing their accounts is advanced. Can it be that the case is worse than we had supposed? Certainly it is conceivable that considerable deceptions might be concealed by a careful cooking of Cost Accounts.

COST ACCOUNTS.

(To the Editor of The Accountant.)

SIR,—Referring to your article in the issue of the 3rd instant respecting Cost Accounts, and the apparent dismay and wrath aroused in the breast of the correspondent in *The Practical Engineer* of the 26th ult. upon the subject of "Engineering Cost Accounts," backed by the editor of that paper, claiming that Cost Accounts is a matter outside of our profession, I certainly maintain that that is erroneous, and such work is well within the duties of a professional accountant.

It is upwards of thirty years ago since I received my first instruction in Cost Accounts from a professional accountant. The accounts were then kept on what had been hitherto known as the Italian system, embracing the Trading and Cost Accounts jointly. The old despised Journal was then the fundamental book of the system, arranged like a Cash Book; on the left hand side Ledger Crs., right hand side Ledger Drs., with columns for Capital Expenditure, Personal Accounts, Property and Expenses. The Day Book was similarly arranged, and as each purchase or sale was entered, the Dr. and Cr. were placed on each side; Departmental Books contained the issues from stock, and departments kept their books of productions; all these transactions were carried out into values, the time was kept and apportioned daily, and the whole was gathered together and journalised monthly.

The auditor thus was necessarily compelled to audit the Cost Accounts as well as the Trading Accounts, owing to the combination. To such perfection were these accounts kept that it was a frequent practice to make up the cost of the work in progress of any particular engine or boiler at an hour's warning, such cost to be inclusive up to the night previous, so that, truly well-organised systems of Cost Accounts at that time formed part and parcel of the accounts of a manufacturing business. But with the exodus of the Italian system, thought at the time to be cumbrous for the payment of accounts, various dissections occurred, separating the Trading Accounts from the Cost Accounts, after which it has been a frequent matter of regret to manufacturers that the results of their costs do not reconcile with their Profit and Loss Accounts.

During my experience, I have found Cost Accounts prepared almost entirely from drawings and specifications, the labour excepted, and there is a work published upon "Engineering Estimates, Costs and Accounts," by Crosby, Lockwood & Son, of London, which bears out this view, but the results are attainable more in the form of estimate quantities. No provision is made for such cases as a workman spoiling any material, and drawing from stock to replace, and such "costs" are more assumptions than facts, which helps to explain the difference arising from the Cost Accounts and the result of the trading.

My view as to Cost Accounts being within the radius of a professional accountant is borne out by Mr. John Mann, jun., C.A., of Glasgow, in his paper given to the Society of the Accountants' Students upon Cost Accounts, and reported in your issues of the 29th of August and the 5th of September 1891, which is entitled "Notes on Cost Records; a Neglected Branch of Accountancy."

Doubtless competition in trading has a tendency to make a "Cost Office" a distinct department. As an instance, take the town of Sheffield, where side by side large firms are producing a staple trade of steel. It would be suicidal policy on the part of these traders to make public the costs of their manufactures, hence the secret and closed chamber of the cost office.

I have been honoured with the confidence of two large firms in that town to design and establish their cost office, and for the purpose of secrecy, I have made the system of costings on double-entry principles entirely separate and apart from the Trading Accounts; but at the end of the financial year the Cost Books have produced a Profit and Loss Account parallel and agreeing to the same figure as their Profit and Loss Account in trading books, thereby guaranteeing the absolute accuracy of the Cost Accounts. For the sake of argument I will admit that a slight technical knowledge is a great assistance in keeping the accounts; but this is easily acquired, for at the present time one of my clerks, after six months' tuition, is now with one of my clients as their established cost clerk, and keeping the accounts to their entire satisfaction.

At the Autumnal Meeting, held at Liverpool last month, during the discussion on Mr. Theodore Gregory's paper on the "Responsibilities of Auditors," Mr. Whinney stated that the figures in the assets of a Balance Sheet should represent facts. Many speakers described their inability of knowing when the stock valuations could be considered facts. I contend that with a complete system of Cost Accounts there should be no difficulty in ascertaining the true value of the stock at the end of the financial year; for assuredly the Cost Accounts contain the value of raw materials, materials in process, and finished goods at their actual cost values; then, so far as stock is concerned, the figures would prove the facts.

I maintain that our profession is fully competent to

master any technical business for the purpose of keeping Cost Accounts, and in my introductory paper (on a series of lectures which I have promised to give to the Manchester Chartered Accountants Students' Society) delivered on the 14th of March 1892, I give the leading headings of the various businesses that should keep a well-arranged system of Cost Accounts.

It is also my intention, in the near future, to give a lecture on "Shipbuilding," illustrated by slides on a screen, showing different parts of the building, from the laying of the keel to the actual completion. The Committee of Lloyds' Registry of Shipping, also the Bureau Veritas, have kindly presented me with their annual book of requirements for the current year, for assistance in the compilation of my paper. Therein will be shown a separate Cost Account which it will be necessary to keep during the construction of a ship.

I fear that I have trespassed largely upon your space; but it is a subject of great importance.

Yours truly,
THOS. PLUMPTON.

Manchester, Nov. 6th 1894.

COST ACCOUNTS.

EVEN as "wisdom is justified of her children," so is our esteemed contemporary, *The Practical Engineer*, obliged by every law of humanity to cover the retreat of its correspondent, whose knowledge of cost accounts has been said to be so "intimate."

Our contemporary has thrown its mantle of prophecy over the childish prattle that we reproduced in our issue of the 3rd inst., and so has been obliged to accept the responsibility of having countenanced views which doubtless it finds itself somewhat put about to justify. The curious feature is, however, that the "writer of intimate knowledge of his subject" is evidently not trusted to make his own reply.

The whole question may perhaps aptly be described as a "storm in a teacup," but it seems a little unfair to suggest that this pigmy storm is one of our creation. We should have thought that no one would have accused us of treating the matter seriously, and our own opinion is that this is precisely what our contemporary takes exception to. We have no desire to embark upon an endless discussion with an adversary so ill qualified to add anything to the information of our readers, but having once started, we do not care to let the matter drop until we have corrected the further misstatements appearing in our contemporary's columns.

Firstly then, we are accused of "committing a logical blunder by distributing a term" which our contemporary "did not distribute." We do not quite realise what the enormity of our crime consists of, nor—to be frank—do we fully comprehend what we have done, and how and when we have done it; but doubtless this point is not of any vast importance, so we will let it go by.

The next error we pointed out is attributed to the compositor. This unfortunate artisan has generally a good deal to answer for, and doubtless deserves much of the blame that is cast upon him; but we put it to our contemporary whether it is likely that he would have set up "the Joint Stock Companies Act of 1866" had its contributor written "The Companies Act 1862." The difference may not seem to be a very material one, but it gives one a fair idea of the "intimate knowledge of his subject" displayed by the contributor. This intimate knowledge seems to be shared by our contemporary, else it would hardly speak of "sections" of "Table A." Articles 86, 92, 93 and 94 are not unfamiliar to us, but they seem a little beside the question at issue, inasmuch as they can hardly be stretched to show that the intention of the Legislature was to prevent the accounts of a company being framed upon lines that should commend themselves to those who have made accountancy their study. It may truly be objected that an accountant cannot properly audit accounts that he himself has kept, but it may fairly be urged that a more effective audit is practicable if the accounts are kept upon scientific lines. We are obliged to our contemporary for its distinction between costs and estimates, but it must be admitted that the distinction is now made for the first time. We, being plain accountants, and not professors of social evolution, are, however, unable to appreciate the connection between the two that appears to be so obvious to our contemporary.

With regard to the form of Cost Book shown on page 689 of our current volume, we are content to leave it to our readers whether it meets the requirements stated or not. We think the form in question a good one, and have, accordingly, published it for the information of those who care to read; but, as we have already pointed out, our article presupposes some little acquaintance with accountancy upon the part of our readers. We do not supply information *and* the brains necessary to understand it at the moderate rate of sixpence a copy.

We do not pretend to dictate to our contemporary upon purely technical matters, and, accordingly, we shall not dispute its statement of what engineers mean by a locomotive yard, etc. Still, it is but fair to add that engineers, like doctors, frequently differ; and the interpretation put upon this term by our contemporary is not universally understood and acknowledged.

With regard to our alleged "gratuitous insult" to "the whole profession," it is perhaps desirable to state that no insult has been offered, and none intended. At the same time, we do not take back one word of the last paragraph in our previous article. Plain men of business will agree with us that no sensible man, actuated by worthy motives, would seek to exclude his auditor from the whole of his confidence, and further, that no subordinate who raises difficulties in the way of the examination of his work is entitled to be considered wholly disinterested. Accountants do not, of course, seek to deprive engineers, or anyone else, of their business, but the large experience and special knowledge of accountants make their advice upon matters of business—and especially in the record of business transactions—of no inconsiderable value. This is a matter that is very generally appreciated, and is receiving increased acknowledgment daily upon all sides. The ideas that find currency in our contemporary are certainly not the ideas entertained by the general body of engineers in this country. If our contemporary wishes to deserve its title "practical," it had better lose no time in joining the enlightened majority.

The Birmingham Chartered Accountant Students' Society.

Some Notes on Cost Accounts.

A Paper read at a meeting of the above Society, by Mr. A. J. Cudworth, F.C.A., *Vice-President.*

My object in taking up the subject of "Cost Accounts" is not to advocate any particular system, or to describe any special methods in great detail, but rather to address myself to the younger students of the Society with the view of helping them, if possible, to understand a little of the nature and uses of Cost Accounts in general. In November 1894 a most valuable lecture was delivered before this Society by Mr. Whitehill, dealing specially with the uses of Cost Accounts for the purposes of an audit, and giving a sample set of Cost Accounts which he regarded as specially useful for that particular purpose. I do not propose to cover at all the same ground as was covered by that lecture, but to treat the subject in a more general and elementary way.

Let us address ourselves first to two questions—

(*a*) What are Cost Accounts? and

(*b*) What are their uses?

The first question, "What are Cost Accounts?" is not by any means so easy to answer as "What is a Profit and Loss "Account?" or "What is a Balance Sheet?"

Cost Accounts may vary very much in form, and they may be kept with very different objects, but to get something like a definition of the term, I think we may say that "a "Cost Account is a statement showing the ascertained or "estimated cost of producing a certain article or class of "articles." I say "ascertained or estimated" because it may be either. It may be an estimate based on previous experience of the cost of an article which it is proposed to manufacture, or it may be a statement of the actual cost of an article already manufactured.

The use of a Cost Account in the first case, where it is of the nature of an estimate, is chiefly to enable the manufacturer to form a judgment as to the price at which he can afford to sell the article when made; or, in the event of the selling price being fixed, whether he can make the article at a reasonable profit. And, further, after the article has been manufactured and sold, it affords an opportunity of comparing the estimated with the actual cost, and, if necessary, revising the estimated cost for future use.

In the case where the cost is ascertained after the article is manufactured and sold, a Cost Account is usually of the nature of an elaborate analysis of the Trading Account and Profit and Loss Account figures, enabling a manufacturer to see on which articles the best profit is made, and the average cost of labour and material in each case, and the results obtained for one period are of course valuable as the basis of estimates for the future.

In the definition of a Cost Account I spoke of it as showing "the cost of producing a certain article, or class of articles." Now, most manufacturers produce repetitions of the same article over and over again. In these cases the cost is usually worked out on the basis of the production of a fixed quantity, say, per ton of coal or iron, per 1,000 of bricks, per hundred gross of pens, &c., as may be most convenient.

The term "Cost Account," I take it, is wide enough to cover either—

1. A memorandum of the supposed cost of producing an article; or

2. An account showing the application of the estimated cost of producing an article to the number of articles made or sold during a particular period; or

3. An account showing, after stock has been taken and the actual profit or loss ascertained, the average cost per article made or sold, divided under such headings as may be most convenient.

Before going further into the subject it may, perhaps, be well for us to consider how far Cost Accounts are matters for Chartered Accountants to deal with; seeing that the figures constituting them, as a rule, form no part of the double-entry system of bookkeeping.

We may have prepared careful Trading and Profit and Loss Accounts showing both purchases and sales, divided under a variety of headings, showing the percentage of gross profit on sales, and a complete analysis of all establishment charges; and we may be inclined to think that these accounts give the manufacturer all the information that he can possibly require. But we frequently find that the result is not so good as the manufacturer expects. He remarks, perhaps, that, whereas we show a gross profit of 26 per cent. on the sales, he reckons to get from 30 to 35 per cent. on most of the articles he sells, and cannot understand the result. It is obvious that, in such a case as that, it is unsatisfactory to allow the difference to pass unexplained; and, I think, a further investigation of the circumstances comes well within the accountant's sphere.

Most manufacturers, I suppose, keep a book, or books, in which calculations of the supposed cost of making the articles which they sell are entered; but I am afraid it is quite the exception when these calculations are thoroughly tested and verified by the accountant.

I do not consider it to be necessarily part of the duty an auditor must perform, before he can certify the accuracy of a Balance Sheet, to go into these matters, although I quite agree with Mr. Whitehill that, where a Cost Account system can be carried out in the complete manner described in his paper, a check is obtained upon the *bonâ fides* of the accounts which it would be impossible to obtain in any other way.

I think, however, that in the numerous cases where such a complete system as that would be impracticable, or where the client might be disinclined to go to the necessary expense, and where the only Cost Account kept is in the form of memoranda of the supposed cost of the various articles sold, the accountant may render a valuable service to his client by testing the figures of the calculation, and pointing out in what respect they appear to require revision at each stocktaking.

We want, therefore, to make up our minds whether our services to our clients are to be restricted solely to certifying the accuracy of the Balance Sheet and Profit and Loss Account, or whether we ought to be able to render further services by going into Cost Account matters which may give the proprietors a better grasp of their business.

In the case of a limited company, I have already said that I do not consider it to be an auditor's duty to insist on Cost Accounts being kept, in order that he may the better satisfy himself of the accuracy of the books.

The duty imposed upon him of exercising reasonable care does not, I think, necessitate his insisting on such a course, though, where Cost Accounts are kept, I think it would be his duty to avail himself of such means of checking the accuracy of the results as the accounts afforded.

It is, then, in the capacity of accountant rather than of auditor that we approach these matters; and, while an ordinary audit fee may not be sufficient to remunerate us for the time involved, I think that where our clients are not unwilling to incur the extra expense of a Cost Account system we shall render them an important service by carrying it out.

As regards our side of the question, it affords, of course, a wider scope for our energies, and it is work of a character demanding the best brain power that we can give to it. There are no general rules such as those which govern any application or development of a double entry system, but each kind of business requires treating in a special way and has to be considered in the light of its special requirements.

It is, therefore, one of the most interesting branches of our work, while at the same time one of the most useful to the community at large.

Let us, then, take an instance, such as that previously mentioned, where the rate of gross profit shown by the Trading Account is very much below what the manufacturer estimates, and see what steps can be taken to explain the difference.

The estimated gross profit is from 30 per cent. to 35 per cent. on the sales, and the actual is only 28 per cent.

We must first enquire how the manufacturer arrives at his estimated 30 per cent. or 35 per cent., and he will very likely produce a book and say: "Well, here, for example, is "my estimate of the cost of such and such an article"—say, in the case of a slate quarry, a ton of best slates.

	£	s	d
Labour, getting slate	1	10	0
,, removing rubbish..	0	5	0
,, day-men	0	4	6
Gunpowder	0	1	6
Royalty	0	2	6
Cartage to station	0	2	0
Depreciation of plant	0	1	6
Total cost	£2	7	0

He will go on to say that the average selling price of best slates, less discounts, has been £3 16s. per ton, thus showing a gross profit of about 35 per cent. Now, when such an account as this is produced it is first of all necessary to see whether, in our Trading or Working Account, we have provided for just the same items of expense, before estimating the gross profit, as the manufacturer or quarry owner has done. It is possible that this may be the case and that other Cost Accounts may be produced for other qualities of slate, all showing a considerably greater gross profit than that shown by the Working Account, and the mystery still remains unsolved.

In a case of this sort, if the Working Account is correct, the Cost Account is obviously at fault, and as the quarry owner very likely bases his selling prices on the supposed cost per ton for raising and carting to the station, it is a very serious matter if this calculation is incorrect.

There are a few simple tests which we can apply which ought to throw some light on the discrepancy without any very serious amount of labour.

We will first make an analysis of sales, giving the quantities sold of each class of slate, say, A., B., and C., and the money value of each. By apportioning the discounts, and dividing the amount by the tonnage, we can soon calculate the average selling price of each class and see whether the price the quarry owner reckoned on is correct. This, however, is not a very likely source of error.

Our next step will be to make an analysis of the wages, as follows:—

Getting slate, Class A.	800 tons	at 30/-	..	£1,200
,, ,, B.	600	,, 25/-	..	750
,, ,, C.	400	,, 20/-	..	400
	1,800			
Removing rubbish ..	..	..	..	680
Day-men ..	..	..	..	420
Total pay	..	..	..	£3,450

Probably the prices paid for getting slate will be found to be quite in order.

The amount paid for removing rubbish is £680, and the total tonnage of slates made is 1,800, thus giving an average of 7s. 6d. per ton, as compared with 5s. per ton provided in the Cost Book. Thus, attention is drawn to the fact that in the present state of the quarry so much rubbish has to be removed in getting to the good slate, that the 5s. which was supposed to cover it is found to be quite inadequate, and this under-estimate of 2s. 6d. a ton on 1,800 tons is equivalent to £225.

The amount paid to day-men—£420—divided by the 1,800 tons of slates made gives an average of very little more than 4s. 6d. a ton, so in this particular the Cost Book figure is fairly substantiated.

The figures for gunpowder and depreciation of plant are arrived at by dividing the total cost by the tonnage of slates *made* in the period, and the cartage by dividing the total cost by the tonnage *sold*. It may be that these figures are found to be fairly accurate; the Royalty Account is least of all likely to be wrong; and so the only matter of importance which has been discovered is the under-estimate of the cost of removing rubbish.

It is evident we have not yet got to the bottom of the

mystery, and our next and final step will be to balance the stock for the period.

We shall require a statement somewhat in the following form:—

STOCK ACCOUNT.

	Class A Tons	Class B Tons	Class C Tons	Total Tons		Class A Tons	Class B Tons	Class C Tons	Total Tons
To Stock on hand, Jan. 1st ..	210	120	160	490	Sales for the half-year ..	740	620	350	1,710
" Total make for half-year, as per Wages Analysis..	800	600	400	1,800	Balance forward, being Stock at June 30th	270	100	210	580
	1,010	720	560	2,290		1,010	720	560	2,290
To Balance forward, being Stock at June 30th ..	270	100	210	580					

Now this statement shows that there ought to be in stock the following:—

	Tons.
Class A	270
,, B	100
,, C	210
	580

But the Stock Book shows the following as in stock:—

	Tons.
Class A	230
,, B	80
,, C	180
	490

There is, therefore, a deficiency of—

	Tons.
Class A	40
,, B	20
,, C	30
	90

It is evident that this deficiency in stock is what accounts for the remaining deficiency in the gross profit. But what does the stock deficiency mean? It means one of three things:—

Either the stock has been entered wrongly in the Stock Book at January 1st or June 30th, or wages have been paid for slates that have not been made, or slates have been removed without being entered in the Day Book.

If the Stock Account balanced satisfactorily at January 1st there can be no question about that, but the matter is so serious that in order to verify the correctness of the Stock Book at June 30th we have the stock taken again, say, a fortnight later, and after allowing for slates made and sold during the fortnight, it is found that the Stock Book figure for June 30th is verified within three or four tons.

The only possible explanations remaining are that wages have been paid for slates which have not been made, or that slates have been sent away without being booked.

The proprietor's suspicions now being aroused in these two directions, special precautions are taken; and it soon comes out that one of the gangers among the quarrymen has been in collusion with the man at the weighing machine, and the weight of slates made by his particular gang of men has habitually been slightly overstated.

Deficiency	Tons	*Excessive Wages Paid*	£
Class A.	40	At 30/-	60
" B.	20	" 25/-	25
" C.	30	" 20/-	30
	90		£115

Thus wages amounting to £115 have been paid for 90 tons of slates which were never raised; the deficiency in the rate of gross profit is explained, and the fraud is discovered.

The result of our investigation, therefore, has been to show that the difference between the estimated and actual rate of gross profit is roughly accounted for by the cost of removing rubbish being under-estimated to the extent of £225, and a fraud in the wages of £115.

It is now obvious how unsatisfactory it would have been if, when our client expressed surprise at the gross profit being less than he estimated, we had allowed the remark to pass without getting to the bottom of it; and I hope it is also clear how exceedingly valuable it is to be able to balance a Stock Account.

In the case of a slate quarry, this is a particularly easy process, although there are often slight complications, owing to the ton sometimes being reckoned as containing more than 20 cwt., which I have thought it unnecessary to go into.

In some businesses the balancing of the stock is almost an impossibility; but when it can be done with tolerable accuracy by the expenditure of a reasonable amount of time and trouble, it should most certainly be done.

You are, of course, familiar with the fact that, in ordinary double-entry bookkeeping, the profit or loss for a period is arrived at by two distinct sets of figures, namely, those contained in the Balance Sheet, and those contained in the Trading Account; and one of the chief values of such a system is that one set of figures proves the others.

But you are aware that the figure of stock usually forms an exception to the rule in this sense—that it appears both in the Balance Sheet and the Trading Account; and, consequently, the figure of stock is the only one with regard to which no kind of check exists.

That being so, if a balanced Stock Account can be kept alongside the double-entry system, it provides a control over the business which cannot otherwise be obtained.

In the particular case which we have examined, it is difficult to see how the fraud in the wages could have been otherwise discovered; and wherever a balanced Stock Account is introduced it will be found that, although the detection of fraud may be an exceptional thing, waste or leakage of some kind, which could not otherwise have been detected, is almost sure to be brought to light.

We may remark, in passing, that a balanced Stock Account is not necessarily a part of a Cost Account system, though the figures required in connection with it are very useful in Cost Account calculations.

Therefore, by all means let a balanced Stock Account be introduced, even if a Cost Account system is not combined with it. If you carefully consider the question of the value of Cost Accounts for the purposes of an audit, as set forth in Mr. Whitehill's paper, I think you will come to the conclusion that it is the balanced Stock Account which gives the Cost Accounts their chief value for that particular purpose.

We have now described how we should set to work to test the difference between an estimated and an actual gross profit in the case of a slate quarry; and the only kind of Cost Account we have referred to is the memorandum of the supposed cost of raising and carting to station of a ton of slates. In this particular case the investigation is a very simple one; and, if the figures were not larger than those given, probably the expenditure of one or two days' extra time in connection with the audit would suffice to give all the required information.

But there are many cases in which such an investigation is a much more difficult matter; and it would be impossible, at the time of the audit, to carry it out unless throughout the period under review special records were kept to facilitate the process.

We come now, therefore, to the use of the term "Cost "Account" in the sense of my second definition, viz.:—

"An account showing the application of the estimated "cost of producing an article to the number of articles "made or sold during a particular period."

In the case of the slate-quarry we assumed, for the sake of simplicity, that only three classes of slates were sold; and you will remember that the matter was further simplified by dividing certain items of cost—such as "removing "rubbish," "gunpowder," &c., equally per ton on all slates without regard to class.

But if we consider the case of a printer, for instance, we shall at once be met by a number of difficulties not presented by the other case.

Our first difficulty is that we can fix on no standard—such as a ton of slates—on which to base our cost calculations.

The printer has no memorandum of the cost of producing a particular article which he turns out in large quantities.

On the contrary, almost every order requires its cost to be separately calculated, and repeat orders are quite the exception.

All printers do, of course, make a calculation of the supposed cost of executing an order before they quote the price at which they will undertake the work, and if at a stocktaking we wish to be able to test the accuracy of these estimates, there is nothing for it but systematically entering in a book from day to day the particulars of those estimates in some form or other.

A convenient method of keeping these records, if the want of privacy is not considered an objection, is by having special columns ruled in the Sales Day Book, so as to record opposite each order the supposed cost of executing the work and the margin of gross profit left.

If a very elaborate analysis of the supposed cost is required, or greater privacy is desired, a special book should be kept in which the orders are re-copied from the Day Book for the purpose of the cost calculations.

In either case it will probably be found convenient to have separate Day Books for the different departments, such as general printing, lithography, and stationery.

Let us take a case which is not too elaborate, but in which for the sake of privacy the costs are entered, not in the Sales Day Book, but in a Cost Journal kept specially for the purpose.

The ruling of the Cost Journal will be somewhat as follows:—

GENERAL PRINTING DEPARTMENT.—COST JOURNAL.

Date	Name	Particulars	Paper	Ink and Color	Other Materials	Productive Wages	Total Cost	Selling Price
1896			s d	s d		s d	s d	£ s d
Jan. 17	Wood Bros...	2,000 Circulars	7 6	6	..	8 6	16 6	1 10 0

In the case shown here an order for 2,000 circulars has been executed and charged to Wood Bros. through the Sales Day Book at 30s.

The item is then re-entered in the Cost Journal, and the estimated cost in paper, ink, and productive wages is entered in the appropriate columns. The total estimated cost is seen to be 16s. 6d., leaving a gross profit of 13s. 6d. The productive wages include all wages which can conveniently be charged on to specific work, but do not include warehousemen, packers, engineer, timekeeper, &c., and in the double entry system the same distinction between productive and non-productive wages must be observed.

Every item in the Day Book must be repeated in the Cost Journal in the manner shown, and all orders executed in the lithography and stationery departments will also be entered in separate Cost Journals ruled with appropriate headings.

At the end of a month we take the totals for paper, ink, etc., shown by the Cost Journals, and incorporate the figures into the double entry system.

For this purpose an ordinary double entry Journal will be found a convenience.

The following may serve as sample entries for a month :—

Date	Particulars	Dr. £	s	d	Cr. £	s	d
1895 Jan. 31	Paper *Cr.*	..			650	0	0
	Sundry Departments *Dr.*, viz. :—						
	General Printing	310	0	0			
	Lithography	120	0	0			
	Stationery	220	0	0			
		£650	0	0	£650	0	0
"	Productive Wages *Cr.*	..			800	0	0
	Sundry Departments *Dr.* viz. :—						
	General Printing	560	0	0			
	Lithography	190	0	0			
	Stationery	50	0	0			
		£800	0	0	£800	0	0

And so on with the totals of the remaining columns of the Cost Journals.

We have thus credited the Materials and Wages Accounts and debited the three departments with the *estimated* amount of materials used and wages paid in each department upon the work turned out in the month.

It now remains to be seen whether the wages paid for the month pretty nearly agree with the amounts charged to the departments.

In the Wages Account on the debit side are the wages paid for the month, and on the credit side the amounts transferred to the departments in accordance with the Cost Journals. We shall have to make allowance for the wages paid on work in progress, but when this is done the account ought to balance very nearly if the work has been properly charged.

Should it not approximately balance, there is evidently something wrong in the system of charging which must be explained, and an analysis of the productive wages, under the headings of Composing, Machining, Folding, etc., may be helpful in localising the leakage. It will be seen, then, that in the event of any serious leakage in the Productive Wages Account attention will be at once called to the fact at the end of a month, and a little investigation will soon suffice to put matters on a more satisfactory basis.

The Material Accounts cannot, of course, be balanced until stock is taken, and if this is only done annually no complete check can be exercised until the end of the year.

The Paper Account, for instance, will commence on the debit side with the paper in stock at the beginning of the year, under which will be entered the purchases for the month of January.

On the credit side will appear the amount of paper used for the month and charged to the departments. The balance of the account should, of course, show the value of the paper in stock on January 31st, taking as in stock the paper used for work then in progress. Thus, although the proper stock-taking may be deferred until the end of the year, we have brought before us each month the amount of paper which *ought* to be in stock; and, without spending much time upon it, it is quite possible for an experienced person to ascertain whether the amount really in stock is about right.

Let us now suppose that the monthly totals of the Cost Journals have been incorporated into the double entry system in the manner described for a complete year, and we come to the question of the stocktaking and Balance Sheet.

A statement of the work in progress will have to be prepared, analysed under the headings of the Cost Journals, showing how much paper, wages, etc., have so far been expended upon the work. These sums will be carried forward as stocks in the various Material and Wages Accounts in the Ledger.

Thus the Paper Account, when closed for the year, will appear as follows :—

Dr. PAPER. *Cr.*

Date	Particulars				Fol.	£	s	d
1895 Jan. 1	To Raw Stock brought forward				..	1,715	16	9
"	" Work in progress brot. forward, viz. :—							
	General Printing ..	£121	10	0				
	Lithography	15	0	0				
	Stationery	30	10	0				
						167	0	0
Jan. 31	" Purchases				..	600	0	0
Feb. 28	" do.				..	710	0	0
Mar. 31	" do.				..	596	0	0
April 30	" do.				..	811	10	0
May 31	" do.				..	515	0	0
June 30	" do.				..	687	0	0
July 31	" do.				..	601	0	0
Aug. 31	" do.				..	728	10	0
Sept. 30	" do.				..	589	0	0
Oct. 31	" do.				..	641	0	0
Nov. 30	" do.				..	733	10	0
Dec. 31	" do.				..	467	0	0
					£	9,562	6	9
1896 Jan. 1	To Raw Stock brought forward				..	1,614	10	0
"	" Work in progress brought forward ..				..	311	16	9

Date	Particulars				Fol.	£	s	d
1895 Jan. 31	By Sundry Departments				J. 17	650	0	0
Feb. 28	" do.				..	765	0	0
Mar. 31	" do.				..	528	0	0
April 30	" do.				..	780	0	0
May 31	" do.				..	656	10	0
June 30	" do.				..	627	10	0
July 31	" do.				..	682	0	0
Aug. 31	" do.				..	591	0	0
Sept. 30	" do.				..	616	0	0
Oct. 31	" do.				..	573	0	0
Nov. 30	" do.				..	648	0	0
Dec. 31	" do.				..	519	0	0
"	" Raw Stock carried forward				..	1,614	10	0
"	" Work in progress forward, viz. :—							
	General Printing ..	£165	0	0				
	Lithography	128	10	0				
	Stationery	18	6	9				
					..	311	16	9
					£	9,562	6	9

The amounts charged to the departments represent the estimated amount of paper used on orders actually executed and passed through the Day Books. The paper used for work in progress has, therefore, not yet been charged to the departments, and must necessarily show as stock in hand carried forward in the Paper Account.

The *wages paid* on work in progress will, in like manner, be carried forward as a stock in the Wages Account.

The raw stock of paper, £1,614 10s., is obtained from the Stock Book as a result of the stocktaking; and it is, of course, quite possible that when this figure is brought into the account a deficiency may appear. After a thorough investigation into the cause of the deficiency it will have to be disposed of—either by charging it to the departments, or by transferring the amount to Profit and Loss Account, under the heading of Paper Deficiency. In the example taken it is supposed to be adjusted in the amount charged to the departments for the month of December.

The other Material and Wages Accounts will also have to be adjusted in a similar way, so as to make the accounts balance; and, thus, at each stocktaking, before we can close the books, every deficiency in Wages or Material Accounts necessarily comes under review.

It ought to be noted that, before the books are closed at the end of the year, any finished stock—consisting of executed orders which have not been delivered, and are, therefore, not passed through the Sales Day Books—should, nevertheless, be entered in the Cost Journals, so that the Material and Wages Accounts may be properly credited in respect of it. It will be found the most convenient course to put the selling price of this finished stock in the selling price column of the Cost Journals, thus crediting the year just ended with the profit on the work. To be consistent we must also show the finished stock at selling price in the Trading Account. As regards the propriety of this, we may remember that the goods have not been made for stock, but to special order, and it is largely a matter of accident whether they are invoiced just before or after the end of the year. If, however, the circumstances are such that it is not desirable to value the stock at selling price, it is still a convenient course to credit the Trading Account with the selling price, so as not to complicate the Cost Account calculations, the discount off the selling price being adjusted through the Profit and Loss Account. It is also a good plan to deduct from the sales in the Trading Account the finished stock at the beginning of the year, and to add that at the end of the year, thus giving a net figure of finished stock *made* during the year. This figure is then useful as a basis on which to calculate the percentages of material, &c., used during the year.

When complete the Trading Account of the general printing department will be as follows:—

GENERAL PRINTING DEPARTMENT.

Dr. TRADING ACCOUNT, JAN. 1ST TO DEC. 31ST 1895. *Cr.*

	£ s d	£ s d		£ s d	£ s d
To Paper	5,170 0 0		By Sales as per Day Books	22,410 0 0	
" Ink and Color	380 0 0		*Less* Finished Stock Jan. 1st 1895	275 0 0	
" Other Materials	760 0 0			22,135 0 0	
" Productive Wages	6,840 0 0	13,150 0 0	*Add* Finished Stock, Dec. 31st 1895	186 0 0	22,321 0 0
" Balance being Gross Profit carried to Profit & Loss Account		9,171 0 0			
		£22,321 0 0			£22,321 0 0

An examination of this account will show that, while it is the product of the double entry system, it accords throughout with the Cost Journal; the item paper, for instance, agreeing with the total of the paper column in that book, and the £13,150 agreeing with the total cost column.

On the other side the figure of sales after adjustment in respect of finished stock, £22,321, agrees with the selling price column of the Cost Journal.

The other departments are treated on just the same principle, and the balance of gross profit in each department is carried to the credit of Profit and Loss Account.

We must remember that it will be necessary to charge to Profit and Loss Account all expenses not provided for in the Cost Journals. Thus, in the case we have taken, all non-productive wages, discounts, and depreciation of machinery must be charged to Profit and Loss Account, as well as all other expenses. Also, in the event of the finished stock not being valued at selling price in the Balance Sheet, the adjustment of the Finished Stock Account will appear as an item in the Profit and Loss Account.

There is nothing else of a special nature in Profit and Loss Account or Balance Sheet, and it is unnecessary, therefore, to give them in detail.

It will now be observed that we have not only got Trading Accounts for every department, showing what gross profit has been earned by each, but these Trading Accounts are supported by Cost Journals showing on which orders that gross profit has been earned, or in the event of deficiencies the extent to which the labour or material was underestimated.

It is impossible, therefore, for a printer, whose books are kept in this manner, to fail to understand the result shown by the Balance Sheet. If there is a weak spot, the finger can be placed upon it without difficulty; and, in my opinion, it is quite as much within the scope of an accountant so to arrange accounts as to draw the attention of his client to any leakage which may exist as to certify the correctness of a Balance Sheet.

Before passing to another system of cost keeping, we may remark that, in the example just taken, scheduling the *cost of each order* forms the basis of the Cost Accounts, and the subsequent incorporation of the Cost Account totals into the double entry system, while a valuable method, is by no means necessary. If it were preferred to keep the two sets of figures quite distinct, it would still be possible to exercise the same checks upon the cost of the work.

It may be well, in order to illustrate the variety of methods which have to be applied to Cost Accounts, just to give a rapid sketch of a business differing very much in character from that of a printer; bearing in mind that it is to be another instance of the use of the term "Cost Account" in the sense of—

"An account showing the application of the estimated "cost of producing an article to the number of articles "made or sold during a particular period."

We will take the case of a sweetmeat manufacturer. Now a moment's consideration will show that, in this case, an attempt to schedule the *cost of each order*—as in the case of the printer—would be a hopelessly elaborate method of procedure; for one order may include small quantities of fifteen or twenty kinds of sweatmeats, each having a separate cost.

The case is necessarily somewhat more elaborate than the last; but we have not time to do more than indicate the general lines on which to work.

The first thing is to fix on a basis for the cost, and we will decide on taking 1 cwt. of sweetmeats as the basis.

We shall have to make a special analysis of the Sales Day Books, so as to ascertain the *weight* of each particular kind of sweetmeat sold during the period; and each particular kind will require a line in the Cost Accounts.

In the case of the printer, we only attempted to make the Cost Accounts show the gross profit; but, in this case, we will endeavour to forecast the net profit as accurately as possible, and thus, by bringing our Cost Accounts out in monthly totals, have an idea how the business is going each month, without the trouble of a stocktaking.

We will divide all the expenses of the business under the following headings:—

1st cost.—Ingredients.

2nd cost.—Packing materials.

Piece wage.

3rd cost.—All expenses other than those included above.

The 1st cost, 2nd cost, and piece wage are worked out for every article sold at the rate of so much per cwt.

The 3rd cost is estimated as accurately as possible, having regard to the amount of the expenses of the previous period. The amount is then divided equally for each month of the period, and the monthly figure for 3rd cost is divided by the number of cwts. of sweets of all kinds sold during the month, giving an average 3rd cost per cwt. for each month.

Our Cost Journal will then appear thus:—

SWEETMEAT COST JOURNAL.

Description of Article	1st Cost	2nd Cost	Piece Wage	3rd Cost	Total Cost per cwt.	Selling Price less Discount	Profit per cwt.	Quantity Sold	Net Profit
	£ s d	£ s d	£ s d	£ s d	£ s d	£ s d	£ s d	cwt. qrs. lbs.	£ s d
Cream Caramels	1 11 0	9 0	8 0	1 5 0	3 13 0	4 0 0	7 0	54 2 0	19 1 6

This account shows that the estimated cost of a cwt. of cream caramels is—

	£	s	d
Ingredients	1	11	0
Packing materials	0	9	0
Piece wage	0	8	0
Other expenses	1	5	0
Total cost	£3	13	0

The selling price is £4 per cwt., thus giving a net profit of 7s. per cwt., and the quantity sold being 54 cwts. 2 qrs. the caramels show a net profit of £19 1s. 6d.

You will observe that by this method the estimated net profit for the period is subdivided over every article sold, and if the result can be made to agree approximately with the actual result the information afforded is most valuable. Not only can you tell in which months the larger part of the profit was made, but to what extent each article has contributed to the result; and the advantage of being able to tell the net profit approximately each month without a stocktaking is also very great.

It is not to be expected that, when first introduced, a system of this kind will give a very accurate result; it will, however, draw attention to mistaken estimates, and when these are revised the results will be more reliable than before. Time does not suffice to describe in detail how Cost Accounts of this character may be tested and compared with the actual result shown at stocktaking.

There is always sure to be a difference in the third cost, as it is impossible accurately to estimate establishment charges beforehand; and when this difference has been adjusted, the first cost, second cost, and piece wage remain to be tested. For this purpose the cost per cwt. of each article under these headings must be multiplied by the weight sold, so as to obtain the money equivalent of the various costs; and we then get a Profit and Loss Account in the following form:—

COMPARATIVE STATEMENT OF RESULTS.

	Cost Account Figures	Actual Figures		Cost Account Figures	Actual Figures
	£ s d	£ s d		£ s d	£ s d
To 1st Cost			By Sales (less Discounts)		
" 2nd Cost					
" Piece Wage					
" 3rd Cost					
Total Cost					
Balance, being Net Profit					

Having now got the money equivalents of the Cost Journals arranged as above, we must proceed to arrange the figures of the Trading and Profit and Loss Accounts on the same lines, so as to be capable of comparison; and we shall then see in what particulars the cost may have been under-estimated, and wherein lies the difference between the estimated and the actual result. We must not spend the necessary time to follow this out, but you will see that it involves, among other things, the elimination of the item of stock from the Trading Account; and we shall not be able to treat the finished stock as we did in the case of the printer, where all the work was made to the order of customers, and the figure was trifling in amount.

The arrangement of the Trading and Profit and Loss Account figures in this form is, of course, merely as a memorandum, and for purposes of comparison only; the Cost Account results in this case not being in any way incorporated into the double entry system. A comparative statement of this kind forms, however, a most valuable adjunct to the Balance Sheet, and, in addition, the monthly results without stocktaking which the system affords are a great advantage.

I have not yet referred to the kind of Cost Account coming under the third definition, viz. :—

" An account showing, after stock has been taken and " the actual profit or loss ascertained, the average cost " per article made or sold, divided under such headings as " may be most convenient."

I do not propose to take an instance of this, as an example is fully worked out in Mr. Whitehill's paper, to which I must refer you for particulars.

The chief advantages are those afforded by the balanced Stock Account and the records of the variations in the average costs and selling prices.

I hope I have said enough now to show how varied Cost Accounts of businesses must necessarily be; not only varied in detail, but varied in the basis on which the system rests.

The printer's system is, of course, only applicable to cases where a separate cost is worked out for each order.

The simplest cases are those where large quantities of the same thing are sold, such as collieries, brickworks, or slate quarries, and the most difficult cases are those in which a great variety of articles are sold.

The importance of Cost Accounts of some kind is apparently now becoming more generally recognised. In the new trade combination adopted by the bedstead and other trades, an Association Cost Book is one of the promin features.

It is, first of all agreed, I believe, among the bedstead-makers that the cost of making a bedstead of a particular pattern is a certain fixed amount made up of a number of items which are set forth in the Cost Book, and whether it costs a particular maker more or less, he is bound by the association cost in quoting his price.

I think that this compulsory Cost Book is one of the most attractive features in these combinations, for many trades have been greatly damaged by persons who have ignorantly sold below cost.

Under the new system the various manufacturers will, if they are wise, keep their books in such a manner as to see whether their own cost is above or below that of the association, and if they do so the Cost Book will be of much greater value to them than could otherwise be the case.

I think it must have struck you that the information afforded by a Cost Account system is just what is wanted where a business is not doing satisfactorily, and an investigation and report is required. Of course, an investigation which begins and ends within a few weeks does not afford the opportunity, as a rule, of going very far into these matters; but in many cases the most helpful thing that an accountant can do is to inaugurate a Cost Account system, have it in operation for six months, and then make his report, when the real cause of failure is almost certain to have been brought to light.

In conclusion, let me ask you to be as practical as possible in your daily work. Do not let figures be mere figures to you, or be satisfied with testing their arithmetical accuracy alone. Always make it your aim to grasp the facts which the figures are supposed to represent, and to thoroughly understand the causes which have produced the results which the figures show. If this be your aim and ambition I think that, whether it may greatly help you in your examinations or not, you will find that the study of Cost Accounts is one which you can not afford to neglect.

Chartered Accountants Students' Society of London.

Chartered Accountants as Experts in Commerce and Manufactures.

By Mr. O. Holt Caldicott, F.C.A

A paper read at a meeting of this Society.

Mr. Chairman and Gentlemen,--I propose to employ the opportunity which your Society has been good enough to afford to me in considering the wider uses of accountancy in its application to the varying requirements of the various trades with which we are, as auditors and accountants, professionally connected. I have on more than one occasion, when it has been my privilege to address meetings of practising accountants and of students' societies, urged the necessity for our acquainting ourselves with many of the technicalities of manufacturing and commercial concerns in order that we may be qualified to speak as experts, not merely in figures and intricate calculations, but also in regard to the cost of production and distribution of various commodities, and in regard to the soundness or unsoundness of our clients' trading, having regard to the special conditions affecting the particular business of each one.

I believe that my professional brethren are not all of my opinion on this point, and that some of them think that we have quite enough to do, and undertake quite sufficient responsibility, if we confine our attention to the figures contained in the books submitted to us, satisfy ourselves of their numerical accuracy, and certify the ultimate result of the trading as it appears upon a proper balancing of the books.

I cannot agree to take this restricted view of our responsibilities or of our utility, and I hope that it will become universally acknowledged by Chartered Accountants that we must do much more than this if we are to take our proper rank and perform our full functions in the midst of this trading community, whose commercial and financial operations are increasing day by day, and amongst whom it is becoming increasingly difficult for the individual to look after his own affairs owing to the diffusion of his capital in consequence of the enormous development of co-operation under the Companies Acts.

Probably the ordinary investor does not discriminate between various certificates or stay to inquire if the accountant giving the certificate has special experience in that particular trade, but the Law Courts are quite disposed to insist upon an auditor's responsibility, and to assume that, in giving a certificate, he claims to speak as an expert.

We certainly hold out our qualification as members of this Institute as a guarantee that we are competent to undertake all the duties of our profession, and we cannot afford to limit the scope of our certificates, but must be prepared to say in effect that we not only speak as accountants, but have a sufficient knowledge of the particular business under consideration to entitle us to express an opinion in reference to it which may be accepted as sound and authoritative.

It may be urged that it is impossible for an accountant to acquire so much knowledge, that he has neither time nor opportunity, that many trades require a life-long experience, and that any attempt to acquire so much technical information could only succeed if each accountant consented to devote his whole attention to one or two trades, and that in this way the profession would be split up into sections of specialists, and that any general test of ability to practise, such as the present examinations, would be impracticable. I think not, and upon reflection I fancy that you will agree with me. I have always thought that the ideal accountant was prepared, at a few moments' notice, to go anywhere and do anything—to undertake the management of a small grocery, or to frame a constitution or administer the affairs of a province; but I am really not asking that the average accountant should be a finished master of all trades. Locality and personal connection have so arranged our business that I think very few of us are professionally concerned in a great variety of trades or professions. It may be that some large offices embrace a wide area; but it will be found that in these the business naturally divides itself into departments, and that no one man is required to understand the technicalities of many and widely-varying industries.

The opportunities of acquiring technical knowledge of trades will not fall very largely to the student during his term of articles. He will have enough to do to master the general principles of his profession, and to qualify himself to answer the legal and accountancy questions at his examinations; and, further, he will not always find his employers' clients willing to give him an opportunity of learning their business; but, if he is observant and thoughtful, the special knowledge of which I speak must come, and my object to-night is to illustrate the mode of applying bookkeeping figures to produce results and furnish information which are of real value to our clients Any such application of figures requires a previous knowledge of the requirements of the particular business, and careful thought as to the information which will furnish the most valuable statistics

Looking back over 30 years' experience I am not satisfied that we have, in this particular direction, made all the progress which might reasonably be expected from us. The fault is not wholly ours. For many years the volume of trade has been rapidly increasing, and traders were for a time content to keep pace with it, but now improved means of production have overtaken demand, and competition has reduced the rate of profit to such an extent that it is necessary to scan very closely every item of cost. Some years ago a successful manufacturer said to me that he used not to trouble about an accountant, that he knew he was making £20,000 a year, and that was good enough for him. He was a type of a large class (I do not mean as to the £20,000 annual profit) who looked round their works, saw that the stock was about as usual, that the works and plant were kept up, that there was the usual ratio between book debts and liabilities, that there was a balance at the bankers, and that some investments had been made during the year; and who would have wondered what more any reasonable man could require? But times have changed, and these happy results cannot be obtained without a much closer attention to details than was necessary in the good old times. What were then large undertakings were in the hands of private owners, who, from long familiarity, were intimately acquainted with their business; but now the corresponding trades either are, or soon will be, in the hands of joint stock companies, and the Chartered Accountant employed as auditor should be competent to inform the directors not only what profit their company has earned, but how it has been earned, and should have such a knowledge of the requirements and values connected with the business which he audits as to enable him to assure the shareholders that the liabilities are accurately stated and the assets truthfully valued, and that the Balance Sheet does in fact represent the actual condition of the company's affairs.

A company's auditor cannot enter into details with his constituents, as when he takes them into his confidence he takes in all the world; but the shareholders and those who may become shareholders will feel more confidence in the certificate if they know the auditor to be qualified by special experience to speak in respect of the business under consideration. I know that there are difficulties. The directors may be disposed to recommend to the shareholders an auditor's fee which will not admit of further inspection of the books than is necessary to verify the figures in the Balance Sheet. In this case I would recommend a little patience, a conscientious study of the business, and unobtrusive assistance to the board, and I think in due time the reward will come

It may happen that the board or the managers resent the auditor's attempt to make himself familiar with details In this case, bearing in mind a recent decision wherein it was held that the auditor must not accept the manager's valuation of stock without satisfying himself that it was properly valued, I should advise persistence or resignation.

I am afraid that I am wandering a little from my original intention, which was to set before you a few accounts relating to different trades, drawn up in such a way as to furnish useful information. These accounts have no novelty or originality to recommend them, and, probably, you are all familiar with other and better forms, but my experience has shown me that few clients have adopted them on their own initiative, and I am led to believe that this simple application of figures to show material facts is not so common as it might be with advantage to many. I have selected a colliery, a metal works, and a tramways company for the purpose of illustration, as the operations are simple and the trades well distributed.

Firstly, as regards a colliery. You may have presented to you for audit the Private Ledger, showing the value of the coal sold, the cost in wages, and a few other items of expenditure, the royalty, and the value of the stock at the beginning and the end of the account.

You may check the Day Books with the Ledgers, you may vouch the sales by the Ticket Books, you may vouch the cash payments, check the Ledger balances and carry through all the details of an audit, but if you do nothing more your certificate is of very little worth.

Colliery accounts are usually kept upon a system which is misleading, as no account is taken of the increase or decrease of the gate-roading during the year—that is to say, a large number of men may have been employed in opening-up roads in the pit for future work, but no credit is taken for the value of their work at stock-taking, but in the following year the coal may be gotten from these roads, which may not be replaced by others. You will see that the first year's result is prejudiced and that the second year's profit is unduly augmented by this operation.

Of course, it would not be wise to pay a larger dividend in the first year because you had opened up some work, but it would be wise to put on record exactly what had been done.

This record appears on the plans of the colliery, and it is worth the auditor's while to inquire what has been done during the year, and, further, to inquire if the mine is going on satisfactorily or if any broken ground has been found, and, generally, as to the prospects of the shareholders having a productive mine for a long term of years.

Of course, if the remainder of the mine were found after a number of prosperous years to consist entirely of disturbed ground, which was not worth working, the loss would, under the decision in the *Val de Travers* case, fall upon capital, and there may be no necessity for providing for such a contingency by the creation of a Reserve Fund, but I think that, if no notice were taken of the altered condition of the pit, a purchaser of shares would not be disposed to exonerate the auditor on the plea that he was not a mining surveyor and that it was no part of his business to examine the pit or the plans.

If there is any expectation of such a catastrophe it is certainly desirable that the auditor should know it, and I think that there are means by which he can know it. The auditor will not know the position of every man in the pit, but he ought to know approximately the rate of wages payable in the district, and the ruling prices for coal, and to be able to say how much per ton the wages amount to, and if the other items of expenditure are reasonable or excessive You will probably find a monthly account, somewhat similar to the one marked A. which is in your hands, in use at every well-managed colliery, and, as auditor, you should see it, and if it is not in use you should have sufficient technical knowledge to introduce it. You will observe that this account does not enter into many details, but condenses the numerous accounts in the Nominal Ledger so as to show the expenditure grouped under a few convenient headings, and the total figure of revenue.

The account is intended for the use of the directors at their monthly meetings, and gives them the results of the preceding months of the financial year in totals and separate results for the last month preceding the meeting, which are then added to the figures of the previous months and the totals given up to date, each item being worked out upon the ton of coal sold.

It is desirable that this account should be supplemented at the end of the year by a further account giving a comparison with the preceding year in the Form B. The conditions of the two years may be widely different, but it is precisely that difference, if there is any, and its effect upon their trade, with which the proprietors ought to be acquainted.

In the illustration which I have given the cost of raising the coal has been very similar in each year, but in the latter year a higher price has been obtained. Unfortunately, the company has not had the full benefit of this increase in price, as less coal has been sold, leaving them with a profit about equal to that of the previous year. Whether this deficiency of output arises from want of energy, scarcity of coal, or defective appliances, it is the business of everyone concerned (including the auditor, if only for his own satisfaction) to ascertain.

In Form C. I give you a similar statement for two years applied to a metal working business, but in this case the items of cost are worked out as a percentage upon the value of the goods sold. It would be more accurate to take a percentage upon the value of the goods manufactured, but in a business producing a great variety of articles, of which a large portion is always in process of manufacture, it would entail a very careful analysis of the stock to ascertain the value of goods actually finished during the year, and in a business where there are no considerable fluctuations in the value of the stock the sales represent the main factor with sufficient accuracy. If I were dealing with blast furnaces or smelting works I should show the cost and selling price per ton. In Form C. a break is made after taking into account the stock at each end of the account, the materials purchased, the productive wages, and the sales, and a gross profit is brought forward, against which are charged all the expenses of management and distribution. There is room for an infinite variety of opinion as to the precise point of expenditure at which gross profit should be calculated, but, in my opinion, it is not worth while to spend much time or ingenuity in a fanciful analysis if you adopt a clear and intelligible line of demarcation and adhere to it year after year.

This account shows a great improvement in prices in 1896, with a correspondingly larger gross profit, and the increased value of the sales reduces the percentage of expenses, so giving the firm a profit of £9,600 instead of £5,850. The only item which has increased is discounts; and, probably, the explanation was that the increased trade made the firm rather short of money, and they allowed some extra discounts for prompt payment.

In Account D. I have given a statement for two years of the working of a tramway, where you will see that every item of receipts and expenditure is worked out per mile run. The information conveyed by this account is that the directors have in the second year given a much more frequent service of trams, running 500,000 miles instead of 400,000, but that their enterprise has not at present been rewarded, their earnings per mile having fallen from 6d. to 5·76d. The line appears to have been very economically worked, and I am afraid that both horses and cars have been to some extent starved. The horsekeep is very low, and I doubt if the amount spent in horses would keep their stud up to a high standard, and I should fear that the cars and permanent way are in need of substantial repairs, which will have to be made as soon as an improved revenue will permit.

I had it in contemplation to introduce some tables relating to gasworks, which perhaps admit of the best statistics of any trade I know, showing the produce of each kind per ton of coal carbonised, and the cost of gas per ton of coal carbonised, per 1,000 feet of gas made, and per 1,000 feet of gas sold, as regards each item of production and distribution; and I could take you through other trades, but I think the forms which I have given will sufficiently illustrate my meaning. I think that we ought to be sufficiently expert in every business whose accounts we audit or compile to claim that our opinion should be accepted as authoritative, and I think that when called in to advise upon any business we ought to enter upon our inquiry either with a prior knowledge of that business or with a natural aptitude and an accumulated experience which will enable us to grasp at once the salient points. We should never neglect an opportunity of seeing a business in actual operation. It is a great help to us to see things made. Cordial intercourse with practical men will always help us, and although we could not take their place and do their work, we can by observation and experience bring before them results which they would not without our aid either know or appreciate at their true worth. I am not sure that *Crede experto* means "The opinion of an expert may be safely accepted;" it may mean, "You may believe a man who has "burnt his fingers;" but I think my translation, though free, is sufficiently accurate for me to take the phrase as my motto for this paper. *Crede experto.* "Rely upon the "Chartered Accountant who is an expert in commerce and "manufactures."

You will see that, in my opinion, we should view accounts not merely as auditors, but as skilled accountants and men of sound commercial experience, who are qualified to advise either owners or intending purchasers, and whose opinion may be accepted with full reliance upon its soundness and accuracy. We also place our services at the command of disputants who have decided to submit their disputes to arbitration; and to any accountant acting as arbitrator a knowledge of the technicalities of the particular business is of inestimable value.

We are told at times that our chief occupation will be taken from us by the compulsory introduction of official auditors. I have not much fear that this can take place. There are, at the present time, about 2,000 practising accountants, assisted by trained clerks, and the number is constantly increasing.

Joint stock companies require their accounts to be audited

at the time most convenient to themselves, and cannot wait for official convenience.

I think that the enormous staff required would be alone a sufficient reason why no Government Department could undertake this duty, but our position is immensely strengthened, if we not only provide the services required by the commercial community at the time when they require them, but in addition we bring to bear upon our investigation an intelligence trained in accounts and trained to apply our knowledge to their special business by our intimate acquaintance with its conditions, only inferior to the experience of those actually employed in carrying it on.

I have purposely restricted my paper within reasonable limits, as I think I may probably be asked to supplement the foregoing remarks by verbal explanations of the tables which I have placed in your hands.

Very hearty votes of thanks were accorded to Mr. Caldicott for his great kindness in reading the paper, and to Mr. Pixley for his presence in the chair.

COLLIERY COMPANY.

A. APPROXIMATE RETURN for the Month ending 31st December 1896.

	Tons	Total for 11 months ending 30th November £ s d	Realised per ton s	d	Total for month of December £ s d	Realised per ton s	d	Total for 12 months ending 31st December £ s d	Average price realised per ton for 12 months s	d
Coal and Ironstone sold for 11 Months ending 30th November	110,000	38,500 0 0	7	0						
Ditto for December	10,000	..	..	..	3,000 0 0	6	0			
Total Sales	120,000	..	..	..	..	..	..	41,500 0 0	6	11
		£38,500 0 0	7	0	£3,000 0 0	6	0	£41,500 0 0	6	11

	Total for 11 months ending 30th November £ s d	Cost per ton s	d	Total for month of December £ s d	Cost per ton s	d	Total for 12 months ending 31st December £ s d	Average cost per ton for 12 months s	d
Cost of raising Coal and Ironstone, viz.:—									
Wages	20,000 0 0	3	7·64	1,500 0 0	3	0·0	21,500 0 0	3	7·[illegible]
Stores	5,100 0 0	..	11·13	510 0 0	1	0·34	5,610 0 0	..	11·2[illegible]
	25,100 0 0	4	6·77	2,010 0 0	4	0·34	27,110 0 0	4	0·22
Royalty (estimated)	2,500 0 0	..	5·45	200 0 0	..	4·80	2,700 0 0	..	5·40
General Charges (estimated)	1,240 0 0	..	2·70	200 0 0	..	4·80	1,440 0 0	..	2·88
Directors' Fees, Salaries, and Office Expenses	1,900 0 0	..	4·15	200 0 0	..	4·80	2,100 0 0	..	4·20
Rent, Rates, &c.	2,000 0 0	..	4·36	300 0 0	..	7·00	2,300 0 0	..	4·60
Depreciation	1,000 0 0	..	2·18	80 0 0	..	1·92	1,080 0 0	..	2·16
Balance, being Surplus subject to Stock	4,760 0 0	..	10·39	10 0 0	..	·34	4,770 0 0	..	9·54
	£38,500 0 0	7	0·00	£3,000 0 0	6	0·00	£41,500 0 0	6	11·00

	£ s d
Balance at 31st December	4,770 0 0
Add Increase in Stock	1,000 0 0
Balance as per Profit and Loss Account	£5,770 0 0

B. COLLIERY TRADE ACCOUNT for the Two Years 1895 and 1896.

	1895 Cost per ton		1895 Amount £ s d	1896 Cost per ton		1896 Amount £ s d
Wages	3	11·86	33,500 0 0	3	7·00	21,500 0 0
Pit Timber ..	..	4·57	3,200 0 0	..	4·20	2,100 0 0
Oil and Grease ..	..	·34	240 0 0	..	·90	450 0 0
Candles	..	·17	120 0 0	..	·10	50 0 0
Horse Keep ..	..	1·72	1,200 0 0	..	2·20	1,100 0 0
Iron and Steel Castings, Rails, &c...	..	1·28	900 0 0	..	1·20	600 0 0
Sundry Stores ..	..	1·94	1,360 0 0	..	2·62	1,310 0 0
Royalty	..	5·00	3,500 0 0	..	5·40	2,700 0 0
Discounts and Allowances ..	..	1·29	900 0 0	..	1·60	800 0 0
Repairs to Plant..	..	·24	170 0 0	..	·48	240 0 0
Trade Charges ..	..	·46	320 0 0	..	·56	280 0 0
Boat and Wagon Hire	..	·16	110 0 0	..	·24	120 0 0
Directors' Fees ..	..	·71	500 0 0	..	1·00	500 0 0
Salaries	..	2·14	1,500 0 0	..	3·00	1,500 0 0
Office Expenses ..	..	·17	120 0 0	.	·20	100 0 0
Rent, Rates, and Taxes	..	3·50	2,450 0 0	..	4·60	2,300 0 0
Reserve for Exhaustion of the Mines	..	1·54	1,080 0 0	..	2·16	1,080 0 0
	6	1·09	51,170 0 0	6	1·46	36,730 0 0
Deduct Increase in Stock	..	1·43	1,000 0 0	..	2·00	1,000 0 0
	5	11·66	50,170 0 0	5	11·46	35,730 0 0
Balance being Profit in twelve months	..	8·34	5,830 0 0	..	11·54	5,770 0 0
	6	8·00	56,000 0 0	6	11·00	41,500 0 0

	1895 Tons	1895 Rate		1895 Amount £ s d	1896 Tons	1896 Rate		1896 Amount £ s d
Coal and Slack sold	168,000 0 0	6	8·00	56,000 0 0	120,000 0 0	6	11·00	41,500 0 0
	168,000 0 0	6	8·00	56,000 0 0	120,000 0 0	6	11·00	41,500 0 0

BRASS-FOUNDRY BUSINESS.

C PROFIT AND LOSS ACCOUNT for the Two Years 1895 and 1896.

	1895 Percentage on Sales	1895 Amount £ s d	1896 Percentage on Sales	1896 Amount £ s d
To Stock at commencement	..	15,000 0 0	..	16,000 0 0
„ Purchases	..	24,000 0 0	..	25,000 0 0
„ Wages	..	22,000 0 0	..	23,000 0 0
„ Gross Profit carried forward	23·73	14,000 0 0	27·70	18,000 0 0
		75,000 0 0		82,000 0 0
To Salaries	6·78	4,000 0 0	6·15	4,000 0 0
„ Travelling	3·05	1,800 0 0	2·77	1,800 0 0
„ Rents, Rates, and Taxes	1·02	600 0 0	·92	600 0 0
„ Trade Charges ..	·68	400 0 0	·76	500 0 0
„ Repairs	·34	200 0 0	·46	300 0 0
„ Discounts	1·27	750 0 0	1·70	1,100 0 0
„ Bad Debts	·68	400 0 0	·15	100 0 0
„ Net Profit	9·91	5,850 0 0	14·79	9,600 0 0
	23·73	14,000 0 0	27·70	18,000 0 0

	1895 Percentage on Sales	1895 Amount £ s d	1896 Percentage on Sales	1896 Amount £ s d
By Sales for 12 months ..	..	59,000 0 0	..	65,000 0 0
„ Stock at end of year..	..	16,000 0 0	..	17,000 0 0
		75,000 0 0		82,000 0 0
By Gross Profit brought forward	23·73	14,000 0 0	27·70	18,000 0 0
	23·73	14,000 0 0	27·70	18,000 0 0

TRAMWAYS COMPANY.

D. PROFIT AND LOSS ACCOUNT for the Years 1895 and 1896.

	1895 Rate per Mile run		1895 Amount £ s d	1896 Rate per Mile run		1896 Amount £ s d
To *Horses*—						
Wages	1·05	..	1,750 0 0	1·08	..	2,250 0 0
Bedding	·04	..	50 0 0	·03	..	70 0 0
Hay	·45	..	750 0 0	·44	..	900 0 0
Corn	·90	..	1,500 0 0	·74	..	1,550 0 0
Stores	·04	..	50 0 0	·02	..	50 0 0
Shoeing and Veterinary	·20	..	300 0 0	·22	..	450 0 0
Horse Renewals ..	·10	2·78	200 0 0	·14	2·67	300 0 0
To *Cars*—						
Wages	·04	..	70 0 0	·04	..	100 0 0
Stores	·01	..	10 0 0	·01	..	20 0 0
Repairs	·10	..	200 0 0	·04	..	100 0 0
Depreciation	·07	·22	120 0 0	·10	·19	200 0 0
To *Traffic*—						
Wages	·40	·40	700 0 0	·45	·45	900 0 0
To *Permanent Way*—						
Materials	·10	..	150 0 0	·12	..	250 0 0
Wages	·03	..	30 0 0	·02	..	60 0 0
Depreciation	·10	·23	220 0 0	·15	·29	300 0 0
To *General*—						
Stationery	·	..	50 0 0	·02	..	60 0 0
Water, Gas, and Office Coal	·0	..	70 0 0	·04	..	90 0 0
Repairs	·	..	100 0 0	·07	..	140 0 0
Rent, Rates, Taxes and Insurance .. .	·20	..	350 0 0	·20	..	400 0 0
Salaries	·06	..	100 0 0	·06	..	120 0 0
Directors' Fees	·20	..	300 0 0	·15	..	300 0 0
Professional Charges ..	02	.	30 0 0	·02	..	60 0 0
Incidental Travelling Expenses ..	·05	..	90 0 0	·05	..	100 0 0
Bank Charges	·02	..	30 0 0	·02	..	40 0 0
Depreciation of Machinery ..	·02	·73	40 0 0	·04	·67	80 0 0
To Balance, being Profit for year	2·24	2·24	3,740 0 0	1·97	1·97	4,110 0 0
	6·60	6·60	11,000 0 0	6·24	6·24	13,000 0 0

	1895 Rate per Mile run		1895 Amount £ s d	1896 Rate per Mile run		1896 Amount £ s d
By Traffic Receipts	6·00	..	10,000 0 0	5·76	..	12,000 0 0
By Sundry Receipts	·06	..	100 0 0	·07	..	150 0 0
By Manure	·03	..	50 0 0	·04	..	90 0 0
By Discounts ..	·07	..	110 0 0	·02	..	40 0 0
By Advertisements ..	·44	..	740 0 0	·35	..	720 0 0
	6·60		11,000 0 0	6·24		13,000 0 0

Mileage, 400,000
Passengers, 2,000,000
1895.

Mileage, 500,000
Passengers, 2,300,000
1896.

Birmingham Chartered Accountant Students' Society.

A New System of Cost-Taking in Trade.

By Mr. W. A. ADDINSELL, A.C.A.

A PAPER read at a meeting of the Society held on Tuesday, December 6th 1898, Mr. G. C. T. PARSONS, F.C.A., in the chair.

BEFORE beginning to give you the reflections which it is my intention to bring before you, I feel that I ought to say what may probably be in your minds already, that the subject is commonly accepted as being peculiar to the one person who is known to be the inventor of the plan, Mr. E. J. Smith. It would be impossible for anyone else to adequately say all that can be said in defence or explanation of the scheme.

I do not wish to claim any credit which does not properly belong to me, so that at the outset I wish you to understand that the contents of my paper are to a great extent the outcome of my association with Mr. Smith, and the result of the many opportunities I have had of hearing his methods of explanation.

I have been requested to express my opinion and give my experience as to what is now generally known as the system of taking out manufacturers' costs first suggested and brought into practical working under the new trade combination scheme of which it is a most important part. In doing so, I wish it to be distinctly understood that in this system there is no attempt to depart from any of the well-known principles, or even methods, of accountancy, neither is it desired on the part of its suggestor to reflect in any way on the methods of auditing which are so well known and accepted all over the country.

The new system became necessary for the simplest of reasons: before trade combination was aimed at manufacturers were supposed to take out their costs of production, and to fix their selling price from the results of such cost-taking. In this work the services of accountants were often sought and their advice presumably followed. The new scheme does not question the value of such advice or indeed attempt to override it in any way. It falls in with the methods, accepts the principles, and applies both. The only difference is that while cost-taking hitherto has been done by single individuals, firms, or companies, the new scheme aims at sinking individuality, and making cost-taking an essential part of the duty of a whole trade, large makers and small, each being subject to the same methods and each being called upon to accept the same results.

The difficulty of this will be at once apparent. It is commonly supposed that there must be a wide difference in the cost of production between the large and the small manufacturer. Curiously enough, however, even authorities disagree upon this question as to which manufacturer possesses the advantage—the large or the small producer. Each one of us must have heard the question many times. There are some who strongly assert that the large maker with his ample capital, his perfect machinery, and his large turnover, must be able to produce at lower cost than his small competitor with insufficient capital, his old-fashioned machinery, if any, and his limited trade. On the other hand, there are many who just as strongly maintain that the maker who spends little, because he has but little to spend, who makes best use of the humble means at his disposal, making up by personal work or supervision for the absence of what might almost be called scientific help, and who, because he has a small turnover, puts up with inexpensive methods and cheap premises, must have an advantage over the more freely-spending large competitor.

In introducing the new scheme it is not assumed that either of the two opinions must be correct. It is rather assumed that as there is a difference of opinion no harm can come of further inquiry under circumstances which give a better opportunity of arriving at right conclusions.

Hitherto it has been left to individual opinion only, either on the part of manufacturers or on the part of the experts engaged by them. The new scheme assumes that only by conference between manufacturers, large and small, and only by comparison after unreserved and frank interchange of ideas and opinions, can truth be ascertained. Such conference and confidence in each other was once impossible. Combination has made it not only possible, but absolutely necessary, and from this has arisen the system, supposed to be new, of taking out costs from comparison of ideas and experience throughout a whole trade, instead of leaving each individual maker to judge entirely for himself.

At a meeting of accountants there will be, I am sure, no need for me to enlarge upon the necessity for manufacturers to ascertain the cost of production before fixing their selling prices. Professionally, it must be to our interest to encourage a practice in which professional advice is necessary or advisable. But, coming to the ethics of the question, there is no likelihood of a division of opinion on a subject of vital importance to commercial prosperity in this or any other country.

Yet it is impossible to properly estimate the importance of this new system without realising the fact that cost-taking is not considered to-day an indispensable factor in carrying on business. We may say it with shame, with hesitation, and in fear of contradiction, but if we are to be honest there are few of us who cannot say it with a clear conscience. I do not wish to pose as an authority, excepting so far as my experience must make me wiser than I was before, but I am, on account of that experience, able to say that there is amongst manufacturers to-day a lamentable ignorance, and in many cases, even absolute indifference, as to the real cost of articles they sell.

This is a deplorable state of things which everybody who values the commercial prosperity of this country must regret.

From this arises most of the cut-throat competition which forces manufacturers to do a large turnover without profit, or with so little that they would earn as much if they were not manufacturers at all. The worst of it is that the ignorant, incompetent, or reckless have the power to force other people to their level. It is not in the power of a single honest manufacturer to raise others to his level, but it is in the power of the dishonest manufacturer to destroy the prosperity of a whole trade.

From a knowledge of this fact, and with a desire to provide a remedy, the new system of trade combination, with its many phases, arose. It is not within my province to-night to discuss any of these, excepting the one which forms the subject of my paper. What I wish to bring before you is the fact that it is now accepted by many trades that the wisest and safest thing to do, if ignorance is to be removed and recklessness restrained or controlled, is to take out costs of production by comparison of opinion and experience and after united conference and discussion.

That this has been difficult to bring about you will all be prepared to hear. The jealous guarding of what are known as trade secrets must be familiar to all of you. It is no libel upon manufacturers to say that in no walk in life has so much jealousy and distrust, to say nothing of dislike, been engendered as between business men of this country. The large maker has regarded the small maker as an interloper whom it was quite fair if possible to destroy, while the small maker has regarded large ones as monopolists whom it was his duty to harass in every possible way. Success in either case has only matured contempt, and failure has only engendered bitterness. Of this buyers have naturally taken every advantage, playing off one maker against another until a common danger has made united action on the part of their victims a necessity. This is perhaps the only reason why Mr. E. J. Smith has been able to persuade manufacturers of all sorts and sizes to sit together at one table and confide their dearly loved secrets to each other.

The notion of self-preservation has been the first impulse, and the discovery that none of them were so bad as was supposed has kept them together after they have once met. As for the so-called "secrets" it has been positively amusing to me to watch the surprise, sometimes consternation, that has come with the revelation that a manufacturing secret—generally speaking—exists in the imagination only. The burden of evidence would seem to show that, whatever secrets there are, are to be found in the works of the small maker—late workman—and not on the works of those who have paid large sums for the purpose of securing them.

This, of course, paves the way for mutual exchange of opinion, and a representative committee sets to work seriously to consider the question of costs. The way in which the work is done has been referred to so many times by Mr. Smith himself, that there is no reason why I should not explain it to you as I have seen it done many times.

The first item to be settled is the price or prices of material used. In some trades, such as the Potteries trades, this can be settled once for all. There is seldom any change in the price of clay and marl, and when there is it is too slight to interfere with the selling prices once a real profit has been secured; in other trades the prices of materials are subject to frequent alterations which have to be provided for. The first thing, however, is to fix for the time, and until further notice, the minimum prices to be set down in a cost sheet for materials used. Thus at the outset we come to a distinct and important departure from the ordinary system adopted in trades, which is that each maker sets down his own prices for materials. He may continue to do this if he does not go below the Association minimum—that is, he may go as much higher as he pleases, but not below. You will at once see that this plan ignores any advantage which one buyer may have over another. Materials are by mutual agreement set down at their real market value. Should one maker with large capital be able to buy better, his advantage is regarded as interest for the use of his capital—not as profit on trading. It is contended that buying forward on the assumption that prices have reached the lowest ebb is simply speculation which probably loses as much as it gains. It is also contended that whatever gain may be secured in this way for a time, cannot be used for the purpose of reducing selling prices. It is well known, for instance, that a maker who buys—say iron—for twelve months forward may in the early part of the year have an advantage over his competitors. If prices go up the advantage will increase, but if they go down those who did not buy forward will have the better of it. But if the speculator has at the beginning lowered his selling prices because he has bought well all his competitors must follow him, even if they lose by it. Should the prices of materials happen to go up, the case gets worse, as it is much easier for one man to lower selling prices by himself than to raise them. The latter requires the consent of the whole trade. The advantages and disadvantages of buying are therefore put out of the question, and all the more readily because it is found, after conference, that very often the smallest makers, with the least capital, and taking the largest credit, can buy just as well as those who buy largely and pay cash. The desire for a large turnover is so strong with most sellers that they will often arrange privately to put the small buyer on the best terms for the purpose of getting his order, and if one will not do it another will.

The first item in the cost schedules is, therefore, the minimum prices at which materials are to be taken, and these are binding upon every member. Should any alteration become necessary, it is done either by this minimum price being altered by circular, or by a resolution to issue another list of selling prices based on the real market value of material for the time being.

The next step is to carefully tabulate every process through which the article manufactured has to pass. This is generally a most interesting task. It is simply astounding to find in some trades how many of these processes have been altogether overlooked by some makers. In the new system every process must be provided for. Even if several processes are put down as one item eventually on the cost sheet, the actual cost of each separately is first ascertained so that the total may be safe.

You will have anticipated the fact, however, that in some trades the nature of the processes varies on different works. Take, for instance, a trade such as the manufacture of earthenware. There are processes known to the trade as throwing, turning, and jiggering. Broadly speaking, the differences are between doing the work with the hands and doing it by machinery. It is true that machinery is used in both, but it is depended upon much less in the one case than the other. The question is therefore raised, must the makers who "jigger" only, or "jigger and turn," put down the same amount for the process as the makers who "throw and "turn"? The difference in nearly every trade is very slight, and is often merely a matter of opinion only, but the question is settled in what I take to be the only practical and sensible way. Is the article when done by the one process worth more in the market than the one done by the other process? Will it bring either a higher price, or command a larger sale? If so, it is assessed on the schedule on a proportionately higher scale. If not, any saving by the cheaper process which turns out as good an article as the dearer one is regarded as a question of management only, and the benefit must be retained by the maker instead of being given away in the selling price. Each member is at liberty to adopt whichever process he pleases, but the one he selects must be charged at the rate provided by the schedules.

I hope I have made this sufficiently clear, but I am afraid the limit of my paper will prevent more elaborate illustration.

You may be inclined to ask: Is not this giving away a trade secret and giving up a trade advantage? My answer is, there is no "secret" about it. The migration of workpeople prevents this. It is purely a matter of opinion as to which is the best method. It is seldom that a manufacturer will change his methods because another maker thinks he has a better one. Moreover, the improvement is generally problematical as the discussion soon shows. As for the advantage, the new method secures it to the right person instead of giving it away. Before he joins an Association the maker in possession of the advantage gives it away to his customers. Afterwards he has to retain it. It is true that he may have done a little more trade, although this is seldom proved, but even if he did, the value of the Association is more to him than the trade thus obtained. It is a favourite saying of the promoter of this system, "You are not in "business for the purpose of making this or that, you are in "business for the purpose of making money—the only proof "of success is your Balance Sheet." Another of his teaching is, "If you have a *real* improvement in your methods, the "law gives you the right to protect it. If you do not protect it you cannot complain if others value it at your own "estimate. If it is not worth protecting it is worth nothing." I may say that it is part of the system to acknowledge and protect patent rights. Sometimes it is done in one way, sometimes in another, by mutual consent, but the right and advantage are never ignored.

You will, of course, remember that the system provides for a trade as a community, and only in special cases does it recognise individuals, excepting as members of an Association.

We will suppose that the prices of materials are fixed and the cost of each process set down in a schedule with a due consideration of waste or loss on each, fixed after comparison and experience. And here I must say that it is my profound conviction that so far a much more accurate and dependable result has been obtained than could possibly have been arrived at by any other method. No matter what may be the experience or ability of any one man, there is no one in business who is altogether independent of the judgment and experience of his competitors. I have found that the most unlikely people are often the most valuable in this work. No trade can go through the processes I have mentioned without being the better for it; even if no Association is formed.

The next matter to be settled is one of the utmost importance, as everyone present will, I am sure, recognise. I allude to the always vexed question of working expenses or dead charges. I have before mentioned the amusement caused by the various ideas always expressed on the matters hitherto dealt with. This, however, is a drop in the ocean compared to what we find when we come to the question of dead charges. It is perfectly true that the first estimate, generally put down on a slip of paper and passed to the chairman for comparison, nearly always varies from 5 per cent. to 35 per cent. Sometimes the difference is even greater. Of course, there is laughter and surprise. Please keep in mind, however, that before this question is reached every process of manufacturing which can be provided for has been dealt with, so that it is comparatively easy to make out a list of those things which have not been included and must therefore come under the head of working expenses. Such a list is handed to each member, and the meeting generally adjourns for a week or two so that each may carefully consider the various items and bring his calculations to the next meeting. When these conclusions are produced it is surprising how near they are to each other. Items which in the past have been wholly forgotten have now been considered. A member is no longer allowed to ignore a charge for rent because the premises are his own freehold. Petty cash is found to be a tangible item. Bad debts have to be considered. Salaries have to be recognised. Interest on capital—surprisingly often totally forgotten—is now included. Selling commission, cash discounts, and other numerous items known to an accountant have all been placed in ghostly array and their true effect on gross profits realised. There will, of course, be some difference still in the estimate, but when all is fairly faced it is not difficult to fix an amount which is safe without being excessive.

Without attempting to defend them now, as time will not permit, allow me to give you one or two conclusions to which I have come on this matter.

(*a*) It is remarkable how many trades come out at 15 per cent. for working expenses. Supposing it were impossible to really ascertain the amount—that is, if one was obliged to guess for any purpose, the safest guess for any trade would be 15 per cent.

(*b*) The common opinion that working expenses vary much according to the size and resources of the manufacturer is a common delusion. For various reasons, which it would take another paper to give, there are compensations on the one hand or the other which equalises the total surprisingly This makes it much easier to fix upon some percentage which can be safely adopted by a whole trade.

(*c*) There is no part of a business which is so little understood by business men as the question of working expenses. Nothing is more responsible for loss in trading than ignorance on this question.

After working expenses have been fixed there are many smaller matters to be attended to before the final question of profit is reached. Allowances to large buyers, merchants, factors, &c., all the incidentals belonging to each trade—these all take time and thought, but all are mutually arranged and the way made clear for the final consideration of the profits which can be safely and properly obtained.

I shall not weary you with personal opinion as to what "a "fair profit" should be. There are, of course, general principles to be considered. The promoter of the scheme would tell you that not one penny profit has been made until interest on capital and proper remuneration for personal services have been fully provided for. After these, it becomes a question as to what is possible and as to what is fair so far as the consumer is concerned. More can be reasonably obtained in one trade than in another. It is not a question which properly belongs to the subject of my paper.

I have but little more to add. You cannot attach too much importance to the fact that the system is intended to supply the wants of a whole trade, not an individual trader. It is a communistic system, and includes all the compromises which are necessary to a commune. It is not claimed that the system is perfect. One of its virtues is that being applicable to a whole trade it cannot be tested by the circumstances of a single business. It aims at the destruction of a suicidal competition by a process of education. It is only one part of a great scheme with many provisions, and extensive ramifications. But whatever the criticism it may meet, it is one of the most important and valuable parts of a plan which can only be judged by results. It will prevent bankruptcy! The business vitality of a nation depends upon its commercial soundness. I know of no better way by which commercial soundness can be secured, than by first teaching commercial people how to arrive at the real cost of production, and insisting upon this as the basis upon which selling prices are to be fixed, and profits obtained.

The Birmingham Chartered Accountant Students' Society.

The Methods of ascertaining Costs in a Factory where a variety of Articles are made, which mostly pass through several Processes in the course of Manufacture, and are turned out in large quantities.

By "COSTER."
(Mr. G. E. GOODE, A.C.A.)

IT is the opinion of all men of sound commercial principles that no business can be carried on to the best advantage unless some method of ascertaining costs is in operation, and that no system of bookkeeping is complete which does not include Cost Accounts.

To a manufacturer especially, Cost Accounts are of the utmost importance: firstly, in assisting him to fix a profitable selling price for the articles he makes, or in determining, where the selling price is fixed, whether he can manufacture to sell at a profit or not; secondly, in enabling him to make a sufficiently accurate estimate of the result of his trading for any period, without the labour which must necessarily be incurred in taking stock and preparing Trading and Profit and Loss Accounts in the usual way; thirdly, as they render possible the making of an elaborate analysis of his Trading and Profit and Loss Accounts, showing the profit or loss made on each contract or on each kind of article.

But although the advantages of keeping proper Cost Accounts are so obvious, it is surprising how many manufacturers pay little attention to them. They imagine they know the costs of their trade, but that they are mistaken is proved by the surprise and disappointment they often feel at the result of their trading.

The enormous extent to which they may err may be shown by the following instance, given by Mr. E. J. Smith. A large committee of a certain class of manufacturers met for the purpose of testing a few of the costs of their particular trade. A very common article was suggested, and after careful consideration the total cost was estimated at £4 17s. 8d. per gross, while at the time the article was being sold at £2 19s. 10d. per gross. The meeting was adjourned for the purpose of allowing each manufacturer to check the figures independently, and ultimately it was unanimously agreed that the estimate made at the first meeting was correct, and that the selling price must be raised to not less than £5 5s. 0d. per gross, in order to show a fair margin of profit.

From this it would seem that it is not always the unscrupulous man who ruins a trade by selling under cost, but often the man, who, through ignorance, sells at a loss.

One of the best features of the trades combinations is the Cost Book, which contains details of the costs of the different articles manufactured in the particular trade agreed upon by the manufacturers among themselves.

With regard to the form Cost Accounts should take, no general rule can be laid down, and no scheme could possibly be devised applicable to all businesses. The system must necessarily vary with the nature of the business. For instance, engineering firms, building contractors, and similar businesses, whose chief trade is in the execution of large contracts, usually keep such accounts as will show the actual net profit or loss made on each contract. Printers, again, use a system whereby the estimated cost and profit or loss on each sale is ascertained. The object of this paper, however, is the consideration of the method which a manufacturer, who produces a number of articles of various kinds, might adopt in order to ascertain his costs, taking into consideration that the articles are turned out in large quantities, and pass through various processes in the course of manufacture.

The Cost Accounts of such a business are of necessity somewhat intricate, and for that reason one does not often find such a scheme as I am about to suggest in operation. I have thought it expedient not to take any particular trade as an example, but to attempt to describe the general lines to be followed in ascertaining the costs of any business fulfilling these conditions.

The first step necessary is to compile a complete list of all the articles manufactured, and to open an Estimate Book, apportioning one or two pages to each article. This book might be ruled somewhat as follows (using the letters A, B, C, &c., for the different materials used, and the numbers 1, 2, 3, &c., for the processes through which the articles pass):—

Description of Article. Estimate of Cost per...........

Date of Estimate	Materials used										Processes							Boxes, Packets, &c.	Total Cost of Production
	A.			B.			C.			&c., &c.	No. 1		No. 2		No. 3		&c., &c.		
	Weight	Price	Value	Weight	Price	Value	Weight	Price	Value		Wages	Expenses	Wages	Expenses	Wages	Expenses			

Each article must then be considered separately, and the cost of its production ascertained as accurately as possible. For this purpose, a basis for making the estimates must be decided upon, either quantity or weight—as per cwt. of sweets, per gross of packets of needles—and an estimate made of the weight of the different materials consumed in the manufacture of this quantity or weight of each article.

These calculations must be made with the greatest care, and should be proved by previous experience and careful experiments. The figures should then be entered in the Estimate Book in the appropriate columns.

The next point for consideration is the fixing of a method for pricing out these weights. This latter must necessarily depend on circumstances. In some cases the actual net prices of the materials used may be ascertained from the Stock Accounts, but generally an estimate must be made. For example, if a manufacturer keeps an average stock of raw materials, approximately equal to one month's consumption, the cost of materials during a given month may be taken at the average net buying price of the previous month.

Carriage inwards should be considered as part of the cost price of these materials.

These prices must now be entered in the Estimate Book and the calculations made giving the value of the different materials used in the manufacture of the fixed quantity or weight of each article.

Having now ascertained the weight and value of the materials, the different processes through which the various articles pass to completion must be tabulated, and the cost of each in wages and expenses estimated. With regard to the wages, where the workpeople are paid a piece wage, it is not difficult to ascertain the actual cost of each process on every article, but where a time wage is paid estimates based on previous experience, and careful experiments and calculations, must be resorted to. Any increase or decrease in the rate of wages paid must be provided for by adjusting the cost under this heading from time to time.

The expenses connected with the processes—as, for instance, the cost of acid, grease, varnish, &c., must be estimated and apportioned to the articles in respect of which they are incurred. These amounts must then be entered in the Estimate Book under the several headings on the various pages.

Lastly, it must be ascertained whether anything else can properly be considered as contributing directly to the cost of any of the articles—as, for instance, boxes, tins, and packets, where goods are sold in boxes, &c.—and in such a case the cost on the given quantity or weight of each article must be ascertained and entered in the appropriate columns of the Estimate Book. The total cost of producing the standard quantity or weight of each article can now be arrived at by adding together the several items entered in the various columns, and this amount should then be entered in the Total Cost of Production Column.

The Estimate Book is now complete, and should be indexed. By reference to it the estimated cost of producing any article made (not reckoning expenses of management and distribution), and how the amount was arrived at, can be ascertained with very little trouble.

These estimates should be revised for each Cost Sheet, and provision made for any rise or fall in price of materials or boxes, &c., or any change in the rate of wages.

Having now obtained a reliable estimate of the cost of producing each of the articles made, the preparation of the Cost Accounts must next claim attention. They will generally take the form of a Cost Sheet drawn up at regular intervals, usually of one month's duration.

The first step necessary for the preparation of the Cost Sheet is to make an elaborate analysis of the sales for the period, showing not only the amount, but also the quantity or weight of each article sold. In order to effect this more readily the Day Books should be ruled with a column for the number or weight sold. This column should be added, and the totals of the analysis, both as to amount and quantity or weight, should exactly agree with the Day Book totals.

It will probably be necessary to make this analysis on loose sheets, and the greatest care should be exercised in order to ensure perfect accuracy. The returned sales must also be analysed in the same manner, and the amounts, quantities, or weights deducted from the sales of the same articles.

The analysis of the net sales must then be entered in detail on the Cost Sheet, which might take some such form as the following:—

FORM OF COST SHEET.

Left-hand side.

Description of Sales	Quantity or Weight sold	Amount of Sales	Estimated Discount on Sales at.... per cent.	Special Discounts on Sundry Articles	Net Amount of Sales	Average Net Selling Price per....	Materials						
							A.		B.		C.		&c.
							Weight	Amount	Weight	Amount	Weight	Amount	&c.
		£ s d	£ s d	£ s d	£ s d	£ s d		£ s d		£ s d		£ s d	

Right-hand side.

Processes							Cost of Tins, Boxes, Packets, &c., where goods are sold in Tins, &c.	Expenses apportioned according to the amount of the Sales	Expenses apportioned according to weight of Sales	Expenses apportioned on any other basis	Total Cost	Cost Price per....	Estimated Net Profit	Estimated Net Loss
No. 1		No. 2		No. 3		&c.								
Wages	Expenses	Wages	Expenses	Wages	Expenses	&c.								
£ s d	£ s d	£ s d	£ s d	£ s d	£ s d		£ s d	£ s d	£ s d	£ s d	£ s d	£ s d	£ s d	£ s d

A calculation should then be made of the percentage of discounts allowed on the sales, and amounts (representing the estimated discount at this rate per cent. on the sales of each article) should be inserted in the Discount Column of the Cost Sheet.

In cases where a special discount is given on certain articles, the amount must be separated from the general discounts and apportioned to those articles in respect of which it is given, and no discount should be deducted from such articles as are sold at a net price.

These amounts should be deducted from the sales, and the remainder will represent the net sales of each article. A few easy calculations will then give the average net selling prices for the period.

The costs of producing the quantity or weight of each article sold, under the various headings, must then be ascertained on the basis of the figures entered in the Estimate Book, and entered on the Cost Sheet in the appropriate columns.

The Cost Sheet will now show the gross profit or loss made on each article. It remains to apportion all the expenses—such as Miscellaneous Wages, Office and Management Salaries and Expenses, Rent, Repairs, Rates and Taxes, Power and Lighting, Advertising, Travellers' Expenses and Commission, Trade Expenses, Depreciation, Interest, Bad Debts, Carriage Outwards, Packing, &c., &c.—in order that the net profit may be ascertained.

The total of the estimated or actual expenses for each period must first be obtained, and the sum distributed over the various articles generally, in proportion to the amount of the sales of each. In the case of Carriage Outwards and Packing, however, the cost may more accurately be considered as varying with the weight of the sales, and should be apportioned accordingly. Again, if very expensive machinery or extensive premises are required in the manufacture of certain of the articles, such articles should bear a rateably greater proportion of the cost of Rent, Repairs, Depreciation, and Interest.

Usually it is difficult to ascertain the actual expenses for each period, and therefore the plan most frequently adopted is to carefully estimate the expenses for the ensuing year at the commencement of each year, including an amount for Bad Debts based on previous years' experience, and to charge a proportionate amount each period on the Cost Sheet.

Sometimes, however, an estimate is made of the percentage of the total expenses on the sales, and an amount charged on this basis; but this method does not usually prove so accurate as the former, especially where the turnover fluctuates to any extent.

Having now decided upon the system to be adopted for charging the expenses, calculations must be made of the cost on the sales of each article, and the amounts entered in the appropriate columns on the Cost Sheet.

The total cost of manufacturing and distributing the sales of the several articles can then be ascertained by adding together the various items, and the amounts should be inserted in the Total Cost Column.

The cost prices should then be calculated and inserted in the Cost Sheet.

A comparison of the "Net Sales" amounts with the "Total Costs" will now show the estimated profit or loss made on each article, and the balance of these profits and losses will represent the estimated net profit or loss on the period's trading. The Weight Columns should also be added, and, where the articles are sold by weight, the total estimated weight of materials consumed should be compared with the weight of the sales, and any difference in excess of the usual waste provided for in the estimates should be investigated, and may lead to the discovery of errors in the Estimate Book, or in the preparation of the Cost Sheet.

The sheet is now complete, and it only remains for the manufacturer to make full use of the information it affords. It shows him not only the approximate result of the period's trading, but also in what proportion each article he makes has contributed to that result.

He will be guided by it in fixing his future price-lists, and in determining whether he shall raise the price or cease the manufacture of such articles as are proved to be unremunerative. He will learn from it which articles it is his policy to push, and his attention will be drawn to the weakest points of his business, and generally he will obtain such a grasp of his trade as will prove of the utmost value to him.

The accuracy or inaccuracy of the Estimate Book and Cost Sheets has not yet, however, been proved in any way, and the means of obtaining this proof next claims attention. It will be effected by comparing the Cost Sheets with the periodical Trading and Profit and Loss Accounts.

At the end of each financial period a Cost Sheet Summary should be prepared by an amalgamation of the Cost Sheets for the period, setting forth the estimated costs under the several headings and the estimated profit or loss in the form of a Trading Account. (See Form I.)

The ordinary Trading Account should then be arranged in a form suitable for comparison, and for this purpose the following departures from the usual course must be made:—

1. The cost of the consumption of each of the materials must be shown on the account, instead of purchases and stocks. The amounts should include carriage inwards, and should be reduced by discounts received, in order to show the actual net cost, as on the Cost Sheets.

2. Only the increase or decrease in the finished stock and work in progress must appear, in order that the consumption may more readily be compared with the make. (This amount should be dissected, and an analysis under the several heads of materials, wages, &c., made, where possible.)

3. The wages in respect of the different processes must be shown separately, and any miscellaneous wages must be included in the expenses.

4. The amount of the consumption of tins, packets, &c., must be shown, as in the case of materials.

5. The expenses must be divided into groups in the same manner as for Cost Sheet purposes.

6. The returns must be deducted from the sales, and the net figure inserted in the account.

7. The discount allowed must be deducted from the net sales on the Trading Account, special discounts on certain articles (if any) being shown as a separate item.

8. Weights, as well as amounts, must be inserted where possible, and a calculation made of the average price of each kind of material used.

When the Trading Account has been arranged in this form (see Form II.) it should be compared in detail with the Summary of the Cost Sheets. (Form I.)

The amount of the difference between the actual and the estimated costs under each heading should then be ascertained by drawing up a statement in tabular form (Form III.), and an account, setting forth particulars of the reconciliation of the Cost Sheet result with the actual, should be prepared. (Form V.)

The details of the Cost Sheet Summary, showing the costs and profit or loss on each article, should now be adjusted in accordance with these differences, in order that a schedule may be prepared showing the exact extent to which each article has contributed to the result of the trading.

A thorough investigation of the items which make up the Reconciliation Account should also be made, and, where it is found necessary, the estimates should be amended for future use.

In this manner, even though unreliable at first, the estimated costs will gradually become more nearly accurate, until at length the manufacturer can place implicit reliance on them and the results shown by the periodical Cost Sheets.

The following sample accounts and statements will, perhaps, show more clearly the method of comparing the Cost Sheets with the Trading Account, and of tracing the various differences to their sources:—

Form I.

Dr. SUMMARY OF COST SHEETS for the Year ending .... *Cr.*

	Weight Tons	Price Per Ton £ s d	£ s d	£ s d
To Materials consumed, viz.:—				
A.	15,123	1 0 0	15,123 0 0	
B.	7,186	4 0 0	28,744 0 0	
C.	3,112	1 10 0	4,668 0 0	
				48,535 0 0
" Wages:—				
Process 1	..	..	20,123 0 0	
" 2	..	..	15,916 0 0	
" 3	..	..	13,126 10 0	
				49,165 10 0
" Expenses of Processes ..	..	..	..	1,066 0 0
" Boxes, Tins, Packets, &c. ..	..	..	..	1,915 0 0
" Expenses apportioned according to Weight of Sales..	..	..	..	3,166 0 0
" Expenses apportioned according to Amount of Sales..	..	..	..	20,894 5 0
" *Balance, being estimated Net Profit*..	..	..	..	14,554 0 0
			£	139,295 15 0
Total estimated weight of Materials consumed ..	25,421			

	Weight Tons	£ s d	£ s d
By Sales, less Returns..	25,326	142,138 10 0	
Less Discounts allowed (estimated at 2 %)	..	2,842 15 0	
			139,295 15 0
N.B.—No special discounts.			
Estimated Deficiency in Weight..	95		
		£	139,295 15 0
	25,421		

Form II.

Dr. TRADING ACCOUNT for the Year ending .... *Cr.*

	Weight Tons	Price Per Ton £ s d	£ s d	£ s d
To Net Cost of Materials consumed:—				
A.	15,712	19 10½	15,613 16 0	
B.	6,980	4 0 6	28,094 10 0	
C.	3,002	1 10 6	4,578 1 0	
				48,286 7 0
„ Wages:—				
Process 1	..	..	21,329 8 0	
„ 2	..	..	16,312 10 0	
„ 3	..	..	12,910 13 0	
				50,552 11 0
(Office and Sundry Wages included in Expenses.)				
„ Expenses of Processes ..	..	.	..	1,329 18 0
„ Boxes, Tins, Packets, &c. ..	..	.	..	1,983 10 0
„ Expenses apportioned according to Weight of Sales..	..	..	..	3,224 0 0
„ Expenses apportioned according to Amount of Sales..	..	..	..	21,415 0 0
„ *Balance, being Net Profit* ..	..	..	..	12,848 9 0
			£	139,639 15 0
Total Weight of Materials consumed	25,694			

	Weight Tons	£ s d	£ s d
By Sales, less Returns..	25,326	142,138 10 0	
Less Discounts allowed ..	..	3,111 5 0	
			139,027 5 0
„ Increase in Finished Stock and Work in progress, analysed:—			
Materials, A.	85	84 10 0	
„ B.	40	161 0 0	
„ C.	15	22 17 6	
Wages, Process 1	..	125 0 0	
„ „ 2	..	90 0 0	
„ „ 3	..	70 0 0	
Expenses of Processes ..	..	10 0 0	
Expenses	..	49 2 6	
			612 10 0
Actual Deficiency in Weight ..	228		
		£	139,639 15 0
	25,694		

Form III.—

COMPARISON OF COST SHEETS' SUMMARY WITH TRADING ACCOUNT.

Description	Amount charged to Trading Account	*Less* Increase in Finished Stock	Net Amount	Amount charged on Cost Sheets	*Surplus* of Net Amount charged to Trading Account over Amount charged on Cost Sheets	*Surplus* of Amount charged on Cost Sheets over Net Amount charged to Trading Account	Remarks
	£ s d	£ s d	£ s d	£ s d	£ s d	£ s d	
A. Materials	15,613 16 0	84 10 0	15,529 6 0	15,123 0 0	406 6 0		
B. „	28,094 10 0	161 0 0	27,933 10 0	28,744 0 0		810 10 0	
C. „	4,578 1 0	22 17 6	4,555 3 6	4,668 0 0		112 16 6	
Wages, Process 1	21,239 8 0	125 0 0	21,204 8 0	20,123 0 0	1,081 8 0		
„ „ 2	16,312 10 0	90 0 0	16,222 10 0	15,916 0 0	306 10 0		
„ „ 3	12,910 13 0	70 0 0	12,840 13 0	13,126 10 0		285 17 0	
Expenses of Processes	1,329 18 0	10 0 0	1,319 18 0	1,066 0 0	253 18 0		
Tins, Boxes, Packets, &c... ..	1,983 10 0		1,983 10 0	1,915 0 0	68 10 0		
Expenses apportioned according to Weight of Sales	3,224 0 0		3,224 0 0	3,166 0 0	58 0 0		
Expenses apportioned according to Amount of Sales	21,415 0 0	49 2 6	21,365 17 6	20,894 5 0	471 12 6		Actual Rate 2½% on Sales
Discounts allowed	3,111 5 0		3,111 5 0	2,842 15 0	268 10 0		
					2,914 14 6	1,209 3 6	
						1,705 11 0	Balance being excess of actual over estimated costs
					£2,914 14 6	£2,914 14 6	

Form IV.—

COMPARISON OF THE ESTIMATED WEIGHT OF MATERIALS CONSUMED WITH THE ACTUAL.

Description of Materials	Weight consumed	*Less* Increase in Finished Stock	Net Weight	Estimated Weight consumed, as per Cost Sheets	*Add* Surplus of Waste over the Estimate	Net Weight	Surplus in Estimating Weight on Cost Sheets	Deficiency in Estimating Weight on Cost Sheets
	tons	tons	tons	tons	tons	tons	tons	tons
A.	15,712	85	15,627	15,123	83	15,206	..	421
B.	6,980	40	6,940	7,186	36	7,222	282	
C.	3,002	15	2,987	3,112	14	3,126	139	

Form V.—

Dr. RECONCILIATION ACCOUNT. *Cr.*

	£ s d	£ s d		£ s d	£ s d
To Waste of Materials in excess of Estimate valued at		248 14 0	By *Net Profit as per Cost Sheets' Summary*		14,554 0 0
(Waste estimated at ⅜%, actually ⅞% on consumption)			" Value of errors in Estimating the Proportion of the different Materials used :		
" Net Under-estimate in Price of Materials		162 18 7½	B. Materials over-estimated ..	1,135 1 0	
" Deficiency in Charging Wages on Cost Sheets :			C. " " ..	211 19 6	
Process 1	1,081 8 0			1,347 0 6	
" 2	306 10 0		*Less* A. " under-estimated ..	418 7 4½	
	1,387 18 0				928 13 1½
Less Surplus " 3	285 17 0				
		102 1 0			
" Deficiency in Charging Expenses of Processes..		253 18 0			
" Deficiency in Charging Boxes, Tins, Packets, &c...		68 10 0			
" Deficiency in Charging Expenses :					
Apportioned according to Weight ..	58 0 0				
" " " Amount ..	471 12 6				
		529 12 6			
" Deficiency in Estimating Discount .. (Actual Rate 2½% ; estimated 2%)		268 10 0			
" *Balance, being Net Profit as per Trading Account*		12,848 9 0			
		£15,482 13 1½			£15,482 13 1½

The mode of the preparation of the Trading Accounts, Forms I. and II., has already been referred to.

Form III. shows the result of the comparison of the Cost Sheet Summary with the Trading Account.

Each of the differences must now be thoroughly investigated, as follows :—

(I.) *Materials.* Form III. reveals the following discrepancies :—

	£ s d
A. Materials apparently under-estimated on Cost Sheets	*406 6 0*
B. " " over-estimated "	*810 10 0*
C. " " " "	*112 16 6*
The net amount over-estimated is therefore	*£517 0 6*

Differences under this heading may arise in any of the following ways :—

(*a*) Errors in bookkeeping or stocktaking.

(*b*) Errors in estimating cost price of materials.

(*c*) Errors in estimating shrinkage or waste, or theft of stock.

(*d*) Errors in estimating weight consumed, or the proportion of the different materials used in the manufacture of the articles.

(*a*) Errors in bookkeeping can only be discovered by a thorough audit of the Trading Accounts. The figures and calculations on each periodical Cost Sheet should always be checked, and, if this had been done, the chance of discovering an error in the Summary Trading Account would be slight. But with regard to the ordinary Trading Account, errors might be found, even though the books were balanced, in the analysis of purchases. For instance, "A" materials might have been analysed as "B," &c.

The stock should always be thoroughly checked, both as to weights, amounts, and analysis. Late invoices should be examined to guard against any stock being omitted, and it should be ascertained that all goods taken into stock have been invoiced and put through the books.

In the example above, special attention might be directed to seeing that no "A" materials have been omitted from stock, and that no "B" materials have been wrongly included.

If Stock Accounts are kept they will, of course, be of great assistance in proving the accuracy of the stock.

(*b*) The amount of the difference due to errors in pricing may now be ascertained as follows :—

A. Materials. Estimated at £1 per ton, actually cost 19s. 10½d. Over-estimate of 1½d. per ton on 15,123 tons = £94 10s. 4½d.

B. Materials. Estimated at £4 per ton, actually cost £4 0s. 6d. Under-estimate of 6d. per ton on 7,186 tons = £179 13s.

C. Materials. Estimated at £1 10s. per ton, actually cost £1 10s. 6d. Under-estimate of 6d. per ton on 3,112 tons = £77 16s.

	£ s d
B. and C. Materials are therefore under-estimated ..	£257 9 0
A. " " over-estimated	94 10 4½
Net under-estimate	£162 18 7½

(*c*) A comparison of the weights of consumption with the weight made shows the following result :—

Actual excess of weight consumed over weight made,	228 tons.
Estimated " " "	95 "
Surplus of actual over estimated deficiency of weight	133 "

This difference may be owing either to an error in calculating the shrinkage or waste, or to errors in bookkeeping, or a theft of stock. If the percentage of the actual deficiency is greatly in excess of the usual, a thorough investigation should be made into the cause of the increase.

On the supposition that the difference is due to an under-estimate, its money value may be ascertained, apportioning, for example, the weight over the different materials proportionately to weight of each consumed, as follows:—

				£ s d	£ s d
A. Materials	83 tons at	0 19 10½	=	82 9 0
B. "	36 "	4 0 6	=	144 18 0
C. "	14 "	1 10 6	=	21 7 0
	133			£248 14 0

The amount under-estimated from this cause may, therefore, be reckoned at £248 14s.

(*d*) A comparison between the estimated and actual weight of each material consumed, taking into consideration the under-estimate of the shrinkage or waste already provided for, will now show the errors in estimating the weight or proportion of the different materials used in the manufacture of the articles. (Form IV.)

These differences should be investigated and taken into account in amending the estimates for the following year. Their money value is ascertained as follows:—

		£ s d		£ s d
B. Materials.	Over-estimate of 282 tons at	4 0 6	=	1,135 1 0
C. "	" 139 "	1 10 6	=	211 19 6
				1,347 0 6
A. "	Under-estimate of 421 "	0 19 10½	=	418 7 4½
	Net over-estimate			£928 13 1½

The net over-estimated cost of materials consumed may, therefore, be explained as follows:—

		£ s d
Over-estimate, owing to errors in estimating weight, or proportion of different materials used		928 13 1½
Less Under-estimate in cost price of materials	£162 18 7½	
Less " in shrinkage or waste	248 14 0	
		411 12 7½
Net over-estimate as per Form III.		517 0 6

(2) *Wages*.—The differences under this heading are as follows (Form III.):—

	£ s d
Process 1. Wages under-estimated on Cost Sheets	*1,081 8 0*
" 2. " " " "	*306 10 0*
" 3. " over-estimated " "	*285 17 0*

The above may be due to any of the following causes:—

(*a*) Errors in estimating cost owing to changes in the rate of wages, or other reasons.

(*b*) Errors in analysing the wages paid under the same headings as on the Cost Sheet. For example, some miscellaneous wages may have been included in Process 1 wages, or Process 2 wages may include amounts which should have been analysed as Process 3.

(*c*) Wages may have been paid for work not actually done, owing to dishonesty of employees. Where piece wages are paid an investigation can easily be made which may lead to the discovery of fraud of this kind.

Unless these differences are cleared up it may be necessary to amend the estimates for the following year in respect of them.

(3) *Expenses of Processes*.—The under-estimate of these expenses may be owing to various causes—for instance, increase in price of materials. If the amount is greater than usual, and no cause for it can be assigned, an investigation should be made, and may lead to the discovery of waste in the factory.

(4) *Tins, Packets, Boxes, &c*.—The discrepancy under this heading should not be large, as an accurate estimate of the cost can usually be made. A difference may arise, however, in consequence of changes in the purchase prices or loss, owing to goods becoming unfit for use, &c.

(5) *Expenses*.—A detailed list of the amounts charged on the Cost Sheets should be compared with the actual figures. This will reveal the reason for the discrepancy under this heading.

(6) *Discounts Allowed*.—The difference between the estimated and actual amounts may be due to a change in the nature of the business, or an alteration in the rate or in the regulations with regard to allowing discount. The average rate for the following year's estimates should be altered to provide for any such change.

The investigation of all the differences is now completed, and an account should be prepared showing how the Cost Sheet's result is reconciled with the Trading Account. (Form V.)

The Reconciliation Account will show what alterations are necessary in order to render more accurate the estimates for the future.

In conclusion, I would express the opinion that a method of ascertaining costs, such as I have endeavoured to explain, will prove of the utmost value to the manufacturer, and amply repay him for the labour involved.

Workshop Administration.

Workshop Administration, with Special Reference to Tracking Work and promptly ascertaining detailed Costs and Profits.

By Mr. DAVID COWAN.

Reprinted by permission from the Transactions of the Institution of Engineers and Shipbuilders in Scotland.

Read 20th March 1900.

MUCH has been done by engineering and other institutions towards the advancement of the scientific and technical branches of the profession, and for the instruction of younger members in knowledge which lies beyond their own experience. There is, however, an apparatus of production that has not received the attention from such institutions which its importance merits—viz., the workshop itself, treated as a whole. This is the more to be regretted, since under the stress of modern conditions a higher complexity of development is called for. The responsibilities of public undertakings are greater than those of individual proprietors. The importance and value of scientific shop management have been more fully realised in America than here. All students of mechanical engineering in their fourth year of study at the Massachusetts Institute of Technology are, among other subjects, required to "study the organisation and rules of the "various departments of an industrial establishment, "both in the office and in the workshop, the conduct of "accounts, the methods of compensating labour and super-"intendence, and the effect on the cost of production, by "different methods of indirect expense."

The purpose of this paper is not to discuss the whole subject of such study, but to induce this Institution if possible to treat the study of shop administration as a branch of the productive art. The consideration of this subject by the Institution does not involve the giving away of matter which is purely private, but the members can, with advantage to themselves and to the community, from their own practice contribute towards the advancement of this much neglected science.

That the subject is sufficiently broad, and that there is ample scope and opportunity for making the administration of productive engineering enterprises a special subject of study, will be gathered from the chart, Fig. 1, which shows a graphic analysis of the more important acts requiring to be performed.

The items specially referred to in this paper are those printed in italics in the chart.

Workshop organisation should have as its fundamental principle unity of action; it should eliminate all guess work, and depend for its efficiency on a constant knowledge of all individual acts. It should be simple in its conception, automatic in its working, and impartial in determining results; it should force instant recognition of "on-cost" fluctuation and the constant comparison of co-rélated cost factors; it should permit of results being obtained in such detail as the special circumstances of each case warrant; and it should be based on those properties which enable analyses to be made at considerable intervals after the work is completed, without making calls on the time of the executive officials.

The more diversified the products of the workshop the more necessary becomes the knowledge of the differences in cost, although the greater the diversity of products the more expensive is the obtaining of that knowledge. Without this knowledge, principals are unable to make themselves intimately acquainted with what is going on, and they cannot, with any degree of confidence, introduce modifications of detailed routine which their judgment would indicate to be necessary.

The prevailing idea regarding shop records is that they are only necessary for determining the selling price of the product. The accountant and his needs for arriving at the final results are considered all important, and it is held that any clerical labour over and above is needless. The important functions of records in pointing out where economies may be effected, production quickened, and supplies regulated, are usually lost sight of; and the practical officials are depended upon for the performance of those functions which ought not properly to devolve upon them in detail.

The selling price of the product is determined not so much by its cost as by competition.

If the manager finds that the cost of an article is too high he must find a means of reducing the cost if he is to continue its manufacture, and this can only be done by reducing the amount or the cost of labour and material, or by reducing the rate of oncost, or both. In order to do any of these intelligently, with a minimum of trouble, he must be provided with fully detailed economic information with regard to the product in all its parts. The personal supervision of the manager may in a small business accomplish these objects, but personal supervision is limited in its range, and when this limit is reached, subordinate authority, in the shape of the "leading-hand," foremen, or heads of departments, becomes a necessity. Then the duties of the principal become those of collecting and recording the *data* needful for formulating the arrangements whereby secondary authorities have the necessary freedom of action under superior control. Clerks without practical knowledge of work, who make *ex post facto* analyses by the aid of foremen, cannot be depended on for collecting the information necessary for efficient administration.

To secure a useful analysis, it is essential that the demands of the administration be anticipated, and the various acts of all the subordinate officials recorded, at the moment of their performance. To ensure accuracy of description, and at the same time reduce as far as possible the volume of such records and the time required for their production, simple symbolic nomenclature covering all the elements in such record is a necessity. This cannot well be entered into here, but is of great importance in the detailed working out of any well-considered scheme of administration. To properly initiate such records implies a constant analysis of the work beforehand, and a continuous record of all the acts by those executive officers who know most about them, at the time of performance, and, if this is properly attended to, a subsequent synthesis is easy.

Generally the acts of a workshop may, for administrative purposes, be divided into two kinds (1) Those of the executive, whose acts result in the continuous expenditure of materials and labour, and the delivery of the finished product; (2) the recording of these acts.

Hitherto, shop records have been usually kept in bound books. The disadvantages of books for this purpose are many—

They can only be used by one person at a time.

The combining of similar entries made at different times and places is laborious.

Effete matter soon obscures current information, so that the longer an entry has escaped attention the more certainly will it continue to be neglected

The use of type-writing machines, mechanical adders, time-recorders, and other labour-saving appliances, is impracticable.

For these reasons it is suggested that the use of books be dispensed with, except for final records, and a "card" system adopted.

Cards lend themselves to the production of a complete system of self-indexing all memoranda, letters, papers, and records of every kind. Such groups of *data* may always be kept in exact order; eliminations and additions can be instantly made without disturbing the sequence. By restricting the entries on each card to *one only*, the number of possible combinations is endless. In this atomic state information may be treated analytically and synthetically, in every form, and for every purpose. Examples of such cards for the records of, and synthesis of, costs are given later. The production of a suitable card for the use of any particular business requires much experience. No makeshift gives any satisfaction.

The first essential in setting on foot a complete system of record is the analysis of the work to be done into distinct objects of expense. This analysis should be full and complete, and should be made at the outset by persons acquainted with the whole process. Diagram, Fig. 2, shows how a customer's order for work may be analysed into special products, and how these products may each in turn be resolved elementally.

Fig. 3 shows an example of a shop specification analysing a product into separate objects of expense.

The shop officials are thus put into simultaneous possession of full details of all work requiring to be performed in connection with the product. These details, arranged and grouped on a systematic basis, are applicable to both office and shop requirements; they promote the smooth working of the establishment, and minimise worry on the part of all concerned. It is a mistake to suppose that such a preliminary analysis, if judiciously carried out, involves any delay in putting the work in hand and passing it through the shop.

A complete specification should embrace all the information necessary for the following purposes, among others:—

(1) The issue of shop orders for work, in terms of processes and operations necessary.
(2) Ordering materials from outside.
(3) Ordering materials from work stores.
(4) Standardising details.
(5) Recording conditions of work in process, packing and forwarding.
(6) Erecting in shop and on sites.
(7) Compiling Cost Accounts.
(8) Permanent records of the special product.
(9) Identifying replacements or repairs.

In practice many more uses, special to individual shops, will become apparent. The specification is the pivot round which the whole mechanism of the establishment revolves. To conveniently embody all this information on the specification involves the use of the symbolic nomenclature already referred to.

The issue, the trail, and the records of authorisations of expense.—An order from a customer to supply him with goods is the source of all production orders. Special products made for the establishment or for stock are treated exactly as customers' orders, and all such orders are entered in the Customers' Order Book and there dissected into separate objects of production. Special care should be exercised in keeping this book in all its details up to date. When this is done it forms a summary showing the condition of all work in hand, as well as a record of all past performances.

The products special to any customer's order being dissected into special production orders, Fig. 2, these may be sub-divided thus:—

Production Orders.—Issued by the office to the manager for the production of complete products, Col. 3, Fig. 4, and Fig. 6.

Sub-production or Shop Orders.—Issued by the managers to the foremen under their charge, for the production of separate members, components, or pieces of a given product, a separate order being issued for each separate object of expense, the whole product being itemised to such an extent as is considered necessary. Should it be necessary to issue the work to more than one department simultaneously, a copy of the shop order with the process special to each department should be given to the respective foremen, Col. 4, Fig. 4. and Fig. 5.

Job Orders.—The authority for the issue of these is the shop order issued to the foremen. The job order is personal to the workmen, and to each operation; it authorises the individual units of expenditure, and specifies the conditions of performance, Col. 7, Fig. 4, and Fig. 7.

Forwarding Orders.—As any product nears completion, such an order is issued by the manager on form, Fig. 8.

Foreman to Foreman Orders.—In many cases the foreman receiving a shop order may require the co-operation or assistance of a foreman in another department, in which case he issues a *shop order* form, a duplicate of which is, of course, sent to the cost office.

Alternatively, the first foreman may hand the *shop order* card originally received by him to the second foreman, and so on, recording receipts and completions at the time of transference. In this way one shop order may serve for the instruction of any number of foremen, but possibly at the expense of time.

Standing Orders.—For shop expenses or oncost. These are dealt with generally in a manner similar to special shop orders, and they may be further sub-divided into orders for components and pieces, a separate job order being issued for each, Fig. 4, Cols. 2 and 3. For the sake of distinction, order cards for standing shop orders may be distinguished by difference in colour, or in some other way.

The manager and foreman are each provided with a card index cabinet, in which they set apart a file for each production order, or for a given number of orders as circumstances render necessary. All orders are issued by the respective executive officers in duplicate, one copy being sent to the cost clerk and the other to the person responsible for the production. The issue of production orders is recorded on the original shop specification. Shop orders are recorded on the production order cards analysing the work. Job orders are recorded on the shop order cards, thus giving trace of all subordinate acts.

On the front of each card its course is recorded by every recipient entering, into the space set apart for the purpose, his name or symbol, and the date of receipt and completion.

On the back of the duplicate cards sent to the cost clerk, are printed the forms for use in ascertaining the cost of the product, Figs. 9, 10, and 11.

It has been assumed that the manager and foremen make out and attend to all "receipts" and "completions" of order cards; but it may easily be conceived how this could be better attended to by a clerk, who, at the same time, may attend to the orders for withdrawing materials from the stores and the time record cards, referred to later on. The offices of timekeeper and job clerk may with advantage be combined. When such a combination is made, the job office should be as nearly central in the shop as possible, and should be fitted with a complete equipment, including a service card index-file. The job clerk and timekeepers should be in the office during the whole hours of work, and the foremen and shop manager should also be on duty the whole time as well.

Records of the Condition of Work.—For the record from time to time of the state of progress of work in the shop the shop specification is used, suitable distinguishing signs being used for the purpose, Fig. 3, Columns 11 to 23 inclusive. These symbols are posted up daily in the shop specification. This is done by a boy, who makes use of the duplicate order cards, "issue," and "completion" records for this purpose. This system of recording the condition of work from time to time is already in use in many of the Glasgow shops in some form or another, and a description has been published in *Engineering.*

The index spaces on the different order cards may also be made to serve the same purpose by crossing out the numbers of such job orders as are completed from day to day.

Elementary Shop Records.—A reference to Fig. 12 will show that the element of shop orders should be as follows:—

(1) Materials—delivered direct.

(2) Materials—drawn from store.

(3) Out-services.

(4) Labour.

Materials.—In most shops, particularly those employed in building the heaviest kinds of machinery, where transportation is an important factor, materials are handled in two ways.

The heavier pieces as received are delivered direct to the job on the shop floor, checked with the delivery note, and a receipt given for the same by the foreman to the storekeeper, shortage or breakage, or other faults, being reported on the same form of card, and steps at once taken for replacement.

The lighter materials are usually bought in quantity, and passed through the rough stores, being retailed in exchange for a requisition made on a "material card," stating the estimated quantity required by the foreman or other responsible person. This card is received by the storekeeper, who fills in the daily serial number, and enters on the card the actual quantity issued, and at the same time enters it in the corresponding stores "journal card"; thereafter the original requisition card is forwarded to the cost clerk, who, after filling in the value, files it away with other cards of the same kind under its job order number.

Credits of material, whether returned to suppliers or to rough stores, are made on "material cards" by making the necessary entry in the credit space. These cards are also sent to the cost clerk, who gives due effect to these credits at the proper time.

Outside Services.—Outside services are paid for either through the Supplier's Journal or the Petty Cash Book. The items are transferred therefrom on "material cards" by the purchasing clerk, or by the cashier, and are dealt with in the same way as material delivered direct, being charged to the shop, or job orders, against which they are issued.

Labour.—Labour is recorded direct on cards, Fig. 13, either by the workmen themselves or by the timekeeper. The time on which the workmen are paid is taken by checks at the shop entrance in the usual way, but before any wages are disbursed, the total time units and values as recorded on the cards must be in agreement with the corresponding time in the Wages Book.

The Cost of the Product.—Whilst the accountant is chiefly concerned with final results, the manager of the shop requires continuous records showing how the current expenditure on the various objects in course of construction is creeping up towards the total estimated cost. Hence, any system of shop accounting to be of real value should, in the first instance, serve this purpose. Before enquiring how this may be obtained, it may be well to define some of the leading terms, since they may have different meanings in different shops.

Prime Cost is the summation of the cost of materials, labour, and outside service, chargeable solely and directly against the product.

Oncost is the indirect expenditure incurred for the purpose of increasing the productive power of labour, and includes every outlay whatever, not chargeable to a specific product. Oncost includes depreciation for tear and wear, obsolescence, and all safeguards of capital against risks and casualties, but the remuneration of capital is not included as oncost.

Gross Cost is the sum of prime cost and oncost.

Nett Cost is the gross cost, less the value, for future use, of any plant or tools made specially for the production of the special product.

Plant includes drawings, patterns, models, moulding-boxes, gauges, and similar appliances for common use, also mandrils, boring bars, &c., which have more or less special value apart from the special product for which they are originally obtained.

Tools include the ordinary loose tools, hammers, chisels, files, reamers, cutters, &c., and also those perishable portions of machines which act directly upon the objects of production, and are subject to consumption from wear during the execution of the order for which they are made, the most important being templates, cradles, jigs, and such like. When tools are consumed in the manufacture of products, these should be charged direct to the work. When consumed in miscellaneous work they should be charged to oncost.

Tools and fixtures when made for a specific job are usually charged in the first instance to the job as such, and afterwards credited at their estimated value for future use.

Machinery includes all prime-movers, shafting, gearing, and machines of all kinds actuated thereby.

Work, as distinguished from plant, is the transformation of materials (stores) by organised labour into products.

Stores (Rough) are materials of every kind on which labour is to be expended for converting into work or stock. These may include finished articles—such as screws, bolts, bright shafting, finished pulleys, finished special parts, and so on.

Stores (Finished) are the parts or components of machines, often made in quantities in shops. These, when completed, are sent into the warehouse to await the demand. Were the same articles purchased from outside they would be classed as rough stores; dealt with as finished stores, they are included in the general term "Stock."

Stock is the finished product resulting from the conversion of stores.

Production Account.—In most establishments, it is usual to keep in the general books a Production Account, to which is debited all expenses whatever, as relative to production, and to which is credited the value of all products, the balance being the profit or loss. The debit side, less balances brought forward, should balance with the total of the cost returns as made on the elementary cards.

Balancing Production and Cost Accounts.—The first step towards accuracy in shop returns is to make sure that the expenditure, represented by the total of all the elementary record cards, agrees with the corresponding charges in Production Account. The routine of this balance is as follows:—

The labour and material cards as they come into the cost office are examined, the prices filled in and extended, and filed in a cost index cabinet, a separate drawer-file being set apart for each product in course of construction; the order of filing being that set out in the shop specifications. Guide cards are inserted between the record cards belonging to each shop order, and these again are cross-indexed by the insertion of tab cards between the records pertaining to each job order. The record cards corresponding to each of the four main divisions of prime cost—viz., materials-charged-direct, materials-charged-through-stores, out-services, and labour—may be distinguished by being made on different coloured papers or otherwise. The credits may also be distinguished in the same manner. All the cards of the same colour corresponding to each job order are collected into one group.

At the end of each balancing period the current-service file-index cabinet is gone over by taking each product in succession, and entering every current shop order number corresponding thereto into the weekly cost sheet. These numbers may be got from the index section of production order card. The corresponding job orders, the number of which may be obtained from the index section of shop order card, are treated in the same manner by entering them in another column, the sequence to be observed being that in shop specification.

Then classify all elementary cards by job orders, and each pack according to elements. Sum up the values and units on the back of the last card in each lot. Next enter their totals in the columns under their corresponding headings, opposite the job-order numbers. When all job entries have been entered for any one shop order, sum up the vertical totals, and the result gives the total of the elements going to make up the prime costs expenditure on that shop order for the week.

Proceed thus to ascertain the expenditure on all shop orders—special and standing—in progress.

Bring forward the gross expenditure from the week preceding. Compute the oncost for the current week in the matter hereinafter indicated, and enter same in its proper column. The cross totals of each line of all the columns give the gross expenditure to date on all current job orders, grouped according to shop orders. The sum of all shop orders gives the cost of the product, grouped according to its members' components and parts as set out by the analysis made in the shop specification.

The total cost of all work in progress and completed during the week is the total expenditure for the week. The vertical grand totals of the columns of the cost sheet should agree with the corresponding totals charged to Production Account through the general books.

These costs of completed work are summarised every four weeks in a suitable register, where all credits are deducted, and where the net cost is set out parallel with the invoice price, the difference between these being, of course, the profit or loss on the respective products.

It will be observed that it is thus practicable to interlock the Shop Costs Account with the accounts kept in the general books. They may, however, be worked independently and parallel with the commercial books. In either case they should agree as regards total expenditure.

So far, attention has been directed only towards determining the cost of shop orders in terms of shop processes, if the order and elementary record cards are properly filled in when the work is initiated, extended detail can always be had when desired, but it is unnecessary to make up the details until they are wanted for some specific purpose.

Oncost.—It has been shown how the prime cost may be determined with accuracy, but the oncost addition which it should carry is always an assumption, usually based on an average of past years, but subject to modifications arising from improvement or otherwise in shop efficiency or other causes. Oncost should be treated like an Insurance Account, the amount of recoveries or credits being equivalent to the insurance premiums, and the actual oncost or debits to the casualties. There is much difference of opinion as to how the oncost should be allocated. The most satisfactory method appears to be to distribute the expense in ratio to the productive labour; and since the lower grades of labour require the greater share of those facilities for which expenses are incurred than do the higher grades, it follows that each class should at least equally share that expense, and that the distribution should be made in terms of the quantities of labour, and not upon labour values. The most fitting unit for this purpose is the hour of direct labour.

Permanent Records.—Cards having been used for the purpose of determining prime cost and oncost of products, they can also be arranged to give the entire cost of any construction, however elaborate. The following is an example of each application of the cost cards to these purposes:—

The Job Order Work Ticket, made on the back of a job order card, shows the cost of the jobs in terms of material, out-services, and labour, Fig. 11.

The Shop Order Work Ticket shows the cost of shop orders in terms of shop processes, and may also be made to show the cost of members by processes, and in terms of materials, out-services, and labour, Fig. 10.

The Production Order Work Ticket shows the cost of the product according to its members, and in terms of materials, out-services, and labour, Fig. 9.

The Consolidated Work Ticket is, as regards nomenclature, a duplicate of the shop specification, Fig. 14, and may be posted up weekly from the cost sheet, or may be posted up on completion of the product, as the special requirements of each shop may determine. As soon as the work ticket is completed, the totals of all separate objects of expense are posted to *comparison cards*, all like items being entered on the same card. These are filed into a permanent record cabinet, and are the base of all sound workshop administration. The consolidated work-tickets may, if it be desirable, be bound up into books. As each product is completed, the total prime cost is transferred from the consolidated work ticket to the net cost return, which is a return of the net cost of all work done during the week; and the total of the credits of the several columns headed with the names of the elemental and oncost items should agree with total debits to Production Account. Another column should show the credits to this account. If the work is correct, both sides of this account should balance.

The advantages arising from such methods of records may be briefly summarised as follows:—

The comparison cards permit of ascertaining how many objects of the like kind are required within a given period, the variations in their costs, and whether the quantities are sufficient to warrant the expense of standardising.

They afford the information necessary for arranging workmen's rates, whether by hour, piece, or premium.

They enable the manager to point out what items can be reduced in cost, and to suggest the methods whereby this may be done.

They are invaluable for estimating purposes.

They avoid transcriptions—the first writing serving all

purposes, except when specific analysis is required; yet the system is so elastic in its working as to yield readily, when, and as required, either classified or elementary detail, or both.

They are available for the valuation of the individual energy of each official or workman, the relative efficiency of the different machine tools, and the comparative value of designs.

Space does not permit of giving examples showing how the latter operations are worked out.

The continuous use of such records, and the wealth of information thus ascertained, will suggest many other uses to which they may be applied.

They are invaluable because reliable.

For ordinary working purposes the compiling of too much detail should be avoided, except in the case where a special study as to the means of reducing the cost of a product, or for the determination of efficiencies; extended analysis is seldom necessary.

Ascertainment of the net profits or losses arising from operating the whole establishment during any given period.—When the general books are designed so as to admit of their summarised results being classified, and the respective totals for each class of entries transferred to a General Check Journal; and if proper Store Journals are kept and means adopted for continuous stock-taking (consequently dispensing with a general annual stock-taking), and if the Day Books or Sectional Journals are written up daily as they should be, a balance of the financial books, showing the profit or loss during any pre-determined period, may be brought out in an hour or two after the closing of the Sectional Journals. The result so obtained should agree with the total profits, less losses, on the completed production orders for the same period, and in order that this may be so it is essential that no profits be taken cognisance of until they are actually earned.

Where there are sources of profit or loss other than completed shop work, this has, of course, to be given effect to in concording the results obtainable by either method.

There is a group of subjects outside either general or cost accounting, bearing upon capital—its protection and renumeration, and a second group bearing on the workshop and office and their methods—which have a most important bearing on the administrations of engineering undertakings, but which space does not even permit me to enumerate. They underlie all that has been already touched upon; they are the fundamentals of financial success, and no study of workshop administration is complete without an examination thereof. This, however, with regret, we are obliged to defer.

General Establishment.—In many of the older shops little attention has been given to matters outside the accommodation which may be described as purely productive. General office accommodation, store rooms, works office, &c., have been looked upon more or less as luxuries and sources of unnecessary expense. Proprietors have ever before them the weekly outlay in wages paid to all kinds of indirect producers, but it is only with difficulty that they can realise the losses arising from waste and leakage. They are particularly careful in the handling of actual cash. They do not object to a book-keeper spending days or weeks in looking for an error of a few pence in his balance, but they are not equally alive to the necessity for supervising other items which just as really represent cash. We are now wakening up to the necessity of eliminating waste in every form. The methods of administration here referred to have this object in view. They demand accurately-balanced records for all items of expense.

These methods can only be introduced gradually into an already established shop. In a new shop they may be introduced at once. In that case they should be so designed as to yield not only that amount of detailed information which the administration finds necessary for ordinary working purposes, but a fully detailed analysis of cost at any future time, or when occasion may require; and the complete scheme should, in the first instance, be formulated by an expert, whether it be for an old or for a new shop, so that the initiatory work may be such that the ultimate arrangement will be harmonious and complete. These reforms cannot be initiated by any manager on his own responsibility, however ambitious he may be to make his mark. They must originate with the principal, who must thoroughly realise their importance. When he does, and resolves on making an earnest effort to transform his business from the conditions of non-homogeneous management to those of complete homogeneity of action, he will require to exercise a good deal of courage and have a stiff backbone; but his anxieties would be much ameliorated had he at his disposal a band of men thoroughly trained both scientifically and technically in the art of management. The old hands who have honestly and conscientiously toiled to build up a business in its early stages under a "leading hand" and "head-of-department" system, which permits of the operation of independent control subject to little or no itemised criticism, are at the outset likely to resent the recording and examination of their individual acts. The march of events will, however, force compliance with the inevitable, and so will arise the necessity for bringing forward a class of men trained in the general principles of administration, and in the scientific and technical principles of design and construction.

The engineer can now, in a large measure, receive his practical training in certain of our Universities and Colleges, and there is a near prospect of these facilities being augmented in our city, when the engineering laboratory in the University is in operation. The Institution of Civil Engineers provides that students, before being admitted to the full privileges of membership, shall show a certain proficiency in theoretical and practical attainments. The accountant has to satisfy his guild of his knowledge of accounting and commercial law. Unfortunately, as yet no provision has been made in this country, so far as the author knows, for securing efficiency in the art of management. As matters now stand, each aspirant for such a position has to pick up his qualifications as best he can; and he has to commence almost every new effort with a ground start. Were he to get a good flying start in the shape of preliminary training in which the fundamental principles are taught, and if he possessed the necessary natural ability, how much more rapidly would he pick up those finishing touches which practical shop and office experience alone can give.

The hope is that the members of this Institution, interested as they are in productive engineering, will bring their influence to bear in order to get our Universities and higher scientific and technical colleges to take this matter in hand, and elevate shop management from the position in which it now stands into the realm of scientific study, so that it may rank in these respects alongside the kindred professions of civil engineering and professional accounting.

The discussion on this paper was adjourned till the next meeting.

(To be continued.)

(The Forms referred to will appear in a subsequent issue.)

Workshop Administration.

Workshop Administration, with Special Reference to Tracking Work and promptly ascertaining detailed Costs and Profits.

By Mr. David Cowan.

Reprinted by permission from the Transactions of the Institution of Engineers and Shipbuilders in Scotland.

Read 20th March 1900.

(*Continued from Page* 92).

The discussion on this paper took place on 24th April 1900.

Mr. Henry A. Mavor (member) considered that this subject was one of primary importance to all engineers. The attention of engineers to the questions raised in the paper had been directed largely to the accounting side, and less to the administration of the shops. He had had the pleasure of making an experiment with the methods defined in Mr. Cowan's paper, not directly on the lines of the paper, but on the principles embodied in it, and, after an experience of nearly a year in working, he found the result was very surprising. Every engineer wanted to be able to feel the pulse of his shop, and see what state any particular piece of work was in—if it was delayed, why it was delayed—and to be able to forecast the date of its completion. Cost came into all administration, because when one grasped the question from the beginning, and had the record carried out in an orderly and systematic fashion, the cost revealed itself automatically and without special attention. No doubt all had been making attempts to find out the cost of their products, and it had generally been found that the information thus obtained, however useful it might be for them in forecasting the cost of future work, was hardly ever available for taking the cost during the progress of the work. Speaking from experience, the system such as he described made it possible to place one's finger upon a sore place quickly. Whenever a mistake or delay in the execution of the work occurred, cards lent themselves to investigation of the causes. Mr. Cowan had described very clearly how necessary it was to fully specify what was to be done, before the work was proceeded with. Some experienced engineers had the view that, to specify everything in full detail before it came into the shop was a waste of time, but there was no greater error. The Americans had worked this out and fully specified every detail, mentioning every operation to be performed and the time it would take, and, so far from being a waste of time, it was that method alone which would produce efficiency in the shop. With the card system, anyone who required an analysis of the work had the whole material at hand without further trouble. It was a mistake to suppose that the introduction of such a system was a saving of labour in the office. He did not think it was anything of the kind. It involved a great deal more labour in the office, but it gave a result which was not attainable by any other means, and the additional labour which was required for manipulating the cards was of a very cheap kind. A small boy would do the work better than a skilled cost clerk on the old system.

Mr. J. R. Richmond (member) said the Institution owed a debt of gratitude to Mr. Cowan. It was curious that in looking over the "Transactions" of the Institution for a number of years back, he had not found a single paper dealing with this particular subject, and he thought it was a very significant thing that at this time Mr. Cowan should have brought it before them; because, in latter-day engineering there was more attention being paid to improvements in shop system than had hitherto been the case. In fact, engineers had come to recognise that method and system were paying factors. In reading over the paper he wished that Mr. Cowan, instead of writing a paper, had written a book on the subject, because he felt that the paper had suffered slightly from limitations of space. At the same time, if Mr. Cowan had done nothing else than cause them to think on this subject, a very valuable result had been obtained; and if it made them go further and induced them to revise their methods according to some of his suggestions, then it had attained even a still more valuable object. No doubt some of the members of the Institution had seen the papers by Mr. Roland in the *Engineering Magazine*, and it was a curious thing about those papers that it seemed that no one could take them *en bloc* and apply them to any particular shop. The same thing might be said about Mr. Cowan's paper. Mr. Cowan did not put it forward as a universal panacea for all the ills that shops were liable to; each particular shop must be studied by itself, because, after all, shop method was systematised common-sense, and they must take each as a problem and apply common-sense to it as well as they could. Regarding the card system, he was very pleased to hear Mr. Mavor speak on this subject, and he hoped that at some future date Mr. Mavor would see his way to put before the Institution, in some detail, the results that he had obtained by the card system. No one that he knew had gone into this subject more deeply or more carefully than Mr. Mavor had, and it would be of considerable value to the Institution to have a paper dealing with shop system and management on the lines he had spoken on. While Mr. Mavor was speaking he was led to think over the application of the card system to a particular shop, and found that if applied in the manner indicated by Mr. Mavor, he would have 135,000 cards in circulation, which seemed to him an unwieldy mass of matter to be dealt with. He thought that some of the disadvantages that Mr. Cowan had spoken of in his paper as applied to books *versus* cards, were rather more fanciful than real. There were many good points about cards in the way of keeping records of patterns and drawings, because when they were used, the card could be taken out and replaced by others if necessary; but a card-cost system was not applicable to all shops.

The discussion was resumed on 15th May 1900.

Mr. John Mann, Junr., M.A., C.A. (visitor), observed that from his professional standpoint as a Chartered Accountant, this subject was of particular interest to him; at the same time, he was afraid anything that he might say would be rather tabooed by the expert engineer, as the tendency was rather to minimise anything that the expert accountant had to say relating to matters of practical engineering. In Cost Accounts, however, the two professions found a common ground, and the expert accountant and the expert engineer had a great deal in common when they dealt with the records and accounts of processes of engineering. For the last ten years it had been to him a kind of hobby to deal with the application of scientific records to Cost Accounts. When he first mooted the question in his own professional Institute in Glasgow, he was laughed at as a faddist in proposing to record at all the intricacies of costing, especially in engineering works. Since then the subject had advanced by leaps and bounds, and within the last two years it had assumed a prominence which ten years ago would have been undreamt of. What appealed to the accountant most of all was the desirability of bringing into agreement the results of the Cost Accounts and the commercial books. To many that might seem an ideal that was quite impossible of attainment; but, speaking from some little experience on the subject, he might say that it was by no means impossible. Often, in ordinary cases, the results the commercial books revealed, which were certified by the Chartered Accountant, were nothing more nor less than an "undiscovered difference" in the books; while, by the addition of a scientific system of costing, these results were traced back to their origin—to the particular contracts or jobs handled throughout the year. The profits, less the losses, could be made to tally within reasonable nearness with the results shown in the commercial books. The very difficult question of "oncost" could not be treated in Cost Accounts by anything more or less than an estimate; and, so far as he remembered, Mr. Cowan had hit upon what seemed to him the only scientific way of dealing with that question—viz., by apportioning the shop expenses by the *time unit*, according to the *time spent* upon particular jobs. The rough and ready way of measuring this was by the *wages spent* upon the different jobs, instead of the hours spent upon them. For all practical purposes, where there were no rapid fluctuations in rates of wages, that method was no doubt sufficiently near; but the scientific measure was the time unit—that was to say, superintendence and general expenses varied in a more or less exact proportion to the time spent upon the work. With regard to the card system, it was to some extent a novelty. He had studied it in one or two different aspects, and, so far as he could see, it was really the introduction of an additional labour saving appliance. It dispensed with a tremendous amount of detail in arriving at results, and arrived at them by a shorthand process, which brushed aside a great many of the elaborate steps in the records. No doubt there were difficulties, and very great difficulties, in introducing the card system into an existing engineering shop, but he thought it was possible by working in stages to gradually arrive at a complete installation of the system, beginning perhaps by a record of the wages, passing on to a record of materials, and finally to a record of the whole processes. The disadvantages were very trifling. One might hear of the loss of cards occasionally, but that was no greater than the omission to make an entry. There was, no doubt, a great deal of stationery required; but that was a mere trifle compared with saving in time and labour in arriving at results. These results were summarised, and presented in what might be called a "graphic" form, which no one who had not seen the system in operation could really appreciate. The important cards were to be found standing up in the drawers, so that one could pick out what he wanted without having the result complicated by an enormous mass of detail. No doubt it might cost a little more money, but he believed, after some experience, that the extra expense would be found to be more than repaid by the promptitude by which the results could be arrived at. Under the old system, in particular cases he had in mind, the Cost Books were always a perfect bugbear, generally with such an amount of work in arrears that they were positively disheartened to tackle it. Under the other system, by the cheapest form of labour, the results were, with comparative ease, always up to date. What he had said was offered under correction, and simply from the layman's point of view—that of the accountant.

FIGURE I. ADMINISTRATION OF

RECORDS OF THE ACTS

- **SALES**
  - Comparisons ...
    - Competing products .. ..
    - Products which serve same purpose .. ..
  - Analysis of Sales .. ..
  - Collection of Accounts due ... .
- **PRODUCTION**
  - *Cost Accounting* ...
    - *Current Costs* .. ..
      - ***Prime costs*** .. ..
        - *Materials*
        - *Out-services*
        - *Labour*
      - ***On-cost*** .. ..
        - *Current expenses*
        - *Safeguarding expenses*
      - ***Credits*** .. ..
        - *Surplus materials*
        - *Plant*
    - *Comparative Costs* ..
      - Like Objects .. .. ..
        - Prime cost
        - On-cost
      - Elementary analyses .. ..
        - Materials
        - Out-services
        - Labour
      - Contracts between .. ..
        - Cost Price
        - Selling Price
    - Comparative Labour Rates .. .. ..
      - Day rates .. .. ..
        - Time values
        - Time units
      - Piece rates .. .. ..
        - Time values
        - Time units
      - Premium rates.. .. ..
        - Time values
        - Time units
- **CAPITAL**
  - General accounting ... ...
    - Statutory .. ..
      - Share Capital .. .. ..
        - Register of members
        - Share ledger
        - Numerical register of members
        - Certificate book
        - Register of Transfers
        - Register of Mortgages
      - Minutes .. ..
        - Board of Directors
        - General meetings
    - Ordinary Business ..
      - Personal .. .. ..
        - Suppliers' customers
      - Impersonal .. .. ..
        - Real
        - Nominal

SALES

- Salesman or Commercial Manager
  - Is directly responsible for ...
    - Estimates for work .. ..
    - Correspondence relative to production .. ..
    - *Analyses of customers' orders* .. ..
    - Orders for supplies .. ..
    - Special reports.. ..
      - On Work tickets .. ..
      - Comparison Cards .. ..
      - Special Subjects .. ..
  - Superintends .. ..
    - Looking for probable customers .. ..
      - Advertising
      - Exhibiting
      - Distributing Catalogues
      - " Printed matter
      - " Display cards
      - " Pictures and models
      - " Photographs
    - Tracking .. .. ..
      - Enquiries
      - Estimates sent out
      - Customers' records
    - Agencies .. .. ..
      - Service records
      - District Maps
      - Financial condition
      - Reports on Sales
      - Reports on quality of business
      - Reports on general standing
  - Is personally responsible for .. ..
    - Reports .. ..
      - Reports on Stocks
      - Special
    - Correspondence .. ..
      - Relative to sales

(This and the following three pages form one.

ENGINEERING WORKSHOPS.

ACTS

- Equipment ...
  - Production ...
    - Machinery .. ..
      - Standard .. .. .. — More or less; Common to all; Kindred undertaking
      - Special to .. .. .. — One operation; Groups of operations
      - Power transmissions .. .. — Shafting — Belting; Ropes — Electric cables
      - General service .. .. — Engines — Boilers; Furnaces, &c.
    - Plant .. .. ..
      - Drawings .. .. .. — Standard; Establishment; Unclassified
      - Patterns.. .. .. .. — Standard; Establishment; Unclassified
      - Fixtures.. .. .. .. — Offices; Shops
    - Tools .. .. — Standard for general use; Special jigs, fixtures; Hand Tools, Implements, and Utensils for general use
    - Supplies .. .. — Rough stores; Finished stores
  - Distribution ...
    - Stock .. .. — Completed products for Sales
- Superintendence ... (The General Manager)
  - Designing, Chief Engineer ..
    - 1st Senior draughtsman .. .. — 1st Junior draughtsman; 2nd do. do.; &c. do do.
    - 2nd do. .. ..
    - &c. do. .. ..
  - Construction ... (Shop Manager)
    - 1st Foreman .. ..
    - 2nd do. .. ..
    - &c. do. .. ..
      - 1st sub-foreman .. .. — 1st Workman; 2nd do.; 3rd do.
      - 2nd do. .. ..
    - Store-keeper, &c. .. ..
- Operating ... (The General Manager)
  - *Issue orders to Engineer relative to*
    - *Current shop orders* ..
      - Prepares all drawings .. ..
      - *Analyses work into separate objects of expense* .. ..
      - *Prepares all shop specifications* .. ..
    - *Standing shop orders* ..
      - *Shop* .. .. — Maintainence; List of Standard parts; " Symbolic nomenclature of machine details; " Rough stores; " Operations of work; " Nos. ranging Men in shops; " Drawings; " Patterns; " Jigs; " Templates; " Fixtures; " &c.
      - Sales .. .. — Cataloguing; Estimating quantities; " Drawings; " Specifications
      - Special .. .. — Diagram from comparison cards; Conduct of all scientific operations; Tests of all products; Photographs, &c.
  - *Issue orders to Shop Manager relative to* ... ...
    - *Special objects of expense, who analyses same and issues orders to foremen for the execution of*
      - *Shop orders* .. : .. — 1. *Job Orders*
      - *Foremen analyses them into and issues to* (1) *Workmen* (2) *Stores* — 2. *Elementary Orders*

FIGURE I.—*Continued.*

ADMINISTRATION OF

IN REGARD TO

PRODUCTION

- Structures ..
  - Work-shops ...
    - For Building Heavy Staple Products ..
      - Wood-working .. .. .. — Pattern-making; Carpentry
      - Smithing .. .. .. — Power forging; Stamping; Hand forging
      - Boiler-making.. .. .. — Preparation for Union; Uniting—; Riveting
      - Machining .. .. .. — Planeing; Milling; Turning; Drilling; Special operations
      - Fitting .. .. — Hand adjustment
      - Erecting inside.. .. .. — Assembling— Pieces into Components; Components into Members; Members into Products
      - Erecting outside .. .. — Building in sitio; Testing; Running; Maintainence under guarantee
      - Painting.. .. .. .. — .. ..
      - Packing, &c. .. .. .. — Home distribution; Export, &c.
    - For Manufacturing Light Components and Pieces .. ..
      - Iron and Steel working .. — Turning, Ordinary; Turning, Forming tools; Turning, Turret Machines; Turning, Chuck work; Screwing; Milling; Gear cutting; Drilling; Grinding and polishing; Scraping; Inspecting; Assembling
      - Brass working .. .. .. — More or less the same as Iron working
    - Services.. .. ..
      - Tool-making .. .. .. — Templates, jigs, fixtures and such like; Cutting tools; Hardening, Tempering, &c.
      - Cutting out and marking off.. — Metals; Timber
      - Prime movers .. .. .. — Engines, motors, &c.; Transmissions
      - Internal transport .. .. — Tramway service; Crane service; Messenger service
      - General .. .. — Water, Light, Heat; Common labour; Cloak-room, Lavatory, &c.
  - Storages ... ...
    - Receiving, checking, inspecting, and clearing materials inwards .. .. .. — Castings, forgings, &c.; Boiler and Smithy materials; General supplies
    - Rough stores .. .. .. — Furnishings; Timber; Smithy iron and steel; Tools; Inflammables; Fuel
    - Finished stores, Warehouse.. — Components and Pieces; Completed products
    - Drawings .. .. .. — All kinds
    - Patterns.. .. .. .. — All kinds
    - Spares .. .. — All kinds

ENGINEERING WORKSHOPS.

- **CAPITAL**
  - Liabilities …
    - Shares .. .. ..
      - Ordinary
      - Preference
    - Borrowed .. ..
      - Mortgages .. .. .. Special Debentures
      - Loans .. .. Bank Overdraft
    - Safeguarding funds ..
      - Depreciations .. .. ..
        - Tear and Wear
        - Obsolescence
      - Risks and Casualties
      - Dividend Equalising
    - Sundry Creditors ..
      - Secured
      - Unsecured
      - Bills Payable
    - Profits .. ..
  - Assets … …
    - Fixed .. .. ..
      - Tangible .. .. ..
        - Land
        - Buildings
        - Equipment
      - Intangible .. .. ..
        - Goodwill
        - Preliminary Expenses
        - Patents
    - Floating .. ..
      - Goods .. ..
        - Stores
        - Products—Stock
      - Sundry Debtors .. ..
        - Good
        - Doubtful
        - Bad
      - Cash .. ..
        - In hand
        - Bills receivable
        - In bank
    - Loss .. ..
  - Economics …
    - Ratios .. .. ..
      - Oncost to Labour
      - Nett Cash to Revenue
      - Capital to Revenue
      - Drawings, value to Revenue
      - Patterns, value to Revenue
      - Loose Tools, value to Revenue
    - Protection against ..
      - Depreciations
      - Risks and Casualties
    - Remuneration .. ..
      - Dividends
      - Interest
- **Offices** …
  - Executive… … General Manager ..
    - Personal Staff
    - Engineer Staff
    - Salesman's Staff
  - Common … … Services.. .. ..
    - Telegraph
    - Telephone
    - Book-room
    - Registration and Filing Room
    - Drawing Store
    - Board, Private, and Waiting Rooms
    - Cloak Rooms
    - Lavatory, W.C., &c.
  - Administrative … Secretary .. ..
    - General accounting and statutory records
    - Cashier
    - *Cost, Accounting, and Shop records*

Mr. Archibald Denny (member) considered there were many in the same position as himself; they could not possibly absorb the paper in one night, or even in many nights, as it was of extreme complexity. They might get a broad general idea, such as Mr. Mann had so well expressed, and doubtless the basis idea of the system was good. While in the United States last year he observed that the card system was being used in every factory which he visited, not only for costing, but for keeping records of costs, and for every kind and description of record one could think of. Some went so far as to keep their Ledger by cards; they had no books at all. When he pointed out that a card could be taken out and the account lost, and with it all means of checking, it was admitted that that was a possible difficulty. In regard to adopting it in his own business, that of a shipbuilder, while he could see how it could be done in other people's business, it was very difficult to see how it could be done in his own. He knew that Mr. Mavor had adopted it in quite another way from what Mr. Mann suggested. Mr. Mavor did not adopt it sectionally, but right away in a single day. He himself was trying to introduce it in Mr. Mann's way, and he began at what Mr. Mavor would think the wrong end, at the records of costs, and instead of having large books with the records of costs, these were now concentrated in ten small cards for each ship. Whether he would succeed in introducing it universally he could not say, but he feared that with their rivetters and gentlemen of that description they might have a little difficulty in accounting for the rivets. That the system was good, and that Mr. Cowan had explained it in a very full manner, he thought there was no doubt, and he was sure that while many like himself felt a difficulty in rewarding Mr. Cowan with a full discussion, they were none the less grateful to him for what he had brought before them.

Mr. Henry A. Mavor (member) said Mr. Denny had mentioned that the cards could be suddenly introduced. That was quite true, but nobody could ever initiate them in a day. The book records might be stopped on any day and the card records started the next day, but the books must have been worked up and a systematic arrangement established before this was possible, because the haphazard method of costs in many places could not be departed from, and a skilled record kept on the following day, without the training of men into systematic keeping of records.

Professor A. Barr, D.Sc. (member), hoped that this was only the first of a number of papers the Institution might receive upon this and kindred subjects. Most sections of engineering work could be as well done in this country as elsewhere, and the Americans were a very long way ahead in the matter of tracing work through the shops and in that which followed from it—the production of work cheaply, more especially where it was of a repetition kind. He had looked into the card system for a considerable length of time with very great interest. He had seen it used in America for almost all purposes. There he saw an index which struck him as being one that would be absolutely impossible to keep on any system whatever other than the card system. Although it was not engineering he might mention it. The Library Bureau of Boston, which was the first to introduce the card system commercially on a large scale, had instituted a record of everybody who applied for life insurance within the United States; and if a person went to any insurance company in America and said that he had never been refused life insurance, all the company had to do was to go to the card catalogue and there his name and his description would be found, and when and where he made the application previously, if his statement were untrue. That would not be possible by any other system than the card system. Each card went into its alphabetical place and could be immediately produced. The Library Bureau itself received intimations from the insurance companies, and a sufficient number of copies were typewritten and put by the Bureau's own staff into their places in the record cabinet of each insurance company. That was an example of how far the system could go. Mr. Mann's remarks were very interesting, and they should not look upon him as discussing the subject from an outside point of view, because it was as much a matter of accounting as it was of engineering. The paper was one which it would be almost impossible to discuss fully at the present moment. It hung very largely upon the card system certainly, but it involved a number of other things which would require a greater amount of consideration than they had been able to give to it. The question of nomenclature was one of the greatest importance, because a good nomenclature would simplify the whole system. He could not say that he altogether liked the nomenclature which Mr. Cowan had proposed for the various divisions of work, but that was simply a detail. He was afraid also that no system of cards could possibly be of general application. What applied to a shipyard must necessarily be somewhat different from what was applicable to an electrical engineer's workshop. In the workshop with which he himself was connected a beginning had been made to introduce the card system, but he would not go now into any details. Mr. Jackson could relate his (the speaker's) experience much better than he could himself. He considered the paper one of the most valuable that had been brought before the Institution.

Mr. H. D. D. Barman (member) agreed with Mr. Mann that it was better to start step by step. He had started with wages cards, and had found them exceedingly simple and of the greatest use, especially for estimating varied classes of work; but he dreaded starting cards for material, where, to carry out the system properly, not only the chief items, of say an engine, had to be dealt with, but also every bolt and nut. The materials for cards should evidently be issued from the drawing office, and he would be glad to have further information of the methods used from those who had already adopted the system.

(*To be continued.*)

Workshop Administration.

Workshop Administration, with Special Reference to Tracking Work and promptly ascertaining detailed Costs and Profits.

By Mr. DAVID COWAN.

Reprinted by permission from the Transactions of the Institution of Engineers and Shipbuilders in Scotland.

Read 20th March 1900.

(*Continued from Page* 120).

Mr. Harold Jackson (member) said it appeared to him that one point mentioned by Mr. Cowan and Mr. Mann should be very much insisted upon in organising a system of Cost Accounts. Everyone knew how accountants insisted upon a search for hours for a penny. It really did not matter whether they found it or not, but they searched diligently for that penny until they found it. On p. 90 (*Acct.*) Mr. Cowan said, "It will be observed that it is thus practicable to interlock the Shop Costs Account with the accounts kept in the general books. They may, however, be worked independently and parallel with the commercial books." In order to ensure Cost Accounts being kept correctly and up to date, he thought it was necessary that they should form an integral part of the commercial books. The diligence spent in searching for the lost penny would then be applied equally to the Cost Accounts. A card system had been adopted in the works with which he was connected, and he had drawn up the cost of that system. As at present in use, the cards would cost one-fortieth of a penny apiece, and each man used on the average two time-cards and one material-card per day, but the number of cards in use might at any time be varied, so as to show operations in more or less detail. They could be arranged to show a whole piece of work on one card, or they could be detailed so as to give the cost of a single piece on one card. There were about 85 men employed, and the total number of cards used per day was about 250, making the total cost of cards per day about 6d. The time taken to check the cards with the men's time record, to affix the various rates of wages, and to allocate the cards to the various jobs, &c., was not more than two hours per day, and the work was done by two boys. On Tuesday morning, at the latest, he had handed to him the allocation of the wages and materials for the week ending on the previous Thursday night, showing that the Cost Accounts were absolutely up to date. Before the system mentioned above was adopted this had never been the case. In order to deal efficiently with the varying prices of material, and to ensure that the correct price was put against material given out for any job, a scheme had been devised which would shortly be put into operation, and, although it appeared somewhat bulky, he believed it could be worked at a very low cost. Mr. Mavor told him that he believed, from his experience, the system would work correctly; and he felt sure it would, but he was not sure that it was not too bulky to be practicable. It was proposed that *every item* of every invoice should be entered on a *separate* card under a reference number. As the invoice came in, the reference number would be written on the card, and on a tag or tags, the latter being sent to the storeman to be affixed to the material in question. The card would also bear the date that the material came in, and the total value and price per unit of the material. On giving out material the reference number would be entered on the card by which the men drew it from the store, and when that card was handed to the boy who priced the cards, he would have simply to refer to the reference number, and there find the correct price per unit. He believed, in that way, it would be possible to cost correctly all the material in the place. It seemed to him very essential that all material, of whatever nature, should be entered and given out in one way only, as where two ways existed there was always the possibility of the same material being treated through both channels, or being forgotten altogether. One great advantage cards gave in furthering this idea, was the possibility of each card being stowed away out of the road as soon as the material entered upon it had been all given out to the job or jobs for which it was intended; with books, such a system as he had sketched would be utterly impracticable.

Correspondence.

Mr. A. D. Smith (member).—It was an easy matter to point out the vastness and expensiveness of Mr. Cowan's system. Shop management nowadays, from its complexity and the keenness of competition, required more and more technical ability on the part of the manager, and he would best succeed in the task who made the *work proper of first importance*, and any system of costing, &c., connected therewith secondary; this he would find to be the first essential of any system which, to quote Mr. Cowan's own words, "is simple in its conception, and automatic in its working." This order of things, however, Mr. Cowan completely reversed. On page 86 (*Acct.*) Mr. Cowan spoke of a manager finding means of reducing the cost of a product. He (Mr. Smith) admitted that a manager now and again might institute particular inquiry into the cost of some piece of machinery, but to continue this minute inquiry at all times added a cost to the product, which defeated the end in view—viz., the cheapening of that product. In the last sentence of the clause already referred to on page 86 (*Acct.*). Mr. Cowan made the following remark:—"Clerks without practical knowledge of "the work, who make *ex post facto* analyses by the aid of "foremen, cannot be depended on for collecting the in-"formation necessary for efficient administration." How would Mr. Cowan make this agree with his remarks on page 88 (*Acct.*)? His whole system depended on clerks, and, in a symbolic system such as his, mistakes were bound to be of no uncommon occurrence; and, further, he might say that a mistake rendered the whole information that had been collected, and the conclusions drawn from it, valueless. Mr. Cowan considered simple symbolic nomenclature necessary to secure a useful analysis. On that point he differed from Mr. Cowan. How had engineering concerns got on without this system so long? The simplicity of the symbol was purely imaginary. For example, let reference be made to Fig. 14, Sheet V. A workman might have been employed fitting a key to a spur wheel for a particular job, but before he could return his time as S.O., 111 B 3, he would have to consult his foreman with respect to the symbolic specification, and to those symbols add another for the operation he had performed. It was possible to imagine the symbolic number to reach 1,000! The advantages of issuing cards instead of books was dealt with on page 87 (*Acct.*). In his opinion, the practical disadvantages were as follows:—

(1) The number of cards to be handled;

(2) The ease with which they were lost;

(3) The labour in turning them over and examining every one of them before the one wanted could be found;

(4) The impossibility of docketing them in such a manner as to ensure their ready accessibility; and

(5) The expense of printing them.

With regard to the subject of a shop specification as described on page 87 (*Acct.*), and illustrated in Fig. 14, Sheet V., Mr. Cowan divided the job into members, components, and pieces, and it would readily be seen that the whole was so interwoven, one piece hanging on another for its symbol, that before the work could be issued to the shop the complete specification required to be written out. This necessarily meant that all the drawings had to be made, and the details all worked out. Great care and no small amount of ingenuity were required to be shown in the construction of such a specification, and how all this could be done without causing the most real and vexatious delays, Mr. Cowan did not seem to have inquired into. When the shop specification had been distributed through the shop various cards had to be written from it. He would only take one example—viz., Fig. 7, Sheet III., job order card. Mr. Cowan said this order was personal to the workmen, and to each operation. Could anyone possibly imagine what this would mean in a large engineering establishment? The number of cards would be fabulous, and the cost of dealing with them in many cases would far outrun the cost of the operation recorded. He would give an example of what he wished to point out. One of the leading hands in a fitting shop required a piece of wood to go across the mouth of a pump barrel, so that he might mark off the holes in the flange. He required first to find his foreman, and together they would consult the symbolic specification, and a card would be written out for the man to present to the foreman patternmaker or joiner. The man then went in search of this foreman, and after he had written out one or more cards the man was given the piece of wood. Returning to his job, he found that he had spent more than half-an-hour, and cost the firm at least 6d. for a piece of wood valued at less than a halfpenny. Mr. Cowan dealt entirely in symbols; his system was simply endless. On page 88 (*Acct.*) he described the symbols for recording the condition of work in the shop. To his mind, it was hardly conceivable that a manager would get any intelligent idea of the condition of work in the shop by wading through a pile of specifications every other day, and tracing out the various symbols. On the subject of oncost, Mr. Cowan said, "Oncost is always an assumption." In this remark Mr. Cowan gave his system away. What was the use of imposing on workmen such an elaborate system of costing, seeing that all methods of ascertaining cost must contain a variable and uncertain amount called "oncost" to be added to material and labour? To make use of the information collected on cards was sufficient work to keep any manager fully employed without time to give a thought to anything else, except that one thought might arise in his mind as he saw the mountain of cards piled up before him. What was the cost of this costing system of Mr. Cowan's?—a question that naturally arose in the mind of anyone who read his paper. By this system a principal might get information on minute details which he had not been in the habit of getting before; but at what cost would it be ascertained? He would have to—

(1) Treble his staff;

(2) Double or perhaps treble his Stationery Account;

(3) Make the costing system of paramount importance;

(4) Demoralise his men by ruining their memories;

(5) Compel them to waste their time learning and consulting on the system;

(6) Retard the work indefinitely at the outset, and all through its progress in the shop; and

ADMINISTRATION OF ENGINEERING WORKSHOPS.

FIGURE 2.

Diagram analysing Customers' Orders for Work into Special Products, and these again into their Elementary Forms.

CUSTOMERS' ORDER FOR WORK	PRODUCTS, Symbolized by three Capital Letters, As P, S, X.	MEMBERS, Symbolized by Arbitary Letters, As A, B, C, &c.	COMPONENTS, Symbolized by Numbering ending in 0, As 10, 20, 50, &c.	PIECES, Symbolized by Digital Numbers, As 1, 2, 3, 11, 19, &c.	ELEMENTS OF EXPENSE
1	2	3	4	5	6
Customers' Orders are divisible into *Products* ..	1st. Product 2nd. Product each being divisible into *Members* .. .. 3rd. Product &c. Product	1st. Member 2nd. Member, each being divisible into *Components* .. 3rd. Member &c. Member	1st. Component 2nd. Component each being divisible into *Pieces* .. .. 3rd. Component &c. Component	1st. Piece 2nd. Piece each being divisible into *Elements* .. 3rd. Piece &c. Piece	1st. Materials, withdrawn direct from outside 2nd. Materials, withdrawn from Stores 3rd. Out-services 4th. Labour 5th. Oncost load

FIGURE 4.

Diagram analysing Customers' Orders for Work into Elementary Shop Orders.

Customers' Orders for Work	Direct and Indirect Expenses	Products—Symbols three Capital Letters, as P, S, X	Objects specially to be worked on. Symbol O.	Character of Expense, Symbol P. or W.	Processes, Symbol T	Operations, Symbol N.	Elementary Shop Orders
1	2	3	4	5	6	7	8
Customers' Orders are referable to	1. Special Orders for Products These can be sub-divided into .. 2. Standing Orders for Maintenance of the Establishment necessary to the performance of work on Special Orders These are classified and	1. Production Order 2. Production Order. authorising expense on a Special Product. This may be referred by Shop Manager to .. .. 3. Production Order &c. Production Order Are sub-divided down to Elements same as the Special Orders	1. Members. The expense thereon being divisible into that on .. .. 2. Components Do. 3. Pieces Do.	1. Work by .. 2. Plant by ..	1. Process by 2. Do. .. 3. Do. &c. Do. 1. Process by 2. Do. 3. Do. .. &c. Do.	1. Operation 2. Operation, The Elementary Forms being .. 3. Do. &c. Do. 1. Operation 2. Do. 3. Operation, The Elementary Forms being .. &c. Do.	1. Materials, withdrawn from Outside 2. Materials, withdrawn from Stores 3. Out-services 4. Labour 1. Materials, withdrawn from Outside 2. Materials, withdrawn from Stores 3. Out-services 4. Labour

ADMINISTRATION OF ENGINEERING WORKSHOPS.

FIGURE 3.

BLANK & COMPANY, LIMITED.

SHOP SPECIFICATION NO. *960* PRODUCTION ORDER NO. *501* DATE *28th January 1899*

S.O.'s Nos.	SYMBOLS: Member's Letters	SYMBOLS: Components Nos. ending in o	SYMBOLS: Pieces, Digits only	SYMBOLS: Same as	Quantity	Full Symbol of Object, P S X. Full Names of Members and Pieces. Full dimensions and all additions afterwards made in Shop	Classes of Materials	Detail Drawing References	Symbols showing condition of Work	CONDITIONS OF WORK — Stores: Rough	Stores: Finished	Processes: Drawing	Pattern-making	Smithing	Boiler-making	Machining	Fitting-ins	Erecting		Painting	Fitting-outs	Order out
1	2	3	4	5	6	7	8	9	10	11	12	13	14	15	16	17	18	19	20	21	22	23
..	A	..	..	..	..	*Machine Body*																
..	A	10	..	..	1	*Main casing, punch gap 36", shear gap 34"*	*Cast Iron*	*A-10*	*Completed,* ×			× *670*	× *671*			× *685*						× *690*
..	A	..	2	..	1	*Cam shaft cover, 8" bore on engine side*	*do.*															
..	..	..	3	..	2	*Bolts for do., 6" × 1¼" dia.*	*Steel*							× *200*		÷ *410*	+ *420*	= *300*				+ *700*
..	A	30	..	..	..	*These assembled*																
..	A	..	4	..	1	*Cam Shaft cover, 10" bore on angle cutter side*	*Cast Steel*	*A-40*				× *897*		× *491*		× *500*	÷ *501*					× *700*
..	..	..	5	..	2	*Bolts for do., 4" × 1¼" dia.*	*Steel*															
..	A	50	..	..	..	*These assembled*																
..	A	..	6	..	2	*Fulcrum pins with collar 12" × 5¼" dia., Collar 6¾" dia. × 2¼" wide*	*Steel*	*A-60*	*In Hand.* =			× *751*		× *690*		= *965*	÷ *706*					
..	..	..	7	..	2	*Taper pins for do., 9" long × 1" dia., thick end*	*do.*															
..	A	70	..	..	..	*These assembled*																
..	A	..	8	..	1	*Punch ram strap ¾" thick × 4" wide*	*Steel*	*A-90*				= *550*										
..	..	..	9	..	1	*Gib and cotter for do.*	*do.*															
..	..	..	11	..	2	*Bolts for do., 3" long × ¾" dia.*	*do.*															
..	A	110	..	..	..	*These assembled*																
..	A	..	12	..	2	*Cover plates for shear slide*	*Cast Iron*	*A-110*	*Ready for Process,* ÷		× *703*	× *560*										
..	..	..	13	..	8	*Pins for securing do., 2" long × ⅞" dia.*	*Steel*															
..	A	130	..	..	..	*These assembled*																
111	A	**230**	..	..	..	*Machine Body assembled*																
..	B	..	..	..		*Cam Shaft with spur wheel*																
..	..	10	..	..	1	*Cam shaft—cam faces chilled*	*Cast Iron*	*B-10*				+ *300*										
..	..	..	2	..	1	*Spur wheel, No. 1407, 42 teeth, 3" pitch, 6" broad, 12" bore, flanged to pitch line*	*Cast Iron*	*B.30*	*Required,* +			+ *307*										
..	..	..	3	..	1	*Key for do., 8" long × 1¼" × ¾"*	*Steel*															
..	B	30	..	..	..	*These assembled*																
116	B	**130**	..	..		*Cam shaft and spur wheel assembled*																
						Total Prime Cost—transferred to Register																

ADMINISTRATION OF ENGINEERING WORKSHOPS.

FIGURE 5.

SHOP Order No.______ Charge prod'n. Order No.______ | Service Index Reference

Issue Job Order for	Aggregate	Members	Components	Pieces
Return Expense on	C.	O.	T.	N.

Job Order No. Index,______

MAKE ONLY ONE ENTRY ON EACH CARD.

Issued by______ Date, __/__/__ Shop Sp'n. No.____

RECEIPTS No.	Mo.	Day	NAMES	COMPLETIONS No	Mo.	Day
			Charged up—Cost Clerk			

REQUIRED—Date.______

DESCRIPTION______

REMARKS______

BLANK & COMPANY LIMITED, GLASGOW.

FIGURE 6.

PRODUCTION Order No. *1001* Charge to Customers' Order No. *650* | Service Index Reference

Issue S.O.'s for	Aggregate	Members	Components	Pieces	
Return Expense on	C.	O.	T.	N.	*27 B*

Shop Order Nos. Index, *101, 107, 110, 112, 114, 116, 118, 119, &c.*

MAKE ONLY ONE ENTRY ON EACH CARD.

Issued by *G. M.* Date, *1* / *7* / *99.* Shop Sp'n. No. *96*

RECEIPTS No.	Mo.	Day	NAMES	COMPLETIONS No.	Mo.	Day
61	*7*	*3*	*Head Draughtsman*	*61*	*8*	*10*
63	*7*	*5*	*Leading Draughtsman*	*63*	*7*	*22*
65	*7*	*12*	*Second Draughtsman*	*65*	*8*	*20*
S M	*7*	*1*	Manager	*S M*	*8*	*25*
S C	*8*	*25*	Sales Book—Sales Clerk	*S C*	*8*	*27*
C C	*8*	*27*	Charged up—Cost Clerk	*C C*	*8*	*29*

REQUIRED—Date, *31 / 12 / 99*

Catalogue Ref'ce., Sec. *I* Page *57* Symbol *P S X*

DESCRIPTION AND REMARKS, *One Punching and Shearing Machine, Lever principle, to punch and shear Steel Plates, 1½" thick, Engine driven.*

SPECIAL FEATURES, *To have Cutters for Steel Angles 6" × 6" × 1", the punch sockets to suit Customer's Standard Taper. Nameplate of Customer.*

To be gummed, after completion, on front page of Shop Specification.

BLANK & COMPANY LIMITED.

ADMINISTRATION OF ENGINEERING WORKSHOPS.

FIGURE 7.

Job Order No.________ Charge to Shop Order No.

Issue Elementary Orders for	Aggregate	Members	Components	Pieces	Service Index Reference
Return Expenditure on	C.	O.	T.	N.	

Material Card—Direct—Index No.________

Do. Rough Stores—Index No.________

Out-Services—Index No.________

Labour—Index No.________

MAKE ONLY ONE ENTRY ON EACH CARD.

Issued by______to______Date,___/___/___Shop Sp'n. No.______

RECEIPTS					COMPLETIONS				
No.	Month	Day	Hour	Minute	No.	Month	Day	Hour	Minute
Charged-up—Cost Clerk									

Description________

Remarks________

Workmen to hold only one Card at one time.

BLANK & COMPANY LIMITED, GLASGOW.

FIGURE 8.

FORWARDING Order No. *1234* Charge to **CUSTOMER'S Order No.** *650*

Issued by *G.M.* Gen. Manager, Sig. and Date, *1st Nov., 1899*

Catalogue Reference, *Sect. I.* Symbol, *P S X*

Packing Instructions, Marks, and Numbers, *All cases to be zinc lined and made air-tight* *Marks, T (3) K.*

Conveying and Forwarding Instructions, *Deliver alongside s s. Burmher, Prince's Dock, Glasgow, to be alongside not later than 5th Jan., 2000.*

Carriage Forward or Paid

Forwarded by *Cameron & Co., Carriers.*

Greatest External Dimensions, ft., ins., ... *7' 6" × 3' 0" × 1' 6"*

Nett Weight of Machinery, cwts., ... *10 2 28*

Gross Weight, " *12 1 17*

RECEIPTS			NAMES	COMPLETIONS		
No.	Mo.	Day		No.	Mo.	Day
S M	*10*	*30*	*Shop Manager's Register*	*S M*	*10*	*30*
101	*11*	*1*	*Foreman Joiner*	*101*	*11*	*5*
108	*11*	*5*	*Foreman Fitter*	*108*	*11*	*10*
S M	*11*	*1*	Shop Manager's Signature and Dates .. C	*S M*	*11*	*15*
S C	*11*	*25*	Shipping Clerk " " " .. C	*S K*	*11*	*20*
S C	*11*	*27*	Sales Clerk, Journal Folio	*S C*	*11*	*25*

On completion, to be gummed on front page of Shop Specification.

BLANK & COMPANY, LIMITED.

(7) He would find in the end that he had got his information in a form which necessitated his reading it by the aid of a symbolic dictionary.

He believed Mr. Cowan's paper only gave the beginning of the system, and that its developments were endless. He would warn the members from being persuaded to try Mr. Cowan's system. He was surprised that Mr. Cowan should have brought up such a subject, as it was tried lately in a well-known engineering works in Glasgow, and had to be abandoned as keeping back the work proper, being too expensive, and altogether unworkable.

Mr. Cowan, in reply, said he did not know that he was exactly in a position to answer the various points raised that night—points that had not exactly been anticipated in his paper. His paper, at the outset, distinctly pointed out that the scheme as there set forth was specially intended for the operation of an engineering shop turning out heavy products. It was further stated that every particular manufacturing business required the scheme modified to suit its own particular wants. The discussion had, irrespective of any of these considerations, proceeded on the assumption that the scheme, as set out in the paper, was a universal panacea for all the ills that engineering works were subject to. That was not so, but he had not the slightest hesitation in saying that the scheme as outlined would work satisfactorily in all manufacturing businesses except a chemical one, when intelligently modified to suit. It required to be modified very considerably for what might be called light work—viz., machines under two tons in weight, such as that carried on by Mr. Mavor—and to a still greater extent would it require to be modified for the work as carried on in a regular factory—for instance, in a concern performing thousands of operations of the same kind in a day, by the aid of machines specially constructed for the performance of each operation. Mr. Denny's work (shipbuilding), on the other hand, differed widely from that of constructing range-finders, as carried on by Mr. Jackson. Still, a system to meet most of Mr. Denny's requirements could, he thought, be devised by one who had a full knowledge of all the underlying principles on which this system of administration was based, and with an opportunity of studying all the intricacies of a shipbuilder's business; but the study would probably require to extend over a year or two before it would be safe to introduce the system into that particular business. One thing required in introducing the system seemed to have been overlooked by all the speakers, unless perhaps by Mr. Mavor—namely, that before any attempt should be made to introduce the use of cards for recording detailed costs, and more particularly for the purpose of keeping these accounts in a concern where heavy materials had to be treated in one way and light materials in another, the general business books should be put in such a condition that they could be worked parallel with the shop accounts; because, under such circumstances, the shop Cost Accounts should form an integral part of the whole scheme of accounting in use by that particular concern. Unless this was done, and all other preliminary arrangements necessary to the system were properly carried out—such as the providing of shop specifications more or less detailed, the setting out of each item of expense separately, the providing of proper office accommodation, and appliances for the use of works-manager, foremen, time-keepers, and job-clerks, also rough stores accommodation of a sufficient kind—they generally failed. If these provisions were not made, most people would get disgusted at the outset, and the not uncommon verdict would be pronounced—the thing would not do. It would do, however, if intelligently gone about at the start. A beginner usually attempted too much, as Mr. Mann properly pointed out. In an old-established concern the process of introduction should be a very gradual one, and the proprietors should not be disappointed although a year or two passed before the system was even properly blocked out, and not in full running for all details. The employment of an expert with a thorough knowledge of the subject would simplify materially the process of its introduction, and might be the means of avoiding the repetition of much which would require to be undone in order to get the scheme into one harmonious whole; but, even with such assistance, the change should be brought about slowly, especially in an old-established shop. In a new shop the system could be started right away. Mr. Mavor had given them to understand that he did not anticipate any great saving in expense in substituting the card system of Cost Accounts for the book system now generally in use. He (Mr. Cowan) did not suppose that many of the members anticipated much lowering in the expense of lighting by introducing the electric light, but most of them who had adopted it did so simply because, by an additional outlay for light, they would get a better return for their money in the form of increased shop output. If Mr. Mavor and others who had adopted the card system of Cost Accounts would be content to accept the same amount of light with regard to the internal economy of their shops as they had to remain satisfied with under the time-honoured book system, they would find that the expense of the card system would not be greater, but probably less. There was, however, no advantage to be gained by making the change unless greater value was obtained in some form or another. The book system did not lend itself to yielding full economic information in regard to a product in all its parts, without incurring an unjustifiable outlay. The card system, on the other hand, did this at a very small outlay, and in a manner which provided just such detail as was wanted in each particular case, and only when it was required, not before. It only demanded that the objects of expense should be defined at the outset, and the items of expense at the time that the work was being performed; the synthesis of expense could then be compiled whenever wanted, and in such form as the administration deemed proper to meet each particular case. Mr. Mavor had informed them that evening that he made his change from books to cards in a day, and that he had as yet scarcely a year's experience of the new system. That being so, it was not surprising that he did not find any saving in expense. In all probability he had been doing much of his work twice over, because his general account books had not been designed specially in anticipation of his introducing the use of cards. Until all were equally efficient the best results could not be looked for.

(To be continued.)

Workshop Administration.

Workshop Administration, with Special Reference to Tracking Work and promptly ascertaining detailed Costs and Profits.

By Mr. DAVID COWAN.

Reprinted by permission from the Transactions of the Institution of Engineers and Shipbuilders in Scotland.
Read 20th March 1900.

(*Continued from Page* 155).

The author felt confident from the flattering way Mr. Mavor had spoken of the advantages that had accrued by the use of the cards during his short trial, that when he (Mr. Mavor) had three or four years more experience, with more perfected arrangements, he would have great reluctance in going back to the older method, if compelled to do so by circumstances outwith his control. Professor Barr had mentioned that cards had been much more largely used in America than in this country. Certainly they had been made use of there to a greater extent than here for records of all kinds; but, on reflection, it would be seen that their use was not altogether new here. In this country one of the most striking instances of their use was in hotels, and it was that which first drew the author's attention to the possibilities of their use. A person sat down to breakfast, ordered his bill, and in a few minutes the waiter presented it. If he examined the hotel books to see how that was done, he found that for each meal there was a separate ticket or card, which, on its receipt at the office, was entered up instantly. Thus, he got his bill when he called for it, and the hotel proprietor had recorded in his books a complete analysis of all services and materials supplied, which he could post the same evening to the secretary of his company, if he desired to do so. What was a railway ticket but a card? By the use of these tickets the receipts were apportioned to the different railways over which the passenger was carried. It was chiefly for this purpose that the railway clearing-house was originally established. One-pound notes were simply cards. The great bulk of the financial business of the world was carried on by the use of loose bank-notes, cheques, and such like. What were these but loose cards? Cards which they were very careful in looking after. They were seldom lost; the loss of a card was equivalent to the omission of an entry, with this difference, that one could tell when a card was lost; but who could tell how many entries had been omitted from book records which were squared by an undefined balance? Engineers for many years had been using cards in the shape of orders for stores, and latterly as "premium tickets." Some had made use of these store orders for grouping the cost of stores according to "blocks of expense," and charging the slump values of these "blocks of expense" into the Cost Books; but it did not appear, until recently, that anybody had the courage to use them directly as an integral part of his accounts. Instead, numerous transcriptions had been preferred. Professor Barr did not altogether approve of the symbolic nomenclature proposed for distinguishing the machine details as exemplified in the paper. He (Mr. Cowan) knew of none better, but doubtless there might be others, not published, which were more suitable for the purpose. He would only mention here a few of the conditions that should be complied with by such a nomenclature, and would be very thankful to any member who should bring before the Institution a scheme which covered the whole and of a simpler character. These requisites of a symbolic nomenclature were:—

(1) Isolation of names, each object having a name which did not belong, or ever could belong, to any other object.
(2) Brevity, simplicity, and clearness in description.
(3) Suggestiveness of the objects dealt with.
(4) Simplicity of use.
(5) A common principle by which substantially the same notation might be determined by independent notators working on the same product.

It was understood that names were more or less scientifically arranged, depending, of course, upon the amount of study and ability expended. Mr. Richmond mentioned that in a particular shop he had in view, 135,000 cards would be in circulation. As each man might use five cards per day—the average in practice was three or four—it would thus appear that Mr. Richmond's shop was employing something like 27,000 men. In such a shop the mass of paper floating about under any system would be difficult to wield; but, if the hands employed only amounted to 1,000, the number of cards floating in the shop would be 135 per man. If this latter figure even represented the true state of the administration or organisation in that shop, it was high time that the searchlight of the card system was thrown upon it, so as to reduce the number of special objects of expense (jobs) floating about the shop in an unfinished condition. It looked very much as if Mr. Richmond was labouring under some misapprehension. Mr. Barman had asked about the use of the material cards. That was too long a subject to be discussed that evening, but if Mr. Barman arranged his general account books properly, and if he referred to the consolidated work-ticket, Fig. 14, he would see that the materials had been divided into two sections—materials delivered direct from outside to the job, and materials delivered from the shop rough stores—and if he recalled that the paper dealt specially with a scheme applicable to heavy work, where the proportion of labour to materials was about four to one, it would be evident that the great bulk of the materials would be charged direct from outside to the job, that from the stores being comparatively small. Separate methods of treatment were required for each class; but the general principle was that all materials were supplied to an order on a requisition card, Fig 12, and that only one entry should be made on each card so as to permit of a full analysis of the expense when required. If the providing of opportunities for analysis was deemed unnecessary, he could make as many entries on each card as he liked, but at the expense of flexibility. Mr. Mann, who modestly put himself down as an outsider, had shown a noble example to the other members of his profession in coming there and bearding the engineer in his den. The union between the accountant and the engineer, in the matter of shop administration, could not be brought about too soon; at present there was too little attention given by practical engineers to the economies of the workshop. The great importance of the accountant's work was generally underrated, because, as usually applied, it proved too cumbersome to set out in full detail all the acts of engineering workshops, to say nothing of the expense. Hence managers had been forced to favour methods savouring more or less of the rule of thumb in tracing the work through the shops. The use of cards altered all that. He (Mr. Cowan) could say from experience that it was quite possible to make the Cost Accounts and the general accounts agree as to balance, and run parallel with each other; and that it was also an easy matter, when one knew how, to devise a system of financial books which would admit of being balanced in two hours after the sub-Journals had been written up and their totals of the different classes of transactions ascertained, and to keep a Balance Ledger in a state of constant balance. Mr. Smith seemed a little at sea in his remarks, and was apparently full of reverence for existing methods. He referred to a trial of the system in a well-known shop as having been abandoned. It was apparent that he did not understand the facts of the case. The assertion was incorrect, and he (Mr. Cowan) was only prevented from replying to his allegations by considerations of not introducing matters of private business into a public discussion. To one point he might, however, refer. Mr. Smith seemed alarmed at the cost of the proposed system, and at the demoralising of his men by ruining their memories. The cost in one establishment where the system had been in operation three years—the work being light, and the proportion of materials to labour four to one—for keeping the general accounts of the establishment and the Cost Accounts of the work, costing about £30,000 per annum, was that of one bookkeeper, one cost clerk, and one boy, and one man acting as time-keeper and store-keeper, or slightly over 1 per cent. on the cost of the work. Regarding the demoralising of the men by ruining their memories, the prime object of the system was to trust nothing to memory, and to trust entirely to written records. By means of the records which the proposed system could furnish, one of the great needs of modern production was met, since the first requisite of agreement between employer and employee was the mutual understanding of one another's views and of the approaches by which they had been reached. Whether the methods proposed to that end would serve this purpose time only would show. Those features of the plan which were in accord with this object would serve their uses, and eventually give place to others still more highly adapted for their purpose. He sincerely hoped and trusted that this was only the beginning of a discussion upon the economic side of industrial engineering. When he came before the Institution it was not so much to give information, but to get information on certain details which required clearing up, presuming that the members were all fully conversant with the economic details of the working of their shops. The paper merely sketched out, and linked together in a general way, both in the text and the diagram Fig. 1, the various processes that had to be dealt with in an engineering business. He hoped that in some manner the Institution would see its way to express itself as to what was wanted in the way of improved shop management, and recognise its value in the same way as was now done by their friends across the water, who not only discussed it in their institutions, but had established institutes for the regular teaching of scientific shop management.

ADMINISTRATION OF ENGINEERING WORKSHOPS.

FIGURE 9.

WORK TICKET	Prime Costs—Products Consolidated		Permanent Index Reference No.
PROD'N. ORDER No.	C.	O.—Full Symbol & Cat. Ref.	

SYMBOLS	Materials Direct			Materials from Stores			Out-Services			Labour			TOTALS			
Members	£	s	d	£	s	d	£	s	d	£	s	d	Hours	£	s	d
A - - - -																
B - - - -																
C - - - -																
D - - - -																
E - - - -																
F - - - -																
G - - - -																
&c. - - - -																
Totals - - - -																
Credits - - - -																
Nett - - - - -																
Comparative Data: Estimated Cost - -																
Comparative Data: Previous Cost - -																
Comparative Data: Cost per Unit: Each, - -																
Comparative Data: Cost per Unit: Cwt., - -																
Comparative Data: Cost per Unit: Sq. ft., - -																

BLANK & COMPANY, LIMITED, GLASGOW.

FIGURE 10.

WORK TICKET	Prime Costs—Members or Components				Permanent Index Reference No.
S. O. No.	C.	O.—Full Symbol	T.	N.	

Dates	13	14	15	16	17	18	19	20	21	
Month / Day	Drawing	Pattern-making	Smith-ing	Boiler-making	Machin-ing	Fitting	Erecting-ins	Erecting-outs	Painting	Processes
										Materials from Outside
										Materials from Stores
										Out-Services
										Labour
										Hours

BLANK & COMPANY, LIMITED, GLASGOW.

ADMINISTRATION OF ENGINEERING WORKSHOPS.

FIGURE 10A.

WORK TICKET	Prime Costs—Members only		Permanent Index Reference No.
	C.	O.—Full Symbol	

PROCESSES		Materials Direct			Materials from Stores			Out-Services			Labour			TOTALS			
Names	Nos.	£	s	d	£	s	d	£	s	d	£	s	d	Hours	£	s	d
Drawing	13																
Pattern-making ..	14																
Smithing	15																
Boiler-making ..	16																
Machining	17																
Fitting	18																
Erecting-ins.. ..	19																
Erecting-outs ..	20																
Painting	21																
Totals	..																
Credits	..																
Totals transferred to Products Ticket	..																

BLANK & COMPANY, LIMITED, GLASGOW.

FIGURE 11.

WORK TICKET J. O. No.	Prime Costs—Processes or Operations				Permanent Index Reference No.
	C.	O.—Full Symbol	T.	N.	

Week ending		Materials Direct Delivery			Materials from Stores			Out-services			Labour			Credits		
Mo.	Day	£	s	d	£	s	d	£	s	d	£	s	d	£	s	d
Totals Transferred to J. O. Ticket																

BLANK & COMPANY, LIMITED, GLASGOW.

ADMINISTRATION OF ENGINEERING WORKSHOPS.

FIGURE 12.

ELEMENTARY MATERIALS AND OUT-SERVICE RECORD No.... Charge to Job Order No.... Service Index Reference

Object of Expense	C.	O.	T.	N.	Service Index Reference
	W.	*A-10*	*20*	*471*	*27 B*

Shop Specification No. *501*

MAKE ONLY ONE ENTRY ON EACH CARD.

ISSUED BY			RECEIVED BY		
NO. OR NAME	MO.	DAY	NO. OR NAME	MO.	DAY
101	*3*	*6*	*189*	*3*	*7*

QUANTITIES	UNIT	RATE	AMOUNT £	s	d
Assumed Quantity ... *1 Piece*	..	..	.	.	.
Actual Quantity ... *123*	*lbs.*	*2d.*	*1*	*-*	*6*

DESCRIPTION, *Shear Steel—24" × 4" × 1",*
for Shear Blades.

REMARKS, *Sawn obliquely to Template.*

BLANK & COMPANY, LIMITED, GLASGOW.

FIGURE 13.

ELEMENTARY TIME RECORD No.... Charge to Job Order No.... Service Index Reference

Object of Expense	C.	O.	T.	N.	Service Index Reference

MAKE ONLY ONE ENTRY ON EACH CARD.

Issued by______ Date,__/__/__ Shop Sp'n. No.______

NAME	Units	Rate	Amount s	d
Hours,				
Units,				

DESCRIPTION,______

REMARKS,______

BLANK & COMPANY, LIMITED, GLASGOW.

ADMINISTRATION OF ENGINEERING WORKSHOPS.

FIGURE 14.

BLANK & COMPANY. LIMITED.

SHOP SPECIFICATION NO. *960* CONSOLIDATED WORK-TICKET NO. *501* DATE *28th January 1899*

S.O.'s Nos.	SYMBOLS: Member's Letters	SYMBOLS: Components Nos. ending in o	SYMBOLS: Pieces, Digits only	Same as	Quantity	Full Symbol of Object, P S X. Full Names of Members and Pieces. Full dimensions and all additions afterwards made in Shop	Classes of Materials	WEIGHTS—LBS.: Rough	WEIGHTS—LBS.: Finished	PRIME COSTS: Materials: Direct from Outside	PRIME COSTS: Materials: Drawn from Stores	PRIME COSTS: Labour: Units, Hours	PRIME COSTS: Labour: Values	PRIME COSTS: Out-Services	PRIME COSTS: Credits	PRIME COSTS: Totals: Plant (P)	PRIME COSTS: Totals: Work (W)	PRIME COSTS: Totals: Gross
1	2	3	4	5	6	7	8	9	10	11	12	13	14	15	16	17	18	19
..	*A*	..	..	..	..	*Machine Body*												
..	*A*	*10*	..	..	*1*	*Main casing, punch gap 36", shear gap 34"*	*Cast Iron*	*12,000*	*11,780*	*25 7 6*	*17 2 6*	*600*	*25 10 6*	*. 2 6*	*. 7 6*	*12 10 .*	*55 5 6*	*67 15 6*
..	*A*	..	*2*	..	*1*	*Cam shaft cover, 8" bore on engine side*	*do.*	*1,150*	*1,120*	*5 . .*	*. 7 6*	*80*	*2 3 6*	..	..	*2 . .*	*5 11 .*	*7 11 .*
..	..	..	*3*	..	*2*	*Bolts for do., 6" × 1¼" dia.*	*Steel*				*. 10 6*	*8*	*. 5 .*	..	..	..	*. 15 6*	*. 15 6*
..	*A*	*30*	..	..	..	*These assembled*				*20 7 6*	*. 18 6*	*688*	*27 19 .*	*. 2 6*	*. 7 6*	*14 10 .*	*61 12 .*	*76 2 .*
..	*A*	..	*4*	..	*1*	*Cam Shaft cover, 10" bore on angle cutter side*	*Cast Steel*	*1,034*	*996*	*4 10 .*	*. 14 7*	*16*	*1 7 6*	*. 5 .*	*. 2 9*	*. 10 .*	*6 4 4*	*6 14 4*
..	..	..	*5*	..	*2*	*Bolts for do., 4" × 1¼" dia.*	*Steel*			..	*. 7 6*	*4*	*. 2 6*	..	..	..	*. 10 .*	*. 10 .*
..	*A*	*50*	..	..	..	*These assembled*				*4 10 .*	*1 2 1*	*20*	*1 10 .*	*. 5 .*	*. 2 9*	*. 10 .*	*6 14 4*	*7 4 4*
..	*A*	..	*6*	..	*2*	*Fulcrum pins with collar 12" × 5¼" dia., Collar 6¾" dia. × 2¼" wide*	*Steel*	*226*	*190*	..	*. 16 6*	*10*	*. 8 9*	*. . 6*	..	..	*1 5 9*	*1 5 9*
..	..	..	*7*	..	*2*	*Taper pins for do., 9" long × 1" dia., thick end*	*do.*			..	*. 7 6*	*5*	*. 3 6*	..	..	..	*. 11 .*	*. 11 .*
..	*A*	*70*	..	..	..	*These assembled*				..	*1 4 .*	*15*	*. 12 3*	*. . 6*	..	..	*1 16 9*	*1 16 9*
..	*A*	..	*8*	..	*1*	*Punch ram strap ¾" thick × 4" wide*	*Steel*	*90*	*75*	..	*. 10 6*	*4*	*. 2 3*	*. 1 .*	*. 5 .*	..	*. 8 9*	*. 8 9*
..	..	..	*9*	..	*1*	*Gib and cotter for do.*	*do.*			..	*. 5 6*	*3*	*. 1 9*	..	..	..	*. 7 3*	*. 7 3*
..	..	..	*11*	..	*2*	*Bolts for do., 3" long × ¾" dia.*	*do.*			*. 8 .*	..	*5*	*. 2 .*	..	..	..	*. 10 .*	*. 10 .*
..	*A*	*110*	..	..	..	*These assembled*				*. 8 .*	*. 16 0*	*12*	*. 6 .*	*. 1 .*	*. 5 .*	..	*1 6 .*	*1 6 .*
..	*A*	..	*12*	..	*2*	*Cover plates for shear slide*	*Cast Iron*	*160*	*145*	..	*. 7 6*	*6*	*. 2 6*	*. . 6*	..	..	*. 10 6*	*. 10 6*
..	..	..	*13*	..	*8*	*Pins for securing do., 2" long × ⅞" dia.*	*Steel*			*. 9 6*	..	*8*	*. 3 6*	..	..	..	*. 13 .*	*. 13 .*
..	*A*	*130*	..	..	..	*These assembled*				*. 9 6*	*7 6*	*14*	*. 6 .*	*. . 6*	..	..	*1 3 6*	*1 3 6*
111	*A*	**230**	..	..	..	*Machine Body assembled*				**35 15 .**	**21 10 1**	**749**	**30 13 3**	**. 9 6**	**. 15 3**	**15 . .**	**72 12 7**	**87 12 7**
..	*B*	..	..	..	..	*Cam Shaft with spur wheel*												
..	..	*10*	..	..	*1*	*Cam shaft—cam faces chilled*	*Cast Iron*	*336*	*310*	*1 1 .*	..	*14*	*. 7 6*	..	..	..	*1 8 6*	*1 8 6*
..	..	.	*2*	..	*1*	*Spur wheel No. 1407, 42 teeth, 3" pitch, 6" broad, 12" bore, flanged to pitch line*	*Cast Iron*	*784*	*770*	*2 2 .*	*. 3 6*	*30*	*. 15 6*	*. 4 6*	..	..	*3 5 6*	*3 5 6*
..	..	..	*3*	..	*1*	*Key for do., 8" long × 1¼" × ¾"*	*Steel*			..	*. 1 6*	*3*	*. 2 .*	..	..	..	*. 3 6*	*. 3 6*
..	*B*	*30*	..	..	..	*These assembled*				*2 2 .*	*. 5 .*	*33*	*. 17 6*	*. 4 6*	..	..	*3 9 .*	*3 9 .*
116	*B*	**130**	..	..	..	*Cam shaft and spur wheel assembled*				*3 3 .*	*. 5 .*	*47*	*1 12 6*	*. 4 6*	..	..	*4 17 6*	*4 17 6*
						Total Prime Cost—transferred to Register				**38 18 .**	**21 15 1**	**796**	**31 18 6**	**. 14 .**	**. 15 3**	**15 . .**	**77 10 1**	**92 10 1**

Cost Accounts.

A LECTURE delivered before the Incorporated Accountants' Students' Society of London, by

MR. A. E. SHOWELL, A.S.A.A.,

CHIEF ACCOUNTANT TO THE SALT UNION, LIMITED.

Mr. A. R. KING FARLOW, President of the Society, occupied the chair.

The LECTURER said: You will, I am sure, all admit that my subject is a very wide and important one, and one to which we cannot direct too much attention. Perhaps it may be said that it is not a matter that so directly affects the professional accountant as many others; still, it is quite possible that some of the student members may find themselves called upon to advise in the starting of manufacturing concerns, or even obtain appointments as accountants to such, and for that reason it is my wish to deal briefly with the general run of a system leading up to the obtaining of accurate Cost Accounts, rather than with any special system which might be suitable to one business and not to another.

The importance of the subject is very much increased by the re-doubled efforts of foreign countries to capture our trade. If we are to retain our trade, we must not only maintain our reputation for quality by keeping up our standard of excellence, and by taking full advantage of the labour-saving appliances and other such economies, but we must also be prepared to cut things very fine in the matter of selling price; and, in order that we may discover where economies can be effected, and where we can cut down to meet competition, it is essential that great care should be exercised in ascertaining the cost of production.

PRIME FACTORS.

The two prime factors in almost all costs are Labour and Material. I therefore propose to deal with my subject under those two main heads.

LABOUR.

The first point to consider is the drawing up of a system for accurately recording the time made by the workman.

RECORDING TIME.

The one which I believe is most usually adopted is the check, or tally system. The workman on arrival at the works passes a time office, and there receives from the foreman or timekeeper a metal tally with his number, which is taken from a board bearing the corresponding number.

From this board the timekeeper enters up his time sheets, recording by a mark those whose tallies have been applied for.

In case of labour paid by time, and where the workpeople do not take meals on the works, the tallies should be deposited in a box each time on leaving the works, and then re-sorted by the timekeeper in readiness for their being applied for on the return from the meals, and the recording process again repeated.

There are also systems of automatic time-recording machines, such as the Bundy, Day, Llewellyn, &c., which are very effectual, and in some instances are to be preferred to the above-mentioned.

PREPARATION OF WAGES SHEETS.

At the end of the week the timekeeper will total up the time made by each employé, and will fill in the rate of pay against each. This he will ascertain from a book which should be kept, wherein is a record of each employé, showing date of engagement, rate of pay, and each successive variation in rate; after which he will make the calculations and sign the sheets as having prepared same and made the calculations. The various foremen or overlookers should then examine the sheets or book, and sign the same as being correct as regards time and rate for the employés under his control. The sheets or book will then be sent to the counting house to be checked by an independent clerk, and in order that any deductions, such as rent, sick fund, &c., may be made, and a cheque for the net amount drawn; or, as in many cases it is preferable, the cheque is drawn for the gross amount of the wages, and the sums deductible paid over to the cashier, and treated as ordinary receipts.

It might be well, in this connection, to warn you of the provisions of the Truck Acts, regulating the question of making any such deductions from wages, and to remind you of the necessity, in all cases where deductions are permitted by the Acts, of getting an agreement signed by each employé, from whom such deductions are made, authorising the same.

ALLOCATION OF TIME.

Where a workman is employed exclusively upon piece-work, or even is paid day wage, and is solely occupied upon one process or class of article, it is a very simple matter to correctly charge off his time to that process or class of article; but where he is employed in various branches—take, for instance, an engineer, who during one day may have done (*a*) repairs to the machinery pertaining to one process in the morning, and has been occupied (*b*) fitting up shafting for driving some new machinery upon the works in the latter part of the day; or, again, has been engaged until dinner time (*c*) upon repairs to a locomotive which has suddenly broken down, and for the remainder of the day upon work connected with (*d*) the manufacture of some article for stock, then very careful apportionment of the time spent will have to be made, so that the correct amount may be charged against each of the following:—(*a*) Maintenance of plant relating to the particular process; (*b*) the works order relating to the cost of erecting the new plant; (*c*) the locomotive repairs account; and (*d*) the stock order number relating to the particular article.

In cases of this nature, the employé must be provided with time boards or slips, whereon to record, at the completion of each job, or when employed upon one job the whole day, then at the end of the day, the nature of the work, or where there is one, a works or stock order number (to both of which I will refer later), and the time occupied. This should be initialled by his own foreman, or by the foreman of the department where the work has been done.

In the case of overtime, where higher rates of pay obtain, special record will have to be made of time thus spent upon the particular job. This is important, not merely from the point of view of the preparation of the wages sheets, but in order that a record may be made of the extra expenditure incurred, so that the principal may be able to judge as to the real necessity of such addition to the cost.

ANALYSIS OF WAGES.

These time boards or slips will be collected each day and entered up by the clerk whose duty it is to prepare the analysis, either on rough sheets, or, for preference, in a waste book ruled across with money columns, using a page, or portion of a page, for each separate process, branch of manufacture, works order or stock number to which the items are chargeable, the cross columns being used for the different classes of workmen employed upon it, as shewn in Form A appended hereto.

WAGES ANALYSIS SUMMARY.

The time clerk will at the end of the week, *i.e.*, the end of the period for which wages are made up, after casting the analysis, enter the same either on loose sheets, which can be press copied in order that he may retain a record, if he has to send same from outlying works, or in a ruled book if the works are concentrated. The gross total of these sheets will, of course, agree with the amount of the weekly wages paid.

Where the nature of the business requires the cost books to be entered up weekly, the summary of analysis sheets can be used for the purpose of posting direct to the prime cost ledgers, being either pasted into guard books or filed in some convenient manner; but when monthly, quarterly, or half-yearly statements of cost are sufficient, much labour may be saved by entering the sheets up week by week in a wages journal, with printed heading down the side for all constant accounts, such as maintenance of plant, repairs and renewals to buildings, locos, waggons, &c., and with the necessary space for expenditure upon works order numbers, stock numbers, and then five, thirteen, or twenty-six money columns for the weekly amounts, a total column, ledger folio and remarks, similar to specimen. (*See* Form B appended.)

I now turn to the other principal factor in Cost Accounts, viz.:—

STORES.

It is of equal importance that there should be a system for the accurate recording of all transactions, whether requisitions, orders, prices, consumption or stocking of stores.

Assuming that there are several sections or branches connected with the works, each of which has its separate stores department, it will be the duty of the chief of each section or department to make out periodically, say weekly, a requisition to the head office for his estimated requirements, sufficiently far ahead to enable their being purchased, in case no stock is on hand at the chief stores. The forms are most convenient, I find, bound in books, paged and perforated, with manifold copying sheets interleaved.

The forms should show in columns, in addition to full description of the article or material, the quantity required, the purpose it is required for, when required by; and also for the guidance of buyers, the date of last supply, and by whom supplied, and a column for remarks.

In some firms the requisitions themselves are put before the principals, but to my mind it is more convenient to have them entered up in a requisition book, and especially if several of the departments and branches are using similar materials; by so doing the various classes of materials can be grouped in entering up the requisition book, and the principal or buyer can see at a glance the total quantity of each commodity required throughout the whole works.

The requisition book, therefore, should have additional columns, showing firm goods are to be obtained from, number of order, quantity ordered, rate, date received, and reference to invoice.

STORES ORDERS.

The goods having been ordered, manifold order books being used, the number of the order and other details will be entered up in the requisition book.

STORES INVOICES.

In cases where the Cost Accounts for each works, branch, or department are kept separately by them, it will be advisable, and in fact necessary, to obtain separate invoices for the quantity of goods sent to each, as much inconvenience and delay would be occasioned by sending an invoice from one department to another for them to mark off their portion.

If the Cost Accounts, however, are all kept at the head office, one invoice is quite sufficient; but it will be necessary for the branch storekeeper, on receipt of goods, to send in an advice form to the head office, giving quantities, and with any remarks as to quality and condition. When the invoice clerk at the head office has marked same off, he will fill in the blank columns on the advice form, the invoice number, firm supplying, rate and value, and return the advice for the departmental storekeeper to complete the necessary entry in his stores received book.

STORES INVOICE BOOK (*kept at head office*).

When the inward invoice clerk first receives the invoice from the vendors, he will number it, and enter the name and amount of same, after deducting trade, but not cash discounts, in a column for "amount of invoice as received" in the stores invoice book. After the advices have come to hand from the various departments that have received the goods, and the various quantities traced and agreed, and the rates and extensions checked, he will enter the amount for which the invoice is passed in a column for that purpose This may or may not agree with the "amount as received" column, according to whether there has been any correction made in the invoice.

This amount will be posted to the credit of the individual firms, and to the debit of a general stores account in the commercial ledger. It may be a convenience to have the right hand side of the opening ruled with analysis columns, so that the amounts relating to each works or department may be entered in separate columns as a check on the departmental stores account, and to facilitate the localisation of errors in the works books.

STORES RECEIVED BOOK (*kept at department*).

This book should be ruled with columns for recording the date, number of invoice, firms supplying, description and quantity of goods, rate, amount, and also stores ledger folio. The amounts will be posted from this book to the debit of the account in the stores ledger for the particular material.

STORES LEDGER (*kept at department*).

This ledger is much the same as the commercial ledger, save that the accounts are with the different classes of materials instead of individuals. Both sides of the account should be ruled for description of goods, rate and amount, whilst the debit or "received" side will in addition have space for name of firm supplying goods.

If the material is received by transfer from another department, or from the chief stores, or if it is material which has been previously issued and returned for any reason, or if it is material recovered from plant, then instead of name of firm supplying, the transfer or returns advice number (which I will deal with later) should be entered.

ISSUE OF STORES.

I will now deal with the issue of stores by the storekeeper. No goods should be allowed to be issued except on a written order from the foreman or manager of the department or branch requiring the same. These orders should be numbered consecutively, and a duplicate retained by the foreman ordering the stores. When the stores are issued, the storekeeper must obtain the foreman's signature to the order form as having received the goods. The order should state distinctly for what purpose the stores are required, *i.e.*, for some process of manufacture, maintenance of plant. buildings, works order number, or stock order number, as the case may be. Cases may arise where stores issued for one purpose, are eventually used for some special reason for another purpose altogether. In such instances the foreman must immediately advise the storekeeper, who will enter such to the credit of the account which was originally debited, and debit the account for the job to which the material was actually applied. Every effort should be made to reduce such cases to a minimum, or errors will creep in.

STORES ISSUED BOOK (*kept at department*).

The storekeeper will record in his stores issued book the full details of the material issued, and from this book he will post the quantity and value to the credit of the account in his stores ledger for the particular material so issued.

STORES ISSUED ANALYSIS.

He will then prepare a periodical analysis, according to the requirements of the business, and to coincide with the period for which the wages analysis is prepared, and send the same to the head office for filing and posting to the prime cost ledgers; or the foreman's orders themselves, with the acknowledgment of receipt of goods duly signed, after having been dealt with and initialled by the storekeeper, may be sent to the head office, and used as the source from which the debits to prime cost arise. In the former case, where the analysis of the stores issued is prepared by the storekeeper, the door is perhaps rather left open to the storekeeper to so adjust his summary of analysis as to cover any irregularities that may have been going on, and it would be desirable, in fact necessary, to periodically test the accuracy of his analysis.

WORKS ORDERS (*issued from head office*).

It is most advisable that a fixed rule be made that no general expenditure, such as maintenance or repairs, alteration or addition to plant, exceeding a certain sum (say £25 or £50) should be put in hand by the foreman or departmental manager, without the preparation of an estimate which should be submitted to the principal, and when approved by him a works order, bearing a distinctive number, should be issued for the work to be done. As I mentioned just now, in dealing with wages, and again with stores, all expenditure on account of that job should be booked by the storekeeper or wages clerk to that particular number.

STOCK ORDERS (*issued from head office*).

In works where articles such as boilers, cranes, waggons, or such like are manufactured, or with smaller articles where a certain number are being made for stock, a stock order should be issued by the principal or manager to the department or departments, to make the same, and for the purpose of ascertaining the actual cost of the particular article, part, or group of articles, all wages expended, or stores issued for the same should be booked to the stock order number.

PROCESSES.

In the case of works, where processes are continuously carried on, such as chemicals, glass, salt, iron, and such like, the wages and stores will be charged off to the particular process, quality, section of work, or other sub-division which the nature of the business requires.

STORES TRANSFERS, ETC. (*used between departments*).

It may be well to mention here that stores issued by the chief stores department to departmental stores should be merely treated as transfers. The storekeeper issuing such should enter the quantities and values in his stores issued book (or if the transactions are frequent in the case of departments, a separate book for transfers may be kept), and post to the credit side of his stores ledger. He should also send to the department receiving the goods a stores transfer, with full details of quantities and values. After verifying same the receiver should enter in his stores received book, or transfer book, in the same way as if the goods had been received from outside merchants, but quoting stores transfer number in place of the name of the merchant, and then return the transfer signed and dated to the issuing department. These transactions being merely departmental, need not be recorded at the head office, unless, as before stated, all the clerical work is done there.

RETURNED STORES.

There will also arise cases, even in the most carefully prepared estimates, when an excess of material is applied for, and a rule should be made that the surplus must in all cases be returned to the storekeeper. There will also be in many trades scrap material and unsuitable or spoiled articles or material, which must be returned to the stores; or, in the case of scrap, come under the control of the storekeeper, although not actually deposited in stores. A form, similar to the stores transfer, should be sent by the foreman returning such to the storekeeper, giving particulars of the job for which the material was originally issued.

SCRAP.

With regard to scrap, the question of pricing presents, at times, a difficulty. But the system I find most effective is to fix a standard for all the usual classes of material, which can be revised periodically by the head office, as the market for such fluctuates. In such cases the storekeeper must enter the quantities and values in his stores received book in the same manner as in the case of transfers, and after having made such entries send the form to the head office, so that it may be correctly dealt with by the costs clerk; or the advices themselves may be sent to the head office direct and treated as quite distinct from ordinary stores.

FUEL AND RAW MATERIAL.

There are, of course, cases where wages and stores are not the largest factors in cost of production. Take, for instance, the works with which I am connected, where fuel is the largest, and consequently one of the most important items, in the cost of production.

In such cases it is necessary to have a complete system whereby the coal, or other raw material, received in bulk, and which cannot, therefore, be passed through stores, is charged off to the particular set of works where it is to be used.

FUEL OR RAW MATERIAL RETURNS.

Returns must be sent in to the head office, giving the name of sender, name of vessel, or number of truck, gross tare and nett weight, remarks as to quality, &c. If any portion is used for other purposes than the actual process of manufacture—say, for instance, coal for locomotives, steamers, offices, cottages, or other distinctive purpose—a periodical return must be made to the head office, so that the same may be dealt with in the proper manner.

FUEL (OR RAW MATERIAL) REGISTERS.

'(*Kept at both department and head office.*)

A register of fuel (or other raw material, whatever it may be) will have to be kept, with columns for date advised, date received, number of advice, name of colliery or merchant, number of waggon or name of boat, weight advised, weight received. The book for the head office will, in addition, require columns for pit price, railway rate, delivered price, and then also analysis columns for weight and value, with headings for the various branches, departments, or processes.

FUEL (OR RAW MATERIAL) INVOICE BOOK.

The fuel invoices will be entered in a book, similar to the stores invoice book already described, with analysis columns.

The total of the fuel invoice book will be posted periodically to the debit of the fuel account for each works, or to a general fuel account, which account will be relieved by the analysis of the fuel received book, the amounts, and if necessary, quantities, being charged off to the various processes in the prime cost ledger, or to the expenses accounts, such as locomotive running, craft working, offices, &c., in the impersonal ledger.

PRIME COST.

Having dealt with the main items which go to make up prime cost in most factories, up to the time of the receipt of advices by the head office, where I am assuming the Cost Accounts are being kept, and with the necessary books for recording these advices, I will endeavour to explain in a general way the method of dealing with the same in the prime cost books.

First of all, let me submit to you suggested rulings for prime cost ledgers. The rulings suitable for one trade are, of course, not necessarily applicable to another; but, speaking generally, one or other of these forms will be a guide, with certain modifications in most cases. (*See* Forms C (1) and C (2) appended.)

(1) For works where an article or number of articles or parts are made to a stock order number.

(2) In works where processes are being carried out and material being manufactured.

Firstly. The wages, after having been dealt with as already described, will be posted, either weekly direct from the analysis sheet sent in by the various departments, or periodically from the wages journal, to the debit of the accounts to which its items relate, and under the various sub-headings showing the different classes of workmen, if deemed necessary, in the prime cost ledger. The total will, of course, be posted to the credit of wages account in the impersonal ledger, and *per contra* the wages cheques which will have been posted to the debit of that account. In the case of general items, such as maintenance of plant, repairs to buildings, &c. (except when chargeable against a process or the manufacture of some regular and exclusive output) will not be posted to the prime cost ledger in the first instance, but to separate accounts in the impersonal books (which can be ruled to record, if necessary, on the self-analysing principle) afterwards to be dealt with by apportionment over the various stock orders, &c.

Secondly.—As in the case of wages, the debits for stores used can be posted to the prime cost ledger, either weekly direct from the stores used analysis sheets (or the stores orders themselves), or these analysis sheets may be summarised in a stores journal similar to the wages journal and posted periodically (monthly, quarterly, or half-yearly) as the circumstances of the trade would indicate to the debit of the respective accounts in the prime cost ledger, and the total to the credit of the general stores account.

The transfer forms relating to returned stores or scrap will have to be journalised, and the items posted to the credit of the various accounts to which they relate, in the prime cost ledger. The debits will be posted to the general stores account; or, if a separate scrap account is kept, then scrap will be posted to the debit of such, in the impersonal ledger.

The expenditure upon works orders (*i.e.*, special expenditure upon works, for which an estimate has been prepared and passed by the principal), should be very closely watched and totalled up week by week, and when the amount is approximating the total authorised by the works order, the principal should be informed by the costs clerk.

Thirdly.—Fuel or other raw material, received in bulk, and not passed through stores, is treated as separate and distinct from ordinary stores, and will be posted to the prime cost accounts periodically, in the same way, from the fuel (or raw material) received book or from the invoice books themselves, if kept on the self-analysing principle. In such cases it is advisable to post the quantities as well as values, so that the consumption of coal (or other raw material) per ton of the manufactured material produced, may be ascertained. This is, of course, a most important point.

Fourthly.—Maintenance and other expenses not directly or exclusively connected with and chargeable to the cost of particular articles, will have to be apportioned over the various stock orders, &c.

In the case of processes, the actual cost of the maintenance of plant, repairs to buildings, and such like, can usually be ascertained, as a distinct set of buildings, or part of building, and separate and special plant are usually employed. But in cases where several classes of trade are carried on under one roof, and the same plant is being used for various stock orders, &c., the apportionment of the cost of upkeep and running must be approximated.

It is impossible to lay down any rule as to the best method of apportioning indirect charges, it being a very much debated point, and one which in itself would require more than the limits of this paper to give anything like adequate consideration. As a rule, however, one or other of the following bases are usually employed:—

- Sales value of articles produced.
- Sales quantity of articles produced.
- Wages expended on articles produced.
- Wages and stores expended on articles produced.
- Time employed on articles produced.
- Estimated life and value of machinery employed in producing.

Similar bases may be adopted in apportioning the wages of foremen, timekeepers, &c.

"Stock Orders" Prime Cost Ledger.

In the case of my specimen ruling for prime cost ledger (C 1) that relating to stock orders and articles for stock, as distinct from processes or bulk goods—the finished articles will be credited to the account when transferred from works and taken into stock at warehouse, as distinct from stores.

Stock and stores must be kept quite distinct, and must not be confused. When completed articles are sent into warehouse, whether they have been manufactured for a special order or for general stock, a warehouse transfer form should be made out by the departmental foreman, giving the full particulars as to weight, &c. The rate and value will then be filled in by the prime cost clerk, and the transfer sent to the warehouseman, who will allot a warehouse number (as distinct from stock order number), and will be entered in the stock books.

The costs clerk will enter the goods and value to the credit of the account for the particular stock order number, or the account for the particular class of article in the prime cost ledger, recording also the warehouse number allotted.

Processes Prime Cost Ledger.

In the other case, specimen ruling (C 2) it is practically only a debit ledger, the space at foot for credits being merely for adjustment of overcharges in wages, returned materials, and so forth.

The real credits for sales are, in this case, better abstracted from the sales journals, which should be ruled on the self-analysing principle, giving quantities, as well as values, of each material. In abstracting the sales, it must, of course, be borne in mind that the stocks at the commencement of the period will require to be deducted, and the stock at the end of the period added, in order to ascertain the make to which the figures in the prime cost ledger apply.

Cost Sheets.

These can be compiled at intervals, as the exigencies of the particular trade demand, columns being ruled for the average cost per ton of each part of the process, which can be subdivided to any extent, according to the detail posted to the prime cost ledger from the subsidiary books. Columns may, if thought advisable, be also provided, for the standing and general charges, rents, rates, management expenses, travellers, bad debts (estimate), advertising and carriage, if included in selling prices. These items will be taken from the various accounts in the impersonal ledger; but as they are mostly of the nature that are unaffected to any appreciable extent by the volume of business done in any particular period, there is no real reason for considering them in comparative costs.

There is just one other matter which I would call attention to, and that is the system in vogue at some factories, what I might call the

Estimate Cost System.

It is adaptable to works where there is a regular steady output of certain articles, packets, boxes, &c. The principal prepares a very carefully detailed estimate, which he enters in an estimate book.

Assume the estimate is for 100,000,000 cigarettes in packets of ten. He heads his estimate book with this quantity. The book has columns for tobacco, paper, packets, boxes, each with weight or number, rate and value; also columns for the various classes of wages and expenses, and total prime cost. He calculates exactly the weight of tobacco which will be required for making this quantity, and prices the same at the rate then ruling, or makes allowance for a probable rise or fall in market during the period of manufacture. The same applies to the other material.

If the wages for the various processes of tube making, cutting, machining, boxing, &c., are paid piece work, the calculations for them will be simple; but, if day wage, he will have to make a careful estimate of the probable output of the person or persons engaged in each process, per hour or per diem.

These estimates are totalled on a cost sheet, as the quantity under each estimate is produced.

The sales are also abstracted from the sales journal, periodically, giving quantities and amount. A column is provided for estimated average discount, and the average net amount realised.

To the costs, as per the estimate, is added the miscellaneous expenses, estimated on the same lines as I referred to just now in dealing with the processes costs sheets. The total cost (estimated) is then ascertained, and the nett profit or loss shown.

These cost sheets are periodically summarised in the form of a trading account, and a comparison of these will often lead to the detection of error, either in estimates or in the account.

In preparing the trading account for comparison, care must be taken as to adjustment of stocks.

In conclusion, gentlemen, let me thank you for the very patient manner in which you have listened to what is, I am afraid, a very imperfectly prepared paper; but if it only has the effect of drawing your attention more seriously to the enormous importance, not only to us accountants and to manufacturers, but to the country generally, of keeping Cost Accounts, it will not have been time wasted.

Discussion.

The Chairman, in calling for a discussion, said: It would be interesting to know Mr. Showell's views as to how far it is the practice in the north for accountants to be employed in institutions checking cost accounts, or whether it is not, in fact, the practice for large concerns to have a separate department and staff under the control of the principals only for these purposes.

The Lecturer: Speaking generally, it is not a matter which the auditors would have to deal with except in certain cases. For instance, in very large concerns, where there is a continuous audit, and where the cost accounts are of supreme importance, the auditors ought to, and often do, check them. Take the case of a chemical works; it would probably be necessary there for the auditor to check the absolute accuracy of the records of the cost department, because they play such an important part in the administration of the business.

Mr. J. M. Fells: I came here to-night rather to listen than to speak, and I was particularly desirous of hearing Mr. Showell's paper, as it was my pleasure to be associated with him in business for a number of years. In point of fact he succeeded to a position which I had held for some time, and consequently I feel a certain amount of paternal pride in hearing him deliver a paper on what I think is the most important practical subject within the realm of accountancy. I was interested in the chairman's enquiry as to whether accountants in the north or elsewhere were called in to consider, discuss, analyse, check or verify the cost accounts of a manufacturer. I do not think they are called in usually for that particular purpose, but the point which is so forcibly borne upon one's mind is the fact that unless the auditor of a manufacturing concern verifies the conclusions shown on the balance-sheet by some independent check, or some independent audit, there can be no certainty whatever that the balance-sheet is not inaccurate. Look at the case of Edison & Swan, Limited, which occurred recently. There £56,000 had been carried forward in the balance-sheet as representing the value of certain work supposed to be in progress, which had in reality been finished for a number of years. I am, of course, quite aware that the auditors who audited those accounts were able to bring forward some very cogent pleas as to the non-discovery of that particular item, but I contend that had the ordinary books of account not merely been supplemented by, but absolutely considered in conjunction with, the manufacturing books of the concern, such a mistake could not possibly have happened. But it is not merely from the point of view of the accuracy of the balance-sheet that one urges so strongly that accurate cost accounts should be kept, but it is also because we find that our keenest and most active rivals in the competition for trade are practically *au fait* with the methods of arriving at costs, and are thus able to obtain orders which English manufacturers for want of that knowledge would pass by. Take the question of the manufacture of matches. We all know, and most of us I think regret, that the firm of Bryant & May has become absorbed in the Diamond Match Company of New York, but if one had read the comments which appeared in connection with this subject of the manufacture of matches in the *Engineer*, and dealing specially with the costs, one would have seen that the American mode of keeping account of costs of manufacture had led to enormous economy being effected in the cost; that is to say, by knowing absolutely and certainly where the heavy expenditure in the manufacture of a particular match was incurred, they were able to apply their ingenuity to the manufacture of machinery which would enable them to considerably reduce the cost. Instances of that kind might be multiplied to a large extent, but I will not delay you now by their repetition. I would only like to say that it is true that many accountants consider these matters as somewhat outside the scope of their work. Well, I myself take a very high view of the function of an accountant. My view is that he has to practically apply economic theory, or rather, perhaps I should put it, that he has to demonstrate economic theory in its practical application. Probably you have seen the very interesting paper of Mr. Victor Branford on "The Correlation of Economics and Accountancy," and I think the more it is brought home to the minds of accountants that their work stands in nearer relation to economics than to mathematics, the sooner we shall find accountants giving their great ability and analytical power to the examination of all those items which make up cost accounts. I agree with Mr. Showell that it is impossible to lay down any general rule that will apply to all classes of business, and it will hardly do for me to say anything too complimentary to Mr. Showell's paper for reasons I have already hinted at. I take it that Mr. Showell has given us the outline of a system which he has proved in actual practice to be successful, and it is, moreover, a system which I had an opportunity of working out in actual practice as well. But there is one thing I noticed, and that was where he dealt with processes, and the specimen rulings he gave us for a prime cost ledger. Now, I cannot see why that record should not for all practical purposes be made much more useful. If the tonnages produced within the given period were worked out in the book itself, so that you might have a continuous record of the cost of manufacture per ton, or the unit whatever it might be, then I think it would be a book of very great service to the manufacturer, for after all one must recollect that the business is not made for the accounts, but that the accounts should be so framed as to meet the requirements of the business. Anything, therefore, that tends to help the business along by giving the manufacturer, or the owner of the business, a greater control over the expenditure, enabling him to detect differences, and enabling him to consider the cost of the various parts of the processes, must be of great assistance and utility to the manufacturer, and must help him to practically carry on his business more successfully than he otherwise could. Railway companies are proverbial sinners in respect to their accounts. Sir Joseph Pease was speaking some two or three months ago at a meeting of the North-Eastern Railway Company, and in the course of his remarks said that he had spoken to the accountant, to the goods manager, to the general manager, and to everybody else immediately concerned, and they were all agreed on one thing, viz., that they could no more "spot" where the increase had arisen in the passenger traffic than they could "spot" the decrease in the goods traffic. This is not at all a desirable state of things. It is very different from the manner in which the American railway companies' accounts are kept. Everybody knows that Mr. Pierpont Morgan, when he first took the railway companies of the United States in hand, gathered together and studied very exhaustively all the statistics he could get at, and as a result he pointed out that by the increase in rates or decrease in cost of one-tenth of a penny per ton per mile the companies would receive some £60,000 or £70,000 a year more. And if one looks at the elaborate accounts of these companies one can see what a great advantage these administrators have over administrators in this country. It may be asked, why should we endeavour to give people information for which they are not eager? Well, I take it that the province of an accountant is to make a man see all the various advantages that arise from a complete system of accounts, and if the accountants would only insist upon their clients being more accurate with regard to what it has hitherto been the fashion to call subsidiary matters, but which are really matters of vital importance, it would undoubtedly open up a new era for accountants, and would also be of great service to manufacturers and traders.

Mr. W. SOUTHWOOD SMITH, F.S.A.A.: In the specimen wages journal I take it that there might be any number of works order numbers set out, and that, if necessary, you would go on page after page in the journal.

The LECTURER: Yes.

Mr. W. STRACHAN, F.S.A.A.: I should like to ask Mr. Showell's opinion with regard to a system of Cost Accounts which I have seen recommended in a lecture delivered in Manchester by one of the members of the Society there. The system was rather different from that advocated by our lecturer, and probably that was on account of its being applied to a different class of business. The business was the one so frequently given as an example in text books, viz., that of a shipbuilder, and instead of using a cost ledger, cost sheets were employed. It seems to me that these cost sheets could be used in a very elastic way; they could be modified in any given case to give a large amount of detail or a small amount, and at the same time they showed the cost price of the individual parts very clearly. If I remember rightly, they were kept somewhat in this form: There were three or more distinct classes of sheets called, say, A, B, C, &c. In the A sheets were incorporated the costs of minor parts, which, when completed, were transferred to the B sheets, anything uncompleted being carried forward to the next month. When the larger operations covered by the B sheets were completed, they were in their turn transferred to the C sheets, and thus the final sheet was made to cover the cost of the whole ship. In that way it was possible by collecting the sheets together which related to any one contract, to get the whole of the details relating to that contract attached together and filed away under an index. Moreover, it showed clearly the cost of every individual part, which was a great advantage, and further it facilitated the delegation of labour, because, there being no book, any number of clerks could work on the sheets. Another matter Mr. Showell referred to, struck me as being of considerable importance. That was the question of excess materials in the hands of workmen after the completion of the particular matter in hand. Mr. Showell said that any such excess should be returned to stock. In one case that came under my notice, that of an electrical engineer, it was the custom for the men to keep on their benches a certain amount of materials for making items such as screws, bolts, nuts, &c., so that when not engaged in other work they might be making goods for stock. Taken altogether they had in this way rather a large amount of stores on their benches, and that seemed to be a difficulty in the way of arriving at a proper costing system. I listened with much pleasure to Mr. Fell's remarks as to the necessity of keeping full and accurate Cost Accounts. He remarked upon the great advance which has been made in America in this direction as compared with this country, and everyone will, I think, agree with what he said. But it is not only with regard to Cost Accounts that the Americans are giving us a lead, but in accountancy matters generally. For instance, they have started in New York, in connection with the University there, a College of Commerce, Finance and Accounts, with professional accountants as lecturers, and the latest report I have seen is to the effect that a scholarship has been founded in connection with that college or school. We, unfortunately, have nothing of that sort in this country to encourage accountancy. I am aware, of course, of the Chair of Commerce in connection with the recently formed Birmingham University, but I hardly think that in its present form it will cover accountancy in the sense that we accountants regard it. I should like to see something more definite done here in that respect, and, I think, it would be well if those who should lead the way in accountancy matters would devote their serious attention to it. What we have to do more particularly in relation to costing is to educate manufacturers to see that it is even more to their interests, than to the interests of accountants, to keep proper Cost Accounts. They usually have their own methods of costing—mental or otherwise—which are very imperfect; in fact, I should think that in the majority of cases where rough and ready calculations are applied, establishment expenses are left out of account altogether, and as these are often heavy, the results arrived at must necessarily be very inaccurate and misleading.

Mr. H. Morgan: From Mr. Showell's paper I gathered that he made the cost ledger a book of account. Would it not be better to make it subsidiary to the other books by opening an account in the general ledger, called "Cost Ledger Account," and one in the cost ledger, called "General Ledger Account," on the self-balancing principle?

The Lecturer: I think it is very advisable to have each set of books self-balancing, and to have a channel account, as it were, in the way you suggest. With regard to Mr. Strachan's remarks as to the sheet system, I cannot say that I am quite conversant with it. I have rather an aversion to sheets because they are so easily lost, but I can see that such a system has its advantages, and for filing purposes, in order to be able to ascertain the details of each particular part of the ship, it might be a very good system, but the great danger I should fear would be that the sheets might be mislaid. As regards materials in the hands of workmen after the completion of the work, I certainly think that where the method mentioned by Mr. Strachan is adopted, it would seriously interfere with the keeping of proper cost accounts, and would be liable to render the results inaccurate. It is far better, I think, that such materials should be returned to stock and re-issued.

In seconding the vote of thanks to the lecturer, Mr. T. Tinner, Student S.A.A., said that he was very much impressed with what Mr. Fells had said as to the development of accountancy in the future, and he thought it should be considered by the two great examining bodies in England whether economics and kindred subjects should not be introduced into the final examination, as was done in Scotland.

Votes of thanks to the Lecturer and Chairman brought the proceedings to a close.

A.—SPECIMEN OF WAGES ANALYSIS BOOK.

(*a*) Maintenance of Plant— Department.

Bricklayers	Joiners	Mechanics	Glaziers	Plumbers	Masons	Painters	Smiths	Rivetters	Total.
£ s. d.	£ s. d.	£ s. d.	£ s. d.	£ s. d.	£ s. d.	£ s. d.	£ s. d.	£ s. d.	£ s. d.

(*b*) New Grinding Mill—W/o. 35.

£ s. d.	£ s. d.	£ s. d.	£ s. d.	£ s. d.	£ s. d.	£ s. d.	£ s. d.	£ s. d.	£ s. d.

(*c*) Works Loco. Repairs (General A/c.).

£ s. d.	£ s. d.	£ s. d.	£ s. d.	£ s. d.	£ s. d.	£ s. d.	£ s. d.	£ s. d.	£ s. d.

(*d*) Stock Order No. 58.

£ s. d.	£ s. d.	£ s. d.	£ s. d.	£ s. d.	£ s. d.	£ s. d.	£ s. d.	£ s. d.	£ s. d.

B.—SPECIMEN WAGES JOURNAL.

	Week Ending.											Total.	Ledger Folio.
	£ s. d.	£ s. d.	£ s. d.	£ s. d.	£ s. d.	£ s. d.	£ s. d.	£ s. d.	£ s. d.	£ s. d.	£ s. d.	£ s. d.	
PROCESS No.													
Foreman													
Fireman													
Mixers													
Loaders													
PROCESS No.													
Foreman													
Fireman													
Mixers													
Loaders													
MAINTENANCE OF PLANT:													
Bricklayers ..													
Fitters													
Joiners													
REPAIRS TO BUILDINGS:													
Bricklayers ..													
Fitters													
Joiners													
Painters													
LOCO. REPAIRS													
WAGGON REPAIRS ..													
WORK'S ORDER No.													
WORK'S ORDER No.													
STOCK ORDER No.													
Foreman													
Fitters													
Joiners													
Smith													
STOCK ORDER No.													

C.—(1.) SPECIMEN RULING FOR PRIME COST LEDGER.

STOCK ORDER No..............

Dr.

Date.	Details of Material, &c.	Jnl.	Fo.	Quantity.				Rate.	Material.	Wages.			
				No.	Cwts.	Qrs.	lbs.			Fore-man.	Fitters.	Joiners.	Smiths.
									£ s. d.	£ s. d.	£ s. d.	£ s. d.	£ s. d.

Dr.—*Continued.* ....DESCRIPTION OF ARTICLE. **Cr.**

Other Disbursements.		Total.	Date.	Details of Articles or Parts.	Stock Transfer No.	Quantity.				Rate.	Amount.
Details.	Amount.					No.	Tons.	Cwts.	Qrs.		
	£ s. d.	£ s. d.									£ s d.

C.—(2.) SPECIMEN RULING FOR PRIME COST LEDGER.

Dr. ....Process. ....Works.

Date.	Jnl.	Fo.	Wages.				Fuel.				Raw Material.			
			Foremen	Firemen.	Mixers.	Loaders.	Quantity.			Amount.	Quantity.			Value.
			£ s. d.	£ s. d.	£ s. d.	£ s. d.	Tons.	Cwts.	Qrs.	£ s. d.	Tons.	Cwts.	Qrs.	£ s. d.
Total Dr. ..		..												
Cr.														
Total Cr. ..		..												
Net Total		..												

Dr.—*Continued.* Month of.... ...., 190......

Maintenance of Plant.			Repairs to Buildings.			Lighting.	Water.	Other Disbursements.		Total.
Wages.	Materials.	Use of Tools.	Wages.	Materials.	Use of Tools.			Details.	Amount.	
£ s. d.	£ s. d.	£ s. d.	£ s. d.	£ s. d.	£ s. d.	£ s. d.	£ s. d.		£ s. d.	£ s. d.
Cr.—*Continued.*										

Glasgow Chartered Accountants Students' Society.

Oncost and its Apportionment.

By Mr. John Urie, C.A.

A meeting of the Glasgow Chartered Accountants' Students' Society was held on 12th December, in the Accountants' Hall, 218 St. Vincent Street, Glasgow, when there was a fair attendance of members.

A paper was read by Mr. John Urie, C.A., on "Oncost and its Apportionment." He said:—You are all familiar with the ordinary form of a Trading and Profit and Loss Account, which shows in more or less detail the sales or production of a business during a stated period, the gross profit made on same, salaries and other expenses deducted, and the resultant net profit or loss. When this account is presented in comparative form it is possible to compare the expenses of one year with another, and trace the items which have resulted in the fluctuations of profits in the years compared. For many businesses a Trading and Profit and Loss Account drawn up in this form is sufficient for all practical purposes; but there are other businesses, particularly engineering and kindred trades, where, in addition to this, it is necessary to ascertain profits or losses made upon the various contracts completed during the year. For this purpose what are known as Cost Accounts are kept. The data for these accounts is very carefully collected and recorded, and the value of these records to the manager of an engineering concern is incalculable. They enable him to get at the true costs of any product, and should provide him with the means of checking waste, either in time or materials. They also serve as a basis for the preparation of estimates for future work, and are a standard by which the cost of similar work can be tested. As so much depends upon these records it is essential that they should be accurate in every detail, otherwise they are of little service.

The three elements in the cost of a job are (1) Direct Wages; (2) Materials and Direct Charges; and (3) Indirect Charges, generally called "Oncost." In this paper I purpose to confine myself to the last of these items—viz., Oncost—what it should include, and how it should be apportioned over contracts, as I consider that this portion of the subject appeals most to accountants, and is that in which our knowledge of the commercial books is likely to be of most service. I propose to deal principally with the Cost Accounts of engineering or kindred trades, as it is in these trades that the greatest attention has been given to the subject, and Cost Accounts have there come to be regarded as an essential part of a proper system of account-keeping. One of the first maxims of a system of Cost Accounts is that all expenses should be, whenever possible, debited direct against a job. In the case of direct Wages and Materials, this can be readily done; but the charges for Rent, Management, Advertising, Office Expenses, and the like cannot be charged direct against any particular job, and must be spread over them all in such a way that each shall bear its proper proportion.

This oncost is generally added as a percentage, sometimes upon the wages alone, sometimes upon the wages and materials, and occasionally upon the materials only. The percentage varies according to the class of business and the basis upon which it is calculated, being sometimes as low as 30 per cent. when calculated upon the combined cost of wages and materials, and as high as 100 per cent. when calculated upon the wages alone. It will, therefore, be readily understood that the oncost in wages forms no inconsiderable part of the total cost, and as much care should be taken to see that it is adequately provided for and properly apportioned as is taken to insure a correct record of the direct wages and materials. The ideal system is that in which the direct wages and materials are properly debited against all jobs, and each receives just its proper proportion of oncost—no job getting too little or too much. In actual practice, however, we find very scant attention often paid to this factor of oncost, and after an elaborate and expensive analysis of the wages and materials, the oncost is apportioned without any proper data and on no defined plan. The accountant is frequently asked by the head of an engineering concern to advise him whether the rate of oncost which he is adding to his jobs is correct. One naturally asks what the rate is, how it has been arrived at, and whether it has been checked in actual practice and found correct. More than likely the reply is—"Oh, I add 50 per cent. to my wages; "I don't know whether this is correct or not, but Mr. "So-and-So adds it and he says that it is about right." This practically means that while he may be satisfied that he obtains a correct record of the wages and materials upon each job, he is entirely in the dark as regards the important item of oncost, and, in the absence of precise information, he has assumed a rate, the accuracy of which he has not checked in any way. It has been very aptly said by a competent critic that "any system of cost-keeping based "on assumption at any material point throws away the "money which it costs to maintain it," and I will go so far as to say that any system of Cost Accounts, however perfect otherwise, which does not admit of a reconciliation between the Cost and Commercial Books, and by which the amount debited to jobs to cover oncost is not periodically compared with the actual indirect charges, is incomplete, imperfect, and will in many cases be quite misleading Further, while it is essential to reconcile the total additions for oncost with the indirect charges, I strongly advocate in a business of any size that the oncost should be divided over the different departments and even in some cases over the machines, and I propose to outline how this may be done.

Oncost may be divided into two broad heads:—(1) Departmental Charges; and (2) General Organisation Expenses. What is known as prime cost is composed of the direct wages and materials on a job. Shop cost is prime cost with the addition of departmental charges, and shop cost, with the addition of the organisation and selling expenses, gives the total or inclusive cost. I may here explain that the word "shop" is used throughout the paper in its technical sense as referring to a department of an engineering concern.

To arrive at the departmental charges we must first decide into how many departments the works should be divided. Suppose we have several departments, such as Foundry, Forge, Pattern-shop, Boiler-shop, Erecting-shop, &c. A book would be started which we should call the Indirect Charges Book. This book is not necessarily part of the Commercial Books, and would generally be supplementary to them for the purpose of analysing expenses. In it, accounts would be opened for each department. If we take the Boiler-shop as a typical case, we would find this account in the Ledger debited with the following:—

(1) All wages expended entirely in the Boiler-shop but not directly chargeable against any particular job.

(2) Cost of up-keep of Boiler-shop, Buildings, machines, and tools, whether the work is done by the firm themselves or by outside firms.

(3) A pre-determined rate to cover depreciation and deterioration of shop, buildings, machines, and tools.

(4) Proportion of power, lighting, and heating.

(5) Water for hydraulic tools, &c.; stores and oils and waste used in Boiler-shop.

(6) Proportion of rent, rates, taxes, and insurance, or, in lieu of rent, interest on capital invested in buildings and plant.

This would give the total Boiler-shop oncost, which would be apportioned, as afterwards explained, over the various work done in the department, and the total of the amounts so debited would be placed to the credit of the "Boiler-shop Indirect Charges Account." If this sum exceeds the debits, then the percentage has been more than sufficient, but if, on the other hand, the debits are greater, then the percentage added has been too little, and in the absence of special circumstances the percentage should be at once increased. It is well, however, to consider the adequacy or otherwise of these percentages, not on the results of a single year, but on the average of two or three years.

By dividing the oncost over different departments and giving each its particular rate, instead of charging it as an overhead percentage over the whole works, we are able to apportion it more in accordance with the facts. Certain work may be completed in a particular shop which may have a low rate of oncost, and it is unfair to load it with the oncost of the other and heavier rated departments; or, again, certain shops have a heavy oncost, and it is but right that the jobs done in these shops should bear the heavier rate of oncost. Oncost is generally apportioned upon the money value of the productive wages. The total amount of the shop oncost—ascertained as already described—is divided by the amount paid in the shop for productive wages, and a rate per cent. is arrived at to cover shop oncost. Thus, suppose the Boiler-shop indirect charges amount to £1,500 and the amount of productive wages in the Boiler-shop is found to be £5,000, then the rate per cent. to be added to cover Boiler-shop oncost would be 30 per cent. A more correct method of apportionment, however, is to base the oncost upon the number of hours of productive time wrought in the shop. Here, instead of dividing the shop oncost by the money value of the labour, we take as the divisor the number of hours of productive time and arrive at a rate per hour to be added. To explain how this second method is more correct, let us take the case of a journeyman and apprentice doing similar work, the journeyman's rate being 1s. per hour and the rate for the apprentice 4d. per hour. Suppose the journeyman does the work in one day while the apprentice takes two days (a day being reckoned as eight hours). Under the first method, the rate of oncost being taken at 50 per cent., this would work out as follows:—

	Wages		Oncost	Total
Journeyman	8/-	+	50 % = 4/-	12/-
Apprentice	5/4	+	50 % = 2/8	8/-

Thus, although the journeyman has taken only half the time of the apprentice, his labour is debited with heavier oncost. By the hourly plan, supposing the rate for oncost to be 6d. per hour, it would work out as follows:—

	Wages		Oncost	Total
Journeyman	8/-	+	8 x 6 = 4/-	12/-
Apprentice	5/4	+	16 x 6 = 8/-	13/4

This makes the apprentice's labour bear the greater proportion of oncost, which is in accordance with facts, as the apprentice would require more use of machines, more floor space, more superintendence, &c., having taken double the time of the journeyman.

The General Establishment Charges would be dealt with similarly to the shop expenses. Thus an account would be opened in the Indirect Charges Book, called General Establishment Charges Account, to the debit of which would be transferred:—

(1) Salaries of Clerks, Manager and Principal Officials, Messengers, Travellers, Gate and Timekeepers.

(The Storekeeper's wages are also generally debited to General Establishment Charges, but an alternative method is to charge these wages against Stores Department, and when stores are charged against jobs add a percentage to the invoice price to cover the running expenses of the store, losses on old stock, and shortages in charging stores against contracts.)

(2) General Stationery, Catalogues, Advertising, Travelling Expenses, and all expenses connected with securing orders.

(3) Discounts and Allowances to Customers, Bad Debts, Discounting Trade Bills, &c.

(4) Proportion of rent, rates, taxes, and insurances applicable to office, postages, telegrams, upkeep, and depreciation of office buildings and furniture.

(5) Cost of maintaining Branch offices or showrooms, &c.

This would give the total amount of General Establishment Charges. We have now to consider by what method —most in accordance with facts—we should apportion this over the contracts. Here again we have our choice of two methods, as the General Establishment Charges may be either apportioned as a percentage upon the shop cost or on the hourly burden principle. The hourly burden is probably the more correct. The prime cost of jobs fluctuates through rises or falls in prices of raw materials and this, under the percentage on shop cost plan, would tend to upset the oncost in a year of violent changes in prices of raw materials. In most cases, however, it would be found incorrect to debit all the different classes of work with the same overhead rate to cover General Establishment Charges, as certain classes of work require more advertising, travelling expenses, correspondence, &c. It is, therefore, advisable to classify the work under two or three heads, and by an analysis of the Expenses Accounts, it will be possible to fix a rate, so that each class of work will receive only its fair proportion, and the total amount debited will square with the total General Establishment Expenses.

These are the general lines upon which, in an engineering establishment, the oncost would be most correctly ascertained and apportioned. There are, however, many points which will arise from time to time in actual practice which will probably call for a modification of the plan which I have outlined. The first exception I would refer to is the Foundry. In the Foundry the wages cost forms a very small proportion of the total cost of the castings produced, and here instead of taking the wages or number of hours as the basis upon which to apportion the oncost, it will be found more equitably calculated upon the tonnage of castings produced, and in the case of a foundry doing castings of various classes, it will be advisable to have different rates of oncost for each class, as they require quite different treatment, and it would not be fair to debit them with the same rates of oncost. Another refinement in oncost apportionment, and one which, I think, will enter very largely into the question in the future, is the spreading of the oncost over the various machines. In recent years there has been quietly going on quite a revolution in the methods of doing certain classes of work, and machines have to a large extent superseded hand labour. The introduction of machines has a direct effect upon oncost. It reduces the number of hours wrought upon a job and increases the oncost. If, therefore, we continue to charge upon the number of hours of man's time, the results got from doing a piece of work in the old way by hand and by machinery would be quite different. To obviate this there has been adopted in many establishments what is known as a machine hour rate. To get at this, each machine is treated as a small department, and is debited with a charge for space, lighting, power, upkeep, depreciation, and capital invested. Dividing this total charge by the normal number of hours which the machine works, a rate per hour is arrived at, at which the machine is charged much the same as a workman. Where this method is adopted it has, of course, an effect upon the shop oncost, as certain of the expenses, instead of being charged against a department, are distributed over the various machines. This method is a little more troublesome to work out, but where any considerable number of machines are employed, the hourly machine rate—corrected by a supplementary rate when the shops are not working full time—is by far the most accurate.

No doubt much of this appears elaborate, but the principle is exceedingly simple. Oncost is an element which must be provided for in all estimates, and Cost Accounts should be designed so as to give accurately, not only the cost of a job in wages and materials, but should also show how the rate on oncost added compares with the actual expenses of the business. To do this the same plan of account-keeping is adopted as in the Commercial Books—viz., Double-entry. This, as you know, involves some extra labour, but ensures accuracy, and I fear we can no more dispense with it in the Cost than we can in the Commercial Books. Many firms are content to prove the oncost in total; and while this is satisfactory as showing that all expenses have been provided for, the slumping of productive and selling expenses and adding to the cost of all jobs by an overhead percentage, is generally misleading and often renders worthless all the time and money spent upon the system. On the other hand, by splitting up the expenses into Shop Expenses and General Establishment Charges, the productive cost of each job is ascertained; and by analysing the General Establishment Charges and spreading them over the jobs according to a proper classification of the articles produced, we bring out in startling fashion the relative profitableness of the different classes of work.

In conclusion, I would like to say a word as to the importance of the subject from the accountant's point of view. In many of the limited companies whose accounts we have to certify, the item "Stock on hand and work in progress" forms no inconsiderable item in the Balance Sheet; and in view of certain legal decisions, I question if an auditor is entitled to take on trust the percentage of oncost added to the work in progress, without ascertaining how it has been arrived at, and what it is supposed to cover. The question of oncost also crops up in the sometimes large item of "Work done for selves." An engineering firm may sometimes, when the books are not too full of orders, carry out large alterations and extensions to their works and plant. In addition to the wages and materials expended in these extensions a percentage is added to cover oncost, and it is possible that a "lean year" may be made "dividend-paying" by a large percentage of oncost being thus capitalised. The correct practice is to add a smaller percentage of oncost to this class of work than to contracts, but this is a matter which requires careful attention when auditing the books of a business of this kind.

The Chartered Accountants Students' Society of Kingston-upon-Hull.

Hints to Students in devising Systems of Engineers' Cost Accounts.

By John B. Bardsley.

Read at a meeting of the Kingston-upon-Hull Chartered Accountants Students' Society, April 2 1902.

It has become almost a cant phrase in commencing a one evening's lecture upon a large and important subject to refer to "time limitations" and their consequences in crippling the lecturer's efforts. And whilst it does seem ridiculous to spend even a moment in emphasising a self-evident fact, it is, I think, desirable, if not necessary, to say once for all that in the time at my disposal what I shall endeavour to give to you is neither an essay on Engineering Works Management, nor a complete system of Engineers' Cost Accounts, nor a lecture on Bookkeeping, though in parts it will embrace portions of all three. And though I myself suggested the title of this paper—or, rather, corrected your Secretary's more ambitious description of what I was requested to give to you—I felt extreme diffidence when I came to face the subject at close quarters, which feeling, I assure you, has deepened each day until now. Though in our own minds we may have a comparatively clear idea of a given subject, when we are compelled to set forth in black and white, in what should be a connected and lucid manner, a presentment of our views, the subject seems to loom upon us in a shape far removed from that clear and sharply-cut outline with which one would like to portray it in an expository essay. My first step, therefore, was to obtain from your Secretary an idea of the "hints" which would be appropriate and acceptable in a meeting of students. I must confess I was staggered by the reply—that I should be expected "to sketch a financial system, go down to first principles in the compilation of Cost Accounts, touch upon "oncost and establishment charges, and demonstrate "how the results shown by the Cost Accounts could be "reconciled with those appearing in the financial books."

The policy of "thorough" could not be carried much further, in my opinion; and your expectations, I am afraid, will not be realised, although I will do what I can to meet them in the time I have. I disclaim, however, any ambition to portray a complete system of Engineers' Cost Accounts to-night. What I hope to accomplish in a modest way is to give to you generally in the course of my remarks some insight into the needs of engineers, for whom, possibly, in the course of your professional career, you may be called upon to devise a scientific system of Cost Accounts. You must not expect from me a comparative study or criticism of other Cost Account systems extant. It would be presumption on my part to criticise the work of able and experienced men, when I am not attempting to set forth a complete system myself. At the same time, you must remember that in effect I shall be describing some features of a system which has stood the test of everyday wear and tear in a busy engineering works, and that I am not theorising only, but giving you my personal experience. In following my remarks some of you may possibly say you are acquainted with different methods, which also have stood the severest of all tests—viz., that of actual experience—and I should not be disposed to gainsay you. I do not claim perfection for anything I may bring to your notice, for I am always myself on the look-out for improvements, and when improvements are found I do more than make a note of them. In each engineering works you have local conditions peculiar to the place to encounter and satisfy, and therefore my reply to any such criticism as that I just referred to is: You must take it for granted that the system I describe to you works well in its environment.

Although it is not an everyday occurrence for a professional accountant to be asked to devise a system of Cost Accounts for an engineering client, he cannot have too close an acquaintanceship with all known systems, in order to enhance the value of his audit, or his advice to his client upon the account-keeping generally. But there is almost as much variety, first, in the nature and magnitude of the undertakings comprehended under the general term of "Engineering Shops"; and, secondly, in the circumstances which surround and may affect each individual place. To devise a system for a new works is comparatively a matter of ease, compared with a similar operation in an old-established place, with its fine old crusted prejudices and unwritten laws and customs. And although no one system may be capable of literal transportation from one engineering establishment (even if in the same line and of the same size) to another, yet the same principles apply in all cases, just as you adapt the theory of double-entry bookkeeping to an infinite variety of commercial enterprises. In conveying my hints, therefore, I came to the conclusion that it would be best to imagine ourselves devising a financial and cost system for some hypothetical works, comprising within itself all the essential departments of a fair-sized engineering establishment, without being too small to prove of no account as an example, or so large as to take us beyond the average experience.

Our task is therefore to take in hand this going concern, and devise a cost system fulfilling the conditions looked upon as essential in any system based upon scientific principles—namely, one capable of agreement and proof with the Financial Books, giving a perfect check on Stocks, the arithmetical accuracy proved by Double-entry, and, moreover, a system containing as one of its salient features my main thesis—viz., that in the Cost Books (devoted, as they must be, primarily to the guidance of the technical staff) all the machinery of account-keeping be rendered as unobtrusive as possible; the proof Double-entry and of Stocks, and in the long run of actually achieved results, and all the wire-pulling and adjustments necessary in the accounting department of such a works as I am imagining being carried out in the Impersonal Ledger or Financial Books generally. Now, in entering such a place, and in taking up your task, you will find that you can learn quite as much as you are able to teach, however great your skill as an accountant; also that there are problems in the internal economy and departmental accounting, towards the solution of which you will require knowledge and experience not always obtainable by the professional accountant. In meeting engineers as a class, you meet men whose education and standing are no less than your own—men fully as accustomed in their daily work to meet and grapple with hard facts, and, moreover, men of an intensely practical habit, knowing exactly what they *want* in Cost Accounts, and possessing a latent suspicion of the "doctrinaire," whether in their own profession or outside of it. I tell you this because I want you to avoid giving any reason inadvertently for remarks such as I have seen from time to time in engineering publications concerning the "pedantic methods of professional accountants," and contemptuous references to "that blessed word" (although it is two) "Double Entry," and "The Trial Balance, which is the sheet anchor of the "average professional accountant, who looks more to "the regularity and symmetry of his ticks than to the "actual needs which Cost Accounts are devised to "satisfy." Do not attach undue importance to these gibes, or allow them to do more than teach you to avoid giving any reason for them. The truest wisdom is shown in trying to understand the needs of the engineering staff, and you must adopt the "put yourself in his place" policy. Now, to satisfy such needs, and still to keep your methods free from the taint of being "doctrinaire," involves that perfection of the art of management which conceals itself. It is at times not inopportune or unhealthy for the professional accountant to ask himself, "Is my client made for me or am I made for my client?" Neither hypothesis is literally correct, but the doubt implied is a useful corrective. So bear in mind that a system has to be fitted to the particular works, and do not expect the place to be revolutionised in order to reflect your genius, because however slow "evolution" may be, it is infinitely to be preferred, and is more lasting and beneficial in its result, than "revolution." To devise a system of Cost Accounts, and adapt it to an extensive engineering establishment with a "past" is a far greater test of skill than elaborating a system for a brand new works. Success in the former case is therefore more creditable, although at times the extreme deliberation with which new steps are taken, and new types evolved, rivals the speed of the evolutionary efforts of Nature herself.

In devising Cost Accounts the tendency on the part of many really clever accountants is to raise to themselves a monument of constructive skill as solidly linked or wedged together as Eddystone Lighthouse, and, having completed their masterpiece, they are apt to fall down and worship it, and look upon engineers as "no class" when they can see neither beauty nor utility in it. A perfect network of books, forms, and accounts may represent power, and by chance efficiency, but it will also mean friction, and it is desirable to avoid that. Without entering into detailed criticism of any particular system, I would just like you to look at the broad outline of the different systems which one meets with—viz., as devised by engineers and as devised by accountants. Amongst engineers, as I told you, you find (in any place of importance) that, as a rule, the responsible technical manager has an excellent idea of what he *requires* in Cost Accounts, and just as "Necessity is the mother of invention"—and engineers are an inventive race—they set to work to get a Cost System which shall satisfy their needs as they see them. These systems vary in excellence and utility, no doubt, just as accountants' systems do, but the published samples I have seen are mainly good in their several ways, and, though cumbrous, are, as Cost Accounts, effective, supposing always that the actual figuring and clerical work is under good supervision and faithfully and accurately performed. But, in my humble opinion, where they sometimes fall short of complete efficiency is in the essential particular of easy verification of results by means of and with the financial books. It is probably my misfortune, but I have not met with any engineers' system which, to my mind, fully satisfies this want. No doubt there are many large engineering establishments where the chief of the accounting department has been without what is known as a "professional training," but who has, notwithstanding, possessed a genius for accountancy, and in such places necessity, primarily, and a slow but sure process of evolution, have sufficed to produce a thoroughly effective system, looked at from anyone's standpoint. But these systems never see the light of the Engineering or Accountancy Press, and exhale their sweetness only in their native air. But they have an advantage over professional accountants' systems in this respect, that the inventor has to work them, and wherever the shoe pinches he is doubtless the sufferer, and quickly eases the pressure and so gets an easy fit. But sometimes, apart from any disadvantage which accrues to the professional accountants' system from his peculiar position, there are inherent faults in his methods, if you will pardon me for saying so. Not in his methods of execution, but in his conception of what is required, or his method of meeting such requirements. The strenuous pursuit of a profession often has a narrowing effect on one's mind. Great experience is doubtless acquired, and a high degree of excellence from a professional standpoint; but just as that signboard artist who was accustomed to paint nothing but rampant lions was once required to depict an angel, and produced a mythological beast, part angelic lion, part leonine angel, so do some accountants, whose minds run in grooves, fail to realise exactly the requirements of their engineering clients. They produce a system perfect in theory, bound to get full marks in any examination, but bearing the mark of the professional accountant, and too full of the machinery of account-keeping to prove a success. You have, in fact, to drop any preconceived opinions of Cost Accounts, and all trammelling effects of ordinary double-entry bookkeeping arranged for strict audit and for protection from nefarious operations on the part of the staff, and in very deed to put yourself in the place of those who use and need every hour of every day the guidance of Cost Accounts.

Broadly speaking, therefore, these are the faults of the two sides: the engineers' systems being incomplete, and therefore frequently misleading and useless, and the accountants' too much trammelled by rigid theory and over-elaboration, and by his failure to use fully that power of mental detachment which he should cultivate assiduously. If called upon, therefore, to assist the engineer, don't raze his edifice to the ground, however humble it may be. You will often disarm prejudice, and be enabled to secure hearty co-operation by extending and perfecting his system, or, at all events, by letting him think so, without trying to drive home into his inner consciousness your sense of his inferiority. The point, therefore, which I want to emphasise is that the engineering manager and his technical staff are those for whom you are prescribing when devising a system of Cost Accounts. You should, therefore, keep a single eye upon their needs, and your watchword all through should be "simplicity *in excelsis*." But, you say, what are those needs? And I will try and tell you. The responsible manager requires to see at any time the exact cost, in wages and material, of each order or contract passing through the shops; also the exact cost in wages and material of repairs and maintenance of or extension of plant, machinery, tools, and buildings, and also exactly how the added percentage made in the Cost Books for covering the Indirect Expenses exceeds or falls short of the expenses themselves. Now this is very simple and comprehensive, and you are doubtless all of you aware of what I tell you. In seeking a first step to simplicity, have you ever noted how all these items are debits, and that it simplifies your Cost Accounts to have no credit side. Therefore, as I have already said, the first point I wish you to note is this—viz., put ***nothing*** in your Cost Accounts beyond the records satisfying the requirements I have mentioned, keeping all Stock Accounts and making all adjustments in your financial books. The financial books in themselves should be entirely self-contained and planned to yield accurate results, without reference to a Cost System. The Cost

System fulfils functions which ought not to be expected of a Financial System (if things are to work smoothly), so do not complicate your Cost Accounts with one single detail of which the financial books can relieve them. You need stock adjustments and various Adjustment Accounts and proof of arithmetical accuracy by double-entry, but you must obtain these essentials outside your Cost System. It is hide-bound insistence upon non-essentials to a Cost System which causes an engineering staff to rail at the orthodoxy of the "hard shell" accountant, and turns his well-meant efforts to anathema.

For such an engineering establishment therefore as the one we are imagining I should institute the following departmental divisions—viz., (1) Foundry, (2) Forge or Smiths' Shop, (3) Boiler Shop, and (4) Engineering Departments and the Sub-departments of Drawing Office and Pattern Shop. Imagine also the products to be heavy and complicated machinery taking months to turn out, and for the ultimate results to show, as this renders extreme accuracy in costing more essential and more difficult than in shops where quicker production and standardisation simplify matters. The first detail, then, you will have to settle is, shall I incorporate my Cost Accounts with the double-entry of the financial system, or shall I not? On this rock alone many efforts at a Cost System are wrecked, therefore determine well in your own mind at the outset your course of procedure. With one or two circumstances reserved, and the needs of the financial and commercial side of the engineering establishment and those of the purely technical side being so different, my advice is do not link the two sets together. I don't say that under no circumstances are you to incorporate your Cost System with the double-entry of the financial books. You must always remain judges of special circumstances yourselves, but speaking for myself, and with such a place to prescribe for as the one we are imagining, I advocate running the two sets of accounts on parallel lines, commencing at the same base, utilising the same data in rather different form, and yielding identical results at any "cut off" *en route*. My guiding principle would be, in brief, to make the Cost Ledgers a minutely detailed Memorandum Account or counterpart of the Total Wages, Materials Purchased, and Expenses Accounts contained in the Impersonal Ledger, excepting, of course, various cash disbursements, each department of the works being self-contained—*i.e.*, each department possessing its detailed Cost Ledger, and in the Impersonal Ledger possessing its distinct Purchases, Wages, and Expenses Accounts. By this means your Cost Accounts are checked by double-entry, because for any given period the totals of Wages, Purchases, and Expenses in the Impersonal Ledger will tally with the summated columns of your Cost Ledger for the same period, always, of course, granting accurate bookkeeping. The Stock Accounts would be kept and agreed in the Impersonal Ledger. You will thus obtain two of the greatest essentials of correct costing—viz., proof of the arithmetical accuracy of the postings—by the double-entry of your Impersonal Ledger and agreement of stocks at any stocktaking period, whilst keeping your Cost Accounts clear of every complicating feature, leaving them a simple narrative of wages and materials expended, and also of the amount added as a percentage or machine rating to meet the indirect or establishment charges. You are all no doubt familiar with the principle involved here, from your experience of Self-Balancing Ledgers, and, in the system I recommend, your Cost Ledger would bear a relationship to the Impersonal Ledger analogous to that of the Purchases and/or Sales Ledgers in a self-balancing system. Now I feel I am treading on very thin ice when I say that part of the advantage of this system is that it might curtail the labour of an audit, as I know what gluttons accountants are for work, so I will only urge its great advantage at audit periods in this way. Supposing you got a check in total on the Cost Ledgers, you would scarcely check them in detail as you might the financial books, but with clear and minutely-detailed costs you could far more easily and completely check the value of the "Work in progress" asset at a balancing period, enabling you perhaps to appraise with all possible accuracy any amount representing an anticipated portion of profit on a contract nearing completion at the making-up date, and also enabling you on the other hand to ascertain if a loss is more or less certain on any piece of unfinished work, rendering necessary some reserve in the financial statements.

Referring now to the departmental divisions I mentioned—viz., Engineering (comprising the Machine, Fitting, and Erecting Shops), Foundry (Iron and Brass), Smiths' Shop or Forge, and Boiler Shop, and the subsidiary Expense Departments of Drawing Office and Pattern Shop—points of difference commence right away. Some engineers' accountants treat pattern shop as a foundry cost, and some include drawing office under engineering. I keep them separate for various reasons. One reason is that the pattern shop does not work for the iron foundry alone. In these days of high speeds and high pressure, engine parts which used to be of cast iron are now cast steel, and as only a very few engineers, and those the most extensive in the land, possess a steel foundry, most engineering firms have to purchase their steel castings from those who make a speciality of such work, and therefore your pattern shop, for important reasons of accuracy, &c., makes the patterns to be sent out to the steel founder, who returns them with the casting. The drawing office also works for each of the departments I have specified, and thus I hold to the convenience on many grounds of the separate treatment I advocate, more especially that the cost of each pattern would be debited to the contract concerned, as also would be the time of every draughtsman spent upon such contract. Now it is quite within possibility that the above departments—Drawing Office, Pattern Shop, Iron Foundry, Smiths' Shop, and perhaps Boiler Shop—might all work together to turn out one engineering job, which finishes up in the Machine, Fitting, and Erecting Shops, being invoiced by the Engineering Department as one item. In this case, each department would transfer the cost of its own product into the Engineering Department Cost Ledger, either at cost—*i.e.*, shop cost, plus a percentage to cover share of Establishment Charges, or at an agreed price. Again, the foundry might turn out a casting, or the smiths' shop a forging, which after more or less machining is sold as a separate part and invoiced by the Engineering Department, the foundry or forge being credited cost (plus Establishment Charges) of the rough casting or forging mentioned. On the other hand, the boiler shop might be a totally distinct business from the Engineering Department, capable of working apart and producing the largest steam-raising plants, as opposed to those instances where the boilers might be integral parts of an engine—such as traction engines, road rollers, locomotives, or stationary engines of the locomotive type. Now no difference in principle is necessary, but to make my purpose clearer I may say I treat the Engineering Department as taking all castings and forgings and patterns, and crediting the separate costs to foundry and forge and pattern shop as if to outside suppliers (but not at a profit rate), but I treat the Boiler Department as a *profit* department, having no connection with the Engineering Department. The chief difference between the two types of boiler-making is that there is more variety in the one I am adopting, as each boiler may differ in detail with every other in size, working pressure, furnace fittings, mountings, and so on, entailing differences in the thickness of plates used, and thus necessitating special direct purchases of plates from the plate-rolling mills, which would be, of course, direct debits to Cost Accounts. In the other case, where boilers are made an integral part of an engine—the type is, as a rule, a standard one—a stock of plates, angles, and other parts is kept from which supplies are obtained, and, being a standardised product, the approximate cost would be known, and the endeavour would be to work at or under such cost. In either case the principle is untouched. It is only the details which vary, and I mention them to render clearer, I hope, my treatment of the case.

Financial Books.

Taking the Financial Books first in order to clear them from our path, I may say I would keep my Cash Book on the columnar principle, in the form of a Cash Journal —a form I much prefer, but which I have not seen in general commercial use excepting in the North-West of England. There is no need to mention this book particularly, except to emphasise the point that I would keep all Ledgers on the self-balancing principle, which partly accounts for the form of the Cash Book. In the Petty Cash Book you will notice a column headed Cost Ledger, which is used for any item of petty cash expenditure, such as Travelling and similar expenses incurred in fitting and erecting, and the appropriate account in the Cost Ledger is debited whenever such expense is a direct charge, and, of course, the Impersonal Ledger Account, representing the departmental production affected, is also debited.

In the Impersonal Ledger I should set apart several sections, one for each department, and in each section I should open separate Wages and Purchases Accounts for each separate head of departmental expenses, in fullest detail, according to requirements, making each department self-contained, and so arranged that the total of wages and purchases and direct departmental expenses shall at any time equal the totals of the postings found in the Cost Ledger for that department.

One of the most important financial books for our present purpose is the Purchase Journal (Form D), and its attendant satellite, the Sundries Analysis Journal (Form D 1). The Purchase Journal is, as you see, quite simple and in common form, with analysis columns on the debit side for each department, also a column for General Store and one for Sundry Expenses. This latter column is for direct and indirect expenses, and, containing as it does an immense variety of items, I abstract it into the Sundries Analysis Journal (Form D 1). This book is a "cut-leaf" book, and contains "an endless vista of vertical columns," as one engineer writer would say—a writer remarkable for the freedom of his criticism of professional accountants—but his gibe is as free from being *à propos* as would be an accountant's gibe at the "endless vista of vertical and horizontal lines" in a fully detailed drawing. These books being the financial books, I claim entire freedom in my treatment of them from the interference of the engineering staff, just as I advocate the fullest consideration of the engineer's convenience in the Cost Books. I am quite aware that some accountants will criticise the book adversely, but I welcome *their* criticism. The book justifies its existence, and I am satisfied with it.

In the Purchase Journal the Store column takes all purchases which cannot be debited direct either to Cost Ledgers or Departmental Stock Accounts. The Foundry columns are Departmental Stock Accounts, as also are the Smiths' Shop and Pattern Shop columns. The columns devoted to Engineering and Boiler Department purchases are kept for *direct* purchases only.

The detail of the purchases is, of course, credited to the separate suppliers' accounts in the Purchases Ledger in the ordinary way, and the total is credited to the Purchases Ledger Account in the Impersonal Ledger.

Here we first touch the Cost Accounts. In order to obviate the risk of omitting to post items of direct purchases or expenses to the Cost Ledger Accounts, I include a folio column for the Materials Cost Ledger, so that direct purchases are debited in the Cost Ledger to the particular contract affected. If these postings of materials are allowed to be made from invoices, there is serious risk of omission or misposting to the Cost Account, as many invoices have to be analysed and subdivided for posting where more than one column is affected. With this method there is none, all postings being called over and agreed in total monthly with the Impersonal Ledger Account. I may remark incidentally that the system of invoice keeping which I favour is, that on entry into the Purchase Journal each invoice receives a number, which is affixed by a stamping machine with large steel type figures, and that the same number (also affixed by this stamp) appears on the line in the Purchase Journal upon which such invoice is entered. These numbers are consecutive, and run for the full financial year, and then revert to 1 again. This number determines the identity of each invoice in any financial year. The entry in the Purchases *Ledger* is referenced to this invoice number, so also is every entry of direct material in the Cost Ledger, Store Ledger, and throughout the entire works. The invoices are filed monthly in card-board box binders in the order of their consecutive numbers, and thus direct and instant reference is had from any part of the Financial or Cost Account System to any required invoice without loss of time.

I have already said that the items which go through the Sundries Analysis Book are items of expense, which, whilst not capable of being debited to any contract, are capable of proper division over each department; but in addition to these, there are other items of expense which cannot be allocated to any particular department, but have to be debited each to its appropriate account in the Impersonal Ledger, and be dealt with under the general term of Establishment Charges or Incidentals. You will require, therefore, separate accounts for such expenses in the Impersonal Ledger—viz., such as Rates and Taxes, Books and Stationery, and Drawing Office Material, Stable Expenses, Directors' Fees, and/or Management Salaries, General Office Expenses, Income Tax, Rent, Insurance, Debenture and Mortgage Interest, Bank Commission, and Interest, and so on. Some accountants prefer to keep these items in one account under some such designation as Establishment Charges Account, but I prefer to keep them separately under their own proper style and title. This method facilitates quick reference to any specific Expense Account—such as Rates or Insurances—and by using a memorandum book in Form C you may keep before you from month to month your exact total expense or liability on Establishment Charges Account, and allocate the monthly total of such charges over all the departments at whatever ratio may be determined upon. Although this book does not belong to the double-entry system, it fulfils a most important function. I shall point this out more fully when I come to Establishment Charges, but its importance consists in this, that though in memorandum form you find from it your total monthly expense not directly chargeable, you also see how each department of the works is affected by such expense, and by a comparison with the sum charged as a machine rating or percentage in the Cost Accounts to cover these Establishment Charges, you ascertain whether you are covering the same or not.

You will see that the ruling of this book provides 13 vertical money columns, and a Description and Date column on the left. By taking one column per month, and taking the Expense Account items from the Impersonal Ledger in the same regular rotation—providing for all expenses accruing or accrued due but not rendered, and also providing for the proper apportionment of all unexpired values of expenses paid in advance—you arrive at the correct total of the month's indirect expenses. This total would then be apportioned to the column for each department at any agreed ratio, and to each of such apportionments you would add the amount already debited to the separate Departmental Expense Accounts for items chargeable direct to departments, and this second total forms the monthly charge against each department. The cross additions of the Establishment Charges (Memo.) Book show the total amount of each Expense Account for any period under any specific heading—such as Interest or Repairs, and so on. This book, I need hardly say, calls for the same care and accuracy in treatment as any book which is included in the double-entry system. The fact that it is a memo. book, and leaves you a fair amount of freedom in its use, must not hide the fact that it is, or should be, a valuable guide in your Cost Accounts.

I shall leave the financial books now, whilst I describe the Cost Books more particularly, but before I do so, may I say that I have not exhausted this side of the subject, but must leave the Sales Day Books and other purely financial books, which do not touch the Cost System, unreferred to. I will add, however, that for each department I would open in the Impersonal Ledger a Trading Account in the usual form, to which at each making-up and stocktaking period (I make up half-yearly) I should transfer the total of each subsidiary account, the balance showing the profit or loss on the working for the period, and the debit side should tally with the total summations shown by the Cost Ledger and Establishment Charges Account for each department.

In dealing with the Cost Books, one department will in principle be found identical with another, only differing in various details. I will therefore take the Engineering Department Costs firstly, as these will afford a comprehensive example, absorbing as they do the subcosts of Foundry, Forge, and Pattern Shops, and if time allows we will take the other Departmental Costs as we encounter them in the Engineering Book.

The first item in Prime Cost is the Wages of Labour, and the process of obtaining in any week, or over any pay period, the wages expenditure on any one contract or order necessitates a reliable method of taking the men's time. There are many methods, each with some feature suitable to the environment of the works, but for such a place as I am imagining I must give my vote to a time-recording clock, by which the workman himself prints on a card or paper strip bearing his official number (a fresh card or strip being provided once or twice a week) the time at which he enters and leaves the works. These clocks are placed either in the time-house or in each department or shop, according to convenience, but always, of course, under careful supervision. The timekeeper fixes these strips weekly in a Guard Book made for the purpose, thus forming a permanent Time Book. The advantages of these mechanical time recorders are many. There is scarcely any risk of collusion between workman or timekeeper, or of dispute in regard to accuracy, and the card or strip stamped by the workman himself forms a reliable base for your wages cost arrangements. I may here remark that if cards are used they furnish the starting-point for a system of cost keeping on the American card system. This is an ingenious system, and rather takes my fancy in various respects, but I am not going to praise or condemn it. I lean rather to evolution than to revolution, and the card system involves radical and sweeping changes. It is easiest tried in a new place. In an old-established works its introduction would necessitate long inception and intelligent co-operation in quarters where at present we do not look for such assistance. But in addition to the time clock, a clerk or clerks—as many as necessary, but as few as possible—go round the works and see each man, and ascertain exactly what work he is engaged upon. This is done at least twice a day, if not oftener, and the results are recorded in a Time Book (see Form L), wherein each man has a Time Account opened in his own name, and which shows at the week end the contracts or orders upon which he has been engaged, the total hours worked, his rate, and the amount of wages earned. In some places numbered cards or boards are used, and the workman puts thereon the particular work or contract upon which he may be engaged, and gets his foreman to vouch his entry by initial or signature. I think, however, that the other method is better on all grounds. It is more certain —that is, you may rely more implicitly upon getting the workman's time debited to the proper order; it saves the time of the foreman, who is a more highly-paid man than the time-clerk, and has very important technical matters to deal with, and therefore is a man whose attention ought to be left undivided for his particular duties, and it avoids giving the men any clerical work to do; and these constitute reasons for separate time-taking not lightly to be disregarded. The time clerk, of course, must understand the work passing through the shops, and be able therefore to judge with accuracy of the *bona fides* of any workmen's statement as to the job he is engaged upon. I need not further dilate upon the great importance to the reliable character of any Costing System of the time clerk's duties. His returns are the very foundation of the wages costs, and an error in taking time not only vitiates or tends to vitiate a particular cost, but is apt to be perpetuated in future estimates. The time as taken by the time clerk is compared and agreed with the man's time as stamped by himself during the week, any discrepancy being, of course, enquired into. These individual Time Accounts for the week are then abstracted from the time clerk's book, not only under the headings of each order or job, or shop repairs upon which he may have been engaged during the week, but sub-divided for each contract, as to whether wages of draughtsmen, fitters, or machine men, or for erecting, packing, labouring, and so on. This abstract is then agreed in total with total wages paid, and forthwith posted to the proper accounts in the Wages Cost Ledger. The Wages Cost Ledger and the Materials Cost Ledger are most important books. Of course, all the books and forms used in any system of accounting where a desired result is the outcome of numerous operations must be equally important. The chain is no stronger than its weakest link, but if I lay any stress upon these books it is simply from the standpoint of importance in design, because of the permanent character of the books and their records. The form of Cost Ledger which I have used for two years past is known as the "Loose Leaf" or Perpetual Ledger —an American importation, and in this case a good one. Even since the purchase of these Ledgers great improvements have been introduced into the arrangement of the locking device, and, so far as my experience of the Ledger goes—viz., for Cost Ledgers and for Shareholders' Ledger and List—I can give the invention an unqualified testimonial. For an Engineer's Cost Ledger the advantages, or some of them, are as follows: In almost any contract, large or small, there will be considerable sub-division of costs required. A number is given to the main contract, and then the same number—with a sub-number or sign perhaps supplemented by description—is given to each part, the cost of which it is desired to separately ascertain. But whatever the number of sub-divisions, it matters not. In the Loose Leaf Ledger you take a leaf for each sub-division, and as soon as the first leaf is full you unlock the book and slip in another at its back, and so on, so that at the completion of this contract you have not only a connected and consecutive narrative of detailed costs, sub-divided to any desired extent, but you have each sub-division by itself, but yet in its appointed place in the main contract; and, further, you can take out the whole of the leaves forming such narrative of costs and separately bind and reference the costs of this contract for future use. This is without interfering either with your Ledger or any other Cost Account in it, and without affecting your financial books in the least. A further advantage is, that on a cost being completed and removed to the transfer file or binder, it leaves the Cost Ledger containing nothing but "live" accounts, and to those of us who have had to wander for days and nights in old style Ledgers, which resemble disused cemeteries more than living assemblies, this advantage will be fully appreciated. Accountants' clerks "meditations" amongst such "tombs" are not always fit for publication.

Now, referring to the form of the two books—Wages and Materials—firstly, the division is a mere matter of convenience, and you may have it all in one book or make it more than two, just as necessity dictates. You will notice first the division of wages into Draughtsmen, Fitters, and so on. These items are posted weekly from the time clerk's abstract of his book, and this book total agrees with the total paid through the financial books and debited to Engineers', Trading, or Production, or Working Account, just as you like to name it. This secures agreement of wages item in both sets of books; but it may not be agreement to a penny. You will inevitably find that the abstracted items do not total exactly to the wages paid, and this is caused through dropping halfpence or reckoning a further halfpenny in subdividing time, therefore it is non-essential. Don't trouble over it, but keep a memorandum "Over" and "Under" Account if you choose, and so agree each week's pay.

Now, passing from the Wages columns, you will observe columns wherein is inserted the time which the particular piece of work has occupied on any particular machine. A charge is here made against the contract for use of this machine, and this is known as the machine rating (and where the wages are not those of a machinist a percentage is added in the column headed "Percentage on Wages"). This machine rating may vary in amount, according to the machine used. For our purposes we make three gradations in our machines (large, medium, and small), each at a different rating, and the time occupied on any such machine computed at the rating for its class extended into the money column, which you see headed "Machine Charge." This is where we first come into contact with Oncost or Establishment Charges. Into the nature of this part of the cost I will not at the moment enter. At present merely note that this is the first place in the Cost System where we come into contact with an estimate instead of dealing with known figures. Now, in order to test the value of this estimate, the cost clerk, at the week-end or month-end, abstracts the column totals for each contract on to Ledger Sheets, showing the grand total of wages and machine rating and percentage on wages charged to each contract or subdivision of a contract. The whole monthly total of this machine charge and percentage is then compared (as I said when describing the financial books) with the book in which I keep in memo. form the actual monthly total of Establishment Charges, and any disagreement is noted for enquiry. I will not stop any longer at the moment over this machine charge or percentage question, but pass on to the "Materials" column in the Wages Cost Ledger. This item is a lump sum weekly transfer from the same contract or sub-contract heading in the "Materials" Cost Ledger, which is thus subsidiary to the Wages Cost Ledger, and which we will now consider. Passing by the merely descriptive columns, you will notice the first division is "Castings." I told you at the beginning the reason why iron and steel castings stand on a different footing in this form, K—viz., that I am dealing as with a works where no iron castings are *purchased* and no steel castings are *made*, few engineering establishments possessing a steel foundry. Taking the columns seriatim, the "Iron" Castings items are posted from the Iron Castings Production Book (Form I). I treat this book as the Foundry Day Book, and debit each item of total cost to the appropriate account in the Materials Cost Ledger in the column for Iron Castings, and the monthly total of such individual postings is carried to the debit of the account in the Impersonal Ledger representing the total purchases for the Engineering Department. Where any foundry work has been done for other departments—such as for Boiler Department, &c.—or where any repairs have been done involving foundry work, the full detail is posted to the Materials Cost Ledger to the Repair or other account affected, and I post the monthly total only of such repairs to the Impersonal Ledger Account. The summations of the detail columns are then credited monthly, viz., the first column giving the Weight of Finished Castings Produced, and the next column headed "Cost of Metal" are credited to the Foundry Purchases Account, the balance of which account will then give the value and weight of pig iron, scrap, &c., remaining in stock, after the allowance for waste has been made. I may here remark that the figure which would appear in the column headed "Cost of Mixture per Ton" is taken from the Cupola Book, to which I will refer later if time permits. The total of wages charged is then credited to Wages Account (the balance of this account then showing wages expended on unfinished work in progress carried forward to the next weekly or monthly Production Account), and the total of the Incidentals column (being the percentage added to prime cost to cover indirect charges) is credited to the Foundry Establishment Charges Account. This completes the postings, and gives a double-entry check on the amounts posted to the Cost Ledger by reason of the Impersonal Ledger being required to balance and the debits in both Ledgers having to agree; but in addition to the above postings I keep a memorandum posting of the total, crediting Total Foundry Production or Sales and debiting Total Purchases and Repairs, as I find this facilitates the work of making up the ordinary aggregate Trading and Profit and Loss Account at making-up periods. It is not, however, essential to go into this latter refinement, but I find it useful for my purposes. An exactly similar book for brass castings is used in the same manner, therefore I have not multiplied forms by giving one for brass castings. Now the next three columns in the Materials Cost Ledger are devoted to items of direct purchases which come through the Purchase Journal—viz., Steel Castings, Sundries (which includes all manner of engine fittings bought from firms who specialise such things), also Railway Carriage, and so on, and any Forgings purchased as distinct from those produced in our own forge. The total of these three columns equals the Engineering Department column in the Purchase Journal, which column is debited in total to Engineering Purchases Account in the Impersonal Ledger. The next column—Forgings ex Smiths' Shop—is posted from the Forge Production Book (Form H), exactly the same as the iron castings, and the next column (Patterns) is posted from the Pattern Shop Production Book, an identical book to that shown by Forms H and I, the treatment in posting being in each case the same.

(To be continued.)

The Chartered Accountants Students' Society of Kingston-upon-Hull.

Hints to Students in devising Systems of Engineers' Cost Accounts.

By John B. Bardsley.

(*Concluded from page* 1061.)

Referring again to the Castings and Forgings columns, there are other reasons than those for facilitating accuracy and proof of agreement in bookkeeping for keeping these records apart. At the completion of a contract an analysis is made of the separate total weights of iron, brass, and steel castings, and iron and steel forgings, so that when the total cost of any contract is analysed and transposed in the book devoted to finished costs an indication is given which shows that for such and such a type of engine or engine part so much of each description of castings or forgings was required; and when cross indexed to the book wherein are aggregated the history of costs of individual parts, such as cylinders, valve boxes, pistons and piston rods, connecting rods, cross-heads, crank shafts, and so on, a useful guide is afforded for checking estimates. The total weight of iron and steel castings and/or forgings in any engine divided into the total contract price gives an idea of the cost per ton on finished weight of such engine or machine. Sometimes, after completing a detailed estimate calculated as carefully as possible, the weight per ton on estimated finished weight is no mean guide as to accuracy in the estimated cost, especially as in many complicated engines and machines important parts which may be duplicated or triplicated in building the engine are reckoned separately in estimating, and sometimes the estimate for one such part might be included alone, when really it should be multiplied by two or three. The value therefore of this apparently rough guide is not to be despised, and is an additional reason for sub-division of castings and forgings.

We have now got as far in our consideration of this Materials Cost Ledger as the last detail column—viz., Goods *ex* Store.

Store.

It is a very important matter for accountants in devising a system of Cost Accounts to provide for a reliable arrangement governing the issue of goods *ex* store. In themselves the items are small and sometimes look insignificant, but in twelve months the aggregate astonishes one, and if no reliable method is pursued the discrepancy at stocktaking time may be great, though where no good system is in vogue the evil effects are not immediately apparent. In dealing with the store I will only take notice of those books which directly affect our Financial and Cost Books, as we are not considering every detail of works management. From the Purchase Journal you find that the total of each month's purchases for store is debited in the Impersonal Ledger to Store Account, and an entry is made when goods are received in the Stores Inward Book (Form E). Each item is here detailed in full as to the nature of the goods, and the total of this book agrees with the total of Store Account debit in the Impersonal Ledger, less, of course, any stock at the commencement. As regards withdrawals from Store, no goods of any description should be delivered by the store-keeper, excepting upon the presentation of an official slip—series numbered and lettered—showing the department of origin, and signed by the foreman of the shop or chargeman of the job. This slip bears the order number of the job, and shows clearly the subject of the requisition. These slips are taken charge of by the cost clerks each morning, and entered at once into the Stores Outward Books—either Form F or G—one book being for all departmental debits, the other for "Direct Supplies" for orders passing through the works, and it is the items contained in this latter book which are posted to this "Goods *ex* Store" column in the Materials Cost Ledger. The items in the Departmental Stores Outward Book are also posted to the Cost Ledger, as accounts are opened in the Cost Ledger for each department (sub-divided to show (1) all Shop Expenses of working the Department, (2) Repairs to and Maintenance of Plant and Machinery, (3) all Building Repairs, and (4) Capital Extensions, including labour charges incurred in getting new machinery fixed and into working order), and the monthly totals are posted to the corresponding account in the Impersonal Ledger.

I need not point out the great value of these detailed accounts of Shop Expenses and Repairs, Capital Extensions, and so on. At the end of any financial period they are most useful, should any question arise on making comparisons with previous financial periods under any particular heading of expense; and, further, should any question arise as to the propriety of any amount representing additional capital expenditure during the period. A reference to these accounts gives the whole detail of Wages and Materials expended for Repairs, Renewals, and Extensions during the financial period, but beyond this the monthly comparison of these expenses (at all events all items of expenditure on Revenue Account) with the amount set aside in the Cost Accounts to cover such charges is invaluable.

Referring again for a few minutes to the Pattern column, the cost of patterns ought to be carefully ascertained, because pattern-making is frequently a heavy item of cost. In some places patterns can be used over and over again, and the cost may then be spread over a period, as long, in fact, as the pattern is usable. In others the first cost is debited ruthlessly to the order for which it is made, and nothing is added to Capital Expenditure in respect of such patterns. I need hardly say to an audience of accountants that any addition to the asset "Patterns and Drawings" should be very rigorously watched. Nothing is so hard to value, excepting perhaps goodwill. In any place where the product is standardised, or repetition work, patterns have a more definite value as compared with another where every fresh order differs, and where it frequently happens that a particular pattern is never used again. The timber, or some of it, may in some cases be used again for other patterns, and so reduce the cost of such patterns. Don't imagine, however, that patterns have not a real value, but it is difficult to appraise. It ranges from firewood value upwards. In any case, where you have to deal with such an expense and such a possible addition to capital expenditure, see that pattern costs are accurately obtained, and also see whether the patterns are likely to be used again or not, as it will guide you in deciding the propriety of treating any portion of pattern costs as an asset.

This brings us to the end of our consideration of the Engineering Department Cost Book and its subsidiary books, at least such consideration as we can give to the subject to-night. I have not made any reference to the detailed costs of the Boiler Works, and I am afraid I cannot do so now, as I wish to make a few remarks on Foundry Costs, which are more intricate than Boiler Works Costs, and I have also still to deal with Establishment Charges. I may say, however, in a sentence that the Boiler Works Costs are as simple as any we have yet touched upon. The time is taken and dealt with, and wages abstracted and posted to the contract affected in the Cost Ledger, and Direct Purchases come through the Journal, and Goods *ex* Store through a Stores Book, and a percentage on Wages or a Time Charge per hour is added to prime cost to cover incidental expenses. All this is simple and straightforward, and the Ledger (a loose leaf one) is posted and abstracted exactly as described in considering the Engineering Department Costs. These costs, therefore, hold nothing out of the ordinary character, and need not detain us. Foundry Costs, however, are somewhat more intricate, and deserve a few words to themselves. You will by now have gathered, from seeing the ruling of the Foundry Day Book, and from the remarks I made explanatory of the use of this book, that the system of Foundry Costs there illustrated is that of ascertaining the exact prime cost of each casting in wages—viz., moulding, plus Cupola Costs (which include cost of metal and fuel used), and the addition of a percentage on moulders' wages to cover the Indirect Expenses or Establishment Charges. The foundry is, as I told you early on, really a branch of the Engineering Department, and all the Foundry Product is taken over by that department at cost—*i.e.*, prime cost, plus a percentage to cover incidentals. Our foundry work is mostly on large, heavy, and frequently very intricate castings, and there is little or no repetition work, except grate-bars and such-like work for the Boiler Department. Thus, the endeavour is to get at the cost of each casting, whatever its size or nature, but in order to check this cost a monthly aggregate Cost Account is made out, and this is compared with the Day Book total for the month, and any variation is investigated. Again, each half-year a general stocktaking is had, and a further proof is afforded as to the accuracy of the separate costs, and also of the correctness of the stocks of pig iron, scrap, and other material. These monthly and half-yearly proofs are essential to accurate Foundry Costs, and they demonstrate the sufficiency or otherwise of the percentage added to cover Indirect Expenses, which always form a large proportion of Foundry Costs. Now, you see by the Foundry Time Book how each moulder's time is taken In this book each moulder has a Time Account, and his time is abstracted on to the Moulders' Sheets, according to the number of orders he has worked upon, each order having as many sheets as needful, all being kept in a Loose Leaf Ledger. Thus the moulding wages expended on each casting are ascertained, and a percentage added to cover Establishment Charges. As regards material, the Cupola foreman keeps a record, and sees that all material going into the cupolas is weighed, and from his daily returns a book is made up by the foundry clerk, showing the exact weight of foundry pig, scrap iron, hæmatite, limestone, cold blast iron, &c., put into each blow. A percentage varying from 4 per cent to 10 per cent. (according to the material used, some pig iron being very dirty) is allowed for waste, and a rate per ton charged for coke used in melting the charge, and for the wages of cupola men and upkeep of cupolas, &c. This rate is based upon experience, and is tested as to results, exactly as all other estimated rates—viz., by keeping Separate Wages and Repair and Coke and Limestone Accounts for the cupolas, and dividing the total of these accounts by total weight of iron melted. From this Cupola Book you will see that you get the amount of metal put into cupola, and the Weight column shows the credit to Pig Iron Stock for metal used. After a casting is lifted out of the sand it is weighed, and the process called fettling or cleaning up the casting is carried out, and then the finished casting is weighed. Thus you have three weights, and are able to check loss in melting per ton, also in fettling, and to reckon your cost per cwt. or ton on the finished weight. The casting is then turned over to the Engineering Department. Now this is all straightforward so far. But there are one or two problems out of the ordinary in Foundry Costs. Before or after a casting goes into the machine shop it may be found to be what is called a "waster," and has to be re-made. Thus there is a dead loss of all wages, fuel, &c., expended on that casting, and if the flaw be not discovered in the foundry, but comes to light in the machine shop after more or less labour has been expended on it in machining, the loss would be increased, so that the foundry has to replace the casting at its own expense, and the machine shop has to bear the loss of wages, &c., in machining as far as it has gone. The foundry, however, gets the metal back, and with a very small addition of new metal the waster casting can be used again by remelting and remoulding. But you naturally ask how the Cost Accounts are concerned, and what is done with the waster casting therein. You will notice one or two considerations to be dealt with in the circumstances I mention. You have to take care that your Stock Account is not deranged by again crediting the weight of the remelted waster through the Cupola Book to Pig Iron Account, unless you had first debited the same, and as this would involve useless labour I deprecate such a course. Then another consideration is, where to debit the cost of replacing the waster—*i.e.*, the further cost of moulding, melting, and all the other descriptions of foundry service which each casting requires. There are several ways of dealing with the various questions which arise, but I think the one which secures all essentials, and at the same time requires the minimum of labour and friction is as follows:—Allow the original cost of the waster to stand in the Cost Books against the contract (including the cost of any machining or fitting, if any incurred), and ignore the cost of material in replacing the waster, debiting only the exact wages cost, plus percentage for Establishment Charges, and charge this up to the contract affected, keeping, however, a Memorandum Account of all wasters, so as to see at any time the average percentage of wasters to sound castings. This percentage of wasters is then considered in any estimate for castings, but a special note made in the contract concerned against the cost of replacing a waster prevents such cost being included in a future estimate for a similar casting, maintaining at the same time the principle of making each contract responsible for its own disasters. Castings will occasionally turn out wasters, despite all the care and skill bestowed on every part of their production. By these means you prevent your Stock Account being deranged, you debit the loss on the waster to the contract for which it was made, and you have an account of all wasters for future guidance, and all this obtained by as little extra labour or friction in the Cost Accounts themselves as is possible. But there is one other feature in foundry work to which I must briefly refer as affecting stocks, and that is the boxes and plates which are used in making some castings, and which are made in the foundry for its own use. Now, when first made, these boxes and plates might be debited to Foundry Loose Plant Account at cost, and, once in existence, they may be used over and over again for many castings, or it may happen that they are only used once —viz., for the particular casting for which they were made —and are then broken up and remelted to make other boxes and plates. Thus you can easily see that not only will your stock of boxes and plates, as part of loose plant, vary from week to week, but your stocks of pig iron are likely to be affected by repeated credits from the Cupola Book, unless, as I mentioned in discussing waster castings, you debit the old boxes and plates as old metal to the stock when broken up and remelted, or ignore the cost of *material* in *new* boxes and plates. I think the easiest and most practical method, keeping in view only essentials, is by taking the exact weight of all boxes and plates at any stocktaking period, and then onwards until the next stocktaking by ignoring the cost of *metal only* in new boxes and plates, but debiting the labour cost and percentage of Indirect Charges to the contract for which the new boxes and/or plates may be required, and then at the following stocktaking period again weighing all boxes and plates on hand and debiting or crediting Pig Iron Stock Account by the amount of any decrease or increase found as compared with the previous period. This method may be attacked by theorists as too rule of thumb. I could easily show you its possible weaknesses myself, but I want to show you direct practical methods which, whilst causing the minimum of friction and labour in the foundry, attain at the same time as many of the desiderata of the thorough-going accountant as is possible in every-day workshop life.

I cannot go further into those questions affecting Foundry Costs, which I should have to deal with if I were giving you a complete scheme of Cost Accounts. I have, however, selected the one or two features in foundry work just dwelt upon, because to keep accurate costs you must have accurate Stock Accounts; and to keep an accurate Stock Account or Accounts of Foundry Materials, you must deal effectively in some manner with the waster question, and also that of boxes and plates broken up an remelted. Hence these few hints, which, I hope, may whet your appetite for further knowledge regarding an interesting branch of accountancy, as Foundry Costs are a study in themselves.

Establishment Charges.

We cannot do much more, I am afraid, then examine the broad outlines of this section, but I will try to show you as briefly as I can what to look for and aim at.

You know, of course, that these charges are those expenses of a manufacturing concern which cannot be allocated to any particular order, and therefore must be spread over the entire production of any given period at some arbitrary ratio. It is easy enough at the end of any financial period to ascertain the ratio of these expenses to the turnover, or to the wages paid, and it is upon the experience gained in one financial period that the arbitrary ratio to which I have referred is based. So, you will see, the problem you have to face at the beginning of any financial period may be stated as follows—viz., At what ratio and upon what valuation may I compute and levy upon the work passing through the various shops a "rate in aid" which shall at the end of the financial period have allocated fairly to the work done therein a sum equal to the Indirect Expenses incurred in the said period? The proposition is easily stated, but by the time you can write "Q.E.D." at the foot of it you will know that it is a really difficult one to solve if faithfully dealt with.

From the forms I have already shown to you earlier on, and from my remarks thereon, you will have gathered the main headings under which I prefer to divide these charges. My principle in dealing with them is, in brief, to avoid in every way lumping items of expense together which are capable of segregation. Do not have a great "Sundries" Account. It degenerates in the hands of even fairly conscientious bookkeepers into a mere *cloaca maxima*, through which any amount of increase in expenditure may escape notice. Much rather, I say, go to the other extreme, and use "hair dividers" in your analyses. I advocate, therefore, opening accounts for every expense which can be included under a representative heading, and in minute detail, in order that any alteration in such expense cannot fail to attract attention. The next essential is to provide for the equitable incidence of these expenses upon the various departments of the works. Upon these two essentials—viz., (*a*) the amount of, or fluctuations in, each kind of Indirect Expense; and (*b*) the separate incidence of each expense upon each part of the works—depends half the value of accurate cost keeping to the responsible manager or managing director. I need say no more concerning the first essential, but in regard to the second—viz., the incidence of these charges upon the various parts of the works—I want to draw your attention to several questions which arise in carrying out the "taxation" or "rating" of each shop. In the first place, you may divide Establishment Charges as a whole into three divisions—viz., (1) Charges which can be debited at once to the department affected (although not to individual contracts)—such as Foremen's and Labourers' Wages, Lighting, Heating, Motive Power, Repairs and Renewals, Depreciation of the Machinery and Plant in a particular shop, Oil, Waste, and all such stores used in a particular shop; (2) charges which cannot be debited to departments singly, but which have to be borne rateably by all—such as Salaries, Directors' and Auditors' Fees, Rents, Rates, Taxes, Insurance, Petty Cash Expenses, Office Expenses, Time Keeper's and Storekeeper's Wages, Stable Expenses, Interest, Travelling Expenses, Postage, Telegrams, Telephone, and so on; and (3) exceptional administrative expenses of any kind which it would be unfair and misleading to debit against any one or two of the departments, and which, in fact, have to come out of the profits of the place as a whole. In some places part of the expenses I have enumerated under (1) might come under (2) particularly Light, Heat, and Motive Power, but electric lighting and driving and meters placed in each department enable these expenses to be divided up in some places with accuracy. But this does not affect the principle, which is endeavouring to arrange your Indirect Charges so that you can ascertain, firstly, true shop cost of any order; secondly, finished cost; thirdly, be able to see the ratio of (3) expenses to your total net profits, or turnover of the whole place. It is not an easy thing, as you will find, to arrange the incidence of the Indirect Charges in section (2) equitably. And yet the endeavour must be made, and you must also be ready to alter whatever arrangements you do make, where from time to time changes in the manner of working the place render elasticity in your methods desirable. You must never lose sight of the end towards which you are struggling in allocating these Indirect Expenses to departments. It is not sufficient merely to say that for any period you have covered by your added percentage the sum total of Establishment Charges. What you are primarily trying to do in covering these charges is ascertaining as nearly as is humanly possible the cost of each order or contract progressing through the works under each heading of expense, so as to show true results in profit or loss on each contract, and also provide reliable data for future estimates. Careful consideration, therefore, is necessary of every Expense Account in the Ledger, and its connection with each of the principal departments and the total of each such account must then be divided up according to the results of your investigation. You can easily perceive, however, that, as your base is a shifting one, you must always be examining it, in case a revision of the mode of charging the Indirect Expenses should prove essential.

You see, therefore, in my division of these Establishment Charges the 1st division items are debited straight away to the Departmental Account affected; and as regards No. 2 division, the items are separately considered, and a certain ratio debited to each department; and the 3rd division items (if any) are separately dealt with apart from Departmental Accounts—*i.e.*, they would form a debit to General Profit and Loss Account. Having determined, therefore, in what proportions the various departments shall contribute to this No. 2 division of the Establishment Charges, you have to go forward and determine how you will proceed in debiting to the orders passing through the shops that portion of the Departmental share which will as nearly as possible represent true cost to that order of such Departmental Expenses. There are several methods. Some favour a simple division of the entire charges, based upon wages and/or materials cost turnover. This is done at the close of any financial period, and affords no guide during the period as to whether the charges are being covered or not. Some other places favour an added percentage on wages and material in the Cost Ledger, and others calculate a percentage on hours worked, and yet a further method is that of a machine rating calculated at per hour and at a fixed price upon all work done on machines. There is naturally a pro and con to each method, and in determining your procedure you must, by a study of the *locus in quo*, conclude which it is best for you to adopt. I find I have to use two or three of these methods. In the Foundry, Boiler Shop, Pattern Shop, and Fitting Shop a percentage on wages is used, also in the Smiths' Shop, with the addition there of a time charge for fires to cover fuel expended, but in the Machine Shop a rating is used varying with the size and nature of the machine. There are critics of each of these methods, and differences of opinion even as to the most correct method of charging your machine rating, and so you will find that whatever you determine upon will be much in the nature of a compromise, and will be dependent upon local conditions. Let us look, however, for a moment at the machine rating method. Of late years the increased use of powerful, expensive, and ingenious machine tools, superseding as they do very largely what used to be skilled handicraft, causes this question of machine rating to receive more attention. The root idea of this rating is that of treating the machine as an account, debiting it with interest on Capital Cost, Depreciation, Upkeep, Oil, Tool Repairs, and a proportion of rent for ground space and building and so on, and crediting the agreed rate per hour for all time worked, which amount, of course, is debited to the job or contract, the result showing the profit or loss on the work done by the machine. I must confess that, personally, I have not yet gone in for statistical luxuries, such as the first part of this method viz., keeping an account current with each machine. In a new place you have a chance of commencing such a system; in an old one the chance is remote, and the advantage sometimes open to question. So that, leaving out the question of a *Dr.* and *Cr.* Account with each machine, the method of debiting the Cost Account with an agreed machine rating, varying with the size and nature of the machine, is a good and reliable method. Moreover, every practical purpose achieved by the first and most elaborate method is equally served by the shortened one. You get in the aggregate every one of the debits to the machines as a whole which I detailed, without the trouble of separate accounts, and your Shop Costs do not suffer in any way at all. One reason given by some engineers in favour of these separate Machine Accounts is that it enables them to vary the depreciation rate, which rate does naturally vary with the character of the machine, whether it runs double-shift or at accelerated speed and so on, and, of course, it enables them in a measure to make provision in their depreciation for obsolescence of any particular machine. There is no subject upon which engineers wax so contemptuously eloquent as the one rate of depreciation upon which the professional accountant depends. But the difference between the two methods is, as you will know, more apparent than real, and it is results which, after all, test both. The engineer is apt to overlook the fact that however depreciation rates may vary, and however quickly some machines live their lives and pass untimely to the scrap heap, that all these different rates are capable of expression in a single rate over a given period, and that rate is the one at which the accountant aims. Therefore where you are unable for any reason to go in for the elaboration referred to, and are compelled to simplify, I say you may use the machine rating in your Cost Accounts as the "rate in aid" of the Incidentals, allowing all Depreciation and so on to fall into the Incidentals Account, and apportioning the total of that account over the various departments. The rate charged may or may not at the end of any given period approximate with accuracy to that figure which, multiplied by the number of hours worked annually, will equal the sum of Interest, Depreciation, Upkeep, Rent, Service, and so on, chargeable against the machine shop. But supposing it should fall short, are you therefore at liberty to raise the rate merely to cover the Incidentals, and thus get the total expense and the total rate in aid to agree? I have said once or twice your Cost Accounts are not merely for the purpose of proving whether profit or loss has accrued on any one order or over a given period. When a cost is ascertained it is summarised and cross indexed in various ways as a basis for future estimates, when similar parts or whole contracts have to be tendered for. If, therefore, you increase your machine rating simply to be able to say the charges have been covered, you may cause future estimates to be so far out of the running as against other firms as to lose the contract for which you are tendering. But you may say, "What is the use of a contract taken at a loss?" I reply, your machine rating cannot safely exceed the price at which you could get similar machining done outside your works. Therefore, if at that said rating you cannot make a profit, the cause of this condition of affairs must be looked for, and not glossed over by the misleading course of an increase in rate. Moreover, if your machine rate is no higher than the price at which an outsider would do the work, it must in some degree be based upon the annual cost of upkeep referred to, even allowing for the differing percentages of Standing Charges in different works. So that either your cost of Upkeep is too great (where a loss is shown by the Trading Account), or the general administrative charges are excessive or abnormal, or the shop may not be worked to its full capacity (from shortness of work or other causes, thus making the percentage of Incidentals a high one), or some other influence is at work, and must be looked for and removed in order to better the trading results. Thus you must look upon your Cost Accounts as a valuable guide and mentor, and not smother the mentor in the ample folds of an increased rating for being a candid friend.

Nothing will do in these cases but a study of each individual case. What you are aiming at is that mathematically perfect ratio which will apportion to each order its proper share of the known and unknown charges; and though you will never reach this mathematical ideal, you must always keep it in view, and let it be your constant aim. Where machine work is the work to be charged, the rating, in my opinion, is the best system to use, and as regards the differences which exist amongst works' managers concerning the percentage on wages or a time rate per hour worked, I consider the time rate the nearer approach to an equitable arrangement as between one contract and another than the percentage on wages, but for various reasons I use all three. You will find in your study of these questions differences of opinion, even as to methods of making a machine rating or time charge, but into these differences we cannot now enter. Briefly recapitulating the whole subject, I feel that I have only dealt in a very superficial manner with the salient points raised, but it is such a complex problem that if I have given any of you an insight only into the underlying principles of Cost Accounts I shall feel satisfied. I have not given you a complete system of Cost Accounts, but I trust you will consider that I have sufficiently sketched the outlines so as to enable expert account keepers like yourselves to fill in the details necessary to completion. You may probably conclude that there is a lot of work for the accountant or chief bookkeeper, whichever you like to call him, and you will be right. There is no royal road to accuracy and complete efficiency in Cost Accounts. It is a plodder's road all the way, and you have to go every inch of it to gain the full reward. Remember also that no system will work itself, and being dependent upon human instruments, many of whom imperfectly realise the part they have to play in ensuring sound results, and very few of whom can really see a system as a whole, constant supervision and regular proof at convenient intervals will be essential to counteract a natural tendency to error. To use the motto of a very successful American magnate, you have to "Organise, deputise, criticise," and you will find great scope for all three faculties, particularly the latter. But in your "organising" don't be trammelled by text-books or other people's systems. There is no chance in the present day for anything unprogressive. In many professions, and particularly, I think, in accountancy, a wise empiricism is to be encouraged—that is to say, the best technical knowledge guided by wide experience. We can learn some lessons in this respect from our American cousins, but although I admit to the full the excellence of many ideas we get from them, I have no sympathy whatever with the cry that our ways will have to be "Americanised." We possess ability, I think, in engineering and accountancy, and in all other subjects, fully equal to theirs, and all we want is to give that ability free play, clearing the obstacle of "precedent" from our path. Although the greater part of what we hear and read concerning the excellence of American talent as compared with English is mere "natural gas," for which the States are so renowned in more senses than one, we do find their guiding principle is to seek for better and still better methods; and in the strenuous future before both engineers and accountants you must bear a strenuous part, and ever bring fresh ideas and improved methods to bear upon the problems of accountancy with which you are sure to meet in your professional life.

Form A.—

Dr. CASH JOURNAL. *Cr.*

Date	Bank	Cash	Purchases Ledger	Impersonal Ledger	Discount	Ledger Folio	Name of Debit Account	Vouch'r No.	Name of Credit Account	Ledger Folio	Discount	Impersonal Ledger	Sales Ledger	Cash	Bank
	£ s d	£ s d	£ s d	£ s d	£ s d						£ s d	£ s d	£ s d	£ s d	£ s d

Form B.—

PETTY CASH—ANALYSIS OF DEBITS.

Cash Received	Date	Details of Payment	Voucher No. or Initial	Total	Foundry	Engineering	Forge	Pattern Shop	Boiler Dept.	Sundry Accounts		Cost Ledger		
										£ s d	Fol.	Order No.	Fol.	
£ s d				£ s d	£ s d	£ s d	£ s d	£ s d	£ s d					£ s d

Form C.— ESTABLISHMENT CHARGES.

MEMORANDUM ACCOUNT.

Date	Description of Expenses & Remarks	Ref. Fol.	Jan.	Feb.	March	April	May	June	July	August	Sept.	Oct.	Nov.	Dec.	Totals
			£ s d	£ s d	£ s d	£ s d	£ s d	£ s d	£ s d	£ s d	£ s d	£ s d	£ s d	£ s d	£ s d

Form D.—

PURCHASE JOURNAL. ANALYSIS OF DEBITS.

Date	Invoice No.	Name of Suppliers	Description of Goods	Weight or Quantity				Detail	Total Credit	Folio Purchases Ledger	Iron Foundry	Brass Foundry	Forge	Pattern Shop	Store	Sundries see Analysis Journal	Cost Ledgers		
																	Engineering	Order No.	Boiler Works
				T.	C.	Q.	L.	£ s d	£ s d		£ s d	£ s d	£ s d	£ s d	£ s d	£ s d	£ s d		£ s d

Form D 1.—

SUNDRIES ANALYSIS JOURNAL.

Date	Invoice No.	Supplier's Name	Description	Quantities and Weight		Coal and Coke							* Stable Expenses		
						Total of Coal and Coke	Fitting Shop	Smiths' Shop	Foundry	Brass Foundry	Machine Shops	Boiler Works	Hay, Corn, &c.	Shoeing, Harness, Repairs, &c.	Veterinary and General
				T. C. Q. lbs.	£ s d	£ s d	£ s d	£ s d	£ s d	£ s d	£ s d	£ s d	£ s d	£ s d	£ s d

Repairs to Buildings, &c.						Machinery and Plant Maintenance and Repairs						Books and Stationery		Drawing Office	Electric Department	
Fitting Shop, &c.	Smiths' Shop	Foundry, &c.	Pattern Shop	Boiler Works	Offices	Fitting Shop	Smiths' Shop	Foundry	Pattern Shop	Machine Shops	Boiler Works	General	Boiler Works	Materials	Purchases of Fittings, &c.	Gas and Water
£ s d	£ s d	£ s d	£ s d	£ s d	£ s d	£ s d	£ s d	£ s d	£ s d	£ s d	£ s d	£ s d	£ s d	£ s d	£ s d	£ s d

* Carriage and Freight.						Advertising			Miscellaneous					Capital Expenditure		
Engineering	Smiths' Shop	Foundry	Brass Foundry	Steel Department	Boiler Works	Sundry	Engineering	Boiler Works	Engineering	Foundry	Smiths' Pattern Shops	Yard and Office	Boiler Works	Description	Imp. Ledger Folio	
£ s d	£ s d	£ s d	£ s d	£ s d	£ s d	£ s d	£ s d	£ s d	£ s d	£ s d	£ s d	£ s d	£ s d			£ s d

*The columns between the two asterisks form a small inset in every opening of the book, which is cut half the width of a page, so that the Date, Suppliers' Name, Quantities, and Weight can be seen.

Form E.—

STORES INWARDS.

Date	Invoice No.	Quantity	Description	Weight	Price	
						£ s d

Form F.—

STORES OUTWARDS.—DIRECT CHARGES.

Date	Foreman's Requisition No.	Order No.	Description	Quantity	Weight	Price		Folio Cost Ledger
					T C Q lbs.		£ s d	

Form G.—

STORES OUTWARDS.

DEPARTMENTAL CHARGES.

Date	Foreman's Requisition No.	Description	Quantity	Weight	Price	Foundry	Engineering	Forge	Pattern Shop	Boiler Department	Sundry Accts.	Led. Folio
				T. C. Q. lbs.	£ s d	£ s d	£ s d	£ s d	£ s d	£ s d	£ s d	

Form H.— SMITHS' SHOP OR FORGE PRODUCTION BOOK.

Week ending ....

Order No.	Description	Finished Weight of Forgings	Rate	Cost of Material	Smiths' and Strikers' Wages	Incidentals added	Cost per Cwt.	Total Cost	Cost Ledger Folio
				£ s d	£ s d	£ s d	£ s d	£ s d	

Form I.—

Order	Description	Finished Weight of Castings	Cupola Cost of Metal per Ton	Metal Melting and Cupola Men's Wages	Wages Moulding	Incidentals added	Rate Cost per Ton	Total Cost	Folio
	Brought forward		£ s d	£ s d	£ s d	£ s d		£ s d	

Form J.—

Name.........................

Description of Contract......................

Contract No ....

Date	Description	Ref. Folio	Wages					Incidentals				Wages Total	Incidentals Total	Materials Total	Grand Total
			Draughtsmen	Fitters	Packing and Fixing	Carters and Labour'rs	Machinists	Hrs	Mach'n.	Machine Charge	Percentage on Wages				
			£ s d	£ s d	£ s d	£ s d	£ s d			£ s d	£ s d	£ s d	£ s d	£ s d	£ s d

Form K.—

Name.. *Description of Contract*..

Contract No. ....

Date	Description of Goods, &c.	Ref. Fo.	Invoice No.	Quantity	Weight	Castings: Iron	Castings: Brass	Steel (Direct Purchases, see Purchase Journal)	Sundries (Direct Purchases, see Purchase Journal)	Forgings: Purchas'd (Direct Purchases, see Purchase Journal)	Forgings: Ex. Smiths' Shop	Patterns	Goods Ex. Store	Total of Materials	Transferred to Cost Ledger Fo.
					T. C. Q. lbs.	£ s d	£ s d	£ s d	£ s d	£ s d	£ s d	£ s d	£ s d	£ s d	

Form L.—

Name..........................

Number........ *Occupation*.............. ....

Order No.	Description	F.	S.	M.	T.	W.	T.	Total Hours	Rate		Ref. Folio
										£ s d	

Form M.—

Week ending..........................

Check No.	Name	Order No.	Drawings No.	Description		F.	S.	M.	T.	W.	T.	Total Hours

* **Form N.—**

Week ending..

Check No.	Name	Order No.	Description	F.	S.	M.	T.	W.	T.	Total Hours	Weight

See note on Form O.

Form O.—

Name.. *Order No*............

....

Date	No. of Smith and Striker	Hours	Rate		Weight	Description of Material	Rate		Total
				£ s d	Cwt. Qrs. lbs.			£ s d	£ s d

* NOTE.—Forms " N " and " O " are Forge Time Book form, and Smiths' form for Cost of Forgings, and as the course of procedure is exactly as for Iron Foundry, no specific mention of these forms is made in the text.

Form P.—

Date..........................190 *off*

Order No.................... *Drawing No*..............

Name ....

Date	Name of Moulder	Hours	Rate		Date	Name of Moulder	Hours	Rate	
				£ s d					£ s d

The Cost Accounts of Small Manufacturers.

IN our issue of the 9th ult. we printed a paper on the above subject, read by Mr. M. WEBSTER JENKINSON, A.C.A., at several meetings of Chartered Accountants Students' Societies during the months of February and March, and we may mention that this paper has since been published in book form by Messrs. GEE & Co., price one shilling. It is thus readily available for the use of those who may have occasion to refer to it, and we venture to think that these are likely to be a somewhat numerous body, bearing in mind the importance of the subject and the manner in which it has been handled.

In dealing with an audience of accountant students, the lecturer was undoubtedly wise in drawing somewhat prominent attention to the futility of relying upon theory alone for the evolution of a system of Cost Accounts suitable to any particular undertaking. It is worth while to bear in mind, however, that the converse holds equally good—that is to say, the practical manufacturer cannot hope to evolve a satisfactory system of costing without the aid of theory. The point is the more worth bearing in mind in that, of the numerous inefficient so-called systems of Cost Accounts in existence, by far the larger number have been evolved by practical manufacturers without the aid of professional accountants, and without regard to the principles of accounting or the necessity of so arranging the accounts as to make them to the largest possible extent self-checking. Of late there is evidence that manufacturers in this country are awakening to some appreciation of the fact that they are at a disadvantage because their accounting methods are not up to date. They do not, however, appear even yet to have realised that, although no wise accountant will attempt to devise a system of costing without first very carefully considering all the practical circumstances of its environment, costing systems are, nevertheless, a department of accounting upon which professional assistance is absolutely necessary, if satisfactory results are to be achieved. Until it is really understood that economy of expenditure increases net profits just as directly as does an enlargement of output, this state of affairs is likely to continue.

For these reasons we do not at all agree with Mr. JENKINSON's statement that the most ignorant manufacturer knows more about costing in his own business than any average Chartered Accountant, and we are convinced that that would not be the experience of the average practitioner. A good many manufacturers think they know all about costing, but those who have studied their systems in the majority of instances come to the conclusion that in a very large number of cases they are totally unacquainted with even the elements of the subject, and that their ideas are as defective in principle as in matters of detail.

With regard to the system, or rather the alternative systems, suggested by the lecturer, if they are really intended to apply to small manufacturers there is no doubt a good deal to be said in favour of the retention of the old-fashioned method of record in bound books. But in the case of manufacturers transacting a business of medium size, and *à fortiori* in the case of large businesses, the necessity for prompt records almost invariably demands the employment, to the largest possible extent, of Card and Loose-leaf methods of accounting; and as under these circumstances a properly-trained bookkeeping staff ought always to be available, there should be no difficulty in utilising these modern methods to the greatest possible extent. Even, however, when the bound-book system is retained, we would deprecate the use of counterfoil Requisitions, in that the manifold system occupies less time in their actual preparation, and further enables copies in any required number to be obtained in exact facsimile of the original; whereas it is notorious that the entries upon a counterfoil are never an exact copy of the original, but invariably an abbreviation, and not infrequently an incorrect one at that.

Another point upon which we feel constrained to join issue is the statement that the Stores Ledger is quite apart from the cost books, and has nothing to do with the financial books. In a sense, this statement is doubtless correct; but it suggests that stores books, cost books, and financial books are entirely independent of each other, and it is only one step from this to a state of affairs in which they are absolutely incapable of being reconciled with each other. The Stores Ledger is directly subsidiary to the financial books, as providing a continuous and detailed record of movements of materials, amplifying and verifying the Materials Accounts in the financial books. Similarly, the cost records amplify and verify the Trading Account. It would thus be more accurate to regard these two as Departmental Ledgers, capable of being balanced independently of the financial books, and of being controlled by the aid of total accounts kept therein.

On the subject of Oncost, Mr. JENKINSON'S comments are of but limited utility, in that they are obviously confined to specific cases. It cannot be too clearly emphasised that no hard and fast system of apportionment can work equally satisfactorily and produce equally accurate results under all conditions.

The concluding portion of the paper, dealing with the auditor's relations to the Cost Accounts, we regard as being specially valuable, but we think the statement that it is no part of the regular duty of an auditor to check the Cost Accounts is too sweeping. It is the regular duty of an auditor to verify the financial books of an undertaking, to the best of his ability, by the aid of the available material. If it be unnecessary to check the Cost Accounts in detail, it is only for the same reason that it is frequently unnecessary to check the financial accounts in detail--namely, because the accounts have been arranged upon a system that is self-checking, and is capable of being controlled by the aid of total accounts. In this connection, however, it is perhaps worth while to mention that probably one of the chief reasons why manufacturers, as a class, seem to like to withhold Cost Accounts from the cognisance of their accountants, is because by that means they are better enabled to keep Secret Reserves, and the manipulation of Secret Reserves, from the knowledge of their auditors. It has been held that such knowledge cannot legally be withheld from the auditor of a company; and, that being so, there can be little doubt that it is the duty of the company auditor to make himself acquainted with all that the Cost Accounts are capable of telling him. The more the Cost Accounts are systematised, the easier will be his task, and the more efficient the manner in which he is able to discharge his statutory duty. This, again, may possibly explain why in some cases there is a disinclination to systematise these important records.

Some Economic Considerations Bearing on Costing.*

By W. R. HAMILTON, J.P., F.C.A.

A LECTURE delivered to the Northern Chartered Accountants Students' Society, December 8th 1909, and the Leicester Chartered Accountants Students' Society, December 15th 1909.

There is a book which once had a vogue, called "Reading without Tears." Even so would I endeavour to write a paper on "Costing without Forms."

Such a task would be well nigh impossible did I set out to put before you a system of costing which could forthwith be put into operation. But I have no such intention—my more modest design is to endeavour to draw your attention to the place which costing occupies in the general conduct of a business—not from the point of view of the accountant, of the counting-house, or of the factory manager, but from that of the active and responsible proprietor or general manager.

A going concern—a business in actual operation—is a serious affair. On one side it is a unit in the vast total of commercial enterprises which maintain the nation; on the other side, it is the very hub of the universe for the proprietor and his family, and perhaps also for many other families whose breadwinners depend on it for their wages. When you see a business—when you get the inside view which we accountants get—try to get to the heart of it. If it is a successful affair, why is it so, when there are opponents on every side? If it is unsuccessful, why does it go down, while others, not visibly superior, stand or grow larger? You will find it an interesting study, none the less, so that you will not find an answer. "The proper study of mankind is man," said Pope, and man is at least as interesting and as elusive when exercising the function of carrying on a business as in any other capacity. Audit his books, if you can; wind him up, if you must; but always remember that you are dealing with an individual—not a machine.

Why does a man cost? The question seems, and indeed is, elementary. Such a question is exactly the one which a business man should put to himself with regard to any action he takes which involves expenditure of money or energy. I do not mean that a man should examine himself each time he is confronted with the question of the desirability or otherwise of putting a stamp on a letter which is going to the post, and should recall the good reason for affixing one. To stamp postal letters, to see that goods are addressed to the purchaser; these are instances of matters of routine, to be settled once for all. But a man should know all the processes he is responsible for, and should, if questioned about them, be able to say: "I do this or that, because if I did not do so this or "that undesirable consequence would follow, and not only "must the thing be done, but I can find no better way of "doing it than the one I employ." This principle of action, I may say in passing, is as useful for accountants as for other people.

To come back to our question, Why does a man cost? In the main, I take it, for two reasons—to obtain a basis for a selling price, and to satisfy himself that the article he produces is produced at the lowest cost. The two reasons do not necessarily hang together, for selling price may be permanently fixed (a year or two represents permanence in business), like a railway rate or a seat at a theatre, or it may be fixed by a general market price, as

* Copyright by W. R. Hamilton, F.C.A.

in the case of corn or leather; so that costing to obtain a selling price is useless, and yet it may be both possible and desirable to know that the article is being produced at its lowest cost.

Keeping in mind these two aims of costing, the next question is, "What *is* cost?" Subdivisions are many—almost as many as there are authorities to make them—but with two main headings I think all will agree. Every service rendered in the business world, whether or not it takes a concrete form, involves some expense specially attributable to the rendering of it, and also involves some share of the general expense of carrying on the business—of those expenses which would go on irrespective of the rendering of this particular service. On the top of these two items of expense there is, of course, something to be reckoned for profit, and this is an element in costing, but whether or not it is to be called a factor in cost is only a matter of words.

It is in manufacturing businesses that the necessity for costing as an aid to selling price really arises. And I think you will find that it is in such businesses that the accountant is of most value to the commercial community. A normal business (1) earns profit, (2) ascertains the amount so earned, and (3) distributes it. A great deal of our work is necessitated by the complex monetary interests incidental to a modern industrial State, and is concerned largely with ascertaining the profit earned by a concern and its proper distribution. Indeed, strictly speaking, this is the beginning and end of auditing. But in the case of a manufacturing concern, we not only perform these two functions; we also help to earn the profit, or we may help if we know our business, and if our client is wise enough to ask us for what we are able to give, and not for more than that.

I propose to deal therefore with manufacturing concerns alone. A strict definition of the term "manufacturing concern" I cannot give; nor, I think, is it specially necessary to do so—the term is well enough understood by us all for the present purpose. All businesses, manufacturing or otherwise, ought to be carried on at the cheapest rate, and for this purpose accurate records of expenditure should be kept, but not all businesses yield from these records a basis for the selling price of individual articles. Thus careful economy is as necessary in a theatre, or an accountant's office, as in any other profit-making concern, but the records of such economical management afford no information as to the cost of a particular seat, or audit. If you doubt this statement as to auditing, let anyone who starts on his own account ask himself what is the cost price of the first audit he secures?

Again, in the vast industry of distribution, whether wholesale or retail, while costing is vital, yet it is also so simple that it need not detain us. If a trader cannot, unaided, elaborate some method of marking his purchases so as to show their cost price, and cannot make a proper addition to the cost for expenses and profit, he is not likely to remain long in business.

Speaking generally, a manufacturing concern, properly conducted, does all in the way of costing that any other concern does, and something more, and therefore with it alone need we deal.

The elements of cost in such a concern are two—(1) the expense specially attributable to the execution of the particular order, and (2) a share of the general expenses of carrying on the business. There is also, of course, the addition to be made for profit. The term "Prime Cost" is one which is often used, but it has no generally accepted precise meaning. In my opinion the term is best used to express what I have just called the expense specially attributable to the execution of a particular order; for here one is on sure ground, or at least on the least uncertain foothold on the slippery path of costing. Thus the execution of an order for so many hundred dozen pairs of boots involves on the part of the manufacturer a certain expenditure on leather, nails, thread, &c., and also on the wages of the people actually engaged in making these particular boots. The material he may, indeed, take from stock; but as he finds it necessary to keep his stock up to a certain standard, its depletion by reason of this order is one of the factors which cause him to replenish it, and therefore, in effect, he has had to buy stock for this particular order. The expenditure on productive wages is also purely due to this order; had it not been executed he would not have employed the labour. There may be other cost specially attributable to the order. For instance, the use of electricity as a motive force has led to a subdivision of power impossible in the case of steam. Where each machine has its own motor the ascertainment of the power used in driving it is possible; and if a certain amount of electrical power can be earmarked to a particular order, the cost of that power enters into the prime cost. Suppose all this expenditure comes to £100, you have there a known sum which, for the moment, is the specific loss caused by this particular transaction. Of course, the manufacturer temporarily loses this sum, only to gain a greater—the amount for which he sells his boots, which we will suppose is £140.

This cost, specifically attributable to a particular order, is, in my opinion, the true prime cost. It is a sum which (as costing goes) is easily ascertainable and easily explained to any business man, and the idea which it implies is one which is already present in his mind. You get an indication of this in the attitude of mind of a creditor in an insolvency. You will find that he generally regards an offer of 15s. or 16s. per £ as one which "gives him his money back again"—he feels that the expense that the debtor put him to in executing the orders out of which his claim arises is being repaid.

After prime cost comes the share of the expenses of carrying on the manufacture and of selling the product. The expenses vary in character from an expense so closely connected with manufacture as repairs to the machinery to one so obviously a cost of selling as a traveller's salary. But they have two points in common, and for purposes of costing these two are essential attributes. In the first place, they all alike are necessarily incurred in carrying on the business; and, in the second place, they are none of them specially attributable to the execution of any one order.

What is the proportion which these standing expenses bear to prime cost? There is, of course, no exact answer to this question, but probably in most manufacturing concerns they range from one-fourth to one-sixth of the prime cost. At any rate we know that when we speak of standing expenses we refer to an expense very much smaller than prime cost, but yet so large that its proper estimation makes all the difference in the result. It is because standing expenses are small in relation to prime cost that the latter is the basis of costing—because they are so large in relation to the profit that they cannot be neglected.

You will notice that my definition of prime cost is a restricted one. Many people consider that motive power, wear and tear of machinery, and the like purely manufacturing expenses should also be included under this head. But directly this is done one gets away from the approximation to fact which the more restricted definition undoubtedly affords, and enters the region of estimates. To my thinking, to confuse a known amount with an estimate is always dangerous. Let the known cost stand forth clearly *as* known, and then make what estimates you please.

In theory the business of a manufacturer is quite easy. He buys his raw material and engages his labour; he keeps an accurate record of his prime cost on each order; to this prime cost he adds the proper percentage for expenses and for profit; the price thus obtained is the proper selling price, and at this rate the goods are sold. Nothing can be simpler—in theory. In practice he is beset by difficulties at every turn and by temptations at many of them. These you must try in some measure to appreciate, for if you would help a person you must endeavour to put yourself in his place.

It is a mistake to think that any factory goes on without a costing system. The thing is impossible, though it is far from impossible that the system is a bad one. The pressing necessity of living—*i.e.*, of making a profit, or of producing a result which for a time at least is mistaken for a profit—forces sound system on the least systematic of men. So far as my experience goes, all manufacturers have some way of arriving at prime cost. Such methods as are employed, however crude, do not depart materially from fact, or would not do so if only they were tightened up so as to provide for possible dishonesty, and, what is far more to be feared, waste through carelessness.

When a manufacturer, however unsatisfactory his system, tells you that the prime cost of any particular article is £10 he is probably right, to the extent that something very near £10 is what that job ***ought*** to have cost, if his factory had been so well organised that there was no leakage from any cause.

Where the unsystematic manufacturer is likely to go wrong in his costing is in this same leakage, but more particularly in estimating the percentage to be added for expenses. Even with the most systematic of men, there is every excuse for going wrong at this point.

Not only is every manufacturer under the necessity of making his factory pay, but, as a general statement, it is correct to say that all businesses do pay. Exceptions there are, and an accountant whose practice includes a good deal of insolvency work may be pardoned if he give undue weight to them. Even so may a detective overestimate the criminality of the population he lives amidst, or a doctor the disease. But in the main, and taking perhaps a longer period than a year as the standard, businesses pay. In other words, the world's work is done. But this fact, comforting though it may be to the onlooker, is of small consolation to the individual manufacturer, who is concerned first and last with his own little corner of the commercial world. There is no law which compels *his* business to pay, and he must fight for his existence. To be successful it is one requirement that he must produce as cheaply as possible, and must call to his assistance in his factory organisation every aid he can obtain.

Not only must the manufacturer produce cheaply; he must also sell cheaply. His natural desire to reduce the cost of production is one which is not necessarily the outcome of competition; for even were there no competition, he would still find it to his interest to reduce cost and thus increase profit. But where the business is competitive the desire for reduced cost is much quickened by the necessity for keeping abreast of rivals—for getting a little ahead of them, if possible. The principal weapon he can use in this warfare is that of price, assuming, of course, that quality is equal. If his price is equal to that of competitors he has a chance; if lower, a good chance. Other factors count such as the personality of the proprietor and his staff, a reputation for prompt delivery, and for delivering goods about the quality of which there will be no doubt. The length of credit given also counts, but that is almost wholly a question of price; the longer the credit the lower is the real price.

That which tells, then, in competitive selling is, first and foremost, *price*. In fixing a price any one manufacturer is working in the dark, so far as concerns his competitors. He generally has a very fair idea of the organisation and working of other similar factories in his neighbourhood, or even of those in his own country; but this avails him little, for he does not know the intimate details which make the difference between success and failure. Still less does he know the financial position of his rivals, unless they are public companies. Even then, as auditors know, there is sometimes more to be learned about a company than the Balance Sheet discloses! What he does know is that the article which he makes is being offered by B. at a certain price, and that he, A., must accept that price or go without work for his factory. It may happen that B. is the most careless of men, who, while thinking he is asking a remunerative price, is in reality selling below his actual cost. Or it may happen that B.'s plant is new while A.'s is old. Or that B. is deliberately selling at a low rate in a desperate endeavour to keep his head above water. Whatever the reason, the result is the same; the buyer asks no questions, but goes where he can buy most cheaply, and A. must conform to this or cease to do business.

Again, it may happen that the time is one of those when trade is depressed all over the world, or in a particular country or neighbourhood owing to some local circumstances. Or his particular trade may be depressed owing to change in demand. This alteration in demand is always going on. I suppose there is never a time when some trade is not depressed for this reason. I do not refer only to fashion changes, such as changes in personal attire. I mean the constantly fluctuating demand due partly to gradual changes in national habit as evidenced by the expenditure, begun within quite recent years, on electric tramways, motor cars, golf, cycles, holidays, &c., and partly to the enormous increase in proprietary articles of daily use. In my young days tea was tea; now one is urged by flaming posters to try A.'s tea, or B.'s, or C.'s. So with a hundred other things—always the same pressure on the public to change from one maker to another.

All these changes must be responded to by the manufacturer. Some way or other he must keep going—*i.e.*, he must continue to make a profit. He may perhaps have to reorganise his factory, to scrap his machinery, to find a new market, or to create a demand for a new article. Something he must do, and it must be something which leaves a margin for him to live on.

If you have followed me so far you will by this time have seen that the problems which beset a manufacturer are many and various, and it may perhaps have struck you, as it certainly has me, that the problem of complete accuracy in costing is not the most important. There is, to be sure, a sense in which the key is as important as the watch, but nevertheless a watch is worth more than the key.

I mentioned at an earlier stage that I believed that a manufacturer has generally a very fair idea of what his prime cost is. In most trades this prime cost is much the greater part of the price which he can under any circumstances hope to obtain. Whatever pressure is put upon him, he is never likely to sell under this prime cost—no man knowingly accepts elevenpence in exchange for a shilling. (I am referring, of course, to normal sales; job lots follow no rule and are small in total.) But the standing expenses are a different matter. It is one thing to admit, as every manufacturer must, that in the long run all standing expenses must come out of selling price realised; but it is quite another matter to admit with regard to each and every order that it must bear its proportion of these expenses. Moreover, it is obvious to anyone who looks on a business as a living concern, and not as mere raw material for statistical information, that it is impossible to fix on a percentage which shall be uniform for all orders. Small wonder is it then that our harassed manufacturer, compelled to conform to a selling price not of his own seeking, often finds a temporary refuge from his troubles in under-estimating the loading necessary for standing expenses. A man has to be very particularly honest if he would refrain from deceiving himself—it is much harder to be truthful to oneself than to one's neighbours—and this question of the proportion of standing expenses to the prime cost offers in times of stress peculiar opportunities for self-deception.

Suppose that you are able to show to a manufacturer by the accounts you have regularly prepared for him that for the past three years his proportion of standing expenses to prime cost has been within a fraction of 20 per cent. in each year. You have told him of something of value to him. It is of importance to him to know the absolute rate, and perhaps of even greater importance to know that the rate, whatever it is, has remained constant, or has gone up or down, as the case may be. The same considerations apply to the ratio which the gross profit bears to the sales—in my opinion, the most valuable information for purposes of internal economy which an accountant can give his client—valuable both absolutely and relatively to other years. When you have given this information you have gone a very little way indeed towards helping him to decide at what price he shall sell, or offer for sale, a given article which he manufactures.

Consider some of the difficulties. First, take the case of a manufacturer who has a good sound business, who is holding his own, and who, while having no monopoly, can find a market for his output, provided he is content with a moderate profit. Such a man is in a position favourable, but not uncommon. But even if he be so happily situated that his competitors do not seriously trouble him, yet that is only so while he keeps within certain definite limits, and always he must keep an eye on his public. While each manufacturer in a trade competes with all the others, there is an equally severe competition going on between one trade and another. Cocoa competes with meat extract, croquet with tennis, books with pictures, beer with whisky and so on. Let the price of A go down and people spend their money on it who previously had patronised B, unless the price of B follows suit. For this reason our manufacturer finds that the uniform percentage which we furnish him with is of no great value in any particular case; he is still under the necessity of selling cheaply, and must consider each case on its merits. Thus one article which he makes may require the use of expensive and perhaps special machinery, while another may require only cheap standard machinery. For this difference an allowance must be made, based on some estimated charge per machine, according to the time spent on it, the number of revolutions, or some other method. Or a particular order may require an unusually large proportion of material to labour, and then, in ordinary circumstances, the percentage would have to be lower than the average. When it comes to the addition for profit, one article may very well bear a larger addition than another, because the public like it better, even though it may cost no more. A variation from standard, too, generally bears a larger profit. Or, again, there may be a leading article knowingly sold at a very low price; and if sprats are sold cheap, so much the more must be added to the price of the herrings.

For all these reasons a manufacturer can only use a uniform percentage as a general idea; it is of little value in individual cases such as I have referred to. And there comes to every manufacturer a time when it is of even less value—the time when trade is slack and orders few—when the difficulty is to get orders at any price, every order being competed for by firms anxious to get work to keep their factories going. In such a time a man may, and does, reduce his wages list by discharging some of his workpeople, or by putting them on short time, but he cannot discharge his premises and plant, which go on costing money in interest and upkeep. Nor can he discharge his staff—foremen, clerks, and sellers. In short, his standing expenses go on much the same. In such circumstances what is a man to do who knows that he must get 25 per cent. in addition to his prime cost to pay his standing expenses, and who also knows that the current price for what he sells does not give him more than 10 per cent.?

The plight of a manufacturer in bad trade is really even worse than suggested above, for this reason: The average percentage to be added to prime cost to provide for standing expenses is, or ought to be, calculated not on actual output, but on normal output. If a man has a more expensive organisation (relatively to his sales) than the average manufacturer in the trade, he must not expect for that reason to get a higher price. Nor if he can manage more cheaply than others need he accept a lower one. To say that his output goes down owing to bad trade is only to say that he is receiving, in his sales, a smaller amount for standing expenses—too little to cover them—so that even if he keeps his price up he is trading at a loss. But it is just when he needs a larger profit that he must be content with a smaller. Here it is in figures. The prime cost of my normal output is £100,000 per annum. My standing expenses (apart from profit) are £25,000 per annum. Therefore, merely to pay my way, I must on the average add 25 per cent. to prime cost, and this addition brings in £25,000. Suppose my output falls so that my prime cost for the year is only £60,000. If to this I add 25 per cent. I only get an addition of £15,000, so that, as my expenses are the same (and they would not be much lower than in a normal year) I am £10,000 to the bad. To get £25,000 out of a prime cost of £60,000 I should have to add not 25 per cent., but 41⅔ per cent. But trade is bad and I cannot maintain my old price, much less get an advance. So I am between the devil and the deep sea. The devil is represented by my state if I hold out for my old price and get no orders, it being clear to me all the time that to call my expenses "standing" expenses is but a sorry joke, for I know full well that, far from standing, they move, they run. The deep sea is represented by my condition if I lower my price and sell for a sum which, while it brings in something, cannot possibly cover my standing expenses. Most people in such circumstances choose the deep sea as the lesser evil, and I think they are right.

It is a comparatively easy matter to command the ship when the weather is fair; it is storm that tries a man. When, figuratively speaking, the tempest is raging a man gets but little help, either as to general policy or a particular course of action, from statistics, however carefully compiled. The one piece of information of value to him is his prime cost. He knows that it can never be anything but a loss to accept orders at a price below prime cost. There is, however, a point of view from which the slightest advance on this represents a profit. For if the expenses go on in any case, anything received towards them is to the good. Indeed the question of applying a portion of standing expenses to particular orders is largely a matter of opinion. I was staying in Zermatt in the latter half of September last. Many of the hotels were closed for the season, and most of the visitors had gone. My particular hotel had only a few guests, not 20 per cent. of its possible number. The incoming from these guests could not possibly pay, were the place charged with its full proportion of expenses over the whole time it was open. But if the proprietor chose—as he apparently did choose—to consider that his season ended on September 15th, and if he spread his standing expenses over a period which ended then, he had his hotel for the next fortnight free of all these expenses, and the few guests paid very well; for, of course, the total charge made to them was much more than the specific outpockets necessitated by their presence.

If I have seemed to draw a somewhat gloomy picture of commercial life, remember that it is not always, or indeed generally, that we have to go by dead reckoning. On most days the sky is clear and an observation can be taken. It is just in the provision of these observations that we accountants can assist, and our assistance will be valuable if we know not only what we can do, but also what we cannot do. But let us above all things get into true relation with the concern we have to do with. It may be true that last year a man's rent amounted to 2.16 of his turnover, while in the preceding year it was only 2.09. But of what use is such information? When you give it to a harassed man immersed in the business of keeping his head above water (if you will pardon the bull), what can you expect but, at the best, indifference? But there is some information he will be really grateful for. If you can find a way of preventing waste; if you can show him an approximate, perhaps even an accurate, way of ascertaining his prime cost; if you can show him the expense of his various processes; if you can show him how his rate of gross profit to sales fluctuates—that this rate is sufficiently high, or impossibly low; that his expenses bear a reasonable, or unreasonable, ratio to his turnover; that a particular group of expenses shows, over some years, a tendency to rise or to fall: if you can show him such information as that you have really helped him. The value of this information, however, is much enhanced by the way in which it is imparted. We may prepare our accounts from the commercial books, and certify them without much regard to the personality of our client. But when he talks to us about internal organisation we have got away from the region of formalities, and though a fact is still a fact it is of more or less importance according to how it is presented. Especially is this so if, as is generally the case in such matters, the fact be that there are no facts, but only presumptions, more or less strong.

Time fails me to deal with many matters which my very general observations have suggested—to me, at least. But there are a few which I must touch on. There are many kinds of manufacture, and though most kinds can be gathered into one of a few groups, yet the difference between the groups is considerable, so far as the application of any internal system of costing is concerned. A factory where weaving is carried on in any of its ramifications is very different from one where bicycles are made. In weaving, the whole product is passed through the loom; certain lengths of cotton, wool, silk, jute, or what not go into the loom, have their relative positions altered, and come out again; what goes in comes out, but in a different form. But a cycle factory is rather a collection of small industries, mostly of an engineering character, whose various outputs are easily so combined as to form a bicycle. Both of these differ from a furniture factory, which is a place where particular pieces of timber go through process after process till the completed table (or whatever it may be) emerges. General engineering work, again, has some of the costing characteristics of cycles and some of those of furniture. And when we come to shipbuilding, or to building in the ordinary use of the word, we have quite another set of conditions, and the possibility—indeed, the necessity—of costing individual jobs. Then there are concerns like tanneries and breweries, where standing expenses are large in relation to prime cost, and that brings difficulties of its own.

I mention these instances only to show how various are the problems, and how impossible it is to dogmatise on the subject of costing. You will find a very good classification in Mr. G. A. Mitchell's book on "Single Cost Accounts" (Volume 47 "ACCOUNTANTS' LIBRARY"). To Mr. Mitchell has been revealed the fact—hidden, I think, from some writers on the subject—that costing should be made for the factory, not the factory for costing.

There are other matters to be considered in relation to any particular business. There is, for instance, the question of departmental profit and division of expenses. It is easy to carry this division to a point at which it ceases to correspond to any useful fact. What, for instance, is the use of splitting up a manager's salary between departments? If a department be shut up, can a portion of the manager be dispensed with? If such divisions have any value it is a relative one only, as between one year and another. They have no absolute value, for they do not answer to facts which confirm past action, or give rise to new—the only facts worth having in business.

Then there are trades where, instead of the selling price being fixed by working from the prime cost forwards, the prime cost is fixed by working from the selling price backwards. Out of cattle one gets meat, bones, hides, and a few other things. An ox complete has a true prime cost, while bones have not, as opposed to meat and hides. If the price of meat is abnormally high ordinary everyday competition will bring down the price of bones, so long as there is no other disturbing factor.

These points do not exhaust the problem, but they may well have exhausted my audience, so I must bring my remarks to a close.

The conclusion of the whole matter is that advice on costing is not to be lightly given. There are many difficulties to face, both in comprehending the nature of the business and in making recommendations likely to be acceptable to the individual proprietor or manager of it. And when we have done our best, and even if it has been recognised that our best is good, yet we have but equipped the vessel with a compass. To navigate it is not ours, nor is it ours to know what storms it may have to contend with. But if it would weather them, its equipment must be complete and must be good of its kind. So far as we have a hand in this equipment let us see that our contribution is of the best. With the students lies the future of the profession. Bring to your chosen calling not only professional knowledge, but an intelligence quickened by a wide outlook on life and a participation in its many activities.

Some Principles of Accounting Affecting Cost Accounts.

By M. Webster Jenkinson, F.C.A.

A paper read before the Leeds, Bradford, and Keighley Associations of Engineers and the Leeds University Engineering Society, on the 14th January 1914; the Sheffield Society of Engineers and Metallurgists on the 26th January 1914; and the Sheffield Chartered Accountants Students' Society on the 4th February 1914.

Files—
The Files—
Office Files—
Oblige me by referring to the files.
Every question man can raise,
Every phrase of every phase
Of that question is on record in the files.

Kipling.

The object of any system of Cost Accounts is primarily to show—

(1) The prime cost or cost of production, so that the manufacturer or contractor may know either the profit or loss on the article or job, or, if not sold, the selling price he should charge.

(2) The analysis of such cost.

The secondary objects are—

(1) To obtain reliable records of work done for future reference.

(2) To detect waste of material or loss of time.

(3) To act as a check on managers and others in authority.

(4) To enable monthly or other periodical returns to be prepared to show the progress of the business.

Only by means of an adequate system of Cost Records can the managing director of a large concern put his finger on the weak spots in the administration; only by use of the Cost Records can orders be obtained in the face of keen competition; only in cases where proper Cost Records are available can it be determined whether or not a profit has been earned.

Cost Records are the files to which reference is made for information upon every question which arises in connection with any job, and " every phrase of every phase " is there to be found.

Many are the occasions when the management are by this means able, as Hamlet puts it,

"To have the engineer
Hoist with his own petard,"

and many the mistakes made in tendering for work which would have been avoided if a little more time had been spent in " referring to the files."

Cost Records deal entirely with the internal management and organisation of the business; Whereas the Financial Accounts might be described as synthetic, collecting all the transactions together in one final statement, the Cost Records are analytic, dissecting and classifying the various component parts of each completed job.

Samuel Smiles once said:—

"We learn wisdom from failure much more than from success. We often discover what *will* do by finding out what will not do."

It is not on record whether Mr. Smiles ever attempted to devise a system of Cost Records for a large works, but certainly the advice he gives is peculiarly suited to those who are called upon to do so.

The chief difficulty in costing is to frame a system applicable to the particular requirements of the undertaking concerned, for although the general underlying principles are always the same, yet the special needs of any two businesses are never alike, the methods of working never exactly the same, the general organisation never on parallel lines.

Each undertaking must be considered on its own merits, and the wide differences in the methods of manufacture employed appreciated, the special circumstances of each case demanding special treatment for each.

And when, on paper, the ideal system is obtained, its practical application will reveal innumerable faults which require rectification; countless points which escaped notice, and for which provision must be made; unforeseen practical difficulties which will put the whole system out of gear.

The only way the cost accountant can find out what *will* do is by finding out what will not do.

Needless to say, however, a complete knowledge of the business and the particular conditions under which it is carried on is essential if successful results are to be attained.

The editor of "The Accountants' Library," in an introductory note, points out that lines of organisation rather than similarity of products provides the clearest basis for a system of Cost Accounts, and the following classification is suggested.

(1) *Multiple Costs.*—Applicable to undertakings where a number of products are involved bearing little or no apparent relation to each other in cost or selling price—such as Engineering Specialities, Cycles, Hosiery, Boots, Furniture, Agricultural Implements—in which standardisation in parts is carried to a high degree of specialisation in manufacturing.

(2) *Terminal Costs.*—Applicable to undertakings where definite contracts are entered into, in which the costing is definite and terminating—such as Engineers, Shipbuilders, Builders, and the like.

(3) *Single Costs.*—Applicable to Breweries, Collieries, Quarries, Mines, and businesses in which there is a natural unit of cost, as the barrel, the ton raised, &c.

(4) *Process Costs.*—Applicable to Chemical Industries, Food Products, &c., in which conversion of material takes place, and there are principal and by-products—such as Tanners, Fellmongers.

(5) *Operating Costs.*—As Railways, Tramways, Gas and Water undertakings, Electricity, and similar industries.

Engineering concerns which obtain orders by contract usually adopt the *Terminal Cost* system, the profit or loss on each order being ascertained.

The *Multiple Cost* system is only applicable to undertakings which can fix upon some common unit which may be taken as the standard of output.

The *Single Cost* method may be used where only a few machines of a standard pattern are manufactured.

In any system of costing it is, however, most desirable that the results shown by the Cost Books should be incorporated in the financial books of the undertaking.

In the case of Terminal Costs the balances on the Work in Progress Accounts should correspond exactly with the balances on the various accounts in the Cost Ledger, thus proving the clerical accuracy of the Cost Records; and only where such agreement of the financial books with the Cost Books is obtainable can the system be considered satisfactory.

The underlying principle of costing is that each item of expense is charged to the particular job or department which benefits thereby; and, where it is not possible for such allocation to be made direct, the expense must be apportioned and charged to each job or department on some equitable basis, according to the benefit each receives.

The following general analysis of a product will illustrate the meaning of the word "cost."

Elements of Cost.

(1) *Materials* and Direct Expenses } Prime Cost
(2) *Labour* }
(3) *Shop Expenses* or Expenses of Production, including :—
- (*a*) Foremen's Wages
- (*b*) Unproductive Wages, such as Storekeeper, Crane Drivers, &c.
- (*c*) Coal and Coke, Power and Water
- (*d*) Rent of Shops
- (*e*) Repairs to Plant and Machinery
- (*f*) Repairs to Buildings
- (*g*) Drawing Office
- (*h*) Lighting
- (*i*) Yard Expenses
- (*j*) Depreciation, &c.

[Items (1)–(3): } Shop Cost]

(4) *Establishment Expenses* or Expenses of Administration and Distribution :—
- (*a*) Rent, Rates, &c., Warehouse
- (*b*) Travellers' Salaries
- (*c*) Office Expenses
- (*d*) Stationery and Printing
- (*e*) Managing Directors' Salaries
- (*f*) Bank Charges

[Items (1)–(4): } Total Cost]

(5) *Trading Profit*

[Items (1)–(5): } Selling Price]

The classification varies in detail in different concerns, but, broadly speaking, the above differentiation is adopted.

Shop Expenses should embrace all expenditure incurred in running the shop, whereas the Establishment Expenses cover items of an administrative character, the distinction between Shop Expenses and Establishment Expenses being that whereas the former is part of the cost of the job, the latter is a charge against manufacturing profits.

The object of this paper is to discuss in some detail the method of ascertaining the amounts to be charged under these heads, but some reference to costing systems generally was necessary as an introduction, in order that subsequent references might be understood.

As already stated the system of Cost Records differs in every business, each must be framed to meet the requirements of each particular case—as the old proverb runs, "Every bird must hatch her own egg."

But from the accountant's standpoint, although differences of opinion as regards detail may exist, the underlying principles which distinguish capital from revenue expenditure are fairly well established; and whilst those connected with the technical side of a concern are apt to think the auditors too liberal in the provision for depreciation, &c., which they advise, and too critical of the valuation placed on the assets, still it should be remembered that dividends once paid can never be regained, and—"Better give the wool than the sheep."

Wages.

The time of all workmen, whether engaged on productive or unproductive work, should be recorded on either a Daily or Weekly Time Sheet, and charged up to some order number.

It is desirable to have a separate Cost Ledger for time spent on capital expenditure or upkeep, accounts being opened for additions to Plant, Repairs to Buildings, Plant Repairs, Unchargeable Time (*e.g.*, cleaning up shops), such items being charged up from the Time Summary Books.

The total amount of wages paid as shown by the Wages Account in the Impersonal Ledger will then correspond with the cost of the total time charged out through the Time Summary Books, and a record should be kept of any differences due to fractions of a penny or overtime, so that an adjustment can be made when the Time Cost Ledgers are reconciled with the financial books.

It is not usually possible to charge up the wages of the Drawing Office to the different jobs, as so much time is spent on tenders for contracts which are not obtained; generally therefore the wages of the draughtsmen are treated as part of the establishment charges, and not as part of the cost of the job.

Materials.

Materials may be divided into three classes :—

(1) Goods and materials purchased direct for a job.
(2) Goods and materials for stock to be charged out subsequently as used.
(3) Small stores for which no proper record can be kept.

As regards goods and materials purchased specially for a job or any work sub-contracted, such expenditure should be analysed in a separate column in the Purchase Journal and the individual items posted to the various accounts in the Materials Cost Ledger.

The total of the columns in the Purchase Ledger are posted to a separate account in the Impersonal Ledger, which at the end of the period is transferred to the Materials Work in Progress Account, thus ensuring that all such expenditure has been actually charged out.

As regards materials taken out of stores it is essential that proper Stock Accounts be kept, and that a Requisition Note is obtained for all stores issued.

The Materials Issued Book should, whenever possible, give some analysis of the various classes of stores used, corresponding to the accounts in the Impersonal Ledger for stores purchased. Although, generally speaking, the accounts in the Stores Ledger record *quantities* only, the stores issued are charged out at cost price, and therefore at stock-taking, in addition to the check obtained by the comparison of the Stock Sheets with the Stores Ledger Account, the accounts in the Impersonal Ledger will show the cost of stores purchased and the cost of the stores issued and of stock remaining, subject, of course, to the necessary adjustments for waste.

A fixed percentage, according to the nature of the job, is usually debited through the Materials Issued Book for small stores of which no record can be kept.

It is very essential, however, that the Stores Accounts and the amounts charged to the Cost Accounts should be reconciled with the financial books, as only by this means can errors and leakages be avoided.

Transfers from one Department to Another.

The principle enunciated by all accountants, that profits must not be anticipated, only being credited when a sale actually takes place, often gives rise to some difficulty when dealing with transfers from one department to another.

Where a product undergoes various processes of manufacture before it reaches a finished or marketable state, and where at each stage in the manufacture part of the products of that department are sold to outside customers, it is impossible to insist that transfers to other departments should be made at the actual cost price.

Not only would one department show a profit at the expense of another department, but, so far as the Cost Accounts were concerned, the results would be misleading, the materials being charged out at less than the actual cost if bought on the open market.

On the other hand, there is a risk—particularly in the case of what may be termed Stock Departments, *i.e.*, departments which merely sell the goods received from other departments—that goods will be valued for Balance Sheet purposes at a price exceeding the cost to the business as a whole, thus anticipating a profit which eventually may never be realised.

In the case of contract jobs, this matter is not of the same importance, provided the whole contract when completed will show a profit, but as regards goods for stock the position is different.

To facilitate the costing arrangements and to show true departmental results, it is generally better to make the transfers at departmental selling price rather than cost price, and then to deduct from the value of the stock at the end of the financial period a sum equal to the amount of profit credited on stock unsold.

The departmental selling price will, however, be less than the price charged to outside customers, as from the latter must be deducted travellers' salaries and commissions, part cost of packing and delivery, part cost of office charges, &c., otherwise the producing department would obtain a wrong percentage of oncost on sales to outside customers, owing to the inclusion of such items of expense, although never suffered in connection with departmental sales.

Proper Interchange Books must, of course, be kept, and the total transfers inwards and outwards reconciled monthly.

Work in Progress Accounts.

Reference has already been made to the desirability of the Cost Books reconciling with the financial books, and this is effected by means of the Work in Progress Accounts, the clerical accuracy of the entries in the Cost Books being likewise proved by these accounts.

Two accounts are opened, viz. :—

Time Work in Progress Account,
Materials Work in Progress Account.

The Time Work in Progress Account shows in the case of terminal costs—

On the debit side—

Wages paid transferred from the Wages Account in the Impersonal Ledger, which amount must agree with the Summary of the Wages charged to the various accounts in the Cost Ledger.

On the credit side—

1.—The cost of time charged out to customers on completed jobs as per Sales Journal.

2.—The cost of time spent on
(1) Additions to Plant.
(2) Repairs to Plant.
(3) Patterns.
(4) Unchargeable time, &c. &c.

as shown in the Cost Ledger, which amounts are transferred from the Work in Progress Account to the debit of the various Impersonal Accounts.

3.—Time spent on uncompleted work, which amount must agree with the summary of the Time Cost Ledger balances.

Similarly, the Materials Work in Progress Account shows—

On the debit side—

(1) Materials used charged to customers' accounts in the Cost Ledger through the Materials Day Book.

(2) Materials charged direct.

(3) Direct expenses.

On the credit side—

1.—Cost of materials charged out on completed jobs as per Sales Journal.

2.—Cost of materials used on
(1) Additions to plant.
(2) Repairs to plant.
(3) Patterns
(4) Unchargeable materials, &c. &c.,

as shown in the Cost Ledger, which amounts are transferred from the Work in Progress Account to the debit of the various Impersonal Accounts.

3.—Time spent on uncompleted work, which amount must agree with the summary of the Materials Cost Ledger balances.

Before closing the Cost Ledgers and completing the Work in Progress Accounts for the period, care must be taken that all the balances represent work actually chargeable to customers, any work done or materials used on jobs for which no charge can be made being transferred to Unchargeable Time or Unchargeable Materials Account.

In the case of concerns which manufacture goods for either stock or customers' orders, and where the costing is not definite or terminating, as in the example given above, the cost of completed work can be ascertained from the Warehouse Stock Books or Output Book and the same method adopted.

Valuation of Stock-in-Trade and Work in Progress.

From the accountant's standpoint the usually accepted basis for the valuation is as follows:—

(1) *Raw Materials* at cost or market price, whichever be the lower, adding carriage and deducting any trade discount or other abatement.

(2) *Partly manufactured goods* or partially completed jobs at prime cost to date, *e.g.*, materials, wages, and direct manufacturing charges.

(3) *Manufactured goods.*—The actual cost of production, including oncost.

To those, however, who have to deal with the valuation from the practical standpoint, some further consideration of the matter is necessary, as it is seldom possible to apply the above rules without certain modifications being made.

In order to ensure accuracy in the taking of stock it is very necessary that preparations should be made some time previously, and that careful instructions should be given both to the managers of each department and to those responsible for the stocktaking.

To prevent errors of omission, and to facilitate comparison with the stocks of previous years, rough Stock Books should be issued, each book being numbered consecutively, and indicating on the cover the exact nature of the stock to be entered therein.

As far as possible each item should be independently checked as regards weight, measurement, number, and price, and each sheet initialled by those responsible for the stocktaking.

The pricing will generally be done in the department, and the extensions made and checked by the counting-house staff.

If it is not practicable to close down during the period of stocktaking, the greatest care must be taken that all material received into or taken out of stock is properly adjusted, clear and definite instructions being given to the stockkeepers beforehand, or confusion is bound to occur.

After the schedule of stores on hand has been prepared the quantities of raw material should be compared with the balances shown in the various accounts in the Stores Ledger, and if serious discrepancies exist an investigation is most necessary, as, apart from the question of theft, it may happen that some loophole in the costing system exists, and that stores are being used on jobs and not charged up, thus nullifying the benefit to be gained from the Cost Records as a medium for future reference.

Where, as generally is the case, raw material has been bought at different prices from various firms, it is impossible to base the valuation on the invoice price, and as such stores will have been charged out on an average monthly basis, it is better to take the average price for the last month of the financial year.

Needless to remark, any old or damaged stock must be taken at its actual worth only.

Objection is sometimes made to the "average" basis, on the ground that if prices have been rising and large stocks have been previously bought in anticipation of such increase, credit is taken for a profit not actually earned. Theoretically this argument is in accordance with the recognised principles of accounting, but it is submitted that, as a matter of fact, in practice the variation is but slight as a rule, and except where large purchases have been made to cover contracts entered into on the basis of the lower or cost price, it is justifiable to value the *stores* on the average price at the time of stocktaking. In case too broad an interpretation be placed upon this statement, it is necessary, to avoid any misapprehension, to point out that where, during the last few weeks, there has been a *sudden rise* in the price of raw material, it would not be justifiable to value large quantities on the higher basis, but where certain stores—say, for example, copper—have been bought for stock earlier in the year, and the price has gone up, and contracts which will absorb all that stock have been entered into subsequently on the basis of the higher price, then there is no objection to the valuation of such copper on the average price if the remaining stores, some of which may have fallen in value since purchase, are similarly treated.

Of course, most firms using large quantities of valuable metal, such as copper, on accepting a contract buy forward to cover the contract at the price at which taken, and in these cases the stock must be valued at the cost price.

The amount of the work in progress, so far as the prime cost is concerned, will, of course, be ascertained from the Cost Ledger, but each account must be examined and compared with the original tender, so that provision may be made for any loss which eventually may accrue.

As already stated, in closing the Cost Ledgers all unchargeable work must be written off, and not treated as an asset.

If the job is for stock, shop oncost only should be added, but if the work is being done for a customer it is permissible to charge both shop and office oncost, calculated on the amount of work done and at the same rate per unit as calculated in the tender.

The latter precaution is necessary, as in certain cases a special low rate may have been provided.

Until a job is half completed it is not usual to take credit for any profit, as it is generally impossible until that stage in the work has been reached to know whether the cost is in accord with the original estimates.

In certain contracts extending over a long period, where it appears that the cost is within the limit calculated, it is not unusual to take credit for a proportion of profit after the job is more than half completed, but as it is possible that the profit anticipated at this stage may, owing to unforeseen circumstances, not be realised, ample provision must be made for contingencies, whilst the amount must not in any case exceed the proportion applicable to the work already done.

Where, however, the job is sufficiently advanced to allow the engineers to estimate the cost to finish, then there is no objection to taking credit for the full contract price, after allowing for such estimated expenditure, plus the oncost and proportion of profit on such further cost and a margin for contingencies.

In the case of firms manufacturing goods for sale, as distinct from contractors who execute work to customers' orders, stock of either finished or partly finished goods must be valued at *cost* without any addition for standing charges or profit, except shop oncost; otherwise, during a period of depression, when orders were scarce and the hands were employed manufacturing for stock, a paper profit might be shown, instead of an actual loss, as the stock might never be realisable at the amount included in the Balance Sheet, the standing charges which were included in the valuation of the stock actually being a loss which should have been charged to the revenue for the year.

Until a sale has actually been effected, or, of course, a contract made for the future delivery of goods already manufactured, credit must never be taken for any profit, as profit can only be made when realisation actually takes place, and the article is exchanged for cash or another commodity of the same value in cash.

Oncost.

Oncost may be defined as—

The amount to be added to *prime cost* (*i.e.*, cost of direct wages, materials, &c.) to provide for dead charges, and it is always a difficult matter to fix upon some basis whereby such expenses may be properly allocated to the various jobs.

In the first place, the actual amount of the dead charges for the year is not known until after the end of the year, and as the oncost charge takes the form of a percentage compared with the turnover, the latter has also to be estimated.

In the case of a factory producing only one class of commodity, it is possible to frame fairly accurate estimates of the oncost charge, but where, as usually is the case, there are various departments undertaking various kinds of work bearing little or no relation to each other, it is a problem requiring very careful calculation and consideration before a proper basis can be ascertained.

Nevertheless, it is little use having an elaborate system of Cost Accounts and allocating exactly the prime cost if the apportionment of the fixed charges is misleading and founded on a wrong hypothesis.

The most satisfactory method, after having estimated the total dead charges for the year, is to apportion the Shop Expenses or Expenses of Production among the various departments or shops, on the basis of the amount of work which should be done by each during the year as shown by past records.

Each works manager then knows that unless he can distribute such amount of dead charge over the various orders or jobs during the year there will be a debit balance to set off against the profit earned on such work. This may be due to the fact that orders do not reach the turnover estimated at the commencement, in which case the works manager is not to blame, and the management must take steps to increase such turnover for the next year, if the department or shop is to bear the same proportion of oncost.

If, however, the turnover estimated has been reached, and the oncost charge is not covered, it indicates that the manager has not been adding sufficient to certain jobs to cover expenses, and that the profits supposed to have been earned in certain cases do not exist.

Merely to fix a general percentage to apply in every case is misleading, as the result may be that some department is overcharged, whilst another shows a paper profit which has not actually been made.

Before an equitable apportionment of the total expenses can be made, the different conditions existing in each part of the works must be considered and each item allocated accordingly.

Thus, one department may occupy considerably more space than another, and must be charged with a greater proportion of the rent and rates. Another shop or department should perhaps bear the larger part of the charge for power and coal. It is a matter which can only be solved by considering the merits of each particular case.

The actual apportionment of the amount charged to the shop or department over the various jobs or orders is best left to the judgment of each works manager; and, if it is desired that the *actual* net profit earned should not be ascertainable by him, the difficulty can always be met by adding a fixed percentage to the amount of the expenses, which subsequently can be written back.

It is usual, however, for the shop oncost, which is added to cover the expenses of production, such as Foremen's Wages, Power, Repairs to Plant, &c., to be treated separately and on a different basis from the office oncost or establishment expenditure, which includes Travellers, Office Expenses, Stationery, and the like, the office oncost generally being provided by a percentage on the shop cost, *i.e.*, prime cost plus shop oncost.

The various methods of calculating the shop oncost are as follows:—

(1) A percentage on prime cost.

(2) A percentage on the cost of labour.

(3) A fixed sum for each hour of time worked by each man.

(4) A fixed sum per hour for each machine.

(5) A fixed sum per unit of weight or quantity, *e.g.*, in a foundry the calculation is based on the weight of the castings.

In most cases, although, of course, there are exceptions, the prime cost is not a reliable basis.

For example, suppose that the cost of two cylinders of exactly the same size is as follows:—

	Brass	Iron.
Material	£40	£10
Labour	10	10
Prime cost	£50	£20

If 40 per cent. be added for oncost the brass cylinder would be charged with £20 and the iron one with £8.

If the price of brass increased so that the materials in the first case cost £50, the oncost to be added would also increase to £24, which, it is self-evident, is misleading.

Although the time basis is apparently the most accurate—at least from the theoretical point of view—it does not follow that in practice it will prove correct, as whereas a skilled man may get a job finished in a certain time, a less competent man at half the wage would take twice as long over similar work.

On the other hand, a job requiring a large amount of unskilled labour should bear a larger percentage of shop oncost than a job on which the wages paid to skilled workmen were the same but the time occupied was one half, as in the former case the cost of superintendence, lighting, &c., would be much greater.

It is for this reason that it is desirable to leave the method of allocation to the works manager.

To base the oncost charge on the hours worked by each machine is only possible where there is little hand labour, but a combination of methods (2) and (4) will undoubtedly in the long run prove the most satisfactory, although not always practicable.

The classification of the elements of cost (*vide* p. 565) is one adopted with slight variations in most cases, but from the costing standpoint it is possible that some additional grouping is desirable as certain of the items often included in the establishment expenses have no relation to the cost of an order or job either directly or indirectly.

For instance, Bad Debts, although seldom avoidable even in the best managed business, have no connection with cost, and although Bad Debts are a charge against profits, for which provision must be made, from the costing standpoint the profit is earned when the goods are delivered and accepted, or the job completed. If in any one year the losses through Bad Debts are heavy, to include such amount in the standing charges in the estimate for the next year is misleading.

Interest on Debentures and Bank Interest, although charges against trading profits, should likewise be omitted, as, if interest is charged at all, such interest must be calculated on the whole of the assets employed, and not merely on a proportion of the capital which has been borrowed because the subscribed capital is insufficient. Directors' Fees other than those of a managing director, Remuneration of Trustees for Debenture-holders, Income Tax, Discount on Bills, Expenses in connection with Annual General Meetings, are other items of a similar character.

Such items might be grouped under a separate heading, such as Financial Oncost; but as they have no relation to the cost of any article or job, it is better to treat them as a charge against the Trading profits earned, as shown by the Cost Accounts, and not to attempt any apportionment.

Some manufacturers are content to know the prime cost, and will not trouble about any proper allocation of the shop and office expenditure, but the knowledge thus obtained is not sufficient.

Professor R. H. Smith suggested in *The Economic Journal*, 1906, that there were three ways of bettering production, viz.:—

(1) By increasing rate of production per time unit.
(2) By decreasing cost of production per time unit.
(3) By decreasing time spent in making and realising value of product.

The standing charges in a business are usually more or less fixed, and although the shop expenditure varies with turnover the increase is not in the same ratio. In a well managed concern, where a strict supervision exists, it is not possible as a rule to effect economies which will reduce the gross amount of the establishment or office oncost charges.

But the relation existing between the cost of production and the oncost charge is a matter of the utmost importance in these competitive days, and a reduction in the percentage can only be attained by

(1) Increasing the total production; or
(2) Increasing the rate of production so that the shop charges will be less.

If, however, the management have no reliable data available, and only have the expenses grouped under convenient headings in one general Trading Account, it is impossible for them to formulate any reliable opinion on the profitable or unprofitable result of any department or job, or to exercise any efficient check on the works management.

Capital Expenditure.

Inasmuch as the charges made against revenue have to be included in the oncost, the allocation of expenditure between capital and revenue is one of some importance.

Capital expenditure may be classified as follows :—

(1) Actual additions, such as new buildings, new plant, or new tools, which did not exist before, and do not replace any similar asset.

(2) Alterations to capital assets producing increased capacity, only a proportion generally being chargeable to capital.

(3) Alterations to capital assets not producing any increased capacity, but allowing a lower cost in output, as, for example, the removal of plant from one position to another, permitting more economical working.

Such expenditure, although productive of benefit in increased revenue to the undertaking, is not strictly a capital charge, being more of the nature of revenue expenditure paid in advance, and the more preferable method, instead of charging the cost to Capital Account, is to open a special account, and spread the expenditure over a term of years.

(4) Special replacements of plant, either to increase capacity or to reduce cost of production, owing to the competition of rival undertakings with more modern installations. To a large extent the cost will represent mere replacement, and the amount by which such replacement exceeds the provision made for depreciation may in some cases be regarded as a Capital loss, provided the deficiency is not due to the inadequacy of the depreciation charged in previous years. If no Reserve Fund is available to meet the loss the amount should be spread over a term of years, but in no case must the value of the scrapped plant be included in the Plant Capital Account, as otherwise the annual revenue charge would be misleading.

(5) Ordinary replacements which are chargeable to Capital Account, provided the plant item replaced is or has been written off out of revenue.

Distinction must, however, be made between the cost of maintenance, consisting of small renewals and repairs, and replacements which are renewals of the whole or some substantial part of the asset.

Maintenance or upkeep charges must always be charged to Revenue or to the Maintenance Equalisation Fund (*vide* p. 575), if one exists. Replacements are only chargeable to revenue to the extent the asset replaced has not been depreciated during its life.

In the case of capital expenditure on works erected by the firm's own workpeople, it is frequently contended that the expenditure charged to Capital Account should represent only the actual out-of-pocket cost, excluding both establishment oncost and interest on capital.

Otherwise, it is argued that, the standing charges of the undertaking being reduced, a paper profit is earned, and made available for distribution as dividend, whereas the accepted doctrine is that dividends can only be paid out of realised profits.

But, however prudent this contention may be from the auditor's standpoint, the fact remains that, provided the cost of works constructed by the firm's own staff does not exceed the cost if erected by an outside contractor, value exists, and it is immaterial whether such value is represented by fixed assets or book debts, so far as the question of value is concerned.

There are two methods of acquiring works or plant, namely, (1) by purchase, (2) by construction ; and the most economical method will naturally be adopted, so that a larger return from the use of such works or plant may be obtained on the fixed capital expended.

If it should be found that the cost of construction has exceeded the cost of purchase in the open market, the difference is a revenue loss as much as if a contract had been made for the construction of the same work for an outside customer at the same price.

It is suggested, however, that the ordinary profit on sale should not be charged, as to some degree such profit represents a profit on selling, *i.e.*, a speculative profit, as compared with a profit on manufacture, representing the interest on the capital employed.

Those who object to interest being included in the capital cost will usually concede that interest on moneys specifically borrowed for the purpose of the construction may be capitalised ; they will admit that interest paid on capital during construction, as allowed by Section 91 of the Companies (Consolidation) Act, 1908, is capital expenditure : and yet, inexplicable as it may seem, they take exception to a company charging the asset with the interest on the capital employed during its construction, if provided out of its own resources.

To take an extreme case as an illustration. A company has a Reserve Fund of £10,000 invested outside the business, producing 4 per cent. per annum.

It decides to erect additional shops, putting in new plant costing £10,000.

What is the difference between—

(1) Borrowing £10,000 at 4 per cent., and charging the interest paid to Construction Account, the investment being left intact and the interest received credited to revenue ; and

(2) Realising the investment as required, using the proceeds for the construction purposes and debiting the Capital Account and crediting revenue with the interest.

If the investment be producing less than 4 per cent. and the cost of borrowing the money exceed 4 per cent., to adopt the former method would be as foolish as financially unsound.

Before the erection of new works or plant, the management take into account the return to be obtained, basing the cost on the purchase price, which includes administrative charges and interest. Assume this cost to be, say, £100, and the return anticipated 5 per cent. If constructed entirely by own capital, instead of purchase, taking only the *direct out-of-pocket* cost, the charge to be capitalised would be (say) £90. To obtain a return of 5 per cent. on such plant it is only necessary to earn £4 10s. per annum, instead of £5, if the plant had been purchased.

If this figure be used in the costs it will therefore be possible to sell cheaper to obtain the return required.

Assume it then becomes necessary to duplicate the plant, and the company being busy the erection of the duplicated plant is made by purchase from an outside vendor.

What is the result? The cost being £100, to produce a return of 5 per cent. on the capital invested, the selling price must be increased so as to earn £5 instead of £4 10s., as formerly.

To those who suggest as an analogy the case of similar plant made for stock, which should, of course, only be valued at cost price, it should be pointed out that unsold stock represents *surplus* articles the sale of which will involve expense, and which are only convertible into money when someone is found who requires such plant for use in a business.

Plant actually in use has a different value in a business which is a going concern to plant in works where the business has ceased to exist, and the fact that such plant is actually being used to produce revenue justifies the constructional cost being taken as the cost of sale to an outsider, provided the latter does neither exceed the lowest market price nor includes any speculative selling profit.

To avoid misapprehension, it must, however, be pointed out that, under the existing company laws, a company is not entitled to pay dividends except out of profits, unless the sanction of the Board of Trade is obtained for the payment of interest during construction (*vide supra*); therefore any interest charged on constructional work debited to Capital Account would, unless it could be set off against interest on borrowed money (including debentures) have to be transferred to Reserve Fund.

Probably, however, the capital for such extensions would be provided by a Reserve Fund created out of profits invested in the business, in which case it is proper to add interest each year on the amount of such fund. Otherwise, on the distribution of such fund as bonus shares, the rate of dividend earned becomes apparently less.

The interest debited on construction can therefore be regarded as part of the amount of interest credited to the Reserve Fund, which actually is the case.

Interest on Capital.

Some divergence of opinion exists as to the desirability of including Interest on Capital in the oncost charge, those who are opposed to the practice arguing that, as interest is merely a form of profit, a portion of the *profits* earned should not be allocated as a charge.

If, however, interest on capital is charged, there are several points which may easily escape attention, and which for comparative purposes may upset the calculations of cost.

In the first place, interest should, if charged at all, be calculated on the whole of the assets employed in the business, less the trade creditors, and excluding unrepresented expenditure, such as Goodwill and Preliminary Expenses.

The capital of a business is not the capital of the proprietors, nor the capital of the proprietors plus the loan capital, but the total assets less the amount of credit obtainable without payment of interest.

As goodwill merely represents the premium paid for the possibility of earning a higher rate of profit in that particular business than if the capital employed in the business were invested in some outside concern, it necessarily follows that for costing purposes the interest thereon is not an element in the cost of the article produced.

Neither are such items as Preliminary Expenses, which are usually written off over a term of years, but which in any case represent expenditure in connection with the form of ownership, and have no relation to the business itself, except so far as the cost of raising capital is concerned.

If interest on capital is charged, no logical objection exists to a charge for the cost of raising such capital, the expenditure under this head, which usually takes the form of discount, representing the present worth of an increased rate of interest.

Of course, if interest on capital is ignored, interest on debentures or other borrowed money must likewise be omitted, as the annual amount paid to debenture-holders merely represents a division of the profits, their legal rights to payment whether the accounts do or do not show a profit not affecting the principle.

The difficulty from the practical standpoint arises when the allocation of the interest charge over the various jobs or departments has to be made.

To obtain *correct* results there must be considered the relative values of the plant and machinery used for each job or order, and the time such plant or machinery is in use; there must be taken into account the periods at which the greatest value of labour is employed; the terms of purchase of the material bought specially for the job must be ascertained; whilst all sales should be calculated to the average due date of payment and the interest adjusted accordingly.

In other words, to calculate the interest apportionable to each job on an absolutely reliable basis would entail more work in the majority of cases than the results obtainable justify.

Nevertheless, to be consistent, if interest is charged on the plant owing to the Annuity or Sinking Fund system of depreciation being adopted, interest should likewise be charged on the labour employed and materials used, it usually being sufficiently near for practical purposes to charge interest each half-year to the average due date.

From the economic standpoint interest may rightly be regarded as an element in the cost of production, and for estimate purposes the manufacturer must take it into account; therefore, provided some satisfactory system of allocation can be determined in each case, more accurate costing results are obtainable by interest being charged to each job.

But for the purposes of ascertaining the profits of a company legally divisible among the members as dividend, it is a recognised principle that anticipated profits are not available, and therefore, interest being only a form of profit, the amount, if any, included in the work in progress must be written back for Balance Sheet purposes.

Depreciation.

The subject of Depreciation is one which affords scope for very great difference of opinion, the divergence of views being largely attributable to the varying meanings in which the term is used.

Depreciation may be defined as the diminution in the value of an asset due to

(1) Wear and tear, or exhaustion of subject-matter.

(2) Natural causes, occasioned by the effluxion of time.

(3) Obsolescence, owing to inventions and the general progress of mankind.

It must always be considered as an element in the cost of manufacture, representing the gradual reduction in the value of the fixed assets employed in the business, and which are consumed in the process of earning revenue; the loss being as much an element in the cost of production as the materials used or the labour employed.

Any estimates of cost or profit made without due regard to the appraisement of loss under this head are both fallacious and misleading.

It is frequently contended that, owing to plant having been maintained in an efficient working condition out of revenue, it is not necessary to provide any further sum for depreciation.

This proposition only holds good, however, in two cases, viz., where the plant wears out so quickly as to need replacement at frequent intervals; and secondly, in large undertakings of a permanent nature affording a wide average of deterioration and renewal over the whole plant.

Although a concern keep its plant in good working order, it must be admitted that there is bound to be some limit to its physical life, whilst all machinery is constantly being superseded by new inventions, and sooner or later the day comes when the old machines have to be "scrapped" and others purchased.

To postpone the charge for renewal until it actually takes place is tantamount to increasing the profits fictitiously during the intervening period by the amount of the annual shrinkage, and to putting the whole burden on the year in which the renewal takes place, with the not infrequent result that a concern finds that it has not the available capital to make the replacements required; and, if the issue of fresh capital for the purpose is impossible, the only alternative is liquidation.

It is not sufficient to consider either the present market value or its present earning power to the concern at the time of the valuation.

Whilst a business is a going concern the value of the plant is its value to that business during the whole period of its life, and in writing off depreciation an attempt is made to distribute the original cost proportionately over the period during which it is earning revenue.

A simple example will serve as an illustration:—A man buys a three-year-old horse. The life of the horse he estimates at twelve years. At the end of each of the first three years he finds that the market value of the horse has increased, whilst its earning capacity is better than when he bought it. At the end of the fourth and fifth year he still considers he could sell it for as much as he gave for it, so until the sixth year he makes no provision for depreciation. What is the result?

During the last four years he must charge against revenue each year approximately one-fourth of the original cost in order to replace the horse at the end of its life, his profits for those years being reduced accordingly; or at the expiration of the twelfth year he will have to find additional capital to purchase a new horse.

The original cost should have been distributed over the whole period, the horse being a fixed asset, a profit being made from use; not a floating asset to be resold and a profit earned by the resale.

It is important to observe that market fluctuations have no bearing on the provision to be made for depreciation.

Depreciation, strictly speaking, is only applicable to wasting assets, although frequently used erroneously when dealing with any fall in exchangeable value, and represents the diminution in the worth of any asset which is not held for the purpose of sale, but for use and occupation, a profit being earned by such use and not by its transfer to a customer at a higher figure than the purchase price.

The actual intrinsic worth at any particular moment is therefore of no account, provided the cost is properly distributed over the whole life of the asset or the period during which it can be profitably used.

Therefore, whilst it is not necessary to give effect to any sudden drop in market worth which may be regarded as a fluctuation due to outside causes, so it is incorrect to set off any appreciation in value against the amount which should be charged for the gradual exhaustion of the original capital outlay owing to depreciation.

To adopt any other principle would result in profits varying enormously, and frequently without real cause.

Obsolescence is a risk for which provision must be made not only on account of the possibility of new and improved plant superseding that existing, but also on account of the fact that the plant itself may become worthless owing to the demand ceasing for the commodity which it produces.

This diminution in value due to external causes is, it is contended by some, a loss of capital for which provision should be made by means of reserves out of *divisible* profits instead of a charge against revenue to be covered by depreciation.

It is impossible, however, to accept this line of argument. Unless the inventive genius of the world suddenly came to a standstill—which in these days of progress and high technical education does not seem probable—new and improved methods of manufacture are *more* likely rather than *less* likely to occur; and unless manufacturers prefer to take the risk that some day they may find they have been living on their capital, they must, as prudent men, regard obsolescence as a liability increasing each year as the plant becomes older, and charge a provision for the risk in their costs.

A fire insurance company knows that each year certain fires will occur, occasioning a certain amount of loss. In one year the losses, compared with the premium income, may be small, in another year heavy; but by taking a series of years an average is obtained, and by providing that average annually proper provision for the risks is obtained.

In the same way the manufacturer must calculate the risk of obsolescence and provide accordingly.

Although for income-tax purposes the Surveyors only allow an *annual* charge for wear and tear, in 1897 the Board of Inland Revenue—in response to a memorial of the Association of Chambers of Commerce of the United Kingdom—issued instructions that, where a claim is made in respect of the introduction of more modern machinery in a factory, no objection is to be taken to the allowance as a deduction from the assessable profits of the year of so much of the cost of replacement as is represented by the existing value of the machinery replaced. The principle of loss through obsolescence being charged to revenue is here admitted, and although, to prevent evasion, the charge to revenue must, for income-tax purposes, be made in the year in which replacement occurs, the manufacturer cannot afford to adopt this method, for, having distributed the whole of the past profits in dividend, the cash required has disappeared, and therefore the replacement would have to be made out of additional capital.

Sometimes, of course, Reserve Funds exist which can be used for the purpose, but such is not the function of a Reserve Fund, as it is submitted that the risk of obsolescence is a known but unascertained liability, and should be taken into account in calculating the cost of production.

Even if the full benefit of the physical life of one machine is obtained, it will generally happen that the replacement of some other machine has to be made sooner than anticipated, thus averaging the loss.

The only excuse for this somewhat full reference to the necessity for depreciation in a paper which has to cover so many points is the fear that English manufacturers do not provide sufficiently for depreciation, and as a result are not able financially to replace their plant in order to keep up to date with their foreign rivals.

There is not the slightest doubt that the Americans are far ahead of the home manufacturers in this respect, and it is because they are in a position to scrap their plant without financial embarrassment when improved methods are introduced that they are able to reduce their costs of production and get orders in open markets, although their labour is costing more.

The English concerns distribute too high dividends compared with the *turnover* done during the good years, so that there is not sufficient reserve capital when it is required; fresh capital is then issued, new plant laid down, and profits again earned; the same process being repeated again and again, until the capital has been so watered that the profits are not sufficient to pay the dividends, and liquidation ensues.

This is the experience of many English industrials which by prudent provision for depreciation would have been flourishing concerns to-day.

In considering the methods to be adopted to provide for depreciation, it is desirable to endeavour to make such charges as constant as possible, as otherwise the costing results cannot be reliable for comparative purposes.

Although it is inevitably misleading to take an average percentage rate covering the whole of the plant, as certain jobs may necessitate the use of special machinery of short life, it is usually impossible to deal with each machine or plant item separately, owing to the amount of detail involved. The most practicable method is to classify the plant. If there are various departments a classification will be made for each department, and then a further classification according to the nature of the plant or machinery.

Of course, in some cases, only the second classification is possible.

In calculating the depreciation to be provided, the following factors have to be taken into account :—

(1) The original cost, or, if not new, its present value in use, having regard to its earning power.

(2) The estimated life, taking into account the functions of the plant, the risk of obsolescence, and the extent to which its ordinary life will be prolonged by renewals of parts and ordinary restoration.

(3) The residual value.

Plant of a general nature generally has a higher residual value than plant erected for some particular purpose, the only value attaching to the latter being that of old metal.

Having ascertained the amount of depreciation to be provided, the method whereby such amount is to be spread over the life varies according to the circumstances of each case, the various methods being as follows :—

(1) *Equal Instalment, or Straight-Line System.*

By this method an equal proportion of the original cost or value is charged to revenue each year. The objection is that in later years, when the cost of repairs becomes more heavy, the charge to revenue increases, whilst the earning capacity may be reduced.

This can be obviated by the creation of a separate Repairs and Renewals Account, or Maintenance Equalisation Fund, as it is sometimes termed, a method always to be recommended, as it allows an average charge to be made each year, instead of, as frequently happens, the cost varying considerably from year to year.

As a general overhauling usually takes place during slack times, the cost in the lean years is heavy, whilst in the fat years, when the plant is working to its full capacity, there is no time to put down for repairs.

From the costing standpoint the average charge is therefore far the most satisfactory.

As the constitution of the Plant Account changes from year to year, it is necessary to keep a statistical record, to ascertain the amount of depreciation to be written off, adjustments being made in the case of sales or plant written off, thus :—

NAME OF PLANT..................

AVERAGE LIFE, 10 YEARS.

Date	Cost	Depreciation Written off for Years ending 31 December										
		1913 1	1914 2	1915 3	1916 4	1917 5	1918 6	1919 7	1920 8	1921 9	1922 10	1923
	£	£	£	£	£	£	£	£	£	£	£	£
1 January 1913 Value at this Date .. .. Estimated Life six years)	6,000	1,000	1,000	1,000	1,000	1,000	1,000					
31 December 1913 Additions for year	500	..	50	50	50	50	50	50	50	50	50	50
31 December 1914 Additions for year	2,000	..	..	200	200	200	200	200	200	200	200	200
31 December 1915 Additions for year	900	..	..	..	90	90	90	90	90	90	90	
Depreciation for 1913		1,000										
Depreciation for 1914			1,050									
Depreciation for 1915				1,250								
Depreciation for 1916					1,340							

Note.—In practice it is desirable to have an extra column showing the value at the end of each year, so that adjustments may be made for any plant sold or scrapped before the expiration of its expected life.

(2) *Reducing Balance or Diminishing Value System.*

Depreciation is charged on the balance standing to the debit of the account at the commencement of the year.

The charge to revenue therefore diminishes each year, but as a much higher rate must be charged, the earlier years are subjected to a heavier burden than really necessary.

Thus, in the case of a machine costing £1,000, with an estimated life of twelve years and a residual value of £100, whereas under the straight-line method £75 would be charged against revenue each year, and the book value at the end of the third year would be £775; under the reducing balance method it would be necessary to use a rate of 17½ per cent., £175 being charged the first year, £144 7s 6d. the second year, and £119 2s. 2d. the third year, when the book value would be only £561 10s. 4d.

In a general Plant Account, where additions are constantly being made, so that the law of average applies, this method is possible, and it may also be used in the case of plant and machinery bought for a special purpose, where the chief benefits will be derived during the early years, but for costing purposes it cannot usually be adopted.

(3) *Annuity System.*

Such an amount is charged to revenue each year as will at the expiration of the life of the asset write off the initial cost plus interest on the capital sunk in the asset.

The asset is presumed to earn a certain amount of interest each year, which is debited to the asset and credited to revenue, and although the gross amount charged is constant, the net cost increases as the capital sunk in the asset diminishes.

Thus, in the case of the machine taken as an example in (2) (*supra*) the first year £50 would be credited to revenue, being 5 per cent. interest on the cost, viz., £1,000 and £106 10s. 7d. charged for depreciation, the net charge therefore being £56 10s. 7d. The second year £47 3s. 6d would be credited for interest and the same amount debited, the net charge being £59 7s. 1d.

The last year the interest would be £9 16s. 10d. and the net charge £96 13s. 9d.

In the case of a lease this method is the most equitable, as the amount paid for a lease is merely the present worth of the annual value for the term of the lease, calculated at the current rate of interest; and, as the amounts are written off, the proportion of the capital invested which is charged to revenue comes back into use in the business, and can earn presumably the same rate of interest as if invested in the lease.

Thus, if a man is willing to pay a rental of £100 per annum, then, taking interest at 5 per cent., he would pay £1,246 for a twenty years' lease, charging his Revenue Account with £100 each year as rent, and crediting interest at 5 per cent. on the annual balance of his investment.

In the recent Telephone Arbitration, the Commissioners refused to recognise this method as the correct one to employ in the case of the valuation of plant as between buyer and seller, and there are certainly practical difficulties in the way of its adoption.

The life of a lease is fixed, and, as already stated, the premium paid is merely rent paid in advance.

But if for any reason the life of the plant fall short of the amount estimated, the whole system fails, and a larger sum has to be written off, owing to the fact that under the annuity method the actual charges are heavier in the later years.

The amount to be spent on repairs and renewals during the life of the machine must also be taken into account, and if the estimate is wrong the calculations will also be incorrect.

Again, the annual value of a lease is usually more or less the amount of the annual rent, and the manufacturer who purchases a lease does not expect to make any profit out of the transaction, the advantage being security of tenure.

But when new plant is put down, a return of more than 5 per cent. is expected on the outlay, particularly in the early years, but the annuity system takes no account of the *actual* revenue which will be derived.

At first sight it might seem that under the equal instalment method, as the charge to revenue each year is the same, a similar objection might be urged, but as the capital invested is reduced each year by the amount of the instalments, the smaller amount employed in the later years is some compensation for the reduction in the earning capacity of the plant and the increased risk of obsolescence.

A purchaser of secondhand plant, having this fact in mind, will seldom pay even half the original cost, less residual value, for plant where half the life has expired, yet under the annuity system the machine costing £1,000, with a life of twelve years, taken as an example (*supra*), would at the end of the sixth year stand in the books at £613 19s. 6d., less £100 residual value.

Mathematically the annuity system is the correct method, but in practice it introduces an unnecessary element of speculation, owing to the fact that the amount set aside varies according to the rate of interest employed, whilst any alteration in the life upsets the calculations.

The income from a lease is a fixed regular sum, the income from plant varies according to outside causes.

The only factors to be taken into consideration in the purchase of a lease are the term and the rate of interest to be employed, and in depreciating the lease the rate of interest used is the same as in making the purchase calculations, whilst the only depreciation arises from effluxion of time; in the case of plant or any other wasting asset the physical decay has to be determined, the depreciation arising from wear and tear, natural decay, and obsolescence; and the rate of interest employed if the annuity system is used, has no relation to the profits derived from use.

It therefore follows that the purchase price of a lease, being merely a question of interest calculations, the unexpired value at the end of any one year is the actual value, whereas, in the case of plant, although the cost is eliminated at the end of the term, at any intermediate stage the book value is not necessarily the true value as a going concern.

Although for the purpose of departmentalisation it is correct to charge interest on the capital employed in the department; although for the purpose of deciding whether certain plant should be scrapped, it may be desirable to calculate the interest on the unexpired cost, which will be lost; for the purpose of fixing the depreciation necessary to reduce a fixed asset to its value to the business as a going concern, the annuity system, depending so largely as it does on the rate of interest to be adopted, is not one to be recommended.

(4) *Sinking Fund System.*

This method is the same as the annuity system, excepting that instead of the various instalments remaining in the business, a fixed sum is set aside, and cash of an equivalent amount specifically invested, and allowed to accumulate at compound interest, so that at the expiration of the life of the asset the cash is available for the purposes of renewal.

Although at first sight the charge to Revenue appears to be less, being in the illustration taken as an example in (3), £56 10s. 7d., instead of £106 10s. 7d., it must be remembered that as the instalments are invested outside the business they are not earning profits, as presumed to be the case under the Annuity System.

Where it is desirable to ensure the provision of capital for renewal, say, for example, of a lease, at the expiration of its life this method is one which should always be adopted.

(5) *Insurance Policy System.*

For practical purposes this method corresponds with the Sinking Fund System, excepting that instead of the investment being made direct an endowment policy with an insurance company is taken out sufficient to produce the amount required at the expiration of the term.

(6) *Estimate System.*

The amount which it is estimated will have to be spent on repairs by renewals during the life of the asset is, for the purpose of the depreciation calculations, added to the original cost, and a fixed proportion of the total debited to revenue each year.

All repairs and renewals will then be charged to the Asset Account instead of to revenue during the term.

The difficulty is to estimate the amount which will have to be spent on repairs, &c., and the preferable method is to adopt the suggestion made on p. 575, and average such expenditure in a separate account.

(7) *Revaluation System.*

To revalue the fixed assets each year, charging any diminution in value after allowing for additions to revenue as representing depreciation, is a method adopted by some engineering firms, but, apart from the cost and labour involved, the system is unsatisfactory, as with the exception of assets of an equal market, or small individual value, the charge to revenue will be unequal, owing to the fluctuation in the market price affecting the result, whereas it is most necessary that depreciation charges should for costing purposes be as constant as possible.

A periodical valuation is, however, always desirable as a check on the sufficiency of the depreciation charged, but it does not follow that because such valuation exceeds the book value the rate employed has been excessive.

In the case of live stock, patents, loose tools, &c., this method may and frequently is adopted, but in other cases it is not advisable.

It is not intended to discuss here the actual rates to be employed, but a few general observations respecting certain assets may be of use.

(1) *Buildings.*

It is often suggested that as buildings are kept in an efficient condition out of revenue it is unnecessary to provide any depreciation. Nevertheless, the most substantial buildings cannot last for ever, and there is always the question of obsolescence. Improved methods of production and organisation often necessitate new buildings, whilst a variety of causes may make removal desirable. The buildings are erected for the purpose of earning revenue, and the turnover done should be charged with the proper proportion of the cost, so that when alterations in the trade necessitate alterations in the situation of the works the change can be effected without capital loss. In other words, account should be taken of the possibility that the works, like the plant, may some time be out of date, although the physical life has not yet expired.

It not infrequently happens that expenditure treated in the financial books as on buildings is actually in relation to the plant.

Alterations in the plant may mean new floors at different levels, or the removal of girders and columns, necessitating considerable expenditure in the reconstruction of the building, and this factor must be taken into account when considering the rate of depreciation to be employed.

In the case of leaseholds the amount paid for the lease will be written off on the Annuity method, and the cost of buildings depreciated at such rate that, although the physical life may exceed the length of the lease, the value will be eliminated during that period.

(2) *Furniture, Fixtures, and Fittings.*

The rate depends very largely on the nature of the asset; but if a large amount has been spent on joinery work, the cost should not be spread over a long period, as the life is generally short, owing to the alterations made from time to time.

(3) *Plant and Machinery.*

The estimation of the life of plant and machinery is entirely a matter for the consideration of the engineers.

Each class of plant has to be considered on its own merits, and in some cases different rates adopted for different machines of the same pattern.

The classification is also a matter depending on circumstances, a frequent division being—

(1) Engines and Boilers.
(2) Shafting.
(3) General machinery.
(4) Special machinery.
(5) Fixed Plant.

Another classification is—

(1) Motive power, including boilers, engines, &c.
(2) Prime movers, such as shafting, pulleys, &c.
(3) Productive plant, such as lathes, saws, steam hammers, &c.
(4) Miscellaneous, including weighing machines, cranes, &c.

The particular circumstances of each case must, however, always be considered. For instance, a low pressure boiler will last much longer than a high pressure boiler, whilst the life of either will be prolonged by the use of a water softening plant.

Engines running day and night will wear out more quickly than those which are afforded periodical rests.

Electric motive power is gradually displacing gas and steam in certain trades, and the risk of obsolescence in such cases, particularly of the shafting, is therefore great.

Other instances could be cited, but the above are sufficient to show that no good purpose can be served by laying down general rates of depreciation, the estimated life being a matter for the decision of experts competent to judge upon the facts of each case.

Where, however, special machinery is put down for some particular job, and it is not expected that it will be of any value subsequently, except as scrap, the whole cost should be charged against that order, less the residual value.

In all well-managed concerns a Plant and Machinery Ledger is kept, an account being opened for each machine, or class of plant or machine.

Additions, repairs and renewals, and other expenses are debited, and depreciation and the amount written off for repairs and renewals credited, so that the cost of running each machine can be readily ascertained.

The Plant and Machinery Ledger does not generally form an integral part of the financial books, being of the nature of a subsidiary Ledger showing the details of the Plant and Machinery Account in the Private Ledger, a summary being made each year and agreed with the Private Ledger total.

The following example illustrates the form of such register:—

PLANT LEDGER.

GAS ENGINE, DON MILL.

PARTICULARS.—*Date Purchased*, 1st January 1913.
Makers, The Universal Engine Co., Lim. *Insurance Policy*, No. 8614. *National Insurance Co.*
Cost, £1,000 *Specification* (Set out details).

Date	Particulars	Fo.	Interest	Additions		Repairs and Renewals		Total
				Time	Materials	Time	Materials	
1913			£ s d	£ s d	£ s d	£ s d	£ s d	£ s d
Jan. 1	To Purchase price	P.J. 61	..	..	..	..	..	1,000 0 0
Oct. 1	" Repairs as per Work in Progress Account..	Cost Sum. 182	..	..	..	18 3 0	16 4 0	34 7 0
Nov. 31	" Jobbers Limited General repairs	P.J. 191	..	..	..	..	15 14 0	15 14 0
Dec. 20	" Patent Starter	..	..	..	10 0 0	..	..	10 0 0
31	" Interest at 5%	JRL. 16	50 0 0	..	..	..	..	50 0 0
			£50 0 0		£10 0 0	£18 3 0	£31 18 0	£1,110 1 0
1913 Dec. 31	To Balance	C.	..		..	..	..	960 0 0

(Continued)

Date	Particulars	Fo.	Repairs and Renewals	Depreciation	Interest	Total
1913			£ s d	£ s d	£ s d	£ s d
Dec. 31	By Trading Account	P.L. 61	50 1 0	50 0 0	50 0 0	150 1 0
	" Balance	C.	..	..	..	960 0 0
						£1,110 1 0

In the above illustration depreciation has been taken at 5 per cent. on original cost, and scrap value ignored.

If the Annuity System of depreciation had been adopted, the column for "Interest" on the right-hand side would be omitted, and the charge for depreciation would then be £73 11s. 8d.

It is assumed, however, that for departmentalisation purposes interest on the reducing value is charged against gross profits and credited to Profit and Loss Account.

The value of the summary of the various accounts for comparative purposes makes this record most desirable in all large undertakings.

(4) *Loose Tools.*

One of the following three methods is usually adopted :—

(1) To revalue the tools each year, charging any diminution to revenue.

(2) To write off about 15 per cent. during each of the first three years, and then, provided the turnover is normal, to charge all renewals to revenue.

(3) To capitalise all renewals and write off about 33⅓ per cent. each year.

(5) *Patterns, Moulds, &c.*

If the cost of the pattern is charged to the customer, the amount must not also be included in Patterns Account. Stock patterns are best valued at intrinsic worth, that is to say, the value of the metal, and in the case of wooden patterns the whole cost written off.

It is frequently contended, however, often with good cause, that the cost of a particular pattern has been heavy, and that, apart from the intrinsic worth, considerable goodwill value attaches thereto.

In the case of patented patterns the value nevertheless is not in the pattern, but in the patent, and the cost of the patent will often include the cost of the pattern.

In other cases, any goodwill value cannot be taken into account beyond the actual cost of making the pattern, and even then the valuation is dependent on the benefit to be derived from future use.

The cost of making patterns will be recorded through the Cost Books and transferred to the Impersonal Ledger. As regards patterns charged out, or the amount debited to a job for the use of patterns, the entry in the Cost Ledger should be made through the medium of a Pattern Day Book, the total being charged to the Work in Progress Account and credited to the Patterns Account in the General Ledger.

Goodwill.

Goodwill was defined by Lord Justice Lindley as "the benefit arising from connection and reputation."

Actually goodwill represents the capitalised value of the profits earned over and above the ordinary rate of interest which the prudent investor would expect from the investment of his money in that particular business after taking into account the risk of capital involved.

The value of the goodwill depends entirely on the profits earned and the probability of those profits being maintained.

The question of the depreciation of the amount stated in a company's Balance Sheet as representing the value of the goodwill is one which frequently arises, but as a matter of fact goodwill cannot depreciate, and although its market value may vary, such changes are due to fluctuation and not to depreciation.

If a company write off its goodwill, the amount set aside is an *appropriation* of realised profits and not a *charge against* profits.

If sufficient profits are, however, earned to provide the directors with enough surplus to allow such appropriation to be made, then it is evident that the goodwill has not decreased in value—if any alteration in value has occurred, the goodwill has appreciated owing to the increased profits.

If, however, the surplus profits are not sufficient for this purpose, then, although the value of the goodwill may be less than the book value, there is no fund available out of which the amount can be written down.

A company is under no legal obligation to write down its goodwill (*Wilmer v. McNamara,* 1895), whether the saleable value has or has not been reduced, and unless the company already has a large Reserve Fund, and desires to retain surplus profits in the business as additional working capital, without calling special attention to the fact, it is preferable to build up a Reserve Fund and show the goodwill at its original cost.

So far as the Cost Accounts are concerned, the question of writing down goodwill is immaterial, as the amount written off cannot be regarded in any way as part of the cost of production.

A case, however, may arise where a company has acquired another business, manufacturing a speciality which has only an expected short life. The amount paid for goodwill under such circumstances corresponds with the amount paid for a patent, and it would therefore be necessary in this event to deal with it accordingly. (*Vide* Patents, below.)

Similarly, where a competitive business has been acquired in order to prevent cutting, and the result is an immediate increase in selling price, it is proper to write off the purchase price, and such amount may in these circumstances be regarded as an element of cost.

But, generally speaking, there is no more obligation on a company to write down goodwill to its saleable value than to write down plant and works to scrap price.

Patents.

The life of a patent is fourteen years, although in exceptional cases an extension may be obtained.

The cost, which includes not only the purchase price or the experimental expenditure, but possibly patterns, advertising, and similar expenses, should therefore, as a general rule, be written off during that period. Unless it is anticipated that full benefits will be enjoyed from the use of the patent during the whole of that time, the full period should not, however, be treated as the life, as it may be that the patent will be worthless or its earning capacity considerably reduced before its nominal life expires.

On the other hand, no appreciable benefit may be obtained during the first two or three years, whilst during the later life of the patent a valuable goodwill may be built up, in which case no depreciation may be necessary.

It is futile to attempt to lay down any general rules, as each patent must be considered on its own merits and depreciated accordingly.

If the removal of the protection given by the patent rights is likely to affect the profit-earning capacities of the article manufactured, provision should be made to cover the capital loss which will accrue, an amount being charged to prime cost which represents the proportion of the original outlay in obtaining the monopoly based on the estimated turnover.

Again, where the nature of the business is such that it it necessary constantly to take out or purchase new patents, the expenditure incurred must be treated as an element of cost, and the same rule applies where minor patents are obtained to protect the original patent.

If, however, a patent is purchased or taken out after considerable experimental expenditure, and proves worthless, the cost should be written off out of profits, but cannot be regarded as part of the prime cost of manufacture of articles under other patents of a different character, the amount written off being an appropriation of and not a charge against profits.

The amount at which any patent is included in a Balance Sheet must not under any circumstances exceed the cost price, and if any revenue is derived from the granting of licences to other persons to use the patent, as such revenue will cease when the life expires, a proportionate amount must be written off. Otherwise, if at the expiration of the life a considerable goodwill value will remain, there is no reason why a company should write off the patent during its life.

It is always desirable, however, to build up a Reserve Fund out of profits equal to the value of such intangible assets as patents, goodwill, &c.

From the above consideration of the subject of depreciation, it will be apparent therefore that, although from the costing standpoint the amount included under the head of "Use of Machinery" in the shop oncost for this item is fixed at the commencement of each year, and occasions but little difficulty in the calculation of the amount to be charged to each job, yet the actual provision to be made in order to estimate such fixed charge is a matter of some complexity, necessitating the greatest care, as any miscalculation will not only alter the costing result, but may materially prejudice the future of the business, affecting as it does both Capital and Revenue Accounts.

Capital Requirements.

The amount of capital required in proportion to turnover varies considerably in different businesses. As a general rule, the book debts in proportion to turnover of a manufacturer supplying products for direct sale to the public are greater than in the case of a contractor or manufacturer whose merchandise will be used for productive purposes and not for sale to the consumer, whilst the former has to keep a larger stock of finished articles, thus requiring a greater amount of working capital in proportion to turnover.

On the other hand, the latter will probably have more capital locked up in fixed assets, against which there is no corresponding credit for amounts due to trade creditors.

The amount of capital required by a manufacturer also varies according to the various stages of manufacture performed. An engineering firm with its own foundry would require considerably more capital than another firm which purchased its castings, not only because of the amount invested in fixed assets, but also because the moulders would be paid week by week, and that amount of capital would be locked up until the job was completed, whereas if the castings are purchased, capital would only be required from the date of payment to the foundry company.

Herein, however, lies the necessity for accurate costing, in order to ascertain whether it is more profitable to factor or manufacture at each stage of production.

The question of markets in relation to capital requirements has also to be considered. Many firms acquire a special reputation in some particular market, and obtain most of their trade in that quarter. The terms of credit, however, vary; and whereas, in one, immediate payment is obtainable, in another three or six months' bills may be customary.

In considering the amount of capital required for a business the following points must be taken into account:

(1) The capital to be sunk in fixed assets.
(2) The working capital needed.
(3) The capital which will be required for unproductive and unrepresented expenditure, such as goodwill.

In determining the amount of working capital it is necessary to consider—

(1) The estimated turnover.
(2) The average credit to be given.
(3) The average credit to be obtained.
(4) The average amount of raw materials either in stores or used on work in progress.
(5) The amount of working expenses.
(6) The average wage bill.

Taking these factors into consideration, the amount of working capital can be ascertained, which, added to the capital invested in fixed assets and unrepresented expenditure, gives the total required, part of which may be raised by debentures or loans, according to circumstances.

Generally speaking, it is not possible to base the estimates on the number of hands employed, except by examination of the records of an exactly similar concern carrying through the same stages of production and trading in the same market.

Conclusion.

The necessity for accurate cost keeping and the application of proper principles of accounting in calculations of productive cost are due not only to increased competition, but also to the alteration in the nature of the ownership of industrial concerns during the last half-century.

When commerce was in the hands of individuals, each of whom carried on business in a small way, it was of small moment whether proper provision was made for depreciation or a correct apportionment of capital and revenue expenditure recorded in the books, provided sufficient cash was available for use when required.

The conditions have, however, changed, and the great bulk of commercial undertakings are in the hands of limited companies, and controlled by a few directors, who are the representatives of the real owners, who take no active part in the administration. The accuracy of the amounts available for distribution as dividend cannot be tested by the shareholders individually, and they are justified in regarding the profits supposed to have been earned as properly attributable to revenue.

It is necessary, therefore, to compute such profits as accurately as possible, and as, usually, the directors themselves do not, with the exception of the managing director, take any actual part in the daily conduct of the business, it is indispensable that the records and statistics available for their consideration should be sufficiently detailed and precise to give them the opportunity of detecting the weak places in the administration.

Cost Accounts not only show the cost of production for the purpose of fixing selling prices and meeting competition, but also indicate the respective advantages of machine and hand labour, and the merits of various types of plant or rival processes.

Without accurate cost records no large commercial undertaking can now be successfully controlled; without due regard to the determination of the provision to be made for the exhaustion of wasting assets no business can be conducted on a sound financial basis.

Unfortunately, in many concerns the calculation of the depreciation is made by "rule of thumb."

Certain fixed percentages are written off because it is assumed that such amount *should* "more than cover the loss under this head." Whilst the financial books are kept with the strictest accuracy and a Trial Balance agreed to a penny; whilst the provisions made for accrued expenses are worked out to the nearest farthing; whilst the calculations in the stock sheets are carefully checked and re-checked, and every item of petty cash expenditure is scrutinised—yet no attempt is made to ascertain with any degree of certainty the extent to which the original capital outlay has diminished in producing the revenue earned.

The cause is attributable to a lack of co-operation between the engineers and the accountants, and not until those responsible for the administration recognise that, by the joint application of the experience of the former and the records of the latter it is possible to determine more correctly the provision to be made, will the present unsatisfactory state of affairs be remedied.

This is an age of specialisation, but the successful management of a concern does not depend alone on the technical knowledge of the controlling spirit, but on his ability to select the right men for the subordinate posts; on his powers of observation and discrimination; on that faculty which enables him to leave details to others, whilst keeping the broad issues before his mind, and on his aptitude for understanding and dealing with human nature.

But although a man possess all these attributes he must have the records of the business before him to enable him to formulate his policy and to assist his judgment, and unless he understand the value of accounts and the construction of the financial statements given to him, he cannot make that use of them which should be the case.

Cost Accounts are the index of the works, but those who use that index must understand the meaning of the text, as without that knowledge the index is useless.

Gladstone said, in a speech at Chester in 1890, that "Technical education is the exaltation of manual "labour, the bringing of manual labour up to the "highest excellence of which it is susceptible," but perfection will not be attained until those responsible for the curriculum recognise that a knowledge of the principles of accounting is as essential to the manufacturer as a knowledge of the technical side of the business in which he is engaged.

It must also always be borne in mind that no business can remain at a standstill, to be successful it must be progressive; and to be progressive it must be built up on a solid foundation that it may be lasting.

Only by a conservative financial policy can this be attained, for the capital which merely exists on paper is simply "dead weight" and unproductive.

The so-called "principles of accounting" are not mere theoretical fads of figure-smiths, but economical conclusions, the truth of which experience will always prove, and as business can only be carried on by the exchange of commodities at a price *exceeding* the cost to the seller it is necessary to apply those "principles" to ascertain what actually is that cost.

Modern business methods are due to evolution in the methods of production, and scientific accounting has been rendered necessary by that change; but

You may figure out in decimals what every job has cost
By systems up-to-date, and scientific;
And demonstrate in units what you've made or what you've lost
And show results reverse of soporific,
But all your calculation
Of expense, depreciation,
And departmental profit-charges—fails
No matter how instructive,
The result is unproductive
If you *don't know* the way to push your SALES.

Importance of True Cost.

By Robert E. Belt, C.P.A.

(From *The Journal of Accountancy*, N.Y.)

An address at the annual meeting of the North Carolina Pine Association, Norfolk, Virginia, 1916.

The subject of costs may not be a very entertaining one, but it is one which should be of great interest to business men, because it relates to information which is essential to the successful conduct of a business. This is a subject that is at present receiving careful attention on the part of many trade associations, and a number of them have achieved marked success in bettering the accounting methods of their members and thereby improving and strengthening their industries in general.

Formerly little attention was paid by manufacturers and by business men to the question of costs. The necessity for a knowledge of costs and its analysis was not so great, as the margins of profits were larger. But to-day margins of profit in most lines are much narrower than formerly and the necessity for the most efficient management and the closest analysis is felt as never before.

It is necessary to-day for a manufacturer's success that he know on what articles he is making a profit and on what he is incurring a loss. Prominent vehicle manufacturers recently made the statement to the Federal Trade Commission that they were forced, for their own protection, to instal an efficient cost system. This cost system showed them, they said, that they had been in the past labouring under wrong impressions. They were surprised to find that where they thought they were making money they were not making it, and that certain lines they were not pushing were affording a far greater percentage of profit than lines they were actively pushing.

A similar instance which came to our attention was the misfortune of a manufacturer of stoves. He had been making two styles, both on a fairly large scale, and on both he considered he was making a profit, as his balance at the end of the year was on the right side of the Ledger and was fairly satisfactory in amount. But for some reason, not clear to him, the one style was selling much better than the other, so he gave orders to his salesman to drop the one to push the good seller. Everything went along well, but at the end of the year things did not come out right. He was at a loss to understand the situation; so he called in an accountant, and, much to the manufacturer's astonishment, the accountant convinced him that the stove he had been pushing had been sold for years at a loss. The only profit he had ever made was on the stove he had slighted, for the reason that it was not selling as readily as the one he had been disposing of at less than cost.

Unfortunately the value and importance of proper cost accounts are often underestimated. So long as the details of a business can be carried in mind, cost records are not so essential, but when this cannot be done it becomes absolutely necessary for the safe conduct of business that cost records be kept. They serve three broad purposes : first, they show the cost of each job or product ; second, they permit the elimination of unprofitable business ; and, third, they establish a correct basis upon which to make future prices. Arbitrarily making a price may result not only in a direct loss but an indirect loss by reason of the demoralising influence in establishing a false price for future business. A manufacturer owes it to his stockholders, his employees, his customers, and his competitors to determine accurately his cost of production. To sell blindly a product of which the complete cost is not known almost invariably produces bad results, not only to the company but to the industry as a whole. Your most dangerous competitor is the man who does not know what his goods cost him.

Another marked advantage of properly kept costs is their value as an index of operating efficiency. With properly prepared cost figures the relative efficiency of the various departments of plants may be watched and compared. The current results obtained in each department may be checked against those obtained in the past, thereby showing increases in efficiency, or the reverse, and the results of improvements in practice. A constant study of properly prepared cost figures will help to bring to light poor and inefficient management and will enable standards to be set for the less efficient departments, based on what actually has been done in departments that are being properly and efficiently administered. In other words, a complete and properly kept cost accounting system will be found to exercise the important and productive function of helping to lower costs and holding them at the lowest practicable level.

In my opinion the day will come when the success of a manufacturer will depend upon the information a complete and accurate system gives him. It will be as essential as good workmen and a good organisation.

This lack of knowledge of the cost of doing business which is so essential to success is a cause of unfair competition, demoralisation and bankruptcy. The fact that our business failures of last year entailed a direct loss to creditors of over $200,000,000 gives some idea of a part of the economic loss which is placed upon the shoulders of the public.

For this reason every chance should be given a weak and tottering concern to get on its feet if it is doing a legitimate business, as the public suffers every time a business goes to the wall, and, conversely, the public is benefited every time a tottering business is saved, if it is a worthy one.

I know I am safe in saying that with better accounting many of our bad business practices would be brought to light and promptly curbed. When accurate results are known to proprietors and to creditors, conditions never become so bad and the losses never so great, as good accounting gives trustworthy information and timely warning.

Undoubtedly ruinous prices are due more to the fact that many manufacturers do not know what their actual costs are than to a desire on their part to sell at prices which do not yield a fair return on the money invested. At times most manufacturers, as a matter of expediency, are obliged to take orders which return little if any profit ; but in the great majority of cases I believe that unprofitable prices are made by manufacturers as a result of their not knowing their total and complete costs of production and distribution.

The trouble is that too many people in figuring profit fail to take into account all the expenses incurred in conducting their business. There's where the trouble comes in. There is no net profit until everything in the way of expense and service is taken care of, including depreciation, taxes, insurance in all its forms, losses from bad debts, price discounts and expense in collecting outstanding receivables. The omission of such items as these is the reason that the final Profit and Loss Account at the end of the year is so often disappointing and so difficult to reconcile with the profit percentage that was added to the supposed cost of the goods.

There are in the United States 250,000 corporations exclusive of banking, railroad and public utility corporations. Of this number, over 100,000, or 40 per cent., do not earn a penny for their stockholders. This shows clearly that there is an unduly large proportion of unsuccessful business in the country.

What is the remedy for this condition? The remedy lies in a large measure in co-operative effort to increase efficiency and to eliminate unintelligent competition.

It is the belief of the Federal Trade Commission that if merchants and manufacturers would agree on some standard practical system of accounting, it would go a long way towards eliminating the unintelligent and destructive competition that is so manifest in many of our industries of to-day.

It is of great importance to the manufacturers of an industry that they agree on the elements or fundamentals of a cost practice, especially to make sure that all the elements of cost are included in their calculations. This is of vital importance. Make sure that you have included in your cost an adequate provision for depreciation and every expense of every description incurred during the year. The test of the accuracy of a cost system is that it dovetails in and co-ordinates with the financial books of account. The cost, then, in the aggregate at least, must be correct.

Production costs, determined by a uniform practice, it has been demonstrated, improve trade conditions to a remarkable degree.

Excellent results are being obtained by trade associations by appointing men to devote their entire time to visiting the concerns that are engaged in their industry, getting acquainted, preaching the gospel of good accounting practice, reconciling differences, and standardising methods. When the person engaged for this work has the subject at heart, is congenial and persuasive and well grounded in the principles of cost accounting, the results in improving the general welfare of the industry are surprising. There should be no selfish motives back of such service. There should be the same willingness and free spirit to help and to aid and bring in line the non-member of an organisation as is manifested toward the member. The non-member is usually the trouble maker. In the interests of the industry, he should be guided by the experience of others. The fallacies and disastrous results of bad business practice should be pointed out to him.

Business men are looking upon activities for the general welfare of their industry in a new light. They are being governed by the single purpose to promote the best interests of the community and of the industry in which they are engaged. They are putting aside sectional differences and there is the broadest and most generous co-operation for the general good. As an example—in the paint industry, one of our largest and most successful establishments has issued a standing invitation to its competitors to inspect its cost records, to adopt its efficiency methods and to profit by its long period of business experience.

The American manufacturer or merchant, generally speaking, is especially in need of such assistance on account of his inexperience to carry on the business in which he engages. We are in this respect at a marked disadvantage as compared with our European competitors. In Europe the business man is brought up in the business that he conducts. He knows his business in all its details, and consequently is thoroughly fitted for his vocation. In America there is a tendency to experiment. The farmer of yesterday becomes the business man of to-day. The lawyer, the doctor, or the day labourer will enter upon a business career in which he has had little or no training. He will depend on the jobber for the selection of his merchandise and on an untrained employee for the care of it. In his effort to attract customers he will mark his goods below the prices of the business man of experience. He is trying to give service for which no adequate provision is made in the margin between cost and selling price. As a consequence there is general demoralisation, for, not only is he wasting his own capital, but, what is worse, he is creating a condition with which the man of experience finds it difficult to contend.

The Federal Trade Commission, under the direction of the Vice-Chairman, Edward N. Hurley, is aiding and co-operating with trade associations and with individual merchants and manufacturers in improving accounting methods and business practice. The preliminary work of the Commission has shown that an amazing number of smaller merchants and manufacturers have no adequate system of determining their cost and that they fix the prices of their goods arbitrarily. Various associations appearing before the Commission have emphasised the necessity for improvement in this direction before competition can be placed upon a sound economic basis.

The lack of a correct knowledge of one's business carries with it various undesirable results. In the first place, the manufacturer is unable to conduct his business upon sound business principles. The results are reprehensible practices as disastrous at times as intentionally unfair methods of competition. In the second place, he severely handicaps himself in that he is unable when seeking credit to produce a correct statement of his financial condition which would enable a banker to extend to him the full credit to which he is entitled. He thereby hampers and limits the possible expansion of his business. The Commission hopes to aid in a constructive way in the correction of these conditions.

The plan, as worked out, is to co-operate with trade associations and others to encourage improvements in accounting methods and business practices, to endorse standard systems of cost accounting for the different lines of trade and industry and to recommend to merchants and manufacturers the adoption of such systems in the interests of better trade conditions. We have for this work experienced accountants and cost experts and the services, in an advisory capacity, of public accountants of national reputation.

If the appropriations of the Commission will permit, it is also contemplated to conduct an educational campaign upon this subject among the small retail merchants and manufacturers, making available to them such data as will enable them more efficiently to conduct their business. In other words, the Commission expects to aid the business man in much the same way that the Department of Agriculture is aiding the farmer. It is felt that this line of activity will be of national significance in its results for the following reasons :—

First. Because individual enterprises will be helped, in that prices will be placed upon a solid basis of fact and a foundation will be laid for the securing of credit, which will result in a normal and healthful expansion of industry.

Second. Because the investor will be benefited, in that he will be able to invest his money with greater safety and a larger assurance of profit.

Third. Because the public will be benefited, in that unintelligent competition, which ultimately reacts upon the public welfare, will be largely eliminated and inefficient methods and practices, which are costly to the public, will be at least partly eradicated.

The Federal Trade Commission is also compiling information for the benefit of business men, embracing every industry of the United States, showing annual sales, capital invested and the return thereon, together with other information which will be of value to business. This will give every man who is engaged in business an opportunity to know whether or not the industry in which he is engaged is in a healthy condition. The industries in which conditions are not found to be healthy will receive particular attention for the purpose of ascertaining the underlying causes. Not only will this information be of practical value to those already engaged in business, but the knowledge of the existence of generally unhealthy conditions will prevent others from investing in an enterprise when the odds are against them.

The Trade Commission believes that with the co-operation of business men it can be of constructive help in assisting to bring about better trade conditions—conditions which will lessen our business death-rate, enable our merchants and manufacturers to compete more intelligently with each other and make them more formidable competitors in the markets of the world.

Fundamentals of a Cost System for Manufacturers.

It is a fact too little realised that an accurate determination of costs is fundamentally related to manufacturing efficiency. More and more concerns are joining the ranks of those who realise the necessity of knowing accurately their costs of manufacturing and selling. Every business man who joins in this work can feel that he is doing his part toward the improvement of business conditions generally and his own business conditions in particular. This bulletin, published by the Federal Trade Commission of Washington, U.S.A., has been prepared with a view to aiding the campaign of education by explaining what a cost system is, how it operates, the results obtained, and the benefits to be derived from its operation.

Objections to Installing Cost Systems.

There are a number of objections in the minds of business men who have not installed costs systems to taking the matter up. One of these is the feeling that exists in the minds of so many that their business is unique and different from any other, and that no system could be devised which would give them true costs. It is unquestionably true that some lines of manufacture lend themselves more readily to the installation of a cost system than others, but it is also true that no line of manufacture is so complicated that a system cannot be devised which will give reasonably accurate results.

The most common objection is that of the cost of installation and the expense of operation. Many manufacturers are of the opinion that a cost system means an interminable amount of detail and red tape, and the assistance of a number of extra clerks. It is true, in many cases, that some extra labour may be required, but not to the extent that the manufacturer fears. There is in nearly every office that is not systematised sufficient unnecessary work done to cut the extra work down to a minimum, and, in fact, in some cases where an office has been systematised, it has not been necessary to employ any extra help at all. If the manufacturer will look upon a cost system as an investment which he expects to produce for him a fair return in the same manner that an investment in improved machinery would, the objection as to the expense is not a valid one. A number of business men think that money spent for stationery is wasted, and that a cheap ready-made book will answer as well as one specially designed for his business. If a 10 dollar book which lasts a year will save half an hour a day for a 12 dollar-a-week clerk as compared with the use of a ready-made book which can be bought for 1 dollar, the additional investment of 9 dollars has brought in a revenue or effected a saving of 39 dollars for the year. This holds true of nearly all specially designed forms as well.

Other business men are of the opinion that they do not need a cost system because they know what their goods cost. They may, and a number of them do have an approximate idea of what their goods cost, but in a large number of instances this supposed knowledge is based on foremen's guesses in advance as to the time necessary to do the work or as to the time spent on the work after it is done. Guesswork is unsafe and poor business practice.

Necessity for Ascertaining True Costs.

Formerly the necessity for the determination of true manufacturing costs was not as imperative as it is to-day. Margins between cost and selling price in most lines were larger. Costs could be ignored except in a general way, and a good return still be made on the investment; but to-day margins of profit in most lines of trade are very much narrower than formerly, and the necessity for the most efficient management and closest analysis is felt as never before.

It is necessary to-day for the business man's success that he know on what articles he is making a profit and on what he is incurring a loss. Competitive conditions are seriously disturbed where losses on one or more articles are recovered by profits on other articles. It is obvious that a manufacturer should not only know the cost of each article he manufactures but that he should see that every article manufactured bears its proper share of factory and general overhead.

Most manufacturing plants have grown to a size which renders personal supervision impossible. The only reliable way, therefore, by which an executive can judge of the efficiency of an organisation is through a system of periodical statistical reports. These reports can only be accurately obtained when a good cost system is in operation.

New methods are being introduced and improved machinery installed in the factory every day, with a view of reducing costs either by the elimination of waste or by increasing efficiency. It is impossible to know whether the introduction of these improvements will reduce costs unless the manufacturer knows not only what his total cost is but exactly what items make up the total. Items of cost are frequently lost track of when the total only is considered, while if these items were properly segregated so as show what they were they could be materially reduced and, in some instances, eliminated altogether.

Exchange of Statistical Information Beneficial.

In the past many manufacturers disliked to give out information concerning their business. To-day the reverse is the case. Trade associations are compiling statistics as to production, shipments, and costs for the benefit of their members, and the manufacturer, instead of trying to keep this information to himself, welcomes the opportunity to supply the data, knowing that his competitors are doing the same thing and that these statistics will be of benefit to himself and to his industry. The Federal Trade Commission is keenly alive to the value of this information.

The Commission is urging manufacturers to determine their costs accurately in the interest of better trade conditions. It believes that anything that is of benefit to an industry is of benefit to the public, and it is also of the opinion that the nearer cost systems approach uniformity the more valuable will be the results.

Many Businesses not Profitable.

A large proportion of manufacturers are not making the money they should. A great number of them are actually losing money.

The purpose of conducting a business is to make money, and the only way to make money is to sell something for more than it costs. The first essential, then, is to know the cost. It is the belief of the Commission that the small margin of profit existing in so many of our industries is due to the ignorance on the part of manufacturers of what their goods actually cost to produce. This ignorance causes them to make unprofitable prices, which the manufacturer who does know his cost is forced to meet to a large extent.

What is Cost?

Cost is defined as the amount or equivalent paid, or charged, or given for anything; loss of any kind, expenditure, outlay, as of money, time, labour.

This equivalent may be in the form of money paid for material or for labour, or for some one of the many kinds of expense or loss that exist in every manufacturing business. It is apparent that cost consists of three elements, viz. material, labour, and expense.

System and its Development.

The problem is to ascertain the amount of each of these elements, and in order to accomplish this in the simplest and most practical manner the manufacturer has recourse to system. System is defined as a regular method or order, a formal arrangement, or a mode of operation governed by general laws or rules.

During the last ten years the best accounting brains in the country have been devoting a great deal of time to the perfection of general laws or rules which will give the desired results with the least effort and expense, and the outcome of their work is what is known as a "Cost System." This provides not only for the determination of the amount of each element of cost properly chargeable to each job or operation, but also provides for an improved method of bookkeeping which causes the books to reflect at all times the true financial and industrial condition of the business and renders possible the preparation of monthly statements of conditions, as well as complete monthly statements of financial and factory operations.

There are, generally speaking, but two distinct methods of manufacture. Each requires a cost system a little different in detail but identical in fundamental principles. The first of these is used in a business where every order is a separate article of manufacture, very often made to order, and the selling price fixed before work is started; and the second is used in a business where the output consists of one or more articles which are being continually produced. For convenience we will designate the cost systems applicable to each as the "Job Cost System" and the "Continuous Production System."

THE JOB COST SYSTEM.

The first step is to provide for giving the factory instructions as to what work is to be done, and a form should be provided which must give the following information: Job number, date, name and address of customer for whom work is to be done, a description of the work to be done, giving sufficient details, specifications as to what material will be needed, and shipping instructions. This form should also have space for the entry of shipments, so that when the work is done the order form will be a complete record. A duplicate of this factory order should be kept in the office, and when the original is sent to the factory the cost clerk opens a job cost sheet under that number.

The job cost sheet should show number, date opened, customer's name, and, in some cases, a brief description of the work is advisable, as it sometimes enables the cost clerk to detect an error in the number shown on the time ticket or material requisition. As all reports are made by job number instead of by name, it is of vital importance that the greatest care be taken to insure the correctness of the numbers on the time tickets and material requisitions. In addition to the above information, the cost sheet should be arranged so as to provide columns for the following: Date, employee's number, hours, amount of pay, machine number, machine hours, requisition number, quantity of material, and cost thereof.

Material.—The first element of cost is material. Material is of two kinds, direct and indirect.

Direct material is that which forms part of some particular job and can be so charged. Indirect material is that which cannot be located as belonging to a particular job, and which is more in the nature of general supplies. This class of material is sometimes termed "expense material," as its ultimate destination is the Expense Account of some department.

Material must be purchased, received, checked, and taken care of until it is required for use, and the general method recommended is as follows:—

A part of the factory should be set aside as a stock room and some employee designated to perform the duties of stock clerk. The stock clerk will keep the stock ledger cards or sheets, one for each article, showing the quantity on hand. These cards should also show the maximum quantity of each article he is to be allowed to carry and also the minimum below which the stock must not be allowed to fall. When the stock reaches the minimum a requisition should be made on the purchasing agent for sufficient quantity to bring the stock up to the maximum and sent to the superintendent or works manager for approval, after which the goods are ordered. When the goods come in they should go to the receiving clerk, who checks them, reports their receipt to the office, and delivers the goods to the stock room, where they remain until requisitioned out.

When the order reaches the factory the first step is to obtain the material, and a requisition should be made on the storeroom for the necessary quantity. This requisition should be numbered and space should be provided thereon for job number or department, date, quantity, description, price, amount, and signature of foreman. The cost clerk extends the amount on the requisition and posts it to the job cost sheet in the space provided, then files it away until the end of the month, when the total for the month must be obtained.

Labour.—The second element of cost is labour, and this, like material, is divided into two classes—direct, or, as it is sometimes called, productive labour, and indirect, or non-productive labour. Direct labour is that which is applied directly to the job and which can be so charged. Indirect labour is that which cannot be located as belonging to any particular job, but must be charged to the expenses of some department.

The general method of handling labour is to have each employee make up a time ticket each day. This ticket, for recording direct labour, should show the employee's name, employee's number, date and hours worked on each job, job number, and machine number, if a machine is used; and in the case of indirect labour the department and nature of the work must be shown in lieu of job number. These time tickets are sent in to the office each day and the direct labour is posted to the job cost sheets and the indirect labour entered on a summary sheet with columns headed by the name of departments, so that the totals can be posted to the Department Expense Account at the end of the month.

The productive hours for each department are entered on another summary, both for man hours and machine hours, which is totalled at the end of the month. If the work is correctly done, the totals on this summary will equal the total of the postings made to the job cost sheets.

Overhead Expense.—The job cost sheet now has entered thereon the first two elements of cost, viz. direct material and direct labour, and the next question is the proper method of handling the third element of cost, which is generally known as "Overhead Expense," or, as it is also called, "Burden." Overhead expense is the expense of every kind connected with the business, none of which can be directly located as belonging to a particular job. These expenses, while part of the cost of a job, are general, so cannot reach the job direct; hence a method must be devised for them to reach the cost sheet in an indirect manner, the method at the same time being so planned that each job will receive its fair proportion of the total.

Before taking up the question of how overhead expense is to be handled, it is necessary to determine just what items constitute overhead. A list of these items and their description must necessarily be very general and subject to change, as items of expense occur in some lines of manufacture which it is necessary to treat as overhead, while the same items in another line can be handled as direct expense.

Overhead may properly be divided into two classes—factory overhead, which consists of items directly belonging to factory operations, and general overhead, which is expense not directly connected with the factory.

As factory overhead is one of the items of total factory cost, the method of handling this will be outlined first.

Departmentalisation Necessary for Proper Distribution of Factory Overhead.

The first step in a fair and equable distribution of factory overhead is a departmentalisation of the business. Every business can be departmentalised to some extent, some more than others, but the subdivision into departments varies so much in the different lines that it is almost impossible to give any definite idea as to what divisions should be made. Generally speaking, it is best to subdivide into departments according to operations of manufacture, although at times, for simplicity, a subdivision which places similar work in the same department regardless of operation is used and has proved satisfactory in a number of cases. By similar work is meant hand workers who use practically the same amount of supplies, machines of similar type, &c. Departmentalising by operations is a little more complicated, as it results in a greater number of departments, because the same or a similar kind of hand work may be done in several departments, and the same holds true of the machine departments.

In a number of lines of manufacture all work can be placed in one department where the unit of production is the same, i.e. with hand workers the unit is the productive man hour, with machine workers the machine hour, and in other departments the unit may be pound, ton, piece, dozen, square feet, yard, &c. In departmentalising a business the fact should be borne in mind that the better the departmental subdivision is made the more accurate will be the cost results.

Fixed Factory Charges.

Building expense, power, insurance, taxes, and depreciation constitute what are generally known as "Fixed Factory Charges," because they are practically fixed, and the factory has nothing to do with either increasing or decreasing them.

Building Expense.

The first requisite of a business is a place in which to work; consequently the first item of overhead is Building Expense or Rent. If the building is owned by the manufacturer, the building expenses consist of insurance, taxes, depreciation, and repairs, together with such other expenses which are general in their nature, but yet are necessary to render the building useful, such as heat, light elevator, janitor, and water. If the building is rented the items of insurance, taxes, depreciation, and repairs are paid by the owner, and in lieu of these is rent. Rent includes a return on the investment in addition to the items named, so when it is desired to make comparisons between plants where the building is owned and where it is rented, the return on the investment must be taken into consideration.

The basis of distribution for all rent charges is the productive or used square feet. The total used square feet divided into the total rent charges gives the charge per used square foot. This result multiplied by the used area of the department gives that department's proportion of the total rent expenses. By used floor space is meant that which is actually in use, exclusive of stairways, passages, elevator space, and idle or unused space.

Power.

The second requisite is power, and this must be obtained either from outside sources or generated in one's own plant. The distribution of power is a little more difficult than that of building expense, and sometimes an arbitrary division based on the opinion of the engineer and superintendent is used, but this method is not recommended. One difficulty in distributing power charges is that very often the same boiler supplies steam for heating and steam for power generating, and it is difficult to say how much for each.

For distributing power charges the factor generally used is found by multiplying the horse-power required by each machine or department by the average hours run by each and dividing the sum into the total power charge. Power distribution is a problem in itself, and it varies so much in different plants that it is impossible to lay down any rules for its solution. Each plant must be treated in an individual manner according to the existing conditions.

Insurance and Taxes.

Insurance and taxes should be distributed on the basis of the actual net value of the equipment in each department. This refers to fire insurance and taxes on the plant only, as boiler insurance is a charge to power, accident insurance is a charge to general factory expense, and the charge for other forms of insurance is determined by the nature of the insurance. Taxes on real estate and plant only are chargeable against manufacturing operations, as taxes on finished goods in stock and franchise taxes are chargeable to general expense, while income-tax is a direct charge to profit and loss.

Depreciation—The Necessity of including in Cost.

Depreciation is one of the most important of all the overhead expenses, because it is generally the largest. There has probably been more written on this subject than any other item of overhead, but there are so many different ways of handling depreciation, some of which are best adapted for one line and some for another, that there is really no recognised standard method. It is universally admitted, however, that depreciation does exist, that it is an element of cost just as much as labour or material, and that any system which does not provide for including it is faulty and one that will not give true costs.

Methods of Determining Depreciation.

One method of handling depreciation, which is unqualifiedly condemned although extensively used, is to wait until the end of the year, and then if the profit and loss statement shows that a good profit has been earned to charge a part of this profit to depreciation. If, on the other hand, the profit and loss statement shows little or no profit, nothing is charged to depreciation. It is difficult to understand how any practical man can take the view that his plant and equipment have not worn out because he has not made a profit, and at the same time have worn out when he has made a profit.

The first step necessary to provide for proper depreciation is to departmentalise the plant values. The next step is to take each kind of equipment or machine and figure its proper depreciation.

There are several methods of determining the amount of depreciation. One is to estimate the scrap value and deduct this figure from the original cost. The difference is then divided by the estimated life of the machine in years, and the result is the annual depreciation on that machine. A modification of this method which is not quite as simple, but really affords no difficulty, is after ascertaining the amount to be charged off during the life of the machine to determine a percentage which, when applied to the net book value of the machine, will leave only the scrap value of the machine on the books at the expiration of its estimated life.

To illustrate: If the initial cost of a machine and equipment is 1,000 dollars and the estimated scrap value is 200 dollars, with an estimated life of 10 years, then 800 dollars is the amount that must be charged into cost during that period, or 80 dollars per year. To attain this result, by using the net value of the machine as a basis, a rate of 15 per cent. would be necessary, which would make the depreciation 15 per cent. on 1,000 dollars, or 150 dollars, the first year; 15 per cent. on 850 dollars, or 127.50 dollars, the second year, &c. The advantage of this method in the interest of normal costs is that the decrease in depreciation charges is ordinarily offset by an increase in repairs.

Variable Factory Charges.

Variable charges or controllable expenses are the final items of factory overhead. These are subdivided departmentally and charged to the Expense Account of each department. Owing to the fact that no two lines of manufacture have the same kinds of expenses, a description of them must be very general. Such items as non-productive labour, repairs, lubricating oils, and miscellaneous supplies are found in nearly all Expense Accounts.

Factory expenses are incurred which cannot be located as belonging to any department, and these items should be charged to an account called "General Factory Expense." This account should be distributed over the Departmental Expense Accounts on some basis which is fair to all, the nature of this distribution varying as to special conditions existing in each particular business. Great care should be taken to prevent anything being charged to the General Account that could possibly be charged to one of the Departmental Accounts, as otherwise, either through carelessness or lack of knowledge, the General Account will become the dumping ground for all items the charge for which is in the least doubt.

Interest.

The question of whether interest on the capital invested is a proper charge against cost of production is one on which there is a marked difference of opinion. The cases where it is considered desirable to include interest in cost may be grouped under two heads:—

1. Where materials have to be stored for long periods while a seasoning process is being completed.
2. Where it is desired to show the effect of variations in the amount of capital employed and the term of employment.

As seasoned material has a higher value than when first purchased, it is apparent that the interest on the capital locked up during the seasoning forms in a sense a direct part of the cost of the material. If the material were purchased in a seasoned condition, a higher price would have to be paid, and this price would at least include interest and other carrying charges.

As some manufacturing processes require the use of expensive equipment, or take a long time to complete, both of which tie up capital, while other processes require neither the equipment nor the time, it is impossible to get true relative costs unless consideration is given to interest on the capital employed.

Cost accountants and industrial engineers, for comparative and statistical purposes, almost unanimously advocate including interest in cost, and so far as interest is included in cost for comparative or statistical purposes it serves a useful purpose.

Auditors, on the other hand, who are more directly interested in the preparation of statements showing the financial condition of a business, take the ground that interest is not an item of cost, and that to include it in cost results in an inflation of inventory values and an anticipation of profits. It is true that including interest in cost does inflate the inventory and is an anticipation of profit by exactly the amount of interest charged to the cost of the goods on hand. In arriving at inventory values, however, the approximate interest which has been charged to the cost of the goods on hand can be readily eliminated.

It is recommended that where interest on the investment is treated as an item of cost that the interest charged to the goods on hand be eliminated from inventory values, and that in preparing profit and loss statements the amount of the interest charged to costs during the period be returned to income under the specific caption "Interest on Investment."

Ascertainment of Normal Cost.

In every manufacturing business it is unquestionably true that in some months items of expense will occur which are not properly chargeable against the cost for that month. For instance, it may be found necessary to make extensive repairs on a machine, which repairs are sufficient for the entire year, and it would be manifestly unfair to include the entire repairs in the costs of any given month. Furthermore, every business has its dull season when its departments are not running more than half time, and this would also result in the actual cost for those months being abnormally high.

These facts lead to the conclusion that what is necessary for the manufacturer to know is not "What did it cost me to produce my goods last month?" but "What "would it have cost me to produce under normal condi-"tions, and how far were my actual costs from normal?" It will be seen that if selling prices are based on actual costs during a busy season when the plant is probably working overtime, the selling prices would be so low that the plant might be literally swamped with work, while conversely, if the selling prices were based on actual costs when the plant was dull, they might be so high that no business whatever could be obtained. It is necessary, therefore, that costs be averaged over a period of time sufficiently long to take in both dull and busy seasons. The method of doing this is to establish a "Reserve for Overhead," and credit this account with the reduction in cost during the busy season and charge it with the increase in cost during the dull season. The balance of this account is closed out to Trading Account, as will be explained later.

Distribution of Overhead to Job Costs.

Having now provided for the recording of the overhead expense, it becomes necessary to provide for charging it to the different jobs. There are several methods of doing this. The first is by charging a percentage on direct labour, but this in many lines results in inaccuracies, and the method has been discarded by a large number of manufacturers, although there are many who still use it owing to its ease of operation. An illustration will show the reason for the inaccuracy of this method. One man receiving 40 cents an hour may be doing handwork, requiring no power, very little floor space, and few supplies. If the overhead rate was 40 per cent., his hour cost would be 40 plus 16, or 56 cents. Another man, receiving the same rate of pay, may be working at a large and expensive machine, being subject to repairs, using power, several times the floor space, and using a quantity of supplies, and his cost would be figured at 56 cents also, although it is probably a fact that the machine he is using cannot be operated for less than 1 dollar an hour. Another fault with this method is that it throws most of the burden on the high-priced man, when, as a matter of fact, and this will be admitted by nearly every practical executive, the high-priced man requires less supervision and wastes less material than the cheaper one, and really should carry a less burden instead of a greater.

There are, however, some lines of manufacture where the direct labour method of distributing overhead can be used to advantage, particularly where the workmen are on a piecework basis or where they receive practically the same wage. In such cases a percentage of direct labour will give good results.

The Productive-Hour Method.

Another method, and the one that is recognised by a majority of manufacturers and accountants as the standard, is what is known as the "Productive-Hour Method." In a plant where practically all the labour is hand labour the man hour is the basis and the total hours divided into the total overhead expense gives a rate per hour, which rate, multiplied by the hours spent on a job, gives the overhead expense chargeable to that job.

In a plant where machines are the producing unit the distribution must be on the basis of the machine hour, and the same method is pursued as in the case of the man hour.

An estimate of overhead expenses should be made at the beginning of the year, based on previous years' experience with such changes as the executive's knowledge of business conditions leads him to make. This figure, divided by the expected output in hours of the machines, gives a normal overhead expense rate to be applied to all work in that department. This rate remains constant until the end of the fiscal year. The following schedule shows the method to be used in establishing this rate :—

Estimated Factory Overhead, 1916.

	Total	Dept. A	Dept. B	Dept. C
Indirect Labour	$7,300.00	$2,500.00	$3,000.00	$1,800.00
Building Expense ..	3,900.00	1,200.00	1,500.00	1,200.00
Power	8,560.00	2,800.00	3,960.00	1,800.00
Insurance	420.00	144.00	192.00	84,00
Taxes	525.00	180 00	240.00	105.00
Depreciation.. ..	2,625.00	900.00	1,200.00	525.00
Repairs	5,400.00	1,500.00	2,700.00	1,200.00
General Factory Expense	4,950.00	1,650.00	2,100.00	1,200.00
Miscellaneous Supplies.	790.00	240.00	360.00	190.00
Miscellaneous Expense	1,818.00	720.00	900.00	198.00
	36,288.00	11,834.00	16,152.00	8,302.00
Yearly Hours Per Unit: 306 Days 8 Hours Each		2,448	2,448	2,448
Less 10 per cent. ..		245	245	245
Net Yearly Hours Per Unit		2,203	2,203	2,203
Number of Units in Department		8	14	25
Yearly Hours per Department		17,624	30,842	55,075
Hourly Overhead Rate ..		67c.	52c.	15c.

Total Factory Cost.

The job cost sheet has now been charged with the three elements of cost, viz. material, labour, and factory overhead expense, and the total of these constitutes factory cost, to which must be added the general overhead.

Shipping, Selling, and General Expenses.

All of the items of factory cost now having been described and the goods completed and placed in the storeroom as finished goods, the next step is the method of handling the shipping, selling, and general expenses of the business.

Shipping Account is charged each month with its proportion of the fixed charges and with labour, supplies, and miscellaneous expense items. The total of this account is closed out to Profit and Loss.

Selling Expense is the next item to be considered. Some include everything under this head that is not charged to the factory. A better plan, though, is to separate the actual selling expense from the general expenses and include in selling only such items as salaries and expenses of the sales force whether on the road or in the office, advertising, catalogues, price lists, the cost of handling cancelled orders, &c.

Under General Expenses are included officers' salaries, office expenses (not including factory clerks), discount on sales, bad debts, bad work, franchise taxes, and other items of a general nature. The item Bad Work included in General Expense is defective work. As every manufacturer has to contend with this item of expense it must be included with the other general expenses.

An estimate of shipping, selling, and general expenses should be made at the beginning of the year. This amount divided by the estimated cost of the total completed work for the year gives a percentage for these items. Applying this rate to the factory cost of a job, the amount which must be added to factory cost to ascertain total cost is readily determined.

The following schedule shows the method of arriving at this rate :—

Estimated Shipping, Selling, and General Expenses.

FOR YEAR 1916

	Total	Distribution		
		Shipping	Selling	General
Building Expense ..	$1,200.00	$600.00		$600.00
Labour	1,500.00	1,500.00		
Salaries	13,200.00		$9,600.00	3,600.00
Officers' Salaries ..	4,800.00			4,800.00
Commissions ..	2,500.00		2,500.00	
Advertising	1,500.00		1,500.00	
Insurance	192.00	12.00		180.00
Taxes	215.00	15.00		200.00
Depreciation.. ..	200.00	100.00		100.00
Repairs	120.00	50.00		70.00
Delivery Expense ..	2,300.00			2,300.00
Discount on Sales ..	1,200.00			1,200.00
Reserve for Bad Debts	750.00			750.00
Miscellaneous Expense	325.00	75.00	100.00	150.00
	30,002.00	2,352.00	13,700.00	13,950.00
Estimated cost of completed work, $120,000 00				
Percentage on Cost..	25%	2%	11.5%	11.5%

Controlling Accounts.

The principles of double-entry are carried out in connection with a cost system by means of what is known as

"Controlling Accounts." The advantage of the controlling principle is that it puts the bookkeeper in position to check up the work of the cost department in totals, or, in other words, to control it. The control system will not detect an error such as posting to the wrong account, but it is an indubitable proof that the cost clerk has posted every item to the proper side of some account. It is hard to exaggerate the importance of this feature in any cost system.

Materials Account is charged with all purchases of materials from the accounts payable or voucher register. The requisitions for the month are totalled and a journal entry effected crediting materials and charging work in process. The balance of the account is the cost of the materials in the stockroom.

Labour Account is charged with the total labour, both direct and indirect. At the end of the month the account is credited with the total labour shown on the cost clerk's labour summaries and work in process charged with the direct labour and the Departmental Expense Accounts with the indirect labour. There will be a credit balance in this account which will represent the amount earned by the employees, but not paid. When the end of a pay period falls on the last day of the month, the account should balance.

The next type of controlling accounts necessary are those which reflect the overhead expenses. Building Expense Account is charged with all expenses of every kind, as heretofore described, and at the end of the month a journal entry is made charging each department with its proportion of the total and crediting Building Expense Account. The entire expense of this account should be absorbed by the Departmental Expense Accounts.

Power Account is handled in exactly the same manner. The entire expense of this account should also be absorbed by the Departmental Expense Accounts.

Insurance is charged with all insurance which applies to the factory, such as fire, accident, boiler, &c. This account is credited each month with one-twelfth of the annual payment and the proper Departmental Account charged. Insurance on stock, either raw material, work in process, or finished goods, is charged to General Expense and Insurance Account credited. The balance of this account is the value of prepaid insurance.

Taxes Account is handled in the same manner as the Insurance Account, but these two accounts should be kept separate.

Depreciation Account is comparatively simple to handle. A journal entry is made each month charging Building Expense, Power, and the Departmental Expense Accounts with the amount of depreciation decided on at the beginning of the year. The credit goes to an account called "Depreciation Reserve," the effect of which is to reduce the book value of the plant and equipment, although it is not a good plan to actually reduce this value on the books. It is better to carry the Reserve Account and let the Plant Accounts remain at the original cost figure.

The Departmental Expense Accounts have now been charged with their proportion of the fixed charges and with the indirect labour. The only other charges are miscellaneous expenses, supplies, and repairs, and these come from the Accounts Payable Register. These Departmental Expense Accounts are now credited with the distributed overhead expense determined by multiplying the number of operating hours by the normal hourly rate, Work in Process Account being charged. This total credit should balance the Expense Accounts, but practically there will be small balances which should be charged or credited at the end of the year to Reserve for Overhead.

Work in Process Account now stands charged with direct material, direct labour, and the departmental overhead expense. It is credited with the cost of all jobs completed during the month, the charge being to Finished Goods Account. The balance of Work in Process Account is the factory cost of incomplete work. The charge to offset this credit is to Finished Goods Account.

When goods are sold, Finished Goods Account is credited with the cost, and Trading Account charged. This figure is what is known as "Cost of Sales." When goods are returned, Trading Account is credited and Finished Goods charged with the cost of the returned goods, so that cost of sales will only be the cost of goods actually sold.

The reserve for overhead is charged or credited to Trading Account, so that the balance of the account is the true gross profit on the goods sold.

The Continuous Production System.

A system for recording the costs of a continuous product is a much simpler one than a system for recording the cost of job work, because in the former costs are figured departmentally or by processes instead of by jobs. The accounts are practically the same, except that there is not the necessity for the same detailed analysis as in the Job Cost System.

The business must be departmentalised as the first step, and the departmental divisions carefully observed, as otherwise true costs will not be obtained. The departmental divisions are different from the job cost divisions, as these should be by processes, regardless as to whether the work is of similar character or not.

Material is handled in the same way in both systems as far as purchases and delivery to stockroom goes, but in a slightly different manner after it is requisitioned out. It will be necessary to open a Material Account for each department. As the material is withdrawn for use these accounts are charged with its cost whether it be purchased raw material, or the finished product of some preceding department. The credit to these accounts will be the cost of the material used on the completed work, and the balance will be the cost of the material used on the work in process.

Labour is handled in the same manner as described in the Job Cost System, except that it is not necessary to differentiate between direct and indirect labour. It is, however, advisable to keep the direct and indirect labour separate in order to get a detailed analysis of cost in each department, so that any leaks which may exist will be brought to light. All labour done in a department is part of the cost of operation of that department and must be taken up in the monthly cost sheets. There will be some general labour, such as foremen, superintendents, &c., whose work must be distributed over several departments. The basis for this distribution depends on the nature of the business. It will be necessary to open Departmental Labour Accounts which will be charged with all labour and credited with the labour cost of the completed material. The balance in these accounts will represent the value of labour done on the work in process.

There should be also an Overhead Expense Account for each department, and these accounts will be charged with their proportion of the fixed charges, with all indirect material or supplies, and with all miscellaneous expense items. The credit to these accounts will be the expense incurred on the work completed, and the balance will be the expenses incurred on the work in process.

At the end of the month a journal entry is made charging a succeeding Department Material Account, or the

Finished Goods Account, as the case may be, with the total cost of the product sent out and crediting each of the departmental accounts with its share of the total cost. When this is done it will be seen that the sum of the balances in these three departmental accounts—namely, Material, Labour, and Expense—will be the cost of the work in process in that department. When a department has completed all the work it has and sent its product to some other department these three accounts should balance.

In some lines of manufacture, where a continuous product is made, it is the practice to issue a Works Production Order to make a certain quantity of goods, and where this practice is used the Job Cost System is used, keeping the cost by order number.

After the goods have reached the Finished Goods Account the method of treatment under the Continuous Production System is identical with the Job Cost System.

Financial and Operating Statements.

The Profit and Loss statement should be so arranged as to reflect the actual results of the period, and the figures shown thereon should not need any explanation or qualification.

For the purpose of giving the executive information as to the operations of his factory it is well to prepare a statement of factory operations. As all the figures are from the books, the preparation of this statement involves very little work and gives valuable information.

A statement of assets and liabilities should also be prepared, and the difference between assets and liabilities must be the figure shown on the Profit and Loss statement as surplus or net profit.

Where goods are purchased for resale the Profit and Loss statement should have another division showing the amount of profit on purchased goods or merchandising separate from the profit earned on manufactured goods. Where this item is small it may be disregarded and merged into manufactured goods, but the best practice is to keep them separate.

The systems outlined are believed to be simple and easy of operation. While a number of details have been explained it must be remembered that the methods outlined are general, and it is not claimed that the outlines as given would fit every business. The one thing above all others that both the manufacturer and the accountant should have in mind in installing a system is simplicity. Simplicity means ease of operation, less liability of error, and, what is equally important, economy of operation.

Ledger Accounts and Statements.

The following schedules show the Ledger Accounts necessary, the trial balance before the closing entries are made, and forms for a Profit and Loss Statement, Statement of Factory Operations, and Balance Sheet. In order to enable ready reference to be made to the various entries numbers have been inserted showing the source of the entry. While the Ledger Accounts show the books as closed, it is not recommended that this be done except at the end of the fiscal year, as statements can be prepared from the Ledger without the accounts being closed.

MATERIALS. 1.

	$ c.		$ c.
Balance	3,000.00	Work in Process (14)	6,484.32
Purchases .. (29)	7,800.00	Balance	4,600.00
Freight and Express (29)	284.32		
	11,084.32		11,084.32
Balance	4,600.00		

LABOUR. 2.

	$ c.		$ c.
Total Pay Roll .. (21)	5,692.28	Balance	200.00
Balance	686.79	Work in Process (14)	4,444.67
		Building Expense (3)	185.00
		Power .. .. (4)	300.00
		Repairs .. (8)	356.40
		General Factory Expense .. (9)	92.60
		Factory Overhead—	
		Department A (10)	246.50
		,, B (11)	251.20
		,, C (12)	185.70
		Shipping .. (21)	117.00
	6,379.07		6,379.07
		Balance	686.79

BUILDING EXPENSE. 3.

	$ c.		$ c.
Labour .. .. (2)	185.00	General Factory Expense .. (9)	76.29
Power (Heat & Light) (4)	84.10	Factory Overhead—	
Insurance .. .. (5)	12.00	Department A. (10)	101.72
Taxes .. .. (6)	20.00	,, B. (11)	127.15
Depreciation .. (7)	40.00	,, C. (12)	101.72
Repairs .. .. (8)	65.00	Shipping .. (21)	50.86
Elevator Expenses (29)	58.00	General Expense (Office) (23)	50.86
Water .. .. (29)	16.50		
Miscellaneous Materials (29)	28.00		
	508.60		508.60

POWER. 4.

	$ c.		$ c.
Labour .. .. (2)	300.00	Building Expense (3)	84.10
Insurance .. .. (5)	8.00	Factory Overhead—	
Taxes .. .. (6)	10.00	Department A (10)	252.30
Depreciation .. (7)	40.00	,, B (11)	336.40
Fuel .. .. (29)	325.00	,, C (12)	168.20
Oils .. .. (29)	45.00		
Water .. .. (29)	38.00		
Repairs and Supplies (29)	75.00		
	841.00		841.00

INSURANCE. 5.

	$ c.		$ c.
Accounts Payable (29)	828.00	Building Expense (3)	12.00
		Power .. (4)	8.00
		Repairs .. (8)	2.00
		Factory Overhead—	
		Department A (10)	12.00
		,, B (11)	16.00
		,, C (12)	7.00
		Shipping .. (21)	1.00
		General Expense (23)	14.00
		Balance	756.00
	828.00		828.00
Balance	756.00		

TAXES. 6.

	$ c.		$ c.
Accounts Payable (29)	1,095.00	Building Expense (3)	20.00
		Power .. .. (4)	10.00
		Repairs .. (8)	2.50
		Factory Overhead—	
		Department A (10)	15.00
		,, B (11)	20.00
		,, C (12)	8.75
		Shipping .. (21)	1.25
		General Expense (23)	16.75
		Balance	1,000.75
	1,095.00		1,095.00
Balance	1,000.75		

DEPRECIATION RESERVE. 7.

	$ c.		$ c.
Balance	1,568.74	Balance	1,240.00
		Building Expense (3)	40.00
		Power .. .. (4)	40.00
		Repairs .. (8)	13.33
		Factory Overhead—	
		Department A (10)	75.00
		,, B (11)	100.00
		,, C (12)	43.75
		Shipping .. (21)	8.33
		General Expense (23)	8.33
	1,568.74		1,568.74
		Balance	1,568.74

REPAIRS. 8.

	$ c.		$ c.
Labour .. .. (2)	356.40	Building Expense (3)	65.00
Insurance .. (5)	2.00	Factory Overhead—	
Taxes .. .. (6)	2.50	Department A (10)	159.00
Depreciation .. (7)	13.33	,, B (11)	247.80
Supplies .. .. (29)	167.00	,, C (12)	115.43
Miscellaneous Expense (29)	48.00	Shipping .. (21)	2.00
	589.23		589.23

GENERAL FACTORY EXPENSE. 9.

	$ c.		$ c.
Labour .. .. (2)	92.60	Factory Overhead—	
Building Expense (3)	76.29	Department A (10)	155.90
Factory Office Expense (29)	265.00	,, B (11)	207.79
Miscellaneous Expense (29)	141.0	,, C (12)	104.30
Miscellaneous Supplies (29)	20.00		
	467.99		467.99

FACTORY OVERHEAD, DEPT. A. 10.

	$ c.		$ c.
Indirect Labour (2)	246.50	Work in Process, 1,802 hours, at 67 cents (14)	1,207.34
Building Expense (3)	101.72		
Power .. .. (4)	252.30		
Insurance .. (5)	12.00		
Taxes .. .. (6)	15.00		
Depreciation .. (7)	75.00		
Repairs .. .. (8)	159.00		
General Factory Expense (9)	155.90		
Miscellaneous—			
Supplies .. (29)	30.00		
Expense .. (29)	75.60		
Reserve for Overhead (13)	*84.32*		
	1,207.34		1,207.34

FACTORY OVERHEAD, DEPT. B. 11.

	$ c.		$ c.
Indirect Labour (2)	251.20	Work in Process, 2,523 Hours, at 52 cents (14)	1,311.96
Building Expense (3)	127.15	*Reserve for Overhead* (13)	*119.78*
Power .. .. (4)	336.40		
Insurance .. (5)	16.00		
Taxes .. .. (6)	20.00		
Depreciation .. (7)	100.00		
Repairs .. .. (8)	247.80		
General Factory Expense (9)	207.79		
Miscellaneous—			
Supplies .. (29)	40.00		
Expense .. (29)	85.40		
	1,431.74		1,431.74

FACTORY OVERHEAD, DEPT. C. 12.

	$ c.		$ c.
Indirect Labour (2)	185.70	Work in Process, 1,418 Hours, at 15 cents (14)	662.70
Building Expense (3)	101.72	*Reserve for Overhead* (13)	153.65
Power .. .. (4)	168.20		
Insurance .. (5)	7.00		
Taxes .. .. (6)	8.75		
Depreciation .. (7)	43.75		
Repairs .. .. (8)	115.43		
General Factory Expense .. (9)	104.30		
Miscellaneous—			
Supplies .. (29)	20.00		
Expense .. (29)	61.50		
	816.35		816.35

RESERVE FOR OVERHEAD. 13.

	$ c.		$ c.
Factory Overhead—		Factory Overhead	
Department B (11)	119.78	Department A (10)	84.32
,, C (12)	153.65	*Trading* .. (20)	*189.11*
	273.43		273.43

WORK IN PROCESS. 14.

	$ c.		$ c.
Balance	2,000.00	Finished Goods (15)	12,086.13
Material .. .. (1)	6,484.32	Balance	4,024.86
Labour .. .. (2)	4,444.67		
Factory Overhead—			
Department A (10)	1,207.34		
,, B (11)	1,311.96		
,, C (12)	662.70		
	16,110.99		16,110.99
Balance	4,024.86		

FINISHED GOODS. 15.

	$ c.		$ c.
Balance	3,754.00	Trading (cost of sales) (20)	8,801.53
Work in process (14)	12,086.13	Balance	7,635.72
Cost of Returns (20)	597.12		
	16,437.25		16,437.25
Balance	7,635.72		

SALES. 16.

	$ c.		$ c.
Sales returns .. (17)	865.20	Accounts receivable (28)	13,485.60
Sales allowances (18)	50.00		
Out freight .. (19)	120.00		
Trading .. .. (20)	*12,450.40*		
	13,485.60		13,485.60

SALES RETURNS. 17.

	$ c.		$ c.
Accounts receivable (28)	865.20	*Sales* .. .. (16)	*865.20*

SALES ALLOWANCES. 18.

	$ c.		$ c.
Accounts receivable (28)	50.00	*Sales* .. .. (16)	*50.00*

OUTBOUND FREIGHT. 19.

	$ c.		$ c.
Accounts payable (29)	120.00	*Sales* .. .. (16)	*120.00*

TRADING. 20.

		$ c.			$ c.
Cost of Sales ..	(15)	8,801.53	Cost of Returns	(15)	597.12
Reserve for Overhead	(13)	189.11	Sales	(16)	12,450.40
Profit and Loss ..	(27)	*4,056.88*			
		13,047.52			13,047.52

SHIPPING. 21.

		$ c.			$ c.
Labour	(2)	117.00	*Profit and Loss*	(27)	*237.19*
Building Expense	(3)	50.86			
Insurance ..	(5)	1.00			
Taxes	(6)	1.25			
Depreciation ..	(7)	8.33			
Repairs ..	(8)	2.00			
Miscellaneous—					
Supplies ..	(29)	50.00			
Expense ..	(29)	6.75			
		237.19			237.19

SELLING EXPENSE. 22.

		$ c.			$ c.
Salaries ..	(29)	800.00	*Profit and Loss*	(27)	*1,120.53*
Commissions ..	(29)	200.00			
Advertising ..	(29)	120.53			
		1,120.53			1,120.53

GENERAL EXPENSE. 23.

		$ c.			$ c.
Building Expense	(3)	50.86	*Profit and Loss*	(27)	*1,180.67*
Insurance ..	(5)	14.00			
Taxes	(6)	16.75			
Depreciation ..	(7)	8.33			
Officers' Salaries	(29)	400.00			
Office Salaries ..	(29)	300.00			
Delivery Expense	(29)	186.43			
Miscellaneous Expense	(29)	204.30			
		1,180.67			1,180.67

DISCOUNT ON PURCHASES. 24.

		$ c.			$ c.
Profit and Loss ..	(27)	*165.40*	Accounts Payable	(29)	165.40

DISCOUNT ON SALES. 25

		$ c.			$ c.
Accounts Receivable	(28)	95.00	*Profit and Loss*	(27)	*95.00*

RESERVE FOR BAD DEBTS. 26.

		$ c.			$ c.
Accounts Receivable	(28)	64.00	Balance		125.00
Balance		131.00	*Profit and Loss*	(27)	70.00
		195.00			195.00
			Balance		131.00

PROFIT AND LOSS. 27.

		$ c.			$ c.
Shipping ..	(21)	237.19	Trading ..	(20)	4,056.88
Selling	(22)	1,120.53	Discount on Purchases	(24)	165.40
General Expense	(23)	1,180.67			
Discount on Sales	(25)	95.00			
Reserve for Bad Debts	(26)	70.00			
Net Profit to Surplus	(36)	*1,518.89*			
		4,222.28			4,222.28

ACCOUNTS RECEIVABLE. 28.

		$ c.			$ c.
Balance		6,000.00	Cash	(30)	9,875.00
Sales	(16)	13,485.60	Returns ..	(17)	865.20
			Sales Allowances	(18)	50.00
			Discount on Sales	(25)	95.00
			Bad Debts ..	(26)	64.00
			Balance		8,536.40
		19,485.60			19,485.60
Balance		8,536.40			

ACCOUNTS PAYABLE. 29.

		$ c.			$ c.
Cash	(30)	15,350.50	Balance		6,250.00
Discount on Purchases	(24)	165.40	Accounts Payable Register		19,499.71
Balance		10,233.81			
		25,749.71			25,749.71
			Balance		10,233.81

CASH. 30.

		$ c.			$ c.
Balance		17,061.00	Accounts Payable	(29)	15,350.50
Accounts Receivable	(28)	9,875.00	Balance		11,585.50
		26,936.00			26,936.00
Balance		11,585.50			

LAND. 31.

		$ c.			
Balance		4,000.00			

BUILDINGS 32.

		$ c.			
Balance		12,000.00			

MACHINERY AND EQUIPMENT. 33.

		$ c.			
Balance		50,000.00			

CAPITAL STOCK. 34.

					$ c.
			Balance		100,000.00

UNISSUED STOCK. 35.

		$ c.			
Balance		15,000.00			

SURPLUS. 36.

		$ c.			$ c.
Balance		6,518.89	Balance		5,000.00
			Profit and Loss	(27)	1,518.89
		6,518.89			6,518.89
			Balance		6,518.89

TRIAL BALANCE (before closing) JANUARY 31st 1916

		$ c.	$ c.
1	Materials	4,600.00	
2	Labour		686.79
5	Insurance	756.00	
6	Taxes	1,000.75	
7	Depreciation Reserve		1,568.74
10	Factory Overhead Dept. A		84.32
11	,, ,, ,, B	119.78	
12	,, ,, ,, C	153.65	
14	Work in Process	4,024.86	
15	Finished Goods	7,635.72	
16	Sales		13,485.60
17	Sales Returns	865.20	
18	Sales Allowances	50.00	
19	Outbound Freight	120.00	
20	Trading	8,204.41	
21	Shipping	237.19	
22	Selling Expense	1,120.53	
23	General Expense	1,180.67	
24	Discount on Purchases		165.40
25	Discount on Sales	95.00	
26	Reserve for Bad Debts		61.00
28	Accounts Receivable	8,536.40	
29	Accounts Payable		10,233.81
30	Cash	11,585.50	
31	Land	4,000.00	
32	Buildings	12,000.00	
33	Machinery and Equipment	50,000.00	
34	Capital Stock		100,000.00
35	Unissued Stock	15,000.00	
36	Surplus		5,000.00
		131,285.66	131,285.66

PROFIT AND LOSS STATEMENT FOR MONTH ENDING JANUARY 31 1916.

		$ c.	$ c.
Gross Sales	(16)		13,485.60
Sales Returns	(17)	865.20	
Sales Allowances	(18)	50.00	
Outbound Freight	(19)	120.00	
			1,035.20
Net Sales			12,450.40
Cost of Sales	(20)	8,204.41	
Reserve for Overhead	(13)	189.11	
			8,393.52
Gross Profit			4,056.88
Shipping	(21)	237.19	
Selling Expense	(22)	1,120.53	
General Expense	(23)	1,180.67	
Discount on Sales	(25)	95.00	
Bad Debts	(26)	70.00	
			2,703.39
Net Earnings			1,353.49
Discount on Purchases	(24)		165.40
Net Profit			1,518.89

STATEMENT OF FACTORY OPERATIONS.
FOR THE MONTH ENDED 31ST JANUARY 1916.
Summary of Factory Operations.

Material—		
Inventory at 1st of Month	$3,000.00	
Purchases	7,800.00	
Freight and Express In	284.32	
Total	11,084.32	
Less Inventory at end of Month	4,600.00	
Direct Material Used		$6,484.32
Direct Labour		4,444.67
Factory Overhead, per detail below.		
Department A	1,207.34	
,, B	1,311.96	
,, C	662.70	
Total Factory Overhead		3,182.00
Total Material, Labour, and Overhead		14,110.99
Add Inventory, 1st of Month:		
Work in Process	2,000.00	
Finished Goods	3,754.00	
		5,754.00
		19,864.99
Less Inventory at End of Month		
Work in Process	4,024.86	
Finished Goods	7,635.72	
		11,660.58
Cost of Sales, per Profit and Loss Statement		8,204.41

SUMMARY OF FACTORY OVERHEAD

Nature of Expense	Total	Department A	Department B	Department C
	$ c.	$ c.	$ c.	$ c.
Building Expense	330.59	101.72	127.15	101.72
Power	756.90	252.30	336.40	168.20
Depreciation	218.75	75.00	100.00	43.75
Insurance	35.00	12.00	16.00	7.00
Taxes	43.75	15.00	20.00	8.75
Shop Repairs	522.23	159.00	247.80	115.43
General Factory Expense	467.99	155.90	207.79	104.30
Miscellaneous Supplies	90.00	30.00	40.00	20.00
Indirect Labour	683.40	246.50	251.20	185.70
Miscellaneous Expense	222.50	75.60	85.40	61.50
Total	3,371.11	1,123.02	1,431.74	816.35
Adjustment in Department Overhead	189.11	84.32	*119.78*	*153.65*
Total Factory Overhead as above	3,182.00	1,207.34	1,311.96	662.70

BALANCE SHEET, 31ST JANUARY 1916.

Current Assets—				
Cash	(30)		$11,585.50	
Accounts Receivable	(28)	$8,536.40		
Less Reserve for Bad Debts	(26)	131.00		
			8,405.40	
Raw Materials	(1)		4,600.00	
Work in Process	(14)		4,024.86	
Finished Goods	(15)		7,635.72	
Total Current Assets				$36,251.48
Deferred Assets—				
Prepaid Insurance	(5)		756.00	
Prepaid Taxes	(6)		1,000.75	
Total Deferred Assets				1,756.75
Capital Assets—				
Land	(31)		4,000.00	
Buildings	(32)	12,000.00		
Machinery and Equipment	(33)	50,000.00		
		62,000.00		
Less Depreciation Reserve	(7)	1,568.74		
			60,431.26	
Total Capital Assets				64,431.26
Total Assets				102,439.49
Current Liabilities—				
Accounts Payable	(29)		10,233.81	
Accrued Wages	(2)		686.79	
Total Current Liabilities				10,920.60
Capital Liabilities—				
Capital Stock	(34)	100,000.00		
Less Unissued Stock	(35)	15,000.00		
			85,000.00	
Surplus	(36)		5,000.00	
Total Capital Liabilities				90,000.00
Net Profit for Month				1,518.89
				$102,439.49

Uses and Advantages of a Cost System.

The prime object of a cost system is to determine costs, to analyse and compare them, and to use them as a basis for making prices. But the uses and advantages go further. A manufacturer from reliable records is able to make clearer and more intelligent statements to his bank and thereby obtain a larger line of credit than he could without them.

Better Direction of Sales Force.

In most every line of manufacture there are some classes of work done on which the manufacturer loses money.

This may be due to the high cost in his own plant, or it may be due to the fact that some competitor is better equipped to make that particular article. A cost system will bring out these facts and will show the manufacturer which lines he should push. Salesmen, like everyone else, are prone to follow the line of least resistance. In salesmanship, the line of least resistance is selling the goods which require the least effort, and in nearly every instance the goods which require the least effort to sell are the least profitable lines. If the selling force know that a line of goods produces little or no profit, and are told to use every effort to push another line, the result will be apparent in the Profit and Loss Account.

Still other manufacturers have customers on their books to whom they have been selling for years, and have been giving some reduction in price or some concession in the way of extra work. A number of these accounts are decidedly unprofitable, and a cost system will bring these to light and put the manufacturer either in a position to raise his prices to a profitable basis or let someone else have the unprofitable business.

Elimination of Waste.

In every manufacturing business there are bound to occur leaks, either of material, labour, or expense. If statistics are kept showing the amount of material necessary to do certain classes of work, the amount of labour, and the amount of overhead expense, an increase in any of these items will be revealed by a comparison, and the executive will be in a position to take the matter up for investigation. It is hardly necessary to say that after a few of these matters have been taken up with the factory the factory people will use a little more care, not only in the use of the material but in the time they spend on the work. A cost system with forms properly designed for giving statistical information is of the greatest aid to factory efficiency.

Cost System an Investment, not an Expense.

A system will not run itself; neither will it in itself reduce costs nor increase efficiency. This is strictly up to the manufacturer himself. A system will give him the information, and, if this information is properly used, he will unquestionably find that his system is not an item of expense, but a very valuable asset.

If a manufacturer purchases a new machine before his old one is worn out, he does so because he expects the amount expended to increase his profits either from economy in operation or from an increase in production. He looks on this as an investment and not an expense. Office methods have been improved to quite as large an extent as machinery, and an investment in improved methods will produce a return just as will an investment in improved machinery.

One of the strongest arguments in favour of installing a practical cost system is the fact that every manufacturer who has installed one and who has operated it for at least a year is firmly convinced that it is a paying proposition

The Federal Trade Commission is urging manufacturers to give the subject of accurate costs the attention it deserves. It has found that unreliable costs of production and distribution cause a great deal of unfair competition and a heavy business death rate.

While the claim is not made that a cost system will save a man from failure, the claim is made that a man who knows where he stands day by day is very much less likely to make a failure of his business than one who is directing his business by guesswork.

The Accountant

THE RECOGNISED WEEKLY ORGAN OF CHARTERED ACCOUNTANTS
AND
ACCOUNTANCY THROUGHOUT THE WORLD.

[Publishing Offices : 34 Moorgate Street, London, E.C.2 Telephone No. 7321 Central.]

VOL. LX.—NEW SERIES.—No. 2308.] SATURDAY, MARCH 1, 1919. [PRICE 9D.

LEADING ARTICLES

Cost Accounts and Accountants.

WE always find a good deal to interest us in the columns of our contemporary *The Efficiency Magazine*, but we cannot altogether agree with the views expressed in the current issue, as to the accountant's place in connection with Costing.

Our contemporary says : "An Accountant should be kept in his place," and "accounting "is a definite job which has to do with records "only, and not with methods, loans, opera- "tions, policies or management" : that it is, in fact, "a matter of statistics." Proceeding, the writer says : "Accounting has on one side "of it costing, and on the other side financing, "but that there is a 'twilight zone' between "accounting and costing, and also between "accounting and finance, and that conse- "quently the accountant sometimes 'gets "out of his place and meddles with costing "and finance, sometimes to the extent of "monopolising all three jobs.'" This, we are told, is "a very serious matter, as the aver- "age accountant is quite unfit to handle "either costs or finance." The writer concludes, "Make your accountant stick to his Ledger; "hire a special clerk for Costings; and consult "your banker on Finance."

It is, of course, very evident all through this that when our contemporary talks of an "accountant," it is not an accountant in the professional sense of the term that is meant, but a bookkeeper. A great many misunderstandings might be avoided, if people could be made to understand that a bookkeeper—and particularly a Ledger clerk—is by no means necessarily an accountant, and, indeed, probably knows little about accountancy; but, after all, the profession can hardly grumble, when it is borne in mind that the term "Accountant" was used as applied to book-keepers, long before there was a profession of accountancy at all. Nevertheless, it is unfortunate that any one in the twentieth century should go so far as to assert that accountants (without particularising what kind of accountant is meant) are "quite unfit" to handle either costs or finance.

It is further open to question whether the alternative advice, that "special clerks" should be engaged for Costings, and that the banker should be consulted on matters of finance, is altogether helpful. If Cost Accounts are worth keeping, they are certainly worth the consideration of someone having a wider outlook and greater experience than any clerk, while the average individual that a business man is likely to see when he goes to his bankers, knows not too much about banking, and certainly little or nothing about finance. Candour compels us to add that it is not every professional accountant who is an expert in either costing or finance, but quite competent experts in either matter are readily to be found among the ranks of professional accountants, and it is certainly not easy to say where else the average manufacturer might look for experts to better advantage.

The war has, of course, brought good costing methods prominently under the public eye. Many manufacturers are to-day keeping Cost Accounts who hardly knew that there were such things five years ago. Many others are thinking of installing a costing system who, five years ago, would have scouted the idea as ridiculous, or at least as not applying to the conditions obtaining in their work. Now there is abroad a healthy spirit of inquiry into the matter, and a disposition to give costing methods a fair trial. This is all to the good, and it is very much to be hoped that this new-found enthusiasm for better methods and more reliable information will not be scotched by the incompetence of so-called experts.

There is something of a danger that a number of persons coming under the category of what our contemporary calls "special clerks," who during the past few years have acquired a certain amount of familiarity with costing methods suitable to some munition undertaking, will, on the strength of this one-sided experience, seek to blossom out into fully qualified "cost accountants." There are as many different kinds of Cost Accounts as there are of manufacturing accounts. The uses of costing, and the objects to be aimed at, vary very considerably according to the nature of each case. No ready-made system of costing is applicable to all kinds of industry, and accordingly it is especially desirable that those designing and installing a new system of costing should, as we have already said, be persons with a wide outlook, and considerable experience. The matter is the more important —and the danger of damage done by incompetent so-called experts is all the more real— because there can be little doubt that, for some years to come at least, the installation of new costing systems is likely to provide the practitioner with a considerable amount of work. Indeed, so evident is this that we learn already certain actuaries are casting envious eyes in the direction of costing and claiming it as their own particular reserve, on the ground that costing is a branch of statistics. In one sense this may be true; but in that same sense it is even truer that all accounting is a branch of statistics, and it may be added that actuaries as such are not sufficiently specialists to deal with accounting matters satisfactorily. In that costing is a still more highly specialised matter, it follows that this argument applies with even greater force to costs. Moreover, it may be pointed out that one of the most important requisites of the cost accountant is that he should be thoroughly alert and broad in his outlook. The mathematical mind but seldom answers to this description.

On the other hand, we do not at all wish to claim any monopoly in connection with costing for professional accountants, as such. The counting-house accounts of a business are primarily concerned with its dealings with the outside world, and with its proprietors. The accounts of its costs department are primarily concerned with its dealings with its own staff. While it is important that the cost records should be sufficiently independent of the works department to ensure their absolute accuracy and impartiality, there must necessarily be complete accord between the works department and cost department before a satisfactory system of costing can be framed, for without such accord it is impossible for the designer of a system to become fully acquainted with the actual conditions he has to face. A properly designed costing system must necessarily be the result of a partnership between operating managers and skilled accountants; but, the system once designed, the operating department should no more seek to influence the accounting records involved than it would tolerate an individual worker attempting to tamper with the records of the time recorder.

Conference on Scientific Costing.

Cost Accountancy : Its Evolution and its Trend.

By J. M. Fells, F.S.A.A.

At the second session on June 5th the chair was taken by Mr. H. R. Cooper, Sopwith Aviation Co., Ltd., and an address on "Cost Accountancy—Its Evolution and its Trend," was delivered by Mr. J. M. Fells, F.S.A.A.

The Chairman, in calling upon the lecturer, said that the first authoritative work on the subject was that of Messrs. Garcke & Fells, and they were looking to Mr. Fells to give them a lead which would crystallise the somewhat diverse opinions to which this conference had listened as to the real function of cost and works accountants, and whether it was possible to draw a line of demarcation between the professional and the works accountant.

Mr. J. M. Fells, who was received with applause, after apologising for having to deliver an address instead of reading a paper—which he had not had time to prepare owing to pressure of work, said: The law which holds good in biology, that "function precedes structure," which, translated into the vernacular, is contained in the proverb "Necessity is the mother of invention," is applicable to the evolution of cost accountancy. There has been some form of it from the beginning of time. Even in cottage and domestic industry—at any rate, in the early days in this country—one found that there was an endeavour on the part of those carrying on those industries to ascertain their costs of production. The introduction of electricity and steam, and the use of machinery—or "congealed labour," as it has been termed by Karl Marx—has led to the very careful and systematic allocation of the various items making up the cost of any product. In that sense I think you will agree that function has preceded the structure of any cost accountancy systems. Unfortunately, however, the same word can be used in many different senses, and does not convey to all minds the same meaning. One can illustrate that by referring to the word "point," which has 88 different definitions in a dictionary which I have seen. With regard to "cost," one finds that it is used interchangeably with other words with which it really has no relation. The matter is one of very considerable importance, for to be progressive you must have a classical nomenclature or terminology which will convey to all persons the same thing in the same way; otherwise you have endless confusion.

There is great confusion in the minds of the majority of people between the words "cost" and "expenditure." It is not understood that the term "cost" is a relative term, having relation to certain units which are produced by that "expenditure." Some 20 years ago, in the Law Courts, I had a controversy with the late Prime Minister, Mr. Asquith, Lord Parmoor, and others, as to the distinction between those two words; fortunately I was able, in that case, to achieve my point by other means.

There is still considerable divergence of view. Quite recently Mr. Justice Lush, in a case in which I had to deal with the same point, said : "I quite agree with the "applicant's witness when he said that 'cost' is not "the same thing as 'expenditure'" in this sense that "larger expenditure may, by leading to a re-arranging "of the conditions of employment, and thereby effecting "economies, be wholly or in part prevented from causing "to those who incur it, larger cost in working. It was "suggested that the words 'cost of working a railway' "have come to have a technical meaning in this Court, "and indicate that the various factors, to which I have "referred, and which are considered in order to ascertain "whether a rate is reasonable will necessarily be con- "sidered in arriving at the cost of working."

The present Lord Terrington had more clear a view as to the difference between the two words. He says : "The first question is what is meant by the expression "'rise in the cost of working the railway' due to "improved labour conditions. It is the first time the "expression has found its way into railway legislation, "but it has been a common formula in the discussions "before this tribunal when hearing complaints under "the Act of 1894, and it has received judicial examina- "tion and interpretation with which the Legislature must "be assumed to have been familiar, but 'expenditure' "and 'cost' in this connection must not be confused; "they are not convertible terms. 'Expenditure' is a "debit factor; it refers to outlay only, and is absolute. "'Cost' is a resultant and comprehensive factor, and is "relative. It embraces economies made as well as "money expended. 'Cost' is unknown until volume is "ascertained, and volume is always fluctuating. To "ascertain the cost of working a railway in comparable "periods, some relative standard or unit of comparison "must be taken. It must, as Lord Collins said, be a "relative figure."

The view of Lord Terrington was not, however, upheld in the Court of Appeal, for the Master of the Rolls stated : "On the part of the traders it is argued that "the phrase 'cost of working the railway' is a term of "art referring to the previous practice under the Act of "1894, that it involves many other factors besides the "labour bill, and that it necessitates a comparison "between two periods, namely, 1911 and 1913. It is "said that there is a fallacy in taking the increases of the "wages bill as a true test, because the labour may be "more efficient by reason of the improved conditions, "and there may be various economies effected. In point "of fact, the evidence is clear that there have been no "such economies. It may, theoretically be true that the "improved conditions may, in the case of certain indi- "vidual workmen, make them more energetic and better "workmen; this, however, is not a practical considera- "tion, dealing, as we are, with some 20,000 workmen, "who are, generally speaking, the same as they were "before."

I would pause here to point out that, of course, the larger number of workmen there were the greater would be the factor of the psychological effect of increased wages on production. Later on, if I have an opportunity, I will deal with the great development that should arise in cost accounting, particularly having regard to what I would call the social and economic conditions of the country, and the estimation of the psychological effect upon production of improvements in conditions of labour. That there is such an improvement with higher wages I am convinced from investigations I have made.

Unfortunately, there is still a great deal of difference as to the meaning of the word "cost," and this has a bearing on certain important matters before the country at the present time. You will have seen in the papers that it has been said that the railways of this country are not in a solvent condition, and that the nation has had to contribute £100,000,000 a year for two years to keep them solvent. That is not only not the fact, but is absolutely contrary to the fact, and the confusion arises from the Minister designate of Railways, Sir Eric Geddes, and Mr. Bonar Law really not understanding the meaning of the terms they used. Sir Eric, in the debate on the second reading of the Bill, said : "The transport systems of this country are financially "in a semi-paralysed state; they are to-day being worked "at a loss of something over £250,000 a day, or "£100,000,000 a year. It may be that this is an estimated "figure, but the best estimate I can give is something "about £90,000,000 or £100,000,000 in increased cost." Later on, even in the same speech, he said : "Last of "all, the taxpayer is paying £100,000,000 a year." Further in the same speech, however, he made this admission : "Up to the time of the Armistice, Government traffic "practically made up the deficit, but since the Armistice "the deficit of the railways has been steadily increasing; "that makes the £90,000,000 or £100,000,000 a year." The Bill passed the second reading on certain representations made by Mr. Bonar Law, and went to Standing Committee; in that committee Sir Eric alluded to this large sum in two or three different ways. First of all he called it "additional cost"; then he alluded to it as a "deficit." Then he said : "I did not call it an 'actual loss'; I have said an 'increased expense,'" so that you see these words, being used interchangeably by Sir Eric, have produced on the minds of the country an absolutely wrong impression.

Mr. Bonar Law was explicit and precise. He said : "There is something like from £90,000,000 to £100,000,000 "which, for two years, has had to be paid out of the "taxation of the country," and he emphasised this later by referring to the "deficit" as an enormous one. Parliamentary proceedings are very much like those in "Alice in Wonderland," where they gave judgment first and ascertained facts apparently afterwards, for two well-known men, Sir Albert Wyon and Sir William Plender, in April last prepared a statement showing the revenue earned of the amount expended on British controlled railways in respect of railway working for the year 1913, and for the period of Government control to 31st December 1918.

In that statement Sir Albert and Sir William, as might be expected, have included estimates for Government traffic not at the rates at which it would have been done for an ordinary trader, but at the pre-war rates for Government traffic, which, of course, were considerably less than the rates passengers and freighters of goods have paid since the war began.

Including that sum, these two accountants point out that the balance of revenue account over expenditure was, in the year 1915, £45,000,000; in the year 1916, £50,000,000; in the year 1917, £55,000,000; and in the year 1918, £46,000,000, and these large balances of revenue over expenditure were earned after including in the accounts for the various years a total sum in the four years of £32,000,000, as an amount set on one side to provide for future renewals of railway rolling stock and permanent way.

A more remarkable instance of the House of Commons voting on a measure in connection with which they had been misinformed could not, I think, have been found.

But this difference between cost and expenditure is elusive unless we adhere to a simple scientific nomenclature. Even Sir Albert and Sir William have themselves dropped, in my opinion, into a fallacy—or at any rate they use the wrong word. Dealing with extra wear and tear, they say the receipts "are subject to provision "for extra wear and tear resulting from the additional "traffic carried. The cost of eventually making good "this wear and tear must be considerable, but cannot be "estimated at present with any degree of accuracy." I think that the word that should have been used is "expense," because they have not dealt with the relative factor of the product of the expenditure, the tons carried, and the number of passengers conveyed.

That leads me to think that in this conference we should suggest, perhaps, the formation of a committee to consider the terminology that should be used in cost accounting, and I am not certain that the word "cost" is in reality the best word to use to convey the meaning which we intend to bring out. "Cost" is in the popular mind associated with the price paid in a shop. Of course, cost price and the price paid in a shop are distinct.

If one were to consider the early history of cost, one would have to go back a very long way. The first time it took very definite shape was probably when, being tired of guild restrictions in the time of Henry VII, a large number of manufacturers migrated into country districts and established industrial communities, in very much the way, 400 or 500 years afterwards, garden cities are suggested as the solution for many industrial evils.

The need for costing has always been recognised, and there have been many systems practised. Each manufacturer who desires to know his cost—and unfortunately a good many have not the wisdom to know its importance—works out a system of costing which answers in his particular trade. The Chairman has kindly alluded to a work in which, in the heyday of my youth, in conjunction with Mr. Emile Garcke, I endeavoured to bring before the public in connective book form for the first time the principles which regulated costing. I was then not aware of a paper read by Mr. F. R. Goddard, Public Accountant of Newcastle, at the Cleveland Institute of Engineers on January 16th 1872, and I am now glad of the opportunity of being able to pay my tribute to that paper. Mr. F. R. Miller, a well-known accountant of Manchester, called my attention to it recently, and gave me the opportunity of perusing it. It is, so far as I know, the first paper dealing with the subject on broad lines of principle. The paper is entitled "The Balance Sheets of Manufacturing Firms. Their Principles and Theories viewed Analytically."

Mr. Goddard uses various terms such as might be used in connection with cost accounting. His great aim seems to be to arrive at what he calls "net cost." This he defines as a system of charging off to each particular engine, order, or contract the amount of raw material used in its manufacture, together with its exact proportion of wages. Then he goes on to oncost and indirect expenses. Charges commonly called "proportional or establishment charges" are such expenses as are incurred in all large concerns in the shape of rents, rates and taxes, salaries, &c. These again are charged off to the engine, order, or contract proportionately. I should like to pay my tribute to Mr. Goddard for the enterprise he showed in 1872, in calling attention to this important matter. I am the more anxious to do so because it becomes all engaged in professional work to recognise the work that other men do. I have gratefully to recognise the many contributions to the literature of this subject since 1887, when I first put pen to paper in this matter. From the gentlemen who have written books and papers I have learned a great deal, and I hope that in their turns they have found successive editions of the original book useful to them.

What do we really mean by "costing"? What is its nature and aim? A little time ago I wrote a paragraph on the subject, which my colleagues of the Cost Accounting Committee at the War Office were good enough to embody in a letter which went before the Army Council. In it I endeavoured to define the advantages which arise from a good system of costing. I said: "Among the advantages arising from the use of accounts of a costing type may be mentioned those arising from the regular "and systematic bringing before the individuals who are "ultimately responsible for expenditure the various "objects on which the expenditure has been incurred, "and the channels through which that expenditure has "been made. The details of the account, although "expressed only in money in the final account, reveal "the commodities used and the services performed, which "are eventually summed up in these terms. By the "agency of cost accounts, it is thus possible to consider "the constituent elements of cost, and by these means "to ascertain the differences which arise from varying "conditions, and to consider methods by which, without "impairing efficiency, either in service or in production, "economies may be effected. Cost accounts also reveal "the differences which arise from varying conditions as "regards supply of commodities or remuneration of labour "in different districts. A knowledge of all these varying "factors is essential to good—that is, to efficient and "economical—administration or management. Without "such data administration and management are either "more or less haphazard, or are carried out on empirical "lines. It is only through the study of comparative "costs that progress in a commercial sense can be "obtained.

"The systematic compilation of cost accounts has the "further advantage of bringing about natural uni-"formity in the methods of accounting with such "variations only as may be necessary owing to the "special circumstances of any locality or any special "class of service or of product.

"Through costing being undertaken as a distinct "function in the accounting system, it is possible to "obtain records of a detailed but general character, "obviating the need of a large number of accounts being "kept individually, and for the information of some "particular branch of administration without considera-"tion of the relation of that particular branch to the "whole undertaking. Cost accounting will thus lead to "the prevention of the duplicating of account-keeping, "and to the elimination of such accounts that are kept "as do not of themselves serve any useful or informa-"tive purpose."

That, of course, was written more particularly with regard to matters of army accounting, for I have the honour of serving on the Cost Accounting Committee at the War Office. Great progress has been made in the direction of standardising the accounts in the Army, and getting cost accounts. Recently, some evening papers have been rather guying the system, and alluding to "Platoons, Ltd." and asking when the War Office was going to declare a dividend. (Laughter.) This subject has been so well dealt with by my colleague, Col. Grimwood, in a recent lecture, that I would not like to pursue it further, save to say that I appreciate very much what he and my other colleagues have done in stimulating what I may call the professional element at the War Office to see the advantage of cost accounting methods. I believe that the result will be of incalculable service to the country, and that those accountants who have remained at the War Office in connection with cost accounting, have rendered very great service to their country, and will themselves see how important is the work they have undertaken.

Then, another branch to which cost accounting should be applied is the relation of the State to its individual citizens. We are probably entering an era in which there will be either municipalisation of many of the large industries, or perhaps some form of nationalisation thereof. It will be particularly incumbent on accountants to throw light on the dark places of the relations between the State and its citizens, not only in matters of taxation, but also in matters in which the State to a certain extent enters into trade or competition with its own citizens,

The war has led to the institution of a system of what are called "Costings." These are not cost systems in the truest and best sense of the word, as they are very often not in accord with, but very largely independent of, the commercial accounts of the firm whose products are costed. Probably it is only a stage in the evolution of proper systems of costing, but many of these costings have to be received with a certain amount of dubiety. One is rather dubious of some of the results produced, and in particular we have to be careful not to encourage indiscriminate contracting or buying by individuals for the State on the basis of cost plus percentage. That way, it seems to me, madness lies, because human nature being what it is, there will be no incentive to reduce the cost. The higher the cost, the higher the percentage, and the higher the profit that will be obtained. If we were all perfect, that system might safely be adopted, but it is fraught with a good deal of danger, and I, as a citizen, would like to enter a protest against the indiscriminate use of this system by the Government, or even by individuals, for all progress consists of obtaining the best possible results for the least possible expenditure of effort, and in the expenditure of effort one includes the element of money, and that which money represents, which is time, which is the only thing that matters. You cannot always measure a thing by money alone; you have to consider it in relation to the time it has taken to produce.

I am not quite certain whether we are right in calling ourselves "cost accountants" or "professional accountants with special knowledge of costing." I think some other and wider term is required. In America many men who perform the function are known as "Production Engineers." Some years ago one of the best known American "Business Doctors" was in England, and came to see me on the question of whether it was possible to institute in this country the profession of Business Doctor. I had regretfully to advise him that I did not think that much progress could be made under that designation in this country.

In some parts of America also, men who perform these services are known as "Consulting Economists." That also, in a conservative country like ours, is not likely to take on. A well-known American writer, dealing with the "Production Engineer," says: "The Production "Engineer, so-called, is also an accountant, but he is "more than that; he is really a Consulting Economist. "He is an accountant who knows, to begin with, the "general economic principles which make for the greatest "efficiency, and who can therefore so direct the account- "ing of the establishment as to find out whether each "and every branch is returning its maximum profit. "Usually, he does not tamper with questions of price; "that is, with the possibility of buying cheaper or "selling dearer, or with the question of getting busi- "ness. He deals principally with the commonplace "economic principles of marginal productivity and "marginal cost."

How can we expect to make any progress in the term "cost accountant" unless we are able to disabuse the public mind of the wrong impressions that it has of the word "cost." or until we can get something like a more accurate definition which will prevent such mistakes being made as have been made by those distinguished M.P.'s and members of the Government to whom I referred? I do not think we shall be able to remove that vagueness about terms unless we set out to reform our terms and make clear what is meant by the term "cost accountancy" and by the term "cost."

There is a further point. and that is the possible danger of over specialisation. Those who do specialise and go deeply into particular branches are rendering great service to those particular branches and to the community. On the other hand there is sometimes a tendency for them to realise the old Shakespearean simile of the dyer's hand "being subdued to that it works in." They see only the system they are interested in, and just as "too far East is West," so a too technical acquaintance with the trade he serves may tend to destroy the accountant's utility, and prevent his making those wisely audacious suggestions which sometimes emanate from men who know their subjects by study and not by the slower movements of practice. I think that there is even an advantage in not knowing a subject too deeply, and being in that state of mind when you do not mind being laughed at for making what may be called a foolish suggestion at all. Therefore, I hope that there will be some who will practise cost accountancy generally, and not in too specialised a form. You must have specialists, of course, just as in medicine and other branches of study and work. I think that the aim of those who do not over specialise is, with as great exactitude as possible, to quantify values and obtain relative comparisons between them, to measure industrial economy and economic forces as affecting production and distribution, and the results of economic tendencies as affecting the community and its group of constituent members.

We should have not merely the idea of quantitative measurement, but also the idea of qualitative analysis. Unless the two go together, you may have misleading results by dealing with quantification only. We have also to be very careful that we do not sacrifice the greater for the lesser object. Absolute arithmetical accuracy is, of course, always desirable, but, if that is obtained by the sacrifice of qualitative analysis, you are not rendering the best service of which you are capable, for slight divergence from arithmetical accuracy produces less evil consequences than does inaccurate grouping or allocation of figures, or the non-severance of the particular from the general. The combination of the like and the unlike may produce absolute arithmetical accuracy, but may result in a "figurative fact," not only absolutely worthless, but positively misleading.

I have alluded to the large field which I think awaits what I must call "cost accounting" in the domain of social service. The economics of the State as a social organism require elucidation from an independent and non-political standpoint by those who possess, as an accountant should possess, a wide knowledge of business in its varieties, methods, and changes, and who are, therefore, specially fitted to consider and advise on the probable financial and commercial effect of proposed legislation: and accountants can also render assistance in making clear to the central authority the methods it should adopt to obtain the advantage of business administration in Government departments.

If one might take a further illustration of the desirability of accountants being consulted before business decisions are come to. I might refer to the recent revelations before the Coal Commission, when it was ascertained that the Coal Controller, without having ascertained the figures, decided to increase the price of coal 2s. 6d. a ton. It was shown afterwards that that advance was absolutely unnecessary, save only from the point of view of indirect taxation as a contribution to the war. It was very unfortunate that the Coal Controller should have come to that decision without having ascertained his facts.

I have notes of other matters I had intended to refer to, but I have detained you long enough. I will just, therefore, thank you for your patience in listening to me (Applause.)

The Chairman moved a vote of thanks to the lecturer. In doing so, he said that there were many points in the lecture that one would like to discuss; for instance, the meaning of the word "cost." A fascinating point was the effect of costing on history. It was pretty well known that, when Philip II of Spain decided to send an armada against Britain, he asked for an estimate of the cost, and owing to the action of the Venetian bankers in raising the rate of interest on loans to Spain, the expenditure was so great that the Armada had to be put off for 18 months, and during that time Elizabeth's Cabinet was able to make the necessary preparations. He had no doubt that they could find many other instances in history. With regard to terms, in one firm in the North of England the works accountant was called the "Financial Manager," and in another he was known as the "Technical Manager."

Mr. E. Miles Taylor, in seconding the vote of thanks, said that very early in his career he obtained the inspiration for his later efforts entirely from the book —more famous in the States than in this country—written by Messrs. Garcke and Fells.

Mr. Owlett asked whether any great difference was proposed to be made in the definition of a costs clerk, who worked upon facts, and an estimator who worked upon the cost clerk's facts to budget for the future.

Mr. Warwick pointed out that in many cases selling price bore no relation to cost, but was simply what the manufacturer could get out of the public.

Mr. Elles-Hill emphasised the necessity of having a fixed nomenclature. At present one man's terms were a foreign language to another man.

Mr. E. Miles Taylor said that when he returned from the United States in 1914, "with more enthusiasm than common sense," he had put up a plate, describing himself as a Chartered Accountant and an "Efficiency Engineer," but the Institute had accused him of using a term which was discreditable to a Chartered Accountant. (Laughter.) With regard to Mr. Warwick's point, manufacturers were experts at getting the maximum price, but many had no knowledge of whether the cost was safely below that figure or not. In many industries a large part of the products were sold at a loss, and the remainder at an unfair profit. Costing was useless unless it dealt with volume instead of price.

The vote of thanks was carried with acclamation.

The lecturer acknowledged the vote. He said that, with regard to estimating future business, on the commercial side and on the technical side these were quite distinct and separate functions. The cost accountant had to provide the material which would enable the estimator to gauge a fair estimate of cost for the future. What was wanted was quantification, not merely in money but in articles used. He thought that the difference was largely similar to that between the accountant and the actuary, the latter being a scientific guesser. With regard to the selling price question, ultimately the cost of production must settle the price, because over a long series of years one could not go on selling at less than the cost of production without going to the workhouse. With regard to the need for a scientific nomenclature, he knew of no profession which was as bad as the accountancy profession in regard to terminology; doctors, architects, and even solicitors, had some terminology which was understood. (Laughter.)

Mr. Ryall said that, on behalf of the Institute of Cost and Works Accountants, he could confirm what had been said as to the difficulty of nomenclature, and would suggest that a member of that body should be on the proposed committee.

A discussion then ensued as to the formation and function of the proposed committee, and a resolution was unanimously passed that a committee should be appointed for the purpose of attempting to fix the nomenclature used by cost accountants, consisting of 12 members, 6 being elected by the present meeting, and invitations being sent to the Institute, the Society, and the Institute of Cost and Works Accountants to nominate two each, making 12 in all.

The following were elected by the meeting:—Lieut.Col. J. Grimwood, D.S.O., and Messrs. J. M. Fells, E. Miles Taylor, Elles-Hill, and H. R. Cooper, with power to co-opt one more.

A vote of thanks to the chairman concluded the proceedings.

The Relationship of Costing to Management.

By James R. Massey.

A lecture delivered at the London School of Economics on 30th April 1919.

This paper is written with the object of defining somewhat of the relationship of costing to management, more particularly in the engineering trade, explaining what costing can do to assist the functioning of management, and what use the management can make of this side of costing in governing and controlling the current operation of the plant.

The routine work of the compilation of factory costs has not been touched on, nor the question of the preparation of basic costs for the guidance of the management in considering questions of lines of apparati, &c., so as to confine the scope of the paper as far as possible to the aspect of costing covered by the title. The preparation of factory costs of product for the management, whether "ideal" or "actual" costs, is connected more closely with the now usually well understood routine of costing.

The term "cost man" is used in the place of "costing," because it is the man who is responsible, practically entirely, for the success of the results rather than the mere system. No system will run a factory, at least commercially; we have very patent evidence of that fact before us in the example of Government Departments—results are obtained, but at what cost? This axiom applies equally to costing as to management.

Every important change that takes place is born of some necessity, and so it is with costing; there is no doubt that the fundamental principles of it must have been used in some form or other, however crudely, from the very commencement of trading in any form, but of late years it has developed more on the lines of an exact science, certain broad principles having come to be recognised as standard and which form a basis on which to build up the individual system.

To account for the development of costing, let us review the circumstances that have given rise to the alteration of its standing. Great changes have come over the engineering trade in the last generation; conditions in the trade have altered very considerably.

Up to about thirty years ago numbers of the large manufacturing businesses were in the hands of their founders, frequently men who had risen from the ranks, in many cases after hard struggles, and who devoted long hours and very close personal supervision to their works, and there was very little that went on in them that escaped their notice. The owner manager of the old order may be said to have carried the whole responsibilities on his own shoulders, but, as an outcome of the vast increase in the variety of product and the growth in the size of individual enterprises, the functions of management have had to be sub-divided; specialists have naturally grown up in each branch who devote the whole of their energies to the perfection of their special line, with, we may say, much greater progress in the efficiency of the trade and at a much quicker rate. Specialisation, as we have all realised, is the basic principle of progress.

The joint-stock principle of carrying on business, now almost universally adopted throughout the trade, has helped in a large degree to bring about these altered conditions of management. Businesses carried on for the benefit of a group of shareholders lose the personal element of the owner-managed concern. Then, again, social conditions have altered so radically: distractions have multiplied exceedingly, and our very habits have altered. We have lost the aptitude for the slogging hard work put in by our forefathers, and tend to lead an easier life. It is not to be contended that this present life is not a better one, but there can be no doubt whatever that business is a loser to some large extent, and other means have grown up to supply the deficiency.

In the old days of the owner-managed concern, when he held all the strings of the business in his own fingers, there was not the same necessity for the strict cost-keeping that is vital to success to-day. Furthermore, we may be quite safe in stating that profits were better, and would stand a certain margin of loss of efficiency in the business without disappearing into nothingness, such as would be likely to happen nowadays under similar conditions owing to the nearer approach of selling price to cost.

Competition was less, both at home and abroad, in those days. We are all well aware of the great competition from the United States of America and Germany that has grown up during the period, and we must look for this factor to increase in severity in the near future, for Japan is making great strides in the field of engineering production; even our own Colonies are progressing towards becoming self-suppliers, if not in some cases our actual competitors in the world's markets, so that the margin between selling price and cost is likely to become less.

Another important factor, connected more with the direct cost of manufacturing, is the alteration that has come over the character of labour and the conditions connected with it. In the old days men settled down in the employ of a firm and brought along their sons to follow in their footsteps; the aspect of the relationship of employer to labour had something of the character of the old patriarchial system about it, but to-day we have very large floating populations in our works, and the increased stringency of Government regulations and the effect of trade union rules and restrictions have tended to reduce the efficiency and output of labour, whilst the expenses of handling and supervising it have gone up considerably.

The only way to meet these adverse conditions is to adopt the most scientific methods of manufacturing, and, not least of all, to obtain the best results for every penny expended in the business.

Having lost to a large extent the personal element in the management of the business, with what are we to replace it? The answer is "costing," and the most scientific costing at that. By the use of the term "scientific" do not imagine that complexity is meant, because the simpler the system that accomplishes the necessary results, the more scientific it is.

Very great interest is taken at the present day in the subject of costing. It has come to be recognised in many circles as one of the main essentials to successful business, but the progress of it has hardly kept pace with the altered conditions in the engineering trade; it has been going through a period of evolution like most good things, and to-day only may be said to be coming into its own. The value and vital necessity of good costing are becoming more generally recognised by the trade every day, and the subject opens up a very interesting and profitable career to bright men who have an aptitude and inclination for the work.

Costing has suffered much depreciation in the eyes of the trade owing to the fact that cost men as a body have been largely untrained, but they themselves have not been so much to blame as circumstances, for there have not been opportunities for the acquisition of knowledge of the subject. To-day most of you would have considerable difficulty in indicating a course of instruction open to the average young man desirous of becoming an efficient exponent of the science.

The subject is confused in many minds with bookkeeping, but it is not bookkeeping, nor is bookkeeping costing. Bookkeeping is the proof of costing, without which it is of very little dependability and consequent worth.

The term "costing" is not an ideal one for the science: "works accounting" is more suitable and explanatory, using the word "accounting" in the literal and not the technical sense. Costing gathers together the salient points in the operation of the plant, and presents them in a condensed and easily assimilable form to the management, as well as compiling the actual factory cost of product.

To do this work efficiently it is obvious that the cost man must have a very fair knowledge of the technicalities of the business, and also be a first-class accountant with a good commercial instinct. Every works is a problem to itself; outlines of general system can be applied, but the details of handling must be worked out by the man himself. Lay-outs, conditions, particular methods of manufacture, different products, working facilities, local customs, and a host of other factors vary, demanding to be taken into account and requiring special treatment to secure the best results.

The real essence of good costing lies in the selection of the right facts and getting them in the quickest and most economical manner. The major importance of the point of speed is particularly emphasised; unless facts are given quickly they are of very little worth to the management, and more often a cause of annoyance. One hears bitter remarks passed in managerial circles on this very score of lateness of information.

The cost man should, of necessity, have every part of the factory open to him and be entitled to investigate all operations and processes in every direction. He, on his part, should see to it that what he requires gives the minimum of clerical work to the actual producers, the foremen and workmen, and try to arrange so that the results assist production rather than hinder it. He should set out to win the confidence of the men in the factory, and always be ready to help by changing methods, where possible, to meet the convenience of foremen and others whenever this can be done without loss to the efficiency of the results; thus the men will come to him with their troubles in connection with the system, to the advantage of both parties.

The cost man is the most confidential man in the shop, and can exercise a very real influence on results by the use of judicious diplomacy. It is very necessary for him to spend a considerable proportion of his time in the shops, and a good man supplies in a very large degree the personal element in manufacturing; his eyes are the eyes of the management, and are the first to see effects and to look for causes; he should know every operation that is carried on in whatsoever corner of the factory, and why and how it is carried on, as well as what is the cost of it; all the multifarious details of the expenses should be thoroughly familiar to him, and he should be able to put his finger upon any item which may have even the remotest connection with the operation of the plant. He should, in effect, be a human card index to the factory for the management.

Having described something of the ground covered by costing, let us consider the management side of the business.

The management is the controlling element of the business, and in most modern works, except in very small ones, the executive responsibility is subdivided under the control of the manager. This arrangement makes for efficiency, as mentioned before, because men who are specialists in their particular branch can be engaged to carry out the general indications of the manager, who is really another specialist carrying out the policy of his board of directors. Although the executive functions of management are subdivided and carried out by specialists, it still remains necessary to co-ordinate their efforts under the control of a manager who directs the policy to be followed, and acts as an arbitrator between the different departments and also as the tangible head of the administration.

The engineers and designers, with the drawing office attached, produce the designs; the purchasing agent provides the material; in many large factories the employment agent supplies the labour; the shop superintendents or managers, with their foremen, do the actual producing; probably a works engineer is charged with the responsibility for the expense and general services of the factory; the accountant handles the financial side of the business; and the cost man gathers together the results of the operations of the other sections of the management and presents them in a clear and impartial form to all those concerned, for their information and guidance.

Thus it will be seen that costing is really and truly a branch of the management, and not one of the least important at that, but, unfortunately, this is not recognised to its full significance in many works in this country. In America the cost man is very highly appreciated and given all support and assistance possible. The money spent on costing is a highly remunerative investment, if judiciously laid out and full advantage taken of the results obtained.

The purely managerial work done by the cost man, apart from the routine work of compiling factory cost of product, consists of the preparation of the periodical returns—weekly, monthly, quarterly, &c.—of the current functioning of the factory. These returns give a very clear insight into the actual conditions obtaining and permit of present investigation and action.

Factory cost records, on the other hand, merely give history of past action, and in a form that is complicated with all sorts of varying factors. Very little action can be taken on them without a considerable amount of investigation of detail, entailing much loss of time. Even then some of the items selected may prove to be due to cases of abnormal conditions which arise from time to time in all shops, and in the others it will possibly be found that the actual occurrence of the default causing excess cost is so long passed that no disciplinary action can be taken, and all moral effect is lost.

It will be worth while to give a description of the main managerial returns and show how they can be used by the management, so as to illustrate more clearly what it is possible for the cost man to do.

First there are the broad facts covering the plant in general, and then there are these same facts in greater detail as relating to the individual sections of the business, together with others particular to such individual sections. The figures used for the compilation of the returns are those produced by the different departments of the works during the carrying out of the routine of paying wages, costkeeping, bookkeeping, &c., so that the head of each department is equally well informed as the manager as to the conditions existing in the part of the business for which he is responsible.

In selecting the method of arrangement of the returns it is the soundest practice to devote a separate form to each main fact, so that when it is under consideration there is more concentration on the point in question.

The main divisions of the facts may be classified under six headings, relating to :—

(1) Labour.
(2) Material.
(3) Expenses.
(4) Defects.
(5) Departments, or units.
(6) Factory costs.

Some specimen forms are shown for rendering the information, and it will be noticed that a number are continuous, either weekly or monthly, for the whole year. This method of continuous returns is very valuable, as it obviously permits of comparing figures over a period in the most convenient manner to the user.

Taking the first item, Labour, a weekly return which is continuous for the year is made up of the number of hourly workers in each department of the factory. The figures are divided under the headings of non-producers and producers.

Each department will keep a continuous weekly record of their non-producers, arranged under categories of occupation, and as to whether on the staff or paid hourly; this will show departmental chief, assistants ditto, engineers, draughtsmen, clerks (office) of different grades, foremen, assistant foremen, shop clerks, storekeepers, labourers, &c. A general summary of these departmental records is made up for the management, showing the total non-producers under each category in the factory, and this summary is continuous for the year, so that the figures may be contrasted.

An explanatory report made up by the cost man should accompany the above summary to account for changes in totals. These returns keep a tight curb on the very vexed question of the number of non-producers in a factory.

The next point in regard to labour is the number of overtime hours worked, and the weekly return of this, also continuous for the year, shows the total hours for each foreman's section, grouped by departments. The hours worked are divided as to non-producers and producers.

Overtime in a factory is an expense that should be subjected to the very closest scrutiny. Having the totals divided as to non-productive and productive work enables investigation to be made as to whether some of the non-productive overtime can be cut out by better organisation during working hours, and by observing the productive overtime, it will be seen if there will be a real gain to the total output, because it is machine work—the machine output is the true "bottle neck" of the factory—or if, possibly, it may be bad organisation on the part of foremen by working handworkers overtime, who will probably have to slack up during the day in a short while to allow the machine workers to catch up.

Overtime is never a success, due to several important factors: the physical effect on the workers; during winter months, and we have unfortunately many of them in this country, overtime is carried on by artificial light, and most frequently only a part of the factory, or even of the particular section working, is illuminated at that; generally there is lack of proper and efficient supervision; probable considerable curtailment of the utility services of the factory, such as cranage, material stores, tool stores, and the possibility of reference to the draughting office. All these points, and others of a similar nature, tend to make for the reduction of efficiency of overtime. There are times when it becomes necessary, even imperative to work overtime, but it will generally be found possible to effect a substantial economy by keeping closely after this item.

The data for this return can be automatically obtained by suitable arrangement of the pay roll, so that the totals will give the statistics correctly divided; the fact that machine workers are supervised by different foremen to the handworkers in practically every factory gives the division under this head.

The report on this return will require a constant knowledge of the conditions in the factory, but the matter for it can be largely obtained by training the foremen to report on unusual conditions at the time of the occurrence.

A further return is that of time lost, compiled departmentally, and this entails some slight additional work in collecting the details, but it is well worth the expenditure for the moral effect that it has on the factory.

Each working hour lost is so much per cent. lost of the possible output of the plant, and every endeavour should be made to trace the causes and reduce the total to the minimum. Time is lost due to various causes: those relating to the man are slackness, sickness, and accidents; those relating to the factory are lack of material, breakdown or shortage of power, breakdown of individual machines, waiting for cranes, work, &c., and it is to be recommended that productive time lost due to internal conditions, although paid for, be included in the return, as well as any time lost by a machine unit standing waiting for labour. The total loss due under the various headings will then be patent, and steps may be taken to remedy the conditions if the particular amount involved justifies the outlay.

The figures for the return are obtained from returns made up by the departments; these show the lost time under each detail heading for every foreman's section, but the return for the management shows them only under the three broad headings of "Men," "Machines," and "Various."

This statistic will be read in conjunction with the overtime return, and might be combined with it but for the fact that it would make the return somewhat unwieldy.

The last return in connection with labour is that of the percentage earned by piece-workers, shown on their time-worked piecework, and should include the amount of the wages earned and the bonus, so that a quarterly summary can be made up.

An increased percentage of earnings spells an increase in the total output for the factory, and a reduction points to the contrary.

The next item on our list is Material, and here there is some slight difference between the small factory and the large one: in the small factory material will be recorded in one account in most instances, the amount being divided between separate Ledgers relating to the different classes of stock carried, whilst in the large factory quite a considerable proportion of the stock will be included in the balances of the departmental accounts. All large factories should be departmentalised, for there is no other method so efficient for controlling them.

The Return on Material shows the monthly balances carried by the various Ledgers representing the general stock, and the balances of the Departmental Controlling Accounts, which include the stock carried by the particular department as well as the value of the work in progress in that part of the shops.

The Purchasing Department will keep a daily record of the value of orders placed, divided similarly by Ledgers and Departments, and the commitments thus arrived at are included in the return alongside the item of stock. The total of these two figures of stock and commitments should bear a strict relation to the amount of work going through the factory.

It would be very illuminative to have the balance at factory cost price, estimated of course, of customers' orders remaining to be completed by the shop, but in many factories this would involve a considerable amount of work in collecting the detail, and it is doubtful if the net commercial result would justify the outlay.

The points that appeal to the management in this question of stocks of materials and work in progress are that more stock, &c., means greater capital investment, greater space occupied to the detriment of convenience in the works, more labour necessary to handle it, and increased liability of direct loss due to deterioration and obsolescence.

The figures of stocks should be read in conjunction with outputs, and these are included in the return, and the comparison then consists of "stocks," "commitments," and "output," the items being added month by month.

The third heading of managerial returns is Expenses, and this is probably the most important of all.

There is no such thing as "expense" or "non-productive," in the strict sense of the words. All legitimate expenditure in the factory is just as necessary to the operation of manufacturing as the time of the workman directly engaged in producing the manufactured article.

If you can conceive a factory producing one article, and one size of it only, then every expenditure of any sort can be charged directly to the cost of producing without any intervening operation of ratios, or other method of loading, and the control of the items of any nature maintained by comparing them as a percentage of the total cost of output. It is possible that there are instances of such plants in existence to-day, even in the engineering trade.

The condition of manufacturing variety of product, and different sizes of it, in the same factory creates the complication of the necessity of separating, as it were, the so-called expenses from the actual direct cost of production for convenience in apportioning them more or less equitably between the different classes and sizes of work produced, and also to maintain a control on the total sum disbursed.

The very unstable nature of many expenses and the rapidity with which the totals creep up necessitate a very careful watch being kept upon them, and the management must have the figures submitted in such a form as to enable fluctuations to be readily inquired into and criticised.

There are two returns, which consist of, first, a monthly statement of the expenditure of the separate departments and expense services of the business under each heading of factory expense. The range of numbers allotted to indicate the separate headings of factory expense is divided into three groups so as to bring together those expenses that relate to the running of the shop sections, and for which the foremen are mainly responsible, those relating to the departments, and for which the departmental head is responsible, and then the group of general expenses of the factory.

The second return is a continuous monthly record of the total expenditure of the factory on each item of expense, and the amounts are divided as to the expenditure on operation and maintenance.

The departments keep a continuous monthly record of their expenditure under each item, which is available for the use of the management as occasion arises.

These two managerial returns are read in conjunction, the source of fluctuations in the total expenditure on the individual items are traced on the monthly return, showing the departmental totals; it is obvious that all fluctuations may not show up on the summary, as there may be compensating reductions for corresponding increases in different departments, but these items will have been noted and remarked upon by the cost man in his report based upon the scrutiny of the departmental returns.

The amount of absorption is contrasted with the actual expenditure on the departmental totals form, and consistent differences—deficit or surplus—are important to take note of. In the one case factory costs are being carried on to the books below their real cost, and in the other case—which, on the face of it, does not look quite so important, and is even considered by some to be on the safe side—the condition is hampering the getting of business by using fictitiously high estimated factory costs.

Of the two conditions, the latter is the more serious; it is possible to retrieve on an order that has been taken on too low an estimated factory cost by the exercising of great care and economy, if the position is realised in time, but nothing can be done in the case of an order that has been lost, and in the meantime an irrecoverable loss of absorption may be accruing in the factory owing to the lost production. This question of absorption is more far-reaching than appears at first sight.

It may be added that the method of distribution of the absorption over different classes of apparati and operations may have a somewhat similar influence to the above mentioned possibilities on the results; the easy method of a flat rate has a tendency to penalise some classes of product to the advantage of others, the result being that some lines may be neglected because they do not show apparently good results, in place of others that are not the real "money getters." This view is one that the cost man should press very strongly upon the management because it is not readily recognised.

Whilst on this question of expenses, a word might be added on the subject of ratios. A low ratio does not always indicate efficiency, nor a high one the opposite condition; it is quite possible to so manipulate the charging of time in the shop as to produce a considerable difference in the ratio without making any alteration in the true conditions. Caution must be used in basing any premises on the point.

We come now to the item of Defects, one that is rarely found to be adequately handled in a great many works, and the total amount of loss due to it not realised. Everyone will agree that it is impossible to carry on a manufacturing plant without continual, in fact daily, losses arising from this source.

Grouped under the heading of defects are the losses arising from defects in materials, defects and mistakes in workmanship, pure accidents, defects in design and specifying, and mistakes in ordering.

The management naturally desire to keep the total loss down to the lowest possible limit. The loss due to defects is not only the net amount of the factory cost of the occurrence but there is the further loss attendant upon the loss of so much saleable product, which should have borne its share of the selling expenses, and produced, in addition, some figure of net profit.

Careful study and investigation of this return will be amply repaid by the discovery from time to time of factors and conditions that can be remeded, as well as by the moral effect produced on the personnel of the factory generally.

The return is made up on two forms: the first shows the total loss in each department under the three broad headings of material, workmanship, and design, the last including all losses in connection with design, specifying, or ordering.

The individual departmental returns, which are continuous monthly and are used also for bookkeeping purposes, show the origin of the responsibility for the loss, such as iron foundry, brass foundry, forge, &c., and the second return for the management is compiled from these, showing the total loss throughout the factory that each separate department is responsible for. Both the managerial returns are also continuous monthly.

The very large amount of money that dribbles away in a business through this channel is difficult to realise until the matter comes to be dealt with on organised lines. The fact of carrying out the system to record these losses, which should include the necessity of the party concerned signing that he accepts responsibility, brings the point up continually before those responsible for the operations in the factory with salutary effect, well worth the trouble involved, apart from the value of the information to the management.

Our fifth point is that of the operation of the different Departments of the factory, and this return is a gathering together of the detail points already reported on other returns, but all brought to a focus in this one, together with such other departmental figures as may be found to be useful. The cost man can here save the management much time by the preparation of a careful report on the comparisons, and including the explanations of abnormal conditions.

The last return deals with the total Factory Costs of completed orders. It consists of a list from each of the departments of the factory showing the result of each order completed during the month, contrasting the actual cost with the estimated cost. Each of these returns is accompanied by a report, prepared by the department concerned, explaining the cases of important differences between the two figures.

The compilation of these lists acts as a guide to those charged with the responsibility of getting out the estimates and brings to light cases of difficult design, as well as ventilating excess cost incurred in the shop.

The cost man can, if the management so desires it, condense the individual departmental reports into one, but it is better that the manager should devote the time to go through the details himself.

These six points or items of managerial returns do not necessarily cover all those of value that might be produced, but they are the main ones, and common to most factories. Certain plants will have special conditions and different types of manufacture, requiring different particulars to efficiently control them, but caution should be exercised in producing returns, for it is very easy to be betrayed into an orgy of statistics; the result in that case is spoilt by watering down. Each fact presented to the management should clearly answer to the question "What will it do?" or, perhaps better still, "What will it permit to be done?" and not to "What will it show?"

If the manager holds a monthly meeting of his departmental heads, and perhaps also of his foremen, the information contained in the managerial returns will provide him with the basis of the material for discussion.

These returns are not the whole story of management; they are merely guides, but good guides, to the trend of affairs in the factory. They will go a long way to assist the management to catch up losses quickly and more certainly, and, consequently, improve results to a large extent. The fact that all this material passes through the hands of the cost man shows in what an important relation he stands to the management.

Dealing with the more personal relations between the cost man and the management, the latter should endeavour to appreciate the former more than is usually found to be the case; encourage him by taking an interest in his work and telling him the moves that have been made as the result of his work. There may be cases where it is not diplomatic to take immediate, or even any, action; this should be explained to him, for there is nothing more deadening to enthusiasm than lack of interest, or apparent lack of it. The cost man is only human after all, and needs some spur to prick him on, and to a good man there is none so effective for this purpose as realisation of achievement of success. Consider the feelings of a man, be he a cost man or any other, who may have put weeks of careful thought and preparation into some work which is put on one side by his superior with about as much interest as the evening paper.

The cost man can be about the most useful man in the whole organisation if he is given the right opportunity and support; a good man may become one of the main factors in building up a successful business, and may enable a good manager to make his reputation, so that the two have considerable common interest. Good costing does not make good management, but good costing is invaluable to good management.

The cost man should live up to his reputation, and never be satisfied that he has reached finality in anything. He should not overload himself with work—that is, detail work; the best piece of advice in this direction ever given the author is, "Never do anything yourself that you can get someone else to do," and the sound common-sense of it becomes more apparent every day. The idea conveyed is not to shirk work, but to organise the work so that all that can be done by cheaper labour is so done, reserving one's energies for the things that others are not capable of doing, but let all beware of the fallacy of trying to "keep things under your own hat," as the saying goes; the man who endeavours to do this is fooling himself all the time and advertising to the world at large that he recognises his own inefficiency and is afraid of competition; he should rather teach his assistants all he can, and learn from them and through their mistakes.

The real mission of the cost man is that of a reformer, and we all know that reformers do not lead very comfortable lives as a rule, but success is a compensation worth striving for, and, on the whole, where the management take interest, the work of costing is intensely interesting.

The author hopes that, while this paper is not by any means the last word on the subject, in the cases where it has the fortune to meet the eye of manager or cost man it will give them to think that there are possibilities realisable that perhaps have not yet been attained.

Costing in Relation to Scientific Management.

By J. H. H. Boyd.

(Director, Costs and Efficiency Methods, Central Stores Department, Ministry of Munitions.)

A lecture delivered before the Industrial Reconstruction Council in the Hall of the Institute of Journalists, Tudor Street, London, E.C., on 13th May 1919, Mr. Baker in the chair.

The Chairman said that they had received a disappointment, having had a telegram from Sir Herbert Austin regretting his inability to attend. It was customary for the chairman to make a few remarks, but they were dropping that on this occasion, and he would ask Mr. Boyd to give his lecture.

The lecturer said :—

It must be a source of gratification to everyone who has taken an interest in this very important question of scientific management to find that the Industrial Reconstruction Council have made it a part of their programme.

In this country we are to-day passing through a period of industrial unrest. There may be divergencies of opinion as to the cause of this, but there can be no difference of opinion as to the necessity for earnest endeavour being made to find a cure.

It would be placing the claim very high to say that scientific management is, in fact, this cure, but it is not going beyond the mark to say that scientific management is one of the most important factors in the cure.

The whole subject of scientific management is intensely interesting, as doubtless those who have attended the previous meetings will have found, and the fact that six different meetings have been arranged to deal with the subject indicates at once the amount of ground which has to be covered before one even gets a grip on really what is meant by the term.

As far as I am concerned this evening, I have to deal with only one of the elements in scientific management—namely, the recording and the use of costs.

There is always a difficulty in handling a subject of this kind, as one is compelled to choose between two courses. That is, a particular form of costing (or cost system) may be described in detail, or one may talk along broad lines avoiding all detail.

The first method is open to the objection that it involves details of routine and the display of forms, graphs, diagrams, &c., and may leave the impression on the hearer's mind that while the system illustrated might be all right for a specific business, it would be useless for the hearer's particular business. In an endeavour to imagine how a particular point would affect a particular business, the hearer may easily miss the main points of principle.

The alternative is to deal only with the broad principles on which any costing system must be founded if it is to properly fulfil its functions, and then to outline what are the main functions.

This method is liable to raise a doubt in the hearer's mind as to whether the theory can be carried out in practice, unless, of course, the hearer has knowledge of the utility of cost records.

As I have decided to deal with the subject on theoretical lines, I will anticipate this criticism by saying that I promise not to make any claim for a costing system this evening which I have not actually experienced or investigated, or which I have not seen fulfilled in practice.

In addition, if time permits, I will give one or two examples of results obtained by scientific management, using a cost system for the purpose of centralised control.

Costs as a Part of Scientific Management.

Briefly, I think costs are the foundation on which scientific management must be built. They enter very largely into the whole structure, and finally they supply the roof. At first sight it might appear that this is a somewhat exaggerated claim, but if we consider what actually happens we may see that, after all, it is quite true.

As long as money remains the medium of exchange, all that is done in business must eventually be expressed in terms of money.

A manager may be an excellent technical man, but he does not, in fact, build his reputation on his ability to do certain technical duties personally, nor does he create much of an impression by showing his directors how well his factory or his office is laid out, if he cannot show that all that he is doing is leading to increased output and, through that, to reduced costs. This is especially true to-day, when he is faced with ever increasing cost in wages and material. The manager of to-day must be more than ever the guiding hand of the whole effort, and not the personal supervisor of petty details. Others must handle details for him ; but he must have facts put before him clearly and concisely, so that he may know in his office that the whole work, from the foreman to the apprentice, is running smoothly and efficiently. A costing system properly based, run, and used, will produce all that he requires for purposes of control.

Before inquiries into the other subjects included under the general heading of scientific management are begun there must be some proof of the necessity for the inquiry. It is perfectly true that one may go into, say, a factory and, by looking round, see the need for improvement, but one cannot gauge the extent of this need until one has it down in figures, and those figures are best obtained from a series of records—commonly called a cost system —which is designed to obtain information regarding output, wages, prices of material, efficiency of performance, &c., and all these facts must be known before one can get a good start on the reconstruction of a business.

Having laid the foundation for improvement in the business by means of careful study of the various elements, it is necessary to have records to show the effect of the introduction of the new methods and to ensure that suggestions are actually being carried out and maintained, and the only way in which this can be satisfactorily done is by having those records so designed that they can be used to record progress right on the spot. The manager should have placed before him, each morning if necessary, brief statements or graphs which show at once all the salient points calling for his attention, and he can thus keep in constant touch with the progress of his reconstruction.

Having introduced new methods, and having established a system of recording all the necessary details to enable a close grip to be kept on the running of the business without the necessity for personal supervision of the actual work, the man responsible can cap all his efforts by showing in hard facts and figures the progress he has made.

The foregoing, although brief and described in somewhat general terms, will, I hope, serve to show the necessity for and the use of the proper recording of costs in the reconstruction and control of any business. I venture to say that the introduction of an efficient cost system into any business where one does not already exist, or where the present one is unsuitable, will almost invariably raise the question of the necessity for inquiry into methods, &c., and ultimately lead to some form of reconstruction and improvement.

Costs Definition.

Now let us look at what we mean when we speak of costs. The word " cost " is very like the word " clerk," inasmuch as it does not convey any definite idea in itself. I have, therefore, prepared a very simple diagram in the shape of an addition in arithmetic.

Wages Cost
Material Cost

Fundamental Cost
Direct Cost

Prime Cost
Departmental Overall Cost

Total Departmental Cost
Administration Overall Cost

Total Cost.

It will be seen that the first little sum shows wages added to material, giving a total of fundamental cost. Fundamental costs are costs which can, in fact, be recorded with accuracy against the operation on which they are actually incurred.

We then have fundamental cost added to direct cost, giving prime cost. Direct costs cannot be allocated with accuracy to any particular operation in a piece of work, but they can be charged direct to the whole of the particular work, and, when added to the fundamental costs, they give prime costs, which are the costs that can with certainty be allocated directly to the work.

Prime cost added to departmental overall cost gives total departmental cost. Departmental overall costs are costs which cannot be charged with accuracy to any particular operation or piece of work, but which can be charged to a particular department.

We then have total departmental cost added to administration overall cost, which gives total cost.

Now, I think, we can be quite clear on what is meant when we speak of costs, and it will be seen that those headings cover all the costs which enter into any business.

The actual term used is of no real moment—for instance, " overall costs " may be more commonly known as " overhead charges," " overhead cost," &c.

Unit Costs.

I can imagine someone saying, " Well, that is all right, " because I already have a record of all these costs. I " have my pay sheets, which show me the amount of " money I have spent in wages ; I have my Purchase " Account, my Stores Balance Sheets, and my Cash " Accounts," &c., which show me the amount of money " I have spent in all these other things." That is true ; one can get from any good system of financial accounting all these items, ***but what one does not get is a grip on whether the amounts which have been spent have been wisely spent.*** That is where the cost system comes in. From a control point of view it is useless knowing only the bulk expenditure. One has to get the expenditure split up and identified with specific units of work, and the information must be available as the expenditure is being made or immediately after it has been made, instead of some considerable time after the money has been spent. As an example :—

A firm building motor-cars would not derive much satisfaction in knowing that after they have made a 100 cars they have spent too much in wages, materials, &c. If they were in keen competition and had to watch carefully the price at which they had to sell the car, then it would be necessary for them to take each particular part and keep a day to day grip on what it was costing them to make each part, so that they could be assured that when the parts were finally assembled and the car produced ready for sale they would not be in the position of having to raise the price of the car or lose money on the transaction without having had the chance of doing something to reduce the cost.

The points to be noted here are :—

(1) Bulk or total costs are insufficient for purposes of control.

(2) Costs must be built up from fundamental cost to the total cost.

(3) Work must be carefully examined and separate records of costs prepared for each operation or group of operations.

(4) The costs for each operation (or group) must be related to appropriate units of work.

(5) Certain costs may, in the first instance, be controlled by units of service rendered before being added to costs expressed per unit of work—for instance, rents, lighting, &c.

(6) The cost records, whatever their shape, must be the telegraphic advice keeping the manager posted on what is happening day by day. Cost records must be " business news."

(7) The preparation of statistics is often looked upon as a system for controlling costs, but there is this vital difference between the two—statistics are simply " business history."

Use of Costs to the Manager.

Let us look now at what a good costing system means to a " live " manager. Time will not permit of my dealing with every point in this connection, and I will, therefore, content myself by taking a few of the principal uses of a costing system.

Imagine the manager as a traveller in a foreign country —a costing system is his map directing him in the right road to travel to reach certain points.

As captain of the ship, the costing system is his chart guiding him into safe channels and warning him of dangerous rocks.

As a general at headquarters, the costing system is the observer who by means of plans, diagrams, and figures, shows him the weak spots and indicates the points of attack.

A costing system enables the manager to make a diagnosis of the business and have diseased parts removed by his practical men or his experts.

It is an indicator as to the necessity for action, and it also shows him whether the necessary action has been taken and whether it has been effective.

Elimination of Waste.

One of the principal uses of the costing system is that it assists in the elimination of waste, which, after all, is the essence of scientific management. As a matter of fact, the introduction of a costing system into a business will, in itself, eliminate waste in wages and in material, &c., simply by introducing the necessity for writing down why and where the expenditure has been incurred. When this is done in conjunction with the study of better methods, and the various other items which are included in scientific management, then one gets the combination which, I hope, in the future will be called —not " scientific management "—but just simply " management."

A costing system may exist and may do good work quite apart from efficiency studies, but the full benefit from a costing system cannot be derived unless the efficiency side is also dealt with, but on the other hand no amount of efficiency work would prove of lasting good without a costing system to control the results.

As an example of where the introduction of a costing system saved money, there was certain work on which tractors were employed. There was no system of immediate control, but statistics were prepared from time to time showing the amount of work which had been done, and so on. A month or six weeks after a system of job cards and other records was brought into use the average acreage of a tractor per day was trebled, and that without any change having been made in the method of doing the work. The saving was due absolutely to the elimination of waste time, and the cutting down of the idle time of the tractors.

Again, in connection with a certain small fleet of tractors, the cost of the repairs per week was cut down by 50 per cent., simply by having recorded what repairs were done, why they were necessary, and what they in fact cost.

There was also considerable saving in petrol and accessories by proper stores accounting which formed part of the costing system.

Idle Time.

I have already mentioned idle time, but I am giving it a separate heading as I wish to draw particular attention to this subject.

How many managers know the amount of idle time in their works or factory? Ask a manager and he will answer, "practically none." Ask, further, how he knows this, and when he has cooled down he will probably tell you that he has eyes which he uses.

It is amazing how many managers rely on the powers of observation either of themselves or their subordinates to eliminate idle time; but get the idle time actually recorded and it will be found that it is probably much in excess of anything they ever imagined.

The obvious objection is that workmen will not have idle time recorded—that it will be dumped into something else; but the costing system can be made sufficiently complete to prevent time being wrongly allocated.

Chase this idle time! Like the will o' the wisp it may flit from point to point and you may never catch it, but at least it disappears. Kill one moment of idle time and it is added to the productive time of the day.

The proper planning of work and the careful fixing of standards will prove how time can be saved and fully utilised, but it is necessary to have records which will show that all that has been planned in this direction is being carried out, and such records are essentially part of a costing system.

Estimates.

A good costing system will keep the manager constantly supplied with up-to-date figures with which he can make estimates and fix prices. There will be no element of uncertainty as to whether his estimate of future expenditure is sound or as to whether a price which he is quoting is too large or too small, when he knows that he is basing his quotations on figures obtained "red-hot" from current work.

Even if the particular class of work for which he is preparing an estimate is not going on at the moment, if he has cost records for similar work done in the past and also records which show the changed conditions in the cost of wages, material, &c., since the work was done formerly, he can prepare an intelligent estimate and feel confident that he is not far out in his conclusions.

Estimates prepared without the aid of cost records must be more or less in the nature of guesswork.

I heard of a case recently in connection with a firm of manufacturers, and by no means an unimportant firm—as a matter of fact their name is practically a household word throughout Great Britain and the Colonies, in connection with their particular manufacture. A customer wrote in giving an order for certain articles to be made and asking a quotation. The request reached the office, a clerk from the office went out into the factory, got hold of the foreman who was responsible for this kind of work, asked him how much he thought it would cost to do the job, took the foreman's word for it, added on a number of different percentages to cover other charges, and then quoted the price. All I can say in connection with that is that I would feel very sorry for the shareholders in this firm if and when they are up against competition. That is a specific case, but I can assure you it is not an unusual one to-day in many of the various big commercial concerns in Great Britain.

Capital and Revenue.

In a business where capital cost and revenue cost are being dealt with, then a costing system is absolutely necessary.

A good example of this is in public utility companies, say railways, gas works, electric supply stations, tramways, telephone companies, and so on. Where capital and revenue work is being carried on day by day, sometimes side by side, and very often by the same gang, then there must be some safe method of allocating the cost correctly to Capital and to Revenue Account if serious consequences are not going to result.

I know that questions of policy very often enter into the decision as to the allocation of certain cost to Capital Account or Revenue Account, but surely it is advisable to get the proper allocation first and make any adjustments which may be necessary afterwards. It is very unsafe to play about with the allocation of cost, as, sooner or later, investigations may be made which may reveal a state of affairs for which the manager may have to accept responsibility. If he has his cost records he can always show just how much of the responsibility is really his.

That matter, I think, is sufficiently clear, and I need not develop it further, but I will just repeat that a good costing system will keep this record as between capital and revenue quite safely.

Depreciation.

Fixing proper rates for depreciation and building up records in respect of depreciation are two of the most difficult points in the accounting of any business.

There are several methods of calculating depreciation charges, and a discussion as to which is the best method would require a meeting to be devoted to this subject alone. I think I am right in saying that any method involving careful study and detailed calculations is generally avoided, and some "get there quickly" method adopted. This may be all right for certain businesses, but where there is a varied plant, and where costs must be solid, the method of calculation should be the subject of serious consideration. To indicate preference for any particular method would probably result in a discussion which would be rather outside the scope of our present meeting. I must, therefore, leave the subject of depreciation with you for your quiet consideration, and with the hope that the importance of this subject in modern business will be fully realised.

The whole point, as far as I am at present concerned, is that cost records are necessary to enable the manager to handle this question properly.

Beware the easy so much per cent. per annum method, based on so called past experience without any cost records.

Running Inventory.

Many times during the life of a business the question arises as to whether the capital value as shown in the books is, in fact, represented by the assets, and the usual way of checking this is to carry out an inventory. Inventories are frightfully expensive and are not always satisfactory. A well designed costing system, however, can be used to maintain a running inventory—that is, it will record all additions to or subtractions from, plant, &c., in quantities and at the same time will record the effect as far as value is concerned. It is then only necessary to check the book value at extended intervals, and during the time between one inventory and another one can feel fairly happy that there is nothing going seriously wrong.

In a workshop or a factory where all plant, &c., is easily viewed this question of maintaining a running inventory is not very important; but in concerns where there is a scattered plant, and where the physical survey of assets is a difficult matter, an inventory kept automatically up to date is something worth while considering, and it can be accomplished by means of the cost records.

The position of a manager who can say at once that his book values are sound is ever so much stronger than that of the manager who must have an inventory made before he can certify his book values.

Progress Records.

It is a common belief that a cost system is only concerned with cost as represented by expenditure of money. This is not right, as it limits the real utility of a cost system which may be made to embrace all records necessary for the manager in the control of the business.

As an example, take records of output; these are absolutely necessary to the manager to enable him to keep a grip on the progress.

Where piece-work rates or payment by results are used, the output per worker must be known for wages calculations.

Where standards have been fixed, output records must be made to arrive at the efficiency per man, per machine, &c., as compared with the standard.

Those output records may be made up quite apart from the records of cost, but it is advisable to have them incorporated in the cost system. There are several reasons for this.

(1) A manager may be entirely satisfied with output as output, but when he sees that to obtain this output he is considerably increasing the cost, he may find it necessary to slow down. To accomplish a huge bulk of work is not always economical, and it is frequently done at the expense of efficiency. If, however, the manager has placed before him the cost, together with the output, he can at once size up the situation.

(2) Workers responsible for compiling output records may have very little interest in the figures, but when they realise that their payment depends on accurate records of the work performed, they will take quite a different view. It is always advisable to get output recorded on the time sheet or job card.

(3) The use of standards does not end with the fixing of the standard. There must be some record of accomplishment as compared with the standard set. Standards are set only after careful study, and they have as their object the fixing of a goal which must be reached before 100 per cent. efficiency can be claimed. Behind all this is the real question—that is, cost—and the record of efficiency in performance is, therefore, one of efficiency in cost, and should be included in the cost records.

It will be seen that a cost return or summary, to be complete, should show:—

(1) Cost in wages, material, &c.
(2) Output.
(3) Standard.
(4) Efficiency.
(5) Cost per unit of output.
(6) Any other information regarding hours, &c., which may be considered necessary in any particular business.

Use of Costs to the Workers.

Now I come to one of the most important points of all. Up to the moment I have been looking at the costing system from the manager's point of view, and when I say "manager" I mean shareholders, directors, &c., whom the manager represents.

Now I want to look at it from the man's point of view. When I say "man" I mean the worker.

Reading the evidence which was submitted during the recent Coal Commission I was very deeply impressed by the fact that, while shoals of figures were produced, there was an element of uncertainty running through them all. When a Government witness came along and said that, had his department had certain figures six months ago which they had to-day, then a levy of something like £25,000,000 would never have been made, he might have gone further and said that the figures which he had to-day would probably be useless six months hence, because while they might be statistics of what happened six months ago, they are not the facts to-day, and they would be very much less the facts in a further six months' time. There we have the great difference between statistics and costs. It is surprising to find that these two terms are frequently considered synonymous; that is a fatal mistake.

Statistics are the history of something which has passed. Costs are the news of what is actually happening at the moment. Statistics may be helpful and interesting, but costs are vital, and, having served their use as costs, may be used again to build up statistics, and because they are proved figures at the time when they are produced their value as statistics is very much enhanced.

I think it safe to say that one of the reasons why statistics have no power of conviction when placed before the worker is simply because they are something which the worker does not grasp, and that is no fault of his. If, however, the worker knew that the figures which were being placed before him were figures in which he himself had produced the fundamentals, and if, in addition, he could be shown exactly what had been added to these fundamentals, then he is looking at something which he can really comprehend.

The relationship between manager and worker is a different thing to-day than it was several years ago, and it is yet in the state of evolution. Let us do all in our power to avoid this becoming revolution.

The manager is now faced with the choice between friction and co-operative working, and to get into sympathetic touch with the worker he must be prepared to produce his cost figures in such a shape that they can be understood by the worker or his representatives.

It is useless talking "up in the air" when discussing wages and their effect on costs, or shorter hours and their effect on output. Facts are solid and can be produced, provided the necessity for accurate unit costing is realised and met.

Sir Robert Horne, Minister of Labour, in a speech at a luncheon at the Aldwych Club, mentioned that the employers in a certain industry had said that the industry could not stand increased costs. That statement was received as such statements have been received for years past. The men did not believe it. It requires elaborate inquiries to convince people as to the truth.

That is the whole point. If the employers had had their costs properly built up they could without any elaborate inquiry place before the men the real facts as they are happening to-day, and the men, I feel quite certain, would at once know that what they were being shown was the truth. The elements of doubt and distrust must be eliminated from the minds of the workers by straightforward dealing with figures of cost.

He mentioned a few things for which the country is striving to-day to make the lot of the workers better—that is, such things as shorter hours, more leisure, a larger share in the fruits of industry, a measure of industrial control. He further went on to say that the employers were prepared to meet their men with a broader mind, and that the general principles, &c., were clearly recognised by everybody. He then said that one might hope in the immediate future that this new spirit would lead to a system of Industrial Councils on which workmen and employers would be represented, where they would sit round a common table and come to common decisions for their common interests.

I want to say, and say as strongly as I possibly can, that all the good intentions underlying Industrial Councils will be absolutely fruitless unless the facts with which the workmen and employers are dealing are fully understood and fully accepted by each.

As far as wages, hours, cost, &c., are concerned the one way in which to obtain those essential facts is by means of a system of accurately recording the costs on each specific kind of work, so that the employer may talk to each man about his own particular job and tell him what each unit of work in that particular job is in fact costing to-day. He can then proceed to build up the cost step by step in such a way that the worker will fully realise just how much, or how little, of the total cost is represented by the amount paid to him in wages.

Conclusion.

All that we may do, all that we may say, regarding the benefits to industry to be derived from scientific management will be of no real value unless we are careful to see that the accounting system in a business is properly organised. I am not going to discuss what I think is a proper organisation, but I would give this word of warning regarding cost accounting.

A cost system cannot be lifted from a book or from one business and placed into another business. Each business must be carefully studied and a system of recording costs adapted to its needs. The system must be built up and not bought ready made. It would be considered rather foolish if a six-foot man bought a ready-made suit of clothes originally intended for a four-foot boy and tried to wear them. That kind of thing is often done with costing systems, and, of course, they do not work, and eventually are dropped as useless.

Once a manager has experienced the use of a proper costing system he will never be without one whatever business he may tackle, and everyone who preaches the gospel of scientific management knows how very important is the accurate preparation and intelligent use of cost records.

The Chairman : I think we are indebted to Mr. Boyd for a useful and very interesting paper. We shall be glad to hear any questions.

Mr. Crossley Jones : With regard to the standards which you put up against your costs, could you give us any idea of the best means of obtaining them ?

A member : I would like to ask if figures are placed before the workers in the way you suggest. It seems to me a new departure.

Mr. J. F. Butterworth : Personally, I should like to thank Mr. Boyd for an eminently sensible and practical paper. I have no question to ask beyond this, in amplification of the methods he has spoken of, whether he has ever heard of the system that is used by many of our American friends, known as graphic control. It consists of a chart on which the various machinery is set out, and it is the duty of a member of the staff to put a small red flag to indicate that a machine is lying idle. He then wants to know how and why, and as quickly as possible. That checks some of the loss of time. Secondly, with regard to his remarks as to railways ; a few years ago the railways in America combined and petitioned the Senate to allow them to raise their rates by some 15 per cent. to 20 per cent., I think it was. This raised a storm in commercial circles, and the result was that the people who were preaching scientific management were able to put before the Inter-State Commission of Washington such a case against the railways that the Senate refused the increase. In other words, they demonstrated to a committee which sat on the subject that if the railways of that country only applied scientific methods there would be no necessity to increase the rates ; inasmuch as the methods they were employing were costing them five million pounds per day. That was proved to the satisfaction of the Commission and the Bill was thrown out. And in connection with that I can mention an interesting fact with regard to our own railways ; a certain American engineer over here had an opportunity of inspecting the locomotive shops of several of our leading lines. I will not mention the names for obvious reasons, but he told me he was astounded to find a difference of no less than 30 per cent. or 40 per cent. in the idle plant. On some lines they had 17 per cent. of the plant awaiting repair. Other lines went up as high as 52 per cent. If that is not a case for inquiry I do not know what is. With reference to his remarks on depreciation, I am at one with him, but I say that if proper standards are adopted in every establishment, machines must be kept in full repair and the difficulty will be minimised and become a decreasing item. Then, as regards output, it may surprise you to know that in some businesses in America the employer has one time-keeper to 32 men. That would give employers here a fit. They find it pays. It also pays well, because of their polyglot labour, to make up their gangs out of people from one country—a gang of Irishmen, another of Englishmen, and so on; and they institute a friendly rivalry between them by constantly telling them what the other gangs have done. That is one of the effects of good time-keeping, and letting the men know what is being done.

Mr. Carlin : We all know that some men will do as much work in four hours as others will in six. I should like the lecturer to explain how that will affect his system.

A member : I should like to know if Mr. Boyd has ever experienced an attitude of suspicion on the part of the workers towards cost records.

Mr. Grant : What value are the records going to be unless you know how long the job should take. I mean the records of the work done in the factory by the mechanics. I suggest that the only way in which it can be done is by a scientific method of rate fixing, which he seems to have missed out entirely in his lecture.

Mr. Crickwood : May I ask the lecturer to what extent cost systems are in operation in this country. I ask that question because Ed. N. Hurley, head of the Merchant Shipping Board, says that in America 10 per cent. or less of the factories are run on a sound cost system. I should like to know to what extent they are used in this country.

Mr. Clemens: There is one point I should like to ask Mr. Boyd. I understand he had the privilege recently of visiting certain manufactories in the North of England, and I should like to know what agreements he found in force between the actual financial accounts and the Cost Account. I think he will find, where the cost system is well done, there is a lack of agreement between the financial and the cost, agreement as far as overhead charges are concerned. In other words, they do not always include in their complete cost everything of overhead charges which should be included.

Mr. Elbourne: With regard to Mr. Boyd's lecture it occurs to me that, in referring to industrial unrest, and seeking a remedy for that unrest, he does not diagnose the position as it is to-day. We are in the midst of an industrial revolution. To use the word "revolution" is not to wave the red flag or use violent methods; and it is not a question of remedy; it is a question of direction, and to give it that direction is the duty of every one who has any responsibility in industry. For me to cover the ground traversed by Mr. Boyd in his lecture would detain you longer than it is reasonable I should attempt to do; but there is to my mind running through this paper a special pleading for the functions of the accountant in charge of the cost accounts that he shall arrogate to himself all statistics. He discredits statistics in general. It seems to me it is a case of special pleading. I suggest that it is part of a propaganda which has emanated from various quarters to claim for the accountant functions which should be accredited to the engineer, plus the accountant. It is the co-ordinating of the two that is needed.. For the accountant to stand up and say he will inform the management what is right and wrong, that he will point out the weak spot, is all nonsense (laughter). They are in this difficulty, that they have no standard except that which is given them by the engineer, and any departure from that standard is something which they are not qualified to criticise. I am not deprecating the value of cost systems, but when output falls per hour they can only point out differences, and I fear there is an attempt to make it an elaborate fault-finding method, whereas what we want is co-ordination. We are to-day faced with the necessity for real facts. I am entirely in agreement with Mr. Boyd that there is a growing need that costs shall be clearly stated and clearly arrived at. To talk of fundamental and direct costs is confusing. Fundamental costs are costs essential, and overhead management is just as essential as the workmen's wages. It confuses thought to break away from the obvious meaning of these words. If he wants to use descriptive terms he can talk of direct costs and secondary costs, and then his "on" costs. But it is perhaps unfair of me to give you a lecture. It is the first time I have come to these meetings, and while that is my loss you will, I hope, forgive me for taking the opportunity to protest against special pleading on behalf of the accountant. The engineer is to be the "star," and they are to help him. (Hear, hear.) There are many details I should like to discuss, but it would be unfair to you to take up your time.

Mr. Whitfield: I should like to ask if Mr. Boyd has actually placed these cost records before the workers, and, if so, what the results have been.

Mr. Charter: The lecturer said that when figures were placed before the workers they were always received with a great amount of suspicion. I want to ask him if he is suggesting that employees should be represented in the office of the firm for which they work when cost records are being prepared?

The Chairman: I think most of you know that I am a trade union secretary. Two questions have been asked as to which Mr. Boyd has not had the same sort of experience that I have. I may say that managers do put figures before their workmen, and the workmen are rightly suspicious of those figures. What happens with your costing system? You send a man down with a watch and he stands over another man watching him work. Now the man who is working is chiefly interested in his job, and in his wages. He begins to exercise his limited imagination and wants to know what is in the wind, because he is afraid that the next thing that will happen will be that he will lose his job. If your costing system is worked on these lines, he is rightly suspicious. That is not Mr. Boyd's view to-night. With regard to figures, I have had figures put before me by engineers and shop managers at one interview, and I have had a copy of these figures supplied to me privately and confidentially, and for my own use, which were used in a second interview before the commercial management and the chairman of the company; and the whole job lot denied as being inaccurate. When we have these experiences we are rightly suspicious of figures put before us. You have a knight in the iron and steel industry saying that the cost of producing a ton of steel is 75 per cent. of the cost of the steel produced. That is one set of figures. We are suspicious of them. You have the Iron and Steel Institute telling the country that these men earn £20 a week, and that that is why you cannot compete with Germany or America. The Smelters' Union reply that the cost of producing a ton of steel is only 8d. per ton. Can any sane man say that such a smelting cost prevents you competing with Germany and America? These are figures; we can pelt each other with figures like that until further orders; but all these figures are used to favour some other body. It might be the general public; it might be the trade union officer or the general manager. It is a game that is played before the public for your entertainment. Mr. Boyd wants to take us one step further and get out the details of that cost, and tell the workman not only how but why; and when you do that the workman will respect you and your figures. (Hear, hear.) So far as we are concerned we have sufficient standing with the employers that if we demand to see their books they will let us. And what are you up against? You are up against that accountant who has such an elaborate set of books that no ordinary mortal can fathom what on earth he is driving at. (Laughter.) That is the secret of the profession. They retain it so that you and I cannot enter in. Notwithstanding all that, I am for scientific management and for a costing system; and in our union, if you come along, you would find us applying this sort of thing. When men lose time we want to know their rate, the time they lost, and we look up the time tables and see that it is just so. That is the kind of thing Mr. Boyd wants. I do not agree with our friend about statistics, because they serve a useful purpose, and I do not think Mr. Boyd objected to their use. But what he says is that you are getting your information from statistics after the fair. You are learning about the failure you know of; but what you want to know is to get in at the beginning before the failure occurred. I have had a pretty wide experience of meeting employers, and on our side we put in accountants to examine the books. Our wages are regulated by the net selling price or net price that the employer receives for the commodity, or group of commodities. We are interested in about 50 sliding scales, and we employ outside accountants. Each side pays its quota, and we do not think it would pay those accountants to make an inaccurate return on a matter of such small importance to them as the net average selling price. We adopt these scientific methods of trying to get right. I am very pleased to be here this evening; I have been keenly interested in the address, and I am now going to ask Mr. Maurice to move a vote of thanks to Mr. Boyd.

Mr. Maurice: I have much pleasure in moving a vote of thanks to Mr. Boyd for the interesting lecture he has given us to-night. It is the fourth of the series, and I think you will agree with me that it has fitted into its place, and has given us just the information we wanted on this question of costing.

Mr. Atkinson: I have great pleasure in seconding the resolution. I have listened with the greatest interest to this paper, because I am in the midst of introducing a costing system into one of the chief Midland industries. I find there is a lot of ignorance, but I am tackling it. Mr. Boyd mentioned the point of idle time. I have found one great difficulty, and that is idle time. We find that if only one furnace or machine is working in a department all the costs go to that machine. In that department we have ten or twenty, and when they are all working the costs come down enormously, while if one is working it bears the whole cost. That, of course, is wrong. It is one of the things I have a great difficulty in getting on to a proper footing. There is one more question I should like to put. When we get round the table discussing questions between employers and workers, and you find two firms are working together and one is paying 20 per cent. dividend and the other nothing, how are you going to get workmen to understand that state of things?

The resolution was carried unanimously.

The lecturer: Mr. Chairman, ladies and gentlemen, I wish to thank you very much for having listened very attentively to what is usually an extremely dry kind of subject. I may say that I felt quite in my element when my friend attacked accountants, because the costs man is always in trouble in one way or another; still, he carries on (laughter). I am taking that point first, because it does want some clearing up. To my mind there are three different kinds of accountant. There are the financial accountant, the stores accountant, and the costs accountant. I have been handling costs for the last twenty years—since I was a boy—in one shape or another, and I have never been attached to any but the engineering or management side; I was never on the financial side of the business at all. The reason of that is that the engineer is an executive officer; he has to do certain jobs. The costs accountant is simply there to do all he possibly can to help the engineer by showing him the result of the work which he is doing. As a matter of fact, where I am at present situated all the figures on which the standards are based, all planning of work, and all that kind of thing, is in fact produced and done by engineers, but what I want to make clear is that I am quite in agreement that the costs accountant is quite a special kind of accountant, and that his mind is in all probability two-thirds technical and one-third accounting. If he is doing his job he is there in an advisory capacity and does not, in any circumstance, usurp the executive power of the engineer or of anybody else. I hope that point is quite clear. The point in regard to statistics was quite clearly answered by the chairman.

With reference to the terms I used, if everybody in this room got up and told me what were the right terms for costing, the reporters would be kept here for a long time. Terms are simply a convenience and are artificial. I use terms which I always have employed and which I understand. I have no objection to your calling a thing anything you like, if you know what it means. The terms I used were intended to indicate that I was building up something from the basis to the top.

The first question put, I think, was as to the method of obtaining standards. The first meeting of this series was on "The Determination of Standards in Scientific Management," and I need not apologise for not being able to answer that question fully in the time available now, since a full meeting and discussion were given up to the subject. The fixing of standards is an element in scientific management which requires study as a subject by itself. I brought standards into my paper because they are necessary and must be used in connection with costing. I would recommend the gentleman who asked the question to try and get a copy of the paper which was given at the first meeting. I understand they are available. He will then probably get some idea of how standards are arrived at.

With regard to the big question of the presentation of figures to the workers, it is not a new departure, as the chairman has quite fully put it to you. Figures have been presented to workers, and that term which I used, of suspicion running through the worker's mind, I really got from what Sir Robert Horne said, and he is the Minister of Labour and ought to know something about the suspicions of the worker. I need not refer to any personal knowledge of the suspicion among workers, but I know that it does exist. What I was pleading for was for the facts to be put down as plain as A B C. Costs require quite a lot of thought and knowledge to build up, and one cannot expect workmen, whose duty it is to do the job, to understand figures fired at them. What I am pleading for, therefore, is this, in the introduction of scientific management let us safeguard all these little points and endeavour to eliminate from the mind of the worker that suspicion, or feeling of suspicion—it may not really be more than a feeling; it may merely be that he says "I do not disbelieve you but I have not been able yet to believe you quite." What I want to do is to encourage him to believe and to do it by being honest.

To the question as to whether I have ever tried to use figures in dealing with workers, the answer is "yes." I have found it extremely satisfactory. For instance, the foreman would be called in and have the cost of doing a certain operation shown to him. He would be told, "Look here, John; you can do that job for such and such "money, and yet yesterday you allowed your men to "charge it so and so, and so you are losing money to the "firm. Why?" John would then go back and say: "I am not going to be on the carpet again. We are going to buck up and keep up to scratch." You can get the same thing from standards. I have often found, when talking to workmen, that if one can transform the figures into money, money is something he can realise, whereas figures are often rather confusing to him. It is only, after all, a method of expression.

With regard to the question concerning graphic control, I personally am a believer in graphic control, because I can always pick up a point much more quickly from a line on a graph than from any method of setting out figures in the form of a statement; and I think that anybody who has used graphs for control purposes will agree that a rise or fall can be seen at once, and the comparison between point and point can be realised at once, very much more quickly from graphs than from statements. It is, of course, advisable to have alongside the graph a statement of the figures, so that you can find what a point on the graph means in figures.

As to the figures of depreciation being included in the standard, that is true, but the point that I was after was rather the method of recording the depreciation readily in the financial books. You may fix your standard and may depreciate according to that, but you have got to have it translated into money so that it will reach the financial accounts, and I was pleading to do that via the costs, as the figure of depreciation is very important when you get the question of costs.

The next question is as to the elimination of waste in the costs system and as to whether that would not be done by standards. The fact is that, as I said, the full use of the costs system can only be obtained when it is used in conjunction with the institution of better methods, the introduction of standards, and the planning of work. Imagine a factory where no time sheets have been kept and no job cards have been carried, and where everybody runs round doing a job in what he thinks is the best way, and the only form of control is that of personal supervision; if you introduce into that factory a system of time-sheets or job cards, even before you have time and bonus standards fixed, you will get a certain amount of elimination of waste time, simply because a man has to write down what he was doing. That is all I say. I do not say that that is the limit of a costs system; I say it will do that incidentally. The full use I have already explained.

Then a question was raised as regards rate fixing being an important point. As a matter of fact, all these points are very important. If you had to fix rates, the first thing you would have to do would be to get standards. The question of rate fixing, however, does not, to my mind, come under the heading of "Costing." Had I been dealing with Lecture No. 3 I might have got on to rate-fixing, but, as I am confined to Costing, I cannot touch it. It is not because I do not know it or want to avoid it, but it is not in the lecture.

Then there is a question as to the extent to which costs systems are being used in this country. That is a question which it is difficult to answer, because it would require more knowledge of what is going on in the country than I have got, but, as I have said, in that tour which I made I found that efficient costs systems were very very rare. I do know that good costs systems are in operation in this country in certain works, but I do not know that costs systems are in full operation throughout the whole of any particular industry. I feel, after the inquiries I made, that there is a very big necessity in this country for an awakening on this question of scientific management, of which costing is only one small part.

Then there was a question as to including all costs in the Costs Accounts. That is absolutely necessary. There must be a reconciliation between the Financial Accounts and the Costs Accounts. The latter must show that they have had through them in detail all the money which is said to have been expended by the business in the course of a period. If the Costs Accounts cannot be—and are not—reconciled and balanced with the Financial Accounts, there is no guarantee that the cost being produced is the real cost. As to the question of idle machinery, I rather think that our friend who spoke about the red flag on the graph rather got that point, but in any case the way to cope with idle time in machines is to take the number of machines you have and the amount of work you are doing on them; fix your standard, record your output; compare the two, and then find out why it is that you are not getting the required output from the machines. If you get your costs records built up in such a way that you have included in them the standard set and the output, giving then the efficiency and also the cost per unit, you have all the elements, so far as I see, which will show up at once any idle time, either of machines or of men. I cannot say at the moment what more is required to cope with idle time. The output record could do that, or the efficiency as compared with the standard set for the workshop.

So far as I have noted, those seem to be the principal questions that were raised, and I simply wish to close by again thanking you for listening and, having listened, inwardly digesting what I have said. Now, having thought the whole thing over, I hope you will go ahead and do something. (Applause.)

The proceedings then terminated.

Costing in Relation to Selling.

By G. T. H. Allen, A.C.I.S.

The third session of the Scientific Costing Conference was held at Anderton's Hotel, London, on June 6th. The chair was taken by Mr. G. Stanhope Pitt, F.S.A.A. (Vice-President of the Society of Incorporated Accountants).

In calling upon Mr. G. T. H. Allen, A.C.I.S., to read his paper on "Costing in Relation to Selling," the Chairman said:—It seems to me that throughout the great war we financial accountants have been so overwhelmed with the large amount of work thrust upon us by the great financial institutions that justice has not been done to this all important question of costing, in the direction of which I believe the future of the accountant's profession very largely lies. I think for this reason that we are greatly indebted to the promoters of this conference on costing for having organised this meeting. It is a remarkable fact that London, although it has, perhaps, a greater reputation for finance, I believe, contains as large a number of factories as many of our great manufacturing towns of the Midlands.

We have been very aptly described as the "surgeons of commerce," and it seems to me that as good surgeons, when we are approaching costing questions, we have to be careful to the last degree to diagnose carefully the complaints which our clients put before us for solution. The natural thing in such circumstances is to localise to the last degree, because only in that way can you successfully diagnose. The greatest help to localising is good accounting. I deplore greatly that I have found throughout London, and in fact wherever I have practised, that the administrative departments are not adequately remunerated, and I think that accountants should do all they possibly can in the direction of persuading their clients of the necessity of adequate remuneration for those men, because only in that way can you obtain first-class men to deal with such a complicated question as costing. After all, it is the man behind the machine that really counts. With these few remarks I call upon Mr. G. T. H. Allen to give us his paper.

The Lecturer: Mr. Miles Taylor asked me to give a paper, but I would much rather call it suggestions for the meeting to discuss. It is entitled "Costing in Relation to Selling."

Costing is the science of tracking expenditure in relation to products made, or services rendered.

Whenever costing is mentioned, it is generally understood as relating to manufacturing activities. At all events, the expression "costing" is not normally associated with purely selling and distributive activities.

It is undoutedly the case that few manufacturers have attempted to analyse selling costs on a scientific basis, and very few retailers know anything at all about their true expense of conducting business.

Present-day competition makes it essential that both manufacturers and retailers should meet competitors' prices with their eyes open.

Bankers invariably make it a condition of loans that an accurate account system be in existence or installed, and maintained. Obviously, this entails suitable classifications, and produces a real knowledge of the cost of doing business as against guesswork.

The analysis of selling expenses is by no means a simple matter. A great many factors of unknown value and varying power have to be considered.

The statement that this or that product is assumed to realise a certain percentage of profit is without any real basis until each of the factors have been carefully investigated on their individual merits.

So far as retailers are concerned, no cost system would be regarded as a commercial success unless the clerical expense were reduced to the minimum. In many lines of business it is difficult to take stock or maintain inventories in such a way that the financial results are of real value.

Many manufacturing and distributing companies maintain a policy of fixed selling prices.

Examples of products sold on an average standard price policy are: branded boots and shoes, branded hosiery, Ingersoll watches, fountain-pens, safety-razors, cameras, automobiles, and proprietary articles of this kind.

This would, to a very large extent, make it unnecessary to tabulate all the differentials for locations, credit terms, trade discounts, interest on stocks held at various points, &c. At the same time, all such variations in true costs of effecting sales should be under constant survey, the result of which may be to counteract or entirely negative fixed-price policy.

The selling activities for both manufacturers and retailers may conveniently be classified in three main groups, which follow the sequence of actual handling from the time the goods are ordered to the time they are sold to the middleman or the public.

The first group, therefore, would track the expenses of purchasing merchanted goods, or, where the company is also the manufacturer, the expense of warehousing or collection from the factory. This group might be sub-divided into:—

- Salaries and Wages;
- Cables, Telegrams, Telephones, &c.;
- General Unclassified;
- Sales Defectives.

The second group would track expenses associated with selling activities prior to the actual delivery stage. This group might be sub-divided for:—

- Rent Charges;
- Interest on Stock and Appliances;
- Insurance on Stock and Appliances;
- A proportion of the advertising expense which the Management may regard as applicable to any particular period;
- Salesmen's and Travellers' expenses;
- Management Salaries;
- Bad Debts;
- General Unclassified.

The third group tracks the expenses of delivery or distribution. The sub-divisions might be:—

- Wages;
- General Unclassified;
- Outside Charges. (This would include railway company's and carriers' bills; hire of vans, motor carriers, and the like, for delivery purposes.)

It is as well to summarise the totals of these three groups, and also show the grand total for operating expenses from warehouse to customer.

There is considerable conflict of opinion among costing students—for I do not wish to pose as an expert in these matters—as to the treatment of sales in relation to expenses incurred in making them effective.

I have not been able to trace in any of the text-books any detailed information regarding the considerable effect which sales defectives and allowances make, when one is endeavouring to express selling expenses as a percentage on sales transactions.

I put it forward as an interesting point for discussion that the amount of net sales—that is to say, the gross sales less returns, allowances for defectives and the like—is not a true basis against which one can associate expenses of purchase, handling, management, and distribution of some larger quantity than is, in fact, shown by the net sales.

The aim of "Scientific Costing in relation to Selling" should be to obtain percentages of the true cost of handling merchandise at each stage from manufacturer to consumer. Obviously, such percentages should be on the total merchandise actually handled.

If for any reason there is double handling, or some of the sales are ineffective or afterwards cancelled or adjusted, such happenings should not be allowed to disturb the true cost of handling the original transactions.

If operating charges are expressed as a percentage on the net sales, then every defective sale has the direct effect of throwing up the percentage for each item of expenditure.

This is a most unfair and unreal representation.

Instead of all these percentages being inflated because of defective sales, one particular account only should be debited in respect of defectives, and the true figures for operating should be left undisturbed.

It may be as well to give an illustration bearing on these points. Definite data may be assumed.

It costs 20s. per ton for purchasing and inspection.

It costs 200s. per ton for general selling expense.

It costs 20s. per ton for delivery expenses.

Total £12 per ton, from warehouse to customer.

Five transactions take place, each for one ton, total cost of handling, £60.

The product is sold for £15 per ton above purchase price—total selling margin £75. Net selling profit £75 - £60 = £15.

These are the true figures, and should not be disturbed because an inefficient salesman delivers the fifth lot which was never, in fact, ordered.

It is clear the £12 worth of expenses incurred on such should have to be charged somewhere.

As a matter of fact, the loss of £12 expenses incurred will wipe out the profit of £3 each on the four other transactions.

If the total expenses of conducting business are thrown up on a basis of net sales, instead of the true figures above quoted of 20s., 200s., and 20s. for purchasing, selling. and distributive expenses respectively, our costing figures will show 25s., 250s., and 25s., total £15, to recover the £60 from the four effective transactions.

The pursuance of such a policy would obviously be fatal from a selling point of view.

Although the true position is that £3 net profit can be won out of normal sales, if the accounting system bases expenses on net sales, no operation profit would be left out of the £15 selling margin, and probably no business would be done at all.

If, however, my suggestion is correct, the £12 lost on the fifth transaction would be debited to sales defectives. A cause would be assigned, and the salesman would rightly be held responsible.

To the extent that this type of accident had to be regarded as normal, there is no objection to its being included as a regular selling expense. The point I wish to make is that sales defectives are charged to a specific account. Only the normal losses would be included in the cost of doing business, and abnormals would be earmarked for action more or less drastic.

It will probably happen that in addition to the loss of operating expenses occasioned by the original transaction, expenses will be incurred for the return of defectives, and this should be an additional direct debit to Defectives Account.

As a matter of fairness, losses arising out of defective sales traceable to faults that should have been picked up by the inspection department should be debited to "Receiving and Inspection Expense."

Where it is the custom, as in the jewellery trade, to despatch goods on approval, the whole of expenses, outward and inward, would be a normal selling expense regardless of whether sales were booked or not.

Costing for selling purposes, therefore, calls for :—

(1) Careful division of expenses into main groups.
(2) Analysis under main groups as far as is reasonable.
(3) Careful examination of comparative data in terms of transactions and also net sales.
(4) The investigation of defectives in an endeavour to distinguish between normals and abnormals, so that normal business is not lost as a result of loading with abnormal losses.
(5) Frequent comparisons of results.
(6) Application of knowledge gained from historical records for the conduct of future business.

I have not attempted within the limits of a paper of this kind—more intended to open the discussion than to cover the very extensive field of sales costing—to discuss the exceedingly large number of variables which must always be considered in trying to illustrate the profit or loss arising out of selling prices.

No less an authority than John Stuart Mill, as long ago as 1848, was careful to point out that although there was a decided tendency for prices to be strictly relative to the cost of production, the pendulum swung both ways, so that at times the public paid for a large profit, and at other times the manufacturer or retailer suffered a considerable loss.

Mills puts it in this way :—"The latent influence by "which the values of things are made to conform in the "long run to the cost of production, is the variation that "would otherwise take place in the supply of the "commodity. The supply would be increased if the thing "continued to sell above the ratio of its cost of production, and would be diminished if it fell below that "ratio."

Coal Industry Commission.

PRECIS OF EVIDENCE ON

The Importance of Efficient Cost Accounting to Coal Industries and the means which should be adopted to secure it.

By M. WEBSTER JENKINSON.

(Fellow of the Institute of Chartered Accountants, Controller of Factory Audit and Costs at the Ministry of Munitions.)

1.—I am a Fellow of the Institute of Chartered Accountants now practising on my own account, but at one time a member of the firm of Hadfield, Riddell & Co., of Sheffield, and subsequently in partnership with the late Sir George Franklin, F.C.A., in London.

In the course of my practice I have been responsible for the audit of collieries, coke oven plants, and coal merchants.

At the Ministry of Munitions, as Controller of Factory Audit and Costs, I have, *inter alia*, been in charge of the audit and costs of all the National Factories, and, with the exception of the explosive factories, have been responsible for the systems of costing introduced.

These systems necessarily vary according to the type of undertaking, and, with the exception of the iron ore mines in Cumberland and Lancashire and certain quarries, the cost system at National Factories, &c., would not be applicable to the coal industry. At one time I was also responsible for the Cost Investigation Department, and carried out investigations into the cost of coke and pig iron.

Value of Efficient Costing.

2.—The value of efficient costing in business administration has not been recognised generally in this country. The main purpose is not merely to determine the production cost in order to fix the selling price, but to give a detailed analysis of how such cost is made up, so that comparison of the various items of expense may be made, and waste and extravagance avoided.

The benefit derived from the costs depends entirely on the extent to which the information thus obtained is used by the management in the control and administration of the business.

Use of Factory Costs by the Ministry of Munitions.

3.—The following procedure was adopted in the Ministry of Munitions to use the cost results obtained from National Factories in the control of such undertakings :—

(*a*) A uniform system of costing was laid down for each class of factory, and printed instructions given showing in detail how the costs were to be compiled so that uniform results could be obtained.

(*b*) The detailed cost returns were forwarded monthly to the department of Factory Audit and Costs, and, after examination, sent to the corresponding Administrative Department so that the technical experts attached to such department could explain the causes of high costs, &c., at factories which showed unfavourable figures.

(*c*) The department of Factory Audit and Costs directed attention to cases of high costs, waste, &c., and these questions were taken up by the Administrative Departments with the factories.

(*d*) In some cases the Administrative Departments circulated the cost results to the factories in comparative form, with the result that the attention of factory managers was directed to economical production.

(The allocation of work was also based, as far as circumstances would allow, on the production cost results of each factory.)

(*e*) A monthly meeting of each Administrative Department was held, when the costs of factories under the control of the department were considered. At this meeting a representative of the Costs of Production (National Factories) Committee and a representative of the Department of Factory Audit and Costs were present.

(*f*) A meeting of the Costs of Production (National Factories) Committee was held each month, when a report of each sub-committee was presented, and any unsatisfactory cost results, after full inquiry into the cause, reported to the financial secretary.

The knowledge afforded by the costing and other efficiency data obtained has been of very great value to the Ministry, giving information as to the actual costs of manufacture which could be used in fixing prices paid to outside contractors and indicating the relative efficiency of the factories in each group.

As the larger part of the work in the National Factories has been of a repetition character, systems of process costing have been possible, and the cost of each operation obtained ; thus showing the relative efficiency of various methods of manufacture or type of operation and the variations each month in the efficiency of each operation at a factory and its efficiency compared with the corresponding operation in other factories in the same group, thus enabling the most economical methods to be adopted.

The value of the cost results is best illustrated by the fact that the introduction of the cost systems was generally strongly opposed at the outset by the factory managers, but when they realised the practical use which could be made of the information contained in the cost returns, they co-operated to the best of their ability in carrying out the system laid down, and frequently asked for more detailed results than originally provided, in order to secure efficient works management.

Colliery Costs.

4.—Probably owing to the fact that the ascertainment of mining costs is comparatively simple, it is usual for most mining concerns to get out costs—generally weekly or fortnightly—but in some cases the Cost Sheets are badly designed, and the results obtained unreliable.

On the other hand, in large collieries there are exceedingly good costing systems in operation, and a valuable fund of statistical information is collected and used by the management for control purposes. In such cases the cost results are usually reconciled with the financial books.

Costing in mines differs from that of the average manufacturer as the selling price of the product does not depend on the production cost, whilst the nature of the product is more or less unchanging, the only variation being in quality.

Nevertheless, an adequate costing system is equally as important to the mine management as to the manufacturer, for whereas the latter can to some extent—as, for example, in the engineering trade—estimate from drawings what each job should cost, the mine manager must rely on his cost returns in order to ascertain the expense of production.

Capital and Revenue expenditure are also going on concurrently and cannot generally be made the subject of separate works orders as in a factory.

The increase in final cost due to extraneous causes, such as flooding, falls of roof, subsidence, geological conditions, and the high costs arising from working thin seams, long distances from coal face, &c., are only brought to light by a scrutiny of the cost returns, and then only can the comparative efficiency of one colliery with another be ascertained.

It is no exaggeration to say that the management of a colliery cannot determine its policy as regards development and extensions of workings, introduction of machinery, markets or retrenchment in production cost, unless complete and accurate cost statistics are available.

Factors which Increase Costs.

5.—In a colliery the factors which increase the costs of production above the normal cost may be divided into two classes, viz. :—

(*a*) Avoidable.
(*b*) Non-avoidable.

The latter, as pointed out in paragraph 4, include such items as flooding, falls of roof, subsidence, and geological conditions, &c.

The "avoidable" costs consist of such items as :—

(*a*) Waste of stores.
(*b*) Idle time of machinery.
(*c*) Inefficient plant or tools.
(*d*) Idle time through breakdowns (not always preventable).
Waiting for material, &c.
(*e*) Faulty works organisation.
(*f*) Waste of power and lighting.
(*g*) Extravagance in administration.
(*h*) Careless buying.
(*i*) Old-fashioned methods of production.
(*j*) Incompetent staff.
(*k*) Inadequate haulage and raising facilities.

Attention is focussed on such factors on the consideration of the cost returns, but it is necessary :—

(1) That the costs be so framed that such items are brought to light.
(2) That the cost results are actually used by a management sufficiently expert to understand the lessons taught by them.

Limitation of Value of Present Cost Results for Comparative Purposes.

6.—The collection of the cost results of a number of collieries for comparative purposes is at present liable to give misleading ideas owing to the diversity of treatment of different items of cost, e.g. :—

(*a*) The allocation of expenditure between Capital and Revenue will not have been made on a uniform basis.
(*b*) Depreciation will have been written off at varying rates.
(*c*) Dead work will be treated differently.
(*d*) Establishment charges will in some cases include interest on borrowed money, which has no relation to the cost of production, and other items representing expenditure of an unproductive character.
(*e*) Selling charges will not always be clearly earmarked, certain expenses being grouped under other headings in the establishment charges.
(*f*) Stores, explosives, pit timber, &c., will sometimes represent purchases during the period, and in other cases quantities actually used.
(*g*) Rents received, bye-product plants, &c., will be treated differently.
(*h*) Coal sent to washing plant, coke ovens, &c., will at some collieries be charged out at a standard (or fixed price) and at other collieries at the market price.

Unification of Cost Returns.

7.—There would appear to be no reason why a standard form of cost return for collieries and their subsidiary operations should not be prescribed by Government in the same way that the forms of accounts for railway companies are laid down (Railway Companies Accounts and Returns Act, 1911).

Such form should only be settled after consultation with the large collieries known to have efficient costing systems in operation, and should generally comply with the requirements set out in the memorandum attached (Appendix 1). A standard cost return could not, however, be prescribed for very small pits, and, in any case, the form would vary in detail in different districts.

The use to be made of such cost returns would depend on the determination of the future of the coal industry, but the following possible uses suggest themselves :—

(*a*) A Costs of Production Committee could be set up in each district to consider the cost results, and, after taking into consideration excessive costs due to unavoidable causes such as flooding, faults, breakdowns, &c., all of which would be noted on the cost returns, such Committee would draw the attention of the management to high costs of production and to savings which could be effected by the use of machines, &c. Technical experts would be sent to inquire into the cause of high costs and find, if possible, a remedy.

(If the present system of ownership continued, such Committees would be formed by the mutual co-operation of the coal-owners in each district, who would share the expense.

The objection might then be raised that the efficient colliery was contributing to make the less efficient more profitable, but in the interests of the coal industry a broader outlook of the mutuality of interests should be taken.)

(*b*) Industrial Councils, composed of representatives of the owners and miners in each district, should be afforded an opportunity to consider the production costs and other efficiency data. If the workers were allowed to study some of the facts relating to the business many misconceptions would be dispelled.
(*c*) A complete digest of the production costs and corresponding selling prices showing details of wages, royalties, wayleaves, and management should be prepared, so that the position of the industry as a whole could be reviewed periodically with a knowledge that the information available had been compiled on a reliable basis.
(*d*) If the mining royalties were fixed on a sliding scale, based on the costs of production (instead of at fixed rates per ton or sliding scales varying with the selling price), the cost returns would form the basis of calculation.
(*e*) In the case of labour disputes it would be very useful to have reliable comparative data of the details of production costs in each district.
(*f*) If statutory powers be taken for Government intervention in the case of collieries which are badly managed, or if the miners are to have any share in the profits of the industry, the adoption of a uniform system of costing would be inevitable.
(*g*) Should any system of control over distribution at pit mouth be formulated, the analysis of the selling and distribution charges of all collieries would necessarily have to be obtained on the same basis to facilitate comparison.

The use to which such cost returns might be put will, however, depend on the future control of the industry, but for illustrative purposes there are examples of *comparative statistics (Appendix 2) obtained by the Ministry of Munitions in the case of the Cumberland and Lancashire Iron Ore Mines (the figures are fictitious).

* Not reproduced.

Coal Merchants' Accounts.

8.—Generally, only the large merchants prepare monthly cost statements showing the expenses of distribution, the accounts of the small men being badly kept and affording little information for management control purposes.

The system of accounting required is exceedingly simple, the expenditure being grouped under various headings in order to show details of the purchase price of coal handled, carriage, and distribution and administrative expenses.

It would not appear feasible to lay down any standard system of accounting that could be enforced by Government, but the various coal merchant associations might arrange for a memorandum to be prepared showing how the accounts should be kept, and the associations might also retain firms of accountants to render assistance to their members in introducing such systems.

Selling Price Fixed by Periodical Cost Investigations.

9.—It has been suggested that the practice of investigating costs as adopted by the Ministry of Munitions in fixing contract prices might be applied to the coal trade in order to determine the price to be paid to the consumer.

Apart from the difficulty of carrying out periodic investigations of this character, a uniform system of accounting would be necessary to facilitate comparison and in fixing prices.

(*a*) Profits or losses on the purchase of material would have to be ignored.
(*b*) Profits from subsidiary operations should not be taken into account.
(*c*) The investigations would have to be carried out by accountants expert in the trade.
(*d*) Percentage limits would have to be agreed for certain overhead charges.
(*e*) Collieries adopting special economical methods of production or producing under particularly favourable circumstances would have to be excluded in calculating the average.

The danger of price fixing on the basis of cost plus a definite fixed profit is that the incentive to economical production is destroyed. The rate of profit should increase as the cost of production decreases if cheap production is obtained by the adoption of economical and efficient methods.

If it be desired to adopt procedure to limit the selling price, the following method might be adopted :—

(1) Appoint Price Committees in each district to fix the maximum selling price in consultation with the representatives of the Trade Association.
(2) Authorise such Price Committees to have investigations of the costs of production made if not satisfied with the figures presented to them.
(3) Appoint an Appeal Council to consider the results of such investigation in case the Trade Association dissented from the price fixed by the Price Committee.
(4) Insist on cost records being kept in a form either prescribed by law or as agreed between the Trade Association and the Price Committee.

Introduction of Cost Systems.

10.—Excepting in the case of large collieries with efficient accounting staffs, a system of costing cannot be introduced merely by forwarding forms of the prescribed returns required and printed instructions explaining the methods of account keeping.

In the majority of concerns the accountants are totally incapable of introducing proper costing systems, and frequently the size of the undertaking would not justify the expense of a whole time highly-skilled accountant.

To produce reliable cost results entails the organisation of the whole accounting on an efficient basis in order to secure the proper allocation of expenditure, and although the final cost returns of a number of concerns may be uniform, the internal records must necessarily vary according to the individual circumstances of each undertaking.

If some system of uniform cost accounting be adopted, it would, therefore, be necessary to appoint advisory accountants in each district who could instruct the accountants at each colliery how the costs were to be kept, and these advisory accountants would have to reorganise the bookkeeping systems to achieve the results desired.

Until the colliery accountants were sufficiently trained, frequent periodical visits would be necessary.

On the other hand, the reorganisation of the accounting systems on an up-to-date basis would in many cases save considerable clerical labour, thus enabling the accountants to devote the time necessary to the preparation of costs.

APPENDIX I.

Basis of Cost Accounts for a Mining Group.

NOTE.—The following suggestions are not intended to deal comprehensively with the details to be given in a colliery cost return, but merely to indicate generally the class of information required to facilitate comparison of the results of a group of mines.

The system of Cost Accounts adopted by any group of mining undertaking should answer the following requirements before the results obtained can be accepted as reliable, viz. :—

(1) It must be capable of reconciliation with the financial books, which should be designed to show a complete analysis of expenditure and revenue.
(NOTE.—This analysis of expenditure in the financial books is essential to an effective examination of costs, as only by a close scrutiny of individual heads of expenditure is it possible to suggest economies and to detect leakages.)
(2) It must be capable of reconciliation with stores and stock records.
(3) It must provide for the elimination of all factors which are not common to all the concerns or to all the periods under review.
(4) It must be so designed that material surface alterations or extensions and improvements in underground workings, as disclosed by the mine plans, will be reflected in the cost returns.
(5) It must provide for the collection of statistical data showing the production per worker under various conditions, time lost, &c.
(6) It must show clearly the results of machinery used (e.g. coal cutters), and bring out separately the detailed costs of washing plants, crushing and screening plants, &c.
The accounts of coke ovens and attached by-product and recovery plants, brick works, workmen's cottages, &c., must, of course, be kept distinct.

In addition to showing the actual cost of "winning" the product an adequate system of Cost Accounts must be in effect practically a monthly "intelligence report" dealing with all matters germane to the working and development of the mine, as well as to the sale of the mine product.

(1) Reconciliation with Books of Account.

(a) *Analysis of Materials and Stores Consumed.*

Headings should appear in the cost returns in respect of each group of materials for which separate stores records are kept, and the figure included as a charge against production each month should be the actual consumption of that material for the period (not the amount purchased during the month). A proper classification of stores is essential if economies are to be effected and waste avoided.

(b) *Analysis of Labour.*

Wages must be analysed so as to disclose the nature of the work upon which the employee is engaged—that is to say, differentiation must be made between surface workers and underground workers, and those classes again sub-divided in accordance with the work upon which they are engaged, the broad principle involved being that the wages of the miners (or to prevent a misunderstanding of this term—the "coal-getters'" or ore-getters' wages) must be kept strictly apart from the wages of all other workers, as only by this means is it possible to get effective comparative figures with regard to the cost of output. A further sub-division of coal-getters' (or ore-getters') wages is necessary as between those working with hand tools and those operating pneumatic borers, cutters, or other mechanical appliances. This is necessary in order to obtain information as to the comparative cost of the different methods of obtaining the product.

(c) *Analysis of Working Expenses (Oncost).*

(Note.—The use of the word "oncost" is avoided because to the layman it is a term capable of misapprehension, while to the professional accountant it leads often to purely academic discussion.)

All working expenses should be analysed in the financial books, and the Cost Accounts be so designed as to include headings for all these accounts or groups of accounts. Economy in respect of working charges is only possible if a detailed analysis of these accounts is made.

(3) Uniformity of Conditions.

(a) *Output.*

Before comparative costs can be of any use as between mine and mine or between period and period a common base for effective comparison must be fixed, i.e. before unit costs can be effectively compared all factors must be eliminated from each case which are not common to all cases under review. For example, it would be unfair to compare the cost of a mine, the product from which is saleable immediately it is brought to the surface, with the cost of a mine the product from which requires to be "washed" before it is saleable in the same category as the former. The figure for output, which is the usual divisor in unit cost for mines, must, therefore, be on a basis common to all the mines in the group. It may be either the actual tonnage brought to the pithead or it may be the saleable or marketable tonnage, according to the conditions ruling.

(b) *Washing Plant, Crushing and Screening Plants.*

Where these subsidiary process plants exist at mines, and the product disposed of obtains a special price, higher than the normal price, as the result of such processes, the raw product as it comes out of the mine should be charged up to these plants at the pithead price, and separate Cost Accounts should be raised to deal with these processes, otherwise the inclusion in the ordinary mining cost returns of the costs of working these processes would completely vitiate effective comparison with other mines where such plants were not in operation.

(c) *Saleable By-Products and other Sales.*

In the ordinary course of mining operations it may happen that limestone or other materials of a marketable nature are brought to the surface in such quantities that they form an appreciable item of revenue. In such cases these sales must be clearly shown distinct from coal or ore sale, otherwise comparison with the costs of other mines where the same conditions did not pertain would be vitiated.

(d) *Coke Ovens.*

In the case of coal mine accounts, separate Cost Accounts must be raised for any coking process and its relative by-products.

The coke ovens will be charged up with coal at the price which that coal would have realised from an ordinary customer in open market. Only by this method will it be possible to judge if the coke ovens are being worked as profitably as similar undertakings not allied to a coal company.

This method has the further advantage of showing where the total profit or loss has been made.

(4) Extraordinary Expenditure.

Expenditure of an extraordinary nature, resulting in alterations in mine plans, should be shown in the cost returns.

For example, if a new shaft is being sunk for, say, ventilation purposes, if the accounts are loosely kept it is possible that the cost may be wrongly included under the head of "wages and materials used upon direct production."

The use of a schedule in the cost returns for extraordinary expenditure (that is to say, for expenditure other than upon direct production or the ordinary normal working of the mine) would keep before the management the progress of all schemes of improvement, exploration, development, or boring work. A periodical examination of the mine plans, which are altered in accordance with the progress of the underground workings, would lead the management to look to the cost returns to disclose under "extraordinary expenditure" the cost of the extensions or alterations disclosed on the plans. This would be the best method of preventing development work being included under ordinary mining costs. Whether the management ultimately might decide to charge the cost of such development work to "Capital" or to "Revenue" is not at the moment relevant.

(5) Statement of Workers' Production Efficiency.

Where mines are similar in character, and where the product obtained is worked under similar conditions, considerable information may be obtained by comparing the average yield per man per day.

When the yield per man per day is less in one mine than the other, the attention of the management is at once attracted and investigation instituted.

Assuming that the basis of comparison is the unit of saleable tonnage, such a difference may be explained by various circumstances, e.g. :—

(a) Actual "slacking" by the getters.
(b) Deadwork.
(c) Machine tools used to a greater extent in one mine than in the other.
(d) Some stoppage of work due to a "fall" or flooding.

The above illustration refers to the yield per miner or ore-getter (i.e. the man actually engaged on getting the mineral).

A similar comparison of the output per man per day for all "underground workers" or for all "surfacemen" will disclose where mines are overstaffed or where slacking prevails.

Further investigation of the unsatisfactory yield per man may lead the management to discover some one factor which is retarding production, such as "inadequate underground haulage" or "inadequate raising facilities."

(6) Comparison of Costs.

Having decided upon the unit of cost, and having determined the common base upon which this unit is to be calculated, the Cost Accounts should afford for purposes of comparison :—

(a) The total cost per ton of any one mine with another.
(b) The cost per ton of any one item of expenditure of one mine with the same item in another mine.
(c) The total cost of each mine per ton month by month.
(d) The true average total cost per ton of the group of mines concerned.

(7) Criticism of Selling Prices.

Although the primary object of cost returns is to show the actual cost of obtaining the marketable product and the analysis of such cost, a complete system of cost returns will also disclose the average prices obtained for the product. By means of this information it will be shown, assuming an equal metallic content, and that other conditions are alike, whether any one mine is selling at a price less than the average obtainable in the group for a product of that quality.

APPENDIX II.

Iron Ore Mines in Cumberland and Lancashire. Memorandum explaining the Composition of Cost Returns and the Method of Utilising the Comparative Figures.*

The following notes upon the cost schedules received by the Ministry of Munitions from the Cumberland and Lancashire Iron Ore Mines will explain the general purport of the cost returns and the use made of the information afforded thereby.

(a) *The Cost Summary* is the principal statement, Schedules 1, 2, 3, 4, and 5 being supplemental statements showing how the details are made up.

(b) *Schedule V* is the workers' efficiency return, indicating the output statistics.

(a) *Cost Summary.*

Column (1)—*Tons Produced.*

The tonnage shown is the actual saleable tonnage—that is to say, in certain cases where the ore contains an excessive proportion of "dirt" the ore has been "washed" in order that the output from all the mines may be compared upon an equal basis.

The total of this column is compared with the totals of previous months, and any decrease or increase in tonnage is noted. The increase or decrease is then traced to see if the result is due to any particular mine or group of mines, or if the increase or decrease is consistent throughout the district.

For example, if a very considerable fall in tonnage is noticed in any one mine which cannot be explained by causes already known at headquarters, such as a fire, flooding, or fault in the workings, the decreased output is notified to the local technical representative, who is required to report upon the reasons for such decrease.

Column (2)—*Wages.*

The percentage of wage cost per ton is compared with the previous month, and differences which cannot be explained by variations in output, recent wage awards, or other causes are reported to the technical representative in the district.

*Figures not reproduced

Column (3)—*Materials.*

The cost per ton of materials is compared with the previous month, and differences which cannot be explained by variations in output, or known variations in price are reported to the technical representative in the district.

Column (4)—*Other Charges.*

Variations in cost per ton are similarly reported where these are unexplainable by conditions known at headquarters.

Column (5)—*Total Cost per Ton of "Raising" Ore.*

It will be noted that, in addition to calculating the total cost of "raising" per ton for each mine, the true average total cost is of use when compared with the figures of the previous month in estimating future expenditure after making allowance for known changes in wages and cost of materials which are likely to occur.

Column (6)—*Profit to Mining Company.*

The figure used of 1s. per ton is merely illustrative of the rates varying according to the terms of the agreement under which the mines were taken over.

Column (7)—*Total Cost to Ministry.*

Column (8)—*Selling Price.*

The average selling price per ton is compared in each case with the average of the previous month. Variations in the selling price obtainable are compared and differences noted. Although these selling prices are "controlled," changes occur in the selling price due to varying metallic content and to the presence of lumpy ores in some cases, which greatly increase values. Any considerable fall in price is at once notified to the technical representative in the district for his investigation and report.

Column (9)—*Other Sales.*

This column shows, distinct from ordinary sales, the proceeds from the sale of sand and limestone extracted in the course of exploration or development work. If these sums were included under the head of "Sales" they might entirely vitiate comparison with selling prices of other mines.

Columns (10 *and* 11)—*Column for Profit and Loss.*

Attention is at once attracted to variations in the cost of production by an increased profit or an increased loss, or by the conversion of a profit into a loss, or *vice versa.*

General Comments.

Mine P.

In the case of this mine, on the summary it will be noted that the output is nil. This is known to be due to flooding, which for the time being stopped productive work.

Mine Q.

The very large cost of "raising" of 77s. 3d. per ton in this mine is known to be due to the reduced production caused by fire.

Mine L.

The comparatively low cost of 24s. 3d. for this mine is traceable to increased production and to recent improvements in the mine management.

(b) *The Workers' Efficiency Return* (*Schedule V*).

The column to which particular attention is devoted by headquarters is "ore raised per ore-getter day." This column refers to the output of the miner upon the ore face, excluding all other underground workers. The average yield per man per day is compared with previous months. The nature of the workings in each mine is known, and the average yield per man is also known. Any fall in this yield is at once noted, and a report called for from the technical representative. Fall in the output may be due to development work, "dead" work, flooding, faults in the ore, &c. &c.

Take another example. Mine S shows a yield per man of 7.2 tons. This increased yield has been found to be due to the use of machine tools in extracting ore.

The main use of this column to the Ministry has been that, through it, it has been possible to check the charging of excessive development work against ordinary productions costs.

(NOTE.—The above examples are, of course, entirely fictitious, and have been merely raised to explain the principle followed in commenting upon variations in costs.)

Some Principles Governing the Ascertainment of Cost.

A LECTURE delivered before the Incorporated Accountants' Students' Society of London, by

MR. JOHN M. FELLS,
INCORPORATED ACCOUNTANT.

Lieut.-Colonel JAMES GRIMWOOD, D.S.O., F.S.A.A., presided, and in introducing the Lecturer referred to the important work which Mr. Fells had done during the war at the War Office, and especially on the Cost Accounting Committee, to which position he was nominated by the Surveyor-General of Supply. He hoped that as a result of the work of that Committee the whole accounts of the Army would be put on a thoroughly sound, commercial, double-entry system, showing the cost of each unit of establishment and sometimes smaller units. He supposed that no profession had been so deeply stirred in regard to the matters which concerned it, during the last four years, as the accountancy profession. Before that time they all felt that the British administrator and the British manufacturer were very slow in accepting cost accounts in any shape or form, but the war had brought out so clearly the advantages of keeping cost accounts that it was difficult now to keep pace with the wants of administrators and manufacturers in establishing the various systems—and their name was legion—of cost accounts. As students of accountancy, therefore, this subject should be put in the forefront of those with which they should be well acquainted.

Mr. JOHN M. FELLS, after a few remarks introductory to his address, said: The flexible fluidity of the English language, although having great advantages from the literary point of view has many drawbacks from the technical point of view, and also from the point of view of the rapprochement of two minds having different connotations for the same words. Until those engaged in various pursuits have agreed the meaning of the terms which they daily use, the compilers of dictionaries are only able to give vague and general connotations to such terms. On that principle I turned up the "New English Dictionary" for a definition of the word "cost," and I found it was given thus: "That which must be given or surrendered in order to acquire, produce, accomplish or maintain something; the price paid for a thing; outlay, expenditure, expenses, charges, expenses of litigation, expenditure of time or labour; that on which money is expended; loss or sacrifice of valued possessions; suffering some penalty; to incur expense; the expenditure to estimate or fix the cost-of production."

AMBIGUOUS WORDS.

I think cost and the word "price" are illustrations of the difficulty to which I have alluded in our not having, in accountancy matters, a nomenclature which is scientific and which conveys the same meaning to all minds. The word "price" unfortunately is subject to the same ambiguity as the word "cost." In the course of my experience I have had to go twice to the House of Lords in connection with the definition of the word "price." It has been held now—and I suppose until we get some more scientific terms adopted it will continue to be held—that "price" can be represented only as money. In the particular case to which I refer it was my duty to prove that if you paid a sum of money and gave somehing else, the real price you paid was the money plus the value of the article that you conveyed at the same time. If, for instance, you exchanged houses and gave an old house for a new one plus £500, the real price of the house was the £500 plus the value of the house you gave. That has been held by the House of Lords not to be so, and the word "price" is considered to be a term that is relative to money only. Then if we take that other word "cost." For many years past, in legal matters, I have endeavoured to convince Judges, and particularly Commissioners of the Railway and Canal Commission Court, that the word "cost" is a relative term. but unfortunately I have not succeeded. Some twenty years ago Mr. Asquith, Mr. Alfred Cripps, the present Lord Parmoor and other Counsel badgered me a good deal to try to get me to agree that the words "expenditure" and "cost" meant the same thing. I have, however, I am glad to say, succeeded in a recent case in getting an opinion—it is a minority judgment—by Sir James Woodhouse, the present Lord Terrington, of what is meant by the expression "rise in the cost of working a railway due to improved labour conditions." He says: "It is the first time the expression 'cost of working the railway' has found its way into railway legislation, but it has been the common formulæ used in the discussions before this tribunal when hearing the complaints under the Act of 1894, and it has received judicial examination and interpretation with which the legislature must be assumed to have been familiar." Then he goes on to say: "But 'expenditure' and 'cost' in this connection must not be confused. They are not convertible terms. Expenditure is a debit factor; it refers to outlay only, and is absolute. 'Cost' is a resultant and comprehensive factor and is relative. It embraces economies made as well as money expended. 'Cost' is unknown until volume is ascertained, and volume is always fluctuating. . . . To ascertain the cost of working a railway in comparable periods some relative standard or unit of comparison must be taken. It must, as Lord Collins said, 'be a relative figure.'" That quotation is, I think, worth placing on record because a great deal more will probably be heard of it in connection with the adjustment of railway matters in the future.

Railway Returns.

Unfortunately even in our own profession the word "cost" is often used somewhat loosely. Thus Sir Albert Wyon and Sir William Plender, in the report which appears in the well known command paper No. 149—a report or statement which has been the cause of a great deal of controversy in the Press and elsewhere—have two notes, and in those two notes they have fallen into error in confusing the two words. They say in their note No. 6 "The cost of making good, maintenance in arrear, is calculated on the basis of expenditure in 1913 increased by 75 per cent. to allow for higher rates of wages and price of material." In their note No. 7 headed "Extra wear and tear" they say: "The above net receipts are subject to provisions for extra wear and tear arising from additional traffic carried. The cost of eventually making good this wear and tear must be considerable but cannot be estimated at present with any degree of accuracy." Then follow figures which I need not trouble you with. But I want to call your attention to the fact that in this case the word "cost" is used in its non-technical sense. There is also an apparent overlapping, either in fact or expression, between the two notes, for if, as stated in note No. 6, the cost of making good maintenance in arrear is calculated on the basis of expenditure in 1913, the ratio of outlay on maintenance to receipts applied to the additional traffic in each of the succeeding years still afford the amount to be provided for the year.

Where the provision of £33,482,262 for arrears on maintenance includes any, and if so, how much provision for extra wear and tear owing to additional traffic is left in doubt by the accountants' carefully worded, but not very explicit note dealing with this "contingency."

What is Cost?

I have thought it worth while to deal at some length with the loose phraseology that is employed with regard to the word "cost," because in the endeavour to lecture on "some principles governing the ascertainment of cost," one has to ascertain first what "cost" itself really is. You will have gathered from what I have said that I take strongly the view that "cost" is purely a relative term, and that it has to be applied as a co-efficient to "expenditure." It really shows what the result of expenditure is. It is the product resulting from expenditure, and not merely the expenditure itself. Now what are the elements which enter into cost? It represents, of course, the sum total of all the expenditure incurred in the production, transport and utilisation of the various commodities concerned. Too often the cost of an article is considered to be merely what is called "first, direct, or prime cost"—practically the expenditure in connection with wages and materials, and none of those other charges which bulk so largely in ascertaining scientifically what is the real cost of production. A further difficulty arises from the fact that there is a great deal of confusion between "cost" and "cost price." One notices it, for instance, in connection with many of the Profiteering Tribunals. If an article is sold for 4s., and the total expenditure by the retailer—including the purchase price for the article—is 2s. 8d., he is obviously making a profit of 50 per cent.; but I notice some of the Tribunals are taking the profit as only 33⅓ per cent. That is to say, they reckon the profits, not upon the expenditure from which that profit results, but on the selling price of the commodity. That is a very fashionable vice, and unfortunately. I think, accountants have been rather lukewarm in allowing that method of calculation to pass. It obviously is not the correct method of calculation, and although it is convenient, and although it has uses to recommend it, I think that it leads to a great deal of misunderstanding, and is not really scientific. Of course, it may be in some cases that, as the logicians would call it, there is an excluded middle term in a calculation of that kind, and if the purchase price by the tradesman is 2s. 8d. and he sells at 4s., he is not really making a profit of 1s. 4d., because his establishment expenses and other factors do enter into his cost of production. That, of course, is quite true, but I think it might be stated otherwise, and the confusion that is created by the present methods of calculation avoided, if we split the word "cost," or qualify it, perhaps I should say, by the use of the various words that represent the different phases of costs.

Costs of Production.

For instance, the cost of production of coal is not, of course, the same thing as the cost to the householder when he takes it out of the coal scuttle; there are many other factors to be brought into that, and there are many intermediate profits also, so that the words "cost of production" require careful separation into the various stages of the costs of production. Whether, instead of using the phrase "cost production," which is not a very happily chosen one, one should use the words "factors of production" is a matter which should receive some attention. My friend, Mr. Garcke, in a very interesting article that appeared in the *Nineteenth Century* in the month of July, dealing with the suggestion that he had to make for the pooling of profits as the solvent of industrial unrest, has dealt with what he calls "the costs of production." He uses the word in the plural, so that it might be quite clear that he is not merely dealing with the cost of production as usually understood. The factors of production he gives—I will not trouble you with all the details—under seven main headings of fixed capital with its sub-headings, "imminent and renewable, circulating capital, rights, power, material, auxiliary services, State and Local Government services," and then he adds an eighth, "contingency services." In that very able article of his, he sets out all the sub-heads under these various headings, and with the accountant's spirit, gives the nature of the outgo or debit against each of these heads. The article is an exceedingly interesting one, as is also the tabulation. If these remarks of mine appear later on in the *Journal*, it might perhaps be well for this tabulation also to be inserted, although I do not, at the moment, propose to deal with it in detail.

"Costs."

Then, what are the costs that we have to ascertain? Broadly, I presume the word "costing" in accountancy circles is looked upon as costing with reference to contracts, with reference to multiple cost, and with reference to process costs. The contract costs are, of course, comparatively simple, but other costs require pretty careful discrimination, so as to make sure that each article produced bears its proper share of charge. I would say in passing that the contract cost seems to me to be very much like the expenditure in connection with matters in which you have no means of ascertaining what is the cost or what is the result of that expenditure. For instance, with regard to sanitation and matters of that kind; obviously you have no unit of cost which you can apply to a main drainage scheme or any of those utility services which make for health and happiness.

With regard to multiple costs the main principle, of course, is that the whole of the expenditure is allocated, as far as possible, directly, and that which cannot be allocated directly, divided in some manner that seems equitable and fair, in relation to the particular processes or the particular product of which you desire to ascertain the cost. The vast majority of the expenditure can probably be allocated directly to some particular article, or some particular thing, or some particular series of transactions; but there are a large number of other items, such as the supply of power, which are not devisible in the same way. I would say parenthetically that perhaps, instead of saying as it does on the paper that I am to give you an address on "Some principles governing the ascertainment of costs," it would be better to say that the address is on "The principles that *should* govern the ascertainment of costs," for I am afraid some of my precepts will go rather ahead of the practice of to-day. But I think I shall be rendering you the greater service by dealing with the matters from that point of view, rather than by dealing with them in a manner referring to the ways used to-day which is very often very imperfect and very unscientific. Passing from that parenthesis, I would say you have, of course, such items to deal with as "joint costs," where you have two or three kinds of things produced very largely by the same processes. In those cases, of course, wherever you can allocate the expenditure to one particular article, or to one of the joint products you should do it; but where that cannot be done one has to find some means, as in the case of power, of distributing it over the various orders, as I may for the moment call them, that are in process at the works at that particular time. This can probably best be done on a time basis, for after all, one might almost say, the real element of value in the world is time. It is the only thing that *is* of value when you come to look at the thing from the ultimate and philosophical standpoint. Therefore, time should enter very largely into all methods of dealing with costing. And not only time, but also what is used in that time.

MACHINERY.

For instance, it would be necessary, and is very desirable from the ultimate economical standpoint and from the point of view of making your costing returns of value not only in quantitative form but also in qualitative form, that we should attempt to distinguish between the use of labour with machinery and the use of labour without machinery. You are thus able to ascertain whether it is better and cheaper to use manual labour or machinery labour, which after all is another form, as Karl Marx put it, of the use of the congealed labour which is inherent in a machine. Therefore you have to deal with the maintenance and upkeep and working of your plant by considering the machine rate hours or the hours you will charge for the use of various classes of machines for particular purposes. Obviously, as the machines will not be used all the time, their full working load for a year will not be used. You have again to discriminate between the machinery hour in use and the idle machinery hour, and by means of the idle machinery hour to get your accounts to balance by taking your idle machinery hour at one rate and your active hour at another, and then, at a given time, distributing your idle machinery costs over the various orders that were in progress during the year.

ULTIMATE COSTS.

A further factor has also to be considered in relation to establishment, marketing, and all the other expenses that really enter into costs in the ultimate sense of the term. The economists have endeavoured to divide costs in various ways, but I think probably not very successfully. Their divisions include prime cost, supplementary costs, total costs, expenses of production, cost of production and cost value. It has been well said that Mill and other economists have in practice used the term "cost of production" in two senses, sometimes to signify the difficulty of production and sometimes to signify the total money outlay that has been incurred in order to induce people to overcome these difficulties and produce the commodities, and "it is through the lax use of these terms that many misunderstandings have resulted and many barren controversies have taken place."

METHODS OF COSTING.

Then if you look at the practical effects of costing methods you will find that they involve that all material in and out of store, and partly manufactured goods, finished products and other stocks have to be recorded in such a manner that balances on hand of each item will be shown continuously. A further point to be borne in mind is that all overhead expenses require careful inspection, so as to prevent charges being grouped under general expenses which can possibly be allocated to departments. In order to avoid redistributing general expenses on an arbitrary basis it is necessary for each department to determine the unit or units of cost suitable to the product. I do not think that in an assembly of students I need deal with the minutiæ of cost. You have that in the text books, but in practice we have to think very carefully, not merely as to the particular method that should be applied to obtain the most accurate results in the different departments or the different undertakings, but also we have to very carefully consider what is the proper unit of cost to be applied in a particular industry or a particular business.

UNITS OF COST.

Unless that unit of cost is chosen very carefully you may have a costing method which will produce most inaccurate results. To take a topical matter, you have Mr. Roberts, the Food Controller, complaining of the increased consumption of food in the United Kingdom since the Armistice. Apparently he has taken the total quantity of food consumed, and not taken into consideration the increased number of persons that, since the Armistice, have been consumers in the United Kingdom. The ration allowance to soldiers, some three millions of whom have been demobilised since the Armistice, was much higher than the ration allowance to civilians, and with the accentuation of appetite which the rations to soldiers has brought about there has been a demand for foodstuffs increased by considerably more than the average of a corresponding number of civilians. Another instance of taking the wrong unit, and one not based upon logical principles, is to be found in connection with the ascertainment of cost in railway working. There the unit adopted has sometimes been on the basis of train mile and in other cases on the basis of engine mile. The train mile represents the number of miles travelled by a train, but the engine mile not only represents the miles run by the engine when attached to the train but the ancillary miles run by the engine. The engine mileage often includes a number of miles not actually run. Thus, if an engine is waiting or standing at a siding on a branch or main line for a period exceeding fifteen minutes, it is credited as if it had been engaged in running miles on the basis of five or six miles to the hour. Of course the true economy in the working of a railway consists of running as small a number of miles as possible to do the required work. In recent years there has been a tendency for railways to load their wagons and vans on more scientific principles, with better relation of bulk to space, than used to be the case. Engines also are now more powerful than heretofore, and there is an increased number of wagons drawn in the train. If the train mile is taken as the unit of cost an anomaly therefore arises: that the more economically and efficiently the railway is worked the greater seems to be the cost. That is to say, the saving in the number of miles run shows an increase of cost in the miles actually run. The adoption of a unit of cost based upon the number of tons run one mile, known as the ton mile—that is, quantity multiplied by distance hauled—obviates the anomaly referred to.

I have here a number of other illustrations in connection with railway matters, but as that is rather a technical subject I do not think I will deal further with it at the moment, except to say that if you get a true system of costing, it is really quite astonishing the information that may be obtained. If the costing accounts are prepared in a scientific way, the information given to the administrators or manufacturers is, or should be, simply invaluable if it is carefully considered by them. To take another case, that with regard to agriculture, for instance, and the question of the valuation of wheat. It is contended by some authorities that the practice adopted in connection with many large estates, of making valuations by means of expert valuers, is unnecessary if proper accounts are kept, and it has been pointed out that mistakes are more likely to arise through valuations than by taking the accounts as shown by the books. Thus many farmers close their books at Michaelmas, just after the wheat has been stacked and before it has been thrashed. The accounts will give the real valuation figure, and in some cases I have found, in agricultural matters, that statistics of costing have been of more value than the expert valuations.

COST ANALYSIS.

I would like, in a discursive way, to hark back and to point out a further dissection which from the practical point of view is very desirable, and that is that in the discrimination between manual labour and machine labour costs that portion of the machine charge which is a fraction of the capital cost of the machines should, if possible, be shown separately, as the capital cost of the machine may vary with the size, and, to some extent, upon the age of the machine. Thus it may be ascertained whether it is better to run with an older machine than to incur the expense of purchasing a newer and more costly type. Then I think, as a governing principle, and particularly if one holds firmly the view that a cost account must not be merely quantitative but also qualitative, that it must be of assistance, not merely as a voucher of the correctness of the accounts, but also in the guidance of the administrators, to bear in mind the economic law of substitution. The cost account of the not far distant future will probably be a conditional cost account; it will have a number of co-efficients. Thus it is absurd, of course, to compare the costs of to-day on a monetary standard with the cost of four or five years ago, and until the principle that has been urged so strongly by Professor Irvine Fisher is adopted, of stabilising monetary valuations, we ought to put in some co-efficients which show that £1 to-day is only the same thing as 10s. four or five years ago. Ultimately the cost account will take probably almost an algebraic form. The great advantage is that in that way our cost accounts, if the accountants prepare them in that fashion, will receive greater respect and greater consideration from the engineers. That is a point to which, I think, we have to pay particular attention now, having regard to the fact that there is an attempt to divorce cost accounting from ordinary accounting, and to consider that engineers and economists are the only fit persons to deal with cost accounting in the ultimate sense. "Cost," expressed in algebraic formulæ, translates general principles into quantitative terms, which is one of the best ways of avoiding ambiguity. But the formulæ, of course, must express quality as well as quantity. That is not the cost account of to-day, but as I said, I thought I should perhaps render you the better service by calling attention to some of the ultimate principles involved in these matters rather than by dealing with that which you can read in the text books dealing with cost accounts. There has been great progress made, however, during the last two decades on this matter, and as the Chairman has well pointed out, greater progress still will probably be made in the future. It is therefore, to use a slang phrase, "up to us" as accountants to see that our return, or that which we give our clients, is not merely in quantitative form. We must help them in the administration of their businesses. We must not consider that the whole matter is settled when we have got the accounts to balance, and think that the "halo of balance," as it has been well termed, covers the whole thing. It is probably better that I should leave other points to be dealt with at some other opportunity, and now deal with some of the practical questions to which your queries will invite attention. (Applause.)

The General Principles of Costing.

By A. Cathles, O.B.E., C.A.

A lecture delivered before the Glasgow Chartered Accountants Students' Society on Wednesday, 11th February 1920, Mr. David Allan Hay, C.A., in the chair.

What is Costing? It is the designation applied to those methods of accounting by the use of which it is possible to ascertain the actual cost of producing and selling each article, or each group of similar articles, that has been manufactured in the business, or of performing services for the business itself, or for other firms, companies, or individuals.

Of what expenditure does the cost of producing and selling consist? It comprises all that expenditure (and the term is used in its widest sense) which will eventually appear in the Manufacturing, Trading, and Profit and Loss Accounts, except such items as are in fact appropriations of profit.

In the financial books the various classes of expenditure are kept in separate accounts, such as Wages, Materials (probably in several main divisions), Heating, Lighting and Power, Sundry Stores, Repairs to Buildings, Repairs to Plant and Machinery, Depreciation of Fixed Assets, Loose Tools, Supervision, Office Salaries, Office Expenses, and so on. For costing purposes the whole of the expenditure is divided into the three main groups (generally known as the "elements of cost") of Wages, Materials, and Oncost, and a system of costing merely consists of the current recording of the expenses in these three groups in such a manner as will facilitate the ascertainment of the proportion of each group which it is equitable to charge to each article or each group of identical articles manufactured, or to each service performed.

There is only one system of costing, just as there is only one system of double-entry bookkeeping. As in the latter so in the former, the names and rulings of forms and books may vary, but there is the one fundamental principle that must be observed. In costing, it is that each minute of each worker's time that is paid for, each pennyworth of material *used* (not purchased), and each penny of other expense incurred, must be so recorded that it will be possible to allocate them to the work in connection with which they are incurred.

Although there is only one system of costing, there are three different methods of grouping the resultant financial statistics, commonly known as:

(1) Job Costing.
(2) Process (or Continuous Production) Costing; and
(3) Operation Costing.

Job Costing is employed where the order is for a single article to be manufactured (e.g. the assembly of a machine, or the building of a ship), or where a definite quantity of articles is to be produced within a comparatively short period. In job costing, little or no useful information can be ascertained until the order is completed, and as cost information is the more valuable the sooner it can be obtained, it will be seen that it would not be suitable to use job costing in connection with the manufacture of a definite quantity (as distinct from a single article) where the time to be taken on the work is to extend over more than, say, a month or six weeks.

Process (or Continuous Production) Costing, as the alternative name implies, is the method of gathering together the expenditure relative to the production of articles that are continuously being made, and in respect of which it may be impossible to give the shop a definite quantity to produce. It is suitable where repetition work is being done, where articles are being turned out in large and reasonably steady quantities, and where the number of operations through which the articles have to pass is not numerous.

Operation Costing is a further analysis of process costing, and is suitable where repetition work is being done, where the operations are numerous, where the quantities handled vary in the different operations, and where rejections are likely to occur after any operation has been performed.

Broadly, these are the principles which govern the decision as to the method of costing to be employed, but as to all rules, so to this, there are exceptions. For example, there is one class of repetition work for which none of the three methods is wholly suitable, and that is where the final product is made up of many different parts, a considerable proportion of which is made on the premises. Such cases will arise in the manufacture of motor cars and aeroplanes, to mention only two; and in these a mixture of job costing and process or operation costing may be found necessary—job costing for the final assembly, and process or operation costing for the making of parts.

It may be accepted as a fact, however, that every business must have the details of its costing system specially arranged to suit its own peculiar circumstances. It is impossible in a lecture, or even in a book, to do more than lay down the fundamental principles which must be observed, for the details of a system that is suitable for, say, the works of John Smith, motor manufacturer, would not be suitable for the works of Robert Brown, motor manufacturer, unless the lay-out of the two factories, the processes carried out therein, and the methods of remuneration of workers, were identical.

Before the principles governing the allocation of the cost elements are considered, it is necessary to touch briefly upon factory organisation, as a proper organisation is absolutely necessary before any system of costing can prove successful.

The average manufacturing business may be said to consist of six different functions :—

(1) Purchasing of materials, parts, stores, &c.
(2) Manufacturing.
(3) Inspecting finished products.
(4) Selling.
(5) Accounting.
(6) Secretarial.

All businesses of average size call for a separate department for each of these functions, each department being in charge of a responsible official who in turn will be responsible for the work of his department to the fountain head only, such fountain head being the managing director, general manager, or proprietor, as the case may be.

The sub-divisions of the various departments are as follows :—

(1) *Purchasing Department.*

According to the necessities of the business, this department is divided into two or more buying sections, each responsible for the purchase of certain commodities. It also has a statistical section whose records facilitate the work of the buying sections.

(2) *Manufacturing Department (under charge of Works Manager).*

An engineering business is the one that calls for the greatest number of sections, which are :—

(*a*) Planning and progress.
(*b*) Labour.
(*c*) Welfare.
(*d*) Engineer.
(*e*) Drawing office.
(*f*) Store-keeping.
(*g*) Production.

The last being sub-divided into various manufacturing departments and tool room.

(3) *Inspection Department.*

This department is conveniently sectionised to correspond with the manufacturing departments whose production requires inspection.

(4) *Sales Department.*

The sections here are :—

(*a*) Advertising.
(*b*) Salesmen.
(*c*) Orders.
(*d*) Invoicing of sales.
(*e*) Statistical.

(5) *Accounting Department.*

In this department the sections are :—

(*a*) Financial books.
(*b*) Timekeeping.
(*c*) Wages.
(*d*) Stores Accounts.
(*e*) Costs.

(6) *Secretarial.*

Here the sections called for are :—

(*a*) Cashier.
(*b*) Registration, transfers, &c.
(*c*) General office.

The two departments that are chiefly concerned with a costing system are those of Manufacturing and Accounting, and the former has two sections that call for further consideration, viz. planning and progress, and store-keeping. The sub-functions of the former are to see that the materials necessary for manufacture are at hand or to instruct their purchase ; to see that the necessary drawings are available for the shop foremen ; to arrange by what shop, on what machines, under which foremen, by what methods, and at what time the work is to be done. In fact, this section, as its name implies, *plans* the work from start to finish, and issues the Orders to the shops to proceed with manufacture. These orders are in writing, are known as Works Orders, and are addressed to the foreman who is to be responsible for the work or for the first part of it. Once the work is on the shops, it is also the duty of this section to record its progress and, if delay arises, to take such steps as are necessary to ensure the return to schedule by time of completion.

The sub-functions of the store-keeping section are those of receiving and issuing materials, parts, and stores, and the proper recording in quantity of such receipts and issues.

It is also the duty of this section to see that stocks are maintained at proper levels and to request the purchase of materials, &c., for this purpose.

Works Orders.

The form of Works Order will vary in different businesses, but whatever the form, provision must be made for the following information :—

(1) Works Order number.
(2) Date of issue of Order.
(3) Foreman's name.
(4) Department.
(5) Description of work to be done.
(6) Specification of material to be used.
(7) Instructions as to delivery when complete.
(8) Date for completion of the work.

These particulars are all filled in and the form signed by the planning section before issue of the order to the foreman. The latter, however, will insert the dates of commencing and finishing the work. The form of Works Order is the same for job, process, or operation costing, and the only way in which the information to be filled in by the planning section will vary is that whereas for job costing a definite quantity for manufacture will be specified, for process and operation costing the quantity shown will be so many per day or per week. In operation costing the various operations to be performed will also be stated. It is necessary that the Works Orders be in quadruplicate, as one copy will be issued to the foreman in the shop ; one to the stores so that the storekeeper may be advised of the materials that will be drawn from him ; one to the cost accountant that he may be advised of the work being undertaken in the shops ; and the fourth copy retained by the planning section that they may have a record of what they have issued and be able to watch the progress of manufacture.

The Works Order issued to the foreman is retained by him until that part of the work under his charge is complete, when the order is passed on to the foreman in charge of the next operation. In process and operation costing, where the operations are in charge of more than one foreman, a copy of the Works Order is issued to each foreman. When the whole order is completed, the Works Order, showing date of completion, is passed to the cost accountant, who, in turn, after abstracting such information as he requires, passes the completed Works Order to the planning section.

In the cost books an account is opened for each Works Order issued, and to that account are posted all allocations of wages, materials, and oncost.

Wages.

All wages, except piece-work wages, are payable in respect of the time the workers spend in the factory, and for this purpose it is necessary to record the times of arrival and departure of each worker. There are several methods of doing this, but the two most common are, in order of up-to-dateness, by means of time recording clocks and by means of discs. In the first case there awaits each worker in a rack alongside of the clock a card bearing his name and number, and by placing this card in a slot in the clock and depressing a lever the time of arrival is stamped on the card. In a similar manner the time of departure is recorded, the mechanism of the clock being so arranged that the stampings can only be made on the appropriate section of the card. The hours of attendance are then calculated and inserted on the card by the timekeeping staff.

Where discs are used the procedure is as follows : The discs are stamped with numbers (each disc one number) to correspond with the numbers of the workers, and are hung upon numbered hooks on a board outside the time office. As each worker arrives he takes from the board the disc bearing his own number and drops it through a slot into a box. The timekeeper clears the box at stated intervals, and on a sheet records the times of arrival of the workers represented by the discs. The discs are then again hung upon the board and a similar procedure is followed on the departure of the workers. As in the case of the clock cards, the hours of attendance are thereafter calculated and same are inserted on the timekeeper's sheet.

From the cards or sheets the total hours for the week are ascertained, the wages are calculated, and the wages sheets or pay-roll compiled.

It will be seen that there is no possibility of finding out from these records the proportion of the wages earned by the workers on each of the various jobs, processes, or operations upon which they have been engaged, and it will be appreciated that such information can only come from the shops or departments where the men have been working. The information is obtained by means of a form, variously called "time sheet," "work ticket," "operation card," &c. Some classes of work call for one form for each worker ; in others it is possible to give the information in respect of a whole gang on one form. The details for which this form provides are :—

(1) Worker's name.
(2) Worker's number.
(3) Date.
(4) Department.
(5) Works Order number.
(6) Operation number.
(7) Description of work.
(8) Time spent on job (distinguishing between ordinary time, overtime, and idle time).

(9) Number of each machine used and hours used.
(10) Number of units produced (where wages are paid on piece-work).

All of that information is filled in either by the worker himself or by the foreman, and the form is signed by the foreman, whose duty it is to see that the details are correct. The forms are then sent by the foreman to the time office, where the number of hours shown as worked by each worker is checked with his hours of attendance as shown by his clock card or by the timekeeper's sheet. This check is very necessary, as it ensures that all time paid for has been accounted for. Thereafter the forms are sent to the cost office, where time and piece-rates are inserted and the wages earned by each worker on each job are calculated and also inserted.

No productive work is done except on Works Orders, and Standing Order numbers are fixed for all the different classes of work done in the factory which cannot be charged direct to any particular Works Order. Such classes of work include that done by foremen in charge of more than one job, process, or operation ; workers engaged on the maintenance and repair of buildings, plant, machinery, &c. ; engineers, and other workers engaged on power plant, stores staff, transport drivers, timekeepers, watchmen, general labour, &c.

All workers paid through the medium of the weekly pay-roll must, in fact, fill up time sheets showing how the time spent by them in the factory has been occupied, and such time sheets must be signed by the foreman or other higher official to whom the individual workers are responsible for the work they do.

When the time sheets are all priced and extended, the hours and wages are listed under the various Works Order or Standing Order numbers, and the total apportionable to each Order number is thereby ascertained. These totals are listed and the grand total of wages earned is obtained.

As the hours shown by all time sheets are agreed with the hours upon which the workers are paid, and as the hours on the time sheets are priced at the same rates as are used for pay-roll purposes, it follows that the money totals of the time sheets should agree with the pay-roll total. In practice, however, these totals rarely agree exactly, owing to the incidence of the odd fractions of pennies discarded or made up on the time sheet calculations. Small differences so arising must be adjusted in the grand summary before the details thereof are used for the purposes of posting to Cost Ledger Accounts.

In the cost books, wages earned on Works Order numbers are posted to their respective job accounts, those under Standing Order numbers to the appropriate Standing Order or Departmental Oncost Accounts.

Materials.

Costing, so far as materials are concerned, really only begins with the issue of material from the factory stores to the shops, but in order that the whole of the materials problem may be appreciated it will be well briefly to consider the history of materials generally up to the time at which they are received into store.

It will be remembered that the responsibility for maintaining the stocks at proper levels rests with the storekeeper, and when the stock of any material requires to be replenished, that official issues a demand or requisition to the Purchasing Department for the necessary goods. Such requisition specifies the class of material and quantity required, the quantity fixed for minimum stock, and the quantity on hand. It also states the date by which delivery is required, and is sent to the Purchasing Department through the works manager in order that the latter, with his more intimate knowledge of the future requirements of the factory, may approve or amend the requisition. When ordering the goods the Purchasing Department prepares the order in quadruplicate, the original going to the supplier, the first copy to stores accountant, the second (unpriced) to the storekeeper, and the other being retained by the Purchasing Department.

When the goods arrive at the factory a record of them is kept on the Goods Received Sheet, which will be ruled to show :—

(1) Date of receipt.
(2) Supplier.
(3) Purchase Order number.
(4) Railway or Delivery.
(5) Truck number.
(6) Cost of carriage (if to pay).
(7) Number of packages.
(8) Class of package.
(9) Quantity or net weight received.
(10) Quality.
(11) Bin Card number.
(12) Stores Ledger folio.
(13) Invoice number and date.

The first eleven columns will be filled in by the storekeeper, that is, up to the Bin Card number, and the remaining two columns (Stores Ledger folio and Invoice number and date) by the stores accountant.

In the Quality column the storekeeper enters "O. K." if the quality is in order, or the report number if the quality is defective. The quality report is made to the Purchasing Department only in the case of defective goods, and the report number on the copy of the Goods Received Sheet received by the stores accountant is an indication to him that the invoice in respect of the goods must not be passed for payment without the sanction of the Purchasing Department.

The storekeeper is responsible for the physical custody of the materials only, and his records are kept in quantities without values. He keeps such records of goods in and out on Bin Cards (sometimes called Stock Cards), one card for each class of material handled. Such cards are headed with a description of the material, and the maximum and minimum stocks, and they are ruled in three division, "in," "out," and "balance." The particulars shown in the "in" columns are (1) date, (2) goods received sheet number, (3) initials (of party making the entry), (4) quantity. In the "out" columns are shown (1) date, (2) requisition number, (3) initials, (4) quantity, and in the "balance" columns, (1) date, (2) quantity. The postings to the "in" columns are made from the Goods Received Sheets, which are numbered serially and are prepared by the storekeeper in triplicate, one copy being retained by him on file in order of date, and the other two copies being sent daily to the Purchasing Department and stores accountant respectively. It is the duty of the Purchasing Department to see that all goods are delivered to time.

On receipt of copy of Goods Received Sheet the stores accountant posts therefrom the quantities received to the debit side of the appropriate Stores Ledger Accounts, the prices and values being posted from the invoices when same are received. Cost of carriage (if any) is entered by stores accountant on the invoices in order that the true cost of the goods may be shown, and the true values are posted to the Stores Ledger Accounts.

Invoices are passed for payment only after the stores accountant has checked them with the copy Purchase Order and with the copy Goods Received Sheet.

Such is the history of the goods up to the time they are in store awaiting issue to the shops, and there now arises great necessity for a careful record of future movements if the proper cost accounts are to be charged with the values of the materials used and if the misuse of material is to be checked.

Issues of goods from store to shops must be made by the storekeeper only on receipt of a proper requisition made out by a duly authorised person. It is usual for the foremen to be authorised to issue requisitions, or same may be prepared by the planning section and issued to the foremen with the Works Orders. The requisitions are orders to the storekeeper to issue to bearer, or to deliver to a shop, for use in connection with a specified Works Order, definite quantities of specific materials. The form is ruled to show :—

(1) Department,
(2) Works (or Standing) Order number,
(3) Operation number,
(4) Date,
(5) Description of material,
(6) Quantity required,

and is signed by the planning section or the foreman, as the case may be. Provision is made for the signature of the person receiving the material and for the insertion by the storekeeper of the Bin Card number when the issue is posted. Columns are also provided for "price" and "value," which are inserted later by the stores accountant.

Requisitions should be numbered serially, and a check should be maintained by the stores accountant to ensure that all requisitions finally reach his department. They are prepared in duplicate, one copy being handed to the storekeeper in exchange for the material and the other being retained by the originating party. At the end of each day the storekeeper sends all requisitions to the stores accountant's office, where they are priced and valued. Each week the values are listed under Works or Standing Order numbers, and by this means the value of materials to be charged to each Cost Account is ascertained. The quantities and values are also listed under class of material to obtain the figures for posting to the credit side of the various Stores Ledger Accounts.

Where the issues of the various materials to each Works Order are numerous, considerable labour may be saved by omitting to price each requisition, by listing each class of material under Works and Standing Order numbers in quantities only, and by pricing the weekly totals only. This method has the additional advantage of giving the total quantity and value of each class of material issued to each Works Order. The total value of the issues each week or month are also entered to the credit of the Materials Control Account, the debit postings to which are obtained from the Purchase Journal monthly totals. This financial control on materials is most useful, necessitating, as it does, a periodical listing of the balances on the Stores Ledger Accounts (the total of which should agree with the balance on the Control Account), and providing proof of the accuracy of the material values charged to the Cost Accounts.

Frequently, it will happen that at the completion of a Works Order, certain material which was issued to it remains in the shop. It is then necessary to have same returned to stores, and for this purpose a "Materials Returned Note" is used. Whereas the requisition represents the debit note to the Works Order, the materials returned note represents the credit note, and it is therefore necessary that it should contain information as to quantity and class of material returned (distinguishing between good and defective material), Works Order number from which returned, signature of foreman and acknowledgment of receipt by storekeeper. This note is serially numbered and made out in duplicate similar to the requisitions, and the return of all to the stores accountant must be checked.

Material passing from one Works Order to another otherwise than through the stores must also be recorded, and for this purpose a "Materials Transfer Note" is used. It contains practically the same information as the Materials Returned Note, with the addition that it will show the Works Order number to which the material is transferred. It is made out in triplicate, and two copies reach the stores accountant—one from the originating foreman direct and the other through the receiving foreman, the remaining copy being retained by the issuing foreman.

Finished products go into store on a "Manufactured Products to Store Note," which is similar to the "Materials Returned Note," and which is treated by the stores accountant in a similar manner.

Most of the recording problems arising in connection with the movement of materials will be easy of solution if the goods are treated as cash would be treated under similar circumstances. In fact, if the store is thought of as a bank and the storekeeper as a banker, it will facilitate matters. A banker does not hand out cash to anyone who asks for it. He requires a cheque (requisition) signed by an accredited party, and endorsed by the party receiving the cash. When paying in cash to a bank one hands with it a pay-in slip ("materials returned note," "manufactured products to store note"), and obtains an acknowledgment. In sending cash to another party one does not just put it in an envelope addressed to that party and post it. No; one sends a note (materials transfer note) stating what it is for, and sees that he gets a receipt. If the workers can be educated to look upon material as being money, a great stride forward will have been made in solving many of the other problems attached to the use and misuse of commodities.

Before passing from this subject it may be well to mention one other matter which, though not strictly part of the costing system, is very closely related thereto. The matter referred to is "stocktaking." The practice of taking stocks of materials annually is out of date and has been superseded by "continuous stocktaking," under which, as is implied by the term, stocktaking is going on all the time. The procedure is for a man or men, acting directly under the instructions of the chief accountant, and responsible to him, to check the stock of certain classes of material each day. The actual quantities in stock are listed, as are also the quantity balances shown by the Bin Cards and Stores Ledger Accounts. If the records are accurate the three will agree, but if they do not agree, investigation is made to trace the error and the necessary action taken to prevent its recurrence. Sufficient staff should be employed on this "stock audit" to ensure that all materials are checked three or four times a year. Some of the advantages of continuous stocktaking over annual stocktaking are that mistakes in the records come under review while still fresh; that the staff engaged on the stores records is impressed with the necessity for accuracy; that pilfering from stores is more quickly brought to notice; and that the disorganisation and loss of time caused by closing down for annual stocktaking are avoided, the book stocks being accepted.

Oncost.

What is oncost? It is all that expenditure connected with the business of which it is impossible to say definitely that it arises out of any particular Works Order. It includes all wages and materials charged to Standing Order numbers, and rent, rates, monthly factory salaries, management, and office salaries and expenses, power, repairs, depreciation, &c.; in fact, all the expenditure that will appear in the Manufacturing, Trading, and Profit and Loss Accounts, with the exception of direct wages and direct material (the methods of charging which to Works Orders have already been explained), and also with the exception of such items as dividends, interest, income-tax, &c., which are really appropriations of profit.

The amount of the oncost expenditure can be ascertained for any given period, but it will be appreciated that, with Works Orders being completed at various odd times, it is not practicable to get down to actualities—that is, to allocate the expenditure over the work done during the period for which such expenditure is incurred.

The opinions of costing experts do not differ much on the treatment of the first two elements of cost—namely, direct wages and materials—for there it is possible to ascertain accurately the proportion of the expenditure that is attributable to each job—but on the allocation of oncost hardly two are of the same mind. On one point, however, all are agreed—namely, that whatever method of allocation is adopted it is at the best only an estimate, an approximation.

The method most commonly used is to allocate all the oncost expenditure to jobs, processes, or operations in proportion to the direct wages charged thereto. Of all methods of oncost allocation this is the simplest, hence perhaps the reason it is so largely used, but it gives results that are very far from true, especially in factories where some operations are performed on machines and others by hand. It will be appreciated that such expenditure as the cost of power consumed by machines, depreciation of machine values, repairs, and maintenance of machines, and rent of space occupied by machines, are all charges which should be borne only by work that is done on the machines. These are usually heavy charges, and if the whole oncost is allocated on the direct wages of the factory, the work that is done by hand will wrongly bear a share of them. Another argument against this method of allocation is that an undue proportion of such charges as supervision is being borne by the work that is done by skilled hands owing to their higher wage rates, and that the work done by the unskilled hands, who actually absorb most of the supervision, is not bearing its fair share.

A second method, namely, allocation in proportion to the hours worked by the men—the man hour method—overcomes to a certain extent the last objection, but leaves out of account the heavy charges due to machinery, and is, therefore, not suitable for factories where both hand and machine work is done. Even by this method supervision is not properly allocated, for a man-hour basis is not much better than a direct wage basis. For this item of expense the truest basis of allocation is probably the man hours divided by the hourly rate of pay in pence.

A third method is to allocate in proportion to the prime cost—i.e. wages plus material. One has only to consider the circumstances of a business where precious metals enter into the manufacture to rule this method out of court, for it is absurd to say that the oncost expenditure incurred in the production of an article in gold is greater than in the production of the same article in silver, by something approaching the difference in the values of the metals.

In the fourth method—the machine-hour method—allocation is on the basis of the number of hours the machines are run. It would appear that this method must have originated in a factory where none of the work was done by hand, as it seems to provide no means of charging oncost on hand work.

These are the four methods chiefly in use throughout the world to-day, and it will have been observed that each and every one of them stands condemned. How, then, is oncost to be allocated ?

Looking down the list of the Nominal Ledger headings of the oncost items, one is struck by the fact that there is no basis common to them all upon which the expenditure can be charged to the various jobs. Some items fluctuate from one cause, some from another, and it is, therefore, necessary to treat the different classes in different ways. The simplest method would be to treat them all in one way, but as the causes of fluctuation are the true basis upon which to allocate, it will be seen that there is no one way that is suitable.

As has been already stated, it is not practicable to allocate to each Works Order its proportion of the actual oncost incurred for the period during which the order is current, and it is therefore necessary to devise some method which will give results that will most nearly approximate to the actual. To this end it is suggested that at the beginning of the year one should budget for the whole year's oncost expenditure —estimates being based upon the experience of the past year adjusted to meet known altered circumstances—and that oncost rates to be charged to Works Orders during the year be fixed on such estimates. The budget should be prepared in detail—that is, under the Nominal Ledger headings, and not in total only—in order that proper control may be maintained by means of comparison between the estimated, the actual, and the recovered expenditure. (By "recovered expenditure" is meant the amount absorbed by charge to Works Orders.)

In considering such a budget, the first thing to strike one will be that it should be first split up over the departments, and that for this purpose such general services as power plant, maintenance staff, stores, stables and garage, &c., should be treated as departments. The charges already appearing for general services should therefore be separated from the others.

Then it is apparent that, in factories employing machinery, certain charges are peculiar to the machines and should be borne only by the work done on them. Such charges are :—

(1) Rent and rates applicable to the space occupied by the machines.
(2) Power consumed by the machines.
(3) Repairs to and maintenance of the machines.
(4) Depreciation of machines.

No other charges of any moment can be said to be peculiar to the machinery, and it would appear, therefore, that these charges should be dealt with separately, and for this purpose they also should be set apart.

There is then left the general oncost expenditure to be divided amongst the departments (including the general service departments), and the basis of this division will vary in any two factories. Each class of expenditure must be considered by itself and the decision made as to the truest basis for distribution. Some may be spread on a wages basis, such as national and workmen's compensation insurance ; some on the weight of materials handled, such as stores expenses and truckers ; some on a capital value basis, such as depreciation of buildings ; and so on. When this distribution is made, the new figures for the general service departments, except those proportions that are peculiar to the machines or capital expenditure, will be distributed over the productive departments on the basis of estimated consumption, and the departmental oncosts thereby obtained will be converted into man-hour rates for the respective departments by dividing the amounts by the estimated number of hours that the men will work therein on productive jobs during the coming year. Likewise, a machine hour rate will be arrived at for each machine by taking the budgeted annual rent, power, maintenance, and depreciation charges in respect of each machine, and dividing it by the estimated number of hours it will run during the year.

The analysis of the time sheets gives the number of hours worked by men and machines on each Works Order, and these hours, multiplied by the appropriate man-hour and machine-hour rates respectively, give the oncost charges to each Works Order. The corresponding credits will appear in the various Departmental Oncost and Machine Rate Accounts.

The fixing of the first year's man-hour and machine-hour rates will involve a considerable amount of labour, but succeeding rates will be fixed without much trouble, for statistics will be available to show the adjustments that are necessary. Altered circumstances may at any time call for alterations in the rates, and it is, therefore, essential that they be properly controlled. This may conveniently be done by preparing monthly statements comparing the estimated expenditure, the actual expenditure, and the amount recovered by means of charge to Works Orders. Provided that the hourly values of partly finished Works Orders does not fluctuate violently at the end of one month, compared with another, the oncost on work in progress may be ignored for the purposes of this control. Otherwise it will be necessary to ascertain it, and in any event it will have to be ascertained at the times when the financial books are closed.

A proper double-entry system of cost books is strongly recommended, and, if adopted, Control Accounts for general and machine rate oncost will be one of the features.

Cost Books.

While the present forms of Manufacturing, Trading, and Profit and Loss Accounts are retained, it will be impossible to combine the ordinary books of account and the cost books, and it is doubtful if such combination is desirable, so long as it is kept in view that the costs (and, therefore, the cost books) must be based upon the entries in the financial books.

The cost books that are necessary are : Journal, Works Order Ledger, and General Cost Ledger. Both ledgers should on the debit side have three columns to allow of the total charges for wages, materials, and oncost on any Works or Standing Order being ascertained without the necessity for analysing the amounts of same. Credits to Works or Standing Order Accounts for material returned to store should be shown in red ink on the debit side of the accounts for a like reason.

The first account to be opened in the General Cost Ledger will be the Nominal Ledger Control Account, which, by means of Journal entries, will be credited with the amounts of the weekly pay-roll, the weekly material issues, and the monthly oncost expenditure, the corresponding debits going to the three accounts for wages, materials, and oncost. The Wages and Materials Accounts will be cleared weekly by transfer direct to the various Works or Standing Order Accounts in accordance with the allocations made; while monthly, or as jobs are completed, oncost will be charged to Works and Standing Orders, and the Departmental Oncost Accounts credited therewith.

The Oncost Account will be cleared monthly by transfers to the various Departmental Oncost Accounts, such transfers being made on the bases already decided upon, and the Departmental Oncost Accounts for service charges will be cleared immediately to the other departmental accounts upon the bases of the actual consumption. Thereafter transfers will be made from the Departmental Oncost Accounts to the various Machine Rate Accounts, and these two classes of accounts will then contain, on the one hand, the actual figures as obtained from the financial books, and, on the other, the estimated amounts charged during the period to the various Works Orders. The balances on these accounts (after adjustment for work in progress) will be the amounts either over or short recovered, and such balances will show at a glance how near to accurate the fixed rates have been to date.

When a Works Order is completed and the final cost thereof is ascertained, the account must be closed. In some businesses it is not considered desirable that the cost office should be aware of the amount of profit made upon each piece of work, and in such case the total cost of the completed Works Orders will be transferred to Departmental Production Accounts in the General Cost Ledger. (These Production Accounts will themselves be closed at the end of financial periods by transfer to the Nominal Ledger Control Account.) Where it is desired to show the profit on each individual job, the Works Order Account will be credited with the sale price (the corresponding debit being to a Departmental Sales Account, which will already have been credited with the amount through the Nominal Ledger Control Account), and the balance will be transferred to a Departmental Profit and Loss Account in the General Cost Ledger. Such Departmental Profit and Loss Accounts will be closed at the end of financial periods by transfer to General Profit and Loss Account, to which account will be transferred also all balances short or over-recovered on the Oncost Accounts. The balance on the General Profit and Loss Account will be transferred to the Nominal Ledger Control Account, which will then show a balance which will be equivalent to the value of work in progress.

. Where goods are made for stock, the total cost will be transferred from the Works Order Account to a Departmental Production Account, which will be credited with subsequent sales, and at the end of the financial period also with the cost of such goods remaining in stock. In such case the balance remaining on the Nominal Ledger Control Account will represent the value of work in progress plus the cost of finished goods in stock.

Where articles made for stock are subsequently used in production, the credit to the Departmental Production Account will be at cost value. Where some are sold and some used, the Departmental Production Account will show this clearly, so that no misconception may arise as to the ratio of profit earned upon the articles sold, and a transfer at the same rate of profit can be made between the Profit and Loss Accounts of the departments concerned, in respect of the goods used.

Just as in all up-to-date accounting systems Control Accounts for all the other ledgers are found in the Nominal or Private Ledger, so in the General Cost Ledger there should be a Control Account for the Works Order Ledger. This Control Account may conveniently be called Work in Progress Account, and should have the three columns for wages, materials, and oncost, thereby showing at any time the analysis of the value of uncompleted Works Orders in the shops.

Costing is but one cog in the wheel of an efficiency system, and some of its functions are apt to be missed or not fully appreciated when it is lifted, as it has been here, out of its natural surroundings. Its importance is only beginning to be realised by manufacturers, only some of whom are now awakening to the fact that it is a money-making proposition all the time. Most manufacturers have the wisdom to have their books properly audited, but perhaps less than 5 per cent. of them have had sufficient foresight to instal a proper costing system. And yet more businesses are ruined through not knowing their costs than fail for lack of an auditor.

For the accounting profession, and more especially for the younger members of it, there is no work that is more interesting than the devising and organising of efficient costing systems; and there is no work that will be more beneficial to the manufacturing businesses of this country, and, therefore, to the community at large.

This class of work provides for the accountant a field of opportunity which is practically virgin soil. It is for him to open it up, sow it, and make it return a splendid harvest of accounts that are quick and live and *not* (as accounts too often are) merely inquests upon long dead figures. The accountant must act as physician, not as coroner.

The organisation of efficiency and costing systems is work worth doing; it is constructive in the best sense of the word, and by taking it up seriously, accountants will raise still higher the status of the profession to which they belong.

The Cost Accountant.

THE OFFICIAL JOURNAL OF THE INSTITUTE OF COST AND WORKS ACCOUNTANTS LIMITED (BY GUARANTEE).

VOL. 1.—No. 1. JUNE, 1921.

Editorial.

Cost Accountancy.

Cost Accountancy is just beginning to receive that recognition which in this country at least, is so tardily given to any advantageous development in business methods.

Unfortunately considerable lack of knowledge is shown by Employers, and even by Cost and Works Accountants themselves, as to the necessary qualifications, the delineation of their duties, and the advantageous application of the results obtained by the employment of properly qualified experts in this science, which embraces so much more than ordinary financial accountancy.

The Cost Accountant, if given full scope for his abilities, holds the key to the whole efficiency of a business, consequently one of his functions is to criticise the working of all the departments of the concern with which he is associated.

The result of this is, that Heads of departments, unless very tactfully handled, have a tendency to withhold information and if possible, hide facts without realising the great assistance which can be obtained from him by giving that full co-operation which is so desirable in every business, and yet so seldom obtained.

A properly qualified Cost Accountant must have had a good technical experience of at least the business with which he is connected. A man with a general knowledge of Accountancy, Book-keeping, experience of organisation, and the installation of card or other systems is not qualified to undertake the. installation of a costing system to produce proper results.

We repeat, with emphasis, that he must have a technical knowledge of, and a practical training in the business with which he is associated.

Too often, more especially in the case of businesses which have grown under the direction of the same man from very small beginnings, the so-called Cost Accountant is merely a clerk, working to the instructions of an employer, neither of them having had the opportunity of obtaining a specialised knowledge of Cost Accountancy, and therefore not realising what great advantages would accrue from a small extension of their system, and a proper application of results.

Manufacturers will often employ in their business, a specialist, such as a trained chemist, and allow, him a free hand, taking full advantage of his services, because they know full well that they have not the requisite knowledge to intelligently interfere in his work. Are they generally equally ready to realise the special function of the Cost Accountant?

Cost and Works Accountants, who are properly qualified, must see that they obtain this recognition, that they are given full scope for their activities, and that the results obtained are so employed as to show to the full their importance, in fact indispensability to industry, so that they may attain that status to which they are justly entitled.

Costing—Principles and Practice.

By Cyril F. Bird, A.C.A.

A lecture delivered before the Chartered Accountant Students Society of London on 9th November 1921.

The ever-increasing importance of Costing in the world of commerce and of finance has, in my opinion, an important bearing on the accountancy profession, because we, as practising members of that profession, and you students as prospective members, are, or should be, *par excellence* the guides and philosophers to those of the trading community who realise the advantages of the introduction and practice of a sound system of Cost Accounts in their businesses. To those who have not seen, or do not see, such advantages, we should endeavour to act as pioneers, and point out the paths of virtue.

My lecture has been called "Costing—Principles and Practice" for a two-fold reason. First, you, as students, should have a clear idea of the fundamental principles of Costing and Cost Accounts, both from the point of view of the tests of your knowledge of the subject which hard-hearted examiners may require of you, and from the point of view of your work after you have satisfied them, when in such work you will probably find it necessary to apply those principles in checking or criticising a system of Cost Accounts already in use, practical or otherwise, or utilise such principles in installing or recommending a system to be adopted. Second, because the opinion is sometimes expressed, quite wrongly, I think, that the installation and keeping of Cost Accounts involves an expenditure either incommensurate with, or in excess of, the advantages derivable therefrom.

It is going to be my endeavour to show you as far as I can, on broad outlines, how the principles of Costing should be applied in and made reconcilable with practice, or, in other words, show how by an intelligent explanation of the principles and a practical application of them, the advantages accruing easily outweigh the expense involved. If accountants can prove this to their clients, that antagonism which in some cases, to a certain extent, unfortunately exists between traders and manufacturers and their accountants can be eliminated, and you, as accountants, will have gone far towards establishing your worth to your clients.

My advice in all matters relative to Cost Accounts and Costing in practice is: "Do not be too theoretical; combine your theory with practical common-sense, which makes sound practice; put yourself in the position of your client, and look at his accounts from his point of view as well as from your own." I might add here that some accountants are inclined to be too theoretical, and that a period of work and service in a commercial concern is, or should be, of great value to accountants; in my own case I was for eight years employed in a large commercial concern, and the experience gained has been invaluable to me.

Brevity is the soul of wit. Try to make simplicity the soul of accountancy. Prove to your clients that

Costing and Cost Accounts can be made quite simple, as well as financially advantageous, and half the battle is won.

The Principles of Costing.—A clear understanding of principles must be the groundwork of all real knowledge and practice of Costing. What then are these underlying principles? I think they can best be explained in this way. A Trading Account is an account drawn up to show a trader or trading concern (which, of course, includes manufacturers) the gross profit on goods purchased, acquired, and/or manufactured for trading purposes, i.e. for intended sale before charging or taking into consideration and account the administrative expenses necessarily incurred in effecting such sale, the Profit or Loss Account showing the profit or loss on such sales after charging these expenses, the object of the Trading Account being to show that the difference between the amount of the sales and the initial cost of goods, together with cost of production, allows sufficient margin fully to cover the expenses incidental to carrying on the business and leave a surplus for private enjoyment. These accounts show profits as a whole, but do not show how such profits are arrived at. Cost Accounts are accounts drawn up to show the cost and profit or loss on each or individual operations which form part of the whole.

Costing may, therefore, be said to be a system of recording by means of and in accounts the total cost of labour employed, materials used, and other expenses incurred in the manufacture of a certain article or commodity or total expenditure on a particular job, contract work or operation (the word "operation" being read with wide significance), and, of course, by arriving at this total cost, the profit or loss on each operation or article is ascertainable.

From these definitions of the principles of Costing one might be inclined to argue: If Cost Accounts show the cost and profit or loss on each operation in trading, a summary of the cost of all operations should furnish the Trading and Profit and Loss Accounts, and there is, therefore, no need for two separate systems of accounts. Theoretically there is not, but a moment's thought will make one realise that there are certain elements of cost which are of necessity of general application to the whole business rather than of particular application to any one single operation, and this being the case it can be seen that although such costs as a whole are ascertainable in fact, the allocation of them to particular operations must be, in the first instance anyhow, by means of estimates, the total of such estimates approximating or equalling the whole cost. The whole principle and utility of Cost Accounts, apart from the advantages derivable therefrom upon completion, which will be dealt with later, is so to keep them that *all* costs are as accurately as is possible allocated to each operation, and the sum total of the costs of all operations equals the total costs of the business or trading as a whole.

You have then a system of accounts which will show the costs and profits of each department, job, operation, or article as well as the profits on the whole business, the first being ascertainable from the Cost Accounts, and the second from the Financial or General Books. It can readily be appreciated that the Financial Books deal with facts, while Cost Accounts deal to some extent with estimates, and the more nearly such estimates approximate actual costs, and the more accurately such estimated costs can be allocated in the Cost Accounts, the greater will be the value of them. I have, so far, dealt with the principles and objects of Cost Accounts. Now a word as to *the advantages* before dealing with the application of principles in practice. At the outset, I venture to suggest that the advantages and utility are as marked in the smallest businesses as in the largest, because in these present times of tightness of money, and need for economy and ever-increasing competition, small individual traders need to subject their trading results to as careful a scrutiny as do the largest concerns. The advantages are really self-evident, but it is often necessary in practice to explain these. It must be of advantage to be able to ascertain the profit and cost of each department or job independently of profits as a whole; by so doing, departments that are not paying can either be dropped or economies effected in the expenses incidental thereto, the Cost Accounts showing which of such expenses are proportionately too high; this, of course, being done either by means of comparison of percentages of each item to the whole over periods, or by means of arriving at a unit of cost for each item.

By means of arriving at the cost of articles, selling prices can be fixed with greater certainty, in order to arrive at percentage of profits, or to realise the desired percentage; and this percentage enables the trader to ascertain whether, for example, he can undersell his competitors and by so doing increase his output, and by such increase maintain his total profits at the figure he requires.

By comparison of labour and materials charged to various jobs, waste of time and stores can be detected and stopped.

Cost Accounts provide valuable information, and in many cases essential data in connection with tendering for contracts, provision of estimates, comparison of results over periods, and necessary or contemplated changes of policy. In practice, all these points should be carefully brought to the notice of clients.

The principles of Costing are applicable to all businesses, but in practice it becomes necessary to determine: (*a*) What class of Cost Account is best adapted to the business concerned, and (*b*) having arrived at such class, what unit of cost will give the most valuable information to the business.

Classes of Cost Accounts.—The conduct of some businesses is such that their trading is comprised and consists of a series of definite and terminating operations, e.g. building a house or building a ship. In others you have operations which are continuous, e.g. railways. In the former, it is necessary to arrive at terminal costs, whilst in the latter operating or working costs are necessary. There are yet again businesses in which cost bears relation to saleable goods independently of manufactured articles known as Single Costs, in which there is a simple and natural unit of cost, e.g. barrels of beer brewed, and businesses in which there is a combination of the two, e.g. manufacture and sale of perambulators or sewing machines, when two units of cost might be required: cost per machine made, and cost per £100 of sales. Then you have what are known as Multiple and Process Costs. In the first cost is required of articles sold, which bear no relation to each other in either cost or selling price, and in the latter, in which the cost is required of each process of a business. It may be, of course, that process and single costs occur in the same businesses, e.g. a company manufacturing a crude substance in which single costs would be required to show the cost per ton of, say, mining the raw material, and also of manufacturing certain other substances or ingredients essential in the process of manufacturing the crude substance, the whole set of accounts furnishing the process cost of the crude. Having arrived at the class of Cost Account and unit of cost applicable to the business concerned, and assuming, for the sake of example, you have been called in to institute a system of Cost Accounts, or advise whether the existing system is sufficient and efficient or requires modification, your next important step is to determine whether it is essential to have entirely separate Cost Accounts, or whether the General Accounts can be so adapted as to provide all the information that is necessary. (This, of course, has a considerable bearing on the point previously raised as to the cost or expense involved in providing or ascertaining costs.) The question as to this depends entirely on the class of business, but as a determining factor, consideration should be given as to what room, if any, there is for discrepancy between the Cost and the General Accounts. Where the items of expenditure or cost in the General Accounts exactly correspond to those which would appear in the Cost Accounts, the required information can easily be obtained by analysing and sub-dividing carefully all expenses, including labour and materials, in such manner that the General Accounts, culminating in the Trading and Profit and Loss Accounts, themselves furnish, in total and in detail, the cost per unit. This would enable the trader to make comparisons over different periods of actual expenditure, item by item or under different heads, and by the provision of "Unit of Cost" columns in the accounts, comparison can be made at the same time of unit costs over, say, the current and previous corresponding periods. It might be said generally that this system is sufficient for all costs that can be classed as operating single or ouput, Multiple and Process Costs, the variation being only in the nature of the unit of cost. When dealing with terminal costs, manufacturing and contract costs, it seems essential that the Cost Accounts should be kept as distinct and separate, for each operation here may be, and should be, looked upon in the light of a separate business requiring its own Profit and Loss Account. In these classes of businesses Cost Accounts can be kept on two systems, one being based on double-entry principles, and the other on single-entry. In both cases it should be considered of first importance that the results shown by the Cost Accounts agree with those shown by the Financial Accounts. Personally, I favour the double-entry system, certainly from the theoretical, and partly from the practical point of view. Let us take the example of manufacturing or job accounts.

As you are all probably aware, total costs are made up of what is known as Flat Cost, Prime Cost, and Oncost, Oncost being divided into Works Oncost and General Oncost, the flat cost including labour and materials and expenses incidental thereto, Prime Cost including Direct Expenses allocatable to labour and materials, i.e. direct expenses of production known as Works Oncost and General Oncost, including indirect expenses of production. Other terms that might be employed are Direct Charges, Standing Charges, and Administrative Charges. By a double-entry system of recording these costs in the Cost Books the cost clerk is able to check the accuracy of his work, and to complete accounts similar to the Financial Accounts. He is also able to keep his accounts parallel with those kept in the counting-house, so that valuable checks on the accuracy of the accounts as a whole are obtainable, stage by stage; and if the two departments are kept quite distinct, assistance is given in the prevention or detection of fraud by one department providing a check on the other. To illustrate this: take our first item of cost in, say, a factory, i.e. Labour. Time-sheets of the men's pay are made up, signed by foremen, and certified by some responsible head. These sheets go first to the counting-house, and are entered by one clerk in the General Wages Book, and are then passed to the cost clerk to be summarised in a Cost Wages Abstract Book, and charged therefrom to the various jobs. From the Wages Book in the counting-house, payment is made by the cashier, and the amounts paid will be posted from the credit of the Cash Book to the debit of Wages Account in the General Ledger. From the Cost Wages Abstract Book the various jobs are debited to Job Accounts in the Cost Ledger, with the wages chargeable thereto, and the periodical totals of the Wages Abstract Book are posted in the Cost Ledger to the credit of Wages Account, this balance, which should agree with the debit to Wages Account in the Financial Books, providing a check on the wages paid. Acting on the same principle, it can be seen that you get what might be termed double double-entry, and the credit balances on the various nominal accounts in the Cost Ledger should agree with the debit balances on similar nominal accounts in the Financial or General Ledgers. Theoretically, of course, this should be so, provided *all* expenses can be accurately allocated to each job; practically, this is only possible as regards direct expenses, and not as regards general oncost, so that it can be said that this system is of considerable practical utility up to certain stages in our building up of costs, and whether the system should be recommended or adopted will depend on circumstances, but it has been quoted as being a system that might with advantage be used. Coming now to the question of General Oncost, which in practice is the great stumbling-block in Costing, and on which so much divergence of opinion exists. It might be said generally that the most practical basis of charging Works Oncost is a percentage on Labour, and not a percentage on Flat Cost (Labour and Materials), because Labour is a more constant quantity, whereas Materials used in Manufacture are liable to wide fluctuations. If the rate of wages varies, such variation is generally more or less permanent, and the rate of Oncost can be correspondingly varied or adjusted. It will be found also in practice that the time occupied by any specified piece of work bears a closer relation to the direct wages expended on it than to the Flat Cost, or Wages and Materials as a whole. Works Oncost is sometimes charged, not on the amount of wages, but on the number of hours expended on the work, and at so much per hour. This has its advantages in greater accuracy, but necessarily increases the work in compiling Wages Abstracts, as the number of hours has to be shown. The principle of, and most practical way of charging General Oncost is by a percentage on the Prime Cost. These percentages are, of course, obtainable from previous periods' Trading and Profit and Loss Accounts. In the case of the first year of a business the percentages would have to be arrived at by consultation with the proprietors of the business, and a good method to adopt is to utilise percentages of a similar class of business, such percentages being subject to adjustments after the first year's Trading and Profit and Loss Accounts had been completed. It is not possible in the time at my disposal to give more than broad outlines of allocations of Costs, but a point to bear in mind is: Allocate as much as you possibly can directly rather than by percentages, as, of course, direct charges or allocations produce most accurate costs. In practice, then, recommend a system whereby expenses can be so directly allocated. For example: If you have separate departments or jobs separately costed, and one item which has to be included in, say, Works Oncost is electric light, power, gas, and water, the amount of which is large, and the procedure has been to take this item on the percentage basis, obviously a more correct method, and more accurate, would be the installation of separate meters for each department, and incidentally such installation might quite effectively reduce expenditure by stopping waste. Many other instances will, doubtless, similarly occur to you.

A few words as to *Units of Cost.* Make these appropriate and useful. For example, say you were costing a large depot which not only received and issued stores but acted also in the capacity of a storing warehouse. It would obviously be insufficient to work your Units of Cost on the basis of tons handled only; the elements of storage should be taken into consideration, and credit given for this in the accounts, so that the accounts prepared could be compared with other establishments of a similar nature. Another illustration: Suppose you were asked to cost the pleasant function that has taken place today at the Guildhall—presumably this is costed in the Lord Mayor's Department of Costs—what unit of cost would you consider would give the most valuable information? It might be costed on the basis of cost per head of banquetters, including guests, or cost per head or body of the banquettees, turtles, fowls, &c., or cost per cover, or from the point of view of the State or the general public at the cost per economic value of output of Ministers' speeches, or per weight of words.

Going back to the question I previously raised as to the possibility of your clients objecting to a Costing system on grounds of expense. In your practice you should endeavour to ascertain if unnecessary work is being done, and if the work can be lessened without any loss of its efficiency and usefulness, by so doing arriving at the minimum of work required—this always pleases clients. Another suggestion that might prove useful: As an auditor of or adviser on Cost Accounts or a Costing system, you might quite easily find it practicable to draw up a Cost Account and an account in the form of debit and credit relative to the expenses incurred in Costing. A Cost Account of the cost of Costing. The expenses would be shown on the debit side of your account, and your credit side could show any actual concrete savings which have been directly attributable to Costing—such as reduction in expenses of administration. You would, by this means, have something concrete to put before your client as an actual profit on the account, and this should be supplemented by taking into consideration and pointing out that, beyond this actual saving, the moral effect is anything but a negligible quantity.

Suggestions have been made that *Cost Accounts should be standardised,* the suggestion, which has evolved, I believe, into practice, originating in the United States of America. Personally, this does not seem to me to be practicable, but then America is the home of standardisation. It might be practicable to standardise Cost Accounts for distinct and separate classes of business, but it appears absolutely impossible to have a standard form of Cost Accounts that could be used for all businesses. Even in distinct and separate classes of businesses many difficulties would arise. Originality and initiative would be lost. Circumstances also so invariably alter cases, and the elements of cost and units of cost in the same class of business might quite reasonably vary. Standardisation of Cost Accounts should, I think, be looked at very warily. The principles of Costing do not vary, and I would say, let a knowledge of these be your groundwork and adapt the principles to the needs of the particular business.

Just a last word. Never be afraid to ask advice of your clients, and discuss with them your views, *as your views,* as well as their views, and get their opinions. If you consider such opinions wrong, try to alter them, or persuade your clients to do so, and show the weak points in their arguments, but be open to all reasonable arguments from their side, remembering that the proprietors of a business should know the business better than you.

I have not been able in the time at my disposal to go fully into details, and have only been able to enunciate broad principles. Costing is a very big and very important subject, and a lecture of this description might well, with advantage, be supplemented by taking the concrete case of an actual business and working through, as a practical example, all the stages of costing such business, and applying to such example the principles I have discussed this evening.

There may be some of you here who have little or no knowledge of Costing, and others who have a considerable experience thereof; the latter, if they feel they have not learnt much more than they already know, will, I feel sure, use a certain amount of that sweet reasonableness which they possess for the sake of the former, who I hope have been instructed and interested, if not amused. And reiteration of well-known principles always helps to make the knowledge of such principles stick

THE NECESSITY FOR SCIENTIFIC COSTING.

Report of the Costing Conference held under the auspices of the Institute of Cost and Works Accountants, at the Holborn Restaurant, on February 3rd, 1922, under the Chairmanship of the Rt. Hon. Lord Weir of Eastwood, P.C., D.L., LL.D.

OPENING THE PROCEEDINGS, the chairman said: Ladies and Gentlemen,—Allow me in the first place to say how very heartily and sincerely I appreciate the honour you have done me in asking me to preside at your conference to-day. Next, I would ask you to refer for a moment to Item 1 on the agenda, because it draws attention to the chairman's opening speech. When I remember that we have to hear a very valuable paper prepared by the Executive Council, next, an address by my old friend, Mr. Mensforth, and then we have to discuss the paper, I think you will agree with me that our programme is quite extensive enough without burdening it with any amateur speech. Accordingly, I propose to confine myself to a very few remarks.

Let me congratulate the Institute most heartily on its courage and enterprise in initiating and organising what I think is the first industrial costing conference ever held in this country. Your Institute, established some three years ago, has in that short period of history, not only achieved remarkable progress against considerable difficulty, and, may I say against a considerable amount of prejudice, but its results have justified most thoroughly the hopes and the aspirations of those pioneer promoters of the Institute, to whom you all owe a very deep debt of gratitude.

The Institute has always had a definite object, which is a great advantage, and that is the creation and fostering of a profession of high industrial status, and unfalteringly it has declined to sacrifice at any time the high standard it originally set. Like all reputable concerns, its growth has been sound and steady rather than spectacular, and that is evidenced by the fact that the highest number of passes for its membership examination has never exceeded 25 per cent. The conference opens very valuable possibilities of a propagandist and educative character. Indeed, I trust that this first conference will be successful and may [illegible]age its promoters to hold an annual Parliamentary Session for the discussion and review of the progress made by the profession. To attempt to-day to emphasise the importance of cost accountancy is, I think, needless. War, and the economic conditions associated with it, gave you the opportunity of justifying the early claims of the pioneers of this Institute as to the value and the function of cost accounts. To-day's conditions of devastating peace confirm the vital importance of the industrial responsibility delegated to your members.

We are witnessing a great process of readjustment of values, and it is unfortunately associated with much hardship. It is becoming clearer that the success and the prosperity of the future must depend to an ever-increasing degree on development and progress in industrial methods and process, both in connection with production and distribution. Any effective industrial policy must involve as one of its main factors a campaign of concentration on securing efficient conditions of production and distribution.

As you can appreciate very readily, a large part of the responsibility devolves on the employers and not on the workmen. Employers must so exercise their directional control and improve their organisation so that waste may be eliminated by ingenuity in method, and imagination should be applied in the process itself. Now, in this campaign of revision of method, every problem for its intelligent solution is associated directly with the work of your profession. The cost accountant and his data should continuously be at the right hand of those in charge of estimating, planning, progress, production, and selling. I am tempted to go further and indicate the necessity for an infinitely closer liaison between the cost accountant and the drawing office and other technical departments. Is it too much to say that the wonderful record of Henry Ford was contributed to more by technical design being continuously subjected to the microscope of works accounting than by any other single factor?

In a gathering of experts I would venture to express the hope that you will avoid the tendency of allowing works accountancy to become unduly academic in its practice and its spirit. The United States have given a large amount of attention to the subject of cost accountancy, and they have produced a voluminous body of literature, which I venture to say is of very varying quality, on the subject.

It is true that in America they regard many questions from a different standpoint than we do in this country, and we may at times question their sense of proportion. A study of their methods never fails to stimulate thought and awaken suggestions. But, surely the essence of any good costing system must be the presentation of only the requisite data for practical use and practical application, rather than the preparation of elaborate returns of great interest to their authors but so comprehensive in their nature as to make their assimilation and application very nearly impossible.

To-day we look back on many acute industrial storms of the last few years. We are experiencing to-day the sufferings and hardship involved by the opportunist character of the settlement of some of these disturbances. They were settlements made in defiance of economic laws and neglect of facts. When we talk of co-operation between capital and labour, such can only be effective if proper data and figures are provided as a result of your work, and then sincere and intelligent action can be based on the influence of that work and those figures.

You have a great future in your profession. It is destined to play a very important part in the solution of the complex and ever-varying industrial problems of the immediate future. Every day the status of the profession is rising and will put you in a better position to exercise your influence. In all your activities I wish your Institute and profession the highest possible success.

Mr. J. C. Todman, F.C.W.A., Member of the Council, then read the paper prepared by the Executive Committee of the Council on the subject,

THE NECESSITY FOR SCIENTIFIC COSTING.

Ten years ago Cost Accountancy was practically unknown to the general public in this country. Cost and Works Accountants had for many years exercised their mysterious functions in obscure corners of great industrial concerns, but their aims, their aspirations, and their achievements were rarely understood or appreciated by the busy world around them.

Nevertheless, their performances amply justified their existence and vindicated the judgment and foresight of the business men to whose shrewdness and enterprise they owed their appointment.

The Great War came and with it the urgent need for securing from all available resources the maximum output of war material at a minimum of cost. Business men recognised the necessity for Scientific Costing as a means to this end, and the application of approved Costing methods to production on a national scale, owing to the action of the Ministry of Munitions, enabled the Government to obtain adequate supplies for carrying on the war.

Scientific Costing was accordingly welcomed up and down the country as a new discovery. It was introduced to an admiring public by a diligent Press, and the advantages of extending its beneficent influence more widely in the field of private enterprise were demonstrated to the satisfaction of all progressive business men. Rarely has an idea secured more effective propaganda and seldom has the object been more deserving.

After the Great War came the chaotic period of so-called Reconstruction. It was like the rush of air which follows in the wake of an express train. Our already disorganised industrial and commercial arrangements were caught in the vortex and completely shattered.

Widespread labour disputes resulted in still higher wages. New Capital was issued at prices which fastened a millstone round the neck of future production. Foreign Exchanges reached figures which brought international trade to a standstill, and there followed a period of industrial and commercial stagnation and widespread unemployment from which we have hardly yet commenced to recover.

Prices rose beyond living memory and resulted in a campaign against Profiteering. This brought Scientific Costing once more into the limelight. This time, however, it was used as a weapon in both camps, and the efforts of Government departments to "set a thief to catch a thief" (figuratively speaking, of course) made Cost and Works Accountants exceedingly busy for a considerable time.

Although the numerous prosecutions to stop Profiteering resulted in comparatively few convictions, there is little doubt that the campaign exercised a restraining influence of great value to the community, and it is fair to assume that, while the use of Scientific Costing methods enabled many business men whose charges were reasonable to vindicate their prices, it also placed in the hands of the Government a very effective means of ascertaining true cost which did not fail to impress potential Profiteers.

The question has been repeatedly asked: "Has interest in Scientific Costing declined since the War?" No doubt, the general public has shown less interest recently owing to the preoccupation of the Press with more exciting topics. But the lessons of the Great War and the subsequent period of Reconstruction have left an indelible impression on the mind of the manufacturer, and the advantages of Scientific Costing, once properly understood, are never likely to be overlooked by business men.

The briefest examination of the main features of a Scientific Costing system will make those advantages apparent. The chief aims of such a scheme are:—

(1). **Determination of True Cost.**
(2). **Provision of a Reliable Basis for Estimates.**
(3). **Control of Stocks and Work in Progress.**
(4). **Valuation of Work in Progress and Semi-finished Products.**
(5). **Provision of Statistical Information for the Guidance of Management.**

The first of these aims is achieved by the installation in the Works of a system of Cost Accounts which charge to the various products every item of material, wages, and overhead expense incurred in running the Works and the necessary offices and distributing units.

This system of Cost Accounts must be complete in itself; no half systems will do. It must account for every penny of expenditure, both Capital and Revenue, and must interlock with the financial books of the Company. Where the nature of the business permits, it must show definitely the progress of the work at stated intervals. Such accounts furnish a reliable basis for pricing products and also an indication of the profit earning (or losing) capacity of each product.

This brings us to the second object of Scientific Costing. Such accounts also provide a reliable basis for estimating the probable cost of prospective products. In certain businesses where prices have always to be fixed in advance of the actual work of production, this is a most important function, and the first object may in such cases be considered subordinate to the second. The development of these two features may be regarded as the primary function of the Cost and Works Accountant. It is, perhaps, hardly necessary to point out that the process of comparing initial estimates with the subsequent true cost of any new product is usually a most instructive operation and one which may be relied upon to demonstrate the value of an efficient system of costing.

The third feature, namely: **Control of Stocks and Work in Progress** is incidental to the first feature. To correctly account for expenditure on materials it is necessary to keep a sharp watch on stocks of raw materials. Such supervision involves the checking of stocks, and sometimes carries with it the work of ensuring that the maximum and minimum stocks are not overstepped. This operates as a check on excessive buying of raw materials. The volume of Work in Progress is indicated by the Cost Accounts, and at this point may be regulated to correspond to the requirements and resources of the business.

The fourth feature, namely, **Valuation of Work in Progress and Semi-finished Products,** is another incidental advantage. In closing the financial accounts for any accounting period, it is, of course, necessary to assign a correct value for Work in Progress, including semi-finished products. The only reliable source from which these values can be obtained is the Cost Accounts, which show the cost of all Materials, Wages, and Overhead expended to date upon the incomplete product.

The importance of this feature varies with different industries, but businesses which carry over from one period to another large contracts only partially completed, may easily misstate their profits by using unreliable valuations for Work in Progress.

The remaining feature, **The Provision of Statistical Information for the Guidance of the Management,** covers a very wide and exceedingly valuable field of usefulness. Some of the chief items may be indicated as follow:—

(a) **Periodical Comparisons** of Costs, carefully analysed and suitably arranged, assist the Management to locate items of undue expenditure. Such comparisons should be made periodically and as frequently as the nature of the business permits.

As applied to Wages, such comparisons reveal any overstaffing of departments, any tendency to increase Unproductive Wages either in total expended or in proportion to productive Wages, and any increase of productive Wages per unit of product.

As applied to **Materials,** such comparisons assist in the elimination of Waste (both seen and unseen). Visible waste may often be controlled directly by supervision, but unseen waste usually requires a properly planned system of Works Accounts to demonstrate its existence and whereabouts.

Applied to **Overhead Expenses** such comparisons direct attention to over-appropriation of floor space and plant by departments. Undue consumption of gas, water, electric current, steam and similar services, may be located and stopped.

Such comparisons are not confined simply to past and present performances. They may be applied to the output and expenditure of different factories producing similar products. This throws into relief the comparative efficiency of the management of the different factories and brings us to the next item, viz.:—

(b) **Comparative Cost of Different Methods.**

Difference in Cost under different Management is generally the result of difference in method. But in any up-to-date business there is usually a constant stream of suggestions forthcoming for investigation. These frequently aim at producing a given result at a lower cost than by the existing method.

Most Cost and Works Accountants will agree that no investigations are so exacting or call for such nicety of handling as comparative costs, especially in regard to the treatment of Overhead Expenses. The prospective saving in wages is usually accompanied by some increase in Overhead Expenses and a just assessment of the latter is essential if a fair comparison of cost is to be made. Any failure in this direction may result in the abandonment of what might be a profitable suggestion or, on the other hand, the adoption of a method which is less profitable than that already in use.

This brings us to another aspect:—

(c) **Determination of Future Manufacturing Policy.**

This differs from the preceding items in degree rather than in essence. It is, in fact, the outcome of a consistent application of the information provided in detail by the foregoing comparisons, and is some indication of the far-reaching character of the advantages to be derived from efficient costing.

This process may simply involve the elimination of losing lines and the pushing of those products which produce profits. Or it may result in an extensive advertising campaign or a surgical operation which lops off a non-paying department, or the migration of a great factory to more congenial surroundings—judged, of course, from an industrial standpoint.

Great economics may be indicated in the matter of distribution or delivery of products by an efficient system of costs. "Is it cheaper or better to deliver by Rail, by Road, or by Water?" is a question which engages much attention at the present time. A few months ago it was Coal versus Oil Fuel. Presently, it may well be the question of erecting factories abroad for the production of goods in the countries where they will be consumed, in order to avoid unfavourable exchanges, prohibitive tariffs, heavy taxation at home, or possibly high rates of wages.

(d) **General Statistics.**

The Cost and Works Accountant is bound to compile for his own guidance much useful information which can be of great value to the general Management and also to the shop or departmental supervision.

Such records include:—

1. Foor-space allocations.
2. Departmental Plant Values for Insurance and other purposes.
3. Machine Running Hours, with percentage of lost time either through absentees, idle time or waste time in the Works (including Road Transport Vehicles).
4. Hand Hours worked, with percentages of lost time.
5. Departmental Output Totals.
6. Fuel Consumption.
7. Package Totals.
8. Waste and By-products with percentages on total output.

So far the advantages of Scientific Costing have been considered chiefly from the standpoint of the individual manufacturer. What advantages can it offer from the standpoint of the various industries and of the community as a whole?

One of the most clearly marked features of the reorganisation of industry and commerce since the recent upheaval is the formation of Masters' Federations in the various industries. The pooling of useful information, the unity of action, and the elimination of unfair competition and price-cutting secured by this means provide adequate justification for this tendency. The question of Cost lies very near the surface of many of these questions, and it is not difficult to foresee the ultimate need for Standardisation, either of costing terms or of principles or of methods, or perhaps of all three, before it becomes possible to discuss comparative costs with any hope of securing really useful results.

The question of Standardisation has been considered at great length and from many points of view. The needs of various industries in this direction differ considerably. In an industry like Printing, it is necessary to standardise in order to secure uniformity of prices amongst thousands of businesses, many of which are comparatively small, and the standardised method must be applicable to all kinds of dissimilar jobs. Another industry producing lines which can be specified exactly, may fix selling prices in committee for the whole trade. Standardisation for such an industry should proceed along the lines of

(1). Definition of terms.
(2). Classification of expenses.
(3). Application of agreed principles.
(4). Adoption of uniform methods.

This would facilitate an exact comparison of costs and estimates, item by item, between the various units in the industry with the object of locating and removing differences which prevent an agreement as to selling prices.

It may not be practicable to secure uniformity of method in Costing in all cases, owing to the disparity of methods employed in the manufacture of similar lines which frequently exists.

It is highly probable that this work of standardisation of costs and the application of uniform methods to each of the units in an industry will in future necessitate the appointment of a Cost and Works Accountant by the Masters' Federation for the industry concerned. The preparation of schedules of comparative costs, showing the component details, and the location of errors and disturbing factors, with the subsequent investigations to which these must inevitably lead, will make it necessary to entrust much valuable and confidential information in the hands of one man. It is hardly necessary to point out how essential it is that he shall be a man of undoubted ability and absolute impartiality.

The necessity for such qualifications will be paramount if ever it becomes usual for wages disputes to be settled by reference to costs. The personal reputation of the Cost Accountant who acts as Statistical Officer to any particular industry may well be an important factor in retaining the confidence of both sides in such disputes. The possibility of such a condition of affairs opens up a prospect in which the profession of Cost and Works Accountant may become one of considerable dignity as well as of inestimable value to the community generally.

The possibilities of general standardisation of Scientific Costing throughout industry as a whole have also received consideration. So far as standardisation of Terms and of general Principles is concerned this appears to be quite practicable. The standardisation of Costing methods, however, is bound to be strictly limited in application owing to the diversity in the methods employed in actual production.

The Council of the Institute has already commenced the work of defining recognised Costing Terms. This is obviously the first step, and until this work is well advanced it will be impossible to discuss the classification and grouping of expenses and the application of principles.

Having briefly indicated the chief advantages of Scientific Costing, it may be well to turn to the Cost and Works Accountant himself and enquire: "What are the qualifications which he should "possess to enable him to discharge successfully "the many important responsibilities laid upon "his shoulders?"

It is fairly obvious that he must possess a very considerable knowledge and experience of general accountancy, not only along the usual beaten tracks of financial accountancy, but also in the direction of setting up special accounts to meet unusual conditions. This calls for a good deal of initiative and aptitude.

But he requires much more than this. He must have a good technical knowledge of the products he is costing. He must be able to examine a finished article and have a shrewd idea of what factors have combined to produce it. He must know fairly accurately what factory conditions make for cost, and he must have or develop a sense of units, so that he can determine what measurements should be employed in each instance as a basis for carrying different overhead expenses. This is a much more important factor in just apportionment than is sometimes realised. He must, therefore, have a good knowledge of factory conditions.

He should also be conversant with the conditions under which the product will be sold. In some industries this has very little significance. In others it involves a knowledge of costs of delivery, and, perhaps, of drawback for import duties paid on raw materials. It may even extend to foreign import duties and delivery expenses on products which are invoiced at prices that cover free delivery, duty paid, to consumer's address in foreign countries.

These qualifications distinguish the Cost and Works Accountant from the financial accountant very clearly. Broadly speaking, his work commences where that of the financial accountant ends. The financial accountant prepares the general Balance Sheet and Trading and Profit and Loss Accounts, and announces that the business has made so much total profit or loss. The Cost and Works Accountant, who might perhaps be referred to as the "Technical Accountant," has to show when, and where, and how, and why that profit or loss has accrued, and to suggest how the profit can be increased or the loss eliminated.

One is tempted to ask: "What indication is there that Cost and Works Accountants realise their great responsibilities and are equipping themselves for the efficient discharge of their duties?"

Cost and Works Accountants, from the very nature of their work, are largely "inside" men. That is to say: they do not usually mix with the outside commercial world in the discharge of their duties as do the buyers and the sellers. Tucked away in their factory fastnesses, they rarely meet other men engaged in work similar to their own, and to this cause may, perhaps, be attributed the very slow development of Scientific Costing in the past and the remarkable disparity in the degree of efficiency and in costing methods encountered in this country—even within the narrow limits of the same industry.

The need for a professional Association, such as the Institute of Cost and Works Accountants, as an Institute for promoting interchange of ideas, for encouraging the development of Costing along scientific lines, and as a focus for the aspirations of Cost and Works Accountants, became manifest, and in response to that demand, the Institute of Cost and Works Accountants was called into existence by a small body of energetic men who possessed the instincts of pioneers and the necessary initiative and executive ability to convert ideals into accomplished fact.

There is every reason for believing that their efforts have succeeded in establishing this Institute on a sound basis, and that it will serve in the future as a lasting monument to their enterprise and a tribute to their devotion to the interests of a rising profession.

No one is admitted to this Institute as a Fellow or Associate without first passing very searching tests in the practice of Scientific Costing and Accountancy, or else producing unquestionable evidence of his or her experience and ability as a practical Cost and Works Accountant. As an indication of the very high standard of merit demanded by the Council from candidates for admission to the Institute, the records show that about 60% of the applications received since its incorporation have been rejected.

By such means the Council seeks to confer upon its members a status of considerable professional value and to extend to the business world a guarantee of security and efficient service.

It has been suggested that many business men who are convinced of the advantages of Scientific Costing have hesitated to adopt such a system because of the cost of installation. Additional expenditure, if any, should be considered in the light of an investment. Provided the system is a comprehensive scheme, the investment will undoubtedly yield a handsome return in the shape of increased efficiency. A close and up-to-date knowledge of the cost of production and the elimination of wastage of time, materials, and overhead expenses, will inevitably follow the installation of an efficient system of Costing.

It is evident that Cost and Works Accountants have a vast amount of work before them. The field of their labours comprises the whole industrial world—a world which is already engaged in a relentless struggle for trade supremacy. The need for their services increases rapidly and grows more urgent.

In the days before us the prize will go to him who knows what his product costs: for Competition will cut out big profits on everything which is not a monopoly, and the margin which separates Success from Failure will be the narrow difference between a small percentage of Profit and an equally small percentage of Loss (applause).

Costing as a Branch of Administration.

By E. T. Elbourne, A.M.I.Mech.E.,
Hon. Director of the Institute of Industrial Administration.

If we consider for a moment the routine of costing, we shall find no difficulty in appreciating that Cost Accounts expressing cost per unit of product in terms of money are only possible as a superstruction on a foundation of administrative records, of which I may mention—

- Employment Records.
- Timekeeping.
- Timebooking.
- Wages Computation.
- Purchase Records.
- Stock Accounts.
- Plant Records.

It may be, I submit, quite reasonably argued that each of these is occasioned by other considerations than the preparation of Cost Accounts; on the other hand, because these records acquire an added significance when there is a costing system, their independence is frequently overlooked.

I trust I shall not seem to be guilty of giving arbitrary meanings to words if I refer to costing as comprising the costing application of administrative records, as well, of course, as the Cost Accounts proper.

I wish, in any case, to break away from the purely departmental conception, because I want the co-ordinating mind to be that of the manager who will make his own arrangements for the execution of the work involved. To put it another way, I would not willingly accept the view that costing comprises only the work carried out by the cost accountant. There can be a costing significance in records that may hardly reach the Cost Department, and I would instance operation efficiency, particularly under a system of payment by results; or again, the matter of rejections during inspection.

These instances serve to illustrate also that costing can be interpreted as truly as a technical issue as an accountancy one, hence it is only the manager who can give to costing its full significance by virtue of his opportunity, and presumed competence, to survey the whole field.

It will serve my purpose if I may discriminate between a cost accounting system and a costing system, though admittedly the more usual conception of a costing system is essentially the preparation of Cost Accounts, no more and no less, which may be accurate in the accountancy sense. In a costing system, as I would ask you to consider it, the statistics of production retain their original significance and do not lose it by a process of accountancy "pulping."

The reason for my striving to get costing recognised as on a very much higher plane than a mere application of bookkeeping is because I am not content, if Cost Accounts be considered as a thermometer, for the manager to be unable to take his own readings, or, alternatively, to take no readings at all and trust to what is sometimes called his practical judgment—arguing it may be that thermometers, anyway, are too expensive.

If, to continue the illustration, you expect a costing system to be a separate instrument of measurement that

Extract from a paper read before the Birmingham Branch of the Institute of Industrial Administration, 26th April 1922.

you use or do not use as you think fit, then probably it will be too expensive because the service it renders will be too detached, requiring too conscious an effort. It is only when costing is an integral part of your administrative methods that it ceases to be a luxury. At the risk of making an erroneous illustration, might I suggest that a costing system properly utilised more nearly resembles a thermostat that automatically cuts off the heat when the temperature rises unduly or maybe releases the sprinklers to put out the fire (to speak in the vulgar tongue, someone getting it in the neck). However, these similes do not cover the ground adequately, and I have yet to meet the costing system that automatically prevents waste without management action.

In truth, I am pleading for the acceptance of costing as a principle of administration and attitude of mind virtually. I want the manager to develop his analytical faculties so that the cost effect of everything that goes on in the works in his charge does find expression in such a way as to enable him to exercise control. After all, truth is essentially comparative knowledge, and real comparison means records rather than impressions. Of course, it is possible for a logical outcome of the analytical attitude to mean an excess of records which defeat their own object. The possibility and danger of over-feeding is, however, no sound argument for not feeding t aall—at least not to me—and we have to find out what amount of feeding gives us health ; and the quantum varies with different people. To follow this simile a little further, a disregard of the consequences of erroneous feeding may be done with impunity by some sturdy individuals while at the other end of the scale are people who are compelled to adopt a very restricted diet, while there is a class apart who have the time and means to be faddists.

Your manager may, therefore, have control of such a sturdy business that he can disregard the consequences of wastefulness or it may be that only the most persistent care will keep things going. The parallel to the faddist is the concern whose manufacturing policy is so thoroughly sound that to indulge in a comparatively elaborate system is no serious charge on the business and affords pleasure and satisfaction if not exactly vital to health.

When I visited the States, twenty years ago, I gained the impression that the development of systems there was evidence of prosperity arising out of sound policy, by concentrating on small ranges of products, rather than the secret of it.

The power to indulge in what might be called fads has doubtless helped managers to arrive at a compromise between extravagance and parsimony that represents efficiency. Out of such an experience the mind acquires a power of discrimination and insight that is not to be won, I believe, any other way.

Speaking in a personal sense, I pin my faith to administration and not to systems, whether they deal with costing or any other branch. Systems, as such, are a means to an end, and the end is the development of the manager's powers of administration. He may change his systems with as little compunction as he changes his personal habits—though a change of system means a change of habit for many others and must be done only after careful deliberation. The point is that it is the resultant effect on the administration of the business that matters. To take the old tag " early to bed, early to rise, makes a man healthy, wealthy, and wise "—it may do, but few of us would say it is a golden rule for all. It may be that at one stage of our lives we would do well to follow it—we certainly think so in our children's case—while at another stage habits might be largely reversed with advantage to results. Whether I am sound or not in this, I am on sure ground in contending that a system, which is habit writ large, is right only so long as it meets our requirements and the system discarded by one manager might be the salvation of another—with due adjustments, shall we say ?

Out of these ruminations may I come to this point—that a costing system is so vital to the control of any enterprise that the development of the system—it may be transformation even ultimately—ought and must not be separated from administration itself.

Some of you here to-night who are responsible cost accountants may wonder where you come in in my scheme of things—actually instead of forcing your way into the administrative area because of the knowledge you have you will be called in by the management as their assistant or delegate in the more statistical and accountancy aspects—you will be required to confirm and supplement with figures the manager's scrutiny of facts.

As cost accountants, I want you to believe that your advancement hinges primarily on the development of costing knowledge by the manager himself.

To you who are managers, may I be allowed to say that except you take up costing as part of your methods of administration you will be unable to carry the burden that the development of social organisation will force upon you. You it is who have already to meet organised labour, and will have still more in future to co-operate with organised labour in the administration of industry.

I will not attempt to visualise the general problem that you may have to face, but this much is clear, that nothing will obviate the necessity of meeting the economic test, and as costing is virtually the economic measure, you must enlarge your methods accordingly and prepare yourselves for living through an even more critical existence as managers in the future than you have had in the past.

COSTING.

THE functions of a factory costing system may be said to be: (1) to assist the works' manager to manage the factory; (2) to provide the administration with facts and figures to enable it to judge of the efficiency of the works management; (3) to provide a comparison between the cost and selling prices of each class of production; and (4) to provide statistics to form the bases of estimates of the cost of new productions of similar nature to past productions.

The primary function must ever be to provide the works' manager with prompt information upon the quantity, quality and cost of the production in such form as will enable him to see quickly just where waste of time, waste of material, and extravagance in his shop overhead expenses are arising. The works' manager is a busy man, and information must reach him in the form which will show him at a glance where anything is wrong. In the presentation of that information, therefore, there is ample scope for the exercise of ingenuity upon the part of the factory accountant. The main facts can best be shown by the use of graphs, but these cannot with efficiency be used indiscriminately to illustrate the mass of the valuable details which arise from a costing system.

The provision, to the managing director and the board, of comparative statistics upon cost of production and services, upon output and upon departmental overhead expenditure, will permit them readily to review the progress of works management, while information upon idle capacity will also materially help them to decide whether the shortage of work is due to their selling policy or sales organisation, or to circumstances beyond their control.

Comparison between true current costs and net selling prices will provide the administration with more up-to-date proof of the profits that are being earned than can be obtained by any other method of accounting. And there is no one in administrative control of a factory who would not sleep better if possessed of that proof.

THE PLACE OF THE COST ACCOUNTANT IN INDUSTRY

By S. Laurence Gill, F.C.W.A., A.C.A.

In this country at any rate, I think we cannot but admit that the business public generally has not yet quite got hold of the idea of that particular kind of accountant known as a Cost Accountant, and I am not sure that even Cost Accountants, themselves, are quite clear as to all the relationships, implications and possibilities of the position. There is more precision and lucidity about the matter in the engineering industry than in any other and the importance of this new profession was accentuated by the Government requirements during the war. In this way, some of the quick blossoming was the result of outside influence; the Cost Accountant was superimposed from the outside on certain industries; he was not altogether a natural and, therefore, a sound growth; unless this development is to be a mere flash in the pan, much spade work is necessary in the education not only of the Cost Accountant himself, but more particularly of the business public, as to his place in industry and his precise use.

The Cost Accountant is the direct outcome of the application of scientific thought to industry; he represents and stands for the scientific idea applied to business management.

The nineteenth century saw an amazing growth of the scientific idea and the substitution in almost all philosophic thought of the rules of logic—observation, experiment, analysis, induction and generalisation—for hearsay evidence and intuition. For one or two decades this attitude carried all before it, and it is not surprising that its application to business methods and organisation—the substitution of scientific ideas for rule of thumb—should have sprung to the front.

Adam Smith, in the late 18th century, in his great treatise on the "Wealth of Nations" was, I suppose, one of the first of distinguished philosophers and economists to draw attention to the extraordinary benefits to be derived from division and specialisation of labour. Once admit this idea, with its first effect of divorcing the industrialist from the agriculturist, and you have the key to the modern organisation of industry and commerce, and a pointer to the place of the Cost Accountant.

The introduction of machinery multiplied the industrial problems of an unprepared world. The manufacturer and the trader leaped into the market, and as any amount of margin existed between the cost of the old hand-made goods and the cost of the new machine-made, they cared little for intensive scientific method—whether of technical production, organisation or costing. In the scramble for profits, little attention was paid to the best way of doing things; labour was cheap; coal was cheap and margins comparatively high. "Get the production and the profits will come," was the creed. Businesses grew up, in a more or less unorganised form, without systematic criticism, or scientific organisation; not only without this, but pooh-poohing the whole idea, and looking upon planning and scientific costing (if they saw them at all) as unnecessary expense. And in the remote hills and valleys of Lancashire and Yorkshire, and I fear in parts of this great city, and other places as well, this feeling is not yet eradicated from the minds of many successful business men. The tradition still lives that the market is world-wide; given ample production, handsome profits are assured. But conditions have altered. The world markets are disorganised, competition, home and foreign, is rampant, production is reduced; profits are elusive, and a somewhat anxious business public is beginning to pull itself together and ask is all well with our business management. Whilst industry needs for its success stabilised markets and exchange, both of which largely depend upon politics, the skill and invention of the technical man, the force and imagination of the enterpriser, it no less needs in my opinion the searching insight, the quick imagination and the marshalling faculties, of the Cost Accountant. The qualities required in a Cost Accountant are other than those usually found in the ordinary business man.

Note how different "pasts" and different temperaments produce different conditions in America and England. In America, the Cost Accountant has come much more quickly into his own than with us, and for obvious reasons. America is the home of mass production. American industry started more from a green field, unhaunted by a past. It is the home of labour-saving devices; it takes naturally to mechanical records. It has been comparatively untrammelled by Trade Union regulation. Money-making is a clearer objective in itself than it is with us. The American takes a pleasure in making his money; the Englishman makes his money that he may enjoy it in other ways; if he can enjoy his garden and his golf, a little motoring, travel or perhaps hunting and shooting, he is content; he is more keenly interested in spending his money than getting it. In America, therefore, there is a ground not only favourable, but thirsting for Cost Accountants. There is a business public keenly alive to his use. He is one of the luminaries of the economic world.

In England, with a few brilliant exceptions, this is not so. England has been pre-eminently the land of *laissez-faire*. England worked out the transition from the small hand industries to the large machine and steam-power factories and workshops. Its people were, and are, comparatively uneducated, though of considerable native grit and shrewdness. Manufacturers, exploiting the great inventions, made immense fortunes in virgin markets by rule-of-thumb methods of management—before cost accountancy was dreamed of. Again, many of our industries are honeycombed and handicapped with the gild traditions belonging to another and a vanished state of society. To-day, the manufacturer and the trade unionist are both rubbing their eyes and cannot believe they are really in a new world. Many of them seem to think that to-morrow, or the day after, the old world conditions will come back to them. Hence, in conservative England, the need for a new profession of Cost Accountants is comparatively unrecognised by either side; the place of the Cost Accountant is either vacant or filled by a comparatively untrained and unenterprising clerk.

How, then, has the new profession come about?

By a process of evolution. As the modern specialised and departmentalised factory has been evolved from the old domestic industries, so the Cost Accountant has been evolved from the old undifferentiated confidential clerk. Going back some centuries to the era before the Industrial Revolution, you will find that the steward of the manor looked after both the legal and accounting affairs of the domain. Gradually, as business increased, separate professions grew up, first the legal, and long afterwards accountancy. Later accountancy became differentiated between the public accountant and the inside official.

As business still expanded into the huge affairs we find on every hand to-day, it became obvious that in many cases the inside official, the old type of cashier, was not equal to these things.

In large companies, it became not unusual for an accountant to be appointed and that accountant was sometimes a "Chartered" Accountant. Speaking as a Chartered Accountant, and one who naturally has a great respect for that profession, I may, perhaps, be allowed to say that unless the Chartered Accountant has had some special opportunities and possesses a combination of qualities considerably different from the usual he does not, for these inside positions, fill the whole of the bill. It became obvious that whilst he was an excellent man to draw up the balance sheet and superintend the finances, for much of the internal work the ordinary Chartered Accountant had not the right type of experience; and it required experience which, as an auditor, he would scarcely ever get. On the other hand, another official was discovered in the recesses of the works called a Cost Clerk. It was then seen that if this man could be given a better general education and a first-rate training in accounts he might become a Cost Accountant. Some favoured individuals got both—a training as a Chartered Accountant and an internal training in costing. The Cost Accountant's relation to a publicly practising Chartered Accountant is that of the specialist to the general practitioner, or perhaps more exactly, the first is allied to specialised *management*, the second, a specialist in pure *finance*. Hence, we have the new Institute of Cost Accountants and I may say unhesitatingly, that in my opinion there is ample room for both professions. The Cost Accountant needs more of the force, enterprise, and agility of the business man, whilst the Chartered Accountant's main characteristic, I believe, should be sober prudence.

I propose now to divide the following remarks under two main heads:—

I. THE COST ACCOUNTANT'S PLACE WITHIN A PARTICULAR FIRM; AND

II. THE CLASS OF INDUSTRY IN WHICH HE WILL BE MOST USEFUL.

I. The Place of a Cost Accountant within an Individual Firm

We cannot understand what should be the place of the Cost Accountant in a particular firm until we know, first, what subject-matter should form his work, and, second, what is the respective relationship to this subject-matter of the Cost Accountant and the other officials, and what is their relationship to one another. The field, the subject-matter, of a Cost Accountant's work is almost every problem of executive control. What do the Executive want to and what should they control? Whilst in the one-man business the controlling genius is in direct touch with every problem and drinks in his knowledge with every breath he draws, in a large concern these things are impossible. The management need to delegate authority and with it responsibility and must introduce some system for the supply of accurate information. In many cases, they need to substitute for a " jumble of unorganised observation " (to use the phrase of a Manchester professor) which leads nowhere, clear-cut, logical and precise thinking—both in the method of organisation and the systematic gathering of information.

What, then, are the main elements requiring this control? I think the following :—

(A) Character of the output.
(B) Labour.
(C) Raw material and its use.
(D) Power: its generation and use.
(E) Fixed expenses or oncost.
(F) Types of equipment.
(G) Stocks (raw material and finished products).
(H) Estimates and selling prices.
(I) Selling expenses.

Some one has recently said " Sound principles emerge from activities." Perhaps the science of costings " has not yet produced an adequate body of tested activity upon which to found theory and practice." But it is growing and already accumulating considerable experience.

The following outlines indicate the kind of help which cost accountancy can give.

(A) *Character of the Output*

By this I mean guiding the trend of business by the comparative profitability of the various products. By the old accounting method if the general profit and loss account showed a balance on the right side everyone was satisfied. This almost invariably concealed losses. It threw no light on the *relative* value of particular directions of work. The furthest it got was to some sort of departmental trading account. The executive of a modern firm must want to know, not only the balance result they have made, but *how* it has been made and where, if anywhere, are their losses. In this way only can they intelligently direct the character of their output. The Cost Accountant is the man who must indicate this.

(B) *Labour*

I am thinking now (and almost all through this paper) of large works. A properly organised administration will have a Labour Department of its own. The Cost Accountant must so arrange the figures of production, speeds of running, rates of pay, departmental or machine labour cost per hour, output per man, that the Labour Department may be in immediate possession of all vital information. He should constantly be associated with the Labour Department in questions of time study. In my opinion, he should countersign all modifications in rates of pay. He may or he may not have anything to say. If he has, he should be listened to respectfully. He should be the first person whom the head of the Labour Department takes into his confidence in discussing methods of remuneration.

(C) *Raw Material*

Here the Cost Accountant has much scope. This material may be divided into two kinds—the subject-matter of treatment (iron, steel, cotton, wool, etc.) or other material applied to it. Two things will trouble him here—fluctuations in the price of the staple commodity and the tracking of waste.

The problems affecting raw material are of a very different nature from those affecting manufacture, and, to my mind, should be carefully separated. If you mix the two, you get hopeless confusion. It should be possible to see whether profits or losses are due to fluctuations in the raw material market or to profits on the process of manufacturing. This, however, is a tricky problem and demands a lecture to itself.

The second point is the tracking of waste. Here again, great differences occur in different industries. In some industries, the waste is colossal and fortunes may be made out of it. The waste material may be sold or it may be put down the drain. It may be the use of *wrong* material or too much material; it may be due to pure carelessness or ignorance. It should be tracked to each department for investigation and action. Here is a whole field for inquiry in itself.

(D) *Power: its generation and use*

Coal is more than ever entitled to its metaphorical title of "black diamonds." Full costs of the generation of steam and its use by each department (or even machine) are required and, if possible, comparative costs between steam and electricity. Here he will encounter much technical detail, and will need the technical assistance of the engineer.

(E) *Fixed Expenses or Oncost*

Here the main things which will interest him are speeds of running, machine hour costs and the cost of idle time.

(F) *Types of Equipment*

Does it pay to perform a particular process by hand or by machine. Does it pay to put in a superior plant at a cost of £5,000 or a useable but inferior variety at £1,000? These are some of his daily questions. The prejudice or the instinct of the Works Manager is not enough.

(G) *Control of Stocks*

The management must keep a close watch on stocks of both raw and manufactured material in total and in detail. These figures are constantly required by the Cost Accountant and it should be his duty to point out excessive quantities and to certify the amounts for balance sheet purposes.

(H) *Estimates and Selling Prices*

Here again the nature of his work will differ with different trades. In trades such as the building trade or many branches of the engineering trade where contracts for jobs are made, he should be in close touch with the estimating department. Quantities should be made out by the technical staff, but the Cost Accountant should check all prices and overhead charges.

In trades where price lists are issued it should be his constant job to watch the margin between cost and list price. It may be essential that he should make elaborate arrangements constantly to do this. It is not his duty to fix a selling price, but he should constantly be consulted. In so far as price represents *cost* of service, he is the man; in so far as it represents *value* of service, the final word must be with the selling manager; similarly, if it is a monopoly or novelty price.

(I) *Selling Expenses*

Another subject which needs the light of day is distribution expenses—often ignored or treated in a slipshod fashion.

The expense of advertising needs careful treatment. A percentage method may in some cases be sufficient, but in others specific items may need to be treated separately.

In short, the Cost Accountant has two main facets to his duties—economy in production and the finding of a sound standard for the criticism of selling prices.

He will be the source of many ideas and must influence the attitude of mind of the management on many problems. This will be so subtle that many things will owe their origin to him which it will be impossible to set out in black and white, and for which he runs the risk, therefore, of never being paid. But he must not be discouraged; he must believe that he will reap if he faint not.

To all these questions he must bring the scientific habit of mind. He must look more clearly into the depths. He must pervade the atmosphere of the workers with his own. As some one has said recently of the scientist, "he must go in exploring; he will come out laden with the fruits of unexpected adventure." He must interpret the past and look into the future. He must not be hookwinked into any facile "yes" or "no," "black" or "white" answers to complex questions: he must weigh arguments from all sides and must not believe that there are only two replies to a question: the full affirmative or the full negative. The answer is generally not so simple as that. He must be ready to go whithersoever the argument leads.

In short, Cost Accountancy means in its highest achievements consummate mastery of the facts and a brilliant power of so co-ordinating them as to bring out new truths.

So much for his duties: what, now, should be the precise relationship between the Cost Accountant and the technical and other officials?

Very little rock-bottom thinking has been done with regard to this. In many firms he has been left to work out his own salvation—to sink or swim as he best could. The Englishman (and the director is no exception to the rule) has a secret horror of exact logical thought. Here he is markedly behind his brother American or West Continental European. He is (though he doesn't recognise it) insular and old fashioned, and he does not like to be forced to think out logical business arrangements, any more than he does the principles of constitutional government. He prefers to let things settle themselves. What should be the Cost Accountant's relation to :—

(A) The Directors or General Managers ;
(B) The Technical or Works Manager ;
(C) The Selling Manager ; and
(D) The Financial Accountant.

The great word here is firstly, secondly and thirdly—co-ordination.

Let us take them separately :—

(A) *Directors or General Managers*

What is the relation of them to him and him to them ? He must be, I think, always the direct agent of the Directors ; no one must come between them. Also, he must be in an absolutely central position, equally with the Secretary and the Financial Accountant. He must survey the *whole* of the activities of the concern from the cost and margin point of view, in detail and in total. All the figures must be arranged with a view to the bringing out of management points.

His position must be a confidential one. He must have the full confidence of the directorate and in turn he must be supported by the full weight of the Board. There must be *mutual* loyalty. *The Board* must make his position known to all whom it may concern. It must not be left to him to tell other people who he is and what he is. This must be done for him.

Second, the Directors must find time to apply their minds to his reports. A well-known text-book says : "Many failures are caused by lack of thorough analysis because those responsible are 'too busy' to investigate." In many cases, time would be more valuably spent systematically working through the Cost Accountant's systematic reports than in the discussion of the indiscriminate questions which so easily fill a Board agenda. The Directors must use the Cost Accountant and use him systematically.

Written reports should be encouraged ; they make for exactness and thoroughness in him who writes and him who reads. Terms and ideas should be thoroughly defined. Loose and unanalysed assumptions are the most prolific causes of misunderstanding. There should be a healthy mixture of written and spoken speech ; the principles and the assumptions should be written, the amplification and the detail may be dealt with by a process of discussion. The Cost Accountant should be specially severe in getting clear the fundamentals of policy and death on the facile, simultaneous holding of contradictory ideas.

(B) *The Technical Manager*

The Cost Accountant must work as a colleague of the technical manager. The position here is a delicate one. It must be made quite clear to the technical man that the Cost Accountant is the representative of the Directors.

If the technical man is sensible, he will take care that he works with the Cost Accountant as a colleague and a friend, and the Cost Accountant must show himself a kindly though firm critic. If there is any suspicion that the technical man is not putting all his cards on the table, or is simply watching the Cost Accountant slip into some trap, the technical man must be made by the Board to know that the Cost Accountant will stand no nonsense, and that affronting him or misleading him is equivalent to affronting and misleading the Board. The Cost Accountant has to take a wider survey, and from a more central point of view, than the technical man. He must know how the work of the technical man fits into the policy of the Board and the Selling Manager. Whilst the Cost Accountant will whole-heartedly assist the technical man, any stupidity or jealousy or idea that the technical man is a born financier or infallible business man must be nipped in the bud. The technical man must learn to distinguish between the duties of a technical *director* and a technical *manager*. The Cost Accountant is the servant of the first, but certainly not of the latter.

(E) *The Selling Manager*

The relationship with the Selling Manager is different again. He is by no means bound to take the Cost Accountant's advice, even if it is offered. His course of action and price policy is between himself and the Board. The Cost Accountant does not so much collect information from him as furnish him with information. Hence, the Selling Manager cannot "queer his pitch" as the technical manager can. Hence, also, as the scope for criticism is not so great as in the case of the technical manager, the likelihood of jealousy and resentment is less. The Cost Accountant cannot apply standards to the Selling Manager's actions—he can always plead market conditions—to the same extent he can to the Works Manager.

(D) *The Financial Accountant*

Here, again, in England so often we have the cart before the horse. The implications of the Cost Accountant's position have not been thought out. I knew an accountant who refused a remunerative position, practically as Cost Accountant, simply because he foresaw endless trouble and antagonism through the Cost Accountant being even nominally under the Financial Accountant. He argued that this was literally putting the cart before the horse, that is, putting a premium on arranging the books without knowing where they are going or what facts they are going to bring out.

The Cost Accountant is, in short, the servant of the Directors (if not, indeed, one of their number), *the equal colleague* of the technical producing and selling managers, but if the work is to be done without overlapping and the whole of the books are to be so arranged as to lead up to the vital cost and management figures, he must have the last say in that arrangement. Some firms have got over this difficulty by making the Cost Accountant the Financial Director and putting both sides under him. But note that it is the *Cost* Accountant, not the Financial Accountant, who is put in this position and that for a reason, namely, that every Cost Accountant must be an accountant, but not every accountant is a Cost Accountant.

There is much to be said for the American practice of putting both officials under another official called the Treasurer.

The promotion to a position as Treasurer should be along the same lines. This may sound revolutionary (it is however already done in some firms), but I am more convinced every day that we and the business public must not be afraid of the implications of our position, but must press for it to be carried to its logical conclusion. This may mean a lot of heart-breaking in very worthy quarters, but the point at stake is too serious for us to be frightened at sentimentality.

What is to be the measure of the Cost Accountant's authority? His authority as to system, record-taking, compilation of figures must be complete; as to the use of his figures he may need a stronger weapon than mild persuasion. It is the duty of *the Board* to let it be known to all whom it may concern that he will be fully supported. This is the Boards' job and not his. In the last resort, he may have to let this authority be felt: generally the mere fact that it is known that he possesses it will be enough. If the technical or selling managers know that the Directors are wobbling or weak-kneed in their support his position will rapidly become an impossible one.

If I am right in my belief that the essential object of modern bookkeeping is the management of the business, and the payment and collection of debts is a secondary, though necessary and important office, it goes without saying that a very proper procedure is to make the Cost Accountant the Financial Director. He would then be present at all Board Meetings: his advice should be constantly taken: no scheme involving finance should be embarked upon without his report (not the Financial Accountant's: whose functions simply relate to the payment and collection of debts and the drawing up of the final Profit and Loss Account and Balance Sheet): and he should have a full voice at the Board.

I said a few moments ago that the great word was co-ordination, and another example of it is in the fact that the duties of the Cost Accountant and the Works Accountant should centre in one person. By this I mean that those other accounting duties which have to do with stock control and internal planning and progress of work should come under the jurisdiction of the same individual: and this for a special reason.

The information required for both costing and progress purposes is to be found in the same production records, and the further fact that, if he is a true Cost Accountant, he is a master of method, make it natural that he should be closely allied with the organisation required for the progress department and that must necessarily be closely allied with planning. In most works there is much room for spade-work and further co-ordination here.

The Cost and Works Accountant is not the planner, but he should be responsible for the organisation and its co-ordination with the other clerical work of the Works.

We come now to

II. The class of Industry in which he will be most useful

This is a wide question, but it may be worth while to spend a few minutes upon it. The principles of Cost Accountancy apply to all trades, but there are not equal opportunities for a separate and specialised official in each or in every type of firm.

In what type of industry is there most a place for Cost Accountants?

We may say at once, negatively, that he will be least useful in purely merchanting businesses, particularly those of raw materials, the price of which fluctuate hourly on the great exchanges of the world, such as the Chicago wheat pit, the New York, New Orleans and Liverpool cotton exchanges, etc., and for two reasons: first, as a cost calculation, the matter is comparatively easy; second, what makes it difficult depends not upon any mathematical or organisation difficulty, but upon innumerable and intangible factors, the assessing of which is the main business of the merchant. Another noteworthy point is that in businesses in which these violently varying raw material prices are an important, though subordinate factor, they will create peculiar difficulties for the Cost Accountant.

His scope of usefulness will begin with the class of people who do something other than move matter to places of increasing utility; people who "get" the material out of the earth, grow it or bring other material and labour to bear on it, transforming it into almost another product.

There is scope for cost accountancy, though rarely for individual Cost Accountants in agriculture and farming of all types—crops, live stock, dairy produce. Costing would not determine the price—it rarely, if ever, does—but it would afford a check on the comparative productivity and profitability of land and kinds of produce.

But leaving this on one side, let us consider for a few moments the other main national industries.

They may be classified as follows:—

(A) Treatment of food-stuffs—flour milling, etc.

(B) The extractive trades—coal, iron, lime, salt, etc.

(C) The engineering trades—from iron and steel furnaces and foundries to machine tools, electrical equipment, motor cars, locomotives, rolling stock, etc.

(D) The chemical trades in all their branches.

(E) The building trades.

(F) The textile trades—whether cotton, wool, flax, silk or jute.

(G) The clothing trades—hats, gloves, boots, hosiery, etc.

(H) The pottery trades.

(I) The shipbuilding trades.

(J) The transport trades—railway, motor carrying, etc.

(K) The publishing and printing trades.

(L) Municipal and Government undertakings—gas, electricity, munition works, dockyards, etc.

In almost all of these there is scope for Cost Accountants.

For the moment I do not wish to distinguish too drastically between the principles of Cost Accountancy and the place for a Cost Accountant, because, though a business might not be large enough to employ the whole time of a fully qualified Cost Accountant, the principles of Cost Accountancy might be used either (*a*) through some other official or (*b*) by employing a consultant. I shall therefore, for the moment, use the words Cost Accountancy and Cost Accountants as interchangeable terms; with the assumption that a separate official will only be employed by the larger firms.

Let us see if we can find any principle which can guide us as to the probable comparative usefulness of cost accountants in different trades. I think we can say that a Cost Accountant will be found useful in direct relation to the increasing complexity of a business.

I know some people believe that the converse is true and that, for instance, whilst costing may very easily, and therefore usefully, be applied to, say, the manufacture of cotton thread, it is not easy, and therefore not useful, to apply it to the textile finishing trades. Here their logic is unsound. Some of these statements are true; their reasoning is a *non sequitur*.

Let us for a moment test this complexity question by reference to a few of the great industries.

Take coal-mining. Suppose you have a colliery which disposes of the whole of its coal at the pit-mouth. Here the problem is simple. The "get" or "output" book with a very rough classification of types of coal, the ground and under-ground wages, royalties, power and other expenses may readily be converted into a cost per ton. If the coal is similar in character this may be sufficient. But in all probability it will not be. If it is not, it will probably vary in cost, partially in accordance with the difficulty of the " get " and partially by reason of sorting operations on the surface. The most costly will probably bring the highest price, but if we are to see the comparative margin on different classes of coal, careful cost accounting, *i.e.*, separation of expenses and products must be provided for.

If we are content with the old method of what we lose on the roundabouts being made up on the swings, all is well. But we may not be.

Take it a stage further and assume that the whole of the coal is not disposed of in its natural state at the pit-mouth, but is subjected to varying processes of distillation, producing coal-tar and the innumerable products of the gas retort and the coke oven, what kind of problem have you for the Cost Accountant here? One of great difficulty it is true, but along with the difficulty grows the necessity.

Take again the production of aniline dyes—often the apex of a whole series of products, some of which are sold off as finished products in themselves. The complexity is multiplied a hundredfold; so is the necessity of accurate costing. The whole of the chemical industry is in the same condition.

In the other extractive industries, a like sequence and growth in the importance and necessity of costing takes place.

Engineering is the classical example of a trade crying out for Cost Accountants, and necessity creating the supply. You have complicated processes; much repetition work in some processes, much individual job work in others, and you have in the Engineer a man who is already used to mathematical problems. It is only natural that Cost Accountancy should have come to its full fruit in this industry. What is extraordinary is that from many text-books you would imagine that engineering is the only trade which had any dealings with Cost Accountancy at all.

The pottery trade is another branch, in which there is much scope and in which I believe progress towards standardisation has been achieved.

Take now the large group of Textile trades. Spinning and Weaving (though I am personally of opinion that much room exists for more refined costing) are by reason of the highly specialised machinery and frequently limited ranges of counts or cloth undertaken by a particular mill or shed, comparatively simple trades, with comparatively little scope for the specialised cost accountant, though costing systems, of a sort, have existed for years. But the finishing trades, whether bleaching, or particularly dyeing or printing, are capable of great variations in methods of manufacture and type of product; there again the scope grows enormously.

Building contractors have for long enough had fairly specialised accounts, but there is further scope for a Cost Accountant with all large firms. Some of F. W. Taylor's historic time-study work was done on brick-laying.

Shipbuilding is another industry in which costing and the Cost Accountant is most important.

The gas undertakings of municipal corporations have been early in the field with fairly well-developed and articulated accounts. Printed unit cost comparisons between various local authorities have been compiled for years. Electricity works are following suit.

In many government undertakings, a similar possibility exists—particularly in dockyards, munition works, etc.

Summing up therefore this division of the paper, one might say that there is almost unlimited scope for the application of the principles of Cost Accountancy in almost every branch of business; there is least in a purely merchanting business, where ***market*** rather than *cost* values are almost everything, and simply distribution expenses with no manufacturing, and *most* in the most complicated businesses with a series of manufacturing processes, distribution expenses and some relation between cost and price. In small concerns, the principles of Cost Accountancy should be applied on the advice of a consultant whilst every large manufacturing concern should have its own specially qualified Cost Accountant.

In fact, one might go so far as to say that the introduction into business of a qualified Cost Accountant is one of the first and most important steps in setting industry on a sound basis. Cost Accountancy is the symbol of careful, exact and systematic thought applied to business affairs. One of its objects is to bring down dizzy and imaginary schemes to solid earth.

One word in closing about the education and training necessary for these things. Some business men think they know enough about accountancy: they have trained themselves. "Self-made men?" says Oliver Wendell Holmes—"Why, yes. Everybody likes and respects self-made men. It is a great deal better to be made in that way than not at all. Your self-made man, whittled into shape by his own jack-knife, deserves more credit, if that is all, than the regular engine-turned article, shaped in the most approved pattern, and French-polished by society and travel." "But," says he, "as to saying one is every way the equal of the other, that is another matter." And there may be home-made accountants and professional accountants. We here expect the "engine-turned" article produced by the Institute.

Whilst there is a special training which is fairly obvious and which the examinations of the Institute provide for, there is another which lies below it, namely, first, a liberal general education, and, second, that general training in experience of life which develops personality. Truth is many-sided; whilst in America personality (except in a few) seems weak and system strong, in Great Britain system is weak and personality strong. With us, thoroughly-organised system, which is typical of all that Cost Accountancy stands for, is the neglected part of the truth; in America, it is the free play of personality.

But here one must put in a "caveat" by saying we must be careful in putting in all these systems that we do not rely *too much* upon mere form. There is meaning in the phrase "*reduced*" to system. Something has escaped. There is something greater in life than system and that is life itself, with all its power of intuition, imagination and innate force. The subconscious is almost always greater than the conscious, and this is where superficial judges so often go wrong.

We want to attract therefore men of a high mentality capable of taking the further polish of the specialised examination subjects.

We want men who are really *men*—well-educated, highly-trained, and with a considerable knowledge of life. Above all things else, the Cost Accountant needs the corrective of a broad humanism. He must correct his view of the mere figures by a continual visualising of the men of flesh and blood beneath. Figures are good servants, but bad masters. He must beware of imagining that he lives in a mathematical world which can be ruled by a mathematical formula.

Someone reminded us the other day in *The Engineer* that Nasmyth, of steam-hammer fame, defined engineering as "common sense applied to material;" so also one could say that cost accountancy is "common sense applied to figures."

We want men of force and character, of imagination and tact. For the highest positions we must have cultivated men of wide reading and knowledge of affairs.

If we are to attract the right type of men to this profession, two things must be done. First, we must point to and get the business public to realise its possibilities, which, for suitable men are, I think, as follows:—

(A) Positions as Cost Accountant in large manufacturing concerns.

(B) Positions as Treasurer of large Companies.

(C) Positions as Financial Directors of large concerns.

(D) Practising Consultants and

(E) Appointments by Trade Federations.

Second, the remuneration must be worthy of the men and their work. They must not be looked upon as mere unproductive staff. They should be paid a large salary and (contrary to the Financial Accountant) a handsome commission on profits. The Financial Accountant's remuneration should be by salary only—first, because he cannot to any material extent influence profits and, second, because in the matter of reserves, etc., he should be entirely uninfluenced by personal considerations. On the other hand, the Cost Accountant's remuneration should be partly by salary and partly by commission on profits; because, in his case, he can influence profits and, second, this mode of payment cannot influence him in any way to the disadvantage of his concern.

(Report of a Lecture delivered before the members of the London and District Branch, on 5th January, 1923.)

THE INSTITUTE OF COST AND WORKS ACCOUNTANTS, LTD.

SECOND ANNUAL COSTING CONFERENCE

Held at the Connaught Rooms, Great Queen Street, W.C.2, on FRIDAY, MARCH 9th, 1923

REPORT OF PROCEEDINGS

MORNING SESSION

SIR HERBERT AUSTIN, K.B.E., M.P., IN THE CHAIR

"STANDARDISATION IN COST ACCOUNTANCY"

The CHAIRMAN: Ladies and Gentlemen, the paper to be read, is a paper worthy of very careful study. At the same time the Institute is relying on the discussion that will follow the paper to naturally add considerable value to the proceedings to-day. Later on in the afternoon a further discussion will take place, and it is hoped that all those Members of the Institute who are present and who consider that they can throw light on the subject that is before the Conference at this Meeting will get up and give the other Members the benefit of their knowledge and experience.

The subject of STANDARDISATION IN COST ACCOUNTANCY is not being put forward by the Institute as something that is quite novel or that has never been attempted before and that has to be looked on with any dread or any kind of fear. It is not new. It has been discussed in the past on many occasions, and it is already in successful operation in at least one of our big trades, the Printing Trade; and from their efforts and from the work that they have done, there is no question that standardisation in a trade is of very great value. I believe the Leather Trade and the Boot Trade have also done a certain amount in that direction; the Cycling and Motor Cycling have done a little; but still there are a very large number of trades in this country to-day where standardisation in their costs would be of very great value, not only to the people directly concerned, but to all those who have business relationship with them.

I need not remind any of you of the great variation there is in the words which we use in describing prime cost. One often calls over expense "overcharges" or at least possibly twenty other names. And standardisation even in the names which we give to our various items of cost, would be a great advantage in itself. There is always a fear in this country—I do not know why—but as a nation we seem to have a great fear of standardisation. I suppose standardisation generally speaking has met with a less cordial reception and has not made the progress in this country comparatively which it has in many other countries, owing to this kind of fear on our part that we might be losing a little of our individuality. Everyone tries to wrap up his own business in his own mind. He fears that if he lets go some knowledge that he has, if he works on the same lines as his fellows, he will be put in a less advantageous position from the point of view of competition. One sees that every day in business life. But while a standardisation of one's cost, standardisation of one's operations, might put one into definite and perhaps very close competition, it would certainly, I am sure, you will agree, be better to know where you are and to be working on a narrow margin than to imagine you were somewhere and perhaps working at a very considerable loss. That is what we want to establish as an Institute. We do not wish to suggest that because our Members, and the businesses and industries to which they belong, adopt the same method of taking out their costs as their competitors, that they are necessarily bound by that fact to any Body in this country to charge more than they consider is necessary under the circumstances; but at any rate, it is good for themselves and good for everybody else that they should know where they are; and it is from that point of view, and that point of view only, that the Institute to-day is discussing the question of standardisation in cost accountancy. In the discussions which take place this morning and this afternoon, I would like to ask the Members to take notice of that particular fact: that we are dealing with the subject of Standardisation in Cost Accountancy as a principle: and while all principles naturally are subject and capable of being discussed in detail, still at the same time I think the discussion ought to take in view the broad lines of standardisation as its theme. By that means, I think we shall be able to arrive at a result that will be beneficial to the Members and to the Institute as a Body.

Ladies and Gentlemen, I do not propose to say anything further at the moment, but I will ask Mr. H. G. Jenkins to read the Paper on "Standardisation in Cost Accountancy," and after the Paper is read, there are two or three Members who wish to open the discussion, and then if we have time, I will ask other Members to join in. (Applause.)

Mr. H. G. JENKINS, F.C.W.A., then read the paper :—

"STANDARDISATION IN COST ACCOUNTANCY"

An appreciation of the benefits which accrue to the individual industrial concern, be it mine, factory, distributing organisation, or public utility service, leads directors to the idea that, if all the other concerns in their own particular branch of industry could be persuaded to adopt the same system of cost accounting, it would create a situation which would be full of advantages. Indeed, there are those who go further, and who envisage the adoption of standardised systems for all industries just in the same way that an orthodox form has been agreed upon for the presentation of financial accounts.

At first sight it would appear relatively easy to introduce such uniformity, and the advantages which would accrue require but little imagination to perceive. Your Council therefore feel that in this important matter they would be performing a service to the community by taking this opportunity of giving a brief survey of the possibility of standardisation in cost accountancy, its advantages, and its difficulties.

It will be generally agreed that one of the principal advantages of an effective costing system lies in the provision of a means of measurement of actual performance against agreed standards; thus the manufacturer is able to compare the cost of one batch of products, against his estimate, or against another batch produced later, and under different conditions, or is enabled to compare the cost of one process, against the cost of another one, involving perhaps greater capital outlay for the production of the same article; he is enabled to set a measure of profit to be earned by each section of his factory, and to compare the actual results with the standard which he has laid down.

It is this function of cost accountancy which possibly makes the idea of standardised systems for one branch of industry so attractive. It would be extremely helpful for manufacturers at the conferences of their trade associations to be able to think and speak in exactly the same terms when dealing with the cost of production; a standard could be set up for the industry, and the factory manager who is unable to achieve such standard of performance could be shown exactly in what direction economies could be effected. It would be of very great value indeed in times of trade depression to make use of cost figures for the purpose of agreeing upon price reductions without resorting to cut-throat policies. Price reductions based upon accurate costs would naturally show each manufacturer exactly what problems he had to face, and to what extent it would be necessary for him to finance his business.

A further advantage of standardisation of costing lies undoubtedly in the advantage which would accrue to industry in collective bargaining with labour. Labour is taking an increasing interest in all questions of cost, and often to-day we find that in their negotiations with individual employers, delegates bring forward examples of cost at competitive firms. This is a very dangerous situation, because, unless labour is made acquainted with the true cost of a product, it is quite obvious that very erroneous conclusions may be drawn, due to the variations in expense apportionment, and also to the amount of direct labour involved; take, for example, two firms, one of which on a large output employs expensive automatic or semi-automatic machinery; the other, with a relatively small output producing the articles with considerably more hand labour.

Appreciating then these obvious advantages which the standardisation of cost accountancy by industries would appear to offer, the difficulties only become apparent when attempt naturally follows to put them into practice. Let it be stated at the outset that the standardisation of cost accounts, and of their form for all industries is not practicable, if for no other reason than the divergence of the nature of the products of industry. Thus, we may distinguish between industries which produce in bulk, industries which produce in detail, and industries the measure of whose output is the service rendered. Obviously, the basis of the cost accounts for these three types of industry are so divergent, and require such different treatment for the examination of results, that uniformity becomes a matter of supreme difficulty.

Dealing then with the minor groups of industry we again encounter technical difficulties in the presentation of uniform accounts, and possibly the principal cause for this lies in the differing natures of the raw materials of each firm's saleable products. Possibly one of the best examples which may be cited is that of the copper industry. In this industry there are factories whose raw material is the ore, in others the ingot, in others again, the first rolling from the ingot, while another group will use large diameter rod, or heavy sheet, working this up into their saleable products. Others again, such as electric cable makers, carry out a number of the processes of copper wire drawing, and apply to them other raw material such as bitumen, india-rubber, cotton, paper and the like, producing a finished article in which are combined not only the processes inherent to the copper trade itself, but others which are allied to the processes employed in totally different industries. Again, in the waterproof garment trade, one factory will work up material which is already dyed and proofed, others will carry out their own dyeing, sending the work out to be proofed, subsequently working it up, alternatively carrying out the dyeing and proofing themselves. Others again, will carry out the making and sewing in their own factory, while the practice of others is to contract with home workers for a considerable amount of their work.

Other factors which vary with different concerns in the same trade include methods of finance, of distribution, and of production, but as will be shown later in the paper, such difficulties are not insuperable, and by agreeing upon certain standards of principle, a measure of uniformity is achievable.

We have to acknowledge that a great deal of work has been done already in certain industries towards agreement upon standard methods of costing. In the Printing Trade the costing system of the Master Printers' Federation is no doubt well known to all members of the Institute, and it is asserted that considerable benefits have already accrued to the industry, although it is admitted that all the members of the Federation are not following in exactitude the lines of procedure laid down in the scheme.

In the Tube Trade, and the Hearth Furniture Trade, and in certain of the chemical industries, a measure of agreement has been arrived at with satisfactory results. In the Electricity Supply Industry the insistence of the Board of Trade upon the publication of accounts in a standardised form has led to uniformity in costing, a process which is interesting as not having been initiated by those in the industry itself.

Encouraged by the success in the Industries enumerated above, other trade associations will doubtless be able to overcome the difficulties inherent to such questions as to what constitutes raw material, and of segregating the costs of the product at different stages of its manufacture, but a further difficulty lies in their path if attempts are made to introduce standardised systems. A system with its blank forms, its analysis sheets, and its statistical returns, is merely a mechanical reminder. It is the mechanism of a procedure which has been agreed upon by the individuals concerned, who have decided that the presentation of certain results is essential to the good conduct of their business. The mechanism by means of which these results are obtainable is a matter of minor importance, a matter of detail which may be well left to each individual to devise according to his own particular local circumstances. To illustrate the difficulty of standardising a system it is only necessary to consider the simple case of time recording. In a very small factory a time note, giving the details of all the work performed during the week, which time note is signed, or even in some cases made out by the foreman, may be perfectly satisfactory, both for the compilation of a pay-roll, and a calculation of job costs, if the foreman be in close enough contact with his men, to ensure the accuracy of these returns. But in a factory employing 1,000 men it becomes necessary not only to have separate cards on which a man records his presence in the factory, which cards are used for the compilation of the pay-roll, but it is also necessary to have job cards for each individual operation, and these may be made out by a time clerk, by the man himself, or may be recorded on a time recording clock, or by means of other mechanism. It is a matter of indifference how this work is carried out so long as the results desirable in accordance with principles are obtained. Due to the nature of the process great differences in system may occur in two factories producing the same article. Thus, we may have inside one factory, bulk or process costing for intermediate products, and operation or detail costing for the final saleable products which are made up of different intermediate products.

Another factory producing only a few of the range of products of the first, may, on the other hand, carry bulk or process costing through to the completion of the finished product. Indeed, it is just at this point where it appears very necessary to come to some agreement in regard to the definition of the principal terms used in cost accountancy.

A cost must always be complete in itself, and may be defined as the sum of all expenses incurred in the making of a saleable product up to the point at which the cost is taken. It therefore must include the cost of all material which appears in the finished product, and which is, therefore, chargeable directly to the cost of that product (being measureable) as well as the cost of possibly some material which, while being directly chargeable to the finished product (that is to say, measureable), may not appear therein, having only been used incidentally to the manufacture. Both of these classes of material may be defined as "direct material." It would also include a certain amount of expense incurred by the use of material purchased and used in the maintenance of the factory in which the work was done, and which, therefore, if more than one product be handled in that factory, can only be apportioned according to some logical method. Such material can be defined as "indirect material." Labour, applied to the saleable products, which bears a measureable ratio in terms of time or cash to the weight or quantity of output, may be defined as "direct labour," and therefore can be charged directly to the cost, whereas "indirect labour" may be defined as such Labour as bears no directly measureable ratio to the weight or quantity of specific products, and which then, again, can only be apportioned according to some logical method. The cost will also include a proportion of those expenses of the factory which do not fall under any of these categories, and which, again, must be apportioned according to logical methods.

Your Council have before them the desirability of standardising the nomenclature of cost accountancy, and while they are not in a position to present a report upon the subject at this date, they desire to take this opportunity of protesting against the use of the terms "productive" and "non-productive" labour, for according to the definition of cost given above all labour in the factory is, or ought to be, included in the total cost of production. In fact, the use of the words "productive and "non-productive" have led to erroneous conceptions of cost and, let it be said in passing, mistaken ideas as to what constitutes good management.

The calculation of the true cost of production, which is a final quantity, appears to be possible by the adoption of standardised principles, but it is obvious that in the obtaining of these results the systems employed need not, and indeed cannot be uniform in the majority of industries.

Having shown the basic differences which make uniformity of costing difficult even in one trade or branch of industry, and having shown the relative unimportance of the standardisation of systems, it remains to show that there are certain principles of good cost accountancy which, if adopted, will enable any group to agree upon a standardised method of presenting their results once they have agreed upon certain fundamentals. These fundamentals should include :—

(A) The definition of what are to be considered "raw materials" of each branch of the trade, and the method to be employed in segregating the costs, so that comparable figures are available for the man who purchases the raw material for certain processes, and for the man who manufactures these intermediate products in his own factory.

(B) The basis or unit for the purpose of comparing cost accounts ; thus the unit may be the actual product in the case of articles which are sold as separate units, the square box as in the biscuit trade, the ton as in the sulphuric acid, and coal industries, the gross as in certain metal trades, the kilowatt hour as in Electricity supply, the therm as in Gas supply, and the ton-mile as in the transport trade. Other units for the purpose of comparison will suggest themselves to particular trades.

(C) The extent to which the financing of the trade is to enter into the costs accounts.

(D) The separation of distribution from manufacturing expense.

Having agreed upon these fundamentals, the authors of this paper have formulated the following principles which will, if adopted, enable industries to go a very long way towards the standardisation of cost accountancy to meet their own particular needs, and should, in the majority of trades achieve their object irrespective of the systems applied. These Principles are :—

1. That cost accounting must be based

upon actual returns, namely, labour costs, material costs, and establishment costs.

2. That there are three fundamental cost accounts for all industries, viz., wages control account, material control account, and establishment charges control account.

3. That being based on actual expenditure, and results being given in terms of cash, the cost accounts must link up with and balance the financial accounts.

4. That cost accountancy distinguishes between factory cost, selling expense, and general administrative expense, and that each of these should be complete in itself, and should be controlled separately to enable the directorate to observe the incidence of profit or loss.

5. That in all industries distinction can be drawn between the standing charges, and running charges. That for all industries the former can be divided into rent expense, administrative or management expense, and fixed charges ; that all the latter will be included in some, if not all, of the following :—

Repairs and maintenance expense, indirect labour, power expense, factory supplies, inter-departmental service expense, and material expense.

The sub-division of these accounts may be different for each industry, with minor sub-divisions for each trade.

6. That cost accountancy distinguishes between detail or product costing, and bulk or process costing.

7. That in introducing cost accounting the successive steps should be :—

(A) Simple recording of time and material.

(B) The calculation of establishment expenses and their control.

(C) The apportionment of expense and its control.

(D) The linking up with financial accounts.

These constitute the major principles. There remain certain minor principles where divergence of practice is possible, and these are as follows :—

1. That work chargeable to plant extensions, or to any of its sub-divisions, should bear its properly calculated share of expense, in that the Capital Account purchases through the Cost Accounts from the factory, and that unless expense be so charged, the factory products suffer in regard to enhanced cost of production to the advantage of the capital assets.

2. That interest on Capital to be expended must always be considered when estimating the cost of new processes or products, but that in the actual cost accounts no interest on capital invested should be included.

3. That the factory when not working to full capacity should only be debited with that portion of the standing expense charges which correspond to the volume of its activity, and that the balance should be shown as a separate debit item, namely the cost of idle time, in order to retain a sound basis for continuous comparison of factory efficiency, and to indicate to directors the loss due to lack of volume of work, which loss must be recovered by increase of sales or in the margin of profit on sales.

This Paper, while laying down certain fundamentals, is intended to serve as a basis of discussion at this Conference. It is quite realised that the subject introduced is far too great to be adequately dealt with even in several volumes, but it is hoped, that accepting what has been definitely laid down, both cost accountants and employers will, in discussion, augment the many points dealt with in this purely superficial manner. One great need of industry in this country at the present time, is the introduction of cost accountancy, not by amateurs, but by properly qualified men, who, with the encouragement and assistance of all those engaged in the industry, will be able to produce results which will enable the directorate to control their businesses scientifically, and efficiently, and thus produce commodities on the most economical basis. This should undoubtedly build up the trade of the country, and tend to eliminate those periods of depression and unemployment, from one of which we are just emerging at the present time. There has been so much amateur work in the past by persons, who, though they are well disposed, do not recognise their ignorance of the principles of cost accountancy, that the introduction of a costing system instead of proving beneficial to a business, has resulted simply in more waste.

It is undoubtedly important that employers as a body should give the costing problem their serious consideration. It may be that they will realise then that the collective employment of a qualified cost accountant for one industry is a necessity; his work would consist, firstly, in explaining and in accomplishing the acceptance of the principles of good cost accountancy; secondly, in advice on systems to give the desired reliable results; and finally, in the preparation of the procedure for the presentation of complete and comparable costs.

ARE COSTS THE BEST BASIS FOR ESTIMATING AND FIXING SELLING PRICES ?

(Two papers read at a Meeting of Members of the Manchester and District Branch of the Institute of Cost and Works Accountants on 20th February, 1923.)

Paper by S. L. Gill, F.C.W.A., A.C.A.

ONE would almost suspect, if one did not know, that this question had come from some branch of the Engineering trade. It could scarcely come from the Raw Produce market, nor from any branch of the Retail trade. The first appears to have little connection with cost, the latter every connection. And to those connected with it, it is, I think, notorious that this question could not come from the Textile trade.

The degree to which costs or costings are a basis for estimating or fixing prices cannot really be seen until we have answered several preliminary questions.

I propose to deal with the question, therefore, under the following heads :—

1. The relation between price and value ;

2. The theoretical economic idea of price ;

3. The actual course of prices in two or three leading industries ; and,

4. An inquiry as to the assistance which scientific costing can give, in its limited sphere, in estimating, fixing or judging the adequacy of a price in particular trades.

1. THE RELATION BETWEEN PRICE AND VALUE

This problem—What is price ? which is a smaller part of the question What is value ? —is indeed a very deep one, and one which we can dream about by the sea-shore on a long summer's day. I do not know whether it is necessary to remind students of to-day of Ruskin's great book " Unto This Last," which deals with this question. It is still worth reading ; the " Cornhill " Magazine refused to continue publishing it, but it marked a turning point in economics. When you ask " What is price ? " you are almost at once brought to a stand by the question " What is value ? " and that in turn tends to " What is wealth ? " and until you determine what wealth is, you have a poor chance to determine what price is, and so, of its connection with Costs. The world is set round with all kinds of values—real and artificial.

In other words, in the realms of philosophy and ethics, with which I suppose we are not intended to deal in these lectures, but which underlie all our problems, the problem of value assumes a different type to what it assumes in economics and business. As, I believe, Lord Morley points out somewhere, " our standard of value changes as life goes on, and we find later much that we counted as trash is pure gold, and much that we thought pure gold is trash." But these fundamental values we must pass by. We are concerned with more ordinary things.

But, in passing, what makes a precious gem valuable ? Its cost of production, or its desirability ? Gainsborough's " The Blue Boy " was sold to America for how much ? £150,000. Was this price based on cost or something else ? Milton received £10 for " Paradise Lost," and his widow another £8. Was this cost price ?—or utility price ?

2. THE THEORETICAL " ECONOMIC " IDEA OF PRICE

Economics talks learnedly of how prices are fixed, and, discarding the accidental fluctuations, strips the process to fundamentals.

" Value " is the first term to be dealt with. This is generally assumed to have two phases— (a) Utility Value, and (b) Cost Value.

Value in the sense of price is not determined until an act of exchange takes place. You may have a quotation, but it does not technically become a price until you have a buyer. A piece of land may have great value, but no price until a bid is made for it or a price put on it by the owner and accepted. The value is latent.

Price is the expression of the money which passes at the point of exchange. This point is determined by some kind of combination of the " x " and " y " which represent respectively utility value and cost.

How does this point come to be fixed ?

The economics text-books will tell us that price is fixed by the law of supply and demand, or more exactly, effective supply and effective demand. What, then, does this mean? What is included in each?

(A) Effective supply:—

1. Quantity or scarcity of commodity.
2. Quality.
3. Transport.
4. Cost of Production.

(B) Effective demand:—

1. Strength of desire for a particular thing.
2. Degrees to which substitutes may be obtained.
3. Quantity of raw produce or manufactured goods available for exchange.

These are all acted upon from every side by international conditions—economic, financial and political—and particularly subject to tariffs and to the course of foreign exchange.

The answer, then, that price is the money for which a thing is bought and sold does not carry us very far. When we ask what that money represents and how that particular amount of money is arrived at, we are in another kingdom. The law of Supply and Demand requires to be interpreted. One can easily ask questions which show the intricacy of this statement. For instance, what is "Supply" of a particular commodity? How near in likeness does an article need to be to be counted as further Supply of the same commodity? To us in England, is "Supply" of a particular product, say cotton, in India or in Nigeria or in the United States, equally important? To what extent do they react on one another? Suppose a large supply of a particular product exists in a particular place, known to the particular inhabitants, but unknown in the place where it is wanted, is this effective supply within the meaning of the term? Again, when we say "Demand"—there is a demand in Russia and parts of Germany at the present moment for great quantities of the necessaries of life; does this demand operate in the Law or not? There is a demand in the sense of a desire by many ladies for silk, and yet they cannot wear it. Why? There is a demand for houses; to what extent is this demand operative (a) on prices, (b) in producing houses? In other words, this Law of Supply and Demand, which sounds so simple, is hedged round by innumerable complications which, whilst they do not render it inoperative, at any rate render its operation most difficult to follow.

Accepting, then, the material value-standards of our times, to what extent in actual business practice may Prices be estimated and fixed on Costs? Speaking very broadly, the general level of Price over a long period and a wide area *must* be fixed by Cost of Production. For a limited time these prices will vary over or below the cost line by the variations in strength of effective demand (which means real demand modified by financial and economic conditions) and by what is known as the "higgling" of the Market. Prof. Marshall says: "As a general rule, the shorter the period which we are considering the greater must be the share of our attention which is given to the influence of demand on value; and the larger the period, the more important will be the influence of cost of production on value." In the great Raw Produce markets, immediate connection between Costs and Price fluctuations, whilst assuredly there, is not very easy to see. Price (say of cotton) seems to be fixed on a basis of estimated average Costs over a wide area, modified by the amount of world Stocks, estimates of the future crops, probable weather, and international demand for consumption. In the Cotton trade, the supply has to be gauged, the probable effects of the ravages of the Boll Weevil, the climatic conditions in the various Southern States of America, the stocks held in the great cotton markets of New Orleans, New York, Liverpool, Le Havre, etc., the Rates of Exchange between America and Europe, the Cost of Freight and Insurance. This is one side of the picture. The next side, the Demand side, depends upon the world demand for cotton cloth. This, in turn, say in Europe, depends on fashion and changes in ladies' dress; in India, on political conditions, and the crops with which the Indian can pay for his cloth. Similar conditions apply elsewhere. It will be seen, therefore, that for the base product of the cotton Textile trade, costs can *not* be the *only* basis of estimating or fixing Prices; and this base will affect the finishing trades also. If they cannot be this, what can they be?

Another important point we shall learn from economics is that the markets of the world may be divided between highly organised markets such as the wheat or cotton market, partially organised markets such as in the yarn trade, and unorganised markets such as in many branches of the chemical and engineering trades. Price is regulated differently in each of these market types.

Another point to remember about price is that many commodities are now the subject of price-rings, which may prevent or modify the ordinary action of the law of supply and demand. There may be also a monopoly price, applying to one firm due to its ability to create a particular article, such as artificial silk; whilst a ring acts almost as a monopolist owner. In both these cases, price bears little relation to individual costs.

Then there is the great question of the effect of speculation—informed speculation and mere gambling,—panic, and the money market.

So much, then, for the theoretical side of the question.

3. The Actual Course of Prices in Two or Three Great Industries

The Lecturer illustrated this point by several Charts showing the course of prices in the Salt Trade, the Coal Trade, and the Cotton Trade.

With regard to the Salt Trade, he pointed out how the price of salt had fallen before the formation of the Salt Union in 1888 to a level which was much below the cost of production. This price rose again not owing to increased costs, and fell again owing to other causes.

In the Coal Trade, it was pointed out that prices rose during the war, firstly, owing to scarcity and increased demand, and, later, wages rose. He pointed out that as an historical fact prices generally rise first, and wages lag behind. In other words, it is not increased cost of production which causes the first rise in prices, but comparative scarcity and increased demand.

With regard to the Cotton Trade, he also pointed out the influence of crop conditions and quantities, and showed a Chart showing the extraordinary rise in Egyptian Cotton to its highest peak in February 1920.

4. An Inquiry as to the Assistance which Scientific Costing can give, in its Limited Sphere, in Estimating, Fixing or Judging the Adequacy of a Selling Price

The staple Manchester Trade is of course that of cotton in all its branches.

The general prevailing idea in this trade is that price is fixed by the demands of the market, and many Manchester men will profess to tell you what a market can afford to pay. The art of bargaining depends upon guessing how much the other man knows. I believe these people to be very largely wrong, and the reason they are wrong is that they take what may be termed the short view rather than the long view. They forget two things :—

1. That the general level of price for a particular article has been fixed over a long period by costs, and,

2. That costs guide them against accepting a price which would result in bankruptcy.

In other words, if you will look deep enough there is a very direct relationship between cost and price. If, then, costs of production are not the sole basis for estimating and fixing selling prices, of what advantage are costings in this connection ?

A proper costing system, showing the cost of individual articles, will show where the best margins are being obtained, and will throw up those cases, if any, where an adverse margin results. They will show that an average price for a number of somewhat similar articles may be sufficient to cover some of them and not to cover others.

In others words, they may lead to a differentiation in the Price List. They point the way to enlightened discrimination between those things which pay and those things which do not pay; it is then up to the Salesman to see whether the price for these things which do not pay can be increased to a sufficient figure ; he will then be able to judge whether selling price can be fixed on cost or not. In many cases, he will find that it cannot be. This is due partly to the ingrained ideas of many foreign customers who cannot be persuaded to give more than a certain price for a particular article. The point comes when a tussle will take place between the salesman and buyer, and it will depend whether the salesman wants the contract more than the buyer wants the goods : or it may be necessary to discontinue that type of work entirely, unless it is simply used as " bait."

Having limited the field in which cost can possibly affect the fixing of price, and understanding these limitations, let us now look at the other side of the picture, and assuming that you have a market in which cost of production is the essential factor in fixing price, let us turn the question another way and ask, Are costings (*i.e.* the " figures indicating the cost ") of use in estimating, fixing or judging a Selling Price? I think the reply to this question is undoubtedly in the affirmative. Speaking in a broad sense, I think cost of production should more frequently fix commodity price, and if this is to be so, scientific accounting based on a scientific classification of commodities with the finest records of direct and indirect expenses, is the best way of determining what this price should be. In other words, this presupposes what are commonly known as Job costs. Job costs may in certain industries represent exactly what the name states, and in every industry in which very much individualistic work takes place, such as building construction and the construction of bridges or large machines, the Job Costs records are essential. In some branches of the Engineering Trade it is quite common in estimating selling prices, where no market price is in existence and a quotation to a specification is to be made, to estimate material and labour required, to add a percentage for fixed charges and profit, and to make a price accordingly. In these cases the Job Costs are not only the best means, they are practically the only means, of fixing a rational selling price. In other trades, one may get either repetition work in groups, or the manufacture of one product. In the first group, the costs require to be grouped under the classes of products ; in the third class, where one type of product only is made, say at a gas works, the sterling costs can be divided by one uniform unit of production. I think personally, as a Cost Accountant, the most interesting variety of business is that which deals with different groups of commodities, such as the dye-making industry. A business which is continually on different jobs must have costings; and divide its costs at the time of estimating under these heads. A business which makes one product is comparatively easy from the Cost Accountant's point of view. The business with the variety of products is much more difficult, has had less scientific costing attention, and demands more intelligence and originality in dealing with its costs.

In practice, I believe that for every manufacturing business a thorough costing system is essential to Selling Management. It is not that prices cannot be fixed another way ; they may be ; but they cannot be estimated without reliable data, and the Selling Manager is unable to direct business into the most profitable channels unless he is kept constantly aware of varying margins on his different classes of product.

Summing up, therefore, I would say :—

(1) Cost of Production is by no means to-day and cannot be the sole factor in fixing price.

(2) Cost of Production from the consumer's and the ethical point of view should much more frequently determine price than it does to-day.

(3) Over a long period, Cost of Production does determine the *general level* of commodity prices.

(4) Over a short period, strength or weakness of demand has greater effect.

(5) The nearer the commodity is to its raw state the less does cost of production govern daily fluctuations in price ; the more completely it is a manufactured article the more is price governed by cost.

(6) In so far as Cost of Production does determine price, a scientific costing system is of the greatest value in ascertaining and displaying the facts.

(7) If the price cannot be fixed by cost, it can at least point the way to an intelligent selling end to the right direction in which to guide the business.

Paper by W. Bryden, F.C.W.A.

The question as to whether "Costs are the best basis for estimating and fixing selling prices" is one of these insidious questions full of trap-holes for anyone who attempts to answer it by a direct negative or affirmative. Apart from its debating possibilities, however, I think the question a particularly suitable one for the consideration of an Association of Specialists such as Cost Accountants, as an attempt to appreciate or define the possibilities or limitations of their work.

If we study the question a minute, it will be seen that it has many similar features to the question of Supply and Demand, which I think or expect has been discussed since the time of King Tutankhamen. We can imagine costs representing the Supply and selling prices representing the Demand. If we could regulate the supply to the demand, then we could regulate the selling prices by the costs, and the question as to whether this was the best basis of estimating and fixing selling prices would become one of practical politics. If we could assume as a condition precedent that supply and demand were exactly complementary, then I do not think we would hesitate in saying that costs were, if not the only fair and equitable way, at least they would be the most practical way of fixing selling prices. I say practical having in mind that it would be the most likely to lead to that mutual satisfaction which is the only sound basis for a healthy and permanent business. Despite the theory and often accepted practice of buying in the cheapest market, I believe few business men would defend such a system if they imagined that it implied buying under cost with possibly ultimate wrecking of the industry. In support of this belief, I would mention that for some years now, not only in this country, but in all industrial countries, we have seen the building up of what has now come to be known as vertical business, that is where industries have amalgamated or absorbed businesses to form a continuous chain of production. Such a development absolutely precludes the possibility of buying under cost and is generally embarked on to ensure control of production and continuity of supplies. I think, therefore, we may say there is no antagonism to profits, and no predominant desire to buy at prices unremunerative to the seller, and it is recognised that a well-established industry working on an economic reasonable basis of profit is the only one likely to give that progressive management and that continuity of service which will provide the maximum amount of satisfaction. Unfortunately, confidence in costs is not such that a purchaser is always willing to negotiate the selling price thereon, and, furthermore, even if confidence were merited, have we any guarantee that they represent economical production ? Could it be established that the highest stage of efficiency had been reached and the figures tabulated the exact cost of production, I do not hesitate to say that they would most certainly form the barometer of selling prices. Such a condition of affairs would carry with it as a corollary that we should then be in the happy position of being able to fix a selling price representing an equitable exchangeable value, and incidentally we would see the Cost Accountant occupying the supreme position of industry, he being the only one capable of defining that ideal price. I say ideal with all reservation, as it is difficult to conceive what consequences might follow thereon. It might lead to stagnation in business, it might stop research and development, it might—well, why should we imagine further, because like all ideals it is never likely to be attained, and so far as we can see prices will continue to be predominantly ruled by the law of supply and demand. To say that supply and demand do not coincide, however, is not to imply that no relation will exist between costs and selling prices, but to my mind it does exclude any idea that there might be only one party to the fixing of the selling price, the producer who has the option of fixing it haphazard, or by an alternative method of reference to cost. Not only so, but we have now had a too long and recent experience where we have seen that the consumer practically dictates the selling price, that is the price at which sales will materialise. That such does not necessarily represent a profitable basis of business we only too truly know, but, on the other hand, we might admit that it has features analogous to a crude expression of the test of efficiency, and by the elimination of the inefficient (which here is used in a narrow sense of those unable to conform to the effective demand) it may allow the ascendancy of the fittest, another often quoted law of economics. If we accepted this as a correct expression of the law we would be implicitly admitting that the fixing of selling prices by the consumer is a natural and logical process, and that therefore, if our costs do not conform to such prices, then they must be made to conform ; in other words, we would arrive at the position that not only are prices not capable of being estimated by costs, but that prices are the standard point, and costs, if considered, have to be regulated and calculated in reference thereto.

To put the matter in another way, a knowledge of the costs not only would not form the best basis of estimating the selling price, but actually would be of very little guide. What I have said so far, however, only illustrates the adage that a little law is a dangerous thing, as no doubt most of you will have noticed that I have only referred to one aspect of the matter. I make no apology for thus apparently dilating on economic laws, as such laws must be kept firmly fixed in our minds and our cost work must be made amenable thereto if they are to reflect economic facts which must be our real costs. By the operation of the law of supply and demand, we know that these two factors by their action and reaction on each other are always tending towards an equilibrium. To mention here the factors or some of the factors which prevent that stability ever being attained, we have wars, pestilence, famine, irregular harvests, over-population, over-production, etc. So in the same way, although costs may never exactly attain a permanent relation to selling prices, they should at all times be tending to develop a par value to one another, whether it be that costs are rising or falling, or selling prices are rising or falling. In the same way as we find fluctuations in the relations of supply and demand, so we find variations in the relation of costs to selling prices. True the divergence occasionally becomes very acute, until comparison almost appears ridiculous if not impossible. To the superficial observer it might then appear that in so far as there is no fixed relation between costs and selling prices, both items being in a constant state of flux and not definitely in parallel to one another, the fixing or estimating of selling prices by reference to cost would not only be valueless but impossible. He might also be tempted to say that the utility of costs were solely limited to a detailed analysis of the profit and loss account. We, as Cost Accountants, would of course at once ask whether it was better that this detailed analysis of profit and loss should be made before or after the event. We would no doubt point out that where conditions exist of incompatibility of costs and selling prices, the most vital need exists for a knowledge of costs to be able to forecast the contingent costs when considering any business offering, and so that one may know the measure of the incompatibility and intelligently decide whether to meet the demand and to what extent, and further to estimate the liability which is being assumed. One does not willingly go out of business, and the invariable rule is to fight on —while there is life there is hope—but the business man is seriously handicapping himself if he carries on without a clear and definite knowledge of the risks he is running. A business man always insures against fire and many other contingent losses, and will devote a considerable amount of ingenuity to anticipate the probable losses he may sustain in such eventualities, so that it would show a surprising lack of consistency if he was prepared in his every-day business to assume losses and commitments without an attempt to foresee the amounts involved. If one suggested to any Executive or Proprietor that the Profit and Loss and Trading Accounts might be dispensed with, I do not hesitate to say that the suggestor would be considered a fit case for admission to institutions where fantasies are the rule; and yet what do such accounts tell us? They merely show the amount of Profit or Loss that may have accrued over a definite period, and generally speaking this in only one net figure. Whether profits have been made on some articles and losses on other articles, or whether losses have been made on all articles, is not shown, and even if they were shown, can there be any doubt that the mere tabulation thereof at the end of an extended period of time is altogether too late and hazardous, and their value practically nil as they would not and could not reflect the tendency. Losses at the beginning of a period may be developing either upwards or downwards, and however detailed the Trading and Profit and Loss Account may be, it can only have a negative value by processes or elimination, until ultimately if the dissection is pursued far enough we arrive at a basis of a crude cost which might enable us to give a Coroner's verdict, but unlikely anything more. I am here assuming, and have so far assumed, that losses have been made, and that accordingly the Proprietor will want to know how he arrived at such a position. But when he does know he has not necessarily cleared himself of all his troubles. He may be still loaded with unremunerative contracts of an unknown liability —perhaps far beyond his capacity—only he does not know, and in any case if he elects to continue in business, as he assuredly will, on what basis is he to continue the struggle and how far can he commit himself? However we view such a condition of affairs, there can be little doubt that although costs may not rule the selling prices, and the basis of the discrepancy between the two may be incapable of exact computation or measurement, costs are absolutely essential and an imperative necessity if suicide or fraudulent bankruptcy is not contemplated.

Coming now to the second aspect of the question where the selling price is a variable one capable of being made amenable to costs, or in other words profits are available and we have to settle the amount thereof, and we have the option of doing so in relation to cost. This aspect, however, carries another problem, as it does not tell us how to fix the selling price even knowing the costs. I am not going to discuss here the question as to what are costs, but will assume that they are a quantity capable of statement at least within practical limits. Having ascertained such figures, at what are we to fix the selling price? We know that various trades and industries have rough and ready ideas of adding 10 per cent., 20 per cent., or other percentage to cost, and while this may be said to be fixing the selling price on the basis of cost, I think what little virtue there may be in it from the practical standpoint of providing a surplus and so justifying the business is nullified from a strict costing standpoint by the indefiniteness of the addition of a standard percentage. The problem to my mind extends to that, knowing the cost, what are the legitimate steps to take to fix the selling price? What are the logical and equitable margins that should be applied? I am aware that in America, where they claim to do everything scientifically, they have devoted a great deal of thought to, and enunciated a number of theories for, the scientific fixing of the profit factor, or the relation of selling prices to costs. That their method of relating selling prices to costs is very elastic and flexible we realise very forcibly when we consider what we obtained for the huge debt they created against this country. Their prices may have been scientifically fixed, but in result they seem little different to what we arrive at by what may I call ordinary business methods. To digress unto abstract theory for a minute, I should like to put forward the idea that costs as generally understood, that is prime cost, factory cost, or commercial cost and the various items that we may or may not include therein, while undoubtedly justified to be called costs from a practical standpoint or as a working hypothesis, there must still be a theoretical cost which covers every phase of human endeavour and every contingency, the costs of enterprise or management and the reward of capital, and while such are impossible of computation or even verbal definition, if such could be ascertained, then they should equal the selling price. In other words, the consumer in this Utopian idea should only be asked to pay the exact equivalent value for the actual services rendered, whether in material or immaterial, direct or indirect forms. If it were possible for mankind to be satisfied, no doubt producers would be satisfied to fix their selling prices on such a basis, but I do not think there can be any question that the general rule is to get as much in excess of cost as can be obtained. I am here referring to costs as accepted in the business. This rule of fixing the selling price of an article at as much as can be got for it might be called the Unwritten Law of Commerce.

Stated so, it might be said that costs do not enter into the question and the fact that the selling price is a certain percentage in excess of cost is irrelevant in so far as the price has been fixed at a supposed utmost limit. This price, however, could only be stable if applied to a limited production opposed to a known limited demand, or in other words, where the volume of output in relation to demand was fixed and invariable. Such conditions do not and cannot exist in industry as we understand it, and we always find that demand can be and is stimulated and increased by reductions in price. We have, therefore, before fixing our selling price not only to know the costs but to visualise the intended output and the potential demand, and the extent to which we would like to develop the output, and what sacrifices of prices will be necessary to create the demand to absorb that output, and the relative aggregate advantage in doing so. To put the matter in A.B.C. language, if an article can be sold at 100 per cent. over cost it is solely due to the volume of the demand, which demand will decrease in intensity as the production increases. The 100 per cent. only represents what can be obtained on one article, but if 75 per cent. can be obtained on each of two articles then a greater aggregate profit is obtained. If the numbers are multiplied, the percentage of profit on each will theoretically decrease, until ultimately we might reach the point that the purchasing parity was not in excess of the cost, or where the margin of profit was reduced disproportionately to the increased output. We see, therefore, that stating that the selling price is what one can get the public to pay, is no more satisfying than to say it should be fixed on a cost basis. We must take into consideration the total volume of output anticipated. To particularise, no doubt Henry Ford produces a cheap car and blazons forth to the world the benefits he has conferred upon mankind by its cheapness, but I am sure his ambitions were not philanthropic and that he actually aimed at the most he could get for the car, but based on a phenomenal output. Were the output reduced possibly he could get more for the cars, which might, however, mean a smaller aggregate profit. We see, therefore, that even where selling prices are flexible and amenable to costs, they are seldom fixed in relation thereto, and if we considered that they should be so fixed, the profit factor will remain undefinable, and even if a scientific formula of profits was available the volume of output would remain indefinite. To say so, however, is not to say that costs are useless, but their greatest and most tangible value will lie in this, that granted a possible unlimited demand or an increasing demand following decreasing prices, we must know the costs, first to know how far prices may be reduced, and second to measure the efficiency factor on profits of increasing output.

To sum up, I would say that Business or Industry is like a Great Adventure or Gamble. Whatever factor we take we find is surrounded by innumerable provisos. Even costs themselves are not capable of exact definition and impossible to foresee on varying volumes of output, without considering the ordinary and extraordinary vicissitudes of life, which always upset even the best laid schemes of mice and men. Costs are, however, one of the factors which can to some extent be translated into pounds, shillings and pence (the alphabet of business), and to the extent to which they can be so predetermined they form a valuable basis upon which to either appraise unremunerative prices or to estimate or fix profitable selling prices.

UNIFORM METHODS OF COSTING

By J. R. Blyth, F.C.W.A.

(Report of a Lecture delivered before the Members of the Sheffield and District Branch of the Institute of Cost and Works Accountants on 5th April, 1923)

In choosing as the subject of my remarks the question of Uniform Costing I was actuated not only by the results of my own experience in the introduction and operation of uniform costing, but also by the opportunities afforded me of observing conditions under which uniform costing would be highly advantageous.

As Cost Accountants, we claim that one of the most urgent needs of British industry is the introduction of modern methods of Cost Accounting. Without this fundamental improvement it will in future be impracticable to develop any industrial undertaking with any degree of security ; for no means will be available of constantly applying the crucial test of whether any development is sound economically and has the elements of commercial success. The same may be said of the operation of a business.

With the exception of those vast industrial enterprises which may be the result of combination of businesses in the same industry, or the integration of a series of industries as in Steel Production, Shipbuilding and Engineering, etc., the large mass of British industry is represented by undertakings that are relatively speaking not large, although too large to be administered successfully by the traditional methods of trained intuition.

The Costing Problem has several peculiar aspects for such industries. Where, for instance, is the necessary skilled advice to be procured without engaging the services of a highly-skilled Cost Accountant who would become a permanent member of the staff ?

To what extent ought Costing to be developed, and what degree of perfection in Costing ought to be aimed at ?

These are the kinds of problems that arise and are more frequently held in abeyance than solved.

It is to such industries that uniform methods of Costing should make a strong appeal once it is realised that uniformity is not only practicable but offers real advantages.

Investigation of existing Costing Systems in any industry will be likely to reveal a good deal of divergence, and one might be led to agree with the statement so often put forward that each business in a given industry is a law unto itself and demands its own special system of costing. This is, of course, quite erroneous ; and it may be equally erroneous to accept the other view that any Costing System, however well thought out, could be rigidly applied throughout an industry.

It is nevertheless true that a large measure of uniformity is not only practicable, but is inseparable from the attainment of a high degree of perfection in costing. This may be illustrated with reference to the derivation of the cost of some specific product or service.

There may be innumerable methods of arriving at some arbitrary approximation to a cost, but there cannot, except by some happy and improbable coincidence, be two correct methods which differ fundamentally. Uniformity in the essentials should, therefore, be quite practicable.

There are two aspects to this question and they may be indicated by the following respective titles, viz. :—

(1) Uniform Methods of Costing.

(2) Uniformity in Cost—not in amount but in relation to what cost includes.

The former would, if completely in operation, embrace the latter, but it is useful to approach the subject in this way, as Uniformity in Cost might be achieved in the early stages before the bigger object had been fully attained.

A few of the advantages that are likely to accrue from the adoption of uniform costing may be indicated :—

(1) Interest would be stimulated in the development of cost finding within each industry, and this would ultimately result in the improvement of costing.

(2) It would also stimulate the use of costing as a function of management and would show the need for costs being

complete and having them brought into focus with the larger commercial problems of a business in place of being considered as incomplete and unrelated statistics.

(3) Uninformed price-cutting would be gradually eliminated, and by this means one of the greatest menaces to successful business would be removed. This would tend to create greater stability, not only in each industry but in industry generally.

(4) Where circulation of costing data had been adopted within a Trade Association, at the various works of a Combination, or even within an industry that recognised the limitations of isolation, a spirit of emulation of the best results would be fostered.

(5) In many industries it would show the impracticability of each of the works in an industry continuing to produce the same large variety of product in face of foreign competition, both at home and abroad. In this connection Uniform Costing should indicate the need for some form of consolidation, or alternatively some co-operative arrangement in production, so that each works might specialise and the advantages of quantity production might accrue.

It would further indicate the need for simplification in manufacture as to variety of product.

If Uniform Costing helped to solve some of the problems of British industry—particularly our older industries—along these lines, it would more than justify itself.

(6) It would gradually build up within an industry a fund of mutual understanding based on solid facts concerning the economics of each industry.

Development of Cost Accounting

I would direct attention to the case of any industry with which you may be familiar and which embodies the characteristics of a large number of small or relatively small businesses each of which is administered on strictly individualistic principles. Take, for example, the so-called metal industries (*i.e.*, the industries engaged with the non-ferrous metals), which are represented by hundreds of relatively small works and a few that have grown to the magnitude of really large undertakings.

The majority of the works had in operation some form of costing, but with few exceptions costing had not been developed beyond the stage of arriving at some approximation to cost and would be concerned with the average cost of the unit of output of a variety of product—differing either in type or in size of the same type.

Assume that each of these manufacturers were left to work out his own costing problem without any co-operation or mutual understanding within the industry, what would be the result ? Progress would in the first instance be exceedingly slow, as there would be no means of stimulating enthusiasm.

It is unlikely, moreover, that each works would engage or be able to engage the services of a highly-skilled Cost Accountant who would be competent to desgin a costing system and put it into operation.

It seems to me, therefore, that the only solution for such industries is to come to some understanding on the matter of uniform methods of costing and agree to work out standard principles to which all might adhere. This can best be accomplished by having a series of Costing Conferences of the Cost Accountants from each of the various works or of a selected number who have made most progress with costing.

By this means it should not be difficult to formulate principles which will represent either the best existing practice or something in advance of the best practice.

In this connection it will probably be found that the services of a central costing officer are desirable, whose duty it would be to visit the various works of a Trade Association or Combination for the purpose of becoming familiar with the processes of manufacture and observing the existing methods of costing so that he might be able to advise as to the best standard methods to be adopted. Such a central officer might be drawn from the industry itself or introduced provided he had a wide range of costing experience and could bring a new point of view to the specific costing problems of the industry with which he was concerned.

These costing conferences, which would be held initially to formulate principles, could in the case of a Trade Association or Combination be developed into a permanent Costing Committee not only to guide and direct the development of costing, but to give skilled advice in the application of Costs.

In reading the Report of the proceedings at the recent Annual Conference of our Institute, when the question of "Standardisation of Cost Accounting" was the subject of discussion, I seemed to detect a failure on the part of some of the contributors to the discussion to appreciate the true purpose of this so-called "Standardisation of Cost Accounting."

While not wishing to play the part of captious critic, I venture to think that the title "Standardisation of Cost Accounting," although self-explanatory to the initiated, might give, and does appear to have given, rise to some misunderstanding. I would suggest that a more correct, or at least safer, term to use is "Uniform Methods of Costing," or, perhaps better still, "Uniform Methods of Cost Finding."

I should like in this connection to emphasise what I consider a most vital point, viz. :—

That the purpose of uniform methods of cost finding is not in any way to interfere with the independent derivation of the true cost at each works, but rather to facilitate this by setting down the best principles.

The purpose of costing is to arrive not only at the truth, but the whole truth, and this ideal should be pursued at each works to at least the same or even a greater degree of finality under uniform methods than when working in isolation, and this irrespective of how irreconcilable the final results may appear to be. Indeed, the fact that the results may be irreconcilable is one of the most potent arguments for the adoption of Uniform Methods of Cost Finding so that it may be ascertained if such disparities are real, and do not arise merely from failure to adopt standard principles or from "Costs" having been brought to different degrees of completeness.

One sometimes sees it recommended in connection with Uniform Costing that such elements of cost as depreciation of plant, metallic loss, or, in fact, any element of cost which may not be precisely determinable over a short period, should be expressed as an average figure—not an average rate per cent. on the Capital Value in the case of depreciation, but as an average allowance in the cost per unit of output. This practice is wholly pernicious in principle. It suppresses the truth at its origin, in place of allowing the truth first to emerge so that the maximum of data may be available in the application of costs as a basis of policy- price fixing or otherwise.

This point may be illustrated as follows :—

Assume two works "A" and "B."

"A" is operating with somewhat old equipment and with a minimum of labour-saving appliances, while "B" has modern equipment and has made a feature of labour-saving appliances.

Under such conditions the provision for wastage of plant values (expressed in terms of the unit of output) might be much greater at "B" than at "A," but might be more than offset by a saving in other elements of cost, *e.g.*, Labour Cost.

One might set it down as a principle that in subjecting Costs to a detailed comparison the interdependence of the different elements of cost should always be kept in mind.

This illustration may serve to prove that the cost at each works must be complete in itself and that the purpose of standardisation is to encourage and promote uniformity of method and not uniformity in resultant cost by any arbitrary means.

One of the ultimate purposes of uniform costing may be to promote efficiency by means of comparison of cost data and so endeavour to reduce all costs to an economic basis, *i.e.*, a basis which will allow of prices being fixed at a generally profitable level which is also sound competitively.

This uniformity in cost, if attainable, must be real ; it must come from internal economy and the elimination of waste, and will be mere make-believe so far as achieved by arbitrary methods in reducing certain of the elements of cost to a common basis.

The Installation of Uniform Methods of Cost Finding

The ideal method of Costing Organisation would seem to consist in first deciding upon the principles, and after having them accepted by all concerned to have them simultaneously introduced at the various works. I may say that I once visualised this taking place in practice, and pictured to myself an advance shoulder to shoulder. On this score I am now disillusioned and find that this unity of action is unusual. I imagine it will more often be found that uniformity will be gradually attained by modification and development of existing methods as the benefits accruing from advancement become gradually apparent. This may mean that uniformity may exist in theory and be only partly effective in practice for a time.

This fact clearly indicates the need for some form of concerted action in bringing before the business community the aims and advantages of Uniform Costing. The action taken by our Council in endeavouring to stimulate interest in this matter is timely, and if followed up should have excellent results.

The initial problem is undoubtedly that of educating those concerned so that a natural apathy to any attempt at interference with established practice may be overcome.

The object in introducing uniform methods of costing may be simply to give to each business engaged in an industry the assurance that each of its competitors has an equally full and accurate knowledge of cost, and that in consequence competition, however keen, will always be carried out with a knowledge of cost, and may ultimately be dictated by cost.

An additional object may either be introduced in the initial stages or adopted at some later stage, viz., the comparison of costs either in total or in detail, so that efficiency in manufacture may be promoted by emulation of the best results shown.

Even where this latter object may not be stated at the outset, I am of opinion that it might well be visualised as a possible development and provision made for its attainment.

This naturally brings one to the basis for organising Uniform Costing, which, of course, may differ in each industry, but which I might illustrate with regard to the non-ferrous metal industries.

In these industries we find that the products pass through several quite distinct processes of manufacture and that different works may take up their raw material at different stages in its progress from the essentially raw product of the mine. Whatever the variations in this respect may be, it will be found that the true basis of organising Costs is the process of manufacture. This will involve division of the works into departments carrying on some homogeneous productive activity, *e.g.*, Refinery, Casting Shops, Piercing Plant, Rolling Mill, Tube Mill, with possibly intermediate processes such as Boring and Turning.

A complete cost of production in each of these departments is derived, and by segregating such departmental costs the cost of production, either of the finished saleable product or of the product at any intermediate stage, becomes available.

The expenses of distribution are clearly distinguished from Cost of Production, and are applied to the finished or at least saleable product.

By this means the Total Costs are comparable, and that under the main headings of Distribution and Production, while a more detailed scrutiny may be carried out by comparing the process costs.

The elements of cost in each process are also clearly distinguished, *e.g.*, Direct Labour by operations, (2) Supplementary Labour in classes, (3) Power, (4) Fuel, (5) Consumable Stores, (6) Minor Tools, (7) Plant and Equipment expense (itemised), (8) Buildings Service (itemised), (9) Interdepartmental Haulage, (10) General Works Charges.

The advantages are as follows :—

(1) Costs are complete.

(2) Costs are capable of comparison to any degree of detail.

(3) The elements of Cost that are Terminable are distinguished from those that are Non-Terminable.

(4) The compilation of standard or normal costs is facilitated.

In taking a basis for the compilation of normal cost it is important that a practical standard of output or load factor be adopted. In an industry with an output the composition of which is continuously changing, as in the metal industries, it is expedient to adopt a standard output or load factor somewhat less than full capacity. A separate standard would be required for each operating department and the above reservation might apply to some or all departments, and that in varying degree. For instance, a mill designed for abnormally heavy work not in constant demand might require a standard considerably below capacity.

In fixing these standards of output it would be essential to have some broad basis of mutual understanding between the different works, but not necessarily the adoption of a uniform ratio to full capacity output. Each department at each works would require to be first considered on its merits. Having done this the question of standards in their broader aspect throughout the industry should be considered so that due weight might be given to matters of general policy in costing and the special circumstances at each works.

Having compiled costs by uniform methods as indicated, the results may in part represent definite costs of a specific product or merely an average of a variety of product diversified by type or by size of the same type. Such average if relating to a limited range of product may be of practical value.

If a section of the works is wholly concerned with the production of a specific product, the costs are not only complete but specific. If this is not the case these departmental or process costs merely provide a preliminary basis for dealing with the internal economy of each department in arriving at specific costs. This will involve sub-departmentalisation on the basis of the various operations in the cycle commonly referred to as a process. It will entail segregation of expense in relation to operating the Drawbenches, Rolling Mills, Annealing Muffles, etc.

The simultaneous accomplishment of uniformity right through to finality in costing is perhaps too much to expect, and indeed would presuppose the existence of a costing organisation of a homogeneous standard of capacity and efficiency. This is not usually the actual position and accordingly uniformity may be achieved gradually.

When our worthy Secretary, Mr. McMurray, extended an invitation to me to address you I chose a subject which I was then unaware would constitute the basis of discussion at the Annual Conference of the Institute; and after such a varied display of oratory I am afraid that my few remarks are rather in the nature of a feeble echo.

I see, for instance, that Mr. Scott Maxwell has referred in not too complimentary terms to that somewhat familiar phenomenon called "Supply and Demand." I seem to have heard this referred to as "the law of supply and demand." I would suggest that a more apt description would be "the Psychology of Supply and Demand." We have all read about the effect upon selling price of, for example, that *rara avis* fresh eggs when the supply is a dozen and the demand is respectively 13 and 11 at different times. The deductions have a resemblance to Micawberian philosophy.

The operation of this so-called law of supply and demand is liable to be so immediate and spectacular in its effect that it appears as a final and ultimate cause. The ratio between supply and demand has become the very corner-stone of the people's economic edifice, and it is the foundation of all their arguments. It may be likened to the exchanges, which after all are merely a barometer. They are a record; but they are not the things recorded.

Psychologically, "supply and demand" have become an obsession and the reason is apparent. The effect upon prices as stated is so rapid and obvious, while the causes that affect and tend to adjust supply to demand are so relatively obscure and slow in their operation that they fail to impress the average man, who does not realise that Cost is the ultimate determining factor of selling price when considered over long periods.

When this fact comes to be generally recognised—and a good deal of progress is being made in this direction—industry and commerce will operate under a stabilising influence that will tend to diminish the element of avoidable risk. Business that is conducted scientifically will cease to be a game of chance.

It took over a year of patient and thoughtful endeavour on the part of many men of varying capacity to design, construct and install the turbines of a modern ocean leviathan. Yet serious destruction and loss of time were occasioned by the careless or malicious dropping of a spanner into the delicate mechanism.

These periodical Trade crises which seem inseparable from abnormal inflation and deflation might be found to have a like obscure origin.

The United States of America, with vivid recollections of the pains of deflation and depression, is now experiencing a rising tide of prosperity. The Americans—but not all of them—are enjoying the delights of inflation. There seems, however, to be arising in the minds of their financial and business magnates a certain amount of misgiving on this score. Will they be able to control the speed and preserve the balance of this vast engine of commerce without the Federal Reserve Board (which is, no doubt, on the look-out for signs of over-trading) having to adjust the Governor as in 1920?

But what has this to do with Uniform Methods of Cost Accounting? Just this:

In American business there is a growing recognition of the value not only of Cost Accounting, but of Uniform Cost Accounting, which is being encouraged for the purpose not only of allowing each business to be more scientifically administered, but so that each industry and the whole of industry may have this stabilising influence in operation.

The Chamber of Commerce of the U.S.A. acts as a co-ordinating body in matters of Uniform Cost Accounting. It collects information from its members periodically as to whether they have adopted Uniform Cost Accounting and, if so, what stage of development has been reached. This information is circulated in the form of a Chart, a copy of which may be of interest. The Chamber publishes bulletins and pamphlets on costing and is prepared to advise its members with regard to the aims and advantages of Uniform Costing.

Here we have an instance of a nation-wide organisation with over one million members making the question of Uniform Costing a vital one in its policy of building up American business on sounder principles.

The British way is different. Whilst our individualism is no more pronounced than the American's, we are more impatient of any interference than they.

To appeal to the individual business man by the customary piecemeal methods can bear fruit very slowly. It will take a generation or longer to have all these innumerable and relatively small businesses arise to the need for cost accounting if there is no co-ordinated effort to come to their aid.

Many of our industries organised in small units are facing competition at present such as they have never had to meet hitherto, and their foreign competitors who have come later into the field and are organised in larger units are no doubt better equipped in many ways. To such of our industries the development of costing is not only a necessity, but a very urgent necessity.

In these remarks I have made a point of emphasising the need for Uniform Costing in industries represented by a large number of small and medium-sized businesses; but I should not like you to assume that I wish to exclude the very largest businesses. In fact, they might benefit most by Uniform Methods of Cost Finding, which, I think, they will be likely substantially to achieve in developing their costing organisation to its full degree of utility, and this they will inevitably do.

STANDARD COSTS

With particular reference to the Sheffield Industries

Report of a Lecture delivered at a Public Meeting held by the Sheffield and District Branch on 16th November, 1923.

By Robert Stelling, Dipl. Ing., F.C.W.A.

If you go to the average commercial library and examine the list of books on Cost Accountancy, I venture to say that the majority will be found to deal almost exclusively with the problems of the general engineering trade, or, at any rate, to take all the examples therefrom. There is a positive reason for this. In the first place, it was in the engineering trade that Scientific Management, of which Scientific Costing is one function, had its origin. Moreover, these products loosely described as "engineering," and which consist in the main of machinery and machine tools, are highly complex products, involving the assembly of large numbers of small parts.

The difficulty and expense incurred in obtaining accurately sufficient data to evaluate the product for estimating and for selling purposes was considerable, yet necessary, but because of its complexity the system remained almost entirely a feature of the general engineering industry, while for other industries making single or simpler products it was held that a much less elaborate procedure was ample to enable a profitable selling price to be fixed. There was a period in the history of industry when the function of Cost Accounting was summed up in the sentence which you will find in so many of our textbooks of to-day, that "The fundamental object of cost accounting is to trace every item of expense to a specific order or process." In other words, to record history in detail.

We distinguish in Cost Finding two main lines of procedure, namely, Order or Terminal Costing and Process Costing. Order costing is usually applied where the identity of a batch or single order can be conveniently maintained until completion. Process costing is applied to continuous manufacture or to cases where a batch loses its identity in the course of production.

Now obviously those firms whose saleable products come within the category of those to which "process costing" is applicable, and which are made in bulk, either continuously or in such a way that batches lose their identity in process (as, for instance, when in an electro-plating vat dozens of articles of different patterns are inserted at one and the same time), could not readily adopt the old cost finding methods of the engineering trade, which was extreme order costing, nor at that stage of the progress of the science could they adapt these methods to their own particular conditions; hence the absence until very recent years of anything approaching a scientific or even a reasonably good costing system in so many of our industries.

But we have passed beyond that stage to-day. Cost Accounting has developed into something more than the mere recording of time, material, and an empirical figure of expense. It has become a science, with its own technique, its fundamental principles, and its accepted good practice.

The science continued to be developed in the engineering industry, principally in America, and notably by British-born or British-trained Accountants! As the result of this development there emerged the recognition of the essentials of Cost Accountancy, of its functions and of its advantages, with the result that the manufacturers of other products began to see their way clear, understanding the principles, to apply the science to their own particular factories.

Let us for a moment examine some of the functions of a scientific cost accounting system, other than that of "tracing every item of expenditure to some specific product or order." These functions may be described as follows:—

(*a*) To report continuously upon the effect of fluctuating market prices of raw materials upon the values of the work-in-progress, the finished stocks, the factory profit and the current cost of the product.

(*b*) To present on a comparative basis information relating to operating efficiencies and preventable waste.

(*c*) To present frequently or continuously the effect of volume of output and orders in hand upon the recovery of establishment charges.

(*d*) To report the effect of all the varying conditions of manufacture upon the normal cost of the product.

(*e*) Finally, to enable a periodical statement of profit and loss and of the financial position to be rendered, say monthly, in order that the directors of a business may exercise the closest possible control over the financial and the general policy.

I do not suggest that all these functions have the same relative importance for each and every factory, nor that these are all the functions of the science. Every case must be judged upon its merits, for Cost Accountancy is and must always be a compromise, and a balance must be struck between the amount of data and detail desirable and the cost of its collection. The functions referred to above appear to me, however, to be particularly important in three, at least, of the trades which have made Sheffield famous, namely, Steel, Cutlery, and Silver.

It may seem strange to group together in this way trades which are so widely dissimilar. Steel smelting and rolling is so obviously a case for Process Costing, whereas the manufacture of Cutlery under new conditions closely approximates engineering production, which has been dealt with in the past, and is dealt with to-day, most efficiently by a system of Order Costing.

But be that as it may, the one principle which it would appear should be applied in these particular cases is that of the application of Standard Costs.

A Standard Cost is a predetermined cost based upon the presence of a given set of conditions. The reservation is most important, and it is in the consideration of the variable conditions of manufacture that the skill of the trained Cost Accountant, as distinct from the purely commercial accountant, comes most prominently to the fore. To give a simple example of varying conditions, the cost of the process of steel smelting will vary according to the condition or temperature of the pig-iron introduced. Whether it is cheaper in the long run to melt and preheat the iron or to introduce it cold is a problem which again must be solved with due regard to the practical conditions and limitations.

Standard costs may be set up for specific operations, such as refining, plating or lacquering, or they may be set up for the production of individual articles, such as ingots, castings, knife blades or coffee pots; for the generating of steam or of electricity, for compressing air or for pumping water.

The application of standard costs is accomplished in the comparison of the actual with the standard, and this may be done in the aggregate, by process, by product, or by department ; these comparisons being so carried out in the accounts that the effect is reflected in those statements of profit or loss, finance, and budgetary predictions which the Cost Accountant will be called upon to present, and which are so very necessary to the intelligent conduct of business to-day.

This is an entirely different thing to comparing actual job costs singly with the estimates, and then laying these on one side and merely accepting the position as shown by the monthly profit and loss account (if such a thing be available) without regard to the realisable value of the finished stocks and work-in-progress. The great advantage of the application of standard costs is that it discloses *tendencies* and thus enables policy to be determined rapidly, undesirable tendencies and their causes being subjected to examination in detail on the exception principle.

The setting up of standards requires the greatest possible care. At every stage consultations must be held and full agreement reached, or else acrimony is bound to arise at a later date if results do not tally with the predetermined figures. The foreman must be consulted as to the effect of varying factory conditions, the technical engineer as to the effect of variations in the specification or analysis of the raw material, the purchasing agent as to the effect of variation in re-order quantities, the salesman as to a sales target, the accountant as to the administration figures, the plant engineer as to the condition of the machinery, etc. These are only some of the varying conditions which the Cost Accountant has to incorporate into a series of formulæ which may be compared with a complex series of simultaneous equations.

It is important, also, when setting up a standard to agree upon the basis of measurement, and here the advantage of a computed standard cost becomes apparent. It conveys far more to the intelligent business man to know that his cost for January is represented by 132, for February by 129, and for March by 136, than to be informed that his cost for January was 87 per cent. of the corresponding cost last year, for February 97½ per cent. of January yet 92 per cent. of February last year.

Standards for labour may be set up on the basis of past records, provided that the conditions are recorded under which they were obtained. It may be they have to be modified to suit new or anticipated conditions. Time study may be necessary to arrive at final values. Where piecework prices rule, these may be taken as standards, but the standards for day workers on production and for indirect labour must be set up as described above.

Direct material standards are relatively easily established, for past records usually exist which are very reliable, both as to quantity and price. Indirect material standards are, however, in another category, and I usually find that an investigation into these standards discloses a large amount of waste.

It is in regard to the standard of establishment expenses that the greatest difficulty is encountered. This standard must be *true for an agreed set of conditions;* it must not be set too high in the hope of being on the right side, for this will seriously affect selling policy. It must not be set too low in the hope of capturing the market, and in the expectation of recovering them through increase in the volume of output. False assumptions such as these two lead to haphazard snap marketing, and weathercock policy is not good business.

Let us take an actual example, such as may be found in hundreds of firms throughout the country, of the usual method of so-called "costing" and see whither it leads us. Such a "costing" is shown in Table I, and this is assumed to be an "estimate" upon which to base selling policy.

TABLE I.

	£	
Materials..	60	
Labour	20	
Prime Cost	80	
Oncost (100% on labour)	20	
Total Cost	£100	
Selling Price	£105	Profit at 5% .. £5

A common practice is to adhere to 100 per cent. charges throughout the year, and to trust that it will cover the Establishment Expenses, or, as I have heard them called, "dead charges."

Going further with our example, we find that for one month the figures extracted from a trial balance might be as shown in Table II.

TABLE II.

	£	£
Wages	814	
Expenses (actual)	758	
Depreciation (monthly quota) ..	65	
Materials issued	2,628	
Sales		3,150
	£4,265	£3,150

What information does this give? It would appear from the ratio of material, labour and expense (if we assume the same ratios exist for all the products of the factory, for the sake of simplicity), that the expenses are £9 above the 100 per cent. on wages, or about 1 per cent. up, and that the labour is £186, or 20 per cent. below the estimate on the basis of the ratio of labour to materials. The data therefore appears to give satisfaction.

Let us carry this a step forward to the usual form of Cost Ledger. In this account the production will be credited at the estimated cost and the account appears as in Table III.

TABLE III.

Dr.	£		*Cr.* £
Nov. To Wages ..	814	By Finished Goods	3,000
To Expenses	758	By Work-in-Progress	1,265
To Depreciation .	65		
To Materials	2,628		
	£4,265		£4,265

Our next step is to analyse the elements of cost and to compare them with the "estimate," and let us assume that the "estimate" tallies with our "standard cost" arrived at on more scientific lines.

Another assumption is made at this stage. It is mathematically correct to assume that if all material is issued at the commencement of a job, and if the flow of work be reasonably regular, then the amount of the work which has been applied to the material issued is at any time equal to half the work which will have been applied when all the material in work at that time has been worked up. On this basis, therefore, as there is £828 of material in work at the month end, the standard labour cost of the work-in-progress will be $\frac{20}{60} \times \frac{828}{2} = £138$.

Table IV. shows our analysis using these standards.

TABLE IV.

	Wages. £	Materials. £	Expenses. £
Total for Month ..	814	2,628	823
Credited by Finished Products	600	1,800	600
Balance	214	828	223
Standard Cost, based on 50% of Material in work	138	828	138
Balance, being LOSS	£76	—	£85

Now in every factory the expense or establishment charges may be divided into two categories, the constant or irreducible expenses, and the expenses which vary directly with the volume of output. How these are computed and controlled is immaterial at this stage; suffice to say that as a rule the constant expense is from 1·4 to 3 times the variable or controllable expense. Let us assume that in the factory under consideration £500 of the £785 represents the constant expense per month. If the factory were working at 93 per cent. of the *standard* capacity, then 7 per cent. of the constant charges would not be recovered in the costs, no matter what the basis of recovery might be. This equals £35, which we designate the loss arising out of unrecovered constant charges due to idle capacity, or, shortly—"Idle Time."

It is not strictly correct to carry expense adjustment into the Work-in-Progress Account, but Cost Accountants will forgive me if I bring it, for the sake of argument, into the Work-in-Progress Account which I now draw up on the basis of the analysis and comparison with standards. This is shown in Table V., in a form quite usual and useful where a good system of order costing is installed.

TABLE V.

Dr.	£		*Cr.* £
To Wages ..	814	By Finished Products at Standard Cost	3,000
To Expenses (actual) ..	758	By Work-in-Progress at standard basis	1,104
To Depreciation (quota)	65	*Loss* due to inefficiency of labour	76
To Materials issued	2,628	*Loss* due to Idle Time	35
	£4,265	*Loss*, being expense charged to excess labour at 100%	76
Gain, being reduction of expense below standard ..	26		
	£4,291		£4,291

We have made a considerable step forward. We know what we have lost due to operating inefficiencies, and due to lack of work, also what we have gained by care of controllable expense. We have ascertained a true value of the Work-in-Progress, reducing the amount from £1,265 to £1,104. This also demonstrates a fallacy only too frequently encountered, possibly due to adopting the methods of ordinary accountancy, in that inefficiencies and losses are wrapped up among the asset figures and are not separated or extracted until they appear at stocktaking, to the great surprise of the directors. It should never be forgotten that *assets and losses appear on one and the same side of the balance sheet.*

We have sold our products for £3,150, therefore making a profit of £150 over our estimate or standard cost, but at the same time we have incurred a gross loss of £161 in the factory, or a net loss of £11 on the two transactions. Where then does the unfortunate manufacturer stand, and what is to be his policy?

The answer is to be found in the scientific application of standards to show *tendencies.* An account should be set out as shown in Table VI., and this is the important feature—capacity as shown from the Idle Time Control Account.

Such a statement would naturally be produced for each line or category of products.

Finally, statements would be drawn up showing variations and their causes. Table VII. shows how this would be achieved for expense control.

Let us carry the idea of standard costs, as applied in this manner, a step further. Does not a standard cost, scientifically calculated along these lines, form the finest basis possible for uniform costing? However the individual expense of each firm may vary, the results and variations due to market fluctuations, wage changes, and the like, can all be considered on a common basis.

TABLE VI.—WORK-IN-PROGRESS ACCOUNT FOR NOVEMBER.

Item.	Standard.	Actual.	Ratio.	Item.	Standard.	Actual.	Ratio.	Loss.
	£	£			£	£		£
To Wages.. ..	738	814	1·103	By Finished Products ..	3,000	3,131	1·044	131
To Materials ..	2,628	2,628	1·000					
To Expense ..	738	823	1·115	By W.I.P. ..	1,104	1,134	1·027	30
Month of Nov. ..	£4,104	£4,265			£4,104	£4,265		£161

the entries can be raised without the laborious work of obtaining the detail cost of each item produced.

This statement shows us that the cost of finished products during November was 4·4 per cent. above the standard, and therefore a 5 per cent. margin would not entail selling at a loss. Further, that the work-in-progress is still above standard cost, and a glance at the individual ratios of excessive cost of labour and expense shows that it is likely to remain high. A selling policy can now be formulated facing all the facts, including the volume of work in hand, and the loss due to idle plant

But whether we consider standard costs from the point of view of a manufacturing association or from that of the individual manufacturer, one salient fact remains: if the standards are truly set and the variations studied *in their relationship to changing conditions,* then policy can be determined on the basis of facts, and the final figures in the balance sheet will correspond with the periodical statements of position and with the predictions of results.

TABLE VII.—PRODUCTION DEPARTMENT M2 EXPENSE REPORT.

Item.	A/C No.	Standard.	Actual.	Ratio.	Percentage Variation due to—: In-efficiency of labour.	Idle time.	Variation in cost of supplies.	Variation in wages.
Repairs to Machinery ..	601	220	231	1·056	+3%	+0	—2·2%	+4·8%
Power, etc.	410	640	602	0·940	+0·4%	+4%	—7·2%	-3·2%

"THE FUNCTION OF COSTING IN INDUSTRIAL RELATIONS."

Mr. H. G. Jenkins, F.C.W.A., M.I.E.E.

The Chairman: "I have to announce with regret that Mr. Jenkins, who should have read the second paper, is unable to be present, but that Mr. Dunkerley, the Honorary Secretary of the Institute, has very kindly undertaken to read it for Mr. Jenkins."

Mr. Dunkerley: "Mr. Chairman, Ladies and Gentlemen,—I have not had an opportunity of reading through the paper since its completion, so I hope you will bear with me."

The Problem.

"The problem of present-day Industrial Relations is so complicated that a solution can only be sought in directions which are hardly understood or appreciated. Some are well-defined and others ill-defined, but that the search is essential to industrial peace and the general welfare of industry is undoubted. It behoves everyone who represents any industrial element, therefore, to investigate the lines upon which he can direct its activities so that he may bring benefits to industry in his own particular field, and add to the sum of human knowledge which is the force by which industrial relations can be improved.

The purpose of this paper is to indicate to what extent the Function of Costing can be used for the purpose of defining and establishing industrial relationship upon a sound economic and psychological basis."

Origin of Costing.

" It is probably true to say that the elements of Costing made their presence felt in that early transaction of mankind when the human brain was first called upon to measure what its efforts were worth so that exchange might be possible without mutual destruction.

It was only during the Great War, when protection against exploitation by some of those whose help was essential to the cause, that it became more generally recognised as a function of industry which could benefit industrial relations."

Ignorance.

" The present state of affairs is largely due to the mistrust which arises from ignorance. Ignorance on all sides ; and in considering this problem it is essential carefully to examine what form this ignorance takes."

Parties to Industry.

" Who are the parties to industry ? They are the Consumer, Capital, Management, Executive, and Labour. It is difficult to decide in what order to take these various parties, but in the order in which they are set out they probably show the most illuminating aspect of the subject with which this paper is concerned."

The Consumer.

" The expenditure of lavish sums on publicity frequently entices him to buy an article at far more than its economic value. He is ignorant of the degree to which he is exploited by these means. He is unaware under what conditions his purchase has been produced. He is frequently unable to determine whether his investment is good or bad. He may have been educated to some degree in the direction of saving or thrift, but he is entirely uneducated in the much more important subject of spending. He is sometimes paying more than an article is worth and at other times demanding a value far in excess of the amount he is prepared to pay. He has no guide, no criterion except the extremely crude one of popularity, which is so fickle as to represent a condition worse than no guide at all."

Work of the Cost Accountant.

" What has already been done in the coal industry and the printing industry indicates quite clearly that here is a field which the Cost Accountant can explore with considerable prospect of contributing to the common welfare. The fluctuations in demand which have contributed to our present industrial difficulties arise partly from the consumer's ignorance as to whether a lower price will be available in the future.

If an examination could be made it would be found that the industrial concerns who have best weathered the storms of the last few years are those whose prices have attained a real relation to cost, and whose customers have not been exploited."

Capital.

" The next party is Capital, which must not be regarded as embracing management. The ignorance of Capital is colossal. Capital controls industry to the greatest extent of all parties. In what direction does its ignorance lie ? It is important in this connection to realise that Capital is really represented by the investment of many and not of few. The individual who contributes to a Friendly Society a weekly sum seldom realises any connection between himself and Capital, and yet that connection is one which induces him to make his contribution. Nor does the individual who insures his life take much interest in the investments from which the Company with which he insures derives its income ? "

The Small Investor.

" Does the individual who is normally referred to as the Small Investor interest himself in the industry with which he is concerned ? How often does he connect the rate of dividend with the industrial conditions which have produced it ? He might regard it differently if, he received with his dividend, let us say from a Coal Mine or a Railway, a statement of the number of human lives lost in accident. Again, with our present legislation, what can the majority of investors, direct or indirect, know of the real conditions of affairs when it is not possible to glean any real information from the balance sheet as published? The plea of greater publicity in this direction which has recently appeared in the financial Press is a sufficient indication of the degree of ignorance of Capital. Many criticisms can be made as to the impossibility of interference by the many, and it cannot be gainsaid that the only practical way, is government by the few, but nevertheless, more information to the investor could only lead to greater knowledge, which, in its turn, must do much to obviate the subordination of all other interests to the payment of dividends."

Publicity.

"Where does the function of costing arise in this connection? It is obvious that the publication of the cost aspect of industrial investment would bring an altogether greater knowledge to Capital and contribute to stability of investment and eliminate much of the speculative element and its influence in Industrial relations. Here the field for the Cost Accountant is wide. He need not give away secrets or help a competitor to increase his competition. That this is possible and will be beneficial is clearly indicated by what has already been done in this direction by our Sister Association in America. Ability to compete does not rest upon the knowledge of what the other fellow is doing, but in the ability to do everything he does better."

Management.

"It may appear extremely presumptuous to suggest that a state of ignorance exists in the case of that body of persons which is directly responsible for the management of industry, but the suggestion loses, I think, its presumption when it is realised that the accusation is not one of general ignorance but of ignorance in a particular direction. Wherein does the ignorance of Management lie? It must be admitted that the great body of management has given little study to the future, and the great number of influences upon which depend not only present but future conditions. Industry in general has grown up relying too much upon 'hit or miss' methods. This has resulted in the entry into industry of individuals with insufficient knowledge of its responsibilities and the prospects of success, and it partly accounts for the number of bankruptcies shown by the official records. The increases there are too frequently blamed to conditions of trade instead of to conditions for which there is no excuse for those who enter the managerial status. It would be foolish to argue that failure can never arise from trade fluctuations but there can be little doubt that a better informed or less ignorant management could have obviated many of the disasters of modern industry.

It is an acknowledged fact that management is seldom in touch to a sufficient degree with the real condition of affairs with the workers otherwise the long tale of success which has attended efforts on the part of Trade Unions for improvements could not be told, nor would have occurred many of the strikes which have so disorganised industry. If there had not been ignorance on the part of management these conditions would not have arisen, for surely they mean, in the majority of instances, a tale of 'penny wise and pound foolish.' It surely cannot be doubted that ignorance of the psychology of industry has been the reason for a great deal of industrial strife coupled as it has been with a failure to realise the trend of industrial relations in time to avoid progress being obtained at a price out of all proportion to its worth."

Executive.

"Is there ignorance in the Executive? The Executive is responsible for the interpretation of the Managerial policy and the direct control of the workers. What is necessary for this interpretation of policy and direction is surely knowledge. Does this knowledge exist? The Executive cannot function correctly unless it has a definite plan and policy. How often does such a plan exist? Even if there is a plan is it one which truly attempts to visualise the future? If it does not how can its interpretation inspire that confidence which is so essential to the leadership of men? What is the great bugbear of labour? In the main, the fear of unemployment, dole or no dole. To the honest man work is desirable, work is essential, as affording him a fair opportunity to win what he can of the amenities of life. The absence of the planning of the future is largely to blame for the high degree of casual employment, and, to some extent, for the high degree of unemployment. Again, in many organisations the Executive consists of disjointed members who are ignorant of the plan, the knowledge of which is essential if they are to see what part they are to fulfil. It is not to be wondered at if, under such circumstances, the result is to foster misunderstanding, to create detachment and to increase lack of trust, and to add a disturbing factor instead of a co-operative factor to the industrial machine.

Here again, to enlarge on the extent to which ignorance exists is not difficult, but it is neces-to pass on to the last element of industry."

The Worker.

" It is certainly not possible any longer to allege ignorance of the worker to the same degree as formerly. It may even be suggested that within his own sphere he is one of the best informed parties to industry. But without his own sphere he has undoubtedly been in darkness, and this shortsighted policy has forced him to combine for his own protection and caused him largely to lose that individuality which has made him so valuable on account of his craftsmanship. He is kept in ignorance, and is not willingly ignorant. It can hardly be doubted that since the introduction of Works Committees which have begun to enlighten him in some directions, the relationship of the workers with the other partners of industry has tended to improve wherever this degree of education has been available. How can he be expected to contribute his part to the industrial fabric if his interest is restricted ? How can he trust capital management, executive, when he is unable to see where they are going and to what extent their responsibilities to him are being performed ? Such information as the rate of dividend or the balance sheet of a public company are the only things which he can, if he desires, come in contact with as an indication of how his confrères in industry have discharged their responsibilities. How can he be expected to gauge the wage that he can anticipate from his efforts unless he has some information to guide him ? Under the circumstances is it to be wondered at if he is easily misled, if he is suspicious of all the information which is given to him, and given to him only under pressure and when every condition is unfavourable to his personal welfare. These factors which are most certainly ignorance are largely responsible for the strained relations of to-day."

Field of Cost Accounting.

" Having reviewed, therefore, under what conditions our industrial troubles are generated it can be assumed that if industrial relations are to be improved we must look in the direction of education. Now this meeting is not for the purpose of trying to decide in what way the present-day industrial evils can be completely overcome but to endeavour to indicate to what degree it is possible for the science of Cost Accounting to contribute its part to improving conditions which all men deplore and which they desire to see improved by every possible means. What is the field of cost accountancy in industrial relations ? It may be defined thus. First to contribute to the formation of a plan and to determine the degree of efficiency in financial terms, to provide information as to the control of cost and price, to bring to management, executive and worker information which will enable them all fully to appreciate the part they play in that part of the industrial machine with which they are concerned.

These are the internal industrial spheres.

In the external sphere of industry to contribute to the sum of knowledge of industrial cost and internal finance to the betterment of the condition of all parties to industry, and assist thereby harmonious relations, and generally to do all possible within their sphere to stabilise industry. It can hardly be doubted that the degree of stabilisation is the real factor in determining the degree of harmony that can exist in industrial relations. All this may be theoretically right and capable of acceptance but the real question is what is the way in which these objects can be accomplished."

Methods.

" It is obviously not possible now to go into detail as to the methods by which the Cost Accountant can accomplish the task which has been outlined as his legitimate function in Industrial Relations. This must vary in each industry and in every type of organisation. It is, however, quite possible broadly to indicate the general principles which govern his work and which provide the means by which he can fulfil his important function."

Planning.

" The first essential of successful business is a plan. .Before the establishment of the complicated organisations of to-day the plan was in the brain of the proprietor, often ill-defined and hardly realised as existing. Modern conditions demand a well-considered detailed plan covering the organisation from beginning to end. The first duty of the Cost Accountant is to act as the convener of the plan. To obtain his information from all sections of the organisation, to co-ordinate and order the details of form of these particular plans, to turn them into financial terms and to produce a budget. Having done so, to determine to what degree such a budget can be supported by the financial resources of the undertaking, to adjust, rearrange the plan by co-operation with the various contributing elements of the organisation so as to be within these resources, and finally to produce a plan which will result in financial success with safety and without stifling enterprise and progress."

Orbit of the Plan.

"This plan must take into consideration every element of the internal finances of the concern for which it is made. It must enable the economic price to be determined, it must provide for the determination of allowable expense, for the necessary reserves for the support of the investment in stock, the maintenance of the plant and manufacturing equipment in an up-to-date and efficient condition and for development of the plant and equipment to meet the development of the business. These are a few of the points. There are many, all within the work and knowledge and capacity of the fully-trained Cost Accountant to undertake and satisfactorily solve, without interfering in any way with the legitimate field of the Financial Accountant. Having made the plan and obtained the consent of the controlling power—the Board of Directors—his duty is then to provide the machinery to control the expenditure within the programme, to provide each element of the organisation with the information as to its allotted task, make such provision as will enable him to determine at short intervals to what degree the plan is being kept and to provide the main control with information in sufficient time to enable deviations to be known and regulated and make use of any advantage over the plan which becomes available to increase the development of the business. The Cost Accountant does not and never can attempt to control the individual activities of any section of the organisation, but he can and does, provide that information which will enable control to be maintained in such a way as to ensure efficiency and prevent disaster.

This plan will, of course, involve the determination of cost, not only of the individual article, which is only partly useful, but in determining cost as related to the effective earning of profit by each individual operation and all operations collectively."

Education.

"It is not sufficient that he should make the plan, advise on the performance and determine the degree to which the plan has been carried out, but he must contribute to the education of the organisation to every possible extent. He must educate every section and part, and, to as great a degree as possible, every individual in the degree to which their personal or sectional efficiency contributes to the success of the whole. He must provide the means of education of every person in the organisation in the essential economics of the business, such as realisation of value, prevention of waste, and efficiency."

Publicity.

"He must preach the gospel of publicity in relation to industrial finance, bring to all grades of manual workers by that publicity, confidence in the management, interest in his job, the sense of achievement, and help him to appreciate that his honest endeavour is essential to his employment, that his co-operation is not only putting profits in the hands of the shareholders but making his employment more secure, and enlighten him in every possible way as to the degree to which he contributes to industry, and, in other words, show the results of his effort so that he may feel the pride of his achievement as an essential part of the whole effort, for without such knowledge no human being can be expected to be content."

Information for the Executive.

"To the Executive he must bring to a great degree the same sort of information as to the manual worker, but with the additional information which will enable it, as the first step to control, to exercise that control with judgment and sincerity, looking at all the problems from the broader aspects than is possible when only one side of the consequence of inefficiency is within their realisation.

All concerned must realise their relative importance to every other section of the organisation. They must be placed in a position to consider their every action in its financial aspect and know out of the co-ordinated experience of cost in relation to effort, where and how to improve the lot of the manual worker and to what extent it is possible to improve his conditions and his interest. These things are only possible when viewed from the broadest aspect which must embrace that of the economic benefit to be obtained."

Help to the Management.

"To the Management, the Cost Accountant in making, watching and tracking the plan can do probably the best work of all in contributing, by his comprehensive knowledge, by his quick determination of the financial aspect of the results, a degree of stability to the managerial policy which without him is not possible. By his long date plans, by his foresight of the future financial difficulties, fend off the worst of all difficulties of management, that of labour turnover, resulting as it does in the necessity for the continuous education of the worker to the job, and bringing in its train mistrust and unemployment, those evils which by their recurrence prevent us from making headway or nullify our best efforts in improving the relationship between capital and labour.

These aspects cover in general terms some part of the contribution which the Cost Accountant can make to the improvement of industrial relations, for, after all, the best way to ensure trust and banish suspicion is for all parties to have sufficient information and knowledge to enable them to realise that they are getting a fair deal. That is to say the worker a fair share of the products of his industry and management honest effort on the part of labour."

Contribution to the external elements of Industry.

" Nothing has yet been said as to the contribution which the Cost Accountant can make to the external elements of industry. This field is one to which, unfortunately, the Cost Accountant has, up to the present, had practically no opportunity to contribute.

During the war the usefulness of the Cost Accountant to the Government who was then the consumer, was amply demonstrated by the extensive use of Cost Accountants in the various Government Departments.

It can scarcely be denied that if the services of the Cost Accountant had been called into use in may of the industrial disputes of recent times, the vexed questions of what industry could afford would have been quickly and positively determined in a manner beyond dispute, and have hastened settlement and provided a more lasting peace than has been possible by the methods used."

Services to Capital.

" To Capital the services of the Cost Accountant can be of the greatest benefit in bringing greater publicity and a greater element of truth into the Balance Sheets and Trading Accounts of our present industrial world, than can ever be possible where the Accountant is not inside the industry and concerned with its daily functioning. Certainly the certification of stocks, as a single example, by the professional Cost Accountant would give Capital greater security and eliminate the dishonest and incompetent adventurer of the industrial world.

Much more can be said of all aspects of the work of the Cost Accountant in industry, but if his operations cover only a small part of the field which has been outlined in this paper, who will say that the function of the Cost Accountant is not essential in every industrial undertaking and that his contribution to the improvement of Industrial Relations can be ignored ? " (Applause.)

COSTING

By H. Julius Lunt, F.C.A., F.C.W.A. A.C.I.S.

The installation of a costing system has two principal functions, the first to find the actual cost of each product, and the second to ascertain the incidence of various expenses so that the cost of future operations can be forecasted and controlled.

THE subject of costing has many aspects and appears in many forms: hardly two businesses, indeed, will carry out the same scheme without modifications to suit individual circumstances.

If it is desired to contrast a system of costing with the system of financial accounts ordinarily in use for the preparation of yearly Profit and Loss Accounts and Balance Sheets it may be said that the yearly accounts aim at showing correctly the result of the year's operations, whereas the aim of the costing is to enable the management to determine what that result shall be.

The practice of costing is recognised as having two principal functions, both of which are regarded by many firms as of equal importance. The most prominent is, of course, the effort to find the actual cost of each product, and the second aim is to ascertain the incidence of various expenses so that the cost of future operations can be forecasted and controlled.

In considering the first of these aims (as in the costing of individual articles) it is necessary to bear in mind that costing does not merely stop at finding the total expenditure necessitated to manufacture a given article, but goes into very considerable detail to show the costs of parts, and operations upon those parts: and it is by constant comparison of details that the ultimate total cost of any product is standardised and the most economical process of manufacture is determined.

It is obviously necessary for this purpose that at every point of the costing the greatest care should be taken to ensure that each item of expenditure is charged up at the point where it is actually incurred. It will not do to charge expenses indiscriminately against products because they show a profit and therefore can stand the charge, as it is said. It is equally necessary when a business is profitable to make sure that in reality each product is making a profit and that some are not, in fact, incurring losses.

Selling Price and Cost

It does not by any means follow that the cost of different products and their values on the market will be in any way proportionate, and therefore it must be borne in mind that selling price is a totally different matter from cost. The selling price of a commodity is determined very much by the demand there is for it, the reputation of the manufacturer or the finish of the article, and the efficiency of the selling organisation, and none of these factors bear any relation to the cost of production.

Expense of Costing Systems

From this conclusion the deduction is sometimes made that in any event the expense of running a costing department will not be remunerative because it does not assist in raising the selling price. To this argument the answer will be that though the mere knowledge of the cost of a product does not enable a manufacturer to get any better price for it, yet if the price is unsatisfactory his knowledge of the cost is a warning to him either to find more economical methods of production or to cease to manufacture, and his business will obviously be more profitable if he discontinues to manufacture articles which are unremunerative rather than continues to manufacture them simply because he does know what they cost.

Estimates and Costs

There is a difference in all cases between an estimate for supplies of a commodity and an account of the cost of that commodity after manufacture. The estimate will be made upon the basis of the prospective cost and will take into account the need which there is for securing orders, the prices at which materials will be obtainable, and to some extent it may pay to undertake to supply goods upon which the usual profit is not earned if the manufacture of such goods will contribute to some extent to pay the standing charges. Such factors, however, do not influence the costing, which must be based upon the cost of material used and labour plus current expense rates sufficient to meet all charges, and, in comparison with the estimate, such a cost will show to what extent the estimated price actually falls short of the price needed to pay the cost of manufacture and to give a satisfactory return upon the capital involved.

Chief Aim

The first aim of costing then is to find the cost of each unit of production whether it is a particular contract or article or a machine consisting of innumerable parts, the cost of each part, and the various operations upon each part, having to be independently determined.

Cost Accounts also serve the following purposes :—

(*a*) They show whether any specific work, article or process results in a profit or a loss.

(*b*) They show whether estimates are being exceeded, or otherwise, *during the course of manufacture.*

(*c*) They assist in forming future estimates.

(*d*) They disclose sources of economies in the comparisons of similar work done at different times.

(*e*) They provide material for periodical profit and loss accounts between stocktaking times.

(*f*) They give detailed information concerning work done, so that it should not be possible to do work at a greater cost than it can be obtained for from an outside source; and so determine that all plant and machinery is operated to the utmost advantage.

(*g*) They facilitate detailed control of expenses.

Cost systems are in many cases designed to take complete records of all the products, but in other

A lecture delivered before the Carlisle Society of Incorporated Accountants on 26th March 1926.

cases the complexity which this would result in makes it necessary to obtain average costs over the whole of the products and to cost individual articles or batches of articles occasionally as necessary. In this case it is just as important to be accurate in the methods adopted, and to compile the necessary particulars with every care.

Prime Cost and Oncost

Expenditure for costing purposes is divided into two main groups—(1) direct and (2) indirect. The direct charges are comprised in the term Prime Cost and include all those expenditures which can be directly associated with a particular job, as direct material and direct labour, e.g. the material and labour which actually form part of and are directly expended upon the job in question, together with any expenses directly incurred for that job, e.g. cost of special tools.

Indirect charges include two main groups—(1) expenses relating to manufacture, and (2) expenses relating to the administration of the business and marketing of the products.

The expenses relating to manufacture are those which are incurred in carrying on the factory, running of plant and machinery, repair and maintenance of plant.

It consequently depends upon the use to which any material is put as to which group it will fall into for costing purposes, and the division is not always easy to determine, at any rate from the financial books. For example, metal may be bought in an engineering business for the purpose of constructing machinery, but in the course of the operations a considerable amount of repair work has to be undertaken both to machinery and tools, and the major part of this repair work is done by the staff of the works. For the purpose of the repairs a quantity of metal would be drawn from the stores and used for the repair operations. It thus becomes necessary to dissect the cost relating to the expenditure upon the metal, the portion which is used for customers' jobs being direct material; and the portion which is used for repairs being indirect material.

In different businesses the same material may belong to different groups and similar analysis will be required in dealing with wages.

The analysis of expenses, which is carried out in the Statistical Department of a large cost office, dissects the expenses over a very wide range of headings and obtains very useful details for the purpose of the management in controlling the expenditure. It is by constant examination and comparison of these details that the statistics are made of real use.

Financial Accounts

In the financial accounts the total of wages is frequently shown under the heading of "wages," and the total of material under the heading of "material." In the costs, however, very considerable dissection is required and the first main dissection is between direct material and indirect material, direct labour and indirect labour, because the direct material and labour are charged as such to specific jobs; indirect charges must be charged by indirect methods, and it is essential that the total of indirect expenses should be accurately determined. If the cost system is not thorough a large proportion of indirect expenses may not be ascertained and possibly may be entirely left uncovered by the costing system. It will thus be seen that a Trading and Profit and Loss Account as commonly supplied does not show the correct dissection between direct and indirect charges for costing purposes.

Job Costs

This method of charging costs against individual jobs by means of direct charges with additions for indirect expenses on the basis of percentage rates or hour rates, based upon hours of labour or direct wages, is known by the general term of "job costing," but it will be found that many businesses are not adapted for record of costs against particular jobs, being more suited to a system of process costs where the different operations that the business carries on form convenient units for costing, the expenditure being dissected over the various operations or processes: and for this purpose costing methods divide themselves into two principal headings—those which work on job cost lines and those which work on process cost lines.

Process Cost

In the process cost groups the principle is to allocate the direct charges to the processes where they are incurred and also to dissect the indirect expenses so as to allocate these as far as possible to the processes for which they are required. Thus the cost of each process is ascertained as regards running expenses, and this may usually be expressed as a rate per lb., per yard, or hundredweight, or in some other unit of quantity or measurement of the material which is passing through the process.

It has to be borne in mind in connection with process costing that there are frequently very heavy losses owing to waste of material, and such losses have to be brought into account as part of the costs of the process. The general plan, therefore, on which process costs are arranged is to charge the process cost account with the material used in the process, also labour and expenses associated with it, to credit the account with by-products (if any) which result, thus arriving at the cost of the product actually obtained. The quantity obtained divided into the cost shown by an account prepared on these lines will give the cost per unit at the end of the process, and the difference between the cost at the commencement and the cost at the end of the process gives the actual cost of conversion of the material or cost of the process.

Cost Accounts are divided into the following classes:—

Single (*or Output*) *Costs*, applicable to businesses supplying a product of a uniform type; the accounts show the cost of a "natural" unit of output, e.g. a ton of coal (in a mining business), a barrel of beer (in a brewery), &c.

Departmental Costs, in which, as the name implies, the cost of each department is obtained separately. This system is employed in businesses which are divided into a number of more or less "watertight" compartments, i.e. departments which are practically little factories in themselves.

Process Costs, employed in chemical works, &c. Where the product passes through a number of distinct processes, which frequently involve conversion of material, the cost accounts give the expense incurred for each process, and the cost of the intermediate and final products.

Terminal Costs, a suitable system for builders and contractors, and in all cases where it is desired to obtain the cost of a number of contracts or undertakings which are entirely distinct and of a non-recurring nature.

Multiple Costs, applicable to businesses where there are complex products which differ considerably in type, and where similar operations are utilised on very different articles, as, for example, in a general engineering firm.

Operating (or Working) Costs, employed by undertakings which produce services rather than goods, e.g. tramways, railways, &c. The unit is a car-mile, passenger-mile, &c., as the case may be.

COSTS

It is naturally impossible in the course of one lecture to describe in detail the costing scheme even of one large business, and in fact a scheme which applies to one business will not apply to another of a different trade, but for the purpose of illustration the case of an engineering works may be taken and a brief description will be possible of practical methods for carrying out the principles which have been explained.

The cost records will be obtained under the Works Order Numbers used in issuing instructions to the works. Separate works order numbers will be usually assigned to each batch of standard parts; each complete machine order; special parts; repair jobs.

In the final cost summaries the cost of each machine will be set out to show the items for each part under the separate headings of labour, material, sundry charges and oncost in each case.

WAGES

The correct booking of time is one of the most important requisites in costing. The two main headings of direct and indirect wages comprise in the first group all labour which can be correctly recorded upon work for customers, for stock parts and machines, or for capital outlay, and in the second group all labour expended upon general services for the works as a whole.

The direct wages are booked to the particular jobs by means of the works order numbers allotted to the work before issue from the planning department.

The indirect wages records are obtained by classifying the workmen according to occupations, when possible, e.g. stores department; and by standing factory expense orders through which dissections of expenses can be compiled in very great detail when desired. The works may be divided into departments and the labour on indirect work separately recorded against each by means of the department number, combined with the factory expense number.

In order to obtain correct record between one job and another the method of booking upon time sheets daily is being superseded in favour of the practice of having a job ticket for each job, whether representing direct labour on piece work, e.g. machinery parts for a customer's order, or indirect labour on expense orders at day rate, e.g. repairs to works plant.

The completed job tickets are collected daily and time on same checked with total time recorded by each employee on entering the works on a weekly time card, so that ultimate agreement between a wages abstract prepared from the job tickets according to the wages on each job and the pay roll prepared from the weekly time cards plus bonuses can be assured.

The postings to costs will be made from the wages abstract and the job notes will ultimately be used for obtaining records of time for rate-fixing purposes.

MATERIAL

The routine for obtaining detailed records of material used on each job comprises the correct allocation of invoices, which should be dissected in the purchases book between special purchases of parts or fittings or special material chargeable to particular jobs; stores materials; and other expenses under the usual headings—works expenses, however, being separated from office expenses as far as possible.

The invoices for special purchases will be identified with the job number to which they relate, and a special folio column should be provided for this purpose and the entry to Costs Accounts will be made accordingly.

Stores materials will be charged to a General Stores Account (or series of such accounts for different classes of goods) in the financial books; and a statistical stores ledger in the stores office will be kept showing an account of each kind and size of material, &c. This ledger may be on cards or loose leaves and will be entered in the first place from the stocktaking records; next from records of goods received which are also debited; then from requisitions by means of which material is issued for use in the works.

On receipt of goods the storekeeper will have careful examination made and report quantity and exact description on his daily goods received sheet to the buyer for the purpose of checking the invoice; and to the progress department to assist in hurrying forward any orders for which the material is urgently required.

No material will be issued without authorised requisitions, which will be either issued to the foreman by the management departments, or prepared by the foreman in accordance with the job specification. In either case the requisition serves as a receipt for the material and is used to enter issues to the credit of the Material Accounts in the stores ledger and to post to Cost Accounts.

The pricing of materials will be done from the prices in the stores ledger and the rule will be to charge at cost price; either actual cost of earliest unexhausted purchase or at average cost price of purchases on hand.

Indirect materials issued for general works service purposes will be similarly recorded and the charges may be dissected as with indirect wages.

In some cases it is not desirable for the storekeeper to be familiar with the prices, and in such a case a price book must be in use.

In addition to the stores ledger it is a useful and common practice to have a card on each lot of material termed a bin card, which shows the quantities received, issued and in stock; the card being altered on each occasion when stock is taken from the bin by the stores labourers. Both the bin cards and the stores ledger serve as records of the stock and are therefore a check upon the storekeeping; they also enable the storekeeper to maintain a control over the quantity of stores, and for the purpose of this control the maximum quantity of stock which must not be exceeded is fixed and noted on the card, as also the minimum quantity which the storekeeper must not allow the stock to fall below without placing an order with the purchase department. On observing that the stock of any article is approaching the minimum quantity the storekeeper informs the buyer and gives him information as to the minimum and maximum stock authorised for that article and the present stock, the rate of consumption, and any special notes which he thinks it necessary to convey.

In order to further assist the storekeeper in maintaining stocks of materials a method of allocation is resorted to. The Planning Department sends a specification of material for each order immediately it is received to the storekeeper so that he can examine the specification and make any preparations necessary for obtaining further stocks. The allocation system further comprises a ledger in which there is an account for materials specially allocated. On one side of each account are recorded the orders for material which are placed with outside firms, giving the date of order, the quantity ordered, and the date of delivery, and on the other side the quantity of material called for by the specifications of the orders which have been received in the works. It is thus possible for the storekeeper to ascertain whether there is sufficient material on order to meet the manufacture of the products which are called for by the customers, and whether delivery needs to be speeded up.

The consumption of indirect material—for example, small tools in an engineering works—can be limited by rationing the quantities which each shop is entitled to draw from the stores week by week, no excess quantities being issued by the storekeeper without specific authorisation.

Other Prime Costs

Other direct charges which form part of the prime cost will be advised by the counting-house.

Small expenses of the nature of workmen's travelling expenses can be definitely charged through petty cash and dealt with by means of a prime cost column in the petty cash book provided with reference column in which the cost number can be inserted by the cost office when the items have been dealt with.

Other charges must be dealt with by indirect means.

Indirect Expenses

Indirect expenses are referred to by various terms such as factory expenses, overhead, burden, oncost; all of these signify the expenses of running the manufacturing operations which can only be allocated by indirect means.

In the first place the works expenses claim consideration because they form part of the cost of manufacture.

Among the methods which are least accurate for charging works expenses to jobs may be mentioned the method of charging a percentage on prime cost, and the method of charging a flat percentage on wages. The first is inaccurate because the cost of the work done upon the jobs does not depend upon the amount of material which the job requires, and therefore the results are bound to be erratic and to bear little relation to the cost of work done; and even if the same material were used in all jobs there would be wide fluctuations due to variations in prices. To some extent the direct wages vary proportionately to the amount of work performed, provided the work is all uniform, none of it entailing expensive processes. In businesses where the output is entirely standard the flat percentage on direct wages may give practically the same result as a series of differential rates in different departments because of the averaging that results in each case, but the type of business to which this can be applied is not extensive, and the results produced in a business which involves numerous manufacturing processes upon a variety of products are very inaccurate, some products being overcharged and others undercharged, in respect of the cost of the manufacturing operations expended upon them. The object of costing is not fulfilled by making an addition to the work produced which equals the amount in total of the indirect expenses; not only must the costing aim at absorbing by means of oncost a total equal to the indirect charges, but the charge against each job should be proportionate to the cost of the work performed upon it.

In order to differentiate between work entailing expensive operations and other work—for example, hand operations—the plan is adopted of using differential rates based either as a percentage on wages in different departments or shops, or hourly rates per hour of direct labour in each department or shop; these rates being arrived at by dissection of the expenses so as to charge in each department the actual expenses for which the department is responsible. The system may be carried further and the charges incidental to the running of particular machines may be grouped so as to arrive at a machine hour rate for the running of each important machine, and by this means the work done upon the machines is charged with a rate per hour for the expenses which are incidental to the running of the tool. The items which are usually included in a machine hour rate on this plan would be a charge for the space occupied by the machine in the building, including rent, rates, fire insurance, building repairs, &c.; a charge for power according to the power required to drive the machine, the cost of repairs incurred and of tools requisite for the machine, with sundry supplies such as oil, cleaning materials, &c.; a charge for depreciation of the machine based on its original cost and useful life, and a charge for interest on the outlay represented by the cost of the machine taken at a fair market rate. The whole of these charges estimated in each case over a period divided by the anticipated number of running hours the machine will actually be at work will give the machine hour rate. If the machine does not actually work for the anticipated number of hours the loss due to idle time will be shown to be the cost for the idle hours at the machine hour rate, subject to any saving that may be made in respect of power, repairs, &c.

The expenses will include service departments such as boilerhouse and running of steam plant for generating electric current; millwrights' and tool-shop departments, which are organised for the repair of machinery and supply of standard tools; similarly, the Stores and Transport Departments; and these all require to be dealt with as composite services. The cost in each case embraces actual wages which have been paid under the different headings, and also the heating, lighting and power used in each case, use of building, depreciation of plant, and so on. These charges require to be assembled in the statistical abstracts of the cost department and then dissected over the various operating departments.

In order to arrive at the charges which are incidental to the operating departments the expenses in the financial accounts require to be allocated by means of a schedule of allocations according to the operating shops responsible, or the works services for which each expense is undertaken. These works services can be grouped under the following heads among others :—Building service, which comprises all the charges entailed in providing a building in which the machines can operate ; power service, which includes all the costs incidental to the production of power ; heating, where heating is done by separate heating apparatus ; hydraulic power service, where there is hydraulic power supplied to machines ; compressed air service ; maintenance departments handling repairs ; stores service ; transport service and welfare. The charges which accrue in the financial accounts are set out in tabular form and the proportions to be allocated to each of the services can be determined according to the scale which is appropriate in each case. Such a scale will be based on actual consumption in the case of power, gas and water, if obtainable ; based on floor space for such items as rent, rates, fire insurance on building ; based on the value of plant for such items as insurance of plant, depreciation of plant ; based on wages in each department for such items as National Insurance, Employers' Liability Insurance; and in cases where the charges vary more in proportion to the number of employees than in proportion to their wages, a distribution of the expenses should be based upon the number of employees engaged in each section.

The charges which are appropriate to the general services are set out in this way and the totals of the general services are apportioned so as to be directly placed against the operating departments, and the allocation schedule when complete will indicate the whole of the works charges allocated to the operating departments, and according to the number of working hours or amount of wages paid in each operating department the appropriate oncost rate as a percentage on wages or rate per hour can be determined.

Cost of Production

The appropriate charge for oncost is then shown on each job ticket and summaries are made to find the total oncost chargeable to each job for posting to the cost ledger.

The details posted to each Cost Account must be carefully checked with the works order and specification to detect omissions or wrong entries.

From the cost ledger as each job is complete transfers are made to cost summaries in the case of special parts for the machine cost accounts ; to finished stores for the cost of stock machines or standard parts, and to completed costs for debit of Trading Account in the case of machines despatched to customers, repair jobs, &c.

Gross Cost

The total of the prime cost and the expenses or oncost relating to manufacturing constitutes the works cost or cost of production of the goods. A general percentage of the cost of production may be added to provide for the expenditure on administration and a separate expense or varying expense for different products or different markets may be added for cost of selling and distribution. Naturally the cost of selling and distribution will depend upon the market in which the goods are sold, and therefore charges for selling and distributing must be investigated from the point of view of the disposal of the products and the costs arranged accordingly.

Work-in-Progress Account

For the convenience of the costing routine a control account is kept known as the Cost Ledger Account or Work-in-Progress Account. This may be a memorandum account merely, or it may be a double-entry account in the cost books to which the various cost ledger nominal accounts are transferred at the close of the trading period.

By another method the account may be a nominal account in the financial books to which the charges for expenditure shown in the various nominal accounts are brought when closing the books.

In either method the same purpose is served.

Here is debited the total from each monthly abstract of direct wages, direct materials used, other direct charges and total oncost charged to jobs : the credits include transfers to finished stock, cost of sales charged to trading, &c. The balance of the account represents the value of work-in-progress agreeing with the open cost accounts in the cost ledger. By the use of this account and a similar Stores Control Account a continuous tally upon the value of stores and work-in-progress is obtained, facilitating the preparation of interim Profit and Loss Accounts.

Budget Forecasts

Another of the important functions of the cost statistical departments is to prepare budget forecasts of the expenditure, which, in the first place, are estimates of expenditure under each of the headings in the financial books ; but these forecasts will be sub-divided so as to indicate the departmenta expenditure under each of the various heading authorised for any department, and a comparison month by month of the departmental expenses with the authorised budget will indicate which departments are exceeding their allowance.

Idle Time

To the extent that the oncost chargeable to the jobs at the rates normally in use falls short during periods of depression of the indirect expenses, the loss caused by idle time arises.

Many standing charges cannot be abolished in spite of the fact that the works is not fully employed, and a dividing line may be drawn between the normal expense which is essentially incurred for the manufacture of the products which are being turned out and the excess of expenses above that normal proportion. This normal proportion represents the expense which would be appropriate to the amount of the commodities in normal times. The surplus expense beyond that normally required to turn out the commodities in hand at the time represents the burden upon the business ; the loss which the business is forced to bear through lack of orders.

Conclusion

The need for detailed costing applies particularly in the case of the largest factories, and in smaller works approximations are very largely depended upon by means of which sufficiently accurate results for practical purposes can be obtained. It is necessary for sufficient care to be taken to detect any losses that are being incurred or to reveal the existence of profitable lines which can be developed. Subject to safeguards for this object considerable approximation in charging indirect expenses becomes inevitable.

Relief in handling routine is obtained in large works by the use of office machinery, adding and calculating machines, addressing, duplicating and tabulating machines, wages pay-roll machines, &c. These contribute to promptitude and efficiency when suitably handled.

In conclusion it may be pointed out that costing represents the display of the cost of the output to meet the point of view of the works manager and salesman ; and it is to serve their ends and to make the costs useful for their purposes that the cost accountant must devote his time and energies.

WHAT I EXPECT OF A COST ACCOUNTANT.

A Lecture by MR. C. G. RENOLD, *Managing Director of Messrs. Hans Renold Ltd., to the Manchester and District Branch, 9th March, 1927.*

In this paper I shall not attempt to deal with methods of cost accounting in detail, nor to discuss points of technique. I am not competent to do so, and I take the title which your Committee has given me as an indication that that is not what you want from me. I am going to discuss the part which the Cost Accountant's department plays in the running of a manufacturing business, the general nature of the duties it should undertake and how it fits into the rest of the organisation. And if I do this from my own point of view, as Managing Director of a manufacturing business, and not from a Cost Accountant's standpoint, I believe I shall be dealing with the subject on the lines desired.

One more word of introduction. I shall not attempt to make my remarks universal in their application. That is to say, I make no claim that the theories I shall put forward, nor the kind of organisation I shall describe, apply with equal force to every kind of business. I have not enough experience of different kinds of business to judge. Although the same elements are present in the running of all manufacturing businesses, the emphasis falls in such different places that very different kinds of organisation are called for. Thus, for instance, the success of a business dealing with small articles made in vast quantities on mass-production lines depends on different features from that of a business making a variety of large plant, and the controlling systems will have to be designed to emphasise different aspects, even though the same basic elements of design, purchase of material, machinery, packing, selling, collecting the money, etc., are present. In some businesses the most important thing to watch is the purchase of material or parts, in others it is machining times, in others it is uniformity of volume of output or continuity of works processes, in others it may be cost of marketing. In each case the cost accounting system will necessarily have a corresponding bias and, while it is important to recognise that there are certain fundamental principles, it is just as important to realise, in the case of any particular business, what its central problem is and to build the system round that as a focus.

I shall, therefore, quite frankly discuss the whole question with reference to the particular business I control, viz., a manufacturing engineering business employing about 1,500 people and making a somewhat narrow range of product, mostly made for stock, and much of it, though not all, made to standardised designs on mass-production lines and sold at fixed prices holding for approximately a year.

Taking our total running expenses as 100, the main groups bear the following proportions :—

Raw material for manufacturing purposes	26
Producing wages—direct producers, inspectors, floor services and departmental supervision	26
Depreciation, shop supplies, tool room and plant maintenance	18
Administration and standing charges ..	14
Selling	16
	100

Or lumped together :—

Material	100
Producing wages	100
Overhead (all other items)	200

From these figures you will see that our biggest problem is concerned with overhead expenses and such questions as keeping up the total volume of business over which to spread them. This emphasises, in addition to control of actual items of expense, the need for a very close consideration of programming and forecasting of business available at various price levels, since our costs depend so very largely on the volume of business we can count on doing.

I will now outline briefly for you the organisation we employ.

There are two main sides to the business—the Making and the Selling—each under a director, with a managing director co-ordinating the two, looking after general policy and watching the working of the whole, particularly from the financial point of view. Directly under the managing director, *i.e.*, outside the groups controlled by the works and sales directors respectively, is the Finance Department, which includes, of course, the cost accountancy.

The works director has six chief assistants, viz. :—

Design Manager, responsible for :—

Design of product, tools and processes.

Rate fixing and time study.

Supply of tools.

Controlling :—

Drawing Office, time study department and tool room.

Inspection Manager, responsible for :—

Inspection of work to Drawing Office limits and specifications.
Inspection of raw material to laboratory specifications.

Production Manager, responsible for :—

The output of the works.
Raw material issues.

Controlling :—

Planning department, raw material stores and all superintendents of manufacturing departments.

Plant Manager, responsible for :—

Maintenance of plant and buildings and general services.

General purchases.

Raw Material Manager, responsible for :—

Purchase of raw material.
Metallurgical specifications.
Heat treatments.

Controlling :—

Metallurgical laboratory.
Purchase department for raw material.
Heat treatment department of works.

Employment Manager, responsible for :—

Conditions of employment.
Engaging, discharging and transferring of employees.
General labour relations and policy, etc.

The sales side is divided primarily into selling and merchandising, selling being sub-divided according to markets.

An important section of the merchandising side is that of the Merchandise Control. The job of this is to convert the fluctuating sales' demand into a relatively steady, long date programme of works production, using the stocks of finished product as the balancing factor. All questions of delivery dates are focussed here.

Our stocks of finished goods represent the largest single item, after fixed assets, among the assets on our Balance Sheet, and on the effectiveness of the work of the Merchandise Control Section depends not only the actual volume of this stock but its usefulness to meet the demand, or, conversely, the amount of writing off on account of obsolescence or overstock which we have to face at the end of the year.

I now come to the part played by the Finance Department in this complex organism. The work which it does may be grouped under the following heads :—

1. Accountancy, financial programmes, costing and prices.

2. Handling of customers' and vendors' accounts, cash and pay roll.

3. General services mainly for other departments in the way of statistics, instructions *re* routines, supply and supervision of stationery and office equipment.

The first point that strikes one about this list—which I have purposely made very general at this stage—is that it involves three quite different kinds of relationships to the rest of the organisation.

The first section—the accountancy, costing, etc.—is concerned with the preparation of information for the guidance of the management. It is not executive, since the resulting action, if any, lies quite outside the Finance Department.

The second section—customers' and vendors' accounts, cash and pay roll—is directly executive. It comprises certain of the steps in the chain of work involved in getting the product made and sold, steps for which the Finance Department is directly responsible and which it actually carries out.

The third section, apart from the statistical services, includes something in the nature of control of certain functions which run through the work of other departments. This functional control also plays a part in both the previous sections. Thus the information on which the accounting and the costing work is done is almost entirely drawn from records made or information supplied by various other departments, and the way in which these records and information is produced must, of necessity, be functionally controlled by the Finance Department, so as to key up with the form of the costs or accounts which are based on it.

Similarly, the handling of customers' and vendors' accounts requires a certain functional control over the form of the invoicing and purchasing routines, and the handling of the pay roll over Employment Department routines. A further complication of relationship comes in even with the executive section of the work, since the collection of customers' accounts must be carried on in close consultation with the Selling Department, so that, on the one hand, selling negotiations with customers shall not be unnecessarily hampered and, on the other hand, that sales efforts shall not be wasted on hopelessly bad payers.

I have said enough to show that the position of the Finance Department is no easy one to define. But that makes it all the more important to attempt to do so.

As I have pointed out, the department has three distinct kinds of work to do, though perhaps it would be better to think of it as two kinds, as the third set of duties which are laid upon it in our organisation are somewhat accidental. They are allocated to this department as a matter of convenience rather than because they are a fundamental part of its work. I will describe this third set briefly and then we can forget about it.

Because of the statistical and calculating equipment of the Finance Department, it is available for general calculation service for other departments. Again it has been found convenient to centralise there the publishing and upkeep of the various instructions regarding routines, organisation charts, classification codes, etc. This does not mean that the Finance Department lays down all such instructions, though in the editing of them for publication it is able to give other departments a great deal of assistance and its criticism is necessary in order to ensure that the whole system of routines and instructions hangs together. Again, as the department using the greatest proportion of the stationery, the purchase and issue of this to the whole place has been placed under its control. This has led to its playing a leading part in the design of all forms.

These are all duties which are very conveniently allocated to the Finance Department, but in other organisations could probably be handled in other ways without impairing the effectiveness of the department's real functions.

Apart from these somewhat accidental duties, the essential functions of the department fall into two classes, viz. :—

1. Preparing financial information for the guidance of the management.

2. Direct executive work—customers' and vendors' accounts, cash and pay roll, etc.

The second part consists of quite definite pieces of work which take their place among what may be called the primary activities of the business—getting the product made and disposed of. I do not propose to discuss this part of the work in detail either, because it presents no very difficult problems of relationship to the rest of the organisation. The problems are mainly ones of accounting technique, though, as I have already pointed out, close contact must be maintained with the Selling Department, the various Purchase Departments and the Employment Department, so that relations with customers, vendors, and labour respectively shall not be disturbed.

I will now direct your attention more particularly to the duties which I have grouped under the first class, viz., the preparation and supply of information from the financial point of view for the guidance of the management. In this sense " management " means, primarily, the managing director or the general manager who is responsible to the board for proposing policy and for the running of the management function. As I have already pointed out, this kind of work is quite distinct in its nature from the other work of the department—the executive side. In the field which we are now considering, the Finance Department acts as a kind of intelligence bureau for the management. Its function, in this respect, is to provide information that is accurate, convenient in form and up to date to enable the management to :—

1. Know the true financial position of the Company *at the moment.*

2. Lay down policy.

3. Judge the results of policy.

4. Measure the effectiveness of the organisation as a whole and of its various parts.

5. Concentrate easily on those high spots in costs in which improvement will bring the greatest return.

The machinery by which these given requirements are met are :—

The system of Accounts.

The Financial Programme.

The Cost System.

It may be desirable to split the accounts into two sets—Company Accounts and Control Accounts. The form of the Company Accounts may be dictated by questions of overall financial policy which may require them to be almost distinct from the Control Accounts. In what follows, therefore, it must be understood that I am dealing with the latter.

The three systems—Control Accounts, Programme and Costs—are complementary parts of one whole system of information and their importance lies, not in the information itself, but in the degree to which it helps the management. This seems to me so obvious as not to need emphasising and yet I think it is sometimes lost sight of. Costs are too often built up by the piling of one abstruse percentage on another, and accounts are compiled with quite arbitrary groupings of expenses and credits, so that the resulting cost and account, while possibly showing correct results, are almost useless as guides to management policy.

Approaching the Accounting, Programming and Costing Systems from the point of view I am here putting forward, certain fundamental principles emerge with regard to them.

In the first place all results should show not only the *actual* position but the position in comparison with the programme or, in the case of costs, with the ideal or " standard."

In the second place, the same main groupings of items must be observed throughout, and the basis for corresponding items in the accounts, the programme, or the costs must be the same. That is to say, a given item or class of expense or credit must always mean the same thing, and be measured at the same level or with the same adjustments, wherever it occurs. Thus, if the charge for handling and storing raw material is dealt with in the *accounts* as a *wages* item, it must not be dealt with in the *cost* system as a *raw material* item. " Raw material " in each case must mean exactly the same thing, and the sum of the raw material in the costs must be the same as the raw material expense shown in the accounts. Or again, if sales are dealt with in the programme at minimum selling value, *i.e.*, as though the maximum trade discount had been allowed throughout, the accounts must also show sales on this basis, as *well* as at the actual value realised. In other words, there must be no elaborate reconciliations to remember in comparing the pictures presented by the Accounts, the Programme and the Costs respectively.

In the third place, the grouping of classes of expense in the Accounts, the Programme and the Cost System should coincide, as far as possible, with the grouping of authority in the organisation. That is to say, the grouping of expenses for Finance Department purposes should be such that for each group or each item there is some definite authority in the organisation that is able to control it, or of whose work it is the measure. Similarly, credits should be so grouped as to correspond with some organic reality in the scheme of running the organisation. Thus, if sales are to be subdivided for the credit side of the Accounts, the subdivision should, if possible, correspond to the subdivisions of the Sales Department.

Fourthly, since the work of the Finance Department is built up on information coming in from all parts of the organisation—invoices, in and out ; time bookings ; attendance records ; stock records ; raw material issues ; shop output returns, etc., etc.—it follows that all of these record systems must be modelled with proper regard to the needs of the Finance Department. They must be based on the same definitions of terms as are used for accounting and costing purposes, the same closing periods must be observed, and groupings must be used which will enable the figures to be incorporated direct into the accounts, etc. This means that for the design of all record systems throughout the organisation which enter, in any way, into the foundations of the costs and the accounts, there must be such a degree of consultation with the Finance Department as amounts practically to a functional control over them by that department.

I will now describe to you, as briefly as I can, the forms of Accounts Programming and Costing that we have adopted, pointing out, as I go along, instances of the four principles I have mentioned. At this point I would remind you again of the kind of business to which these apply, viz., a manufacturing engineering business, making articles that are largely standardised, made mostly for stock, and sold at prices that should remain fixed for a year. I would also remind you that I am primarily dealing with the Control Accounts and ignoring the Company or Shareholders' Accounts.

The Control Accounts comprise the following :—

1. Activity Trading Account.
2. Periodic Balance Sheet.
3. Departmental Accounts.
4. Functional Accounts.

Each of them deals with a "four-week month," which we call a "period."

Behind these there is, of course, a background of many other accounts and records, needed for the collection of the elements that build up into the above accounts.

The Activity Trading Account (see Fig. 1), as its name implies, is a financial measure of the results of the activity of the company, undistorted by adjustments or corrections dictated by accounting or financial policy, and undisturbed by the accidental concentration of expenses at certain periods. Thus, work-in-progress changes are valued as though they were sales and certain items of expense are accrued to avoid jerks.

This account includes, moreover, two sets of statistics, in addition to the financial measure of the period's trading. In the first place, it gives the figures of shop production and of sales, both expressed as minimum selling value, and given both as totals and analysed under the main products. For all these figures, the programme figures are also given, on the same basis of valuation, for comparison.

In the second place, it shows, against the expenses actually incurred, the expenses that should have sufficed for the activity actually performed, if the work had been done at standard efficiency. These are the expenses allowed by the standard costs, and these again are given both for the total expenses and the expenses divided out over the main products and departments.

I should explain at this point that the manufacturing departments are organised, in the main, by product rather than by process, so that the analysis of expenses by *department*, referred to above, gives, at the same time, the analysis by *product*, up to the producing expense level, thus giving a running check on costs.

Coming to the trading account proper, the credits and expenses are given in totals, alongside the programme figures, and are also divided out over the main departments, which division, as already explained, gives at the same time an analysis by product.

The headings throughout are arranged to coincide with divisions of the organisation, so that it is possible to go from each item to one, or more, official who controls it in actual working, and who may be held responsible for it. I will run through the headings used and illustrate this, and other points.

CREDITS COMPRISE—

Sales, for which the sales director is responsible. They are given at invoice value ; the comparison between this and the sales minimum selling value, given in the statistics already mentioned, shows the extent to which the sales director is giving the maximum discount allowed.

Change in work-in-progress—Merchandise, at minimum selling value, for which the sales director through Merchandise Control Section, is responsible.

Change in work-in-progress—Shop, at minimum selling value, for which the works director through output manager through Planning Section, is responsible.

EXPENSES COMPRISE—

Material—main manufacturing—for which works director through material manager, is responsible.

Other manufacturing—for which works director through Special Purchase Section, is responsible.

Less credit for scrap.—Purchase Department, under plant manager, under works director, responsible for collection, disposal and price.

Wages — Producing.—Works director responsible. (Analysis in Departmental Accounts is necessary to bring home the control of this item in detail.)

Holiday Pay.—An accrued item, dealt with separately to reconcile actual wage bill with the full wage charge in the costs.

Depreciation.—An accrued figure ; responsibility lies with a decision of the Board on rates, and applied by Finance Department.

Supplies—Tools.—Responsibility of works director, through design manager.

Other.—Responsibility of works director, through plant manager.

The above are sub-totalled as Producing Expenses.

FIG. 1.

HANS RENOLD LTD.

ACTIVITY TRADING ACCOUNT

SERIES	FINANCIAL YEAR
0·1	PERIOD No.

ACTIVITY AT M.S.V. AND CREDITS	SUMMARY: PROGRAM	SUMMARY: ACTUAL	PRODUCING GROUP: SHOULDERED BUSH	BUSH ROLLER: SMALL PITCH	BUSH ROLLER: OTHER, ODD., HOLLOW STUD	INVERTED TOOTH: SMALL PITCH	INVERTED TOOTH: LARGE PITCH	MORTISE	BLOCK AND ACCESS	WHEEL	SEMI-PRODUCING: TOOL ROOM	SEMI-PRODUCING: WORKS SERVICE	ADM'N	SELLING	UNC'TD	TOTAL	WAGES OF CAPITAL
PRODUCTION — PROGRAM																	
PRODUCTION — ACTUAL																	
DELIVERIES — PROGRAM																	
DELIVERIES — ACTUAL																	
SALES — PROGRAM																	
SALES — ACTUAL																	
SALES AT INVOICE VALUE																	
DISCOUNT ALLOWANCE																	
CHANGE W.I.P. AT M.S.V. — SHOP																	
MERCHANDISE																	
TOTAL CREDIT FOR ACTIVITY																	

(ANALYSIS BY PRODUCT AND ORGANISATION GROUP)

EXPENSES	SUMMARY		ANALYSIS													TOTAL	
MATERIAL — CHAIN																	
OTHER																	
CR. FOR SCRAP																	
WAGES — PRODUCING ETC.																	
INSPECTION																	
HOL. PAY																	
DEPRECIATION																	
SUPPLIES — TOOLS																	
OTHER																	
OTHER																	
PRODUCING TOTAL																	
SEMI-PRODUCING																	
CR. FOR TOOLS																	
CR. FOR WORK DONE																	
ADMINISTRATION																	TO COVER CAPITAL EMPLOYED
SELLING, PUBLICITY A/C CLASS																	
UNCONTROLLED																	
TOTAL EXPENSES																	

			EXPENSE ALLOWANCES FOR ACTIVITY PERFORMED BASED ON STANDARD COSTS														
TOTAL CREDITS																	
SURPLUS OR DEFICIT																	EARNABLE AT TASK EFFICIENCY
CUM'L SURPLUS OR DEFICIT																	

ENTERED	CHECKED	APPROVED	PERIOD No.	FINANCIAL YEAR	SERIES No. 0·1	ACTIVITY TRADING ACCOUNT

QUANTITY BASIS	HANS RENOLD LTD	No OF WORKING WEEKS	SERIES No	PROGRAM No	FINANCIAL YEAR
PRICE BASIS	PROGRAM ACTIVITY TRADING STATEMENT		T1	ISSUE No	PERIOD

ACTIVITY UNIT = 1000	ANALYSIS BY PRODUCT GROUP																				TOTAL UNIT = 1	PERIODIC AVERAGE (4 FULL WEEKS)			% OF MINIMUM SELLING VALUE		% TO PRODUCING WAGES	
	HOLLOW STUD		SHOULDERED BUSH		BUSH ROLLER SMALL PITCH		BLOCK		BUSH ROLLER MED LARGE & EXTENDED		INVERTED TOOTH SMALL PITCH		INVERTED TOOTH LARGE PITCH		MORTISE		ODD & ACCESS		WHEEL									
		% PREV PROG		% PREV PROG		% PREV PROG		% PREV PROG		% PREV PROG		% PREV PROG		% PREV PROG		% PREV PROG		% PREV PROG		% PREV PROG		CURRENT PROGRAM	PREVIOUS PROGRAM	% CURRENT TO PREVIOUS	CURRENT PROGRAM	PREVIOUS PROGRAM	CURRENT PROGRAM	PREVIOUS PROGRAM
PRODUCTION FEETAGE																												
MIN. S.Y.																												
DELIVERIES FEETAGE																												
MIN. S.Y.																												
SALES FEETAGE																												
MIN. S.Y.																												
CHANGE W I P AT M.S.W. SHOP																												
MERCHANDISE																												

EXPENSES UNIT = 1	EXPENSE ALLOWANCES FOR ACTIVITY PLANNED										SUMMARY							
MATERIAL CHAIN																		
OTHER																		
CR FOR SCRAP																		
WAGES PRODUCING, ETC.																		
INSPECTION																		
HOL. PAY																		
DEPRECIATION																		
SUPPLIES TOOLS																		
OTHER,																		
OTHER																		
PRODUCING TOTAL																		
SEMI-PRODUCING																		
ADMINISTRATION																		
SELLING																		
UNCONTROLLED																		
TOTAL EXPENSES																		
SURPLUS OR DEFICIT BASED ON																		
WAGES OF CAPITAL QUOTA ON COST SCALE																		
10 % ON CAPITAL EMPLOYED																		

ENTERED	CHECKED	APPROVED	FINANCIAL YEAR	PERIOD No	SERIES No.	
			192 -2		T1	PROGRAM ACTIVITY TRADING STATEMENT

SEMI-PRODUCING EXPENSES.

(=*Tool Room and Work Services Departments*).—Responsibility of works director, through design and plant managers jointly; for division between them we go to the Departmental Accounts.

Less Credit for work done on Tools and Capital Account.—Shown in this way to enable the whole tool charge to be included among the producing expenses above and the whole expense of the Tool Room and Works Services to be shown here.

Administration. Running expenses of;—D.O. and various head offices under works director; Finance Department under managing director and finance manager; Directors and their offices.

Selling.—Responsibility of sales director.

Uncontrolled.—Items like bank interest and taxation which cannot be brought within the control of any section of the organisation.

It will be realised from what I have said that this Activity Trading Account, together with the statistics which are incorporated with it, provides not only a complete picture of the results of our trading, but also it tells us how we stand in comparison to our expectations, and indicates the department or officer concerned in any point needing investigation. Throughout, like is always compared with like, and all adjustments that are used are made so as to bring the items into coincidence with management realities.

The *Periodic Balance Sheet* is a modification, period by period, of the last company annual balance sheet, in the light of the subsequent periodic activity trading accounts, and incorporates such adjustments as that for bringing the valuation of stocks down from selling value, as used in the Activity Trading Account, to the company balance sheet basis.

The *Departmental Accounts* are Activity Trading Accounts for the main producing departments, the semi-producing departments and the selling department. In the case of the first, the expenses are shown in two distinct stages: first up to the level controlled by the head of the department, and then, as an addition, the expenses of other departments for processes that are not carried out in the department itself. The credits are arrived at by multiplying the *output* by the *standard cost* obtained from the Cost System.

This arrangement serves a double purpose In the first place, the head of the department has an account which, up to a certain level, deals only with what he can himself control and gives, in this way, a measure of his success. The whole account is also a check on the correctness of our costs. These accounts " key up " fully, and without reconciliations, both with the main Activity Trading Account and with the Cost System.

In the case of the semi-producing departments the expenses are all under the control of the head and so do not need showing in two stages. They are, however, analysed in several different ways, *e.g.*, by class of expense—material, wages, etc.—by departmental section, by class of work done and by department for which the work is done. The credits are made up partly by the value of the tools made and work done on capital account, and partly by an allowance for maintenance work based on the percentage included in the cost system for this, applied to the level of activity actually ruling in the shops. This arrangement both sets an expense task to the department and provides a running check on the cost system percentages.

The account for the Selling Department is similar in idea. The expenses are analysed in various ways and compared with the programme. The credits are, as in the previous cases, in the nature of allowable expenses based on the cost system percentage for selling applied to the level of activity obtaining.

The *Functional Accounts* are expense analyses only, of those departments, like inspection, whose work runs through a number of other departments. The comparison in these cases is not between expenses and credits, but between actual expenses and programmed expenses. The expenses " key up " with all the other accounts and the functional accounts coincide with subdivisions of authority in the organisation and are used, like the departmental accounts, to judge the work of some particular official.

THE PROGRAMME.

This is a forecast of the Trading Accounts for half a year's or a year's four weekly periods, together with a programme of capital expenditure and a forecast of the cash position resulting from the two.

The programme is based on very carefully compiled forecasts of probable sales, built up from reports from agents, branch offices, etc., and criticised in the light of statistics going back over a number of years. The sales forecasts take account of seasonal effects and holiday periods, of which we have careful records. Sales forecasts are, of course, largely affected by price policy and one or two trial forecasts, with different price policies, may have to be made. Having arrived at our sales forecast and expressed it both as volume and value, the state of our finished stocks is considered and stock policies proposed. The sales forecasts, modified by the stock policy for each class of product, gives us the level of production required from the various works departments. Having arrived at the production programme, period by period, the expenses that will be necessary for it can be laid down up to the producing level, from our Cost System. The rest of the expenses are put in from a consideration of their existing level, modified as may be necessary according to the relation which the proposed activity bears to that then current.

This gives us a means of reviewing conveniently our overhead expenses and of *planning* them in relation to the expected activity. Instead of treating our overhead as some kind of inevitable, more or less fixed, percentage on our wages or some other measure of shop activity, we decide what amount of overhead we can afford for the expected shop activity and how this amount can be most usefully distributed, and so set ourselves expense tasks for each class of overhead expense. The amount and distribution of overhead expenses laid down in this way are also used for the percentages to be used in the costs for the period in question. Having got our forecast of expenses, as described, the forecast of credits follows from the sales forecasts, plus the stock changes decided on. From these expenses and credits a programme trading account is made up, showing the expected position period by period for the half year, or the full year as the case may be, and the expected "*activity*" profit, period by period. While the above programme is in preparation, estimates are being prepared by all departments of the capital expenditure which they desire during the same interval as the programme. These estimates are examined and an approved Capital Expenditure Budget arrived at. From this and the results of the Trading Programme, the expected changes in the cash position, period by period, are arrived at, and by further corrections forecasting the end of the year adjustments, particularly with regard to stock depreciation, a forecast of the Company Balance Sheet is prepared.

In all this work the Finance Department acts as focus, editor and publisher. The responsibility for the sales forecasts rests, of course, with the Sales Department, and the proposed expense allowances for the programmed works activity have to be accepted by the works director, and the various items of overhead expense by the various directors concerned. The various steps in producing the programme cannot, of course, be completed seriatim as the result depends on so many inter-related factors. These steps have in fact largely to be taken simultaneously and trial results obtained based on various assumptions, *e.g.*, as to prices, publicity policy, expense reduction efforts, etc., and it is the work of the Finance Department to work up these trial programmes and to indicate to the sales and works groups the probable effects of the policies they have in mind.

THE COSTING SYSTEM.

This follows the same line as the Control Accounts—that is to say, while the Control Accounts show the expenses incurred by the various sections of the organisation, the Cost System shows the amount of expense, grouped in exactly the same way, incurred in respect of a given product. For our products other than those few that are on a jobbing basis, full cost studies are made once a year or once in two years. The keying up of the Cost System with the accounts gives us a running check as to the degree to which we are departing from our costs, so that we are not left in ignorance of real costs in the interval. The cost items up to the producing level are based on a time study investigation into the times for each process and the material required. The various other items of expense—semi-producing, administration and selling—are put on as percentages derived from the proportions for the total of these expenses in the programme. That is to say, our costs are standard costs, which are correct—

1. As long as the producing departments maintain their standard efficiencies.

2. As long as the total activity conforms to the programme. If it falls below, the costs do not bring up enough to cover the overhead; if it exceeds the programme, they bring up more than is needed.

The Departmental Accounts keep the management informed as to whether the producing departments are living up to their part of the cost, and the expense-allowance-for-activity-performed part of the Activity Trading Account tells us to what extent the actual activity is bringing up the necessary amounts to meet the actual expenses of the various overhead departments.

I will now recall the four principles I laid down with regard to the Accounting and Costing Systems and comment briefly on their application to the schemes I have been describing.

The first was the necessity for comparing actual results with programmed figures.

This is done for every main figure in the Activity Trading Account. In the Departmental Accounts, the credits are really a programme, *i.e.*, they are the expenses that were allowed for in the assumptions on which the programme was compiled.

I might mention here, without going into details, that quite elaborate steps are taken to adjust the programme period by period to the situation, as it appears at short range. If this were not done, the programme would be so out of date by the end of its term as to be useless as a measure. But even here, the adjusted programmes must always be able to be compared easily with the original programme.

The second principle was to keep the same basis for each item, no matter where it appears, whether in the Activity Trading Account, a departmental or functional account, the Programme or the Cost System. If an item appears in more than one place, it must always mean the same thing. We lay great stress on this in our system and it has taken a long process to get there, first of reconciliations and then of defining our bases and modifying our organisation, so as to obviate the need for reconciliations. I suggest that there is no single feature so likely to mar the usefulness of cost and accounting systems to the management of a business as the need for complex reconciliations.

The third principle was that the structure of the accounts and costs should coincide with the structure of the organisation. Accounting items should be so grouped and built up that each item or each group is the measure of the work of some definite organisation group under a known authority. I have stressed this point throughout my description, and will only add that to arrive at this position is not the task of the Cost Accountant alone. Both the structure of the organisation and the scheme of the accounts may need modifying, and the two should be considered together. The necessity for doing this points, even if nothing else did, to the wide outlook called for from the head of the Finance Department.

The fourth principle referred to the need for keying up together, and with the accounts, all records and routines throughout the place. What I have already said about keying up is sufficient to show what has been done. We aim at eliminating all the odds and ends of records that are so often kept for the private information of this or that foreman or manager, by himself. If a record is worth having at all, it must be brought into line with all other similar records and be on the recognised bases as regards time conditions, units of value, of measure and nomenclature, etc.

I will now summarise the points I have been dealing with.

In the first place I described an organisation suited to a particular type of manufacturing engineering business.

I then outlined the work done by the Finance Department, grouping it under three heads and emphasised that the relation of the department to the rest of the organisation was a very different one with regard to each kind of work, viz. :—

For the first.—The supply of information ; it was an intelligence bureau for the management.

For the second.—It was an executive department ; and

For the third.—It was a service department to many other departments and exercised a functional control over many of the routines and records in other departments.

I then proceeded to consider in some detail the nature of the work of the first class, pointing out that it was epitomised in the production of the

Control Accounts.

Programme.

Costs.

The importance of these lay in the degree to which they assisted the management ; they were not an end in themselves, and I laid down four principles which seemed to me to be fundamental, if they are to serve their proper purpose. These were :—

1. Comparing results with programmes.
2. Uniformity of basis for similar items, no matter where they appear ; a given item must always mean the same thing.
3. Making the grouping of accounting and costing items correspond to the groupings of the organisation and the distribution of authority.
4. Keying up all records throughout the organisation with the accounting and cost records.

And finally I described to you in some detail the forms of our main Control Accounts, the Programme and the Cost System, in order to illustrate the application of the above principles.

I have now described the work I expect from a Cost Accountant, and the relations of his department to the rest of the organisation ; but in case you feel that I have only partially answered the original question, I will add a few words as to the qualities which it seems to me most important that he should possess.

I am not now speaking of technical proficiency —of course he must have that—but of his more general qualities of mind and personality. Two qualities or groups of qualities seem to me to be of outstanding importance. In the first place, he must have a passion for facts and truth. This must, however, be exercised with tact and sympathy, and above all, with single-mindedness. It must not degenerate into mere inquisitiveness, still less into " catching people out." He must not be a " busy-body," nor a detective, nor a lawyer trying to prove a case. He must be like a scientist studying the health of a community : he wants the facts, he wants them in their true relations and undisturbed by personalities, and he wants them for the ultimate good of the community itself.

And secondly, he must not get lost in figures and abstractions, but be able to see these and deal with them as symbols representing real life. It is the actual facts of management that matter ; the Cost Accountant's systems are only tools for sorting and clarifying these. He must, in short, always be able to *see the facts behind the figures*.

It is, of course, possible to continue the list of necessary qualities almost endlessly ; but the two groups which I have tried to indicate will go a good long way, combined with proficiency in the technique of accountancy and costing methods, to provide me with " what I expect of a Cost Accountant."

* * *

THE USE OF GRAPHICS IN COST ACCOUNTANCY.*

By T. GERALD ROSE, M.I.Mech.E., Technical Adviser to the Managing Director of Linotype and Machinery, Ltd., Altrincham, Cheshire.

(This paper, illustrated by lantern slides, was given before a Meeting of the Manchester and District Branch of the Institute of Cost and Works Accountants on 7th November, 1929.)

THE increase of interest recently to be observed in graphical methods of demonstrating facts in business is the subject of some satisfaction to those who have for years been using this particular method, especially when combined with the growing tendency to more scientific methods of administration and management.

First in one direction, and then in another, advances can be noted—here in the illustration of popular articles by means of curves, and there by the inclusion of chapters on business graphics in books of management. The latest step which has come to my attention in this connection—a step which to me seems as significant as any—consists in the embodiment in the I.C.W.A. Final Examination of Costing, Parts 3 and 4, of the following question :—

> " 8. Prepare a set of charts and briefly describe how they may be used to enable the Management effectively to control the factory and direct the sales organisation."

Considering that six questions out of eight have to be answered, and the time allowed for the whole is only three hours, it is obvious to anyone with knowledge of the subject of graphical control that the candidate is asked to attempt what is, on the face of it, impossible, since the average time allowed per question amounts to half an hour.

However, the Institute is to be congratulated on being, so far as I am aware, the first controlling body to include in their examination a definite question dealing with the value of graphical control to the management. Other Institutions certainly make references to graphics in their examination syllabus, but only from a general point of view. The inclusion, therefore, of this question points to the fact that the Institute of Cost and Works Accountants has been the first to appreciate the value of graphical methods to those who are concerned with the control and management of a business.

This is, however, only as it should be. The cost accountant exists in order to analyse what is going on in a business from the practical point of view of profit or loss. To him accountancy is only a means by which he obtains the facts for which he is searching, and it is his duty and his privilege to metamorphose the dry bones of statistical returns, which rattle so dismally in most companies, into a useful and efficient member of the administrative staff. To accomplish this miracle there is only one effective way, and that is the graphical method. Statistics will always remain statistics, and reports will always remain reports ; analysing statistics, even to the trained accountant, is by no means an easy task, and the study of reports is to the average manager a weariness to the flesh and a temptation to sleep. He takes up the wad of foolscap with the intention of skimming through it as quickly as possible and making a note of those things which seem to him important—and in most Reports the points which are important could be typed in a few sentences in the margins themselves. Most of you will be familiar with a certain scientific paper with a somewhat deceptive title in which the gist of scientific articles is presented to the reader shorn of all unnecessary verbiage. To read these paragraphs is an education in the art of précis writing, and when one realises that in a great number of cases the useful idea at the back of a five-thousand-word article can be expressed in a sentence of twenty-five or thirty words, one appreciates why many managing directors become so weary of the bulky Report neatly bound in brown paper, compiled by an enthusiastic assistant who feels he will not be considered as having done his job properly unless he can show something of a solid nature as a result of his work.

Cost accountancy, more than any other profession perhaps, exists in order to investigate commercial facts and to present statements. The average managing director, or general manager, has had no training in accountancy, and although he could not have attained his position without a good working knowledge of costs and accountancy in general, he is in most cases unaware of the lengths to which inventions in office machinery can enable the modern cost accountant to go in the analysis of statistics and the preparation of comparisons. But the years pass and with them the older generation. The younger men who are gradually coming on to take the directorial positions at the top are more in touch with the recent developments of modern business practice. They are not going to be satisfied for long with having an expensive and complicated outfit of office machinery and yet getting from it only the same information as they got before it was installed, even though that information may be prepared and placed before them in anything from half to one-tenth of the time previously taken. In the old days one was lucky to get a cost a month after a job was finished. Nowadays one can have a cost placed before one all the time the work is going on, correct to within twenty-four hours of the progress made. But the managing director of the future is not going to rest content with that. The mere fact that his costs can be prepared and placed before him so rapidly will give him more time to investigate, and the pile of accurate and up-to-date costs before him will bring with them the logical demand for some equally efficient summary by which he can see how these costs are locked up with the other items which contribute to the well-being of his works and his company. Of the costs before him, so many are well below the estimate, so many are on the border line, and one or two are perhaps above. How is this going to affect his total profits for the year if things go on as they are going ? What is the reason for the excess where his cost is coming out above the estimate ? How much of his order-book is composed of work of this type on which he is making little or nothing ? What was the sales' quota for that particular line ? How are the salesmen keeping up to the quota, and would it be wise to circularise all the selling agencies with a view to withdrawing that particular line as much as possible from the market ? These and many others are the queries which develop one by one from analyses which are provided by the cost accountant, and by the very fact of their magnitude and diversity these problems become exceedingly difficult to administrate in any clear and effective fashion. Consequently the cost accountant who is making a legitimate effort to become the right-hand man of the managing director, advising him as to the wisest course to pursue in view of the facts which are being continually disclosed by the statistics, must make a serious effort to find the simplest and most effective way of laying those statistics clearly before his chief. This is where he will find the graphical method the best—and, in fact, the only one by which he can obtain a full hearing for what he has to say. Lines, bars and circles, are all at his disposal to be made into pictures from which the busy man at the head of affairs can obtain an instant impression of what is going on ; and where a report would be skimmed through, or a pile of statistics pushed impatiently on one side after a superficial survey, a chart will be accepted and appreciated because the whole situation can be taken in at a glance.

For that reason I should like to see the Institute go still further and make the subject of graphical methods in cost accountancy not an optional question, to be answered in half an hour, but a definite part of the syllabus, with a section in the Examinations entirely of its own. It is not as if it is susceptible of different solutions by specialists who disagree among themselves as to the principles upon which it should be carried out. There is to-day in existence a definite technique of graphics, not only of the methods and principles on which these charts should be drawn up, but also of the lines upon which the cost accountant should go to work in order to lay the foundation for an interlocked graphical control of the business under consideration. Ten years ago the excuse might have been put forward that there were no effective principles, methods, or squared paper available. To-day, however, the whole theory of business graphics has been surveyed and worked out, whilst there is no difficulty in obtaining standard chart papers in convenient sizes, punched to fit standard ring binders, and divided into every scale or design which the accountant can require to carry out his work properly. Every circumstance, therefore, that is required to build up a proper system of business graphics is available ready for use, and it remains only for those in authority to insist that the principles should be studied and developed. The best way to attain this is probably by means of the unsatisfactory, but perhaps necessary, method of including management graphics as a subject to itself in the syllabus of Examinations, and definitely insisting that those taking the Examination shall prepare for and pass in this subject. Once this has been done, and it is perhaps not too much to hope that the Institute of Costs and Works Accountants will be the first to do it, the advantages of graphical methods in management will steadily become more obvious, and we shall have added a new and very valuable weapon to our business armoury.

Since in my paper to-night I have been asked to deal more with control by graphical methods than with the graphics themselves, I do not intend to discuss in any detail the different types of chart available. As, however, there may be some amongst you who have not had much experience of this type of work, or who may not be aware of certain modern developments, I propose to show a number of slides of different types of chart, so that you may perhaps better be able to understand references that I may make later.

(Here followed lantern-slides illustrating 35 different kinds of charts.)

Some years ago I had the opportunity of examining the results of a company which had done fairly well during the boom days and, when the slump came, made a loss, like many others. Those in charge of the business were not at all clear as to why this had occurred, and although the managing director had various charts showing the results of the monthly working, they were so involved that no manager could possibly have obtained any results from them. For my own interest I worked out the trend of the direct labour, the output and the sales, and the position then become perfectly clear. What had in fact occurred was that the sales during the boom period had greatly exceeded the output, which had lagged behind owing to the difficulty in getting suitable labour. When the labour was available and the ouptut had risen, the sales had already begun to fall off, and, owing to the fact that the management could not clearly see what was happening, the labour was not reduced in time; production overran the sales to a considerable extent, stocks were piled up, and at the conclusion of the year the company showed a loss. Had some form of graphical control been in use, the position would have been obvious and the production could have been reduced in time to break level on the year's working.

I do not wish to deal to-night with graphical demonstrations of balance sheet problems, or the charting of accountancy questions arising from allocation of overheads and expenses. I want to try to outline to you the skeleton of a graphical control by means of which a managing director can make sure just how affairs are going with his concern, and so avoid trouble of the nature just described. The preparation of this graphical control would, naturally, fall to the lot of his adviser, the cost accountant, whose duty it would also be to see that the necessary statistics were forthcoming promptly by the correct dates. This form of control has been proved to be invaluable in actual use, and although there remains much research work still to be done, the following description may be of assistance to some of you in introducing something of the same nature.

In every well-managed concern a statement is made covering the results of each month. Such statements can be voluminous and involved, often running to thirty or forty foolscap pages, which may not link up with each other in any logical sequence. It is necessary, therefore, to make some kind of sub-division of these statements, and when this is undertaken, it will almost certainly be found that it is not possible to obtain a satisfactory result merely by transferring to squared paper a summary of these existing statements. A "control," to be effective, must take account of certain things which do not affect the accountancy side, and, therefore, the various important factors must be picked out from here and there and combined together in a logical manner. For the purpose of developing our company control to-night we will classify the items to be reviewed into four sections, as follows:—

1. Trading Result.
2. Business Position.
3. Financial Position.
4. The Sales Pound.

Before going into these four sections in detail, it may be as well to point out that a complete company control is essentially made up of two classes of charted results, which might be designated "primary" and "secondary" respectively. The primary control consists only of the final results, vital figures which can all be got into a quarto sheet of paper. The secondary control takes each section of the primary and analyses it into its component factors, so that the reason for a change in the trend of some primary item can be immediately located amongst the charts of the secondary group. This is done in order to avoid confusing the mind of the executive chief with a vast number of charts; the main object of the primary control should be to present the salient facts of the business month by month in the absolute minimum of space, leaving the multitudinous questions which subsequently arise to be dealt with by the secondary control.

SECTION I.—TRADING RESULT FOR PAST MONTH.

Obviously the first thing required here is the net profit or loss which has resulted from the month's working. The main questions which arise are :—

(A) What has been the profit or loss for the past month ?

(B) How does that profit or loss compare with previous months ?

(C) Is the result to date better or worse than for the same period last year ?

(D) Is the trend of profit-earning upward or downward ?

All these questions are answered at once by an ordinary Z chart built up on the " net

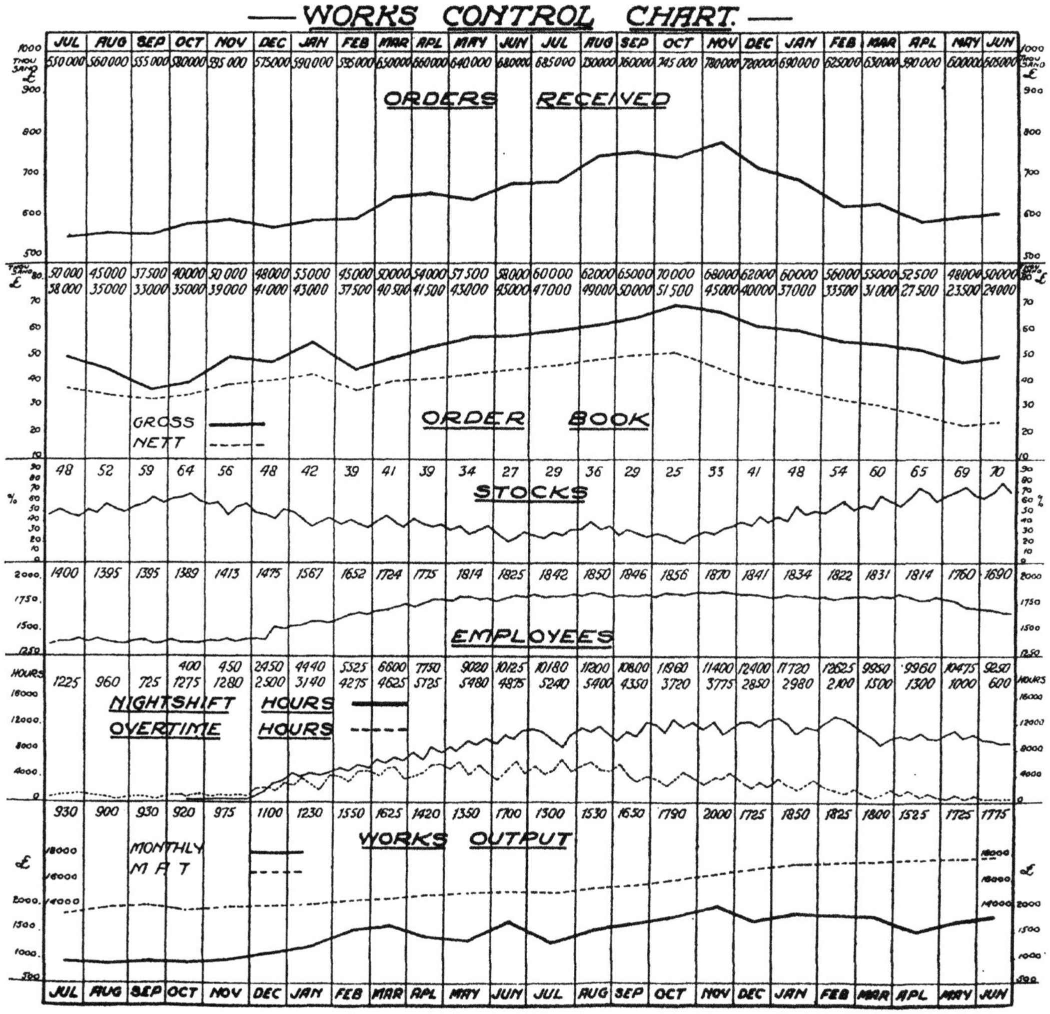

profits" monthly results. The "current" line answers (A) and (B); the "cumulative" line when compared with the chart for the previous year gives (C); and (D) is clearly indicated by the "moving annual total." Further inquiries as to how the profit is divided amongst the various manufacturing departments or subsidiary companies can be answered from the secondary control charts; they should not be included in the primary group.

SECTION 2.—BUSINESS POSITION OF THE COMPANY.

Having reviewed his profits—or losses—for the past month, the managing director's thoughts naturally turn to the present and future, so as to consider whether the situation is likely to alter. For this review he requires :—

(A) What is the state of the order-book for the 1st of the new month?

(B) What did Sales amount to for past month, and what is Sales' forecast?

(C) What did Deliveries amount to for past month, and what is Delivery forecast?

(A) The order-book, or the amount of work ahead of the company, is a matter of considerable importance in the management of affairs. In most businesses there will be a certain "normal" level for all classes of work entered in the order-book and the policy of the company must be based to a considerable extent upon whether the order-book stands above or below the normal level. This is even more marked in the case of the Works order-book, with which we shall deal later.

Concerns marketing an article for which quick delivery is asked will usually be found to have a small order-book, the amount being based on the maximum delay which the customer will accept when he places his order. Hence with such businesses the delivery promise limits the amount of orders received, and if the order-book is to be increased the turnover will have to increase, since the "number of days' work ahead" remains the same. On investigation it will be found that some businesses doing a large annual turnover run year after year with a remarkably small order-book—small if expressed in terms of "output per working day." Many a managing director would be alarmed if told his company had only two weeks' work in front of it. Yet the two weeks' work, like the widow's cruse, is never exhausted.

(B) *Sales for the past month and Sales' Forecast.*

This will be best met by a Z-chart for total sales; the m.a.t. line will give the trend of the sales as a whole, and the "current" line will show the results month by month, the slope of the "cumulative" line giving a clear indication as to what is likely to be turned over for the year.

Sales' forecasting, as far as the statistical side is concerned, becomes an easy matter, as the current Z-chart is placed on top of the Z-charts for previous years and the two compared on a luminous background. You will note I have said "as far as the statistical side is concerned" —this was because the selling problems of an organisation are usually very much more erratic than the manufacturing ones, and statistics of previous results cannot always be regarded as trustworthy. In certain businesses there is a distinct seasonal trend, and by very careful sales' forecasting, and setting quotas for all districts and products, a remarkably close estimate can be made of probable sales for some months in advance. On the other hand, there are some businesses which by their nature make it extremely difficult to forecast sales accurately. Even in these cases, however, Z-charts of past years' sales give some indication of what has occurred; to what extent they are of value, however, must rest on the discretion of the managing director who is studying them.

(C) *Deliveries for the past month and Delivery Forecasts.*

The delivery results can be dealt with from invoices in precisely the same manner as the sales' results mentioned above—Z-charts showing how affairs are going forward, and acting as a comparative basis for past years. In the case where a Works is concerned, however, forecasting deliveries is usually a fairly simple job, provided the practice of valuing the Works' output is in use, since it is then an easy matter to bring down the output to a "value per working day" basis and so provide an accurate comparison from month to month. The relation between the delivery value per working day and the number of men employed, night shift, overtime, etc., is soon found after a little experience, and so from the number of employees in the place the deliveries can be fairly accurately forecasted.

It may be as well, perhaps, to point out here that the control of deliveries often does not lie within the power of the manufacturing departments; goods may be completed and then held up because the customer cannot accept them. An abnormal case of this kind would result in a heavy drop in delivery value, which would show up badly against a normal result in the sales; but the managing director would have already noticed that his figure for "work completed awaiting delivery," shown on the order-book chart, had considerably increased, and this would have given him the key to the drop in the deliveries. Had the "work completed awaiting delivery" remained at approximately the same figure, he would then have known that the drop in deliveries meant some serious hold-up in the manufacturing departments.

(D) *Inventory Turnover and Monthly Investment.*

So many items of interest refer back to the turnover that it is as well to include it on the primary control chart. By adapting the scales the inventory can be shown on the same section without confusion, and from a comparison of the two figures involved the monthly investment can be calculated. As it will be the object of the management to keep the inventory down, and shorten the turnover period, it is clear that improvement in this direction is indicated by the figure in the "months column" becoming smaller.

SECTION 3.—FINANCIAL POSITION OF THE COMPANY.

This section is, perhaps, more difficult than the others to define, as certain items which may be of the utmost importance to one company may be negligible to another. For instance, the rise of an overdraft may mean liquidation to one concern; to another a decrease in "bills payable" is imperative if ruin is to be avoided. Yet to a third both these items are unimportant.

To lay out a control scheme, however, it is best to consider the needs of a company in a normal financial position, and leave the abnormal items to be the subject of a special investigation, and additional charts.

Probably the question as to what are the most important facts for a managing director to watch in connection with the financial position of his company would provide as much difference of opinion as any other section of this control. Quite apart from the actual financial position of the company requiring special safeguards, there is, in addition, the personal preferences which have been developed from financial experience obtained in different ways. It is of the utmost importance to reduce the primary control items to the lowest possible number and only to choose those which, by their variation, can point a direct finger at any change in the company's position for better or worse.

To start with, let us take:—

(A) "*Net Worth.*"

This, as you are aware, is "the difference between all the assets and all the liabilities," and can be obtained from the monthly interim balance sheets. In itself, without investigation it indicates very little, but once the state of affairs represented by the "net worth" figure has been clearly realised, the variation in this figure from month to month will indicate whether the position is improving or getting worse.

(B) *Ratio of Net Profits to "Net Worth."*

This figure gives an indication of the successful working of the company, *i.e.*, that x profits have been made over a twelve months' trading period of the company, starting with a net worth of y. Since, as we have previously seen, we can obtain the net worth of the company each month, we can also obtain a monthly ratio of net profits to net worth by using the moving annual total of the net profits in calculation. A moment's thought will show that since the moving annual total at the end of twelve months corresponds with the cumulative figure for that twelve months, any figure which is usually taken out annually can also be taken out monthly by using the moving annual total. I would draw your attention to this valuable fact. It is a common thing for accountants, and those interested in management, to consider that there are certain figures which are not available except as annual results. The particular case which we are discussing is one of these, since, obviously, it would be useless to compare the *monthly* net profit with the net worth. If, on the other hand, we take the moving annual total of the net profits, we obtain the effect of a financial year perpetually moving forward, and by the time we have arrived at the twelfth month, which forms the conclusion of the actual financial year under review, we have subtracted all the old months, and are therefore left with the current twelve-monthly period.

(C) *Ratio of Trading Profit to Turnover.*

Here, again, we use the moving annual total in both cases, and the figure that results gives the trend of the earnings on the turnover under review. I think it will be conceded that this is a figure of sufficient importance from the financial point of view as to be admitted to the primary control list.

(D) *Ratio of Trading Profits to the Total Capital Employed.*

This figure has been described as the real measure of the operating efficiency of a business, and since the trading profit figure is taken, the result is not confused by any fixed charges which have no bearing upon the trading efficiency of the company as a whole. In this case we use the moving annual total of the trading profits, compared with the capital used in the production of the net profits. This figure is, of course, obtained from the monthly interim balance sheets.

(E) *Ratio of Factory Cost to Turnover.*

This is a ratio which requires careful watching, as if the turnover rises, the factory cost should fall. This is by no means a foregone conclusion, as it naturally depends upon the exact causes at the back of the turnover rise. It is as well, therefore, to control this item in order to be sure that full advantage is obtained from a turnover rise.

As you are aware, there are a vast number of other management ratios in existence, and anyone with an ingenious mind and a leaning towards finance could continue the development of these ratios almost indefinitely. It therefore becomes necessary to pick out only those of the greatest importance and reduce their number as much as possible. The ones that I have chosen are all, at any rate, important, and may serve as a basis for our control.

SECTION 4.—THE SALES POUND.

Returning now to the first section, we there recorded the profit or loss made for the month. In every pound sterling of sales a profit has been made, let us say, of 2s. The remaining 18s. has therefore been expended on manufacturing and selling the goods. If this expense could have been reduced to 17s., the profit would have been 3s. instead of 2s. It is therefore of primary importance to the managing director to know how his Sales Pound has been made up each month, for once he takes the basis of the Sales Pound in his analysis of the results of his company he can begin to build up the structure from which action can be taken; and this, after all, is the reason why we are taking so much trouble. Analysis is only a means, not an end.

Every pound of sales is made up of so much fixed charges, so much company overhead, so much manufacturing expense, so much manufacturing cost, and so much profit; and under these five headings we can group the whole of the moneys shown in the profit and loss account. Once we have this clearly set down in the primary control, the further analysis under each section can be left to the secondary control.

The profit is the portion of the Sales Pound which we shall watch throughout our control, in order to make sure that the profits of the company are not falling off. The whole value of watching the Sales Pound lies in the little section at the top of the bar which shows the profit. The other four sections can expand or contract, but the profit section should not contract—or, if it does, it must be by arrangement.

It is obvious that the total sales will have a very considerable bearing upon the make up of the Sales Pound, since, as the sales go up, the profits will rise, and therefore the percentage amount representing, say, the fixed charges in the Sales Pound will become less. The *sum* representing the fixed charges may not, however, have varied at all, and it should, therefore, be borne in mind that we are dealing throughout with percentages and not with sterling results. These actual results must always be available for inspection in the secondary control chart; the percentage forms the basis of comparison from which our investigations would start.

CONCLUSION—COMPANY CONTROL.

Having now chosen a number of selected items under the above four sections, it remains for us to combine them into a control. The four sections can all be drawn out on a large sheet of paper, one beneath the other, registering by the monthly divisions; and as the points are plotted month by month, and as the curves grow across the chart field, the managing director has under his survey, at a glance, the complete story of the fortunes of the business which he controls.

It would serve little purpose for me to elaborate at length on paper the information that can be obtained from the slide of this that I present. It has been built up from imaginary figures, and, therefore, is certainly by no means as interesting as the genuine article which it represents. You will appreciate the fact that the genuine article is of a private and confidential nature, and that no company would agree to their results being made the subject of public illustration. The example, however, will probably serve its purpose to show how as one curve rises another falls, and how, once the conditions surrounding the genesis of each curve have been thoroughly appreciated, the behaviour of that curve can enable the reader to see at once whether all is going well.

I do not wish to imply that the study of these single charts alone is sufficient; it is clear that the primary figures must be so condensed that the secondary charts must always be available for instant reference if the position is to be thoroughly clear. The net worth may improve, and yet be due to an unhealthy factor. The primary control does not show this, it is true, but the secondary control, which would show the position of the assets, should immediately give an indication of this suspicious item. Apart from this, one is surely justified in assuming that the managing director for whom this control is intended would be personally cognisant of a fact of that nature.

WORKS CONTROL.

The cost accountant is concerned chiefly with the Works at the present time, and the Works Control deals with certain items which are not financial. Here we shall need to analyse not only the money side of the business, but the various items connected with Works management, and collate them in such a fashion that a picture can be obtained as to how the general affairs of the Works are going on. We have the order-book, the orders received, orders delivered, the materials purchased, the stocks of all kinds, the direct and indirect labour, the overtime and night shift, and the output of the Works, and these are all matters to which careful consideration must be given. If the Works as a whole is to function as an efficient machine, all these items must be tuned together so as to run in perfect unison.

Once again we must pick out the items which are vital to the primary control, and leave the rest to the secondary control chart book for reference when necessary. For this purpose, therefore, we take :—

(A) *The moving Annual Total of Orders Received at the Works.*

This item is the manufacturing charter of the Works. The movements of almost every factor in Works management are based upon it. There is always a time lag between the reception of orders and the release of them to the Works as goods for manufacture; and it is best, therefore, to acknowledge that this difference exists, and to start, for the purpose of Works' Control, with the orders which have been passed for manufacture to the Works. In addition, the value will be stated in Works cost allowance figures (*i.e.*, estimated factory cost) and not in actual selling values, which alters matters considerably.

The moving annual total here gives the trend of the orders received, and by watching this curve we can forecast whether the orders are likely to fall or rise, and whether a greater or a less effort will be expected in the near future to keep the order-book at its normal level.

(B) *Total Order-book, Gross and Net.*

The gross order-book is found by taking the Works cost allowance value of all orders on the books not yet delivered, and the net order-book is found by subtracting from the gross order-book the value of all work completed by the manufacturing departments but not yet delivered. For subsequent control purposes it is necessary to differentiate clearly between these two figures, since an order-book which is high in gross value and low in net value may give an altogether untrue impression as to the amount of work ahead of the manufacturing side. When the difference between the two books is high, it is clear that there is some hitch with regard to deliveries; either work has been put in hand before its correct date, or for some reason customers cannot accept delivery. It is clearly in the interest of every company to keep the difference between the gross and net order-books as small as possible, since all work completed but not delivered represents moneys paid out for material and labour which cannot be recovered until the goods have been delivered and invoiced. Moreover, if the work is completed by the manufacturing departments and not despatched, it is blocking up useful productive floor area and may be a real hindrance to further productive work being put in hand.

From the net order-book figure can be deduced the stage when overtime or night shift should be put on or taken off; and taken as a whole the order-book is the clearest business indication as to whether the manufacturing and selling sides of the organisation are running in unison or one falling behind the other. It is one of the main foundations of the Works Control.

The gross and net order-books can either be expressed as a compound "bar" chart or as a double line chart. There is no objection to the latter being used, as obviously the two lines can never cross; and the distance between the two lines would show the amount of work which is completed and awaiting delivery—hence the closer together the two lines, the better.

(C) *Stocks available.*

We included in the company control a financial figure for the total value of the stocks on the company's books. If possible, the figures should be taken in the Works Control not as a financial one, but as a physical one, based upon the authorised stocks which have been laid down for the various classes of goods manufactured. Where no manufacturing to stock takes place this figure, naturally, falls out, but the great majority of companies who work on batch production endeavour to provide quick deliveries for their customers by holding a certain amount of stock ready for immediate delivery. In this case, therefore, the best practice is to set certain definite limits for each class of stock which the company have decided to hold, and then credit the Works with 100 per cent. efficiency if every item is reported complete. Individual stocks in excess of the authorised figure are not allowed to count, and stocks below the authorised figure represent a deduction from the 100 per cent. possible. In this manner the rise and fall of the "stock" line represents the success or failure of the Works manager to keep his stocks up to the correct level; the secondary control, naturally, would provide information as to which items were short and which were complete. It will be seen when we come to discuss control as a whole that the percentage of permissible stocks held is of considerable value to us in visualising the position.

(D) *Employees.*

(E) *Overtime and Night Shift.*

These items show clearly how the personnel, and what might be called the reserve effort, are moving, and are clearly necessary in order to review the situation.

(F) *Works' Output per Working Day.*

Certain fortunate companies are in the position of working to a thirteen-period year, each period having four weeks, and a precisely similar number of working days. This is of considerable assistance to the whole of the management as far as direct comparison is concerned. The great majority of firms, however, have been running too long on the old system to wish to upset the comparison with past records by making a change, and in this case a very simple basis of comparison is taken in the shape of the working day. Once this basis has been taken, the lengths of the months, numbers of Saturdays and Sundays, the incidence of holidays, and so forth, are of no importance; and once the monthly figures have been got out, it is a matter of a few minutes to supply a set of results calculated on the P.W.D. basis.

As far as the Works' output is concerned, we require the "moving annual total" in order that we may see whether the trend of results is upwards or downwards, and we also require the individual monthly results reduced to a working-day basis, so that we can make sure that the monthly result is what it should be, having in view the number of employees and the amount of night shift and overtime.

We have now six sections from which we can develop our Works' Control; and from the accompanying slide it will be seen how these items can be watched in their relative rise and fall. If the orders received rise and the Works' effort is not sufficient to meet the call, the order-book, naturally, rises as well. The stocks fall at the same time, since they are drawn on to meet the increase in sales. It is clear from the output per working day, and from the fact that the moving annual total of the orders received has an upward trend, that the Works' effort, which is known to be efficient—*i.e.*, nothing more can be got from the men already employed—is not enough. Instructions, therefore, go out to take on more hands, and the total employees' curve begins to rise. This increase is reflected in a similar rise to the night shift curve. Meanwhile the situation is being met by excessive overtime—a bad practice, but better than losing orders—and this is immediately brought out on the overtime curve.

The months pass and the situation begins to right itself. The orders received keep steadily rising, but the total employees' curve having risen to meet it, the order-book has dropped to a reasonable position. The stocks are beginning to come back again and the overtime and night shift are also coming back to normal. The output per working day from the Works has risen accordingly. In other words, the situation is once again in balance, and should continue so until the orders begin to fall off. This may quite possibly be due to seasonable conditions, and the picture then reverses itself. The order-book begins to drop; the stocks begin to rise; and the net order-book reaches a dangerously low level. Immediately the Works manager follows this by reducing the total employees, the night shift falls, the overtime comes down to the minimum, and the Works' output per working day returns to a lower figure.

What I have been describing to you is not a fancy theory; it is a system which has been tried out and has been proved to work even more smoothly than the authors had ever dared to expect. It provides a perfectly clear picture from month to month of the position of the Works, and coupled with prompt and efficient cost accountancy, it provides a safeguard which should put the fortunes of any Works in which it is used completely beyond the dangers and pitfalls that so often surround the manufacturing centre. It has, of course, no bearing upon the sales. The collapse of the sales is a matter entirely outside the Works' Control; but it guarantees that should that collapse of the sales take place, the loss to the company can be reduced to its absolute minimum, and the position can be watched month by month so that there is no possibility of excessive stocks or of labour hanging on waiting for work. If a catastrophe has occurred, the best thing to be done is to minimise the evil nature of the results; and this is what the system of Works' Control which I have just described to you genuinely can do.

Management in itself is a science which it is very difficult, indeed almost impossible, to define. It demands what might almost be called a sixth sense, in which experience, analysis, commonsense and foresight all play their part. Above all, it demands time and thought—and herein lies the greatest obstacle to the development of the higher degree of management. Those on whose shoulders the burden should rest have usually so little time for quiet thought and for study, and those who, by virtue of their less responsible positions, can be given the time to think, so seldom possess the experience or the foresight, though they may possess the power of analysis, and commonsense in addition. This is the gulf that must be bridged, and it may take many years before we can get across. It would be unfair to blame those now in positions of authority who appear to take little interest in such matters. You should not censure a man for not buying your goods if you yourself do not know what you are trying to sell. If better management, based on intelligent and analytical control, is to take the place gradually of management based solely on experience and personality, those to whom the higher form of management is profoundly interesting must have something definite and constructive to offer; something that can be put forward in simple terms; something that is not hedged about too much with accountancy technicalities—something which, above all, really *does* produce better results than can be obtained by the older method. This is surely where the cost accountant has such an illimitable field of usefulness—for him merely to produce accurate costs and to provide meticulous analyses is only scratching at the surface. Something better than this must be done if the benefits of the analytical work upon which cost accountancy is based are to be given their real scope. Merely to analyse, to allocate, to summarise, is merely to keep on tramping along the well-beaten circular path which only leads back to the starting-point. Until the cost accountant appreciates this, there is little hope for any "control" such as I have been trying to describe. You may, perhaps, have noticed that there is no real cost accountancy in this paper at all. In the Company Control we have certain financial figures which could be obtained from the chief accountant's office, and in the Works' Control we have no reference whatever to costs. Yet it is to the cost accountant that the manager looks to obtain prompt and accurate statistical returns, and it is to the cost accountant, I hope, that the manager will look in the future for general advice as to the control of his concern. To his costing work, therefore, the cost accountant must add the faculty of looking at statistical control as a whole; and if in what I have been describing there is no curve which has reference to pure cost accountancy, it is due to the fact that the actual cost accountancy curves find their own place in the secondary chart books upon which the primary control is built. Without cost accountancy nothing of this control could exist. The very first curve that we discussed in the Company Control—*i.e.*, the moving annual total of the net profits—must be based upon cost accountancy figures, and the secondary charts behind this primary figure would show how these net profits were made up, which lines were profitable and which were not, and which items should form the main basis of the Sales' programme.

If, therefore, we are to have intelligent analytical management in the future, we must look to the cost accountant to provide that solid basis of practical facts upon which the structure can be built. The manager may be able to visualise a scheme of control by means of which he could direct his business; but to turn that vision into a working commonsense reality he needs all the assistance, all the experience, and all the energy that the modern cost accountant can provide. I have spoken to-night from the manager's point of view; the cost accountant's part is in your hands. I can only hope, therefore, that the suggestions which I have put forward in this paper may be of some slight assistance in the task that lies before you.

THE ECONOMICS OF COST ACCOUNTING.

By E. D. McCallum, M.A., Lecturer in Economics, Armstrong College, in the University of Durham.

(Lecture delivered on the 21st January to the Newcastle and District Branch of the Institute of Cost and Works Accountants.)

There are two dangers of almost equal significance to which the specialist in any one branch of knowledge is liable to be exposed. There is, on the one hand, the tendency to belittle the activities and results of specialists in other or even allied fields, and on the other, the temptation to apply to studies outside his own and upon material which is altogether inadequately understood, methods of reasoning, analysis and observation upon which he has learned to place reliance as a result of experience gained in his own field. To succumb to the first, apart from the narrowness of outlook which it suggests, is to run the risk of making specialist studies unbalanced and to leave their results in a state of suspended animation from which they can only be rescued by a wider synthesis which seeks to co-ordinate results achieved by specialists in different branches of work. The specialist, of course, has served his purpose but his disregard for, or his scepticism of the value of the work of others, is easily liable to reduce the significance and importance of his own. To succumb to the second, is to rush, unqualified, into fields of work where angels fear to tread, and to invite legitimate doubt as to whether such a fool can be trusted as a guide even on his own ground.

Between the Scylla of over-specialisation and the Charybdis of incompetent intrusion, students of economics of the present generation have, on the whole, steered a successful course. From the first of these dangers economists have been saved by the clear realisation of the complexities of economic life. The student of economics is almost continuously aware of the influence which activities completely outside the strictly economic sphere exercise upon the subject matter of his inquiries. Accordingly, in order that the conclusions which he reaches may as far as possible be consistent with the world as it exists, he is ever on the alert for developments in other fields of work, especially if these developments are likely to be of use in aiding his study towards the goal of all science, namely, greater precision in generalisation. In consequence, it may well be doubted if there is any other branch of knowledge which so much teaches its devotees to be tolerant of the work of specialists in other fields.

From the other danger, which has been distinguished, economists too have been remarkably free. Keenly aware of the complexities which surround their own subject and warned by the fate in other fields of enthusiasts less cautious than themselves, they are wary of expressing dogmatic opinions upon subjects with which they cannot claim first hand acquaintance.

It may seem to some that in discussing the subject which I have undertaken to present, a tyro in economics in the praiseworthy attempt to convince Cost Accountants of the economist's interest in the subject of Accounting and particularly in that branch of it known as Cost Accounting, is certain to commit the folly of assuming a knowledge of a highly technical and difficult subject with which, in fact, he is altogether unacquainted. If it was the purpose of this discussion to analyse and determine the difficulties which beset the Cost Accountant in the actual application in accounting practice of the abstract conceptions of economic theory, such an inference would be completely justified. I am only too conscious, however, of the danger and difficulties of any such attempt, and the object of this paper is the much safer and much less contentious one of suggesting to you (1) the nature of the economic problems and conceptions with which Cost Accounting and economics, each in its own separate way, has to deal, (2) the gain which would result to each of these subjects from a fuller co-operation between them and (3) the lasting and cumulative benefit which the community would be almost certain to achieve from the co-operation between the Cost Accountant and the economist.

I.

Let us look for a moment at the first of these aspects, namely, the nature of the economic conceptions which are common both to Cost Accounting and economic theory.

The central problem of economic theory is to

provide a rational explanation of the forces which regulate value. That is, it is the aim of this branch of economic theory not only to account for the rates at which different commodities and services exchange for one another but further, to provide such an explanation of the influences which determine them as will serve as a guide to the future. It is not enough that the ratio of exchange existing between different commodities and services, or, if you prefer to think of the matter in terms of some common medium of exchange, that the existing system of prices should be explained. Explanation is but the first step by which the economist, like all other seekers after truth, hopes to attain to prediction. If economic reasoning and analysis is to be of service it must be able to go a step farther and provide the basis upon which, apart from disturbing conditions, future movements may be foretold with some degree of accuracy. Now in the course of the last century and a half, considerable progress has been made by successive thinkers in providing an organon of thought capable of explaining the existing price system and of suggesting the considerations of which account must be taken in forecasting not only future movements of prices but also changes in the direction of economic phenomena generally. Now no small part of the progress which economic science has made is due to a clearer understanding of the importance of the part played by "cost of production" in the regulation of value. It would take me too far from the subject before us to outline the various stages by which this clearer understanding has been achieved. For those interested in the subject, I may refer to the works of Professor Edwin Cannan—a recognised master in this field. It must suffice for me, therefore, to say that the notion of "marginal cost of production" due to the late Professor Alfred Marshall and developed by his successor Professor A. C. Pigou, at Cambridge, has been one of the gateways to the progress which economics has made in the last generation. By "marginal cost of production" economics means broadly the costs of production which are entailed by producers (1) who are just on the margin of doubt whether to increase by a little the production of the commodity or the rendering of a service in which they are interested and (2) who may be contemplating an incursion into some industrial activity toward which they are tempted by current price. Now modern economic theory teaches us that if we are to understand the causes which regulate value it is to this "margin" that we must go in order to watch the play of the forces which govern value.

Another step in the same direction was made when it came to be recognised that cost of production and marginal cost of production vary in different ways in different industries. Although economists had no actual statistical data upon which to base their opinions, general observation over the course of the development of industry was sufficient to indicate this truth to them. Accordingly, in order to facilitate their exposition of the causes which determine value and prices, economists divide industries into three broad, but still hypothetical, classes, namely, (1) industries of increasing cost or diminishing return; (2) industries of decreasing cost or increasing return; and (3) industries of constant cost or constant return. By an increasing cost industry is meant, broadly, an industry in which additional increments of output of equal size can be obtained only at a greater outlay of labour and sacrifice, while by a decreasing cost industry is meant one in which, as a result of the so-called economies of large-scale production, additional equal units of output can be obtained at a less expenditure of effort and sacrifice. The agricultural and extractive industries, such as mining, are generally regarded as examples of the first class of industry and the manufacturing industries are taken to represent the second class. If an industry can be imagined in which one stage is conducted under the influence of increasing cost and another stage under the influence of decreasing cost, and if the increasing costs at one stage are exactly counterbalanced by decreasing costs at the other, then the industry is said to be one of constant cost.

Now you will readily appreciate the significance from the Cost Accounting point of view of these developments in the field of economic theory. As I understand it, it is precisely with the problem of cost in a somewhat narrower connotation that Cost Accounting deals. Just as economics seeks to explain the value of any commodity or service by tracing the factors which constitute the cost at which that commodity or service is obtained for the community, so it is the aim of Cost Accounting to trace and allocate by product, job, department or process the component items of cost for some particular business. The practical difficulties in the way of the realisation of the aims of his subject are, I suppose, known only adequately to the experienced Cost Accountant. Certain items, in the classification of cost with which the practice of business and perhaps the reasonings of economic theory have provided Cost Accounting, can be traced and allocated with a high degree of certainty. Other items on the other hand, are difficult to isolate and even when isolated present problems with varying solution in their allocation. Thus the so-called " direct costs," or " prime costs " such as direct wages, materials, and even power, present few difficulties, but the trouble begins when the items which constitute the " indirect costs " or " overhead costs " have to be singled out and allocated. Apparently, items which must be included at certain times for certain purposes, must be excluded at other times for other purposes. Thus, for example, the answer to the question whether allowance must be made for interest upon capital invested in a business, in estimating for contracts, will vary according to the stage in the trade cycle through which industry is passing. In a business or industry which is clearly operating under conditions of decreasing cost it will happen that, in times of bad trade with low prices, the items of overhead cost will bear heaviest per unit of output. In such cases, and for short periods only, it may be legitimate as well as necessary to exclude interest on capital. But in times of good trade when prices tend to be high and cost per unit of output low, interest on investment must rank for its place as an item of cost. In the long run, of course, there can be no doubt about the matter. The continual flow of resources into industry is dependent upon the reward which investors and savers secure for making the necessary provision. A check to this reward will soon bring about a reduction of resources devoted to any particular purpose.

Now just as it is the object of the economist to suggest the distribution of resources and efforts which yields a maximum return, so it is the object of the Cost Accountant to achieve this result within his particular domain. Under the influence of the " principle of substitution," that is, the tendency to substitute the more efficient for the less efficient means to an end, the forces in the economic world are constantly tending towards a position of equilibrium at which nothing can be gained by a rearrangement of resources and efforts. The operation of the mechanism by which this equilibrium is achieved has been greatly improved by the advent of Cost Accounting. Cost Accounting indicates clearly the line along which expansion can be profitably undertaken, as well as suggesting the limits beyond which, at any particular time, it would be unprofitable to proceed further in any particular business or process. Here we have indicated the practical significance of Cost Accounting as it affects the welfare of the community but we will leave it for the moment and return to it in the third section of this paper.

II.

It will be evident from what has been said that economics and Cost Accounting each in its own way is concerned with the same general problems. It would seem indispensable, therefore, that these subjects should co-operate and that results achieved in the one would be useful in aiding the progress of the other. Let us look briefly at the ways in which each can be of service to the other.

The aid which Cost Accounting can render to the economist is great indeed. The Cost Accountant in his daily task is working with the raw material upon which economic theory is dependent and without which its progress towards precision is impossible. Necessarily, therefore, any co-operation between these subjects which would place at the disposal of the economist the cost statistics which form the bricks of which a large part of the edifice of economic theory is constructed, would be of immeasurable service. Professor Marshall has said that statistics are the straw of which the economist's bricks are made. Now in recent years an ever increasing supply of this statistical straw has been made available to enquirers into the problems of economic life, but there are many gaps to be filled. Not least of these is the almost complete lack of reliable statistical information concerning costs of production in different industries to say nothing of different costs in different districts and different types and sizes of plant. The economist, of course, is fully aware that there may be a legitimate objection on the part of those immediately concerned with the direction of business to the detailed publicity which the enthusiast might well demand. He finds it difficult to believe, however, that in this country no further progress towards making available the valuable statistical information contained in the files of business concerns can or should be made. No economist would ask for the widespread publication of the intimate details of the individual business, whether public or private, but he thinks, and with good reason, that there could be no objection to the publication by industries of abstracts and summaries of the materials which the individual business within each industrial group collects in the course of its daily operation. In this country, in the case of one of the great industries namely coal, some such publicity has been secured. In the U.S.A. a great deal of statistical information concerning cost of production in different industries has been published through the agency of the Federal Trade Commission and its predecessor, the Bureau of Corporations. Difficulties, of course, are sure to be encountered. But the mere existence of difficulties ought to be no reason for failing to make the attempt. The history of the attempts of the Bureau of Corporations in the U.S.A. to secure the data which it required in its investigations is instructive. In the course of a pre-war inquiry into the steel industry the Bureau had occasion to require returns to be made concerning detailed cost of production in that industry. The first difficulty which the Bureau encountered, and this is one which would confront many industries in this country even in the year of grace 1930, was that of securing comparability in the returns collected. A uniform system of accounts had to be devised and, in the case of concerns innocent of Cost Accounting methods, experts from the Bureau had to be sent to the plants concerned in order to instruct officials in the art, or science, of Cost Accounting. Another objection, safely overcome by the Bureau, and this is the objection of which most is heard in this over-conservative country of ours, is that the position of the individual business is revealed in the publication of the final result. For that belief there is, of course, no real foundation whatsoever. It is really surprising to know the extent to which detailed information can be published without making it possible for the outsider or the competitor to discover, even approximately, the position of individual businesses. In the investigation to which I have referred, statistical information concerning cost of production was finally made public in great detail. Items of cost, such as materials, labour, superintendence, administrative charges, etc., were published for every stage in the process of steel production from the raw materials to the finished rolled products, not only for the industry as a whole, but by districts and by large and small concerns respectively. Indeed, in the case of the U.S. Steel Corporation data on these lines was published plant by plant without revealing the identity of any one of them. This kind of work was continued by the Federal Trade Commission under the direction of the War Industries Board, through the later years of the war for other industries besides that of steel. In the case of steel, these figures were continued after the war and published by the F.T.C. Unfortunately some of the concerns which were making returns to the Commission took advantage of the legal position and secured in the Courts an injunction restraining the Commission from requiring returns of cost data. The basis of the objection to making returns is difficult to see. No company figures were revealed. One would not care to think that the concerns were anxious to hide data which would, if handed over to other departments of the Government, expose their liability to higher taxation than that which they were paying.

Much remains to be done in this country in the direction of the developments which I have indicated to have taken place in the U.S.A. An increasing realisation of the value of publicity is urgently required among business men in this country. To members of the Accounting profession, in all its branches, belongs the duty of encouraging this realisation, not only on behalf of the community as a whole, but on behalf of industry in particular and of the business man himself.

Statistics, *en masse*, are becoming increasingly available concerning many aspects of industrial and social life, but those concerning business activity or business success are still lacking. If business men were more willing, through their respective industrial associations or federations, to permit the publication of much of the material which the Cost Accountant handles, the economist and the statistician would be enabled to increase the precision of their work by having constantly available the means of providing the statistical verification of their theories. Many of the " economic boxes " which Professor Clapham has declared rightly to be empty, might then soon come to be filled with some degree of accuracy. If the economist's desire to fill the boxes, which he knows only too well are as yet empty, is to be realised, it is to the Cost Accountant in the end that the economist must turn for material, and it is to him, in no small measure, that he now looks for help and support.

Next, what in return can economics do for

Cost Accounting? I will not take time to elaborate in detail the benefits which I am certain must accrue to the technique and practice of Cost Accounting from an increasing understanding of economic principles. What I have said earlier will be sufficient to indicate the high degree of mutuality which exists between Cost Accounting and economics. Sir Josiah Stamp has stated that " the development of accountancy " (and the same can be said with even greater force of Cost Accounting) " with the evolution of industry and society is going to be better if its received principles are shot through with light from other angles than the legal, the financial and the technical."

In many respects the light which Cost Accounting can receive from economic theory is likely to be illuminating. I have seen it remarked, by a Cost Accountant, that more losses have been incurred by the application to businesses of systems of Cost Accounting which were altogether unsuited to them than by failure to install any system of Cost Accounting whatsoever. In such cases it appears to the outsider that Cost Accounting wrongly applied is proving a bad master instead of a good servant. Cost Accounting is much more likely to be a good servant if it is used by a person who has a clear understanding of the nature of economic problems and the conceptions and practical significance of economic principles than by one who is altogether unversed in the intricacies of this branch of knowledge. Without some such understanding, no matter how it may have been gained, I doubt if the material which Cost Accountants collect so painfully can be used intelligibly and be made to do the work which it ought to be able to perform. Later I shall indicate the significance and the importance of the practical application of accepted economic opinion.

III.

And now we come to a brief consideration of some of the ways in which the community as a whole might be expected to derive benefit from the closer co-operation between these two important subjects.

In the first place this co-operation might be expected to secure results which would enable a wiser and more profitable use to be made of economic resources. Modern economic theory teaches that the National Dividend or Income is likely to be greatest when resources alike of capital and labour are so distributed that the return which they receive at the margin of profitable application is everywhere equal. Now, without precise information concerning the relative attractiveness of different possible lines of investment of resources, the distribution which the working of the economic system, under the influence of competition, actually achieves, cannot but be a mere rough approximation to the theoretically desired distribution.

Secondly the waste which misapplication of resources brings about in normal times is greatly increased in times of industrial boom. " The almost furious industrial energy of a boom period spends its excesses in wastes and inefficiencies, and speculation and extravagance, and fails to result in anything like a proportionate rise in the country's total production of actual goods," writes L. D. Edie. Business needs, and needs urgently, some guide in the welter of rapid change which comes about in the modern economic world, and the basis of such guidance is to be found largely in the cost experience of industry. " If the efficiency of management were stabilised the hectic efforts of great prosperity would be unnecessary, and if enough concerns were capably managed all of the time, a major step forward towards the prevention of violent depression would have been taken." For this purpose an index of managerial efficiency is required. Few will doubt the truth of E. N. Hurley's assertion, quoted by Edie, that " intelligent Cost Accounting lies at the basis of efficient management " and that " inefficient practices in our (American) industries . . . are almost invariably due to lack of adequate information." In order therefore that this purpose may be achieved the following requirements must be met: (1) The institution of scientific cost systems in every considerable business and industry. It is commonly maintained that even in 1930 many concerns are without definite knowledge of the actual costs at which their products are produced. (2) That where Cost Accounting is carried on it should be used in a manner to control operating efficiency. " Cost records which are merely records of past achievements are scarcely worth the expense of collection." (Edie.) (3) Uniformity of cost system throughout each particular trade or industry is essential. Only by this means is comparison possible between different producers in the same business.

Thirdly, improved distribution of resources between different occupations or industries and between different times is not the only way in which the community may benefit from increasing co-operation between economics and

Cost Accounting. Much too can be gained by influencing the actual forms of economic organisation. Thus, whether resources are better devoted to large or small concerns in an industry, can at present only be answered deductively or by trusting implicitly in inferences drawn from the actual tendencies of the time. But so far as I know there is no authentic or conclusive answer possible to the question whether or no large amalgamations are likely to prove more efficient than small ones. Now as Mr. H. D. Henderson has said, "It is hardly too much to say that the issue as to whether the size of the typical business unit will continue to become larger and larger, or whether it has already overshot the point of maximum efficiency will turn largely upon the capacity of accounting (he is writing of 'comparative costing') to supply large and complex undertakings with some accurate instruments of detailed financial measurement."

Finally, the practical working out of certain economic policies depends entirely upon the successful co-operation between Cost Accounting and Economics. The truth of this opinion was verified abundantly during the war both in this country and abroad. Let me prove it by referring briefly to the work of the War Industries Board of the U.S.A. As a result of war conditions it became necessary for the Federal Government of the U.S.A. and for the Government of this country, to undertake the control of price. To that end in the United States the Federal Trade Commission was required to collect information concerning the cost of production of all the principal commodities necessary for the effective production of war materials. In order to determine the price to be declared for individual products the Government authorities had to work out the quantity of each product, which it estimated was required. Having made this calculation, it had next to decide the level at which prices would have to be fixed in order to call out that amount. Clearly the price fixed would have to be high enough to call out that part of the total output which just brought the production at that price up to the quantity which the authorities estimated to be necessary. In other words, the data provided by the Cost Accountant was interpreted in the light of the "marginal cost" principle of economic theory.

In the same way many other aspects of economic policy depend or ought to depend upon the results of investigations worked out by Accountants and economists in co-operation. There are many signs, evidence of which is to be found, for example, in the work of the Royal Commission on the Coal Industry of 1925, and the Colwyn Committee on National Debt and Taxation of 1927, that in this country the need for co-operation is being realised. Accordingly, therefore, economists and Accountants may renew their faith in their own work and at the same time look to the future of this partnership with increasing confidence and goodwill.

NINTH NATIONAL COST CONFERENCE,

SHEFFIELD,

24th-25th, OCTOBER, 1930.

MEMBERS' SESSION: SATURDAY MORNING, 25th OCTOBER, 1930.

Chairman : Councillor W. H. STALKER, F.C.W.A., A.S.A.A. (Chairman of the Council of the Institute of Cost and Works Accountants).

THE DEVELOPMENT OF COST ACCOUNTING TOWARDS BUDGETARY CONTROL.

The CHAIRMAN (Mr. W. H. Stalker, F.C.W.A., A.S.A.A.) : Gentlemen, we have now reached the last meeting in connection with this Conference, and I am not going to take up your time by making any introductory remarks. We are going to get straight away on to business, and ask these three gentlemen to say what they wish to say, and then the discussion will be open for as many as possible to take part. If you will please make your remarks short, terse, and to the point, then I am sure we shall all get the greatest amount of benefit from this morning's meeting. The subject is " The Development of Cost Accounting towards Budgetary Control," and I will ask Mr. W. B. Walker to give us his paper.

Mr. W. B. WALKER, F.C.W.A. : Having been asked to open the discussion on " The Development of Cost Accounting towards Budgetary Control," I find myself in dire need of the dictionary of definitions which, in confidence, I am given to understand is in course of preparation ; because, when this title is examined closely, it seems to embrace so many aspects of a Cost Accountant's job (both real and imaginary) that one almost shirks the responsibility of saying anything on the subject.

The title would suggest that cost accounting has been, and possibly is still, in the process of development and in that process has moved, or been attracted, from the original position it occupied, towards budgetary control. I am inclined to think that this is so, because, in the past, accounting concerned itself far too much with ancient history and what had happened—no matter how long ago—rather than with what was happening or likely to happen in the near future.

If you will permit an analogy of the tenses—past, present and future—the old-fashioned accounts showed what had actually happened, the modern cost accounts should show what is really happening, and budget accounts should show what is likely to happen.

I should like to suggest a definition of cost accounting simply in order that some of the misconceptions of the words " Budgetary Control " may be cleared away. Here is the definition : " Cost accounting is that phase of specialised accounting which presents an accurate picture of the happenings within the factory in such a way that the management is able to be kept aware of them almost from day to day."

You will note that the definition does not mention control.

The Cost Accountant cannot be said to control a business from his cost accounts, as usually the control is vested in others, and his job finishes when he has presented his picture. He can control his own department (or any other work which happens to be assigned to him) but his control is not exercised as Cost Accountant. In just the same way the Cost Accountant may exercise considerable influence in the preparation of a budget : he may have a considerable amount of work to do in its compilation, and be held responsible for its publication; but he cannot be said to control the budget.

I would suggest, therefore, that the title in one sense should read "The Development of Cost Accounting towards Budgetary Accounting in the sense of enabling the Cost Accountant to satisfactorily perform his duties and present a picture of both the actual happenings and the probable happenings"; and secondly, "Accounting, backwards and forwards, as an aid to management and direction, in the sense that it enables management and direction of a business to be effective."

By "management," I mean the actual task of control—the employment and putting to work of all the available means by which the ultimate objects are achieved; and by "direction" I mean that part of administration which concerns itself with the aims, objects and shaping of policy.

I believe that cost accounting and budget accounting are both necessary, and are complementary each to the other; and no business can be really effectively managed without them.

There is a tendency for administration to try and define its problems ahead, to anticipate its difficulties, to remove them if possible or, at any rate, have a plan of action ready should problems arise, and not be floundering when action is required. This planning is not new: it has been going on for centuries, but whereas each department or function did its planning with or without regard to another department or function, it is now quite common to co-ordinate this planning for all departments or functions at one stated time.

To be of any use as a complete picture, the sectional pieces which form the whole must be measured on a common basis. This co-ordinated planning must be in financial terms. And because a budget is of most use in shaping policy, and because cost accounting is of most use in determining how nearly the pre-determined policy has been adhered to, it is imperative that these two forms of accounting should be presented in identical terms to supply both management and direction requirements.

What has been the development of cost accounting? Without being too precise, I would prefer to deal with the development of, first, Costing, and then Accounting.

The most important *cost* developments, I think, are:—

The improved accuracy in the fundamental or basic elements of cost, and in the distribution of overheads;

The speed of completion;

The improved display of cost, and the reduction in the cost of "cost getting";

The realisation of the limitations of any one system in obtaining the same degree of accuracy when applied to varying ranges of products and conditions.

The most important *accounting* developments are, I think:—

The realisation that the account can be made to be a most effective instrument of management; and

The realisation that to become an effective instrument of management the account must be accurate; easy to understand by the "non-accountant"; easy of comparison; sensitive to changes in conditions and efficiency; a picture of what can truly be said to represent what Is and not what WAS; and must point out and place the responsibility, the credit or the blame.

What have been the developments in budgetary control?

The realisation that budget accounting is simply forward cost accounting;

Its use as a means of evaluating alternative schemes, such as the effect of volume on possible price;

The maintenance of organisation balance; and

Its assistance in allowing administration and management to think out problems, agree major policies as a comprehensive whole, and then be free to undertake other work.

I could enlarge on each of the several points and phases of development indicated, and shall be pleased to do so if called on and time permits.

This I must say before concluding.

Cost accounting in the sense of accounting for what *has* happened, will rapidly become standardised and easy.

The Cost Accountant can *choose* between being a master of BOTH cost and budgetary accounting; a specialist in detecting waste and inefficiencies; a consultant on ways and means of improving the profit ratio; OR, he can miss his opportunity, lose his status and undo most of what has been done.

COST ACCOUNTS FROM THE PROFESSIONAL ACCOUNTANT'S POINT OF VIEW.

By WILLIAM ANNAN, M.A., C.A., F.C.W.A., Professor of Accounting and Business Method in the Edinburgh University.

[The following paper was read by Professor Annan at the International Congress on Accounting, held in New York in September, 1929. His opinion that cost accounts may in the future fall within the purview of the auditor, and his views as to the relationship of the Cost Accountant to the Financial Accountant, will be of special interest.—EDITOR.]

"*Practice is a more intricate and desperate business than the toughest theorising.*"—R. L. STEVENSON.

COST Accounts in Great Britain are popularly regarded as a product of the Great War. Doubtless the needs of the war focussed attention on them, but Cost Accounts existed in Britain, as elsewhere, long before those needs arose. Indeed, ever since mankind commenced to trade and use money, Cost Accounts of some kind, however crude, must have been part of the ordinary business routine. How, otherwise, could prices be fixed? When a merchant puts tickets on his goods showing the prices they have cost him and the prices he is to sell them at, he is virtually keeping Cost Accounts. What the war did was to show that haphazard and unscientific costing systems were in use in the industrial establishments, great and small, throughout the country, and that rule-of-thumb methods were only too common.

In a foreword to a book on Costing, Lord Weir, one of Britain's greatest industrialists, says: "There are many questions in regard to industrial economies which are now dealt with as matters of opinion, while much more properly they could be regarded as matters of fact. Intelligent costing can provide the facts, and on their existence industry will come more and more to rely for stability and confidence." Until comparatively recently "intelligent costing" on both sides of the Atlantic was conspicuous by its absence. It is not so long ago that an investigation into a quarter of a million businesses by the United States Government disclosed the melancholy fact that only 5 per cent. of them knew the cost of their products. It is safe to say that if a similar investigation had been made in Great Britain the result would have been equally unsatisfactory. Before the present movement towards amalgamation began, a past President of the Federation of British Industries, when asked what was wrong with British industry, said: "England is still conspicuous for small-scale enterprise with its innumerable isolated manufacturing concerns scattered up and down the country, with tradition-rotten methods and insufficient costing system, each jealously guarding as knowledge beyond price the details of its inadequate operations." These are hard words, but there is a large measure of truth in them.

Through the new Companies Act a penalty is being placed on Limited Liability Companies which do not keep certain books of Account. This is a step in the right direction. It will give some protection to shareholders and to those who trade with Limited Liability Companies, but it falls far short of the ideal, which envisages a proper costing system as well as a proper financial system for every business. Those who ignore the call for cost accounts are cultivating and increasing, probably unwittingly, the speculative element which is present to a certain extent in every business. To fix a price without scientifically ascertaining the cost is to make a shot in the dark; it is as great a gamble as the Turf, but with less excuse, because of the great responsibility to find steady work for their employees that devolves on those who venture to control a business.

Before the war the British professional Accountant had, generally speaking, been fully occupied in audit work. Up to 1914 the growth of the Accounting profession had practically synchronised with the growth of Limited Liability Companies, the audit of whose accounts is compulsory. During the war, however, professional Accountants in Great Britain were given a grand opportunity. They were engaged to install costing systems where none existed, to extend or alter existing systems, and generally to supervise on behalf of the Government the accounting and finance of national and privately-owned factories of various kinds. The opportunity was unique, and the profession rose to the occasion. The members thus employed were fortunate in being given a chance to put their theories into practice, and that they did so to the great advantage of the nation, as well as of those more directly concerned, has been publicly acknowledged.

A number of the younger members of the profession who were enlisted in this work found the practical side of a modern business so congenial that they have remained in the particular concern with which they were associated, or have been promoted to posts of a similar nature in other concerns. A number of the older members acted as advisers of the Government, and apparently impressed those concerned, for they were invited to join Boards of Directors of commercial and industrial undertakings, and that practice has developed.

Special taxation had the effect of increasing the demands on the profession during the war, and the continuing high rates of Income and Super Tax have helped to keep Accountants busy since the war, but the post-war call for more scientific business management, involving *inter alia* an exact and dependable system of costing, is a more important feature for Accountants than taxation, and presents as great an opportunity for service as taxation and audit work combined. The opportunity exists, but has only been taken advantage of to a very limited extent, so far as I can ascertain.

This leads us to ask: "What are professional Accountants doing towards providing the facts for intelligent costing?" Is it the fault of the professional Accountant that Cost Accounting has made so little progress? Or does the blame rest with the manufacturer and trader in assuming that costing is a sphere of his own, and that the services of the Accountant should be confined to the financial records? The answer to these questions, I think, lies in the old law of supply and demand; service or supply is always forthcoming to meet a demand. Demand again often arises through necessity, and the necessity in this case has arisen (1) through the natural expansion of trade, following upon new inventions that practically annihilate time and distance, and (2) through competition becoming world-wide. So far as Great Britain is concerned, when that country was the workshop of the world, costs were of secondary importance to its manufacturers, but when other countries entered the field (largely, be it noted, with machinery supplied by Britain) and were fostered by their own protective tariffs, scientific price-fixing became a vital consideration. Cost-finding, as the basis of price-fixing and for checking waste and reducing costs, has become a necessity, and the experience gained during the war showed the comparative ease with which it could be accomplished. When manufacturers become convinced that cost accounts are absolutely essential, and that they can be supplied by or under the guidance of professional Accountants, then will such Accountants' services be in demand for that purpose.

Meantime, at all events, it can be said that the profession took the call for cost accounts seriously. Soon after the war was ended, the various Societies of Accountants in Britain, having sensed the demand for a wider knowledge of such accounts, included the subject in their examination syllabuses. In order to qualify for admission to his society, an apprentice or articled clerk must now have an intimate knowledge of the theory of Cost Accounting. Whatever may be the attitude of the older members of the profession, there is little doubt that, as the younger members come into practice, there will be an ever-increasing tendency on the part of the professional Accountant, whether acting as auditor or on the staff of a business, to inquire into the adequacy of the costing system in operation, and to suggest the introduction of a system where none exists. This kind of work is more constructive than audit work, and as such it appeals to many young Accountants' minds in a way that audit work does not. It is true that only a theoretical knowledge is required of professional Accountant students; that is all that can be expected of them under present conditions, because during their apprenticeship they seldom, if ever, get the opportunity of handling cost accounts in the same way as they obtain practical experience in the other branches of their profession, such as the preparation of balance sheets, insolvencies, taxation questions, etc. At the same time, if the student is thoroughly grounded in the fundamentals of costing, he will have little difficulty in applying his knowledge to introduce a system in simple cases, and in testing the effectiveness of an existing system where operations are more involved. This exclusion of cost accounts from the purview of the auditor, however, is probably only a temporary phase. There are indications that it will soon pass.

The auditor of a company has the privilege

of suggesting the best kind of records to be kept, and the best way to apply them for the benefit of his client's business. To keep pace with the rapid development of the science of accounting he must be prepared to render a further service. No longer can his service be limited to the ordinary check on the accuracy of the financial accounts. Everyone agrees that a proper system of cost accounts is one of the best kind of records, and, indeed, is a paramount necessity in modern business. Running a business without such a system has been likened to an attempt to steer a ship without a compass, but it is something worse. It is like trying to set a course without a chart. The Accountant is not concerned with the steering of the ship or the setting of the course. His duty is to provide the chart from which the captain sets his course, and our present concern is how he can best fulfil this duty.

For one thing, he can frame financial accounts in such a way as will give readily the figures required for costing and estimating. If he has a knowledge of the rules on which scientific costing is based, and appreciates the need, he will have no difficulty in doing this. He will show in the Manufacturing Account the prime cost elements (material used and productive wages) and the factory burdens or oncost. In the Profit and Loss Account he will show the sales and the cost of selling and delivery. All these items will be properly grouped. They will be in separate accounts instead of the usual jumble of figures all in one account, commencing with the whole stock-in-trade (raw material and finished goods) at the beginning on one side of the account, and the same at the end on the other side, and a heterogeneous mass of wages and expenses in between. Professional Accountants are not blameless on this point, and the lack of uniformity in form is inexcusable. So is the lack of uniformity in terminology. A uniform classification of expenditure in each industry would be helpful in many ways. Without it no reliable comparisons can be made. Each member of the industry is a law unto himself, and there can be no common fund of statistics available for the general benefit of the industry so long as this state of matters exists.

For another thing, with the aid of the management he can distinguish in the accounts between factory expenses and selling expenses, and in each case also distinguish between fixed and fluctuating expenses. Under a costing system it is necessary to ascertain the total factory expense, or oncost, for the purpose of allocating it over the various products or processes. It is probably a refinement to distinguish between fixed and fluctuating expenses, but by doing so the manufacturer can be provided with information which he can put to good account if he is shown the way. He will readily appreciate the axiom that the greater the production the smaller will be the percentage which requires to be added in order to recover the portion of the expenses which is fixed, and conversely, the smaller the production the greater the percentage charge must be for recovery of fixed oncost; also that the fluctuating expenses will more or less vary with the production. If he is shown the relation which each of these kinds of expenses bears to, say, the productive wages, and the effect on his costs of increasing the productive wages by one-quarter or by one-half, he will be in a position to determine with some degree of accuracy how far it will be safe to reduce prices without decreasing profits. Further, if he is shown the ratio which his selling expenses bear to his sales, he can determine how much increased sales he must secure to meet a prospective increase in such expenses.

The following table shows the effect on factory cost of increased orders for sales, on the assumption that the fixed oncost has been properly ascertained, and that no increase occurs therein, although the production of the factory is increased. It is also assumed that the fluctuating oncost will increase in direct proportion to the increased output, although in practice some of the expenses do not rise in the same ratio, and a further saving will result. The table shows that, on an article involving £100 of Productive Wages, without sacrificing any factory profit, the price can be reduced by £8, provided 25 per cent. more work for the factory is secured, and by £13⅓ if 50 per cent. more work is secured.

The figures contained in the upper part of the table are the totals that would be shown in a suitably framed Manufacturing and Trading Account. In that account, as it is generally presented to-day, it would be impossible to get all these figures. With some trouble, items (A) and (B), and possibly the aggregate of (C) and (D), might be ascertained, but very seldom is the information given to distinguish between (C) and (D).

In the hands of an intelligent manager, a table of this kind is of unquestionable value. In a time of bad trade, it will enable him to decide what limit of price he can accept to ensure the recovery of all or part of his oncost; whether he should reduce the price in order to obtain extra orders; and by how much the price can be reduced without loss of actual profit.

	(1) *Present Output*	(2) *Increased Volume of Wages* ($\frac{1}{4}$)	(3) *Increased Volume of Wages* ($\frac{1}{2}$)
(A) Cost of material used	£10,000	£12,500	£15,000
(B) Productive (or direct) wages	50,000	62,500	75,000
Factory oncost:			
(C) Fixed	20,000	20,000	20,000
(D) Fluctuating ...	30,000	37,500	45,000
Factory Cost ...	£110,000	£132,500	£155,000
Factory cost of article with uniform prime cost of £120, made up of £20 material and £100 productive (direct) wages :—			
Prime cost ...	£120	£120	£120
Fixed oncost:			
(1) $\frac{20,000}{50,000} \times 100$	40		
(2) $\frac{20,000}{62,500} \times 100$		32	
(3) $\frac{20,000}{75,000} \times 100$			$26\frac{2}{3}$
Fluctuating oncost—60 per cent. on direct wages ...	60	60	60
	£220	£212	£$206\frac{2}{3}$
Reduction...		£8	£$13\frac{1}{3}$

No doubt it takes time and trouble to collate the figures for a statement of this kind, but only for the first occasion; once the figures are obtained, it is a comparatively simple matter to arrive at the corresponding figures in subsequent years. That is only a sample of the kind of information every manufacturer ought to have, and his Accountant should offer to supply it, or, at any rate to suggest how it might be obtained. I do not think an auditor should hesitate to make offers or suggestions of this kind. My experience is that they are welcomed and appreciated. If the family physician observes symptoms of illness other than those he has been called in to treat, he does not hesitate to point out the trouble and prescribe for it.

Again, careful comparison should be made of the results shown by the costing system with those shown by the financial accounts. Full use is not being made of the system unless this is done. Indeed, this is where many costing systems fail—it is the rock on which many of them go to pieces. Through a fault in the system, the costing records of work produced during the year may show in the aggregate an amount of profit appreciably larger than the net result shown by the financial accounts. In such a case there is a natural feeling of resentment on the part of the owner, and an inclination to scrap the system and its author forthwith. An auditor has therefore to be careful how he approaches the question of introducing a costing system. He must be sure there is no flaw in it, and he must see that it is properly put into practice and kept up to date.

In introducing a costing system to a business, the main feature on which cost depends must first be ascertained. In one business it may be material, in another wages, in a third factory oncost, while in a fourth it may be the marketing expense. The means of ascertaining the cost will vary according to which of those features is of greatest importance. It may safely be said, however, that in a manufacturing business the ascertainment of the true amount of oncost, and the application of it in the costing system, will most likely be the pivot on which the system will turn. The more complex the operations the greater will be the number of mechanical appliances in use, and the greater will be the oncost. Manufacturers have learned that low oncost in itself does not mean efficiency. Low oncost often spells abnormally high direct wages, whereas an efficient organisation may mean a comparatively high oncost but relatively low wage bill, and correspondingly more profitable results.

With his knowledge of accounting and business method, the professional Accountant should be able to guide the manufacturer in compiling his table of oncost. It is wrong to infer that oncost and out-of-pocket expenses are synonymous. More than actual money spent must be recovered before it can be said that any sale or work done has resulted in a profit. Reserves for outstanding expenses must be taken into account as well as expenses actually paid. An adequate allowance for depreciation on plant is of prime importance. Some manufacturers seem to think that depreciation is not an expense, but something to be written off out of profits, if and when there are sufficient profits to do so. Others, in Great Britain, at all events, are apparently satisfied with an allowance limited to the meagre rates allowed for wear and tear by the Government for income tax purposes. But the true conception of the matter is, of course, that as nearly as possible each item of plant should be written off over the period of its life, regardless of the amount of profit made or of the whims and fancies of the taxing authorities.

As regards the vexed question of interest on capital, the weight of opinion seems to be in favour of including in oncost a gilt-edged security rate on the capital employed in the service for which the cost is being calculated. The principle on which this view is based is that the return from capital sunk in an industry is bi-partite, the first portion being the equivalent of a dividend on a safe marketable security, and the second portion an additional dividend or bonus commensurate with the extra risk which is being taken by investing in an industrial undertaking. In any case, if interest on capital is not included in the cost, it must be added somehow to the figures that go to make up the selling price. Otherwise there will be no profit out of which to pay interest or dividend on the capital employed.

The reconciliation of the cost accounts with the financial accounts is the most troublesome part of the system, and the trouble centres round the application of the overheads, or oncost as we term them in Britain. There are three elements of cost—wages, material and oncost. Wages are easily reconciled; the amount spent on productive wages can be traced exactly from the wages sheets to the cost accounts. Material is more difficult to reconcile because of fluctuations in price, wastage, and the issuing of small quantities, but it is possible by averaging the price, and allowing for wastage, etc., to keep the difference within reasonable limits.

The factors that control the reconciliation of the oncost are more elusive. It is here that practice clashes with theory. In theory, as described in most of the text-books on Costing, recovery of factory oncost, other than any small portion referable and added to material, is achieved by adding a percentage to productive or direct wages, the addition being made on the money value, or on the number of man-hours worked, or through machine rates. To arrive at the amount to be added, the factors generally adopted are (1) the total of the productive wages paid in the previous year, and (2) the total expenditure on oncost for the same period. For example, if (1) amounts to £10,000 and (2) to £7,500, 75 per cent. would be added to the productive wages in each individual costing in the succeeding year. And if the total productive wage bill in that year did amount to £10,000, and if the oncost did amount to £7,500, all would be well—the oncost would be duly recovered, and the aggregate of the costing results would tally with the financial results. But if the oncosts increased to £8,000, and the productive wages dropped to £8,000, it is obvious that an addition of 75 per cent. would not meet the case. It would require an addition to productive wages of 100 per cent. to recover the oncost under these conditions, and unless 100 per cent. was added and recovered in the price charged for the goods costed, the financial results and the costing results would not agree.

That is a simple illustration, but one that may quite well occur. Other more complex illustrations might be given if space permitted. The point I wish to emphasise is that theory must be subordinated to practice, and be subject to adjustment as and when conditions change. Changes in conditions must be given effect to as soon as possible after they occur. There must be no slow-motion pictures in the costing department. But it may be argued that there is no sense in burdening costs with high rates of oncost, necessitated by increased oncost or a reduced productive wage bill, or both, for the simple reason that it will serve no purpose where there is a fixed market price for the goods, or that it will drive the firm out of the market if an increased price, based on the higher costs, is demanded for the goods.

Manufacturers recognise this difficulty, and they and their Accountants have evolved a solution in the form of what are known as "standard costs." "Standard costs" must not be confused with "standardised costs." These expressions themselves show the poverty of the present-day Accountants' vocabulary and the need for uniformity in terms. Standardised costs, or standardisation of costs as it is sometimes called, mean a system of cost-finding based upon a certain form or standard for a particular industry. For example, the printing trade in Great Britain, as well as in America, has for long had a standard form or system which it publishes and recommends its members to use. Standard costs, on the other hand, are what a manufacturer sets up for himself for the purpose of fixing a reasonable price for his products, and showing what he must aim at if he is to carry on his factory profitably. Another and a better name for the same thing, used largely, I believe, in America, is "budgeting." Probably the best term would be "budget costs."

Such costs are framed on the basis of what the particular factory involved is likely to be called upon to produce within the limit of its capacity in a given time, taking into account current prices of material, current rates of wages, an estimate of the amount of the oncost, and the general conditions of the market. Safety demands that this "budget" should not be based on the full capacity of the factory, but on a reasonable percentage of that capacity In a new business the manager must do the best he can to forecast the probable output, but in an established business the forecast will be based on previous years' records. For example, the past history of a business will show what sales may be expected, what volume of production or output must be aimed at, and what the cost of such production in wages, material, oncost and selling expenses is likely to be. This can all be tabulated in a form to show monthly, or in four-weekly periods, what the progress in the factory and selling department ought to be, if the standard based on previous experience is to be maintained. The insertion in this table of the actual results in each period in the current year will show how far short, or in excess, of the standard these results are. It is a shortage of output that must be guarded against, and it is disastrous to go on until the end of the year, as so many concerns do, before ascertaining that there has been a shortage. A table like this puts the management on guard against the evil of underproduction, and a timely warning sent to the selling department may avert danger before it is too late.

Moreover, the table can be departmentalised, and the comparative figures will form an effective test on the efficiency of the departmental managers. A further step is taken by some costing experts in budgeting or planning individual costs in the same manner, and comparing them with actual costs as the work or job proceeds. The great essential in such is to have the actual cost records well up to date, daily if possible. One writer, explaining such a system, advocates what he calls a "telegram" notice from the costing department to the departmental manager if and when it is discovered that the actual cost, ascertained daily, is tending to exceed the budgeted cost, and he claims that these "telegrams" have been instrumental in reducing losses on specific jobs to a minimum.

The professional Accountant can guide his client on questions of this kind; he may save him from disappointment at facts not fitting in with theory at the end of the day. To provide "intelligent costing" skill and perseverence are required. Schools, colleges and offices must provide the training for acquiring the skill, intelligence and perseverance, and this they are attempting. Universities have opened their doors to the students of Commerce. A beginning has been made, but there is plenty of room for development. The future heads of business can have their commercial office training supplemented by courses in Accounting and Business Method, Business Organisation, Commercial Law, Economics and Modern Languages. The student who graduates as a Bachelor of Commerce in the Edinburgh University, for example, is taught, amongst other things, the value of cost accounts and business statistics. The Scottish Chartered Accountant must qualify in the same subjects. The Bachelor of Commerce and the Chartered Accountant will doubtless put their knowledge to use if, and when, they go into commerce. So should the Chartered Accountant who remains in the profession. Let us hope the owners of businesses will give him the chance.

The demand for costs has within recent years brought into being in Great Britain the Institute of Cost and Works Accountants, whose chief object is to secure and maintain due recognition of the status of the profession of Cost and Works Accountancy, and whose broad function is "to supply swift and constant information scientifically gained by which the selling price may be profitably fixed." During its ten years' existence this Institute has done excellent work; its Members and Associates, numbering over 700, are mostly employed in the larger works throughout the country, and form an important link in the chain connecting the factory with the office. Where the business is not large enough to justify the employment of a full-time Accountant, the professional Accountant with a knowledge of costing can provide the necessary statistics, or advise as to how they should be obtained. The advent of the Cost Accountant need not alarm the general professional Accountant. The two professions are complementary to each other. The Cost Accountant in a factory is the right hand of the manager, just as the professional Accountant is the guide, philosopher and friend of the administrator of the business. The Cost Accountant is the chronicler of events in the factory, and his statistics, if properly compiled, will help to eliminate waste and reduce production costs. The professional Accountant, as auditor or advisory Accountant, should see that full use is made of these statistics from an administrative point of view.

The training of a professional Accountant does not specially fit him for the work of a Works Cost Accountant, but he can, at any rate, learn to appreciate the principles which the Cost Accountant observes in his practice. On the other hand, the training and practice of a professional Accountant fit him for assisting the administrator of a business, and the demand for such assistance is growing. Openings of this kind are becoming more numerous. As in the professions of Medicine and Science, specialisation is becoming more common. Many young men train as Accountants with the intention of going into commerce when they are qualified. For such, a close acquaintance with costing is eminently desirable, and young Accountants bent on a commercial life cannot do better than take the Cost and Works Accountants' course of examinations as an extra, not so much with the view of their ultimately becoming Cost and Works Accountants, as with the idea that they will, as Secretary, Director, Accountant, or in other similar post, better appreciate the cost accounting work and the application of it to the general administrative work of a business.

The Managing Director, of course, is primarily responsible for the administrative work; the success of the business depends on him and on his fellow members of the Board of Directors. But, as already mentioned, it has been found that a professional Accountant with a knowledge of costing and factory organisation is a useful person to have on the Board, and the demand is there to prove it. In this demand, and in the call for young professional Accountants with a knowledge and experience of the working of cost accounts, there are world wide openings for the profession.

This is only natural, because the professional Accountant, through the kind of training and experience he receives, is the natural "daily help" to the man of business. In carrying out the audit work of different kinds of businesses, he cannot but observe the strong points and the weak spots in their administration. He becomes an expert business critic, and if he can also claim to be expert at analysing costs, he is practically indispensable to the modern man of business.

As an auditor he can be of great service to his constituents. The terms of the certificate on the Balance Sheet of a limited company in Great Britain indicate the general scope of the usual audit. It is a certificate of the accuracy of the Balance Sheet, as shown by the books, and that entails a laborious checking of the entries in the books and the vouchers instructing them. So far that is excellent, but there is a vast amount of service, beyond checking the arithmetical accuracy of the entries, that a live auditor can render to his clients if he is given the opportunity.

For example, he can, and often does, suggest improvements in the method of recording the entries so as to eliminate useless information and provide more important details; in the adoption of time-saving devices in clerical work; in making timely use of the statistics available to save waste and reduce costs; and, above all, in advising on the reliability and accuracy of the costing system. It is a common experience for an auditor to find books kept on a system entirely out of date, and containing masses of statistics compiled with laborious effort that are of little value from the management point of view. The manager fails to reap the benefit of them because they are not made for him, or because he does not know how to apply them.

"The bookkeeper should aim at giving in the books the 'fullest information in the right place, and in the best way,' and the manager should know where to get it."* This assumes a manager with a mind capable of appreciating the value of figures. Statistics will go far, but they will not of themselves save a business that is controlled by an inefficient manager.

Unhappily, it is not yet the universal rule to expect this kind of work from the auditor. It is not so long ago that auditors were looked upon by business men as a necessary evil. That day has passed, and they are recognised as at least of some help. The soul of the auditor is apt to become dead, and his work mechanical, if he is confined simply to the task of verifying arithmetical accuracy.

The profession has been accused of not aiding the advancement of Economic Science as it

* *Management Book-keeping*. By T. J. Millar, M.A., LL.B., C.A., Edinburgh.

ought. The answer to this is that the confidential nature of an auditor's work prevents him from making public the statistics he has acquired of any business in the course of his practice. Until the time arrives, as doubtless it will, when each trade or industry in a country can appreciate the wealth that lies in the aggregation of each individual member's statistics, and takes steps to collate this wealth of information for the common good, the most practical service the profession can render is by each member placing at the disposal of his clients the accumulated experience and knowledge he has acquired in the course of his practice. And not the least valuable experience he can offer lies in the sphere of Cost Accounting and its relation to ordinary business finance and administration. As an analyst of costs, he may produce cures when all other means have failed. Pioneer work has already been done in this line, but not to a great extent, and the opportunity to extend the service lies before the youth of the profession. It is a fertile field, and there is a golden harvest awaiting the labourer who enters it.

GENERAL PRINCIPLES OF FACTORY COSTING

By Percy H. Walker, Incorporated Accountant

The elimination of waste and concentration on the more remunerative forms of production is one of the most obvious ways in which industry may be assisted, and the accountant who instals an efficient costing system may feel that he is of real productive use to his client. The author of this lecture outlines the general principles of factory costing, dealing more particularly with systems which he has met in actual use in successful undertakings.

OF all the many ways in which the professional accountant can be of real productive use to his client, I think that of installing an efficient system of costing is the one which makes the readiest appeal to the client.

As Sir Mark Webster Jenkinson quoted some years ago, "accurate and efficient records are quite as important to a business as are charts and compasses to a ship at sea, showing the location of the shoals which menace disaster, indicating the channels in which the water is deep and safe and pointing out surely and steadily the course to be followed."

I propose in my paper this evening to outline the general principles which govern all systems of factory costing and to deal more especially with terminal costs as applied to shipbuilding and engineering works, and multiple costs as applied to printers' costs, these being two classes of costs of which I have had considerable experience.

Professor Alfred Marshall states in his book on "Industry and Trade" that the use of systematic analysis as an engine of business first attracted general attention as the result of the dissatisfaction with the crudity of customary methods of making up cost accounts, which claimed to show, but did not in reality show, the total charges to be attributed to each particular class of product as contrasted with accurate cost accounting but which the path of each element of labour or material is traced so as to show how much is lost.

He also points out that the movements towards the general application of scientific methods in business management and administration were pioneered by the study of cost accounts.

With such a sponsor as Professor Marshall there is no need for me to dilate upon the importance of the subject, but I will go straight on to the subject matter of my paper.

I propose in the first place to define what costing really is, its primary objects and the various useful purposes it served, together with the more general methods in actual use for arriving at results.

To quote Professor Marshall again, costing can be defined as the statistical analysis of production.

Having fixed our definition, the natural sequence of events takes us to the question of "what are the objects of cost accounts." It may be said that there are two main objects which all costs accounts aim at fulfilling :—

(1) To give the prime and actual cost of each unit or article manufactured or contract completed.
(2) To give the lowest price at which a manufacturer can supply such unit or article to give a reasonable return on his outlay or at which a contractor can quote for a job.

I want to lay special emphasis on the fundamental difference between these two objects, especially in view of the subsequent remarks I may make on interest on capital and similar items.

Any efficient costing system will also serve the following purposes, but they cannot, I think, be held to be the primary objects, but rather the secondary purposes which automatically arise out of such primary objects :—

(1) That all stores purchased are duly received and accounted for ;
(2) That the buying has or has not been judicious ;
(3) The departmental cost of each article or unit ;
(4) The comparative expenditure and result of each department.

The use to which the results obtained can be put, the advantages of having the information are so obvious as not to need elaboration, the outstanding one being that the company or the proprietor of a business can see which of the departments or which class of article is the most costly to run or the most profitable to turn out, and can eliminate the one and concentrate on the other.

Components of Cost

The component factors of all cost accounts are the same, the only difference being in the method of ascertaining and combining them. Let us first consider what these factors are, viz. labour, materials, overhead charge.

The overhead charges are divisible in a number of ways, such as between office and works expenses, or administrative and distributive expenses, but the three main factors can be traced in every cost account.

All costing systems can be classified under the following heads :—

(1) *Single Costs*, as in the case of a colliery or steel works where the labour and overhead charges are distributed on the output, the unit being the ton of coal or steel produced.
(2) *Process Costing*, as in the case of a dye works, where it is necessary to find the cost of the work done in each process, the unit being the output in process.
(3) *Operation Costs*, as in the case of a tramway or railway, where the cost of a specified amount of work done is required, and the unit is the car-mile and passenger-mile, or train-mile and ton-mile.
(4) *Terminal or Job Cost*, as in the case of a shipbuilder, engineer or contractor where the cost of each completed job is required and the unit is the ship or contract.

A lecture delivered before the Incorporated Accountants Students' Society of London and District on 10th March 1931.

(5) *Multiple Cost*, as in the case of a printing works, where it is necessary to know the cost of a job by stages, together with cost of the finished job, the unit of cost being the job batch or operation.

(6) *Departmental Costs*, as in the case of a retail business, or clothing factory where only the cost of running each department is required, and the department itself is the unit of cost.

As I stated in my opening remarks, I propose to deal especially with terminal and multiple costs, these, in my opinion, presenting the greatest obstacles to both the student and the practising accountant, and also being the two classes of costs in which I have had most practical experience. Let us, therefore, take terminal costs first and consider the various factors, the best and most usual methods of recording them, and, finally, how the cost accounts can be reconciled with the financial books.

As already stated, all costs are composed of three factors :—

Labour, Material, Overhead Charge,

and we will deal with them in that order.

LABOUR

I want to lay it down as an axiom at this point that, under normal conditions, the governing factor in the cost of any job is the time occupied in carrying out the work. By normal conditions I intend to convey not only normal labour conditions, but the existence of the necessary plant to carry out the work. If this is admitted, and I think it will be, it is obvious that an accurate record must be kept of the time spent and wages paid to the particular men engaged on the work. For the direct productive labour on the job any of the systems by which a man is timed into the works in the morning and out and back at midday and out again at night, and preserves a record of how his time has been spent during these periods, can be adopted.

It is often contended that the interests of employer and employed are necessarily so antagonistic that payment of wages on the time work basis only is unsatisfactory.

This has resulted in a number of systems being evolved for what is in effect payment by results. Of course, any such system of payment by results to be permanently effective must possess the following characteristics :—

From the national point of view it must be ready to increase the rate of output not only without increasing the labour cost, but by actually reducing it, whilst from the workman's point of view the reward to the man must be in accordance with and commensurate with such increased rate of production, and from the employer's point of view it should be capable of quick, easy and safe introduction and operation.

Probably the best-known method of payment by results is piece-work, but there are also the various premium bonus systems which have been introduced at the big engineering works.

The whole idea of a premium bonus system is that in contrast to the piece-work system where the man receives a definite price for a definite amount of work, in the premium bonus system he receives a definite bonus based on the time he saves off the time which has been allowed for completing the job.

Given a fair basis of comparison, any bonus system will undoubtedly operate to increase the time rate of production without increasing the labour cost, and will, at the same time, directly reward the workman for his increased rate of production.

The idea of a premium bonus scheme is, of course, increased output and it is often thought, especially by the workmen themselves, that this increased output is entirely due to the workman's own unaided efforts. Actually it is the result of the combination of two factors : (1) on the part of the workmen in increased industry, care, thoughtfulness and foresight and the wisdom arising from increasing age and experience in economising time and methods all stimulated by adequate, direct and immediate reward ; (2) on the part of the employer in providing better facilities, equipment, special small tools, more power, improved lighting, better supply of materials and the numerous little helps of various kinds arising out of a better and more intelligent organisation, efforts continually applied and always operative because of the stimulating effect of the knowledge that by helping the workmen to save time and increase output, the employer is therefore helping to a reduction in his labour costs and thereby obtains his reward.

It would be interesting if we contrasted at this stage some of the different methods.

If we look at what is known as the " Halsey " Premium Bonus System, we find that their method is to fix a standard time for the job, deduct from this the time taken and divide the result by two and treat this as bonus hours, or, to put it more briefly, to treat half the time saved as being bonus hours.

The " Rowan " system, which was introduced into Messrs. David Rowan & Co., Marine Engineers, of Glasgow, is to take the time taken, multiply it by the time saved and divide it by the time taken, plus the time saved, which is merely the time taken multiplied by time saved and divided by time allowed.

The time allowed is the average time which the average workman—neither the quickest nor the slowest—takes to do the job under ordinary time rate conditions, when giving a fair rate of output for his time wages, whilst the premium or bonus paid to the workman is that amount in hours which he received for such saving on the time allowed as he may effect and is over and above the actual hours he took to do the job.

Thus, if the standard time to do a job is 100 hours and the workman does it in 80 hours, he saves 20 hours or 20 per cent. of the time allowed. He, therefore, gets a bonus of 20 per cent. of the time he took, i.e. 20 per cent. of 80 hours and is paid for 96 hours for 80 hours' work.

In the " Halsey " system he gets a bonus of half time saved and if he did the same job in 80 hours he would be paid for 90 as compared with 96 in the " Rowan " system.

The " Halsey " system was introduced by the American engineer, F. A. Halsey, in 1890, and was adopted by Messrs. Weir, of Cathcart, and is sometimes known as the " Weir System."

Another system which is very clearly explained in a booklet which they have issued is that introduced by Professor Barr, Professor of Engineering, Glasgow University, and a partner in the firm of Barr and Stroud, of Glasgow, the well-known range-finder manufacturers. Their booklet gives very excellent comparison of the various methods of remunerating labour and I cannot do better than quote what it says. I do not, however, agree with all the conclusions they draw, their reference to profit sharing being to my mind based on a complete miscomprehension of the underlying principles of profit sharing and co-partnership schemes.

"(1) *Time Work System.*

This system of paying wages is unsatisfactory for the following reasons :—

(*a*) There is no direct inducement to the employee to work harder than will just satisfy his employer.

(*b*) There is no direct inducement to the employee to find better ways of doing the work in hand, as he naturally enough argues that the benefit arising therefrom will go, as a rule, to the employer.

(*c*) Owing to the necessity of paying the least efficient workmen a certain minimum wage, an employer cannot afford to pay a first-class man a wage equal to his merit.

(*d*) The employer constantly thinks that his employees do not work as hard or as attentively as they should. Very often he misjudges them from a momentary glance, since it is evident he cannot be watching them all day, and this feeling, together with the suspicions which it arouses, strains the relations between the two."

"(2) *Piecework System.*

One way out of the difficulties of the 'time-work system' is the adoption of the 'piece-work' system and in certain classes of work it answers well; but it, too, has at least one very serious objection, viz. that known as 'cutting of rates.' That is to say, when a workman becomes very efficient at piecework, his pay becomes very high, while it may be necessary for the employer, from competition, or other cause, to reduce the selling price of his product. If he has still to pay the same price per piece to his employee, it is evident that he cannot reduce his selling price beyond a certain point; he, therefore, reduces the piece-work rate, and immediately trouble ensues. In consequence of this cutting—which, with unscrupulous employers, is often resorted to without any just cause—the piece workman soon gets to know the point to which he may go without having his rate cut, and no longer works his hardest but limits his output to keep below that point. This system has led to many bitter disputes."

"(3) *Profit-Sharing System.*

The system of profit-sharing by dividing amongst employees at given times a certain proportion of the profits is, perhaps, the worst system of any, though it has worked satisfactorily in some individual cases.

The following reasons against it may be stated: (*a*) Profits are not directly made by employees nor are employees directly responsible for losses: bad management of the commercial department and excessive expenditure in 'oncost' charges may account for losses or diminished profits, and over these the employee has no control, and it is unfair that he should suffer from them. On the other hand, profits may be made by outside means, distinct from pure manufacturing, and it is not right that the employee should participate in these, since he has done nothing to earn them. (*b*) It is obviously impossible to allow everybody access to the business books, and hence the employee has to be content with a statement of divisible profits which he is unable to verify. (*c*) No special inducement is given to a good workman as he shares just the same as an indifferent or lazy one the profits which he has helped to make. (*d*) No profits are available for distribution till the end of some long period, usually a year."

"*Premium System.*

In the hope of overcoming the difficulties of the systems mentioned, the premium system has been devised, and it is believed it offers a satisfactory solution of most of them. It is in use in many shops in this country and in America, and works most satisfactorily. The results obtained in many shops have been printed in the 'American Machinist' and elsewhere, and all testify to the benefits to be derived from the system.

The system may be briefly described thus: Each man is paid a regular time rate of wages, but when a job is given out a certain time is allowed for each operation to be completed; if the operation is completed in less time, the employee becomes entitled to a premium varying in amount with the time saved. It will be evident from the above that while the employee may increase his wages, he cannot lose money by introduction of the system.

The system possesses two main advantages: (*a*) That it enables a workman to increase his wages by his own individual effort, and the increase is immediately added to his wages; (*b*) The increased wages to the workman means also a reduced cost of production to the employer, and hence there is no inducement to 'cut rates.'"

"*The 'Barr' System.*

The details of the system are as follows: The amount of premium bears the same relation to the ordinary wages due for the time taken to complete an operation, as the time saved bears to the time allowed—for instance, suppose four hours be allowed in which to complete an operation, and it is completed in two hours the time saved is two hours; the premium would thus be two-fourths (one-half) of the wages due; i.e., if the rate of pay be 6d. per hour, the employee would receive 1s. 6d. instead of 1. od. for the two hours worked (= rate of 9d. per hour); or if the same operation was finished on one hour, the time saved would be three hours, or three-fourths of the time allowed, and the premium would be three-fourths of the wages due—10½d. for one hour's work (= a rate of 10½d. per hour). Small fractions, where these occur, are thrown in to the advantage of the workman.

The following conditions would be observed: (1) The time allowed for any job will be fixed by the manager and heads of departments, and will be, as near as can be estimated, the time which an average workman would take to complete the work. Should it be found to be underestimated, it will be reconsidered before a similar job is again put in hand; but except in special circumstances, such as the introduction of new methods of working, or an obvious error in calculation, the time allowed will not be reduced. There will thus be every inducement to the employees to do the work in the least possible time. (2) The time allowed will include all time necessary to procure tools, set up machines, and obtain material for doing the job; but, of course, in the case of any extraordinary cause of delay, the time so lost will be added to the time allowed. (3) All work will be checked and passed by the foreman or shop inspector before being accepted, and the premium will only be paid after the work has been found satisfactory. In the case of dispute, the matter would be referred to the manager, whose decision will be final as to quality of workmanship. (4) In the case of overtime, the premium will be calculated on the wages due for the actual time worked, without taking the extra half-wages into account.

The largest premiums will be earned by those workmen who arrange their work systematically and who keep their tools in good order, and work their machines in a scientific manner, rather than by those who 'hash.' It must not be forgotten that in this class of work, quality is the first essential, and quantity the second. It is possible, however, to produce both.

The reasons for introducing the system were as follows :—*First*, to reduce the cost of production of output. By so doing they expect to be able to procure more work, thereby employing more hands, and also to enable the company to meet that competition which is every day becoming keener. *Secondly*, to increase earnings. In every shop into which the system has been introduced, it has resulted in a considerable increase in the earnings of the employees. It cannot in any case reduce the earnings, in fact a a general rise has taken place, due to the premiums. *Thirdly*, to stimulate the employees to take a greater interest in their work. With an immediate prospect of deserved reward, better methods of doing many jobs will be devised. *Fourthly*, to sustain and improve the efficiency of the plant. The system will lead to the employees suggesting improvements and pointing out defects in machinery and tools which can and should be immediately remedied."

Returning to the payment of *Time Work*, we will consider some of the more usual ways of recording the men's time.

There is what is known as the "Tally" system, where a man deposits his metal disc or tally on coming in and picks it up on going out. The timekeeper notes the time these discs are deposited and picked up and has to ascertain what the men were engaged upon in the meantime.

Another system, which is still largely in vogue in shipyards and drydocks, is a time board which is handed to the man when he comes in, the timekeeper recording his time in a book and on the board, which is whitewashed, the man records the jobs done and the time spent on each one. This board is given in at night, copied into the timebook and wages abstract next day, re-whitened and re-issued. In the meantime a second board is issued for the alternate days and is dealt with in the same way. The great weakness of this system is the lack of permanent record. The best system I have encountered and one which I have recently installed, a specimen of which I shall be pleased to circulate for your inspection, is based on a time card used in connection with a time-recording clock. Each man has a definite number, which he retains as long as he is in the employ of the firm. Two cards, bearing his number, are issued each week, one for Monday, Wednesday and Friday, and another for Tuesday, Thursday and Saturday. The front of the card shows his time of entering and leaving the works and the back the jobs on which he was engaged.

On leaving the yard or works on Monday night he clocks off and leaves his card with the timekeeper and draws his card for Tuesday. Monday's card is thus left with the timekeeper all day Tuesday, who checks the man's apportionment of his time with the time shown on the front of the card, according to the clock. If this is correct he enters it upon the time-sheet showing the analysis of the hours to the various jobs. This card is then ready for re-issue on Wednesday. For the purpose of ease in analysis, each job has a distinctive number and the clerk making up the wages sheets deals with them by number and is not interested in what the job is for. At the end of the week, the time-sheet is sent in to the pay office where rates of pay are inserted and the amount due to each man calculated out and analysed to the various jobs.

The total of the analysis of the wages sheets must agree with the wages paid and is carried to the wages journal. It is merely a memorandum and does not form part of the books of account.

The difficulty now arises, how can you charge the indirect or non-productive labour to the respective jobs. This will include foremen, timekeepers, storekeepers, yard and work cleaners and draughtsmen, and my experience has been that the best method is to divide the amount paid each workman over the various jobs in the ratio the direct wages on the particular job bore to the total direct labour for the week.

Another method which is almost as effective, is to charge all indirect or non-productive wages to establishment charges. They are then charged to the job in whatever method is adopted for allocating establishment charges.

Material

In dealing with this factor it must be borne in mind that it may consist of raw materials, complete parts purchased, or partly completed parts purchased, and as a general rule is dealt with in one of the following two ways, namely :—

Either sent direct to the contract or department or taken into the stores to be used as required. In the first place it should be debited direct to the contract or department and in the second place to the stores account, a delivery note being signed by the storekeeper or foreman. Care should be taken that material is debited at the actual cost price, any trade discounts being deducted from the amount of the invoice payable. Where material is taken from the stores, a requisition note bearing a distinctive number of the contract or job for which it is required should be given, signed by the foreman of the department and also by the workman to whom it is delivered. Some firms pass all materials through the stores whether the actual materials had gone through the storeroom or direct to the job. Material ordered in excess of what is actually required should be returned to the storeroom with a stores returned note, which should be signed by the foreman.

We have in the delivery note, requisition and store returned notes, the sources from which the stores accounts and the contract or department accounts are compiled.

The storekeeper incorporates this in his store delivery book, giving the job number and the quantity and description of the material. This book is then sent to the counting house to price up the material which is then placed to the debit of the various jobs.

In the system I have recently installed, specimen forms of which I have before me, the stores delivery book is kept in loose-leaf form, each leaf being in triplicate and a separate sheet is allocated to each job. These sheets are entered up in quantities only, by the storekeeper in triplicate. All three copies are sent to the office or counting house, and there priced out. One copy is filed away and becomes a stores issued book, the second copy is filed away with the other dockets relating to the cost of the particular job and the third copy is ready for production in those cases in which the work is done on the net cost and percentage basis. In addition to this a stores issued and received book is kept which is really a stock ledger. All goods as they are received are debited from the invoices, both quantities and value being shown, and the weekly totals of the sheets previously mentioned are posted to the credit. This book is divided into sections, a separate section being kept for each class of material, the advantage being that the stock in hand at any given date of any class of material can be obtained from this book.

An excellent method of dealing with material in the case of a factory turning out standardised parts or articles is one in which the estimating department makes up at the start of a job, a detailed estimate of the quantity of each class of material which should be required ; a blue print is made of this estimate and sent to the storekeeper in charge of each particular store. The foreman or workman who requires material from the store is only allowed to draw the quantities stated in the estimate. Should the workman require more material than is provided for in the estimate, he must report the matter to the estimating department who will then investigate the question and find out whether an error has been made in the estimate or whether the workman carrying out the work has been extravagant in the use of the material. By this means a very close check is kept on material in stock and it prevents what is a very common source of wastage, namely :—the workman drawing more material than is actually needed in order to be on the safe side and save the trouble of going for further supplies.

Scrap material received from any particular job should be sold and the amount realised credited to the department or job to which the material was originally charged.

While we are on the question of material, I would like to deal with the subject of handling charges. Many firms in making out their costs add amounts varying from 1½ per cent. in the case of steel plates and angles and 7 per cent. in the case of paints and similar items for handling. My own personal opinion is that it is so difficult to earmark the actual handling charges of any particular class of material that the better method is to treat this item to the indirect or establishment charges and charge the material in each case at actual cost without any addition.

Indirect Charges

We now come to the third factor of our cost, namely the indirect or establishment charges. This is the most difficult factor to arrive at and is one in the treatment of which there is considerable difference of opinion.

We have to cover in this remaining factor the whole of the indirect cost of running our factory or works exclusive of those items which have already been charged direct to the job, in other words, all those items of expense which appear in the profit and loss account and are incurred in the earning of the profit. I use the expression " incurred in the earning of the profit " as distinct from those items which are allocations of the profit after it has been made.

You will remember that I stated the primary objects of cost accounts were to ascertain first the actual cost of each article or contract, and the second the lowest price at which it was safe to carry it out and I remarked that the two objects were frequently confused.

As an example of this confusion we have the contention urged by so many authorities on costing that interest on capital should be considered as an item of indirect cost. If the object of your cost accounts is merely to give you the lowest price to quote, then, of course, I agree that interest on capital must be considered, but if we are endeavouring to ascertain the actual cost of the article manufactured or contract carried out, then interest on capital must not be considered.

The whole of the capital raised, whether as ordinary share capital, mortgage debentures or overdraft at the bank, is represented on the other side of our balance sheet by various assets of the business.

As we provide for the maintenance, repairs and running of these assets in the indirect charges, we should not also allow interest on the capital which purchased them. Interest on capital in whatever form raised is an allocation of the profits after they have been made and not a charge incurred in the earning of profits. The fact that mortgage debentures, for instance, carry with them a definite charge or lien on some particular asset sometimes leads to the assumption that interest on the debenture should be treated differently to interest on capital, but I think I have made it clear that debentures being merely capital and represented by assets, the manner in which the interest is provided for does not affect the principle.

No one would reasonably argue that the dividend declared on the ordinary shares at the end of a trading period, as a result of the profits made by selling the articles produced, is a charge against the cost of production and the position is exactly the same with the interest on debentures or interest on capital raised as an overdraft at the bank.

The indirect charges are sometimes further subdivided between factory oncosts and establishment charges. Factory oncosts would include :—

(1) Rent, rates and taxes of factory.
(2) Depreciation of plant, machinery and tools.
(3) Depreciation of patterns and designs.
(4) Motive power, lighting and heating.
(5) Superintendence and clerical assistance.
(6) Un-productive wages, such as timekeeper, storekeeper and cleaning of factory.

Whilst under the head of establishment charges we have the cost of administration and distribution which would include :—

(1) Salaries of manager, clerks and directors.
(2) Rent, rates and taxes of office or showrooms and office expenses.
(3) Traveller's wages and expenses.

If merely departmental results are required, the apportionment and allocation of these items is simple, but if the indirect cost per job or article is required, one of the following methods can be adopted :—

(1) The most usual method is to take the wages paid on any particular job and use this as the sole factor on which to distribute all the indirect charges. Where the work done is of a general nature and the whole of the firm's facilities are more or less equally occupied on the one class of work, this method is absolutely sound.

The only point where there is some difference of opinion is whether the indirect expenses should be distributed in proportion of the time spent or the wages paid. This must be governed largely by the class of workmen employed. Where they are all more or less skilled workmen it makes but little difference, but where a number of apprentices are employed it is obvious that a very different cost may be obtained working on the two different factors.

One may have an expert workman who will execute a job in half the time required by another, but for which he will receive double wages. In each case the same amount of wages will be paid, but as regards the wear and tear and cost of superintendence and other charges the inferior workman has probably cost more than the expert as he has wasted material and destroyed more tools than the other.

Against this, however, in every factory there must be some apprentices and inferior hands, and I am of the opinion that it is unfair to inflate the cost of any particular job simply because one or more of these men happen to have been entrusted with the work.

As already stated, where the whole, or practically the whole of the work done in any department is of such character that it is unimportant how it is distributed among the men, it is more correct to apportion the charges according to the wages paid.

Where the work is of a varied nature so that economy can be effected by allotting certain portions to those men earning a lower rate of pay and other portions to men earning a higher rate of pay, the more correct method is to apportion the indirect charges according to the time occupied.

(2) To distribute the departmental charges on the factor of labour, giving what is known as the " factory oncost " and then distributing the administrative charges on the total of the labour " factory oncost " and material. There are certain arguments in favour of this method, but it possesses weaknesses which I will deal with in the next method.

(3) To distribute the whole of the indirect charges on the factor of labour and material. There is an obvious fallacy in this method which to some extent applied to the second method, as a rise or fall in the market price of any particular material does not of itself affect the amount of indirect charges on the job. Whilst any increase in the cost of labour is directly reflected in the indirect charges, the same cannot be argued in the case of material.

It is obvious, and was particularly so during the period of the war, that some individual or class of the community may make a corner in particular classes of material, the prices of which at once jump up to an absurd figure. The indirect charges on any job are the same as when the material stood at a normal price, inversely owing to a larger supply of the material coming on the market, the price drops.

Here again the indirect charges are not really affected. As I have already said, broadly speaking, the labour factor is the safest one on which to distribute the indirect charges.

(4) Where a manufacturing concern has certain plant or machinery which is only used in certain jobs, if we take the whole of the indirect charges, which include the maintenance, repair and depreciation of all the machinery and plant, and distribute them evenly on the factor of labour, it will be seen that the cost of those jobs on which the special machinery or plant is not used is being unduly inflated by the cost of running such machinery or plant, to the benefit of those jobs where they are specially used. In order to avoid this undue inflation of the cost of certain jobs, a variety of methods is adopted. One is to take the floor space occupied by each particular machine or class of machines and base the charges for the use of the machine or class of machine on that figure. This method is all right if all the machines are of the same type or pattern, but in many cases the more up to date a machine is, and generally speaking, the more expensive it is, the smaller the floor space it occupies. It will be seen, therefore, that the old and sometimes more or less obsolete machine occupies a larger floor space than the new and more compact machine, and consequently a higher charge is made for its use.

The best method which I have come across is to take a fixed rate of so much per centum on the capital value of the machine used.

This capital value is from time to time written down as the machine becomes less efficient and consequently the job is charged with a proper proportion of the cost of running the machine in use based on the efficiency of that machine.

It cannot be too strongly urged that in writing down the capital value of the plant, obsolescence must be taken into account even more than wear and tear. The amount so charged is carried to the credit of the general establishment charges and the amount distributed, for those jobs which the machines are not used is only the remaining balance which cannot be allocated to any particular job.

(5) Apportioning the indirect charges on labour and material in a varying percentage according to the ratio of labour to material on each particular job. For this purpose a curve or graph is prepared and in those cases where the ratio of labour to material is high, the highest rate is applied, dropping as the ratio of material rises.

I want now to turn to the other class of costs, namely multiple costs, and I cannot do better than outline very briefly the system adopted by the Master Printers' Association.

The printing trade was one of the first to realise the necessity of a scientific costing system for quotation purposes, but they have, in my opinion, always sacrificed the idea of obtaining the actual cost of the work done to that of obtaining the safe figure at which they can quote for work.

The first system they tried was that of adding a fixed percentage sufficient to cover all general expenses, based on the previous year's profit and loss account, to wages and material alike. It was soon found that the printer adopting this system was out of the market when quoting against a competitor working on a more scientific system on all orders containing much material and little labour, although he would secure most of those orders where there was much labour and little material.

This system was then abandoned and that of taking material at practically cost price and adding a fixed percentage to labour sufficient to cover all other expenses, adopted.

This was found to have the reverse failing to the system previously mentioned, and the system, as finally approved by the Master Printers' Congress at London in February 1913, was on the following lines :—

(1) The cost per hour (if the work is done on time, or per piece unit if the work is done on piece-work rates) must be found for each process in the business.

(2) This hour or piece unit cost, should cover all expenses of wages and general expenses, viz. idle time, rent, rates, taxes, selling expenses and interest on capital.

(3) A percentage sufficient to cover the cost of warehousing, handling and selling should be added to the net cost of the material.

(4) The individual cost of each job on the above basis should be ascertained, to which should be added a reasonable amount for net profit.

(5) The above hour costs should be automatically checked at recurring intervals, so that the printer may know that the hourly rates on which he is working are covering the cost of production.

You will, no doubt, observe the confusion I have already mentioned between the primary and secondary object of cost accounts very marked here, as they include both interest on capital and a reasonable amount for net profit.

A series of statements is compiled, the first of which is called "statement of expenses." In this statement we get from our profit and loss account the following items :—rent, rates, taxes, light, heat and water.

These are divided between the composition room, machine room and the paper or material stock room, according to the floor space occupied.

POWER

This is divided between the machine room and the binding room, according to the amount used.

DEPRECIATION

This is divided between the composition room, machine room, and binding room, and is charged at 10 per cent. on the value of the plant in each department.

FIRE INSURANCE

This is divided over the four departments according to the floor space and contents.

WORKMEN'S COMPENSATION

This is divided according to the wages paid in each department.

REPAIRS AND RENEWALS, MACHINERY AND PLANT

This, of course, is divided according to the actual amount spent in each department.

DIRECT DEPARTMENTAL SUNDRIES

These, of course, are charged direct to the department in which they accrue.

ALL OTHER GENERAL EXPENSES

These are not divided to any particular department, but are put to overhead expenses and dealt with in the next statement.

In order to see how the remaining overhead expenses can be recovered, a statement is made out on the following lines, viz. total wages paid for the year, add direct departmental expenses which gives the total departmental cost. To these are added the overhead expenses recovered on departmental expenses plus wages, which gives us the total which has to be spread over the hours worked to give us our hourly rate. If we add to this the materials plus 10 per cent. for handling, we should arrive at the estimated expenditure for the year.

The next step is to compile a statement of the cost of production, each week, which is made up as follows :—

Wages actually paid including national insurance, add departmental expenses, which gives us the total direct departmental cost for each department. To this is added a proportion of the overhead expenses, giving us the total departmental cost for the week.

The next stage is to obtain what is known as value of production. We get from each department a daily docket, which gives the number of hours worked on each job in each process by each worker, whose time is chargeable. The docket shows both the number of hours worked on each job, and the number of non-chargeable hours. These dockets are entered up on a form which provides in each department for the daily analysis of chargeable and non-chargeable hours. At the end of the week the chargeable hours or piece units of each process must be totalled and multiplied by the determined rates or the piece wages totalled and a percentage added.

The method of finding these rates, i.e. the hourly rate, is as follows :—

COMPOSING DEPARTMENT

If the department works on time, the total chargeable hours is divided into the total departmental cost, i.e. into the total wages paid, plus departmental expenses, plus proportion of overhead expenses.

If the department is doing piece-work, only the thousands of ens set out should be divided into the departmental cost.

The result is the cost per hour on time or cost per thousand ens on piece.

If the department works on both piece and time and it is impossible to make a separate department for each, the cost per 1,000 ens and per hour can be arrived at as follows :—

Find the number of chargeable hours for time work, also the number of thousands of ens set on piece and add three quarters of the number of thousands to the number of chargeable hours. This is, of course, because the average compositor will set up approximately 1,000 ens in three quarters of an hour.

The total of these two is divided in the usual way into the cost of production and gives the cost per chargeable hour for time work or per 1,000 ens on piece.

MACHINE UNITS

A unit representing machine hour costs must be found for each machine. This unit will cover all the expenses of the department, with the exception of the wages of the minder and the feeder of each machine and to this unit hour cost a sum must be added to cover such wages of minder and feeder.

The method of arriving at this machine hour cost is as follows :—

A statement is compiled giving the following data :—

Numbers and names of various machines.

Number of units for each machine, using £50 or any part of £50 as a unit.

Average number of hours machine is in use in the week.

Multiplying the number of units by the average number of hours we get to total hour units per week.

We have already obtained the average weekly total departmental cost. From this we deduct the wages paid to the minder and feeder, and dividing the balance by the total of hour units for each week, we get the hourly unit value. Dividing this by the number of units represented by the cost of each machine, we get a separate hourly unit value for each machine.

We now have to apportion our minders' and feeders' wages which we do by taking the total weekly wages paid for each machine and dividing it by the number of hours the machine is in use.

The result is then added to the hourly unit rate and gives us the machine hourly rate.

We now take the chargeable hours (i.e. the actual hours charged on job cost sheets), in each department and multiply by the hourly rates. This gives us the value of production and the difference between the total departmental cost and the value of production shows whether the department is busy or slack and covering costs or not.

I do not propose to dwell on the method of connecting up our cost ledger with our financial books but would merely point out that such an agreement is advisable.

Let me lay particular stress on the point that while the costs accounts should be connected with the financial accounts and balanced with them they form no part of such accounts and should not be mixed with them.

I have confined my remarks this evening entirely to the general principles of factory costing and all the systems I have touched upon are those I have met in actual use in successful undertakings.

The elimination of waste and the concentration on the more remunerative forms of production will do more to help industry than any of the so-called schemes of rationalisation, and I can only hope that by indicating some of the ways in which we can enable the producer to do this, I may have helped some of the students present to fit themselves to become in reality what Mr. Stanhope Pitt so aptly described us as, " Physicians of Commerce."

The Cost Accountant

The Official Journal of the Institute of Cost and Works Accountants (Limited by Guarantee)

VOL. 11.—NO. 11. APRIL, 1932.

EDITORIAL

THE COST ACCOUNTANT AND LABOUR PROBLEMS

THE ever-widening recognition of the science of costing as one of the most important aids to efficient management, and the increasing weight of executive responsibility which falls to the Cost Accountant, mean that labour problems have to be viewed by him from new angles. It is the merest platitude to remark that labour is an important component of cost and, therefore, that the bases of its remuneration and the methods by which its expense can be accurately booked or apportioned to jobs or to processes form an inalienable part of the normal concerns of the Cost Accountant. When, however, he attains executive responsibility, or is placed in the position of giving expert advice on which sound executive action shall be based, he is in a position in which the treatment of labour problems involves a good deal more than arithmetical computation. He must have a sound knowledge of labour organisation, of the methods of labour negotiation and, above all, be possessed of a shrewd insight into human psychology. There are few industrial undertakings in which great advances both in economy and in efficiency cannot be secured by improvement of the labour factor. This calls for work in many directions. There are the study of means of enabling the worker to do the work with the minimum of effort—motion study, and the study of problems of fatigue—apart from consideration of actual methods and appliances. There are questions of demarcation and of class, age and sex of labour. Then there is the ever-present problem of inducing the worker to do his best, of begetting confidence and co-operation and of killing the "ca'-canny" spirit; and this problem is indissolubly linked up with the ultimate problem—that of actual pay; how much is to be paid, and how and for what it is to be paid. It is in connection with this latter group of problems that some of the most difficult and most remunerative work in industry is to be done, and ever will need to be done. There is no universal specific with which to medicate the maladies of wage systems. Each problem or group of problems demands careful and meticulous investigation and the fashioning of sound policies, based on the particular circumstances of the case, with breadth of vision and with foresight. The satisfactory introduction of changes can seldom be effected without patient negotiation involving the overcoming of opposition by persuasion, by a concessive and tolerant spirit, and by opportune and persistent advance towards a predetermined goal—the equivalent in industrial life of the peaceful penetration sometimes so successfully practised in the sphere of international affairs.

In view of the importance of competence in dealing with labour matters, the question of acquisition of experience and training in this connection is one that calls for careful attention. There can be little doubt that the most effective training for dealing with certain aspects of labour questions is that of actually serving an apprenticeship in the shops. This experience enables problems to be seen from the standpoint of the worker, and the true significance of the minor jealousies and prejudices, which otherwise bewilder, can be understood; and the effects of the existence of "fat" and of "lean" prices and of opportunities for favouritism can be appreciated at their source. It would be a mistake to conclude that actual workshop training, however advantageous it may be, is indispensable ; or that it provides a complete education in these matters. It forms merely a sound foundation for the necessary fabric of knowledge and experience. Systems of wage payment involve highly specialised scientific study—a study which is amply repaid ; and it must not be overlooked that in connection with labour there is a large and increasing volume of statutory requirements to be mastered and complied with. The aspiring Cost Accountant will not fail to utilise every opportunity to equip himself to deal effectively and progressively with labour problems. Such problems, apart from their intrinsic importance, have a fascination resulting from their indissoluble association with actual human contact. " The proper study of mankind is man."

THE MEASUREMENT AND CONTROL OF INDUSTRIAL ACTIVITY BY COST STANDARDS—(b) APPLICATION AND INTERPRETATION

By L. Staniforth, A.C.W.A.

(*Cost Accountant, Messrs. Brotherton & Co., Ltd., Leeds*)

A Paper submitted at the Twelfth National Cost Conference at London, on Friday, 20th October, 1933.

The work of a Cost Accountant has been likened to that of an X-ray specialist, and in a sense this is a true comparison; accurately compiled and graphically displayed costs of production in the hands of a business executive may perform a similar function to that of an X-ray photograph in the hands of a surgeon. But if you take as your motto "Costing is the X-ray of Commerce," be sure that the picture presented is a true representation of the business you are analysing. A group of inconsistent reports is as useless to the head of a manufacturing concern as a blurred X-ray photograph to a surgeon in making his diagnosis.

There are two radically different methods of presenting costs; many undertakings still adhere to the earlier plan of compiling costs after the work has been completed, thus delaying information until it is of little value. By the later, and more valuable method, costs are prepared *before* the work is undertaken.

The advantages of the second method are obvious. Not only must the facts be ascertained before the work is begun or during process of manufacture, but the figures finally tabulated are the real costs divided as to each unit, whether a single element or collated from a thousand separate elements (1) into standard expenses and (2) into avoidable loss. An analysis of costs so stated facilitates elimination of inefficient conditions, expenses being constantly standardised at new levels—and wastes, etc., in excess of standards, constantly removed.

In earlier days the farmer planted seed, fertilised it with manure and trusted to nature to do the rest. The modern farmer predetermines conditions, selects and tests special seed in advance, feeds the soil with chemically adjusted fertiliser, irrigates scientifically, and trusts less to nature.

Similar methods may be applied in practically all manufacturing concerns, but information presented to the executive must be given promptly and be up to date. The management is thus enabled to overcome adverse tendencies which would not be brought to light if, say, quarterly or six monthly statements were relied upon.

Too many comparative statistics may be as harmful as too few, if they cloud issues and prevent the management from seeing clearly the major relations between cause and effect in cost. Too few comparative statistics may not present sufficient information to give the management a comprehensive grasp of costs. The same kinds of comparative statistics cannot, however, be of equal value in all industries. In this, as in all things, judgment must be used. The most that can be done is to point the way and leave the individual to determine the plan best suited to his conditions.

If a company owns factories in various parts of the country, and makes similar products in each factory, an opportunity occurs to compare the intermediate and final costs of the processes. When using comparative statements care should be taken to ascertain the conditions at each point.

Such factors as district coal prices, wages rates, carriage charges on raw materials and finished products, disposal of effluent, and, in some cases, atmospheric conditions, must be considered carefully when preparing comparative statements.

In one works the factory may generate its own electricity, in another the power may be bought from the local municipal undertaking. Charges for suitable water in some districts are higher than in others, and in some cases the works have their own wells where water is pumped at a lower cost. Even at two works possessing their own wells, the cost of treating the water before it is suitable for consumption may vary, and this would have a direct bearing on comparative statements.

Standards required for factories applying job costing, and those applying process costing may differ greatly.

The standards required for job costing may be simple in their application as compared with the standards in process costing.

As you are aware, job costing is the costing of an individual job or piece of work, sometimes referred to as terminal costing.

The standards may be fixed as a comparison with the value of the order or on previous cost

The term Process Costing is used when the product is manufactured by means of a sequence of operations.

The chemical trade affords a good example of process costing and the application of standards is an essential part of each element of production. All chemicals have what is known as a molecular weight according to the elements contained therein. In theory, the combination of chemical raw materials by mixing, distilling or fusing transforms them into another product which has the same total molecular weight as the original materials used. A simple example of this may be helpful :—

	Sulphuric acid		Salt		Hydro-chloric acid		Sodium sulphate
Raw materials	H_2SO_4	+	2NaCl	=	2Hcl	+	Na_2SO_4
Molecular weight ...	98	+	117	=	73	+	142
	(Total 215)				(Total 215)		

It will be observed that a definite amount of hydrochloric acid *should* be made from a fixed amount of sulphuric acid and salt if the plant works at 100 per cent. efficiency. The chemical equation is, therefore, used as the standard, and the resultant product compared as a percentage of the theoretical yield.

The standard need not necessarily be the theoretical chemical yield, although it is advisable to use this if available.

In some industries it is not possible to arrive at a reliable theoretical quantity, and in these cases the best results obtained during the previous working year may be taken as the standard. It naturally follows that if the same standard is used throughout, a comparison of the results in the same process will show whether progress is being made and continued, or the reverse.

The question of how far the investigation based on comparison between actual and standard costs or yields should be pursued by the cost accountant is important.

The duty of the cost accountant is to check conversion of raw materials through various stages to the finished products, and to ascertain the cost of the direct and the indirect expenses. The cost accountant should, therefore, have an intimate knowledge of the business with which he is connected, and be able to point out where inefficiency arises or excess cost occurs. To enable him to do this he must collabórate with the foreman, engineer or departmental head, and give the management a clear and concise comparison of his findings.

If the production efficiency is ascertained at each stage in the process the cost per unit will be automatically controlled. A low output or yield as compared with the fixed standard may cause some anxiety to the manager. The cost accountant should be able to point out at what stage inefficiency occurs, thus relieving the executive of carrying out a long investigation.

Low yield and outputs may be due to various reasons, and one point which is worthy of special interest is the check obtained by the use of automatic recorders.

These instruments are suitable for use in most industries where liquids and gases are made, and may be described briefly as follows:

A chart divided into twenty-four hourly sections is placed on a circular turntable which, propelled by a clock motor, makes one complete revolution each day. A steel needle, impregnated with ink, is attached by means of an arm to the clock and this needle traces variations on the chart. Various types of instrument record temperatures, pressures, inches of vacuum, quantities of water, revolutions, etc.

Such recorders give to the cost accountant actual working results, and when these are compared with the standards often point out the reason for the low output.

In a factory where automatic recorders are impracticable, the cost accountant should use efficiency accounts at each stage in the process. A study of these individual accounts may bring to light a bottle neck in the process and thus enable the cause of the loss of production to be ascertained and recorded.

The accountant should be prepared to go into the works and to follow up low outputs and yields. The reason can in most cases be traced if the question is carefully studied.

Inefficiencies in outputs and yields are immediately brought to the notice of the management by means of the correct use of the detailed statistics of the cost accountant.

Some by-products are practically of the same value as the main product for the production of which the plant was constructed, and thus the checking of the yields and the allocation of the items of expense present one of the greatest difficulties in process costing.

Each works having by-products should be considered on its merits, as it is only in very exceptional cases where the expenses can be definitely allocated.

If we take the distillation of crude tar, we have an example of the manufacture of by-products at practically every stage in the process.

Crude tar is purchased from gas works and is distilled in several specially constructed processes. At each stage some of the oils and solids are finished ready for delivery to the customer, and also in the same process by-products are sent forward for further distillation.

The crude tar is tested before it enters the original process and we thus ascertain the standard production.

At each process credit is given for the finished products made for delivery, and also for the constituent values of the by-products.

These constituent values are debited to the subsequent process and a similar account is made up until the final stage is reached. The information available from these accounts is :—

(1) The quantities passing through each department, whether finished or by-products, thus making it possible to prepare departmental cost and efficiency accounts.

(2) The actual loss through evaporation, bad work or leakages at each stage of the process.

(3) A summary at all the stages will show the *total* yields of finished products from the original raw material (crude tar), due allowance having been made for the by-products and stocks at each stage.

This total yield may be compared with the standards fixed by the laboratory.

Generally, service charges account for a considerable proportion of the total cost, and economy in the use of services is essential to secure a satisfactory manufacturing cost. Do not be satisfied merely to express the cost of services per unit of manufacture. The cost of producing the services is an item which should be controlled.

Steam costs are a big factor in many industries. The checking and recording of the costs under this heading may be divided into two sections :—

(*a*) The cost of producing the steam ;

(*b*) The economical consumption of the steam after it has been produced.

It is necessary to keep a check on the quantity of water charged to the meters by means of recording instruments or calibrated tanks, and to ascertain the cost of fuel, labour, etc., at the boilers, and express this cost per 1,000 gallons water evaporated.

The checking and control of steam costs when used for different purposes or in different departments call for careful consideration. Where it is not possible to arrive by the process of elimination at the amount of steam used, the works engineer should determine the quantity of steam used per hour in each of the processes, together with the throughput during that period. This can be ascertained by means of a portable meter, or calculated according to the quantity of exhaust steam. The cost of producing the steam and the *normal* cost of steam at each stage is thus obtained.

A comparison, therefore, of the actual cost of producing the steam with the value of the consumption will show the excess cost of this service.

This method may be adopted for any plant running several processes. The cost per 1,000 gallons of water evaporated checks the efficiency of the steam production, and the percentage excess cost (or saving) brings to light variations in steam consumption ; of course the unit allowances vary with the cost of producing steam each period.

Study also the use of fuel economisers, mechanical stokers, CO_2 recorders, water temperature recorders, gas temperature recorders and steam pressure recorders.

It may be thought that such matters are the concern of the engineer only, but it can be stated with assurance that if economies are to be effected a general knowledge of these matters is essential to the cost accountant.

When commenting on the comparison of like conditions, the question of the differences in the costs of water was referred to. In some industries water plays an important part in the cost of services and its economical use is essential. In addition to steam raising, water is used for process work and for cooling purposes. A check should be kept on the quantities used, and an endeavour made to point out where waste water can be employed for other purposes.

The advisability of having electric meters in various departments of the factory is a point well worth consideration.

In some factories the recording and checking of spoiled work can be done with little difficulty. In an engineering works the passer often is able to detect defective work by examination, and in most cases can trace the reason by means of his personal knowledge of the process.

In cases where the resultant product differs in form from the original material, the question becomes more difficult. A standard quantity of materials is put into the process and when the final product is obtained the result may show a loss as compared with the standard figure. This loss may take the form of a lower weight or strength. The extent of the loss is ascertained by investigation into the quantities and strengths of the materials used, the time taken in the process as compared with normal figures, the records of the temperatures or pressures at which the plant worked, the test and quantity of the waste, or possibly on the quantities of services (steam, water, etc.) used.

The loss due to unused facilities may be considerable if no check is kept upon the time the plant is worked.

Here also, standards of time should be fixed and the actual results compared.

Again, the use of automatic recording instruments is one of the methods to determine the loss of plant time.

Recently it was desired to increase the production of a certain product by 20 per cent. every 24 hours. This product had to undergo four distinct operations before it was ready for sale. From a time study of each batch in each stage of manufacture it was possible to prepare a fresh schedule giving the necessary increased production in the same plant.

On another occasion it was noticed that production on one unit of plant was much quicker and gave far better yields than on a second unit, both processes being similar from a plant point of view.

Upon investigation it was found that whereas in the unit giving better production the temperature kept very steady and never exceeded a certain limit, the temperature in the second unit was rather erratic and at times rose to a comparatively high degree, causing decomposition.

This difference was discussed with the engineer in charge and the second unit made to conform to the first, thus increasing the efficiency. As the chief variations occurred during the night shift it is probable that, had temperature recorders not been used, the variation on the second unit would never have been found, and the loss would have continued.

Records of individual plant performances should be taken, and where it is not practicable to take these automatically, some type of " flow sheet " should be used to see that all facilities are used to the fullest extent.

A study of these records will also bring to light idle time.

Many companies have found a shortage of liquid capital due to the carrying of heavy stocks of raw materials and work in progress.

In addition to the locked-up capital not earning any interest, there is always the tendency for materials to deteriorate in value, due to the length of time kept in process. One should not wait until the periodical physical stocktaking is due before consideration is given to the amount of work in process of manufacture.

It is expedient to study the capacity of the plant and refer to the time records to ascertain the period required for the raw material to go through all stages of manufacture, and to make a monthly tabulation of the raw materials consumed, using the standards already stated, and express these crude materials as finished products.

After allowing for the normal working loss, a comparison with the finished commodities actually produced will show the quantity of the work in process at any time.

It may be found that one particular process invariably has a comparatively large quantity of materials unfinished. See that the capacities of each unit of plant are balanced in relation to each other, and that the first unit of your plant is not making more than the unit controlling the final stage.

As can be readily understood, a low yield in a process may be primarily due to keeping unnecessary stocks of unstable raw materials.

Investigate this point and keep such stocks at a minimum.

Only when standards are obsolete through alteration in process should they be altered.

The standard of molecular weights already referred to remains constant throughout.

Standards based on the best result during the previous year need not necessarily be altered even though the efficiency exceeds 100 per cent. The figures are merely comparative and show the variation in the efficiency. Standards based on laboratory tests are fixed for each batch of material.

If cost data are to be used to the full extent in an organisation, it is necessary that those whom they concern should be impressed with a proper sense of their value. Many executives tolerate cost figures ; many are enthusiastic about their compilation but weak in their use ; few appreciate fully the ways in which cost data can be used to guide the policy of a business.

The cost accountant who can bring to an organisation a full sense of the usefulness of costs is an important factor in its success.

Different methods of appeal are necessary for

different types of minds. Some men are unable to appreciate the meaning of tables of figures; others are too impatient to concentrate upon figures and thoroughly reason out their meaning. Graphic charts present facts in a pictorial manner and make them easy to understand. Rising or falling curves disclose tendencies in a striking manner.

In a large concern there is no better method of recording the details than by use of a tabulating machine using the punched card system. The details of materials consumed, departmental wages, power costs, maintenance stores, deliveries, etc., can all be recorded from the original documents. By use of sorting and tabulating machines the final results only are printed for prompt presentation to the management.

Results should be presented to each departmental head according to his responsibility, and he should be kept informed of the fluctuations of the costs, output and efficiency of his particular plant. The cost accountant will find that investigations are simplified by such cooperation, and periodical meetings of departmental heads to discuss costs tend to promote a friendly rivalry in the works, resulting in increased efficiency all round.

By a correct use of the comparison of the output with the standards already referred to, excesses in cost and variations in yield can be traced to the department concerned.

Calculate the increased cost or excess in money value; the departmental manager will understand this better than a tabulation of tons, gallons or lbs. as the case may be.

Standard costs are predetermined figures which are believed to represent conditions to which it is hoped that actual costs may be made to conform.

The building up of standard costs naturally requires an exceptional amount of careful research and foresight if the standards are to be anything like correct. Marketing conditions, financing methods, selling methods, purchasing power, mechanical equipment, production capacities and labour conditions all have an influence on standards and must be taken into consideration.

Whether standards are set for specific order costs only, or for all activities, makes little difference in the scope of the examination on which the standards are based. Standards are used as a basis of comparison with actual costs in order to discover the extent to which the actual cost or yield varies from the standards, and to determine the reasons for variations. As a result of such comparison it is possible to remedy deficiencies and to bring costs and yields more nearly into agreement with the standards.

Many concerns have to sell ahead and to budget for the purchase of cargoes of raw materials.

Here, a correct interpretation of standard costs is of the greatest value.

Selling prices are usually fixed on the costs shown when the plant works at a certain percentage capacity. Standard costs show that any output above the standard capacity is produced at a reduced cost. Lower costs based on the use of " over normal capacity " provide an added incentive for the sales force.

In conclusion, it cannot be emphasised too strongly that the correct application and interpretation of cost standards play a very important part in industry.

* * * *

BUDGETARY CONTROL—A REVIEW

By ROLAND DUNKERLEY, F.C.W.A.

Director and General Manager, Quilt Manufacturers, Ltd.; late Comptroller, The United Steel Companies, Ltd., Great Britain.

In this paper, submitted to the 6th International Congress for Scientific Management, Mr. Dunkerley reviews the experience of many and varied industries in the installation, compilation, and application of budgetary control principles. Information has been collected by means of questionnaires, and the answers thereto are presented in the form of appendices. It represents the accumulated experiences of some of the leading firms in this country.

HISTORICAL

It does not seem possible to lay down a general ruling on the literal interpretation of the term "Budgetary Control." Other terms have been suggested as alternatives, but, whatever the name, its chief characteristic in actual practice is that it has substituted considered intention for opportunism in management.

In July, 1930, an International Conference on Budgetary Control was held in Geneva, and, in connection therewith, a great amount of information was collected on the theories underlying the use of budgetary control as one of the aspects of management. Since that time there have been numerous other literary contributions to the subject, in many cases dealing with it on theoretical lines, and, in a few cases, putting forward points arising out of individual experience as applied to some particular company or industry. The author feels, therefore, that it may be taken for granted that the theories underlying budgetary control are now firmly established, and are widely known.

In 1933, meetings were held under the ægis of the Management Research Groups, and an endeavour made to consolidate the position by recording information on the practical experience of a number of the leading firms in this country. Early in 1934, another conference of a similar nature was held, but covering an even greater variety of industries. By permission of the directors and executives of these and a number of other companies, the author has been able to draw on these experiences. The surveys include such diverse industries as confectionery, hosiery, motor vehicle (both heavy and light), boot and shoe, musical instruments, patent medicines, heavy steel, glass, light engineering, and rubber, and cover a range from relatively small firms to large combines.

In the early conference, a questionnaire was drawn up as providing a suitable method of collecting and co-ordinating evidence and experience, and this method has been adopted for the purposes of the present review. It is felt that a synopsis presented in this form gives the most ready means of disseminating experience of the actual practical uses of this aspect of scientific management.

Appendix I gives a copy of the questionnaire issued by the Management Research Groups and a synopsis of the replies, from which it will be seen that these mainly dealt with the type of budgets, the bases on which they were compiled, who should prepare them, and such other experience as was then available.

Appendix II, which to some extent overlaps on Appendix I, gives up-to-date information regarding the experience of the wider field of firms using budgetary control, and deals mainly with the difficulties of compilation, the uses made of budgets, and, particularly, with the advantages gained by the use of the system.

In both appendices an endeavour has been made to divide the firms into two representative groups. Experience has shown that this division has an important bearing on how far budgetary control can be taken. The two groups are :—

(*a*) National Distributors, *i.e.*, industries which deal more or less directly with the public ; and

(*b*) Basic Producers, *i.e.*, those who supply materials to other industries for further work to be done on them.

These are shown on the appendices as groups (*a*) and (*b*), and, whilst the division cannot be so sharply drawn, it will be apparent, from the information given, that the difficulties of the two groups are quite distinct.

BUDGET PREPARATION

The question of the responsibility for the preparation of budgets has been the subject of a large amount of theorising. Experience has shown the necessity for the compilation of the budgets to be in the hands of those responsible in the business for the various functions to which budgeting is applied, especially in large concerns, but there may be more concentration in medium or small concerns. It seems, however, to have been firmly established that the co-ordination is mainly carried out on the accounting side, but the cost accountancy aspect must predominate throughout.

The consensus of opinion is that the cost of installing a system of budgetary control is negligible compared with the benefits to be obtained, and, generally, little or no extra cost is required to operate it.

The period of time during which a budget forecast is effective appears to vary very considerably. The light motor vehicle, rubber, and confectionery industries indicate that a basis budget covering a complete year is possible, although some variation at intervals is necessary.

On the other hand, the heavy-steel industries find a three-monthly budget the limit, and of that not more than two months can be regarded as really reliable; the general practice is to re-budget every month for three months ahead.

It has previously been indicated that the preparation of the individual budgets needs to be in the hands of various officials with some co-ordinating centre. Naturally, the various budgets bring their own problems both of compilation and of use. Whilst at the moment the co-ordinating centre is usually an accounting officer, the necessity for co-operation between sections is gradually forcing the setting up of budgetary control committees.

In commenting on the various budgets, the author has endeavoured to indicate the outstanding points brought out by the questionnaire and the various conferences. Details of individual companies' experiences are indicated in the appendices.

SALES BUDGET

In the exchange of experiences on budgetary control, the effect of the accuracy of the sales budget upon the other budgets is very apparent. It is in the sales budget that the two types of industries previously mentioned show their main differences, for since the characteristics of the several industries are so varied, it is obvious that methods of compilation are also of necessity varied.

In one type of business, sales are very largely made from stock, and forecasts in these cases can more easily be established from a consideration of fundamental trends than in those types whose sales are industrial. Hence we find such businesses pushing ahead with market research, studying and endeavouring to mould fashion tendencies, and, keying up with these activities, close attention is paid to the subject of publicity and advertising.

By the very nature of these businesses, decisions must be made a considerable time beforehand as to what is to be manufactured; this necessitates budgets covering a fairly lengthy period, twelve-months budgets being reasonably possible.

The budgeting difficulties which have to be faced are :--

(*a*) The effect of failure accurately to anticipate demand;

(*b*) The necessity to provide for changing the class of product to meet altered conditions; and

(*c*) Estimating the probable reserve allowance which will be required to provide for unusual demands in some of the main-line products, special lines or seasonal specialities.

These difficulties are met by frequent detailed revision of quotas, and especially of individual lines.

The industrial types of businesses do not adhere so closely to a fundamental trend as the other class, since, in many cases, their interests are more widely spread. Whilst advertising can be of help in promoting sales, it does not take the same leading place in directing demand as in industries catering for direct national consumption. Basic producers are followers rather than leaders of demand, and, therefore, past experience has been found to be their soundest guide in forecasting probable demand.

Unfortunately, past experience does not give the lead for accurate dates of probable changes in demand, nor does it give any indication of the source of such demand. Knowledge of general trade conditions, and the state of the contract and order books, must, of necessity, be the main guide. In these businesses, under such conditions, it is not surprising to find that budgets three months ahead are the usual order, and that as sales are very often made first and the goods manufactured afterwards, their various budgets require to be altered at comparatively short intervals.

It seems possible, in all types of businesses, to budget for a fairly substantial bulk of the sales with some degree of accuracy, but it is the fluctuation of the demand for specials and the variations of the seasonal fashion, and fill-up lines which are the chief difficulties.

Budgeting by "classes" and "quantities of products" seems fairly general, but whilst there is an obvious movement to extend this to "areas" and "districts," and even to individual "salesmen"—where it can often be tied up with quotas—this is, so far, not generally carried out.

Because it is vital, the comparison of actual sales with budgeted sales is made at short intervals, in many cases daily, often weekly, and in no case at longer intervals than monthly.

The benefits of the setting up of a quota or objective cannot be over-emphasised as a means of providing a standard against which to judge sales efficiency, but there is the additional benefit that the compilation of the budgets compels complete and regular surveys of classes, quantities, districts, and trends, and also directs attention to all lines of products and not to a special few.

Where sales are from stock, budgets bring in their train reviews of stocks, and reduce to a minimum the dangers of excesses or shortages. Any possibility of taking orders over manufacturing capacity can be seen, or, conversely, Works production can be modified to suit the actual demands before the dangerous condition of over-production is reached. Budgets call attention to the lines which are falling off and indicate where sales pressure is needed, or, alternatively, where unoccupied plant can be utilised for other lines of products.

Perhaps the greatest effect of sales budgets has been to make the sales personnel "profit conscious." The effect of price variations upon profits is thrust forward, as well as the effect of the greater or lesser demand for individual lines, showing that the maintaining of "quantity budgets" does not necessarily mean the same amount of profit. This has brought forcibly home the dangers of loading shop production with uneconomic fill-up lines.

All these points are brought before the sales executive before the event, and as one company states, "it enables the Sales Manager to time special efforts whilst still watching the ordinary everyday routine business."

Business Statistics

One important side-line which has developed out of the use of budgetary control, and the necessity for accurate sales and purchases budgets, has been the demand for external statistical and economic information.

Attempts to forecast trade, both home and export, have revealed :—

(*a*) That there is no standard system of headings by the various statistical bureaux of different countries ;

(*b*) That the statistics of imports and exports of this country are given in omnibus divisions ; and

(*c*) That there is a fairly considerable time lag in the issue of detailed statistics.

The last pertains particularly to statistics issued by the various industries. There appears to be still a great reluctance to issue co-ordinated statistics with reference to particular industries. The nearest approach on these lines is the Census of Production ; but this is only taken at relatively long periods, and, even in this case, details are not published until many months afterwards.

Interdependence of industries demands knowledge of each other's business, more to-day than ever, and particularly where the industry is one which supplies manufactures to another for subsequent work. This lack of information regarding other industries is one of the chief difficulties which exist in this country for long-range sales and purchase budgeting.

Production Budget

The production budget, also, is not an easy one to prepare.

Where sales are from stock, the programmes are influenced by the stock position, which, taken in conjunction with the sales budget, gives leads which will allow orders to be placed on the manufacturing departments to take the fullest advantages of long runs. The chief difficulty lies in forecasting the variations which must be catered for. All the industries contributing their experience make mention of this, and it is safe to say that no budget is subject to more frequent revisions, while long-range budgeting is only possible in a few types of industries. Pressure of sales demands must always predominate.

Variations are mainly due to the impossibility of correctly forecasting sales by type or variety of product, either through fashion or similar changes, abnormal demands or influx of orders for non-standard lines. Experience would indicate that the allowance of production capacity to permit of variations enables these difficulties

National Distributors

APPENDIX 1 (a)

Question	Firm No. 1. Confectionery	Firm No. 2. Hosiery	Firm No. 4. Motor Vehicles Light	Firm No. 8. Motor Vehicles Heavy
1. **What budgets do you prepare? How often and for what purpose? (a) Trading and P. and L. Budgets. (b) Capital Expenditure Budgets. (c) Financial or Cash Budgets. What supplementary estimates do you prepare in connexion with building up the above three budgets?**	(a) Yes. (b) Yes. (c) Yes. The main supplementary estimate is a Major Sales Plan prepared early in December and covering the following year	(a) Annual budget prepared at the beginning of each year and divided into two half-yearly ones, which are again divided into four-weekly ones. (b) Quinquennial and annual budget prepared. (c) Annual and four-weekly periodical budgets are prepared, the latter being progressive.	A Master Sales Budget is prepared giving quantities and periods with values, and showing rise and fall of stores and stock. A Financial Budget is prepared at the same time translating this to time with local costs and monetary resultants: progressive oncost is outlined.	(a) Yes annually. (b) Yes in advance for contemplated extensions. (c) Yes—quarterly. Supplementary estimates are prepared only when necessary.
2. How often are budgets revised?	The budget is not revised unless some major alteration is made to the Sales Plan. The effect of any deviation from the budget can be assessed, and it is not found necessary to alter the original forecast.	Principally half-yearly, but a review does take place as soon as it is possible to get a reasonable indication from the position of forward orders.	Only revised if financial or national disasters are looming	No stated period—as and when circumstances warrant.
3. **Who is responsible for the preparation of the budgets? If committees are responsible, of which executives are they composed?**	Functional Managers are provided with a statement of the planned sales for the following year and estimate their expenditure based on past experience and expected volume of sales. All Expense Budgets are sent to the Chief Accountant, who criticizes them and raises points with Functional Managers. All subsidiary companies budget on standard lines.	(a) By the Assistant Managing Director and Secretary. (b) By a committee composed of Director and Secretary. (c) By the Secretary.	The Control Office.	Chief Accountant, who obtains necessary data from chief executives.
4. **Is the year for budget purposes split into periods three-monthly, monthly, four-weekly, weekly, etc.?**	The year is split up into thirteen four-weekly periods; the Sales Plan is further divided weekly.	Half-yearly and thirteen four-weekly periods	The year is divided into thirteen periods of twenty-eight days each	Four-weekly and weekly periods.
5. **On what basis do you complete your Sales Budgets, etc.— (a) On past records? (b) Field reports—on conditions? (c) On a basis of economic production and insisting on this being attained?**	(a) Yes. (b) Yes. (c) No—rather are they planned to consumer demand. The plant is designed to produce economically what it is considered the public will buy readily. Demand can, of course, be influenced to some extent by advertising.	On past records and current information	The Master Sales Budget is based on (c) tempered by accumulated knowledge of market variants and field experience	(a) No. (b) Yes. (c) No.
6. **Have you an annual or long-date Capital Expenditure Budget and if so, what variations from this are allowed?**	An annual Capital Expenditure Budget is set up, the main purpose being to gauge financial requirements for the year. Changes in products, technique, etc., may, however, involve expenditure which has not been planned.	Yes—quinquennial and annual.	No.	Yes—in advance for contemplated extensions.
7. **Is the sanction for capital expenditure decided on a profit-showing basis? If not, on what other factors?**	Yes—in all changes of procedure, improvement of methods, etc., a return in the form of a saving or reduced costs equal to 25 per cent. of the capital value is looked for.	Capital expenditure is sanctioned either on an established or an anticipated demand. The quinquennial budget is provided primarily for the replacement of obsolete machinery, either due to discontinued demand or improvements.	Yes—when investigation points to the necessity for improved methods, or required expansion, such expenditure is all voted upon measured facts having a profit basis.	
8. **Has the installation of budgetary control involved you in much, if any, additional expense?**	So far as it is possible to say, no extra expense has been incurred	Difficult to say, as most of the necessary records and information are compiled as a matter of routine	Budgetary control, as applied, has created a large proportional saving. Executive and office mechanism costs have retired in a proportion greatly exceeding original practice.	No.
9. (a) **How far down is the comparison made between budgets and the actual results? (b) What investigations are carried out when variations from budgets occur? (c) How soon after the actual results is comparison possible?**	Close comparison is made, the responsible Functional Manager being called upon to explain any wide deviations. In important cases the services of departments peculiarly equipped for such investigations are made use of (e.g. Office Planning Department or Comparison Department).	*Budget No.* 1, so far as percentage of sales is concerned, does not present any great difficulty, but the amount of profit, depending as it does on the sales, is very different. *Budget No.* 2 is reasonably accurate, except that a certain amount of latitude is and must be allowed to provide for unseen developments. *Budget No.* 3 is also reasonably accurate. (c) Actual results can be compared with budget within three weeks.	(a) and (b) Comparison with budget instructions is maintained daily throughout every strata of activity, from marketing to manufacture. Processing is subject to inspection, and check on the spot by time elapsed to account for cost. Correction necessary is made immediately. Time elapsed and mechanical factors are analysed continuously by machine. Production and financial figures in bulk are compared daily by one or more directors and the Comptroller. They are also reviewed weekly at a meeting of executives. (c) Comparison in detail in any field is possible almost at any moment.	(a) As far as necessary to reconcile differences between actual and budget. (b) All excess expenditure is closely examined in detail, and reductions in income are closely investigated. (c) Expenditure summarized monthly and weekly within a few days. Sales—within a few days of each monthly period.
10. **Exactly what use is made of the budgets by the management?**	Used by executives as a control instrument. To the management, the budgets represent their tasks, and by constantly watching them some help is gained in achieving these tasks.	—	The twelve-months' budget epitomizes company purpose and policy under absolutely every heading, including export trade, and controls action down to such details as the number of man-hours to be worked each day, with the attendant direct and indirect finance. Budget provisions control all activities, from those of higher executives to those of trainees.	Generally speaking, the budget is used as a medium of control.

Basic Producers

APPENDIX I (b)

Question	Firm No 10. Steel	Firm No. 11. Glass	Firm No. 14. Rubber
1. **What budgets do you prepare? How often and for what purpose?** (a) **Trading and P. and L. Budgets.** (b) **Capital Expenditure Budgets.** (c) **Financial or Cash Budgets.** **What supplementary estimates do you prepare in connexion with building up the above three budgets?**	(a) Yes—compiled every four weeks for current and two subsequent periods. (b) and (c) Yes—compiled each month for current and two subsequent months. *Supplementary estimates used.*—Sales Budget of qualities, quantities and realizations, purchases of raw materials, fuels, etc., works expenses, salaries, wages and stocks, etc.	Financial P. and L. Budgets—prepared half-yearly. Sales—quarterly, but subject to continuous revision. Raw Materials, Purchase, and Consumption Budgets—prepared each month to cover the next three months. Capital Expenditure—a continuous budget built up from separate sanctions.	(a) Yes (b) Yes } prepared annually. (c) Yes The following supplementary estimates are prepared: Sales, Stocks, Production Programme, Raw Material Requirements, Labour Requirements, Works and Administrative Expenses, etc.
2. **How often are budgets revised?**	Owing to industry's general policy of buying hand to mouth by customers, it is found necessary to revise budgets each period.	Budgets are on the basis of quarterly periods; hence a complete revision automatically takes place each quarter.	(a) and (c)—quarterly. (b) – bi-annually.
3. **Who is responsible for the preparation of the budgets? If committees are responsible, of which executives are they composed?**	Responsibility is shared by the Sales and Works Management, and co-ordination is through the accounting side of each individual company. Combined co-ordination is through the Comptroller at Head Office.	The management of each department prepare their own budget, having regard to the general programme. Persons preparing Works budgets are responsible to the Works General Manager. General budgets are prepared by the managers concerned for the approval of the Sales Director and Technical Director, etc.	Each unit is responsible for the preparation of its own budget. The co-ordination is done by the Accounts section, and finally the Controller o Finance is responsible for the Master Budget. All allied companies budget on standard lines.
4. **Is the year for budget purposes split into periods three-monthly, monthly, four-weekly, weekly, etc.?**	Budgets are for four-weekly periods (thirteen budgets during the year).	The year is divided into three-monthly periods, which are subdivided into monthly periods.	The year is divided into quarters to coincide with the accounting periods.
5. **On what basis do you complete your Sales Budgets, etc.—** (a) **On past records?** (b) **Field reports—on conditions?** (c) **On a basis of economic production and insisting on this being attained?**	(a) Yes. (b) Field reports and estimates as such have not yet been fully developed. (c) Minimum economic quantities required to operate the plant are important factors, as plants are large units dependent on heat and incapable of being put on and off at short notice.	(a) Yes. (b) Yes. (c) Although economic production is kept in view, it is impossible to insist or dictate.	Sales to manufacturers are based on a study of individual manufacturer's own anticipation of their business for the ensuing year. Public statistics are of considerable value in estimating replacement sales.
6. **Have you an annual or long-date Capital Expenditure Budget, and if so, what variations from this are allowed?**	No—but occasionally long-date schemes of foreshadowed development are called for. These, however, are only on very general lines, giving an idea of the amounts involved, etc. These schemes are by no means final, and authority to spend is not given at this stage.	The main capital jobs are the subject of detailed consideration about a year ahead, but no definite budget is actually prepared.	Yes—prepared annually. The approval of this budget, however, does not represent authority to spend.
7. **Is the sanction for capital expenditure decided on a profit-showing basis? If not, on what other factors?**	Mainly yes—having regard to the facts of: (a) The expenditure leading to economies of manufacture. (b) Service to customers. (c) Improvement of products. (d) Development of present products. (e) Development of present business by increasing the manufacturing capacity. (f) New manufactures and completely new plants.	Yes—in the main, with the following factors also taken into account: (a) Necessity to keep abreast of technical developments. (b) General programme of capital reconstruction. (c) Resulting economies in manufacture.	Yes—except in cases where the expenditure is for improving quality, development, or other policy reasons.
8. **Has the installation of budgetary control involved you in much, if any, additional expense?**	Practically none. The installation of budgetary control synchronized with a period of reorganization.	Not so far, but complete budgetary control throughout the company has not yet been installed.	No
9. (a) **How far down is the comparison made between budgets and the actual results?** (b) **What investigations are carried out when variations from budgets occur?** (c) **How soon after the actual results is comparison possible?**	(a) and (b) From the trading results right back through the natural order to the individual elements of cost. (c) Cash is reconciled within a few days of the end of the month, and trading results are known and compared within one to five days of the end of the period.	(a) In matters of manufacture immediate comparison is essential, and so far as is possible, this is carried out. With Sales a quarterly comparison is probably the minimum practicable period. (b) Managers are asked to explain any substantial discrepancies between estimates and actual expenditure	(a) and (b) Explanation is called for when the final results of any unit show wide variation from the budget. (c) Comparison with budget is made immediately the actual results are available
10. **Exactly what use is made of the budgets by the management?**	(a) To indicate trend of trade from the point of view of quantity and price. (b) Research of markets. (c) Policy regarding forced sales. (d) Regulation of stock. (e) Speeding up of manufacture and deliveries when necessary. (f) Control of production costs. (g) To dictate or change general policies as may be revealed.	Expenditure is thoroughly scrutinized before being incurred. Output is regulated within certain periods. The budget is of definite value in limiting maintenance and service expenditure	For the purpose of control, and have been found valuable in co-ordinating the efforts of the whole organization and in deciding policy

to correct budgeting to be overcome. Deficiencies of raw-material supplies and usual manufacturing problems appear to present no special budgeting difficulties, since past experience is a very ready guide.

In some of the basic industries where production only follows the receipt of actual orders, past experience must, of necessity, be the influencing factor. Some of these industries work on order books not more than three or four days ahead, in some cases with the order book changing whilst the particular material is actually being produced. In these cases, detailed production budgeting is impossible, but budgeting as a whole is possible. Since the production budget must form the basis for the trading and profit-and-loss budgets, the experience of the compilation of these shows that this apparent impossibility for satisfactory budgeting can be, and is, surmounted.

The advantages of the production budget are enumerated in the experiences recorded in the appendices. The chief of these would seem to be the opportunity provided for planning production programmes to allow for steady flow and economical production by long runs, with all the attendant advantages to costs. Stock orders can be programmed with confidence in order to obviate peak loads. These long runs give opportunity for piece work and bonus rates to be established.

The predetermining of overhead expenses for budgetary control purposes seems to be generally practised. These form part of standard costs, and as such have been set up to vary according to the production load on the Works.

Two important matters have been mentioned in the experiences, *i.e.*, the opportunity which the necessary review of production budgets gives to :—

(*a*) The study of machine or plant capacity, which focuses attention on the necessity for additional plant before the production demand arrives ; and

(*b*) The calling of attention to possible idle capacity to invoke further sales effort or the introduction of new lines.

The production budget has proved in practice to be the connecting link between manufacturing interest in sales and sales interest in production.

Purchasing Budget

The purchasing budget follows the production budget in logical sequence, and since the latter indicates quantity demand, the difficulty of compilation of the purchasing budget is mainly that of price forecasting.

A review of the experiences shows that purchasing on the basis of a budget is largely confined to bulk purchases of raw materials, and here its advantages are very apparent. With a sales and production budget prepared, it is possible for the purchasing agent to take a long-range view, and this is very helpful when large contracts are being contemplated to obtain competitive prices. The dangers of over-buying are minimised, and the advantages of buying material on contract basis for what may be termed non-standard lines by realising probable demand have become possible.

The forecasting of price trends has forced more detailed studies of markets, and the fixing ahead of material prices enables price variations to be easily translated into cost of production and effect on profit margins. Besides acting as a measure of the Purchasing Department's efficiency, budgets are used to incite that department's interest into the vital matter of the influence of purchasing on the costs of production.

Stock Budget

Stock budgets in some industries more or less " happen," *i.e.*, stock is an accident resulting from the effect of production overrunning sales demand.

The difficulty in forecasting stocks is one of allowing sufficiently for the variations. In the heavy industries the influence of economic manufacturing qualities and the necessity for completing the manufacture once production is commenced is very great. This budget is, therefore, of the utmost importance, since balances, over and above immediate demands, must be transferred to stock, and high values are often involved. The benefits of the long-range view given by budgetary control, in helping to decide possible absorption, assist the decision of " to make or not to make," and (in the case of raw materials) " to buy or not to buy."

In the industries where sales are mainly made from stock, the building up of the stock budget provides opportunities for detailed review, both of past and forecasted sales, and so influences the decision whether the production budget needs to be cut or increased.

One company, with long-range stock policy, minimises the necessity for frequent re-budgeting by dealing with the effect of varying stock levels and prices as follows : basis quantities and prices are agreed, and adjustments are made for any variation by adding percentages to these bases.

In every business the question of obsolete and slow-moving stocks is important. Stock budgets, by indicating future stock values, call attention to any growth, and so demand review. Action to " job off," apply sales pressure, or cut down production can be taken without waiting for visual review or periodic physical stocktaking to show the necessity.

Financial Budgets

Capital expenditure budgets must, in some trades and industries, be for several years ahead, but these are really the subject of a separate sphere of budgeting, and it is not the author's intention to enlarge on this aspect, but rather to assume that such expenditure when budgeted for is covered by the necessary inclusions in the cash budget and trading profit-and-loss budget.

Providing that a scientific cost system is in operation, the trading, profit-and-loss, and cash budgets do not present any great difficulty, since they largely consist of translating the other budgets into terms of money. Experience in time lag is the essential feature of cash budgets, as is also the knowledge of anticipated capital expenditure and payments for advertising. The influence of the stock budget on the forecasted liquid cash position is thrown into relief.

All successful budgetary control systems are backed up by a sound cost system, and by this is meant, not only a system which builds up figures, but one which provides information for those figures to be translated into reports for action. For budget purposes, the employment of " standard costs " and the setting up of standard overhead expenses varying with shop load are now the general practice. One firm describes this aspect as of paramount importance.

Application

Throughout the whole study of the experiences set out in the appendices, there stands the salient thought that the ideal of " fixing a budget and adhering strictly to it in every phase " cannot be applied in practice. Common sense has shown the necessity for reviewing all budgets continually and modifying them as circumstances demand. This, on the face of it, may seem to vitiate the benefits of budgetary control, but the reverse is the case if the revisions of the budget are the subject of investigation, report, and study by the management.

There do not appear to be any golden rules which can be explicitly followed in preparing budgets, but undoubtedly the sales budget is the keystone of the structure, and the profit-and-loss budget the objective. As one company points out, " the fact that we are trying to earn a dividend for our shareholders is not always obvious to the executive." Budgets keep the objective well to the fore.

Undoubtedly, the preparation of budgets and the study of the actual results against those anticipated does make people think, and demands, in many cases, that they think as a group. This, in its turn, has the effect of turning a number of individuals into a team, with all its attendant advantages.

A good many reasons have been advanced for the introduction of budgetary control as an aid to management, but they all appear to boil down to the same three main points :—

1. To enable managements to decide their forward policy with some indication of what the results of that policy will be. This enables them to be wise before the event, not after. Budgets eliminate the element of surprise and of taking risks blindfolded.
2. To provide an objective against which to measure the efforts of executives and be a starting-off point for investigations and reports to be of a constructive nature. By means of budgets, it is relatively easy to locate weaknesses and to take action accordingly.
3. To provide stimuli and to emphasise the benefits of collective effort by showing the interdependence of one section on another. There is a considerable danger to-day of busy executives being apt to regard their own particular sphere as an end in itself.

Profits are the objective of business, and budgetary control, by allowing an estimate of these to be made in advance, has enabled managements to direct attention to this objective. It has stimulated the attention of all executives to the desired end, and has, as a result, widened the interest and co-ordinated the effort.

Conclusions

Summing up the experience of the firms contributing to the questionnaires, one could say that all are extracting considerable benefits from the use of budgetary control. Some, like the light motor-car and confectionery industries, are going a long way towards full exploitation of the underlying theories ; others, in the basic industries, are finding budgetary control of value, even in their limited sphere. Throughout, it is abundantly clear that adjustment of the principles necessary to meet the varying demands of the numerous industries does not in any way vitiate the benefits to be obtained from the installation and working of a budgetary control system.

It has been applied with sound business commonsense and adapted to the needs of large firms and small ; to the direct distributor, as well as to the basic supplier, who is several stages away from the consumer ; to the varying stages of sales, purchasing, and manufacture as well as to the financial side ; and through all it has demonstrated itself as a valuable aid to scientific management.

Budgetary control is not, and cannot be, a substitute for management. It will not eliminate the necessity for making decisions nor enable managements to avoid any responsibilities attaching to its office, but it will be found to be an effective aid to that efficient management which commands success.

THE MEASUREMENT OF ECONOMIC FACTORS IN COSTING—I

by ***W. Y. Dunnigan***

The Economic Factors

The experience of the difficult economic conditions which have perplexed industry during the post-war depression years has emphasized the need of a fuller knowledge of the varying behaviour of costs and prices under changing economic conditions, and the individual business which has a thorough knowledge of the extent to which it is affected by such changes, although unable individually to make any impression on them, is at least in the position to take any steps that may be possible to maintain stability against the economic pressure which they exert. It may be worth while, therefore, to consider the possibility of developing a scheme of cost analysis which would enable these problems to be studied by the individual business as affecting itself, and the present article is intended as a suggestion of the technique which may be employed in such a study under conditions of process costing.

The problem of the depression from the point of view of industry has been the disequilibrium of costs and prices, and resulting from this, the burden of idle capacity. As these factors, therefore, together with that of the economy of works operating expenditure, are the fundamental factors governing the stability of a manufacturing business, the scheme of analysis suggested is an attempt to provide a systematic quantitative measurement of them as a constant guide to the degree of stability being maintained. There are thus four principal factors which may disturb the economic equilibrium of a business or department, namely (1) the supply prices of the cost elements; (2) the sales prices of the products; (3) the load factor, or ratio of the actual production to the equilibrium production (which in effect measures the cost of idle capacity); and (4) the economy of the operating expenditure.

The stability of an industry as a whole may be measured by the degree of equilibrium between the average supply price of the cost elements and the average selling price of the products, an average manufacturing efficiency for the industry being assumed, but from the point of view of the individual business not only is a reasonable degree of equilibrium between factors (1) and (2) a condition precedent to profitable working, but factors (3) and (4) are equally important as their operation determines the extent of the deviation of the factory's efficiency from the average efficiency of the industry, and consequently the competitive power of the business. Generally speaking, factors (1) and (2) may be regarded as external factors and (3) and (4) internal factors.

Supply Price Index

In any cost comparison for the purpose of measuring the efficiency of the business provision must be made for eliminating the external influence of the price factors. This implies the construction of price index numbers. As will be seen later it would be necessary for the purpose of this analysis to estimate normal costs and prices for the various products and the price index numbers would therefore be fixed, as far as possible, on the same basis as these estimates. The basis would probably be an actual past period or average, modified for known or probable changes.

The most useful index of supply prices would be obtained by providing on the prime records for extending the charge at the base rate as well as at the current rate. For example, on all wages cards the hours would be extended at the base rate as well as the current rate, on material requisitions and invoices quantities would be extended at the base price as well as the current price, and similar provision would be made on the records for other charges.

The difference between the total base value and total current value would be the net average value of the fluctuations in the supply prices of the cost elements. In other words, taking the total base value equal to 100, the total current value divided by the total base value would provide an index of the average

Form I

Supply Price Index

S.O. No.............. Dept...

	Month...............................			
	Base Value	Current Value	Gain/*Loss*	Index
Direct Materials—				
....				
....				
....				
....				
....				
Direct Wages				
Indirect Wages				
Supervision				
Power Services				
Maintenance				
Miscellaneous Charges				
Totals				

supply price. An index could, of course, be calculated thus for any group of charges and in fact group indices would be necessary in order to analyse the gain or loss on the standard groups of expenditure. It may be noted that the index thus calculated is, in effect, an average of the supply prices weighted by the current quantities.

Form I (p. 13) illustrates the form on which the supply price index may be compiled. As the prime records would, in any case, be arranged in order of sub-departments and expense headings for posting to the cost ledger, while thus arranged the base values and current values could be listed and posted to the departmental index sheets. These sheets would then be summarised to give a main department or factory total.

Sales Price Index

Although a normal selling price may be estimated for each product, both as a basis for comparison and for quotations, it does not follow that this price will be rigidly adhered to by sales department in quotations. The sales policy of discriminating between different markets is well known and the selling price with which the factory has to endeavour to maintain equilibrium is, therefore, the average of a number of prices. Obviously, the average selling price realised in any month may not, and possibly rarely will, be the normal average which may only be realised over a period. To calculate the difference, therefore, between the average current selling price each month and the estimated normal average, for the purpose of comparison and analysis, a sales price index would require to be constructed.

Form II illustrates the form on which a sales price index may be calculated. There would be a sheet like this for each product, the production of the products at each stage would be entered and the value of materials and departmental expenditure extended at both the basis and current prices. The gain or loss would be carried out and the index calculated. The product sheets would then be summarised to give a main department or factory total.

Form II

Sales Price Index

S.O. No. .... Product. ....

	Month.						
	Production	Basis Price	Value	Current Price	Value	*Gain/Loss*	Index
Materials—							
....							
....							
....							
....							
Departmental Expenditure—							
Sub-Dept.							
„							
„							
„							
„							
....							
Totals							

Datum Cost Curves

By load factor is meant the ratio of the actual production to the production level at which cost price and selling price are equal, i.e. in equilibrium. In a plant in which, due to a large amount of fixed or relatively inelastic expenditure, the law of decreasing cost operates, while on the other hand, the selling price is fixed by the market, this equilibrium position may be illustrated graphically thus :—

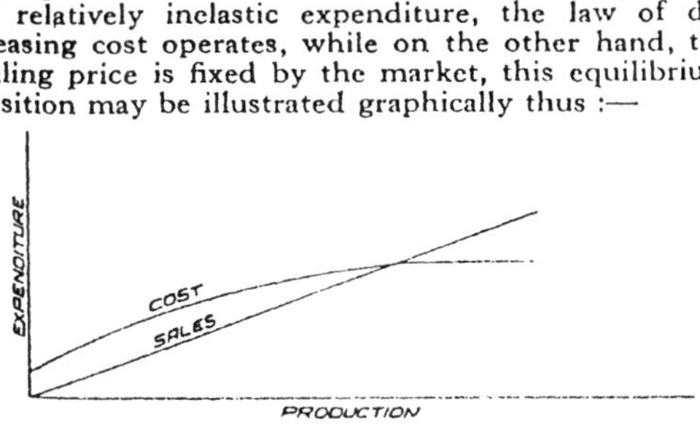

The lessening gradient of the cost curve indicates the economy of increasing production when a considerable part of the oncost is fixed or relatively fixed. The diagonal sales line indicates a fixed selling price per unit irrespective of the volume of production. The point of intersection indicates the production level at which the market value of the production equals its production cost. It will be seen from the graph that when the volume of production increases beyond this point of equilibrium the sales value of the production is greater than its cost, and when production falls short of the equilibrium amount its sales value is less than the production cost. In other words, if this equilibrium volume of production be regarded as normal, then there will be a gain on abnormal production and a loss on subnormal production even although the expenditure on the particular volume of production may, from the operating point of view, be quite normal. This is the gain or loss meant as being due to the " load factor."

It is obvious, therefore, that if it were practicable, first, to construct a cost curve for each sub-department showing the production cost at any level throughout the range of the department's capacity, and secondly, to open up the factory selling prices of the products into departmental rates, the economic equilibrium of each sub-department could be determined. Having thus determined the equilibrium production and corresponding equilibrium expenditure, the estimated normal sales value of any volume of production would be obtained by multiplying by the equilibrium rate per unit. The difference between the sales value and normal cost measured along the expenditure axis would be the gain or loss attributable to the " load factor."

A curve of normal cost would also provide a standard for measuring the economy of the actual operating expenditure of a department. As the cost curve would represent, as accurately as may be estimated, the expenditure normally required to produce any quantity of production within the capacity of the department, any fluctuation of the actual expenditure (subject to correction by the supply price factor) from this normal could be held accountable to the manager responsible for the operation of the department.

It will be seen from the foregoing that the basis of the analysis into " load factor efficiency " and " operating efficiency " would be departmental cost curves. These curves would, theoretically, be meant to represent normal cost schedules, but as absolute normal is practically impossible to determine with certainty, they could only be regarded as an estimated normal. Without being absolutely normal, however, they could be adopted as a basis for the measurement of fluctuations and could, therefore, be described as " datum curves." The use of this term in place of " normal " would prevent the curves being interpreted too strictly and thus, perhaps, misleading. They could, alternatively, be termed " estimated normal cost curves."

Whether there should be a curve for each item of expense or a curve for the total departmental expenditure would be a question both of the labour involved and accuracy expected. One curve for a total expenditure covering over a dozen items of varying degrees of elasticity would possibly prove not very satisfactory, while on the other hand it is doubtful if the accuracy with which the departmental expense items could be estimated individually would justify the construction of individual curves. The practical limit of accuracy would most likely be to group the items, thus allowing a certain amount of averaging out. The groups might be such as the following :—

(*a*) Wages.

(*b*) Supervision.

(*c*) Power Services.

(*d*) Maintenance.

(*e*) Miscellaneous Charges.

The next step is the crux of the whole problem, namely, the compiling of the data for the plotting of the curves. Simply to plot the cost of past years would, in many cases where large items such as repairs and renewals occur periodically, still leave a problem of curve-fitting to spots widely dispersed. Further, the curves must represent prevailing conditions and these may not be the same as in the past. The most practical method would appear to be to compile expert estimates at about half-a-dozen production levels, showing the expenditure of each expense group at each production level, the object being that these estimates would be sufficient to determine the curve. For the purpose of actually drawing the curve the spots provided by the estimates could be doubled by interpolation.

Having constructed the datum curves the next step would be to determine the equilibrium position of each sub-department. This may be calculated from either the production or the average selling price. To calculate from the production, the estimated total finished production of the various products which it was planned to achieve during a certain period, say a year, would be analysed to give the corresponding total production for the various sub-departments. This production read off the sub-department cost curve would give the estimated normal cost of production.

As this would be the cost adopted as the basis for quotations it would therefore be the cost at which production would require to average out to maintain equilibrium with the selling value. To calculate equilibrium from the selling price the average market price of an estimated total finished production would be calculated, analysed into the rates for the constituent processes, and the productions corresponding to these rates read off from the cost curves. The equilibrium production and equilibrium cost calculated in either of these ways would be the standard of comparison. The total productions and average selling and cost rates referred to above being the aggregates and averages respectively of a number of different products would, of course, require to be factored (or weighted) totals and averages, and the basis on which these may be calculated will be discussed in the next article.

(*To be continued*)

THE MEASUREMENT OF ECONOMIC FACTORS IN COSTING—II

by **W. Y. Dunnigan**

Factor Basis for Products and Departments

As the production of a department will generally consist of a number of products of different values, a total actual weight of production could not be used for comparison purposes as, owing to the varying proportions of the different products being manufactured from month to month, the productions between which a comparison was being attempted would not necessarily refer to the same thing. Factors would, therefore, have to be allocated to the products in order that, no matter what the composition of the production may be, it could be calculated to a comparable total.

The method of fixing these factors would be to select a particular product as the base product and calculate the ratio of the cost of every other product to this base product. To be strictly accurate the cost on which the ratios should be calculated would be that of the expense group or total expense being compared, which would mean, of course, that there would be a separate production total for each expense group and also for the total. In view of the work involved, however, a more approximate basis of factoring may be deemed sufficient. For example, a sufficiently practical result may be obtained by factoring on the basis of the unit cost of the total of one or two items making up a large proportion of the departmental expenditure, e.g. wages and maintenance.

Having allocated factors to the products in each sub-department in order to obtain a uniform production total, factors would then be allocated to the sub-departments in order to aggregate their productions into a uniform total for the main department or factory. The base of these sub-departmental factors would be an arbitrary selection, the most likely choice being a principal process or the packing process. The aggregate production of the various processes would thus be expressed in terms of the production of the selected process.

Departmental Analysis

From the cost and sales curves the load factor efficiency and operating efficiency would be calculated as illustrated in the following graph.

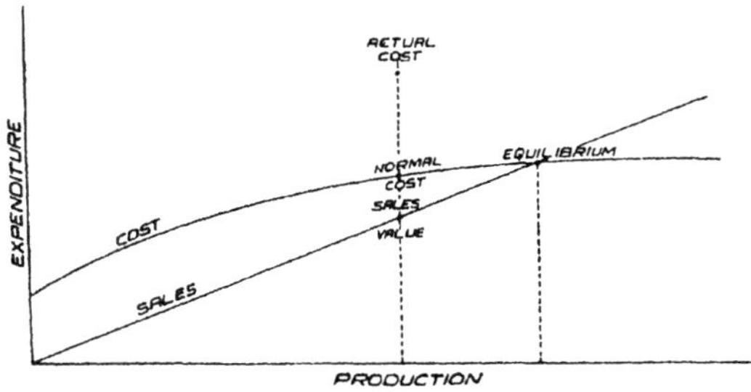

In the illustration the production is assumed to be less than the equilibrium amount and therefore the sales value is less than normal cost, the difference from the point " sales value " to the point " normal cost," measured along the expenditure axis, representing the loss due to the load factor. The amount measured from the point " normal cost " to the point " actual cost " would (after actual cost had been corrected by supply price factor) represent loss on account of operating efficiency. This analysis would be made for each sub-department and, if possible, for each expense group in each sub-department, and the departmental figures aggregated to give main department or factory totals.

Form III shows how the departmental analysis may be compiled. The total actual sales and normal sales values would be obtained from the summary of the sales price index. The normal cost would be obtained from the graph (or table of graph values) and the actual expenditure from the cost ledger.

These figures would be in totals for the department or in group totals according to the extent to which the analysis was carried. The sales price gain or loss would be the difference between the actual sales value and normal sales value ; the supply price gain or loss would be obtained by applying the supply price index (or factor) to the actual cost ; the load factor gain or loss would be the difference between the normal sales value and the normal cost ; and the operating efficiency would be the difference between the normal cost and actual cost.

Form III

Departmental Cost Analysis

S.O. No................ Department..

	Month...............................					
		Equilibrium	Actual	Factored	Index	
Production—						
Product............						
,, ...						
,, ...						
,, ...						
,, ...						
,, ...						
,, ...						
,, ...						
,, ...						
,, ...						

Form III—*continued.*

	Current Sales	Normal Sales	Normal Cost	Actual Cost	Gain/*Loss*				
					Sales Price	Supply Price	Load Factor	Operating Efficiency	Total
Departmental Expenditure—									
Direct Wages ..									
Dept. Wages									
Supervision									
Power Services ..									
Maintenance									
Misc. Charges ..									

Form IV

PRODUCT COST ANALYSIS

S.O. No................ Product..

	Month...............................					
		Actual Production	Product Factor	Factored Production	Dept. Factor	
Production—						
Sub-Dept...........						
,, ...						
,, ...						
,, ...						
,, ...						
,, ...						
,, ...						
,, ...						

	Current Sales	Normal Sales	Normal Cost	Actual Cost	Gain/*Loss*				
					Sales Price	Supply Price	Load Factor	Operating Efficiency	Total
Materials—									
....									
....									
....									
....									
....									
....									
....									
Departmental Expenditure—									
Sub-Dept.									
,, ...									
,, ...									
,, ...									
,, ...									
,, ...									

Product Analysis

With the data already accumulated a sort of cross-analysis may be made to show the allocation of the factors analysed over the products. Form IV shows how the analysis would be calculated for each product.

The actual productions and actual expenditures of each process would be obtained from the product cost accounts. Each process production would be multiplied by its product factor to obtain the production in terms of the departmental standard. This would be entered in the factored column and in turn be multiplied by the departmental factor to enable the various process productions to be aggregated. The " actual sales " and " normal sales " columns would be filled in from the sales price index statement for the product, and the " normal cost " would be obtained by allocating the normal column on the departmental cost analysis over the factored production for the department.

The gains or losses would then be obtained from these columns as already explained, viz. the difference between " actual sales " and " normal sales " = gain or loss on sales price ; the supply price index applied to the " actual cost "=gain or loss on supply price ; the difference between " normal sales " and " normal cost "=gain or loss on load factor ; and the difference between " normal cost " and " actual cost "=gain or loss on operating efficiency.

The fixing of standard costs for direct materials would be done with reference to individual products and would be a comparatively straightforward matter as more definite data is usually available for estimating the cost of a product. In the case of direct materials normal sales and normal cost would probably be synonymous and there would, therefore, be no load factor efficiency. There may be a difference between normal cost and actual cost, however, due to fluctuations in the supply prices and efficiency of usage of materials. These two factors may be evaluated by applying the supply price index for each material to the actual cost and obtaining the gain or loss due to the supply price factor. The balance of the difference between normal cost and actual cost could then probably be regarded as due to operating efficiency.

Final Statements

The final summary of the analysis in a form suitable for presentation to a board or management committee meeting is illustrated on Form V. The compiling of this statement from the summary statements of the departmental and product analysis respectively is obvious.

Form V

..........................Department—June 1935

STATEMENT OF DEPARTMENTAL AND PRODUCT ANALYSIS

Departmental Cost Analysis.

	Equilibrium	Actual	Index
PRODUCTION			

	Current Sales	Normal Sales	Normal Cost	Actual Cost	Gain/*Loss* Sales Price	Supply Price	Load Factor	Operating Efficiency	Total
Departmental Expenditure— Sub-Dept.									
,, ...									
,, ...									
,, ...									
,, ...									
,, ...									

Product Cost Analysis.

	Current Sales	Normal Sales	Normal Cost	Actual Cost	Gain/*Loss* Sales Price	Supply Price	Load Factor	Operating Efficiency	Total
Materials— Product									
,, ...									
,, ...									
,, ...									
,, ...									
,, ...									

Product Cost Analysis—continued.

	Current Sales	Normal Sales	Normal Cost	Actual Cost	Gain/*Loss*				
					Sales Price	Supply Price	Load Factor	Operating Efficiency	Total
Departmental Expenditure—									
Product									
,, ...									
,, ...									
,, ...									
,, ...									
,, ...									

In addition to providing an analysis of the price fluctuations, load factor efficiency and operating efficiency, other features of a scheme of cost analysis on the foregoing lines may be mentioned briefly, as follows :—

(1) *Standard costs.* By means of the product factors and equilibrium costs in each sub-department a standard cost for each product could be built up. The equilibrium production divided into the corresponding expenditure would give the unit cost for the process in terms of the base product. By applying the product factors to this unit cost the unit cost of each of the other products would be obtained. Having done this for each sub-department the addition of the departmental rates (plus, of course, the material estimates) would give the finished cost of the product.

Many factory managers would maintain that the standard should be based on the cost which is normal to the current volume of production instead of on the equilibrium cost on the ground that they have no concern with fluctuations due to prices and load factor efficiency, these being more properly the responsibility of the purchase and sales departments or general management. To adopt the current production basis, however, would usually mean calculating a new standard each month, and in any case the difference between the equilibrium cost and cost normal to the current production is evaluated on the analysis statements.

(2) *Differential costs.* It is frequently necessary in most businesses to make an estimate of the cost of a product, not on the basis of normal or average cost, but on the basis of the cost of " added production," i.e. the additional cost incurred in producing a certain additional quantity of the product assuming production already at a certain level. This is generally known as differential cost which simply means the difference in cost between producing the additional production and not producing it. In the present scheme this information may be found as the difference between two points on the curve of normal cost (or may be read from a table of the graph values) and the cost so obtained corrected by the supply price index.

(3) *Divisional control.* It may be observed that the factors studied coincide with the functions of the main divisions of a business, namely, (*a*) purchasing, (*b*) sales, and (*c*) operating, and the analysis of the gain or loss, therefore, would provide an index of the efficiency of these divisions. A statement of the supply price index would show the trend of, and value of changes in, the prices of material supplies ; the gains or losses by departments on account of operating efficiency would show where investigation was required by the departmental managers ; and the gains or losses on account of load factor and sales prices would provide a guide to sales policy.

The foregoing scheme suggests the recognition of two facts as being essential in a real analysis of cost. First, that such an analysis is not a matter of splitting up the cost figures to account for every penny of expenditure, but consists of tracing out and measuring, broadly but with reasonable approximation, the ultimate factors which govern cost. These, it is suggested, will be found to be largely of an economic nature, and for the practical purposes of an individual established concern may be defined as shown above. Secondly, the essential features of the technique to be employed in measuring these factors must be the application of (*a*) the principle of factoring (which is the basis of index numbers) for aggregating the sub-department productions, and (*b*) cost curves for establishing standards at varying levels of production. Along these lines appears to lie the development of modern cost analysis.

COSTING TERMINOLOGY

(Issued by the authority of the Council of the Institute of Cost and Works Accountants)

MANY busy and eventful years have passed since the Council of the Institute of Cost and Works Accountants undertook the task of preparing a terminology suitable for cost accounting purposes. Although numerous difficulties have been encountered, this important work has proceeded through various stages until it has now reached a point where it is possible to lay before our readers a list of approved terms and definitions.

This list is neither comprehensive nor final. Probably it never will be, for like all other forms of living language, costing terminology must evolve and develop in response to the needs of the profession and in accordance with business requirements. The work of investigation and selection which has resulted in this list of terms and definitions must be succeeded by a more continuous process of elimination, addition and modification at the hands of a standing committee to be appointed for the purpose. The publication of this list is, indeed, the first step in this subsequent process, and in order to make it as effective as possible every member and registered student of the Institute is now invited to examine each definition carefully and to notify the Secretary by the end of April of any suggestions for modifications, additions or eliminations.

It may be helpful to include here a word as to the intentions of the Council with regard to this list of terms and definitions. The Council feels that it can with every confidence invite the cordial co-operation of all its members and registered students in the work of establishing this terminology as the accepted basis of the professional language of Cost Accountancy. It is realised that at the outset some difficulty may occasionally be experienced by those who are more or less committed in their business relations to terms and definitions which are not in entire agreement with this official code. It is hoped, however, that anyone so placed will find it possible to effect any necessary changes gradually, so that more or less universal conformity shall be ultimately attained. It cannot, however, be too strongly emphasised that the Council has no intention of imposing upon its members and students, or upon the business world generally, a code of terms and definitions which has not withstood the test of wide publicity. It is therefore hoped that members and students will assist in this work by sending in their suggestions as early as possible and by making them constructive and specific.

For students who are preparing for the Institute examinations and for all tutors and lecturers who are responsible for their studies, this list of terms and definitions has special importance. It should be borne in mind that all examination questions set by the Board of Examiners will in future be worded in strict accordance with this code and that all examiners will have the approved terminology well in mind when awarding marks for the answers sent in by candidates. A thorough working knowledge of the new terms and definitions will therefore assist candidates, not only in understanding the questions they have to answer, but also in expressing their answers in orthodox language.

A number of supplementary terms are under review and a subsequent list will be issued at a later date.

Accountancy

The process of analysing, classifying and recording transactions and operations in terms of time, quantity or money.

Administration Expense *(see also Overhead)*

The expense of formulating, directing and controlling the policy, organisation and operations of a business.

Administration Overhead *(see Overhead)*

All-In Costs *(see Cost, Total)*

Alligation

A method for determining the proportions of different materials to be used in a mixture to produce (*a*) a specified aggregate price, or (*b*) a required specific gravity.

Amortisation

The gradual extinction of a liability, usually by means of a sinking fund; also the process of spreading over a fixed period the depreciation in value of wasting assets, such as leases and royalties.

Apportionment of Works Expense

The allocation of works expense to departments, services, producing units, materials, etc.

Appreciation

The increase in value of assets.

Appropriation of Stock (*see Material Allocation*)

Audit (*see also Cost Audit*)

An examination and, as far as possible, a verification, of the correctness of accounts.

Auxiliary Supplies (*see Material, Indirect*)

" Batch " Costing

The type of costing where the work is handled in batches which are used as the unit for costing.

Bill of Material (*see Specification of Materials*)

Bin Tag (or Card)

A tag attached to a bin, stack, container, etc., which identifies the contents, indicates the material symbol (if any) and quantity in hand. It may also record the receipts and issues, the maximum and minimum quantities to be stocked, and the ordering level (*q.v.*).

Bonus (*see Payment by Results*)

Book Value

The value of an asset as recorded in the books of the business.

Budgetary Control

The systematic control of business operations by means of pre-determined standards prepared in minute detail and assembled into a comprehensive programme, in order to provide a basis of comparison with actual performances and costs, with the object of attaining the final results indicated in the programme.

Bulk Material

Material not in unit form directly suited to the work in hand ; *e.g.*, Bar, Tube, Sheet, and material which is measurable only by weight or volume.

" Bunch " Costing (*see " Batch " Costing*)

Burden (*see Overhead*)

Capital Services

The provision of fixed assets which comprise the earning capacity of a factory or business.

Chargeable Expense (*see Direct Expense*)

Chargeable Time (*see Labour, Direct*)

Clock Card

A card on which time recording machines record the workers' time in and out or the time when they start and finish different jobs.

Code (*see also Stores Code*)

A series of symbols by which (*a*) expenses are analysed, classified and assembled for allocation or (*b*) units of production are identified for classification and assembly

Collective Payment by Results

Collective remuneration for work performed by a group of workers, usually distributed to the individual workers on a pre-determined basis.

Commercial Cost (*see Selling Expense and Distribution Expense*)

Component

A constituent part which by assembly with other parts helps to form a complete product or a sub-assembly thereof.

Consumable Stores

Indirect Material (*q.v.*) chargeable as Overheads, *e.g.* Lubricants, Waste, Canteen and Ambulance supplies, etc.

Contract System of Wage Payment

The agreement between employers and employees for a fixed price for the accomplishment of a given task.

Control Accounts (*see also Cost Control Account*)

Accounts which constitute the links between the Cost Accounts and the Financial Books and ensure their interlocking.

Conversion Cost

The cost of converting raw materials into prepared materials or finished products, exclusive of the cost of raw materials.

Co-Partnership

The acquisition by an employee of shares in the firm or company by which he is employed. In some cases the shares cannot become the absolute property of the employee but represent a token by which a division of profits may be made.

Cost

The value in terms of money of the efforts, utilities, risks and abstinences which comprise Real Cost (*q.v.*).

Cost Allocation

The distribution of cost to units, processes, services or products in the proportions in which they have incurred it.

Cost Audit

The examination and verification of the correctness of cost accounts and calculations and of the methods used in their preparation.

Cost Control Account

A cost account which :

(*a*) indicates at any time, the state of work in progress, stock in hand, etc., not readily ascertainable by physical inspection ; and so

(*b*) provides a check on the appropriation of materials, wages and expenses

Cost, Elements of

The main divisions into which total cost is divided, *i.e.* materials, wages, expense

Cost of Labour (*see Labour, Cost of*)

Cost of Material (*see Material, Cost of*)

Cost of Production

Prime Cost (*q.v.*) plus Production Overhead(*q.v.*).

Cost-Plus Contracts (*see " Time and Lime "*)

Cost, Real

The efforts expended, the utilities consumed, the risks incurred and the abstinence endured in providing a commodity or service, expressed as such instead of in terms of their money value.

Cost Sheet

The form on which are assembled the costs of a specific product, order, job, unit or service.

Cost Summary Card (*see Cost Sheet*)

Cost, Total

The sum of all items which comprise the cost of production, administration, selling and distribution.

Cost Unit

The quantity upon which cost can be conveniently allocated or determined.

Costing

Comprises the following :

(*a*) the allocation of expenditure to cost accounts relating to services, production centres and departments ;
(*b*) the assembly and classification of records relating to output, operations, processes and to the use of facilities ;
(*c*) the determination of actual and standard costs of products, orders, jobs and other cost units by means of the above information ;
(*d*) the investigation, measurement and explanation of differences between actual and standard costs and performances ;
(*e*) the examination of schemes and proposals from the standpoint of cost and of their probable effect upon sales, selling prices, profits and working conditions ;
(*f*) the presentation of such information in a lucid and convenient form ;
(*g*) the interpretation and explanation of all cost records, information and results in terms most suitable for the control and administration of the business concerned.

Daywork or Day Rate Wage System

The method of remunerating labour on a time basis.

Defective Work Charges

The cost of rectifying faulty work caused by defects in design, material, workmanship or management.

Defective Work Report

A statement detailing the extent and causes of defective work , sometimes including suggestions for its prevention or remedy.

Deferred Charges

Prepaid items of expense, such as Rates, Taxes, Insurances, Interest and Discount, Subscriptions and Membership Fees, Railway Season Tickets, Royalties, Patent Fees, etc., which not being wholly consumed in the current accounting period, have unabsorbed balances to be carried forward to the ensuing periods.

Deferred Credits

Income received during the current period on account of the ensuing period to which they are to be credited.

Deferred Maintenance

Normal or abnormal repair work or upkeep of buildings or equipment which should be performed and charged in the current accountancy period, but which for various reasons is deferred to a subsequent period.

Delivery Note

(1) A form of request to receive goods, which may or may not contain a detailed description.
(2) An advice of goods to be received.

Departmental Charges

The allocation of Overhead to workshops, departments, production centres or services.

Departmentalisation

The organisation of a business and the classification of its expenditure, functions and operations on the basis of departments, production centres and services.

Depletion

The exhaustion which takes place in natural resources when raw materials are extracted from mines, quarries, clay beds, gravel banks, etc., and when the normal fertility of agricultural land is diminished.

Depreciation

Normal deterioration in value which takes place during the life of an asset

Depreciation-Repair Reserve Method

A method for making periodical provision of uniform amount to cover the depreciation and cost of repairs of an asset based upon its estimated life. The estimated number of years is divided into the original cost of the asset, less the estimated ultimate scrap value, plus the estimated cost of repairs, the result being used as a flat charge to cover all repairs and depreciation for each year of the estimated life.

Despatch Note or Order

An instruction to the Forwarding Department to despatch goods.

Differential Piece-Rate System

A method of remuneration in which a scale of quantities is first determined and piece rates are fixed which are applicable to each quantity, differentiation being on a sliding scale.

Direct Charges (*see Direct Expense*)

Direct Cost (*see Prime Cost*)

Direct Departmental Expenses

All items of cost other than materials and wages which can be charged directly to specific departments; such as: rent, rates, gas, water, light, heat, power and salaries.

Direct Expense

All items of cost other than materials and wages not forming part of the normal production overhead, that are incurred on specific products, production units or services.

Direct Goods Account

An account to which are charged materials purchased for a specific cost unit.

Direct Labour (*see Labour, Direct*)

Direct Production Time (*see also Labour, Cost of*)

The measure of Direct Labour in terms of time.

Direct Wages (*see also Labour, Direct*)

The measure of Direct Labour expressed in terms of money.

Distribution Expense (*see also Overhead*)

The expense of distributing finished products; including those of warehouse and stock rooms for finished goods; carriage outwards; road transport outwards; freight outwards; sales depôts; provision and upkeep of outer containers (returnable and non-returnable).

Distribution Overhead (*see Overhead*)

Dockets

Generally used as a description of a label, tag, card or form. This term is not specifically descriptive of any particular document and is sometimes loosely applied to Bin Cards, Stores requisitions, Piece work contracts, Time cards, etc.

Establishment Charges or Expenses (*see Overhead*)

Expense

The third element of cost, which combines with Materials and Wages to produce Total Cost.

Expense Allocation

The process of distributing items of expense to the appropriate products, services, production centres, etc.

Expense Material (*see Material, Indirect*)

Expense Order (*see Standing Order Number*)

Facilities

Services and Equipment.

Factory Expense (*see Overhead*)

Factory General Charges (*see Overhead*)

Factory Indirect Expense (*see Overhead*)

Factory Cost or Works Cost (*see Cost of Production*)

Factory Order (*see Production Order*)

Factory Overhead or oncost (*see Overhead*)

Financial Budget (*see Budgetary Control*)

Finished Material Waste

Comprises:

(*a*) Avoidable waste, such as deterioration of finished stock due to faulty methods of storing, handling, etc.

(*b*) Unavoidable waste, such as waste in finished stock due to shrinkage and deterioration caused by obsolescence, evaporation and lapse of time.

Finished Parts

Items or sub-assemblies awaiting final assembly or sale.

Finished Parts Stock Record

A record indicating the quantity, and in some cases the value, of each class of finished part and its location in the stores.

Finished Stock (Manufactured Stock or Completed Stock)

The completed product awaiting sale or despatch.

Finished Stock Record

The record of finished stock received into store.

Finished Stores (*see Finished Stock*)

Fixed Assets

The permanent equipment of an undertaking.

Fixed Capital (*see Fixed Assets*)

Fixed Charges (or Expenses)

Expenses that do not vary substantially with the volume of trade or output.

Fixed Factory Charges (*see Fixed Charges*)

Fixed Plant

Plant, machinery and other equipment fixed in a definite position.

Flat Cost (*see Prime Cost*)

Floating Assets

"Those assets which in the ordinary course of business are continually changing and which are intended either for consumption in the ordinary process of manufacture or trading operations or for sale, and such intermediate forms (Book Debts, Bills Receivable, etc.) as they may take in the process of conversion into cash.

"Cash and all forms of temporary investment are also included under this heading." (*Dicksee.*)

General Expense or Charges (*see Overhead*)

Goods in Process (*see Work in Progress*)

Guarantee Pay

The amount by which the earnings of an individual (who has been employed on a system of payment by results for a period of a week or less) fall short of the value of that period calculated at his time rate, where it is the recognised practice to guarantee time rate.

Hour Cost (*see Hourly Rate*)

Hourly Burden System (*see Hourly Rate*)

Hourly Rate

The rate per hour to be charged to a manual or machine operation to charge overhead expenses. It may also include direct labour.

Idle Labour Expense (*see Waiting Time*)

Idle Time (*see Waiting Time*)

Interlocking System (*see also Control Accounts*)

A system by which the reconciliation of the Cost Accounts with the financial books is ensured.

Inventory

A detailed record of buildings, plant, stock, etc., indicating its state at any particular time, together with any similar information which may be required.

Invoice Allocation

Instructions recorded on the invoice itself, or on an attached slip, indicating the account or accounts to which the purchase or expense is to be charged.

Job Card

The card on which is entered a record of the time spent on any particular operation or job. In addition, the job card may contain details of the operations performed.

Job Costing

The method of costing jobs or contracts which are kept separate from other jobs or contracts during manufacture or construction.

Job Number

The identification number and/or symbol allotted to each job for :

(*a*) tracing and location purposes ;
(*b*) costing.

Job Rate

A pre-arranged basis of payment for the accomplishment of a specified task.

Labour, Cost of

The wages paid for direct and indirect labour expended in rendering a service or in the production of a product or any component or part thereof.

Labour, Direct

Labour expended in altering the composition, condition, conformation or construction of the product.

Labour, Indirect

Labour expended which does not alter the composition, condition, conformation or construction of the product.

Loose Plant or Loose Tools

Machinery and Tools required for manufacture, which have no fixed or definite location in the factory and can be moved freely from one part to another.

Machine Card (*see also Plant Record*)

A card for recording output per machine and, if required, stoppages, breakdowns, and repairs. It may also record date of purchase, price and value for depreciation purposes.

Machine Rate (*see Hourly Rate*)

Machine Unit System (*see Hourly Rate*)

Machinery Account (*see Plant Record*)

Maintenance Expenses

Expenses incurred in the upkeep and preservation in running order of fixed assets (*q.v.*).

Management Expenses (*see Administration Expense*)

Manufacturing Budget (*see Budgetary Control*)

Manufacturing Cost (*see Cost of Production*)

Manufacturing Expenses (*see Overhead*)

Manufacturing Order (*see Production Order*)

Mass Production

The production in large quantities of standardised products with the primary object of reducing cost. The essential features are a constant and uninterrupted flow of work, the use of labour-saving tools and equipment specially designed for specific operations, and the subdivision of processes into their simplest forms to avoid loss of output due to loss of time in changing over from one operation to another.

Material Abstract or Analysis

A classified record of issues from and returns to store, both direct and indirect, under :

(*a*) Cost unit or standing order number ;
(*b*) description or code ;
(*c*) quantity ;
(*d*) value.

Material Allocation

The setting aside of material for a specific order or production programme.

Material Appropriation (*see Material Allocation*)

Material Control

Comprises the purchasing, receiving, storing and issuing of every kind of material, with effective checks to prevent misappropriation and waste.

Material Controlling Account (*see Cost Control Account*)

Material, Cost of

The value of direct and indirect materials consumed in rendering a service or in the production of a product or any component or part thereof.

Material, Direct

Material that forms part of the product.

Material Expense (or Service)

Expenses incurred in the purchase, receipt, storage and transport of material.

Material, Indirect

Material which cannot be identified as part of the product.

Material Prime Cost (*see Prime Cost*)

Material Requisition (*see Stores Requisition*)

Material Service (*see Material Expense*)

Material Transfer (*see Transfer Note*)

Maximum and Minimum Stock (*see Bin Tag*)

Multiple Costing

A method of costing by aggregates where a great variety of articles is produced.

Net Production Cost (*see Cost of Production*)

Non-Chargeable Time or Material (*see Labour, Indirect, and Material, Indirect*)

Non-Productive Departments (*see Service Department*)

Non-Productive Expense Labour (*see Labour, Indirect*)

Non-Productive Labour (*see Labour, Indirect*)

Non-Productive Order (*see Standing Order Number*)

Normal Cost

A Standard Cost for which normal working loads and other working conditions have been taken as the standard.

Obsolescence

The natural process by which assets diminish in value owing to supersession or causes other than wear and tear.

On Charges (*see Overhead*)

Oncost (*see Overhead*)

Operating Cost

Cost incurred in rendering a service or maintaining an undertaking such as Railways, Tramways, Carriers or Gas, Electricity and Water Supplies.

Operation Costing

Method of costing by operations applicable to quantity or mass production.

Ordering Level

The point in the reduction of a stock commodity where action to replenish should be taken.

Output Cost (*see Unit Costing*)

Outside Labour (*see also Outworker*)

Work performed by sub-contractors. Also labour undertaken on a piecework basis by workers in certain industries and trades in their own homes.

Outworker

An employee working outside the precincts of the factory.

Overhead

The cost of indirect material, indirect labour and indirect expense.
Overhead may be subdivided into :

(*a*) Production Overhead.
(*b*) Selling Overhead.
(*c*) Distribution Overhead.
(*d*) Administration Overhead.

The component items of Overhead having been assembled under the above headings, the totals are then distributed in such a manner as will ensure their recovery in equitable proportions through each individual cost unit.
Overheads are sometimes referred to as : Burden, Oncost, Establishment Charge, General Expense and Indirect Expense.

(*a*) PRODUCTION OVERHEAD (*also referred to as Factory Overhead and Works Overhead*)

All indirect expenditure incurred by the factory from the receipt of the raw material until the finished product is placed in the warehouse ready for despatch.

(*b*) SELLING OVERHEAD

Includes all expenditure incurred in soliciting and securing orders, including advertising and publicity, also in the offices in corresponding with customers, in receiving and putting forward orders, in invoicing, in crediting returns and in keeping sales ledgers.

(*c*) DISTRIBUTION OVERHEAD

Expenditure incurred on the product and its containers from the time it is placed in the warehouse ready for despatch until it reaches its final destination, including all outward transport, inward transport of returned empties, etc., cost of maintaining outlying sales depôts, and the receipt, handling and reconditioning of returned empty packages.

(*d*) ADMINISTRATION OVERHEAD

Expenditure incurred in formulating, directing and controlling the policy, organisation and operations of a business.

Part-Finished Stock

Work in progress which has not reached the stage of completion as a part or component.

Pay-Off Note

Notification to the Pay Office of the wages due to an employee on the termination of his employment.

Pay Roll (*see Wages Sheet*)

Pay Roll Analysis (*see Wages Sheet Analysis*)

Pay Slip (*see Wage Ticket*)

Payment by Results

Remuneration for increased effort, *e.g.* by means of piecework, premium bonus or similar system
Straight piecework is the simplest example of payment by results, and consists of a flat payment per unit of output.
Premium Bonus is a term applied to any system whereby the payment per unit of output varies according to the worker's total output in a given time and the bonus is an addition to the time rate and is based on the increased output or on the saving of time on a definite time allowance

Permanent Assets (*see Fixed Assets*)

Perpetual Inventory

A method of recording Store balances after every receipt and issue, to facilitate regular checking with quantities actually in store and thereby obviate closing down for stock-taking.

Piece Rates (*see Piecework Price*)

Piecework (*see Payment by Results*)

Piecework Balance

The difference between piecework earnings and the value of the time taken calculated at standard time rates.

Piecework Price

The amount fixed for the performance of a specific job or operation.

Plant (*see Fixed Plant and Loose Plant or Loose Tools*)

Plant Record

A classified record of fixed and loose plant by units and/or groups, giving details, *e.g.* origin, cost, date of purchase, depreciation and repairs, and location.

Pre-Determined Cost (*see also Standard Costing*)

Cost computed in advance of production by reference to a specification of all factors affecting cost. A pre-determined cost may become a Standard Cost.

Premium Bonus (*see Payment by Results*)

Preparation Expense

Expense incurred on an order before manufacture is commenced.

Prime Cost

Those direct items of cost which, entering into and forming part of the product, are charged directly to the product, *i.e.* :

(*a*) Direct Material ;
(*b*) Direct Labour ;
(*c*) Direct Expense.

Process Costing

A method of costing applied to manufacture carried on by processes which have one or more of the following features :—

(*a*) That the product of one process becomes the material of a subsequent process ;
(*b*) That different products (including by-products) are produced simultaneously at the same process.
(*c*) That products (ultimately differing only in shape or form) are not distinguishable one from another during one or more of the processes of the series to complete the manufacture.

Process Material

Materials which can be traced as a part of one or more of the products of the process.

Production Cost (*see Cost of Production*)

Production Efficiency

The ratio of Actual Cost or actual time to Standard Cost or standard time.

Production Expense (*see Overhead*)

Production Note

An intimation from the factory to the office of the completion of work or an operation.

Production Order

Written instructions to the factory detailing work to be put in hand.

Production Overhead or Oncost (*see Overhead*)

Production Service

A standing aid to production which is available at all times, is applicable generally and is used as required, *e.g.* power supply, etc.

Productive Department

A department in which the saleable product is manufactured, as distinguished from service departments (*q.v.*), which are ancillary thereto.

Productive Expense (*see Overhead*)

Productive Hour Method (*see Hourly Rate*)

Productive Labour (*see Labour, Direct*)

Productive Material (*see Material, Direct*)

Productive Wages (*see Labour, Direct*)

Raw Material

Material purchased either in a natural or prepared condition.

Recipe Costing (*see Standard Costing*)

Residual Value (*see Scrap Value*)

Running Cost or Running Charge (*see Operating Cost*)

Scrap Material

Material, raw or manufactured, residual or other, which is useless for its original purpose.

Scrap Value

The value of an asset at the end of its useful life, or of an article which is no longer wanted.

Secondary Labour (*see Labour, Indirect*)

Secondary Material (*see Material, Indirect*)

Secondary Wages (*see Labour, Indirect*)

Selling Cost (*see also Cost, Total*)

Comprises Prime Cost (*q.v.*) and all Overheads (*q.v.*).

Selling Expense (*see also Overhead*)

All expenses incurred in obtaining orders and marketing commodities or services, including such items as sales office expenditure ; travellers' salaries, commission and expenses ; catalogues, price lists and advertisements ; samples and patterns of saleable lines ; discounts allowed.

Selling Overhead (*see Overhead*)

Service Department
A department which provides facilities which are ancillary to production and distribution.

Services
Facilities which are provided to assist the production and distribution departments

Shop Burden (*see Overhead*)

Shop Charges (*see Overhead*)

Shop Cost (*see Cost of Production*)

Single (Output) Costing
A method of ascertaining cost where only one commodity is produced.

Specification of Materials
Details of raw or prepared materials required for a unit of production

Spoilage, Cost of (*see Defective Work Charges*)

Standard Costing
The determination of costs of standard products, produced in standard quantities under standard conditions which may be normal or otherwise.

Standing Expenses or Standing Charges (*see Fixed Charges*)

Standing Order Number
A permanent classification number (or code) to which a particular type of expense is charged

Standing Time (*see Waiting Time*)

Stock Account (*see Stores Ledger*)

Stock Control (*see Material Control*)

Stock Debit Note (*see Production Note*)

Stock Issued Book (*see Stock Record*)

Stock Order
Written instructions to the factory detailing work to be manufactured for stock.

Stock Received Book (*see Stock Record*)

Stock Record (*see also Bin Tag or Card*)
Statistical and descriptive information as to the stock of all kinds of raw and prepared materials and of the receipts and issues of same. It may include records of quantities ordered for future delivery and of appropriations for work in hand ; it may also be subdivided into sections relating to :
(*a*) receipts ;
(*b*) issues ;
(*c*) balances.

Stock Requisition
A request from the Storekeeper for the replenishment of stock.

Stores Account (*see Stores Ledger*)

Stores Balance Card (*see Stock Record*)

Stores Code
A series of symbols indicating the various descriptions, sizes and qualities of materials.

Stores Debit Note
A permit to return to the Storekeeper raw material, finished parts or other stores no longer required in the factory.

Stores Issued Warrant (*see Stores Requisition*)

Stores Ledger
A record of quantities and values of stores received and issued, assembled under commodities.

Stores Requisition
An authorisation to the Storekeeper to issue raw material, prepared material, finished parts or other stores.

Stores Returned Warrant (*see Stores Debit Note*)

Stores Withdrawal Note (*see Stores Requisition*)

Swarf (*see Scrap Material*)

Syllabus Order (*see Standing Order Number*)

Symbols (*see Code*)

Terminal Costing (*see Job Costing*)

" Time and Lime "
A term applied to contracts placed on the basis of cost. This basis was originally employed in connection with bricklaying and similar work, but its use was extended to various kinds of contract work during the Great War Sometimes referred to as " Cost-plus contracts."

Time Booking (*see Work Card*)

Time Card (*see Work Card*)

Time Clock or Time Recorder (*see also Clock Card*)
An instrument for recording workers' time It may be used for recording each employee's times of arrival and departure and, if required, the time of starting and finishing each job or operation

Time Docket (*see Work Card*)

Time Rate
The rate of wages paid to a worker on a time basis.

Time Record (*see Work Card*)

Time Sheet (*see Work Card*)

Time Slip (*see Work Card*)

Transfer Note or Voucher
A document for adjusting charges when material or work in progress on an order has been appropriated to another order

Unabsorbed Expense
The excess of the total actual overhead over and above the amounts charged to orders, jobs or other cost units by pre-determined rates of absorption.

Uniform Costing
The use of the same costing methods for different factories in the same industry or combine.

Unit Costing
A method of costing by an all-round unit of production where manufacture is continuous and the units are identical. It may be combined with process, operation or batch costing.

Unit of Cost (*see Cost Unit*)

Unproductive Labour (*see Labour, Indirect*)

Unproductive Material (*see Material, Indirect*)

Unproductive Time (*see Labour, Indirect*)

Wage Ticket
A summary of the make up of the gross and net wages payable to an employee and corresponding to the amount on the wages sheet (*q.v.*)

Wages (*see also Labour, Direct and Labour, Indirect*)
The remuneration of labour expressed in terms of money.

Wages Abstract (*see Wages Analysis*)

Wages Analysis
Dissection, classification and assembly of wages earned under the various orders for :
(*a*) Production ;
(*b*) Overhead ;
(*c*) Capital Services.

Wages Sheet
A summarised statement of wages payable to the employees. It usually details in addition :
(*a*) State Insurance deductions ;
(*b*) Other deductions or additions (if any) ;
(*c*) Employers' State Insurance contributions ;
(*d*) Extra payment for overtime.

Wages Sheet Analysis
A dissection or summary by departments, shops, etc., of certain statistics recorded on the wage sheets, *e.g.* the number of employees, average wages, overtime hours, lost time, etc.

Wages Summary (*see Work Card and Wages Analysis*)

Waiting Time
Time spent by an employee when standing by for reasons beyond his control, *e.g.* waiting for instructions, power, materials, tools, etc.

Waste (*see also Scrap Material*)
Any form of loss in material, labour, overheads or product.

Wear and Tear (*see Depreciation*)

Work Card
The record of an operation, stating quantity, time occupied, and the order chargeable.

Work in Process (*see Work in Progress*)

Work in Progress
Work in hand and not ready for despatch from the factory.

Work Ticket (*see Production Order*)

Working (Operating) Cost (*see Operating Cost*)

Working Order (*see Production Order*)

Works Charges (*see Overhead*)

Works Cost (*see Cost of Production*)

Works Expenditure (*see Overhead*)

Works Expense (*see Overhead*)

Works Order (*see Production Order*)

Works Overhead or Oncost (*see Overhead*)

SOME NOTES ON THE EARLY LITERATURE AND DEVELOPMENT OF COST ACCOUNTING IN GREAT BRITAIN—I

by Ronald S. Edwards

(Assistant Lecturer in Accounting and Business Administration, London School of Economics.)

Industrial and Commercial Background

In reviewing the early development of cost accounting Professor A. C. Littleton (1) observes that "in the last analysis (it) represents the influence of the industrial revolution upon double-entry bookkeeping . . . " Until the 19th century accounting problems were not beyond the competence of the bookkeeper trained in the rather simple rules of "double-entry." It was necessary to record only the purchase and sale of goods, together with warehouse and distribution expenses, and to summarise the result of the transactions for the year in the form of a profit and loss account. If a merchant dealt in several different commodities it was very simple for his bookkeeper to keep separate accounts for each type of goods carrying the profit or loss on each to the profit and loss account. Or, if he sent consignments overseas he could record the details of the disposal of each consignment, and the various expenses incidental thereto in one account, and show the profit thereon. The bookkeeping literature of the 18th and 19th centuries abounds with examples of consignment accounts, voyage accounts and accounts showing the profit on the sale of different types of commodities by the same business. These types of transactions had required recording for centuries and Italian, German, Dutch, French and English writers have left a legacy of textbooks to show that the needs of the day were met.

Most manufacturing activities were equally easy to cater for until power machinery and the growth of communications revolutionised industry. While industrial technique was simple and the size of the undertaking small no difficulty was experienced in recording transactions such as the purchase of raw material, the hiring of a few labourers, and small workshop expenses. With the development of iron manufacture, engineering, coal mining and the textiles, the accountants' problems began.

The invention of the steam engine, the new canals and roads, the work of Darby and Cort in making possible the use of coal instead of charcoal for both smelting and refining, enabled the iron industry to expand rapidly. Imports ceased, and exports began by the end of the 18th century. The size of the business was no longer limited by the available water supply, and all processes could be combined in one place. Furnace, forge and mill were brought together.

> "The typical concern of the new era was integrated in its structure: it mined the ore and coal, smelted, refined, rolled and slit the iron into its finished form of plates and rods. From this time onward, therefore, very large capitals began to be sunk in the industry; and in 1812, to give an example of one locality, there were in the neighbourhood of Birmingham no fewer than ten ironworks, each of which had cost over £50,000 to establish. It was by no means uncommon to find 300 or 500 men employed in a single works, apart from the colliers and others connected with the supply of raw material."(2)

By about 1833 one quarter of the cost of bar iron was said to consist of interest on the capital sunk in the plant. (3)

> "In times of bad trade works were continued so long as the selling price of the iron would cover even a little more than the prime costs of production—raw material and labour. Competition in sales was consequently felt to be harmful, and there was a strong incentive for iron masters to combine with the object of maintaining prices." (4)

Here, then, were a number of problems which accounting had not previously faced. A series of costly processes between the raw material and the finished product, a dead weight of fixed cost which could not be shifted in bad times, a large body of labour to be paid and watched. The iron master would want to have details of his raw materials on hand at all times in order to be sure that production was not going to be held up; on the other hand he would wish to see that capital was not being tied up unnecessarily by holding stocks which were too large. He would require information as to the expenditure and output of the different processes, in order to keep a check on waste and inefficiency. He would need a system of check in order to prevent the fraud and error possible with a large pay roll. In ascertaining his profit or loss at the end of the year, the problem of depreciation of the factory and plant would arise. Lastly it would be necessary to know the minimum to which prices should be cut in bad times and this would involve a knowledge of the variable, or so-called "prime" costs, per unit of output. The problem of "overhead" had come into being.

The coal-mining industry also offered accounting problems, following its rapid growth.

> "By 1750 it had generally outgrown the stage of profitable exploitation on a small scale. The sinking of shafts, the construction of side galleries, ventilation, pumping out, raising the coal to the surface and the accompanying engineering and tool-making services were among the operations which required a large capital investment."(5)

By 1789 one French coal-mining company employed 4,000, and was using a dozen steam engines. (6) The

(1) Accounting Evolution to 1900—page 360.

(2) T. S. Ashton—Iron and Steel in the Industrial Revolution, page 100.

(3) T. S. Ashton, op. cit., page 163.

(4) T. S. Ashton, op. cit., page 164.

(5) Knight, Barnes & Flugel—Econ. History of Europe, page 354.

(6) Op. cit., page 355.

deepening of shafts, the extension of the area of operation, the employment of power machinery, iron rails from the pits to the canals, and a six fold increase in output in Britain between 1795 and 1854 (7)—all suggest that accounting routine would have to fulfil new roles. The " fixed cost " problem again appears, and in addition the accounting department will have to supply the machinery for dealing with a large pay roll, for detailing output figures, for recording the costs of each seam, for showing the various expenses of production on a tonnage basis. It will have to provide some of the information on which the management could decide whether to extend the various workings, or whether to sink new shafts. In preparing the annual profit and loss account, there arises the difficulty of deciding how to treat irrevocable development costs.

The most fruitful field for cost accounting problems should, however, be found in the engineering trades because estimating and tendering for contracts is important.

> " Engineering is the most modern of all the great industrial groups. Since it is engaged in providing the equipment for mechanical transport and for power driven productive plants, together with apparatus for lighting, heating and drainage, it could not exist save in a highly developed economic system . . ."(8)

The production of stationary steam engines was important during the last quarter of the 18th century. Specialist firms were producing textile machinery in the first quarter of the 19th century. Locomotives and railway equipment appeared in the thirties. From the middle of the century steamships and marine engines became of great importance. According to Clapham :

> " by 1820-30 the professional purveyor of machines made with the help of other machines, the true mechanical engineer of the modern world, was just coming into existence—in Lancashire and London where the demand was at its maximum."(9)

The engineering firm was not as a rule large ; in 1824-5 Bramah controlled about 100 men and Galloway about the same number, but these were comparatively big employers. It is hardly likely that accounting difficulties were important until about the middle of the century.

It is only one step from estimating and tendering to what is known as job or contract costing. Having made a quotation and accepted a contract based on it, the engineer would require some means of collecting details of the costs of executing the contract in order to ascertain the profit or loss thereon, and to provide information for future estimates. It is in connection with this type of work that the most discussed problems of cost accounting arose—the allocation of overhead cost to jobs and contracts, the inclusion or exclusion of interest as a cost, the estimation of profit on unfinished contracts, and the decision as to whether cost accounts should be part of the system of general accounting or should be completely separate.

From about 1770 until 1840 the principal textile trades—cotton and wool—were in process of transformation to factory industries owing to machine inventions. By the end of this period machine tools of precision and trained engineers were able to supply machinery of a character which would hasten the change over from manual work to power. After 1835 the power loom spread rapidly, and the position of the hand loom weaver became desperate.(10) The transformation was easier and more rapid in the newer industry of cotton manufacture than in the older organised system of domestic production of woollen goods. However, once the change over had taken place and capital had been sunk in factory and plant, we should expect the problems of overhead cost and accounting for processes to loom up.

The first part of the industrial revolution brought its crop of industrial accounting problems, mainly as a result of the introduction of machine processes. The second development in the Revolution was the growth of communications, which by enlarging the market for manufactured goods and ensuring steady supplies of raw materials, resulted in the growth of the large scale industrial unit. The increase in size of the industrial unit brought in its train a crop of problems concerning organisation and control, planning production, coordinating departments. It became even more important to watch movements in output, costs and overhead expenditure, department by department and product by product. The commercial exploitation of by-products in a number of industries brought accountants face to face with " joint costs," which are particularly apparent in industrial chemistry. By 1830 Charles Tennant, of Glasgow, had a works covering ten acres of ground, the main products being sulphuric acid, chloride of lime, soda and soap. Muspratt at Liverpool in 1823 started the first important works for the manufacture of soda by the Leblanc process.(11) Railways which made large scale industrial development possible combined practically all the problems—joint costs, integrated processes, depreciation and obsolescence, heavy fixed investment and the control of a widespread organisation.

To study the early development of systematic recording of commercial transactions, one would naturally examine the documents and books of those countries which first predominated in the trading world, the greatest harvest would be obtained from the Italian works. Similarly, in tracing the beginnings of industrial accounting one would work among the material provided by those nations which were first faced with

(7) Mrs. Knowles—Industrial and Commercial Revolution, page 71.

(8) G. C. Allen—British Industries and their Organisation, page 134.

(9) J. H. Clapham—Economic History 1820-1850—(Britain on the Eve of the Railway Age), page 152.

(10) See Knowles—Industrial and Commercial Revolutions, pages 56-57.

(11) J. H. Clapham—Economic History 1820-1850 (Britain on the Eve of the Railway Age), pages 147-8.

industrial problems. Britain was of course the first great industrial nation, and she must have been faced with practically all the great industrial accounting problems during the first three quarters of the 19th century. Later, of course, America and Germany needed to examine the same questions, but with different emphasis depending on the direction of industrial development in those countries.

(To be continued)

SOME NOTES ON THE EARLY LITERATURE AND DEVELOPMENT OF COST ACCOUNTING IN GREAT BRITAIN—II

by Ronald S. Edwards

(Assistant Lecturer in Accounting and Business Administration, London School of Economics.)

British Cost Accounting Literature Prior to 1870

Publications which can be said to deal with cost or industrial accounting in this country before 1870 are conspicuous by their rarity. The bulk of the literature deals entirely with the accounts of merchants and few writers paid any attention to the needs of manufacturers or agriculturists.

In 1697 John Collins wrote a book called " The Perfect Method of Merchants Accompts,"* published in London. It contained a set of dyers' accounts, and this is possibly the first work in English on bookkeeping to recognise that the requirements of industrial accounting are not exactly the same as those of commercial accounting. Collins takes dyeing as his example and produces a raw material account dealing with both quantities and values. The incoming material is debited and, when used, it passes from the credit side of the material account to the debit of the process account, i.e. the dyehouse account, to which all the costs of dyeing are debited. Both of the accounts are set out below. The example is important because it shows application of " double entry " to *internal* transactions, namely, the movement of materials.

The following amusing note appears at the end of the book—" This book is so well corrected, that there is not found above one penny error in the sums, and that in the Ship question : Punctuations, if wanting, the reader may supply."

It may not be usual to regard the accounts of a landed estate as cost accounting or industrial accounting in the wider sense, but some of the problems are very similar. It would be desirable, for instance, to know the results of any farms run by the estate, to see that losses are not unwittingly being subsidised by other sources of income. Again, some means should be available for tracing foodstuffs and other commodities to see whether they are used by the household, consumed by the farms, sold or otherwise

* Collins had published " An Introduction to Merchants Accompts " in 1652 which was reprinted in 1664 without alteration; the Fire, however, consumed the greater part of the impression.

THE LEIDGER OF THE DYE-HOUSE PARTABLE ACCOUNT

	Argal Dr.	l s d
1664 Jan. 15	To Stock of *Adam Barker* for 10 Cask Weighing, viz. :— C qrs. l 90 00 27 at 30s. ..	135 07 00
1665 June 10	To Cash for 5 Cask .. 80 00 00 at 30s. ..	120 00 00
	170 00 27	
	To the Dye-house for the neat gains ..	1 09 00
		256 16 00

THE LEIDGER OF THE DYE-HOUSE PARTABLE ACCOUNT

	Argal Cr. C qrs. l	l s d
1665 June 7	By Cash for 2 Csks. weight .. 18 00 00 Sold to J.H. At 32s. per c. – – –	28 16 00
	By the Dye-house for .. .. 72 00 00 spent as per Particulars at 30s. .. – – –	108 00 00
	By Goods remaining for 80 00 00 left at 30s. ..	120 00 00
	Lost in weight .. 00 00 27	000 00 00
	170 00 27	256 16 00

THE LEIDGER OF THE DYE-HOUSE PARTABLE ACCOUNT

Dye-house or loss. Dr.	l s d	l s d
To Wares for sundry Commodities spent, viz. in a Year ending the 29th December 1665		
To Coals for 40 Chaulder	40 00 00	
To Argal for 72 C	108 00 00	
To Allom for 2 Tuns	50 00 00	
To Brazil Wood for 1 Tun	28 00 00	
To Coucheaneel for 40l as 30s. ..	60 00 00	
To the said for 15l at 28s.	21 00 00	
To Fustick for 18C at 6s. 8d.	6 00 00	
To Coppras for 3 h.h.	8 00 00	
To Mather for 68C Crop at 4l ..	272 00 00	
To Shumack for 10 Baggs	56 08 00	
To Island Woad for 3 Tuns	45 00 00	
To Spanish Indico for 3 Cask ..	100 16 00	795 04 00
To Stock of Adam Barker for a Year's Rent ..		100 00 00
To John Garthwait for an Abatement		13 04
To Cash for the Total of Sundry Disbursements in the outward Column		664 12 03
To the Stocks of the Partners for the Dividend, being the neat gains of one Year's Trade		497 10 09
		2,058 00 04

THE LEIDGER OF THE DYE-HOUSE PARTABLE ACCOUNT

Per Contra Dye-house or Profit. Cr.	l s d
By Argal for the neat gains	1 09 00
By Coucheaneel for the said	4 00 00
By Mather gained thereby	3 08 00
By Bayes for the like	100 00 00
By Goods remaining for divers loose Goods left that are charged to Account in the Disbursements per Contra	10 00 00
By John Garthwait for Earnings	1,406 13 04
By Jericho Cudworth for the said..	532 10 00
	2,058 00 04

disposed of. In 1714 a book was devoted to these problems by an anonymous writer who styled himself " A Person of Honour," and his work " The Gentleman Accomptant." Incidentally the author has been identified as the Hon. Roger North, author of the well-known " Lives of the Norths."* The writer was aware of the importance of showing the results of each undertaking separately. Therefore, wages and all expenses except small incidentals are divided up between various accounts. For instance, there is an account for " husbandry " which is debited with opening stock, labour, utensils, wagons, seed, and also with horses which have been taken over from the personal equipment of the estate owner (the equipment account being credited). The husbandry account is credited with sales and closing stock, and the balance is transferred to profit and loss. Thus the result of " husbandry " is separately assessed.

Another account segregates the results of a particular farm, and a third shows the profit or loss on " Grazing and Dairy." This last account is reproduced below† as it should be observed how it is debited with Lambs which have been transferred from the " Flock Account " and is credited with the household consumption.

1708-9		Accompt of Grazing and Dairy .. .. *Dr.*		l	s	d
Jan. 1	f.	To the Personal Estate, the Stock	1	130		
25	ak.	To the Steward's Cash, for Stock bought	23	64	10	
Aug. 5	av.	To the Flocks, for Thirty Lambs to Pasture ..	10	6		
Dec. 30	cs.	To Accompt Profit and Loss, advanced in this Accompt	30	159	5	8
				359	15	8

1708-9		Per Contra .. *Cr.*		l	s	d
Mar. 17	n.	By Accompt House-keeping, for Cattel spent ..	4	12	6	
25	s.	By House-keeper's Cash, for Butter and Cheese ..	22	8		
	t.	By Cash, for Twenty Weathers sold	2	17		
May 21	ae.	By House-keeping, for Beasts spent	4	21	2	
Aug. 1	am.	By House-keeper's Cash, for Butter and Cheese ..	22	10	12	
Spt. 30	as.	By Ditto, for like	22	4	17	8
Oct. 7	an.	By House-keeping, for Cattel spent	4	29	18	
Nov.28	ay.	By Ditto, the Sum of Dairy Profits, and Swine spent	4	95		
30	az.	By Ditto, killed and spent, Cattel	4	22		
Dec.30	bb.	By House-keeper's Cash, Butter and Cheese sold ..	23	9		
	cp.	By Accompt Balances, the Stock resting	31	130		
				359	15	8

Another document which deserves reproduction is the weekly statement showing how the labourers have been employed, " a tabular method of keeping a check upon them with the greatest ease,"* " the knowledge that such an accompt as this is kept, is sufficient to keep men to true reckoning, lest they lose their credit and their work . . ."† It also gives information which can form a basis for future contracts with the men.

Workmen's N'ms	Monday Nov. 8, 1709	Tuesday 9	Wednesday 10	Thursday 11	Friday 12	Saturday 13
A.B.		Lopping of Trees	Same		Filling Gravel	Half the same
C.D.	Dyking, by the Rod	Same	Same	Same	Same	Half the same
E.F.	Dyking, by the Rod	Same	Same	Same	Same	Half the same both done 12 Rod
G.H.	Helping in the Garden	Same	Cutting and Pruning	Same	Same	Same
J.K.	Filling the Gravel-Cart	Digging Gravel	Same	Same	Same	Helping in the Garden

In the words of the author this type of accounting was " useful to gentlemen and to some necessary; commendable in all, and fruitless to none."‡

John Mair, an eighteenth century schoolmaster, whose publications on bookkeeping ran into many editions, included in his " Bookkeeping Modernised," 1768, an example of the accounts of a landed estate, but they show no improvement on those prepared by the " Person of Honour " and, therefore, none of the accounts are reproduced here.

In 1750 James Dodson, " Teacher of the Mathematics," published " The Accountant or The Method of Bookkeeping," which work contains an example of accounts for a shoe-maker. Certain of the combined waste book and journal entries and ledger accounts are reproduced because they show clearly the processes through which the materials went, and the division into different types of shoes. Moreover, they portray a good accounting control over materials. The first two journal entries describe the conversion of leather into soles and heels of different types, and into upper leathers and quarters. Presumably the value of the shoemaker's time is included in the costs transferred, because the leather account shows a profit. The next two journal entries show the delivery of soles and heels and upper leathers, &c., to journeymen to be made up. The imparting accounts are credited and the workmen are debited. Then when the workmen return the materials in the form of pumps and shoes the fifth journal entry credits them with the cost of materials and their own wages and debits the finished goods account with the full amount. Apparently the sums paid to the workmen on account are not the exact amounts due to them, as there are small balances on the personal accounts.

* Murray—Chapters in the History of Bookkeeping—262.

† The examples reproduced are from the 2nd Edition, published 1715.

* *Gentleman Accomptant*: page 208. † Do. page 210.

‡ Op. cit. 4.

Decem. 28

Finished the cutting out of 20 Hides, into Men's Soles and Heels, viz. :—

				l	s	d
48 Pair of Soles and Heels at 3s. 4d. each	18	0	0			
54 ,, 3s. ,,	8	2	0			
72 ,, 2s. 6d. ,,	9	0	0			
84 ,, 2s. 2d. ,,	9	2	0			
138 ,, 1s. 7d. ,,	10	18	6			
				45	2	6

Soles and Heels, Debtor ; Leather, Creditor.

Decem. 29

Finished the Cutting out of 50 Skins into Men's Upper Leathers and Quarters, viz. :—

				l	s	d
48 Pair of Upper Leathers, &c. at 1s. 7d.	13	16	0			
54 ,, 1s. 5d.	3	16	6			
72 ,, 1s. 3d.	4	10	0			
84 ,, 1s. 2d.	4	18	0			
117 ,, 1s. 0d.	5	17	0			
				22	17	6

Upper Leathers and Quarters, Debtor ; Leather, Creditor.

Delivered to the following Workmen, from the 25th Decemb. to the 2d of January 1747 as follows, viz. :—

	Pairs of Men's Soles & Heels, at											
	3s 4d	3s 0d	2s 6d	2s 2d	1s 7d	l	s	d	l	s	d
To A. Bell	2	1				0	9	8			
,, C. Dent		2	2			0	11	0			
,, E. Ford			1	3		0	9	0			
,, G. Hill				2	4	0	10	8			
,, J. King					5	0	7	11			
	2	3	3	5	9				2	8	3

The particular Persons, Debtor ; Men's Soles and Heels, Creditor.

	Pairs of Men's Upper Leathers, &c., at—										
	1s 7d	1s 5d	1s 3d	1s 2d	1s 0d	l	s	d	l	s	d
To A. Bell	2	1				0	4	7			
,, C. Dent		2	2			0	5	4			
,, E. Ford			1	3		0	4	9			
,, G. Hill				2	4	0	6	4			
,, J. King					5	0	5	0			
	2	3	3	5	9				1	6	0

The particular Persons, Debtor ; Men's Upper Leathers, &c., Creditor.

Received from the following Workmen from the 25th of December to the 2d of January, 1747 :—

	Men's Pumps			Men's Shoes							
	Dbl. Chan	Sgl. Chan.	T'nd.	Best	Ord.						
	7s 6d.	6s 0d	5s 6d	5s 0d	4s 0d	l	s	d	l	s	d
A. Bell ..	2	1				1	1	0			
C. Dent ..		1	1				11	6			
E. Ford ..			1	2			15	6			
G. Hill ..				2	2		18	0			
J. King ..					3		12	0			
	2	2	2	4	5				3	18	0

Men's Shoes, Debtor ; The particular Persons, Creditor.

Paid to the said Workmen from the 25th of December to the 2d of January 1747 :—

To—	Dec. 30			Dec. 31			Jan. 2								
	l	s	d	l	s	d	l	s	d	l	s	d	l	s	d
A. Bell	0	2	0	0	2	0	0	2	5	0	6	5			
C. Dent				0	1	0	0	3	0	0	4	0			
E. Ford	0	1	0	0	1	0	0	2	6	0	4	6			
G. Hill	0	2	0				0	3	0	0	5	0			
J. King							0	3	6	0	3	6			
													1	3	5

The particular Persons, Debtor ; Cash, Creditor.

Dodson considered that :

"An intelligent tradesman may easily use the preceding accounts as a model, whereby to form his own books : In doing which, he may enter the delivery of materials, and the receipt of them manufactured, on opposite pages of a book kept for that purpose ; the sale of goods in the shop, for ready money, may make another separate book ; and the payments to workmen, a third."

TRADESMAN'S ACCOMPT

Sold in the shop for Ready Money, from the 25th December to the 2d of January 1747

Men's Shoes																						
Double Ch. Pumps				Single Ch. Pumps				Turned Pumps				Shoes				Ordinary Shoes						
Pair	l	s	d	Pair	l	s	d	Pair	l	s	d	Pair	l	s	d	Pair	l	s	d	l	s	d
1		8	0	1		6	9	2		12	0	1		5	6	1		4	4			
2		15	10	1		6	6	1		6	3	1		5	4	1		4	6			
1		8	6	1		7	0	3		17	6	1		5	8	1		4	3			
				4	1	5	6					3		16	0	2		8	8			
												2		11	0	3		13	0			
												1		5	8	4		17	0			
																5	1	1	0			
4	1	12	4	7	2	5	9	6	1	15	9	9	2	9	2	17	3	12	9	11	15	9

In the same work there appear some estate accounts set out in considerable detail. They show little difference in principle from the examples by the "Person of Honour" and John Mair, but it is worth noting that the "Home Farm Account" which is debited with the farm costs is also charged with the wear of implements and husbandry which is transferred from the credit side of the implements account.

TRADESMAN'S LEIDGER

Debtor LEATHER

1747		Hides	Skins	l	s	d
Dec. 25	To Stock	20	50	67	10	0
Jan. 1	To George Dresskin ..	12	—	28	10	0
2	To Profit and Loss ..	—	—	0	10	0
		32	50	96	10	0

Per Contra *Creditor*

1747		Hides	Skins	l	s	d
Dec. 28	By Soles and Heels ..	20	—	45	2	6
29	By Upper Leathers, &c...	—	50	22	17	6
Jan. 2	By Balance	12	—	28	10	0
		32	50	96	10	0

Debtor MEN'S SHOES

1747		Pumps Dbl. Ch.	Pumps Sgle. Ch.	Pumps T'd	Shoes Best	Shoes Ord.	l	s	d
Dec. 25	To Stock ..	18	12	24	36	42	34	7	0
Jan. 2	To Sundries	2	2	2	4	5	3	18	0
	To Profit and Loss ..	—	—	—	—	—	1	3	9
		20	14	26	40	47	39	8	9

Per Contra *Creditor*

1747		Pumps Dbl. Ch.	Pumps Sgle. Ch.	Pumps T'd	Shoes Best	Shoes Ord.	l	s	d
Dec. 31	By Henry Hotpress	—	—	—	12	12	5	13	0
Jan. 1	By Careless Spendthrift	—	—	1	—	—	0	6	6
2	By Cash ..	4	7	6	9	17	11	15	9
7	By Balance ..	16	7	19	19	18	21	13	6
		20	14	26	40	47	39	8	9

Debtor MEN'S SOLES AND HEELS

1747		At 3s 4d	At 3s 0d	At 2s 6d	At 2s 2d	At 1s 7d	l	s	d
Dec. 28	To Leather..	48	54	72	84	138	45	2	6

Per Contra *Creditor*

1747		At 3s 4d	At 3s 0d	At 2s 6d	At 2s 2d	At 1s 7d	l	s	d
Jan. 2	By Sundries ..	2	3	3	5	9	2	8	3
7	By Balance ..	46	51	69	79	129	42	14	3
		48	54	72	84	138	45	2	6

Debtor MEN'S UPPER

1747		At 1s 7d	At 1s 5d	At 1s 3d	At 1s 2d	At 1s 0d	l	s	d
Dec. 29	To Leather..	48	54	72	84	117	22	17	6

LEATHERS AND QUARTERS *Creditor*

1747		At 1s 7d	At 1s 5d	At 1s 3d	At 1s 2d	At 1s 0d	l	s	d
Jan. 2	By Sundries ..	2	3	3	5	9	1	6	0
	By Balance ..	46	51	69	79	108	21	11	6
		48	54	72	84	117	22	17	6

TRADESMAN'S LEIDGER

Debtor ADAM BELL

1747		Pairs	l	s	d
Jan 2	To 3 Pair of Soles and Heels ..	—	0	9	8
3	To Upper Leathers, &c.	3	0	4	7
4	To Cash	—	0	6	5
7	To Balance, due to him	—	0	0	4
		3	1	1	0

Per Contra *Creditor*

1747		Pairs	l	s	d
Jan. 2	By Men's Shoes	3	1	1	0

Debtor CHRISTOPHER DENT

1747		Pairs	l	s	d
Jan. 2	To 4 Pair of Soles and Heels ..	—	0	11	0
3	To Upper Leathers, &c.	4	0	5	4
4	To Cash	—	0	4	0
		4	1	0	4

Per Contra *Creditor*

1747		Pairs	l	s	d
Jan. 2	By Men's Shoes	2	0	11	6
	By Balance, for Materials unfinished	2	0	8	2
	By Balance, overpaid him ..	—	0	0	8
		4	1	0	4

Debtor PROFIT AND LOSS

1747		l	s	d
Dec 29	To Traffick Sealand, abated to him ..	0	7	0
Jan. 2	To Stock	2	1	1
		2	8	1

Per Contra *Creditor*

1747		l	s	d
Jan. 2	By Leather	0	10	0
	By Men's Shoes	1	3	9
	By Women's Shoes	0	8	5
	By Children's Shoes	0	5	11
		2	8	1

In 1777 there was published at York "The Accomptants' Oracle" by Wardhaugh Thompson, "many years an Accomptant in London." The last chapter of this work is devoted to the accounts of manufacturers.* The example taken is "thread-hosiery" manufacture and in order to simplify matters the writer assumed that all the flax bought was of the same quality and price and also that the hose made were all of one size. Two subsidiary books are necessary, a spinners' book and a weavers' book, which are required in order to relieve the ledger of the

* Thompson—page 243.

great amount of detail which would appear if each spinner and weaver had a separate account. Thus in the ledger there is only a general or total account for spinners, and another for weavers. The writer was dealing, of course, with the domestic system and he assumed that the spinners, weavers, trimmer and dyer brought in their work weekly and the bleacher once a month.

The accounts set out by Thompson are worthy of note because they show the materials moving from process to process acquiring costs as they move. The following is the first page of journal entries—

			l s d
	..............April 1st, 1777..............		
1	Flax Debtor to cash, 28l.		
0	Paid for 5 cwt. at 5l. 12s. per cwt.		28 00 00
	....................2nd....................		
1	Spinners accompt Debtor to flax, 5l.		
1	Delivered 100 lb. at 1s. per lb. to sundry persons as per spinners book		5 00 00
	....................9th....................		
1	Brown linen yarn (scower'd) Debtor to sundries, 6l 13s. 4d.		
1	To spinners accompt, for 200 hanks, received in exchange for 50 lb. of flax	12 10 0	
	To cash, for spinning and scowering	4 3 4	
	Amounting in the whole to about 8d. per hank.		6 13 04
1	Brown linen yarn (unscowered) Debtor to sundries, 5l 16s. 8d.		
1	To spinners accompt, for 200 hanks, received in exchange for 50 lb. of flax, at 1s. per lb. ..	12 10 0	
0	To cash, for spinning, at 1s. 4d. per lb.	3 6 8	
	Amounting now in the whole to 7d. per hank.		5 16 08
1	Spinners accompt Debtor to flax, 5l.		
1	Delivered 100 lb. to sundries, as per spinning book, at 1s. per lb.		5 00 00
	Sundries Debtors to brown linen yarn (scower'd) 6l 13s. 4d.		
1	James Green, for 100 hanks to dye at 8d.	13 6 8	
2	Weavers' acc. for 100 ditto, as per weavers book	3 6 8	
1			6 13 04
1	Thomas White Debtor to brown linen yarn (unscowered), 5l 16s. 8d.		
1	Delivered him 200 to bleach, at 7d. per hank ..		5 16 08
	....................16th....................		
1	Brown linen yarn (scower'd) *Dr.* to sundries, 6l 13s. 4d.		
1	To spinners accompt, for 200 hanks, received in exchange for 50 lb. of flax	12 10 0	
0	To cash, for spinning and scowering	4 3 4	
	Amounting in the whole to about 8d. per hank.		6 13 04

The first entry brings the flax into stock. In the second, some of it is transferred to the spinners' account at cost price. The next two entries show the yarn returned from the spinners, part scoured and part unscoured. The spinners' account is relieved of the cost of the flax debited to it and the yarn accounts are charged with cost of the flax and the cost of spinning. The cost price per hank is worked out for both scoured and unscoured yarn. The sixth entry deals with scoured yarn being sent out, some to be dyed and some woven. A later journal entry shows the yarn returned dyed, and valued at 10d. per hank, and another entry, reproduced below, sets out the return of the woven hose, the total cost per pair being calculated, and the weavers' account duly relieved of the cost of yarn previously debited to it.

			l s d
	....................April 16th....................		
2	Brown thread hose (undress'd) Debtor to sundries, 7l 8s. 8d.		
2	To weavers accompt, for 5 doz. 2 pr. in exchange for 100 hanks of scower'd yarn	13 6 0	
0	To cash, for weaving, at 1s. 4d. per pair	4 2 8	
	Amounting in the whole to about 2s. 4⅞d. per pair.		7 08 08

Some of the ledger accounts are reproduced in order to clarify the explanations given above. It will be observed that this early writer had appreciated the importance of showing the building up of the cost of an article going through a series of processes. Moreover, he knew the bookkeeping technique necessary to handle this sort of work.

LEDGER

Year & Month		cwt	lb.	l	s	d
	FLAX (ready dress'd)		*Dr.*			
1777 Apr. 1	To Cash, at 5l 12s. per cwt. for	5	560	28	00	00
		5	560	28	00	00

Year & Month		cwt.	lb.	l	s	d
	CONTRA		*Cr.*			
1777 Apr. 2	By Spinners Accompt delivered, at 1s. per lb.		100	5	00	00
9	By Do., at 1s. per lb.		100	5	00	00
16	By Do., at 1s. per lb.		200	10	00	00
	By Balance, at 1s. per lb. ..		160	8	00	00
		5	560	28	00	00

Year & Month		lb.	l	s	d
	SPINNERS ACCOMPT (as per SPINNERS BOOK)	*Dr.*			
1777 Apr. 2	To Flax, at 1s. per lb. for ..	100	5	00	00
9	To Do. at 1s. per lb. for ..	100	5	00	00
16	To Do. at 1s. per lb. for ..	200	10	00	00
		400	20	00	00

Year & Month		lb.	l	s	d
	CONTRA	*Cr.*			
1777 Apr. 9	By Brown linen yarn (scower'd) in return for flax, at 1s. per lb. for	50	2	10	00
	By Do. (unscower'd) at 1s. per lb. for	50	2	10	00
16	By Do. (scower'd) return for flax, at 1s. per lb. for ..	50	2	10	00
16	By Do. (unscower'd) return for flax, at 1s. per lb. for ..	50	2	10	00
23	By Do. (scower'd) return for flax, at 1s. per lb. for ..	100	5	00	00
	By Balance, at 1s. per lb. for ..	100	5	00	00
		400	20	00	00

LEDGER | LEDGER

Year & Month	Brown Linen Yarn (Scower'd)	Dr. hks.	l	s	d	Year & Month	Contra	Cr. hks.	l	s	d
1777 Apr 9	To Sundries as per Journal, at 8d. per hank for	200	6	13	04	1777 Apr. 9	By Sundries as per Journal, at 8d. per hank for	200	6	13	04
16	To Do. as per do. at 8d. per hank for	200	6	13	04	16	By Weavers Accompt (as per weavers book) delivered at 8d. per hank	200	6	13	04
23	To Do. as per do at 8d. per hank for	400	13	06	08	30	By Do. (as per do.) delivered at 8d. per hank	400	13	06	08
		800	26	13	04			800	26	13	04

Year & Month	Brown Linen Yarn (Unscower'd)	Dr. hks.	l	s	d	Year & Month	Contra	Cr. hks.	l	s	d
1777 Apr. 1	To Sundries as per Journal, at 7d. per hank	200	5	16	08	1777 Apr. 9	By T. White, bleacher, delivered him at 7d. per hank ..	200	5	16	08
16	To Do., at 7d. per do. ..	200	5	16	08		By Balance remaining, at 7d. per hank	200	5	16	08
		400	11	13	04			400	11	13	04

Year & Month	James Green, Dyer	Dr. hks.	l	s	d	Year & Month	Contra	Cr. hks.	l	s	d
1777 Apr. 9	To Brown Linen Yarn (scower'd) at 8d. per hank for ..	100	3	06	08	1777 Apr. 16	By Blue Linen Yarn, at 10d. per hank	100	4	03	04
	To Balance, due to him for dying			16	08						
		100	4	03	04			100	4	03	04

Year & Month	Thomas White, Bleacher	Dr. hks.	l	s	d	Year & Month	Contra	Cr. hks.	l	s	d
1777 Apr. 9	To Brown Linen Yarn (unscower'd) at 7d. per hank	200	5	16	08	1777 May 9	By Linen Yarn (white) received back bleached	200	5	16	08

Year & Month	Weavers' Accompt (as per Weaver's Book)	Dr. hks.	l	s	d	Year & Month	Contra	Cr. hks.	l	s	d
1777 Apr. 9	To Brown Linen Yarn (scower'd) at 8d. per hank	100	3	06	08	1777 Apr. 16	By Brown Thread Hose (undress'd) received for ..	99	3	06	00
16	To Do., do., at 8d. per hank ..	200	6	13	04	23	By Do., do., received for ..	200	6	13	04
30	To Do., do., at 8d. per do. ..	400	13	06	08	May 9	By Do., do., received for ..	400	13	06	08
							By Balance remaining, as per Weavers Book	1			08
		700	23	06	08			700	23	06	08

Year & Month	Blue Linen Yarn	Dr. hks.	l	s	d	Year & Month	Contra	Cr. hks.	l	s	d
1777 Apr. 16	To J. Green (dyer), received of him dyed at 10d. ..	100	4	03	04	1777 May 25	By mix'd Thread (blue and white) at 10d. per hank, for	50	2	01	08
							By Balance at 10d. per hank, for	50	2	01	08
		100	4	03	04			100	4	03	04

Year & Month	George Forster (Trimmer)	Dr. doz. pr.	l	s	d	Year & Month	Contra	Cr. doz. pr.	l	s	d
1777 Apr. 16	To Brown Thread Hose (undress'd) delivered to trim, valued at about 2s. 5d. per pair, for	5 2	7	08	08	1777 Apr. 23	By Brown Thread Hose (dress'd) received	5 2	7	08	08
30	To Do. (undress'd) delivered him to trim	10 6	14	18	08	May 9	By Do., do., received	10 6	14	18	08
May 16	To Do., do., delivered him to trim	10 6	14	18	08		By Balance remaining in his hands	10 6	14	18	08
		26 2	37	06	00			26 2	37	06	00

Year & Month	White Linen Yarn	Dr. hks.	l	s	d	Year & Month	Contra	Cr. hks.	l	s	d
1777 May 9	To Sundries as per Journal, at 9d. per hank	200	7	10	00	1777 May 25	By Mixed Thread (blue and white) at 9d. per hank for ..	100	3	15	00
							By Balance, at 9d. per hank ..	100	3	15	00
		200	7	10	00			200	7	10	00

Year & Month	Mixed Thread (Blue & White Twisted)	Dr. lb. oz.	l	s	d	Year & Month	Contra	Cr. lb. oz.	l	s	d
1777 May 25	To Sundries as per Journal at near 3s. 1½d. per lb. ..	27 8	5	16	08		By Balance, at near 3s. 1½d. per b. for	27 8	5	16	08

Year & Month	LEDGER		l	s	d	Year & Month	LEDGER		l	s	d
	BROWN THREAD HOSE (Undress'd)	*Dr.* doz. pr.					CONTRA	*Cr.* doz. pr.			
1777 Apr. 16	To Sundries as per Journal at near 2s. 5d. per pair ..	5 2	7	08	08	1777 Apr. 16	By George Forster, delivered him to trim	5 2	7	08	08
23	To Sundries as per do. at about 2s. 5d. per pair	10 6	14	18	08	30	By Do.	10 6	14	18	08
May 9	To Sundries as per do. at about 2s. 5d. per pair	21	29	17	04	May 16	By Do.	10 6	14	18	08
							By Balance, at about 2s. 5d. per pair for	10 6	14	18	08
		36 8	52	04	08			36 8	52	04	08
	BROWN THREAD HOSE (Dress'd)	*Dr.* doz. pr.					CONTRA	*Cr.* doz. pr.			
1777 Apr. 23	To Sundries as per Journal at about 2s. 7d. per pair ..	5 2	7	18	08	1777	By Balance, at about 2s. 7d. per pair for	15 8	23	18	04
May 9	To Sundries as per do. at about 2s. 7d. per do.	10 6	15	19	08						
		15 8	23	18	04			15 8	23	18	04

Folios have been omitted in reproduction.

(To be continued)

SOME NOTES ON THE EARLY LITERATURE AND DEVELOPMENT OF COST ACCOUNTING IN GREAT BRITAIN—III

by Ronald S. Edwards

(Assistant Lecturer in Accounting and Business Administration, London School of Economics.)

It must be remembered that it was not internal process movements which Thompson was handling; all these transactions were with outsiders and there was no question of dividing up the costs of a factory, the domestic system did not require this. Nevertheless, both Dodson and Thompson were clearly capable of providing textbooks equal to the needs of their day. They wrote before the advent of the factory and power machinery. It is very unlikely that the book-keeping methods they describe were in general use. These early writers were doubtless pioneers in a field which remained unreceptive for more than a century. It is more probable that the following passage from Robert Hamilton's " Introduction to Merchandise " describes more accurately the general practice of the day :—

> " Artificers and manufacturers sometimes keep only a day book and ledger ; the former, for entering goods sold, or work done on credit ; the latter, for personal accompts ; and perhaps a cash book and an invoice book."*

This Professor of Philosophy, in the Marischal College, Aberdeen, included a chapter on " Tradesmen's Accompts " in his book which was published in 1788. He was dissatisfied with contemporary practice and maintained that—

> " A more complete method is necessary for exhibiting the materials used, the work done, and the profit acquired."†

The writer went on to say that the subsidiary books most useful are :—

(1) A book of materials where the quantities purchased and consumed are entered.

(2) A book of work where the quantities of materials delivered to journeymen, the quantities of wrought goods received in return, the dates of the delivery and return, the value of the materials and wages, and the value of the wrought goods are entered in separate columns. This certainly looks like a cost ledger.

(3) A book of wages for the names of the employees, the work they are engaged on, the number of days and rate per day, or the quantity of work done and the rate when paid by the piece.

In the ledger Hamilton wished to see separate accounts for the different expenses of the business, such as materials, wages, " upholding machinery," rents, &c., and also a

> " general accompt of the trade or manufacture. To the Dr. of this accompt, the balances of the accompts of materials, and other expences, are transferred at the end of the year ; on the Cr. the value of goods manufactured each month is entered. The balance shows the gain or loss, allowance being made for the value of goods not yet completely manufactured, and therefore not entered on the Cr."

He also wanted

> " One or more accompts for manufactured goods, where the quantity made is entered monthly on the Dr. and the monthly sales on the Cr., these accompts will balance by the value on hand, if the prices be constant ; but, if the prices vary, the balance compared with the value on hand, per inventory, will show the gain or loss by the alteration."

It appears that the " general accompt " is a " work-in-progress " account which is credited with goods manufactured at their expected selling value.

This writer from the academic world* went even further.

> " When a person is engaged in several branches of manufacture, whether on different materials, or on the same materials through several successive stages, he should keep his books in such a manner as to exhibit the gain or loss on each.
>
> " Take the example of a linen manufacturer who purchases or imports rough flax, dresses it by his own servants, and sells such kinds as do not suit his purpose ; delivers the rest to be spun, and receives the yarn from the spinners ; weaves part in his own workhouse by journeymen and delivers the rest to other weavers ; gives out the linen to be bleached, and receives and sells it when white.
>
> " If all these branches of business were necessarily connected and the manufacturer had no other choice than to purchase the rough flax, and carry on the successive operations, it would be sufficient to keep his books in a form that should exhibit the gain or loss on the whole ; but if he has an opportunity of beginning or desisting at any stage of the manufacture, his books should exhibit the gain or loss on each operation separately."

We are given no details of the particular application, and the number and form of the subsidiary books as these " will be different, according to the nature and extent of the business." However, from the clarity of other examples in the same book, one might well believe that Dr. Hamilton could have put his general principles into practice.

In a chapter devoted to Farmers' Accompts, Hamilton describes subsidiary books which the farmer should keep for " recording the progress of his operations, and exhibiting the success of his management." One of these is a " Field Book " where several pages are allotted for each field. The expenses and income from each field are recorded here, so that by a comparison of successive years, the success of the different manures, rotations, and methods of treatment may be easily compared. He then sets out the following specimen which shows the success of a rotation of wheat, barley, and hay after a fallow and plentiful manure.

* 2nd Ed., p. 486.

† Op. cit., 2nd Ed., 486.

* Hamilton was a political economist and mathematician.

† Op. cit., 491.

Date	No. 1. *Westfield*, Soil light loam.		Expence l s d	Produce l s d
1772	10 Acres. rent 30s. ll15.			
	Fallow			
Jan. 20 to 24	12 yokings ploughing			
May 18 to 21	10 do. do.			
30	2 do. harrowing			
June 15 to 18	10 do. ploughing			
	do. do. across			
20	3 do. harrowing			
	37 yokings at 2s.	13 14 0		
	100 loads dung at 3s.	15 0 0		
	200 bushels lime at 2s.	20 0 0		
	Carried forward		38 14 0	
	Wheat			
Aug. 15 to 19	10 yokings ploughing			
20 to 21	2 yokings harrowing			
	12 yokings at 2s.	1l 4 0		
20 to 21	Sown 4 qtrs. at 42s.	8 8 0		
Oct. 15	draining	4 0		
1773 Mar. 12	weeding	6 8		
Aug. 1 to 5	reaping, at 5s. per acre	2 10 0		
			12 12 8	
	120 threaves wheat			
Nov. 20	40 quarters at 42s.			84 0 0
	4 quarters per acre			
	10 returns per feed			
	Barley			
Oct. 1 to 4	11 yokings ploughing			
Mar. 15	10 do. do.			
Apr. 1	2 do. harrowing			
15 to 18	9 do. ploughing			
19	2 do. harrowing			
	34 yokings at 2s.	13 8 0		
19	sown 5 qtrs. barley at 25s.	6 5 0		
20	breaking clods	15 0		
1774 Aug. 8	reaping at 5s. per acre	2 10 0		
			12 18 0	
	150 threaves barley			
Dec. 1	28 qtrs. barley at 24s.			33 12 0
	2.8 qtrs. per acre			
	5.6 returns per feed			
	Hay			
	1 qr. 4 bush. rye grass sown with the barley, at 4s. bushel	12 8 0		
1775	200 lb. clover-feed at 6d.	5 0 0		
June 1	mowing at 2s. per acre	1 0 0		
20	winning and stacking	2 10 0		
			10 18 0	
Sept. 30	32 loads hay at £1 5s.	140 0 0		
	3.2 loads per acre			
	12 oxen pastured on the soggage 6 weeks, at 2s. per week	7 4 0		
				47 4 0
	Four years rent ..		60 0 0	
			135 2 8	164 16 0

"To ascertain the expense of a yoking, add the charge of maintaining and upholding the cattle, the purchase and repairs of ploughs, harrows, harness, &c., and divide the sum by the number of yokings in a year; to the quotient add the daily wages of the servant, and the sum is the expense per yoking. The number of yokings in the year will be found from the journal. If the servant be paid by the year, his wages and maintenance may be divided by 300, allowing 65 days for Sundays, holidays and accidents. The expense of reaping an acre is computed by dividing the whole expense of the harvest by the number of acres."

It is difficult to account for the absence of works on industrial accountancy during the next eighty or ninety years. Books on commercial accounts were turned out by the dozen, but with one or two slight exceptions writers on accounting neglected the problems of the industrial community at a time when the latter was being revolutionised by power, the factory system and the growth of communications. One of the exceptions was a work by F. W. Cronhelm in 1818, entitled "Double Entry by Single." This book was mainly devoted to reducing the labour required to effect double entry, but the writer also deals with a set of manufacturers' books for which he chooses as an example the business of a woollen manufacturer. The chapter commenced with some observations to the effect that owing to the numerous processes through which his goods pass, the manufacturer is unable to keep his accounts as systematically as the wholesale dealer or merchant. But the writer regarded the difficulty as applying solely to *quantities* of goods,

> "and in no respect to the accounts, which in all businesses are composed of expenditure and returns, receipts and payments. These particulars the manufacturer can ascertain as easily as the merchant; and, therefore, he may with equal facility systematise his accounts."*

Accordingly, the warehouse ledger is divided into three parts. In the first we have accounts which record on the debit side the wool purchased and on the credit side its transfer to the manufacturing, in the second the wool transferred to manufacturing is shown on the debit side, and on the credit the finished goods are transferred to the debit of the third set of accounts which are in turn credited with sales. Thus, there is a perpetual inventory of raw materials, work-in-progress and finished goods in quantity, but there is no record of values.

In the ledger there is a "merchandise account," on the debit side of which appear the opening inventory, purchases of raw materials, and the wages and petty expenses each week summarised as follows :—

Sorting, carding, spinning, &c., as per Book A.

Weaving, milling, &c., as per book B.

Dressing, finishing, packing, &c., as per Book C.

(Books A., B. and C. are apparently kept by Overlookers.†)

In addition, all other expenses such as salaries, discounts, interest, postages, taxes, carriage, and dyeing, are debited. On the credit side appear the sales and

* Cronhelm—p. 125.

† Op. cit.—127.

closing inventory. No attempt is made to collect the costs of each process systematically, this account being nothing more than a detailed trading account with no useful grouping or classification of data.

Cronhelm seemed less able to deal with the accounting difficulties of industry than the eighteenth-century writers in this country, yet nobody in the first half of the nineteenth century improved on his work.

The following remarks are taken from G. Jackson's work entitled " Check Journal."*

" And in manufacturing concerns, the quantity of raw materials consumed should be made to correspond with that of the articles manufactured. For which purpose, it will be necessary to open accounts for each ; for the steam apparatus ; and for the workmen's wages in every branch ; which last should be done by a proper classification of the *printed weekly papers*. At the close of the year, the amount of all these, together with the charges, under their various heads, are concentrated by being brought to the debit of the general factory ; while the produce, in its several kinds, is carried to the credit of this account."

The author does not support this note with any examples, but the reference to " printed weekly papers " is interesting—the raw material of a costing system.

This barren period is not complete without mention of two other slight works, the first of which was by F. C. Krep in 1858 and entitled " Statistical Bookkeeping." In his " special system " for manufacturers he does not get beyond books for raw materials and finished goods in quantities and kinds with two columns for each material. In the first column appears the quantity of raw material purchased or finished goods produced, and in the second, the quantity of raw material used or finished goods sold. The other work is entitled " Bookkeeping for the Tanning Trade,"† by J. Sawyer, who was a bookkeeper. His rather vague remarks on the valuation of finished stock and work-in-progress throw a little light on the inability of contemporary practice to deal with industrial accounting problems.

" The recognised principle that stock should be valued at cost price (unless depreciated in value) and that no profit should be estimated unless realised, much less upon goods only partly manufactured, and subject further to the contingency of a falling market, may be questioned if applicable to the case in question. Upon this plan, it would be necessary to value all hides in process of tanning, and the produce thereof, at their cost price, to which would be added the cost of tanning material consumed, the proportion of wages disbursed for the attendant labour, and a sum for rent and expenses. But, *apart from the insuperable difficulties attending this*, there are reasons why a tanner is justified, to some extent, in estimating a profit upon goods in process of manufacture, and in connection with which his time, skill, capital and labour have for a period of six months been brought into requisition."

It is clear that this writer could not tackle costing problems, although one may have a certain amount of sympathy with his objection to the slavish rule of not " anticipating profit."

Such is the relevant British literature of a period of great industrial change. It would appear that the late eighteenth century had produced an accounting technique adequate to deal with industry built up on the domestic system, but the Industrial Revolution had not yet brought in its train an accounting service aimed at resolving the " fixed cost problem."

(*To be continued*)

* 5th Edition, 1836, p. 133.
† 2nd Ed., 1862.

SOME NOTES ON THE EARLY LITERATURE AND DEVELOPMENT OF COST ACCOUNTING IN GREAT BRITAIN—IV

by Ronald S. Edwards

(Assistant Lecturer in Accounting and Business Administration, London School of Economics.)

In the first decade of this period industrial accounting began to attract attention in published work. Doubtless during the previous three-quarters of a century those who were engaged in manufacturing concerns were groping with the accounting problems which cannot be dissociated from large-scale undertakings.

We have, for example, the records of the firm of Boulton and Watt, which have been examined from the standpoint of business organisation by Dr. Erich Roll.* The transition of this firm from engineering consultants to manufacturers, culminating in the building of the Soho foundry in 1795, led to changes in the accounting records and the introduction of "a great number of new books of a statistical character."† These apparently included :—

(1) A Forgers' and Fitters' Book controlling the movements of metal.

(2) A Fitting Book designed for the recording of the cost of the time spent in fitting up engine parts.

(3) An Abstract Book for analysing costs over different departments.

According to Roll, records were kept to enable the calculation of the actual profit realised on each engine, but although it seems that indirect and overhead costs were tabulated in considerable detail, "no information is available concerning the way in which they were apportioned for each job."‡ We are also told that profits and losses were allocated between departments ; the bookkeeping in use would certainly have permitted the costs of the departments to be ascertained, but it is difficult to see how the apportionment of the profit could have been made. Professor J. G. Smith suggests in an introduction to Dr. Roll's work that "the Soho system of costing is superior to that employed in very many successful concerns to-day." This assertion cannot be examined unless we know the criterion by which Professor Smith judges costing systems.

There is a tradition in the British business world that as little information should be disclosed as possible in order to hinder competition. This attitude was extended to methods of accounting control, and, as a result, little published work came into existence during the first eighty years of the century to witness the growth of industrial accounting. If manufacturers developed methods which they found satisfactory they were at no pains to act as benefactors to the rest of the business world by disclosing them. John Mann,* writing in 1903, discussing the origin of costing, said that cost methods were generally kept secret, but

> "a more liberal spirit is gaining ground generally, as it is seen that publicity as to principles aids each manufacturer in ascertaining his actual costs, leads to sound accounting, and therefore tends in time to lessen 'price cutting'—a piece of commercial cruelty which sometimes happens from sheer ignorance of actual cost."†

So far as the engineering trades are concerned it is probable that business in the first three-quarters of the century was so good that manufacturers paid little attention to costing methods. While the demand for machinery was great and the supply of engineers limited, there was no pressing need for economy, but in the course of time brains and capital were attracted, and competition became keener. To quote an editorial in *Engineering* written in 1891,‡ on Practical Prime Costs :—

> "The present-day conditions of the engineering and manufacturing trades, as regards keenness of competition and consequent narrowness of profit, render this subject of an increased importance."

Up to 20 years ago conditions were different, it pointed out

> "Selling prices could generally be fixed at figures leaving good margins, and a 'rough and ready' cost of a certain article or piece of work, upon which could generally be fixed a fancy profit, with a liberal contingency allowance, was as a rule found all that was required. . . . It is during the past 15 or 20 years that prime costing has been developed to the elaborate systems in operation in many of our large and well-managed firms.

Nevertheless, there had been some who had seen the value of accurate costing much earlier. Charles Babbage—a Cambridge don—pointed out in 1832 that

> "it is of great importance to know the precise expense of every process, as well as of the wear and tear of machinery which is due to it."§

In 1869 a leading article in the *Engineer* deplored the inaccuracies of engineers' estimates, and pointed out that one

> "right within 20 per cent. of the actual cost, is, however, regarded as a very good estimate, and one reflecting much credit on the engineer and all concerned." "There is no good treatise on the subject . . ."

A letter to the editor of this same periodical in 1870 wanted to know if any correspondent knew of a "good system of getting out cost price."** To which a London correspondent replied that an advertiser in the *Engineer* had installed for him a cost system, and he had

* An early Experiment in Industrial Organisation.
† Op. cit., p. 244.
‡ Op. cit., p. 249.

*" Encyclopædia of Accounting."
†" Cost Records and Factory Accounts—Encyclopædia of Accounting, 1903."
‡" Engineering," 4th December 1891—p. 665.
§" On the Economy of Machinery and Manufactures "—164.
**" Engineer "—25th November 1870.

"no hesitation in stating that a more correct and simple plan could not possibly be devised, and every penny that is paid for wages and all material used is properly charged to each job, and the proportion of unappropriated labour and material is shown as a fixed charge on each job. I can see the cost of the work at a glance, merely by adding a few columns of figures. The books necessary for the system cost me about £10, and the fee paid to the advertiser £10 10s."*

This letter apparently aroused considerable interest for in another letter† the same correspondent said that he had received "numerous replies from all parts of the country," and as he had not time to deal with them all he gave the name of the advertiser responsible for the system—Montague Whitmore, 41 Clerkenwell Green, London. Apparently nothing is known about this accountant, and it seems he has left no published work. Another correspondent, a cost clerk, suggested that

"there are few practical cost clerks who have a fair idea how to get at the real cost of a locomotive engine, or any other distinct piece of machinery."

He went on to say that the only way to acquire the secret of this subject was to offer "a fair remuneration" to a cost clerk !‡

Two of the early writers on cost accounting whose works are important have testified that cost methods were bad. Sir John Mann has told the present writer that even very large industrial concerns had no adequate knowledge of the relationship between direct and indirect costs. In the experience of this authority, one of the earliest firms to work seriously on these problems was an electrical engineering business which, being new, attempted to evolve a new type of accounting. Another concern which engaged his firm was a wholesale cloth house which financed many dressmakers. The accountants had to go round to the various dressmakers, installing simple costing systems, and comparing costs, in order to advise the wholesaler whether to continue supporting the retail business. Mr. G. P. Norton's work, which will be referred to later

"was actually written with a view of systematising bookkeeping in the manufacturing industries, which at that time was in a very chaotic state."**

Doubtless some engineering firms were possessed of systems which were more or less adequate, and which were based on the principles which are still applied. A correspondent writing in the *Engineer* on 23rd December 1870, sketching the broad outlines of a system, pointed out that

"the entire outlay for all purposes may be said to be direct or indirect, according as the disbursements can be charged at once to the various jobs in hand, or only to interim accounts, from which they are deducted from time to time in portions, as may be required for the fulfilment of the work."

*"Engineer"—16th December 1870.
†"Engineer"—23rd December 1870.
‡"Engineer"—9th December 1870.
**Letter from Mr. Norton.

The letter went on to say that it is the latter class of items which cause difficulty,

"as they vary from year to year, in unequal ratio with the rest of the expenditure, unless the business fluctuates to a very small extent."

Further, as the total of indirect cost is different in different departments, it would be incorrect to charge work with a general percentage of expenses throughout; each department must bear its share and, therefore, the accounts of each department must be kept separate. Lastly, he emphasised the importance of agreeing costs in total. This correspondent was apparently familiar with a job costing system which must have been in advance of most, and it is a pity that he considered it too arduous to describe the account books in detail.

During the Proceedings on 16th January 1873 of the Cleveland Institution of Engineers, a paper entitled "Balance Sheets of Manufacturing Firms" was given by F. R. Goddard, a Newcastle accountant. In discussing the various assets appearing on a Balance Sheet, the speaker dealt with "Work in Progress." This led him to explain briefly that

"Net Cost is the system of charging off to each particular engine, order or contract, the amount of raw material used in its manufacture, together with its exact proportion of wages and charges, and of crediting respectively your accounts representing such materials and wages regularly."

The cost accounts are also to be debited with a charge for tools based on

"the value of the time charged to the jobs in the various departments, the same being regulated with due regard to the class of tools used in such departments, should the same be fitters, smiths, pattern makers, &c."

Establishment charges such as rent, rates, taxes, salaries, &c., are allocated as a percentage of total cost. This uninspiring paper is probably typical of the practical work of the period.

In 1878 a Manchester public accountant, Thomas Battersby, published a short book entitled "The Perfect Double Entry Bookkeeper and the Perfect Prime Cost and Profit Demonstrator (on the Departmental System) for Iron and Brass Founders, Machinists, Engineers, Shipbuilders, Manufacturers, &c." We are indebted to this writer for a review of the methods of costing then current. His remarks are quoted *in extenso* :—*

Review of the Various Methods in General Use

There is great dissimilarity in the methods in general use, and they are remarkable for this fact, that the prime cost rates charged for tools and workmen are fixed on no definite principle; and, consequently, they vary according to the opinions of different men. And even where the rates are said to be fixed according to the respective values of the tools this has been done in the absence of data of working expenses; and therefore it is not very probable that they are correct.

The following are some of the methods seen in use by the author:—

*Battersby—34.

1. The workmen are rated at the actual wages paid them, and 100 per cent. is added for the use of tools and all expenses; and 25 per cent. is added on the total and materials purchased for profit, which gives the selling price.

2. The lathes and tools are rated at a *uniform* price, viz. the workman's wages plus 2s. per day for the lathe or tool; and all the workmen—pattern makers, fitters and carpenters—are rated at the wages paid them; and 25 per cent. is added on the total for indirect expenses and profit, and 25 per cent. is also added on materials purchased, which gives the selling price.

3. The workmen are rated at the wages paid them, and a percentage is added on the total for the use of tools and all expenses, and on this and materials is added the profit, which gives the selling price. (The expenses are summarised, and the percentage that they bear to the total yearly sales of machinery is the percentage charged on wages in every contract.)

4. Every tool is rated according to the purchase price and the power, &c., required to work it, plus the workman's wages, and every workman is rated at the wages paid him, and a percentage for indirect expenses and profit is added on the total and on materials purchased, which gives the selling price. (These rates, however, are not worked out on correct principles, as the direct expenses are not taken into account, and therefore the rates are to a great extent assumed).

5. The rates for lathes and tools are fixed by the managing partner, according to the purchase price, and these rates are used as the selling prices, both for contract work and jobbing work. In fixing the rates the principal has no further data than the purchase price and his own opinion to guide him, and he does not consider it necessary to have other than *selling rates*, for the simple reason that every contract is made up at these rates, and a deduction taken off the total, in estimating contract work. This deduction, no doubt, varies according to circumstances, the object being to secure the order with the least possible deduction; but it must be evident that this method is most uncertain and unsatisfactory, and cannot but lead to disappointment and loss.

6. *Piece Work*.—On the first cost of materials and wages paid (which is easily ascertained where piece work is the rule), a percentage is added for the use of tools and working expenses, and a percentage on the whole for profit. (The expenses are ascertained from nominal ledger accounts, and the total sales of machinery from the sales book, and the *percentage of expenses* to the sales is calculated, and added as before stated. This method is tested by summarising all the prime costs and the selling prices for the year, and comparing the gain with the profit as per balance-sheet, and their agreement is said to corroborate the prime cost method.

Lastly, where the method is that of charging a total percentage on the first cost of materials and wages, to cover expenses and profit, the *amount* of percentage varies very considerably in different establishments, according to the opinions of the principals.

These various methods have been first adopted for want of a correct system; and they are continued because they are in keeping with the old styles, and are the easiest ways of arriving at general results. It is supposed that the rates and percentages adopted are sufficient to cover expenses, upholding and profit. The expenses have not been ascertained from the bookkeeping, and in the absence of these data, the only course is that of adopting certain rates and percentages, based merely upon opinion and assumption.

Now if the expenses are not known it is pure assumption to say that certain percentages, or certain rates for tools and workmen, are what is needed to work a business successfully, or because others adopt certain percentages that they must be applicable to every case. It is well known that expenses differ very materially in establishments, and it is important that every firm should know what they are, so as to apply them and gain the advantages that a low percentage gives in every case. And, moreover, it is wrong in principle to apply the expenses by an average percentage on the total cost of materials and wages, as is the general method in use.

The above methods have these defects: they ignore the difference between materials and labour in relation to the working expenses, they confuse prime cost and profit, and, consequently, are so deceptive in effect, that more or less profit is charged than would be charged if prime cost and profit were worked out on correct principles and distinct in their natural order; in short, there is no true theory brought to bear upon the application of the expenses and profit, and the consequence is that whilst the *nature* of the work and the *expenses* are *similar* in all engineering establishments there is great variety in the methods in general use, and many of these methods do not even approach to correctness.

For his own prime cost and profit system the author enumerates the following six advantages.

(1) It shows the actual cost of work as a whole or in detail.

(2) It furnishes important data from which to estimate work.

(3) It shows by comparison whether work is costing too much, and in which department it occurs.

(4) It systematically applies and controls the percentages of profit.

(5) It secures a manufacturer against loss arising from this branch of his business, and it prevents *excess* of profit—extremes equally disastrous in effect.

(6) It is a wise and timely balance-sheet. It is the manufacturer's guide and surety, and consequently a continual source of safety and satisfaction.

The definition of prime cost is curious. It includes materials, wages, working and upholding and general expenses. The working and upholding expenses make up the net prime cost and the general expenses make up the gross prime cost of production. Thus expenses are divided according as they are directly applicable to departments or indirectly incurred for the business as a whole. Methods of absorbing oncost are foreshadowed; for instance, in the power department every tool must be rated per day at its prime cost value—which is regulated by the purchase price, the amount of steam power used, and the proportion of direct expenses that its cost bears to the aggregate expenses in its department. In the labour department every workman must be rated per day at his prime cost value—which is regulated by his wages and the proportion of expenses that the average number of workmen bears to the aggregate expenses in his department. The terminology and language is very muddled, but it is clear that Battersby was trying to set up methods for tackling the problem of overhead costs, and that he had in mind labour rates and machine rates inclusive of fixed costs.

There is a description of the method of ascertaining the cost of castings per ton in an iron foundry. The melting cost is obtained, including depreciation, direct departmental expenses, furnacemen's wages and steam power and the whole is divided by the weight of castings. To this is added the cost of pig-iron and moulders' and labourers' wages. More interesting are the statements for calculating prime cost of the steam power department per indicated horse power per year, and for calculating the inclusive rate per day for power, lathes and tools. It will be seen that the total cost of machine upkeep is divided between individual machines on the basis of capital value, and power cost is added on the basis of horse power. When wages are added, we have the total which Battersby wants. Incidentally, he says nothing about interest on capital tied up in the plant.

MACHINERY DEPARTMENTS

STEAM-POWER DEPARTMENT

Total value of Engine, Boilers, and Gearing £.... ....
No. of indicated horse-power No.. ...
To....% for yearly depreciation.. ..£
,, Direct expenses, viz. coal, wages, &c., as per the Perfect Double Entry Bookkeeper .. ..
,, Direct expenses and upholding account, as per the Direct and Indirect Expenses Book .. ..

Total yearly cost .. ..£

Which, divided by the number of indicated horse-power given out, gives the prime cost per horse-power per year.

POWER DEPARTMENT—LATHES AND TOOLS

Total value of Tools .. ..£........
To....% for yearly depreciation.. ..£
,, Direct expenses, viz. tools and steel for upholding and repairs, belting, grindstones, oil, waste, &c., as per direct expenses and upholding account in the Direct and Indirect Expenses Book ..

Total cost of tools per year .. ..£

Equals....% per £ value of tools ..
Then No. 1 Tool, valued at £.... at ....% per £, equals its yearly cost .. ..£
....horse-power required to work it, at per horse .. ..

Total cost per year of No. 1 Tool ..£

Which, divided by the number of working days, gives its prime cost per day; which, added to the workman's wages, gives the prime cost rate per day to be charged upon work.

(A register of the numbers and prime cost rates of the tools is kept for reference.)

In the "smiths'" department, a daily rate is set up for "smith and striker" and the following is the method adopted to arrive at the rate:—

SMITHS' DEPARTMENT

Total value of Tools .. .. £.......
To....% for yearly depreciation.. ..£
,, Direct expenses, viz. coal, &c., as per the Perfect Double Entry Bookkeeper ..
,, Direct expenses, viz. tools and steel for upholding and repairs, as per direct expenses and upholding account in the Direct and Indirect Expenses Book ..
,, ...horse-power required, at per horse..

Total cost per year .. .. ..£

Or £......... per day, which, divided by the number of smiths, gives cost per day for smith and striker, which, added to the workmen's wages, gives their prime cost rate per day to be charged upon work.

Indirect expenses, that is to say, those which cannot be attributed directly to departments, are applied to contracts by a uniform percentage based upon wages. In his example wages are £10,000 and salaries, rent, rates and taxes, gas, water and general expenses, £1,500, giving 15 per cent. as the proportion of expenses to wages.

A number of subsidiary books used in the "Prime Cost system" are described and specimens are sold with the book—for an extra sum. There is nothing outstanding about them; they analyse materials and wages over jobs, the totals being collected in a prime cost book in which each contract has a separate heading. The information in this book is transferred to a private cost book in which the additions for indirect expenses are made, and selling price and profit are shown. The writer emphasises the fact that the costing progresses at the same rate as the work.

It seems that no attempt is made to "tie in" the prime cost books in total with the financial books. In fact, Battersby points out that "when similar machines are constantly made, it may be sufficient to record an occasional cost."* The claim that the system is "self corroborative through the yearly balance-sheet"† seems untenable. There is, in

*Op. cit., p. 42.
†Op. cit., p. 43.

the financial ledger, an account headed " Machinery, which collects the departmental costs of manufacture on the debit side, including castings produced which have been transferred from the ironfoundry account. This account is credited with sales and with the balance of stock on hand. The profit is carried to profit and loss account when the general expenses, including depreciation of machinery, &c., are set against it.

There is much that is obscure in this book, but nevertheless it is noteworthy as an attempt to bring into job costing expenses which cannot be directly traceable to individual contracts.

(To be continued)

SOME NOTES ON THE EARLY LITERATURE AND DEVELOPMENT OF COST ACCOUNTING IN GREAT BRITAIN—V

by Ronald S. Edwards

(Assistant Lecturer in Accounting and Business Administration, London School of Economics.)

The Progress of Cost Accounting in Great Britain between 1870 and 1890

Another note appearing during the 'seventies is to be found in " Practical Bookkeeping,"* by F. H. Carter, a Scottish accountant. A chapter is devoted to the " cost book " system for mines, quarries, &c., which the author had apparently seen working in practice and which aimed at costing the different workings, galleries, or levels separately. Cost sheets are prepared showing for each gallery (in a slate quarry) the costs of labour, tools, transport and sundry expenses in detail for each month. Additional columns are shown for the cost per ton of rock removed, and per ton of slate produced, for comparative purposes. General expense or oncost has a cost sheet of its own, the expenses are itemised, a column for each month being shown. These expenses are also shown in pence per ton of rock removed and slates produced. The oncost is then added to the cost of each gallery in proportion to tonnage. Carter thought a great deal of this system as a method of control for detecting " mismanagement, extravagance or fraud," and for avoiding losses incurred in continuing unprofitable workings. Incidentally, it may be noted that the term " oncost " to cover general expenses was used very early in connection with mining.

In 1885, Sydney Saker, who styled himself " builders' accountant," published a book on builders' bookkeeping. He describes two books, one for day work and the other for contracts. There is an account for each job or contract which is debited with materials, labour and incidental direct expenses and credited with the price of the contract ; the difference between the two sides being profit. These books are not in any way " tied in " with the financial ledger. In the latter there is a trade account to which all expenses are debited, and sales, stock, and work-in-progress credited. No reconciliation between the contract books and the ledger is given, and the trade account is not classified in any way, salaries, wages, rent, bad debts, interest, discount and petty cash all being thrown together. This book is probably fairly representative of builders' accounting at the time it was written. A. H. Gibson in a lecture, reported in *The Accountant* of 11th June 1887, confirmed this view, while stating his own desire to make " prime costing " part of the double-entry system of accounts. However, he made no attempt to allocate overhead expenses such as rent, rates, general wages, salaries, and depreciation. Gibson distinguished between job or contract costing and process costing, and in respect of the latter shows cost sheets with the total and unit process costs for each main product (tweed and serge) in a woollen industry example. He touched on the fringe of the difficulty of allocating charges like " Engine and machinery expenses " and " general charges," but he thinks " a little patience " will overcome these difficulties.

This decade, however, provides us with two works which have stood the test of time. In 1887 the first edition of " Factory Accounts," by Garcke and Fells, appeared. This book, the combined work of an engineer and an accountant, was claimed to be the first systematised statement for English readers of the principles regulating factory accounts. The authors said that the subject of prime cost admitted of very varied treatment ; they defined the term prime cost as " original and direct cost." They suggested that in some trades—

> " it may be a matter of convenience to include in the cost of production a proportion of indirect expenses, and a charge for depreciation on plant and buildings, but in no case should it comprise interest on capital or profit."

There is, however, a statement which the present writer regards as of considerable significance :—

> " When the indirect charges and depreciation are of a more or less fixed character, it is probably sufficient to know the cost of an article in wages and materials only, but if the indirect expenses and wear and tear of plant form a more direct element in the cost of production, it would be highly desirable to apportion such items among the various operations or departments, either as the business consists of an aggregation of processes differing from each other in character, or of a number of branches each, *sui generis*, comprising a multitude of similar processes."

This statement remained largely unaltered throughout the seven editions. In the seventh edition there is an interesting footnote† dealing with a criticism from Professor W. J. Ashley who complained that the authors " seemed specifically to exclude establishment expenses and interest as items in the cost of production." The authors agreed that these charges must be elements in the cost of production in the wider sense, but they desired to point out that " from the commercial standpoint of a manufacturer desirous under competitive conditions of obtaining business data on which he could act as to the price of the product, establishment expenses, and in some measure, interest, would not be regarded as items in the cost of production of particular commodities in so far as it regulates price." It is clear that Garcke & Fells were groping towards the con-

* 2nd Edition 1874.

† Garcke & Fells- p. 119.

Dr. MANUFACTURING ACCOUNT SECTION I **Cr.**

1884		£ s d	£ s d	£ s d
Jan. 1	To Stock on Hand		33,683 12 11	
Dec. 31	,, Material		36,969 15 7	
	,, Outwork		5,261 3 11	
	,, Packing Materials		225 17 5	
	,, Carriage		942 14 3	
				77,083 4 1
	,, Pattern Making (cost exclusive of Material) ..			1,337 3 4
	,, Processes of Manufacture, at Trade Prices, viz. :—			
	Woollen Spinning Department :			
	Condensing and Spinning	4,046 7 10		
	Twisting	110 11 7		
	Winding	205 6 8		
			4,362 6 1	
	Worsted Combing and Spinning Department :			
	Combing	2,350 7 6		
	Spinning	4,602 11 9		
			6,952 19 3	
	Weaving Department :			
	Warping and Winding ..	507 10 9		
	Weaving	14,960 17 8		
			15,468 8 5	
	Dyeing Department :			
	Dyeing Woollen Materials	560 5 3		
	,, Tops	309 10 10		
	,, Yarns	850 16 3		
	,, Pieces	3,650 7 10		
	Extracting	50 10 6		
			5,421 10 8	
	Finishing Department :			
	Scouring	1,148 6 11		
	Mending	2,296 4 2		
	Finishing	2,014 2 3		
			5,458 13 4	
				37,663 17 9
				116,084 5 2
	,, Balance—Gross Selling Profit to Section II ..			10,203 18 2
				£ 126,288 3 4

1884		£ s d
Dec. 31	By Sales	93,721 3 7
	,, Commission Work	364 11 8
	,, Stock on Hand	32,202 8 1
		£ 126,288 3 4

MANUFACTURING ACCOUNT

SECTION II

Date	Dr.	£ s d	£ s d
1884 Dec. 31	To *Warehouse and Office Standing Expenses, viz.:—*		
	Stables	112 14 0	
	Rent, Rates, Taxes, Gas and Insurance	363 1 0	
	Incidentals	200 0 0	
	Salaries, Warehouse and Office	532 12 0	
	Traveller's Salary and Expenses	1,218 8 10	
	Commission	319 13 4	
	Depreciation of Fittings ..	10 0 0	
			2,756 9 2
	,, *General Charges, viz.:—*		
	Bank Charges	257 16 11	
	Discount on Sales ..	1,789 4 7	
	Bad Debts	149 15 7	
			2,196 17 1
	,, *Net Profit as per Trading Account*		10,039 0 8
			£14,992 6 11

Date	Cr.	Wages and Expenses, as per analysis page 196 £ s d	Work done as per Section I £ s d	Profit £ s d	£ s d
1884 Dec. 31	By *Gross Selling Profit from Section I*				10,203 18 2
	,, *Profit on Departments, viz.:—* ..				
	,, Woollen Spinning ..	3,957 1 11	4,362 6 1	405 4 2	
	,, Worsted Combing and Spinning ..	6,307 17 2	6,952 19 3	645 2 1	
	,, Weaving ..	13,488 13 0	15,468 8 5	1,979 15 5	
	,, Dyeing ..	4,976 4 9	5,421 10 8	445 5 11	
	,, Finishing ..	4,873 3 1	5,458 13 4	585 10 3	
		£33,602 19 11	37,663 17 9	4,060 17 10	4,060 17 10
	,, Discount on Purchases				727 10 11
					£14,992 6 11

cept of fixed cost or "economic rent."* but they were apparently much confused, for in working out machine rates they included fixed charges such as a proportion of rent and depreciation. For the purpose of comparing different machines, they desired to include interest on capital tied up. Unfortunately, they did not keep clear the important distinction between costs before capital is sunk, and after. Nevertheless it was pointed out that the classification of the constituent elements of cost is dependent upon the determination of what information it is desired to obtain, and what particular purpose it is hoped to serve. Again, in the seventh edition it was noted that cost is a relative term, and reference was made to a case before the Railway and Canal Commission Court in 1916, where a minority judgment held that expenditure was a debit factor which referred to outlay only, and was absolute, whilst cost was a resultant and comprehensive factor and was relative.

But turning back to the first edition, it should be stated that the writers used a "Prime Cost Ledger," where an account for each job appeared. In addition, there were accounts showing the prime cost of maintenance and additions to plant and machinery. Other expenditure such as storekeepers, gatemen, &c., may be recorded under a heading "General Charges" in the Prime Cost Ledger, and may be summarised—

> "for the purpose of distributing their incidence, and a ratio established between them and the total amount of the wages expended on the various orders during the same period."

The authors agreed that "labour hours" might form a better basis of distribution, and they also discussed a machine hour rate based on the whole life of the asset, with the cost modified for maintenance and residual value. A plant ledger in modern form is described, and this is credited with the value of machine hours debited to the cost ledger. Incidentally, total accounts are not kept in the stores, prime cost and stock ledgers (in the first edition); agreement at the end of a period must be by abstracts. However, the authors are in favour of including the commercial and manufacturing accounts in one co-ordinated system, stores and raw materials being transferred to prime cost accounts, finished goods being transferred from prime cost accounts to finished goods accounts, and from thence to the trading account on sale. The administrative mechanism is described for dealing with the cost records, and there are discussions of time tickets, wage allocations, and stores warrants.

In English literature "Garcke and Fells" repre-

* On p. 74 (1st Ed.), speaking of Establishment Expenses (clerks, office rent, stationery, &c.), they suggest that there is no advantage in distributing these as "they do not vary proportionately with the volume of business . . . ." The establishment charges are, in the aggregate, more or less constant, while the manufacturing costs fluctuate with the cost of labour and the price of material. To distribute the charges over the articles manufactured would, therefore, have the effect of disproportionately reducing the cost of production with every increase, and the reverse with every diminution of business."

sents an important landmark, yet it is disappointing that so many of the terms used are obscure ; for instance, greater clarity regarding the difference between production and establishment expenses, indirect and direct costs would have helped the reader. However, this is a fault of practically all the literature down to date. The criticism in the review in *The Accountant** was that the book was more theoretical than practical, that it was pedantic and involved, " in the nature of a work on political economy." Moreover, the claim that stock balances should be as readily ascertainable as cash balances was regarded as an unattainable ideal.

On the other hand, " Textile Manufacturers' Bookkeeping," by Norton, first published in 1889, received quite a good review. Mr. G. P. Norton was (and still is) a practising accountant. His remarks on the position of manufacturers' bookkeeping at the time when his book first appeared have already been mentioned. As opposed to Garcke & Fells, Norton preferred that the commercial and manufacturing accounts should be kept separate, regarding the latter as purely supplementary to the trading account. Incidentally, Norton's trading account is divided into three sections. The first is credited with sales and debited with materials, direct wages and carriage, i.e. variable expenses. The balance is carried down to Part II, which is credited with discount on purchases. On the debit side of this section are three groups of expenses, standing expenses of the mill, standing expenses of the warehouse and office, and general charges comprising bank charges, discount on sales and bad debts. Again the balance is carried down to a third section to which is debited interest on loans and capital and income-tax. In favour of his classification of expenses, Norton argued that a change in the relationship between sales and the expenses in the first section will be the result of altered prices, whereas any variation in the standing expenses in Section II, unless there is a violent change in output, is held to be due to economy or extravagance. This, of course, is only a broad generalisation, and the author warned readers of the necessity for considering volume as well as value, having regard to price changes.

The cost records, which are quite separate from the commercial accounts, are designed to allocate costs to departments and processes, the reason for this being that each process in the woollen trade would have been executed by an outside specialist at a trade price. It was, therefore, desirable to compare actual cost with the trade price. The cost records were summarised in the manufacturing account, which was not part of the double-entry system but which was designed to show the same information as the trading account, but in a different form. The expenditure is analysed to departments on analysis sheets and supported by a material and wage analysis. Standing expenses of the mill are an interesting subject for allocation, and Norton shows considerable care in this matter. Power is allocated according to machinery turned in each department, floor space is the basis for allocating rent, rates and taxes. Depreciation of machinery can be calculated separately for each department. While on the subject of depreciation, it is worth noting that Norton mentions as one of its causes the reduction in the " cost of labour and material."

When checking the cost of pieces after they are made and for costing ranges, it is regarded as necessary to add something for pattern-making and warehouse and general expenses. For this purpose it is suggested that non-manufacturing charges be distributed over work done in the weaving and subsequent departments. The charges might be distributed on wages paid, but the author says that this would require additional calculations. Therefore, " aggregate value of work done" in the processes is mentioned as the basis to use.

The manufacturing account is well worth reproducing. It will be observed that in the first section the sales are set against the materials used and carriage. Then follow the various processes in logical order, but trade prices are given, not actual costs. Hence the balance of this section shows the profit which could have been made if all the work had been farmed out (except pattern-making, which is at actual cost). Section II then receives the balance from Section I. This section is credited with the difference between the actual departmental expenses and the trade price, thus showing the profit on each manufacturing department. The section is then credited with discount on purchases and debited with warehouse and office standing expenses and general charges, the net profit then agreeing with the balance of the second section of the trading acconut.

This method of bringing into the accounts the trade prices of processes as a footrule to measure actual results, is the earliest example of standard costing which the present writer has been able to discover.

The period which we have just examined is one of pioneer work in this country following the emptiness of the previous eighty years. When we come to compare it with the efforts on the Continent, it will be clear that its results are not worthy of a flourish of trumpets, nevertheless a beginning had been made although America was soon to take over the lead.

(To be concluded).

* 1888—p 278.

SOME NOTES ON THE EARLY LITERATURE AND DEVELOPMENT OF COST ACCOUNTING IN GREAT BRITAIN—VI

by R. S. Edwards

(Assistant Lecturer in Accounting and Business Administration, London School of Economics)

The Discussion of Oncost and its Allocation

(*Continued from p.* 316)

The subject of overhead or oncost had been discussed in Britain before 1890,* but it had certainly not taken the centre of the platform; emphasis had been on prime cost. Methods of dividing up costs over departments had been worked out in fair detail, for example by Norton, but the overhead of an engineering works was another matter. Garcke and Fells were aware of the problem and their attitude has already been described, but they were not tackling the large fixed costs of a modern engineering works in the early editions of their book. In the review of the first edition of this volume, in *The Accountant Students' Journal*, 1st July 1887, it was suggested that indirect expenses, maintenance, indirect wages, renewals and depreciation should be charged "in properly apportioned amounts to the cost." Office rent and salaries were best unappropriated, it said. In 1890 an anonymous writer, "A General Manager," published a work entitled "Engineering Estimates, Costs and Accounts." He described the elements of cost and pointed out that many of the indirect expenses would vary with the direct skilled labour employed; on the other hand he agreed that rent, rates and insurance vary little from year to year, but in spite of this he regarded direct wages as the best all-round basis for allocating oncost. "A remark that applies to every department and that is sufficiently obvious, is that these percentages will be higher when there is little doing than when business is good."† Interest on capital, he thought, should be included in the overhead.

In 1891, a contribution to the literature of costing was made by John Mann, in a paper entitled, "Notes on Cost Records." In discussing overhead cost he analysed it into (*a*) buying costs which vary with the cost of goods bought; (*b*) selling expenses which vary with sales; and (*c*) production expenses. So far as production expenses are concerned he dismissed quantity or value of material as a suitable basis for allocation, and gave examples of the fallacies which result from using prime cost as a basis. He pointed out the danger of allocating expenses on the basis of wages where some workers are paid more than others and summed up the position by stating that production expenses vary with time. Some proposals were put forward for a machine hour rate which, so far as the writer is aware, were the first to be made in this country.

In the same year G. P. Norton gave a lecture* in which he pointed out the difficulty of separating the more variable from the less variable expenses. He agreed that division must be to some extent arbitrary, but regarded it as desirable to keep standing expenses distinct and separate. Nobody seemed quite clear as to how or why overhead should be allocated, but the general opinion seemed to be that it should be done somehow. A correspondent in *The Accountant* in 1892† asked how oncost should be allocated in estimating for a Government contract.

By the 90's cost accounts were beginning to form part of the general textbooks on accounting. Part III of Dicksee's "Bookkeeping for Accountant Students," published in 1893 included an example of a cost ledger for a builder. Oncost is discussed and Dicksee stated that he regarded "time" as the best basis of allocation, but added that "wages" are more generally taken as the basis in practice. Lisle's "Accounting in Theory and Practice," published six years later included a chapter on cost accounts. Engineers were also emphasising the importance of carefully maintained records. In 1894 there was published‡ a description of a set of engineering cost accounts, and in dealing with depreciation the writer suggested the maintenance of a sort of plant ledger affording "a convenient summary of charges which are arrived at in detail, and according to the special circumstances of each machine or class of machinery." Earlier, in 1891, an editorial in the same journal had suggested a plant charge book, showing a fixed charge per hour for each piece of plant.§

By the turn of the century the flow of literature on cost accounts and particularly on the allocation of overhead was increasing rapidly. David Cowan** in 1901 was arguing that rent and remuneration of capital should not be included in oncost as "most people look upon the money so invested as a speculation . . ." He divided works oncost into departmental shop charges and general shop charges as some jobs do not go through all departments. Stores expenses he would recover in the price of the stores issued to jobs. He warned us that as establishment charges are, to a large extent, fixed and independent of output, any oncost factor applied to estimating or comparison would be misleading. He proposed to set up shop hour rates based on an "average over a series of past years representative

* The term "oncost" is actually very old. In Scottish collieries it was in common use before the middle of the 17th century. It was used mainly to indicate costs other than hewing. For example, these items appear under the heading of oncost in 17th century colliery records—"Horses and Mens charges at mending of coal gate and sea gate"; "New sink charges"; "Wrights wages." (See Nef on the "Rise of the British Coal Industry.")

† p. 53.

* Reported—*Accountant*, 1891, p. 762.

† Reported—*Accountant*, 1891, p. 773.

‡ "Engineering" (January-June, p. 68).

§ "Engineering" (January-June, p. 665)

** *Accountant*—p. 1242.

of the trade cycle." Shop charges would be debited to a shop charges compensating account; this account would be credited with oncost allocated so that in years of good trade the account would show a credit balance and in bad years a debit balance. In 1903 H. S. Garry* advocated treating as a dead charge the cost of excess capacity. His paper was interesting as an attempt to divide up actual cost into standard cost, excess cost and increase in cost due to excess capacity. In the same year the "Encyclopædia of Accounting" was published; it included a thoughtful contribution on oncost by John Mann. He explained how the enormous increase in capital permanently invested in manufacturing industries meant that "the reducible and controllable factors . . . tend to decrease, the fixed and irreducible factors to increase." Discussing the policy of selling under total cost he expressed the view that "if it is done in full knowledge and as part of a set policy of extension it may be defensible; if it is done through ignorance or carelessness it is inexcusable." Following a survey of the various methods of allocating oncost comes this pregnant remark: "When a manufacturer or engineer is prepared to devote a little time and thought to the study of his oncost problems, he will find that valuable results will readily be reached by the separation of the fixed and fluctuating elements of expense."

By this time practically all the problems which are discussed in modern works had been dealt with. An article in 1906 by John Whitmore† provides quite as detailed and good an analysis as we get to-day. The changed attitude to the whole subject is well expressed in a review by *The Accountant* of the 5th Edition of Garcke and Fells—"Suffice it to say that it possesses the material advantage of being founded upon practice rather than theory . . ." The 5th edition did not differ greatly from the 1st edition which had been criticised as altogether too theoretical. The scoffers had been silenced and cost accounting had come to stay.

I do not propose to thread my way through the literature of costing up to the present day—it would be a formidable task and little would be gained. I do not think that in the last 30 years cost accountants have added much to the theory of their subject. A survey of British literature up to the beginning of the 20th century has shown that the writers by this time had thought of practically all the difficulties, but it is true that most of them they did not solve. Unfortunately this is equally true to-day; the important discussions of cost theory have taken place among the economists. What is now required is a closer co-operation between economists and cost accountants.

* *Accountant*—p. 954. † *Accountant*—1906.

THE TREATMENT OF ONCOST IN COST ACCOUNTS

There has recently been published a book, entitled "Some Modern Business Problems,"* containing a series of special lectures given last winter by members of the staff of the London School of Economics on various topics connected with business administration. Two of the lectures are of special interest to the accounting profession: "Some Modern Difficulties in the Measurement of Profits," by Mr. Stanley W. Rowland, and "The Rationale of Cost Accounting," by Mr. R. S. Edwards. Both of these are valuable contributions to accounting literature, and we hope to review them, along with the rest of the essays, at an early date. Mr. Edwards, however, deals with his subject in a manner that may, perhaps, appear unorthodox and controversial to many of our readers, and therefore his paper seems to demand fuller criticism than is possible in the course of a short review.

Mr. Edwards' lecture (a précis of which appeared on p. 389 of our issue dated 13th March 1937) can perhaps be reduced to the following propositions :—

(1) The expensive and laborious process of collecting cost figures is only justifiable if these figures are of genuine value to the management of a business. To be of genuine value, they must be of such a nature as to influence policy ; they may do so, both in a narrow technical sense, by pointing to the most economical methods of production, or in a broader sense, as when they indicate what level of output is likely to yield the greatest profit.

(2) The cost figures to which the management should pay closest attention are the additional expenses due to additional operations. Thus the extra disbursements which are made necessary by the acceptance of another job, by the introduction of a new process, or by the opening of a new department, are all of vital importance. No matter how they ought to be classified later, in the first place such additional costs can all be thought of as prime (or "variable," "direct," or "fluctuating") costs, since they can still be avoided if the proposed operations are not carried out.

Oncost (otherwise known as "fixed," "supplementary," or "overhead" cost) is expenditure to which, at a given point of time, a business is inevitably committed whether or not particular operations are carried out. (Some examples will be given later, illustrating this concept further, and showing in what respects it differs from that normally accepted by accountants.)

(3) The selling prices that a business can charge for its goods are fixed by general market conditions. In "good times," the prices may be higher than the cost accountant's figures. In "bad times," on the other hand, prices lower than these figures must often be accepted if the enterprise is to carry on ; so long as the extra revenue is greater than the prime cost of producing the goods, the enterprise is better off to accept the order (and thus to obtain some surplus wherewith to meet the fixed charges) than to refuse it.

(4) If proposition (3) is correct, there is no point in allocating oncosts over each job, &c., either when estimates are being drawn up, or when cost accounts are being prepared after the completion of the order. Prime costs are the only things that matter. The process of allocating oncost is (as every accountant familiar with complicated methods, like the "machine-hour" system, will readily agree) expensive both in money and time. It merely results in "averaged" long-run costs, which, in the light of the foregoing analysis, would appear to be of little or no value.

(5) A number of other interesting conclusions may be reached if the foregoing propositions are accepted. For example, the long-standing controversies as to the correct method of charging out stock to jobs, and as to whether interest is a cost, will finally be settled. Also, the question of whether cost accounts should be kept on a double-entry system that is "tied in" with the financial books can be re-examined in a new light.

(6) In certain cases—for instance, when there are joint- or by-products—a system of costing that attempts to allocate oncost may be not only useless, but positively misleading.

(7) Having regard to these conclusions, cost accountants should, instead of spending so much time on the process of averaging costs, concentrate on their true sphere of usefulness—namely, estimating the variations in cost that follow expansion or contraction of output.

Mr. Edwards' general views as to the nature of costs are, of course, based on theory that has come to be widely accepted by economists. In many cases, too, men of affairs have been driven to the unpleasant conclusion that their best business policy during times of trade depression is to cut prices as much as may be necessary (so long as prime costs are recovered) rather than to insist on getting back the cost accountant's total figures for a job and thus perhaps lose even more trade. Writers on costing subjects, however, have seldom done more than imply that such is the case. Mr. Edwards has made explicit what has hitherto been only implicit in accounting literature. He has attached fundamental importance to limitations that have usually been dismissed as trivial. And he is, so far as we are aware, the first person who has applied economic analysis to the problems of the cost office thoroughly, and has thus been led to ask whether the process of allocating overhead charges ought not to be abandoned, or, at least, reduced to the simplest possible basis.

Such contentions may come as something of a shock to many of our readers, and in particular to those who have been trained in the orthodox school, where costing is often taught in a manner calculated to suggest that there can be no doubt as to the wisdom of setting up elaborate methods of oncost allocation an attitude which has been strengthened by the propaganda of trade associations, since the latter have often been at pains to impress their members with the desirability of adopting uniform costing systems that pay great attention to oncost. Nevertheless, we feel sure that all our readers will wish to examine Mr. Edwards' views carefully, and to criticise his con-

* Published by Longmans Green & Co. Ltd., 7s. 6d. net, post free 8s

clusions impartially; the prevalence of the error (if error it is) that he has revealed in present methods makes such an examination imperative.

It would be difficult not to agree with the proposition that the overwhelmingly important factor when any fresh piece of work is being planned is the additional cost of this work, and that, at such moments, the fixed overhead costs are of minor interest. But are we also to agree with the corollary that the whole process of allocating oncosts, both in estimates and records, should be abandoned? Is conventional practice in fact so useless and misleading as not to be worth the expense involved? If so, why is it that usually the first act of a " business doctor," when he reorganises an inefficient undertaking, is to introduce one of the conventional costing systems? Is he merely making confusion worse confounded?

Before a convincing answer to these questions can be attempted, some discussion as to the nature of the items that are in practice called oncosts seems necessary. A little thought will suffice to show that, in most enterprises, the term is used somewhat loosely, and covers expenses that are far from homogeneous. As Mr. Edwards points out, the long period and the short period must be carefully differentiated; an expense may be part of the prime cost of running a factory for a year, and yet be an oncost so far as any minor piece of work is concerned. When, in the course of preparing an estimate, a cost accountant adds his "oncost" figure (however calculated) to his " prime costs," he is trying to make allowance for such highly diversified factors as lubricating oil, bad debts, power, repairs to buildings, depreciation, and the manager's salary. Despite the fact that these items are treated as oncosts, many of them are, in reality, wholly or partly prime costs. The amount of lubricating oil used bears a definite relationship to the quantity of work performed. Probably the bad debts provision ought also to be regarded as a prime cost. (If the enterprise insured itself with an outside body against bad debts, the premium would tend to fluctuate with the amount of business done; and an enterprise that creates its own provision is really insuring internally, and so should adopt a similar principle with regard to the annual charge, much as a contract-bridge player estimates risks in terms of fractions of tricks.) Power and repairs to buildings may or may not be prime costs, according to the conditions of the individual factory; nevertheless, the bills for these items usually show at least some tendency to increase when extra jobs are done. Depreciation is partly a fixed cost, since machines will deteriorate even if left standing idle, and is partly a " user " cost which varies with the quantity of work. The manager's salary may or may not be a true fixed cost, according to circumstances.

In many cases, it may be noted, the distinction between prime costs and oncosts does not rest on the type of function performed, but on the terms of the legal contract by which the enterprise undertakes to buy the productive factors. Thus, if a business agrees not to dismiss its works manager without giving him three months' notice, his next quarter's salary at any point of time is a fixed cost and might rightly be disregarded should tenders need to be proffered in a very adverse market; but, if acceptance of these tenders would force the business to continue to employ the manager for, say, five months (and if he would otherwise have been laid off till trade recovered), then his salary for the extra two months is a prime cost, and the business would lose money if it did not allow for this outlay in making its estimates.

Another source of complication is to be found in the fact (carefully pointed out by Mr. Edwards) that men and equipment have usually alternative uses, and need not always stand idle if any particular contract is lost. A short gap of time may be filled by increasing stocks of parts, by repairing and extending equipment, by accepting less profitable work, and so on. Thus, suppose £100 is paid as rent for a given department. If no alternative use can be made of the premises, the enterprise may at a pinch disregard the £100 when estimating; but if the premises could be sub-let for £60, the latter figure cannot be disregarded, because it is really a prime cost (according to the economist's definition).

We might indicate many other circumstances under which the so-called " fixed oncost " is, in fact, a variable amount that fluctuates according to the quantity of work done. For example, in a case that was brought to our attention recently, the manager's salary appeared to be a true fixed cost, and so was left out of account during the preparation of estimates for certain new activities which were to be undertaken in addition to the normal work; but because the manager had the new duties to perform, he could no longer supervise the old operations as fully as before, with the result that their costs rose noticeably. Our readers will doubtless be able to adduce many similar instances from their own experience.

The foregoing examples will suffice to emphasise the important fact that the usual classification of oncosts is not in accordance with Mr. Edwards' strict definition; most of the items fluctuate in greater or less degree when changes in output take place. Probably because of the practical difficulties involved, the accountant has felt unable to divide oncosts in the more logical fashion of the economics textbook. At best, he has split them up into " fixed " and " fluctuating " items (an arrangement which may on occasion be helpful, but which is apt to give a deceptive air of simplicity to the position, for, as has been shown above, all expenses fluctuate if the proposed change in output be sufficiently large). Nothing that Mr. Edwards says is in opposition to this view; on the contrary, he explains the situation accurately, and indeed adds that many true prime costs are, because of their smallness, not worthy of separate treatment among the direct expenses, and so must, for the sake of convenience, be classed with the oncosts.

We can see now why it is that the conventional costing methods, although perhaps based on faulty reasoning, have not in fact been as disastrous as might at first sight have been supposed. If, during periods of depression, quotations were made at a figure only slightly in excess of " prime costs " as normally estimated (i.e. direct labour and material, sometimes plus a few easily traced expenses), a loss would usually be inevitable, since many items among the disregarded " oncosts " are really prime costs, and rise whenever extra work is done. An estimating system that rigidly insists on the addition of some margin for this factor is therefore a valuable safeguard; the error in classification tends to cancel the error in logic.

On the other hand, it is one thing to point out that an illogical system has, as the result of a happy accident, probably not done much harm, and quite another to justify its continued use. Accountants must recognise the lack of logic and consider whether improvements are not possible. To be of maximum service, estimates ought to show a prime cost figure that includes not only materials and labour, but also the amount by which the fluctuating oncosts will increase if the extra work is done. In many cases—particularly until research along new lines has been done—this amount may not be capable of ascertainment with any degree of accuracy; under such circumstances, the management will presumably be able only to hazard a guess as to the correct figure. Such a procedure savours of surrender. Nevertheless, guess-work is probably no more misleading, and is certainly a great deal cheaper than calculations based on fallacious over-simplification. Once the theoretical background is firmly grasped, cost accountants will doubtless be able to work out a new and more logical technique which will throw light on the most important question facing all enterprises, namely, the outlays necessitated by different levels of production. The discovery of this fresh technique may prove to be a difficult task, but it will be an interesting and valuable one, which may be of profound service to many types of business. Incidentally, we cannot but regret that Mr. Edwards' essay does not make any concrete suggestions in this connection.

Two explanations as to the origins of the present confusion in costing theory may present themselves to the thoughtful reader. The first is provided by an analysis of the methods of teaching the subject, the second by historical considerations. They are as follows:—

(1) By far the greatest part of the typical textbook on costing is devoted to job costs. The reasons are obvious; the matter is of vital interest to many industries; and the easiest way for a teacher to introduce his students to costing is by an exhaustive treatment of this branch of the subject, which is attractive on account of its simplicity. We do not for one moment wish to minimise the importance of job costs, or to belittle the skill of the instructor who prefers to start with the easy rather than the difficult. But we would venture to suggest that this emphasis is apt to result in all of us being given a distorted view of fundamental issues; for, later on, when we wish to consider abstract questions, such as those discussed here, nine times out of ten we test the strength of the various arguments that are brought forward chiefly by considering their applicability to job costs. But the latter are in practice confined to relatively few enterprises. Moreover, what is true in this narrow field may not be true elsewhere. Mr. Edwards' essay provides an illuminating illustration of the point. While his contentions may have a wide general validity, they tend to seem much less convincing if they are tested only in the light of the experience gained by industries using job costs. Let us consider, for example, the case of the printer who carries out orders at a prearranged price. If a fall in the demand for such work takes place, the trade might be able, as a result of having impressed its members with the importance of allowing for fixed costs in estimates, to prevent quotations from sinking very far; printers would then find that they had unintentionally come to occupy a position very like that of members of a ring for keeping up prices. (Incidentally, however, it should be noted that the continued high prices would affect other industries adversely, and so might be bad for the country as a whole; and also that the printers would themselves be injured if the fall in demand proved to be permanent, because in this case they would eventually discover that they had only postponed the evil day on which some firms would have to be squeezed out of business altogether, while in the meantime the high prices might have caused a marked decline in orders.)

Where jobs costs are concerned, then, an industry may be able to insist on the recovery of fixed oncosts without ill results to itself. But the average business does not use job costs. Its trade does not lie in accepting single orders at an agreed price. Instead, it produces large batches of articles for a speculative market. If we wish to illustrate costing procedure by reference to the printing trade, we should take as our example, not the firm that is preparing estimates for a given job, but the firm that is engaged, say, on a book-publishing venture. In this case, the facts are fundamentally different from those detailed in the preceding paragraph. The price may be varied enormously, with marked effects on demand; at five guineas, the circulation might be limited to one hundred copies, whereas at half-a-crown perhaps a hundred thousand could be sold. The cost problems will in this case be very different from those facing the printer who works only to order; and clearly the procedure outlined by Mr. Edwards, in which attention is concentrated on the extra costs at different levels of activity, is here the only one of any value.

(2) History provides us with another explanation as to why the cost accountant should have overlooked the economist's teaching. If the ordinary process of buying and selling in a competitive market for any reason ceases to be desirable, and a business is asked to fulfil orders, not at figures fixed by competition, but at "fair" prices, no basis of charging seems possible except one that allocates fixed oncosts in some prearranged way. This situation is sometimes met with, we believe, in the shipbuilding industry. The buyers of ships are anxious, above all things, that their vessels should be seaworthy, and so, to avoid the risk of the construction work being scamped, the builders are allowed to charge whatever the new ship costs, plus a percentage for profit; in such cases, the cost accounts are usually audited by representatives of the buyer. And, as is public knowledge at the moment, during periods of intense activity in the making of munitions, the British Government adopts a similar principle, believing that in so doing it will prevent "profiteering." Not only is much of the present rearmament programme being carried out on some such understanding, but the Ministry of Munitions, in the Great War, frequently gave enormous contracts on a "cost plus" basis, and as a result was forced to insist on the widespread introduction of costing methods, where hitherto there had been none. These particular

methods all aimed at the discovery of the average cost of the units of output, that is to say, at the careful allocation and " recovery " of all fixed oncosts. Most modern costing systems grew from this beginning; and unfortunately accountants did not recognise that the situation obtaining from 1914 to 1918 was ideally simplified, and would no longer be met with when competitive selling was resumed. We suggest that this is the secret behind the adoption of a mental attitude that now seems difficult to justify.

We trust that this appreciation and criticism of Mr. Edwards' essay will lead those of our readers who have specialised in costing to consider whether, and to what extent, accepted methods are faulty and in need of modification. Clearly, his theories can be adequately weighed only by persons who are willing to think in terms of economic analysis; and therefore, even if his essay has done nothing more, it has served to emphasise the practical, everyday importance to accountants of obtaining a thorough grounding in a subject that is all too often dismissed as irrelevant.

The Cost Accountant

The Official Journal of the Institute of Cost and Works Accountants (Limited by Guarantee)

Vol. 17.—No. 6. November, 1937.

COST ACCOUNTING THEORY

In our issue of May last we published an epitome of a lecture delivered by Mr. Ronald S. Edwards (Assistant Lecturer in Accounting and Business Administration, London School of Economics), and in a recent issue of *The Accountant*,* there appears a critical review of the lecture as contained in "Some Modern Business Problems."† The article is, in our judgment, of sufficient importance to justify the suggestion that every member and registered student of the Institute of Cost and Works Accountants ought to read it, and read it with a perfectly open mind.

Elsewhere Mr. Edwards has stated that in his opinion Cost Accountants have not added much to the theory of cost accounting during the past thirty years, and he maintains that a survey of British literature up to the beginning of the twentieth century has shown that writers on cost accounting by this time had thought of all the difficulties, but had failed to solve most of them—a statement which he regards as being equally true to-day.

It is perhaps as well to bear in mind that in the study of costs themselves there are, quite apart from purely theoretical aspects, fundamental differences to be observed which are best illustrated by the number of different persons who deal with costs, all of whom deal with them for different purposes. To name two examples only—the Cost Accountant and the Economist.

The Cost Accountant is required to furnish detailed information which will serve as a guide to management in a great variety of circumstances and on many divergent questions of policy, all differing in varying degrees, in the several undertakings within each separate industry. The Economist, on the other hand, is concerned, mainly, with the effect of costs on prices under natural competitive conditions, or under monopolistic competition. In other words, the Cost Accountant is required to deal with everyday problems arising in a multitude of factories, organisations, and industries, the dominating factor therein being human nature with all its vagaries, its frailties, its susceptibilities and its prejudices, influenced to a large extent by the social and political conditions in the world of affairs outside. The Economist deals with theory under certain postulated conditions as distinct from, and often opposed to, practical realities.

We are quite prepared to admit that one of the features which many Cost Accountants are apt to lose sight of is that of differentiating between long-run and short-run fluctuations and, moreover, that they often fail to realise that certain items of expense may form part of the prime cost of running

* *The Accountant*, 23rd October, 1937

† *Longmans, Green & Co., Ltd.* 7s. 6d.

a factory for a year, or any other fiscal period, and yet be an overhead expense so far as a minor operation is concerned. This contention is supported in the review of our contemporary, *The Accountant*, where such highly diversified items as lubricating oil, bad-debts, power, repairs to buildings, depreciation, and manager's salary are cited as being generally regarded as overheads, although many of them are actually, wholly, or in part, prime costs.

It must in fairness be stated, however, that there are great variations in the usage of the term Prime Cost in industrial and commercial activities, and that Economists usually apply the term in a narrow and restricted sense and that other costs, which are often regarded by them as supplementary costs, differ only in degree from prime costs.

It is reasonable to argue that lubricating oil consumed, for example, bears a direct relationship to the volume of work done, even though for purposes of cost accounting the expenditure involved would be covered by the phrase " cost of consumable stores " and, as such, in ninety-nine out of every hundred cases, would be regarded as an indirect material cost and not as a prime cost. On the other hand, how can the provision for bad-debts be considered as a prime cost ?

It can be, and is, argued that if an enterprise insured its bad debts with an outside agency the premium payable would be calculated to fluctuate in accordance with the volume of business done ; and a concern insuring its bad-debts within its own financial control should adopt a similar principle in recovering the annual liability, even to allocating the amount in proportion to the turnover represented by any specific line of product, or to the product of any given department. In such a case it would clearly be regarded as a prime cost.

We have a great admiration for the work of Mr. Ronald S. Edwards, and his " *Notes on the Early Literature and Development of Cost Accounting in Great Britain* " is a valuable contribution to research. In this connection we would mention that in the conclusion of these notes Mr. Edwards states that " the important discussions of cost theory have taken place among the Economists. What is now required is a closer co-operation between Economists and Cost Accountants " Very few of our readers will disagree with this conclusion and if, as we hope they may, our comments serve to stimulate thought and thereby result in an application of economic analysis on the part of Cost Accountants to their own particular work, we shall have contributed in no small measure to the desired co-operation.

WILL YOUR COSTING SYSTEM STAND UP TO THE TEST OF RISING PRICES ?

Two Papers submitted at the Sixteenth National Cost Conference in London, on Saturday, 2nd October, 1937.

First Paper, by F. W. H. SAUNDERS, A.C.W.A., (*Cost Accountant, Peek Frean & Co. Ltd., London*).

1. It is perhaps a platitude to say that the costing system which cannot respond to changing conditions is worse than useless—that it is a delusion and a snare. Yet we need constantly to remind ourselves that the system which lacks flexibility, no matter how well it functions under normal conditions, will inevitably go to pieces under the new strains and stresses which under abnormal conditions are bound to arise.

2. This was the supreme lesson of the post-war depression, when the problem of the half-filled shop and the falling load factor compelled us to set up standard costs in place of the actual costs previously used as a basis for price fixing. We need always to ask ourselves whether our methods of costing are so just and rational that they will remain good and true through all the changing scenes of economic life. We cannot rest assured that our costing system will not let us down, unless we know beyond all shadow of doubt that it is founded on right principles and that it is free from all those faults and fallacies which even to-day are frequently encountered in badly constructed systems. The power to make immediate response to changing conditions is the hall-mark of the reliable costing system.

3. There are special reasons for directing attention to this subject at the present time. Drastic changes in values in the markets of the world are already throwing costs out of balance. In our own country recent events have produced a pronounced instability of prices. During the war period and particularly soon after the conclusion of the war, prices soared to surprising levels ; then came the slump, with prices falling rapidly and now they have risen once more with almost equal rapidity. The amount of the changes has not been constant as between commodities. This is due, in a large measure, to the many artificial conditions created in various countries in their efforts to weather the political and economic storms.

4. Proper cost finding has had to respond to the difficulties and demands of all these variations. I emphasise the expression " proper cost finding " because much figuring done under the guise of costing is not costing at all. Rule of thumb methods that were good enough in pre-war days have been incapable of meeting post-war conditions. New theories have been developed to meet new situations, and costing would have progressed much more slowly had it not been for the stimulating influences produced by prolonged periods of instability. Necessity is ever the mother of invention and costing is no exception to this rule.

5. Now with all these disturbing factors in mind the obvious question is, has your costing system been so designed as to bring to the notice of the management the true facts of cost variations ? Are you really convinced by its conclusions ?

6. It is often suggested that, provided all the expenses shown in the profit and loss account are absorbed into the costs, then the methods used are justified. We have even heard it stated and defended that, for all practical purposes, overhead expenses can be allocated on the basis of an average percentage calculated upon direct materials and direct wages. It is true that some substantial businesses appear to be satisfied with such figures but I question whether either the customer or the selling organisation is going to be as easily satisfied, in the long run, with prices based upon such dubious methods.

7. How can a business executive be convinced by such primitive methods when material prices vary disproportionately, or when the labour and material content of the various commodities is inconstant ? The cost of raw material in a particular article may be increased without making any difference to the cost of labour expended in its manufacture or to the amount of overhead expense per article except, perhaps, in some very small degree.

8. In this age of mechanical appliances and mass production, overhead expenses represent a much greater part of the cost than used to be the case. Highly automatic devices have displaced labour to a remarkable extent, either by dispensing with it almost entirely or by enabling much cheaper grades of labour to be used. The ratio of fixed to variable expenses has increased

substantially as a consequence. Overhead expenses must therefore become a matter of major concern. Their incidence must be understood and accurate methods of absorbing them in costs must be applied.

9. Time is doubtless one of the most important factors in cost. Since so many expenses are fixed, the cheapness of production per unit is largely dependent upon volume of output during the time available. When work was performed principally by hand, the measurement of labour probably provided a reasonably precise measurement of time for the purpose of distributing other expenses. But there are few industries where conditions have remained sufficiently unchanged to justify the use of such methods to-day.

10. Much is claimed for short cuts and general averages in costing on grounds of simplicity and expediency, but these facilities, without reasonable accuracy must surely lead to disaster unless protected by monopoly or some other artificial factor. Costing may not be an exact science but its methods must be logical if it is to be of real value. It must inspire confidence and present something more than just a rough idea of the position if it is to achieve its purpose of guiding policy and development. We must not be slaves to expediency, ever hoping that things will work out all right on the average. Even if they happen to do so in normal times they will certainly fail when abnormal conditions arise.

11. Materials permeate the average business throughout. They form the base of the product; they are consumed in manufacture in various ways; they enter into production, overhead, selling and distribution expenses. If they rise in price, then most elements of the business are involved in some way, according to the degree to which materials are used.

12. Rising material prices usually herald a boom in the industries immediately concerned and the wages paid for the trades within them tend to rise. Similar trades in other industries follow automatically.

13. It seems inevitable that as material prices and wages rise, and so affect profits, there must be some compensating economy or, alternatively, an adjustment to selling prices. Assuming free competition, there can be no doubt that the firm employing sound methods of costing will be in a vastly superior position when seeking and accepting orders, quite apart from any advantages which accrue from efficient internal control. Even though trade practice may cause prices to be fixed arbitrarily, that is no justification for arbitrary costing.

14. Industry, commerce and politics are so interdependent nowadays that movements in one are bound to produce repercussions in the others. We have seen the effects of increased demands for armaments. Following the oconomic law of supply and demand, the prices of metals increased almost immediately. This provided the opportunity for certain other material prices to follow their example, and that opportunity has not been lost.

15. My interests are particularly concerned with food manufacturing industries, covering a fairly wide field of activity, and this is the position as I have experienced it. The costs of most ingredients have advanced, but by no means consistently. In some cases they have also fluctuated violently because of irregular buying and seasonal influences. Machinery and maintenance materials, coal and petrol are dearer. Higher prices have to be paid for the wide variety of packing and packaging materials used. Certain grades of employees have received wage increases. Coincident with these changes there has been a revolution in the style of packing demanded, largely owing to the new methods of retail distribution to the consumer. This has increased substantially the proportion of materials and labour in the packing of the product. Then, in order to cover the increased costs, selling prices have been adjusted.

16. The natural consequence of these changes is the stimulation of fresh ideas in production and marketing. Any tendency to lethargy and contentment that may have been induced by a period of reasonably steady trading conditions is quickly dismissed and there is a definite urge for alternative methods and materials, and for other economies to combat the upward tendency of costs. The extent to which these many changes affect each type of article produced or each process, can be assessed only by carefully devised detailed costing conducted on a basis which is thoroughly rational and reliable.

17. At this stage numerous questions arise. Which lines really require price increases? Can this one be left unaltered in the hope that a possible increase in its sales will nullify the higher cost at present experienced? How are the services affected? Is it worth while performing certain work on the premises or contracting for it outside? Alterations to

selling prices may upset the proportions of trade—in fact they may be intended so to do.

18. This situation must be typical of many industries to-day and manufacturers are faced with these and the many other costing problems arising from it. Are we equipped to deal with them ? How can we meet the need for proper cost finding ? Would a system of percentages on wages and/or materials provide us with any real security ? Experience derived from many different types of industry has repeatedly answered this question with an emphatic negative.

19. Three main requirements seem to emerge :

(*a*) A plan of proposed activity ;

(*b*) The translation of the plan into terms of cost ;

(*c*) A proper record under cost headings of past and present costs with due regard to fixed and variable expenses.

20. Requirement (*a*) implies a budget and I can hardly imagine any progressive business being conducted to-day without some planning for the present and future. There are difficulties, without question, but a plan of campaign, with an anticipation of its goal, is essential in any responsible adventure.

21. Having prepared the budget, the next step is requirement (*b*) and standard costs are the obvious inference.

22. Carefully constructed standard costs, which account for expenses as they are really incurred, provide the most useful guide to management that costing technique has yet devised. They enable the budget to be interpreted throughout the activities of the business, and they afford a very practicable means of anticipating and knowing the effect of rising prices, as well as any other change. The consideration of cost is automatically simplified and we are forewarned and forearmed because the standards ascertained show what is to be expected from the application of the plan.

23. By studying the variations from the standards set we are in the desirable position of having revealed to us those matters really requiring attention and adjustment. If a cost is increased the cause can be ascertained and we can see whether it is due to rising prices, avoidable excesses or otherwise.

24. The third item (*c*) involves the setting up of a suitably designed system of cost accounting and it is essential to the other two requirements. Experience and reliable data are required for both budgeting and standard costs.

25. The cost accounts will render invaluable aid in this connection by providing a correct view of the trend of the business over convenient trading cycles, whilst showing up the results produced by seasonal fluctuations and other disturbing factors. At the same time they must be framed so as to call attention quickly to any sudden changes.

26. The correct distribution of overhead expenses in standard costs must depend upon the constant reference to actual costs, so that modifications necessitated by changing conditions may be applied as soon as they occur.

27. Provision must be made to separate the cost of departments, service, processes, etc., so that the effect of rising prices may be seen clearly and explained thereby.

28. For instance, an increase in the price of coal should cause an increase in the cost of steam. If, at the same time, the quantity of steam produced happens to be reduced, the total cost may be less. The real position may therefore be hidden unless exposed by accurate cost accounting, which would separate the individual expenses of the service for expression upon an appropriate unit.

29. Maintenance provides another example. As the mechanisation of production develops so must the cost of maintenance be expected to rise. Cost accounts will localise the increases and provide a segregation of the contributing factors. It can then be seen to what extent rising prices of materials are responsible and how much arises from other causes.

30. I have no doubt that there are many sceptics who are quite convinced that their particular business does not lend itself to the methods advocated. We are apt to consider, not unnaturally, that our own problems are quite different from those of other people, and that their theories are not applicable in our case. Is there any justification for such an attitude ?

31. There is no record showing how far standard costs have been brought into use as compared with the diverse types of industry that exist. Perhaps, one day, this Institute may consider a census of methods practicable and valuable. I feel sure that the results would serve to dismiss the doubts of many, and also to inspire the remainder.

COSTING—MARGINAL AND CONVENTIONAL

By J. A. Reece, B.Sc.(Econ.), A.C.W.A.

Marginal Costing

All Cost Accountants are familiar with such problems as the following: "Shall I renew my agreement with a cartage contractor to deliver for £1 a ton my next year's potato crop to dealers, or shall I hire and run myself a lorry for delivering them?" They would probably look upon this as costing but not part of the costing system. In the example given the calculation might be as follows:—

Cost of Delivery:	£	£
(*a*) Using a cartage contractor:		
300 tons at £1 a ton ...		300
(*b*) Hiring a lorry:		
Hire of lorry	40	
Driver's wages	100	
Running expenses	100	
		240
Addition to Profit by Hire of Lorry		60

(*N.B.*—It is assumed that any extra administration would be done by existing staff.)

Out and out exponents of Marginal Costing consider that this approach alone deserves the attention of Cost Accountants. They would increase the number of these inquiries and devise new forms of record to facilitate answering them, and they would abandon conventional costing. (It sometimes seems that they wish to use this approach for the business as a whole in place of periodical final accounts.) A fair examination of their arguments shows them to be (in theory at least) not so extravagant as appears at first sight. In order to make their claims clear the problem set out above will be examined more closely. It will be noticed that:—

(1) Alternatives in the future are being considered in order to see which will add most to future profit;

(2) Only those factors liable to vary are brought into the calculation;

(3) As at the time of the costing the selected alternative and the profit are both in the future, they are forecasts, not facts;

(4) If the best forecast is to be made, accurate past statistics of the potato market, of lorry performance, and of price trends must be used.

Is it possible that such considerations define the whole field of usefulness of the Cost Accountant? The choice of one out of several alternatives *must* be the only object of anyone who wishes to act. This is difficult to explain but self-evident when appreciated. To revert to a previous method after a costly unsuccessful experiment will not bring back the lost profit: the failure may provide data on which decisions to transfer the responsible staff may be based.

Every problem of management (*i.e.*, maximising profit) can be put in this form. For instance, production methods may be compared, but it is only when we decide to substitute one for another, starting on a certain date, that extra profit can arise. Before this a decision had to be made that it was worth while spending time discussing the problem instead of perhaps using the time to initiate a sales campaign. Marginal costing is applied directly at this vital point of decision, asks for a technical description of the alternatives and seeks to provide general methods of accurately forecasting their respective effects on future profits. For this purpose ample suitable statistics must be available, but these may bear little or no resemblance to the records contained in a conventional costing system.

Advantages of Marginal Costing:

(1) The importance of concentrating on the object of the business, viz., to make the most profit starting from the position we are in now, is stressed.

(2) The costs obtained bear directly on the problem concerned, and there is no danger of using previously prepared costs in an inappropriate manner.

(3) The insistence on the availability of accurate technical data and market statistics means that these are also available for engineers and salesmen in considering their own problems.

Disadvantages of Marginal Costing:

(1) It is not clear who would control such a system, as it appears to cover management as a whole and not only figure work.

(2) The details of a complete system have, it is believed, still to be worked out. Too much time might have to be spent on such individual treatment.

(3) It does not provide for the control (*i.e.*, "policing") of men and materials, and subsidiary methods would presumably have to be used for this purpose.

It will be noted that many of the methods of Marginal Costing are already part of the stock-in-trade of the Cost Accountant, though in a limited and secondary way. The question is—is it right to attempt to raise these fragments into a new system to replace the conventional one ?

Conventional Costing

Conventional costing is detailed accounting. An accountant examining a well-kept costing system feels at home. He finds the double-entry system giving a trial balance and leading to the totals in the financial accounts. Allocation of overheads is familiar practice, and variation accounts make standard costs part of the well-known system. Uniform costing recalls obligatory public utility accounts and his own efforts to make business accounts more informative. Engineers may have helped to start modern costing, but accounting methods have not only been adopted but are also widely assumed in text-books and at conferences.

Advantages of Conventional Costing :

(1) The whole of the costs are accounted for, giving a check on loss and a basis on which Management may ask questions calculated to disclose inefficiency.

(2) In highly developed standard costing systems the Management can (in theory) put its finger automatically on the responsible agent.

(3) Help is given to the Management without the presumption to instruct them in the imponderables such as political issues and the judgment of men.

(4) Especially important is the sense of fairness engendered. A reasonable standard is set for the head of a department and this can be discussed if he feels the burden is too great to allow him to make that profit on which he will be judged.

Disadvantages of Conventional Costing :

(1) There is a danger that the cost of an article will be looked upon as something as absolute as weight or volume, whereas the allocation of overheads is necessarily arbitrary and even a small change in output may have different direct costs from the existing average direct cost of output.

(2) Objects may be lost sight of, the system becoming an end in itself.

(3) Average costs may lead to operation on cost levels that do not represent maximum profit.

(4) Management may be short of the full information it requires in facing new problems.

Conclusion

The above discussion roughly represents the impact of economics on cost accounting. Little general literature could be found except articles in THE COST ACCOUNTANT and *Accountant* and especially work by the Accounting Research Association, apart from works on theoretical economics.

The present note is suggestive only, and certainly contains many errors, but it was thought worth while to set out a scheme of approach to this too little considered topic.

COSTING—MARGINAL AND CONVENTIONAL

By F. L. Impey

Mr. J. A. Reece attracts my attention by his article on Marginal and Conventional Costing,* because he assumes too little experience and too short a life for Marginal Costing. For more than twenty years we have employed what is now called " Marginal Costing " in my business, and out of this experience I can say that our costing controls are no different in name and purpose from those employed by Cost Accountants using the conventional methods. Mr. Reece appears to exaggerate differences between Marginal and Conventional Costing ; for in fact the aims of both are the same and the methods of accounting are the same except in the treatment of fixed expenses.

Though not usually made a part of Marginal Costing, it is advisable to evolve a unit of manufacture to use as a measuring rod of fixed expenses in all departments.

Marginal Costing implies the division of the expenses into fixed and variable and the stripping of the fixed expenses from the " cost " of the article. If this is successfully carried out, the cost of the article will include only the out-of-pocket expenses or, to put it in another way, only those costs which would not be incurred if the " marginal " unit of production were not produced and sold. This has a very practical bearing on price policy. How many concerns have secondary lines of production which, by conventional methods, show very little " profit " or even a " loss," but which in fact produce substantial contributions towards unavoidable fixed expenses ? And again, when the factory is under-employed, how much easier it is, if you know the marginal cost, to decide at what price it is worth while to take a special order rather than to refuse it. The fixed expenses cannot be allocated to individual products with any show of logic, and the attempt to do so merely obscures the important facts, namely the out-of-pocket costs.

In the " Advantages " of Marginal Costing, Mr. Reece says nothing of the advantages of the exclusion of fixed charges, which in conventional costing tend to swamp the costs and smother serious errors. On the other hand, in " Disadvantage " 3, he says that " It does not provide for the control of men and materials." Emphatically this is wrong ; by concentrating on the out-of-pocket costs it provides for sounder control of all cost items than does conventional costing.

* *Published in* The Cost Accountant, *Oct.-Nov.*, 1940.

The underlying purpose of Marginal Costing is to provide a cost which is stripped of all fixed expenses, and while output required of the factory in a given period is kept within reasonable limits of planned production, say between a minimum of 85 per cent. and a maximum of 115 per cent., it may be said with certainty—

(*a*) That the difference between the Sales Price and the Marginal Cost Price is the Margin, the whole of which is available for the payment of fixed expenses ;

(*b*) That after the fixed expenses are paid, the whole surplus remaining is net profit.

I should like to add to Mr. Reece's List of the advantages of Marginal Costing—

(1) The marginal cost of articles exclusive of fixed expense is a safe guide to pricing, especially when it is possible to relate fixed expense to the article at a rate per unit of manufacture ;

(2) As the fixed expenses are separated from cost of material, wages and variable expenses in the cost accounts of services, a closer and more reliable supervision of the controllable cost of the services is obtained.

The disadvantages of conventional costing are—

(1) Quotations are liable to be given at prices too high to be competitive or too low to be profitable ;

(2) The Management is liable to push the sale of article A as more profitable than article B, while the true position may be the reverse, thus leading to errors of policy ;

(3) If costs are befogged they cannot be measured against a precise standard and are almost sure to be higher than they should be.

(4) In a period of business recession, the losses due to working below capacity may be disastrous, and without marginal costs and the separation of fixed from variable expenses such losses are very difficult to calculate.

The change of method of accounting is by no means disturbing or disruptive. There is, however, a complete change in the methods of price control, and recovery of fixed expenses. Attention should, I think, be directed to the task of learning this new technique by the executives of the business.

The Cost Accountant

The Official Journal of the Institute of Cost and Works Accountants
(Limited by Guarantee)

22. — No. 3 FEBRUARY–MARCH, 1943.

THE DEVELOPMENT OF COST ACCOUNTING

WITH post-war planning, the implementing of the Atlantic Charter, and the serious task of preparing for peace time activities occupying so much attention in the economic, social and financial spheres, it is of the utmost importance that Cost Accountants should be directing their attention to the development and the application of cost accounting principles and technique so that they may be ready effectively to play their part when a return to peace time trading is made possible.

It is generally accepted that prosperity will not immediately follow the end of the war ; on the contrary, it is considered in many well informed quarters that for a considerable period after its termination we shall all be relatively poorer ; that industry, and commerce generally, will be compelled to operate on narrower margins of profit than was the case either before or during the war. How then can the application of costing technique assist in rehabilitation ? In what direction may we look for development ?

There appear to be two closely allied directions in which development may be possible, and these two may, for all practical purposes, be regarded as one. This does not imply, however, that they are in detail just one and the same, or that the terms themselves are synonymous. We refer to the application of Budgetary Control and Standard Costs.

It is often argued, probably with more prejudice than conviction, that it is impossible effectively to instal and operate a system of Standard Costs under conditions of price instability—conditions which are likely to exist for some time after the end of the war. This contention may be true within more or less narrow limits, but the difficulties encountered ought not to be regarded as insurmountable.

Let us look at the definitions of the terms so that we may rightly appraise their relative merits and note how closely the two aspects of control are bound together. The definitions placed side by side are worthy of careful examination :—

BUDGETARY CONTROL	STANDARD COSTING
The systematic control of business operations by means of pre-determined standards prepared in minute detail and assembled into a comprehensive programme, in order to provide a basis of comparison with actual performances and costs.	The determination of costs of standard products, produced in standard quantities under standard conditions which may be normal or otherwise.

Not for a moment is it to be assumed that the foregoing definitions are regarded as incapable of improvement, and it will be surprising if criticisms, as well as suggestions for improvements, are not received. Nevertheless, the two definitions have been accepted by the

Institute and are included in its published terminology.

While the vocabulary of standard costs is recognised, it is surprising to find the varying interpretations placed upon it—interpretations which, in a number of cases, might be said to distort its real meaning and purpose. The understanding of the theory of standard costing is only that of absorbing an idea which is intended to assist us in our thinking. When studying the application of the theory we may reach a point where we are faced with a stumbling block. But stumbling-blocks, to Cost Accountants, are simply obstacles which have to be overcome. If the theory upon which a principle is based be mastered and kept in mind, it will always be a useful instrument in one's mental equipment.

Standard costs can never be said to be permanent. By their very nature they must be subject to revision from time to time. They have been characterised as "common-sense costs"; figures which reflect the best judgment of management as to what costs ought to be if the business were operated with a high degree of efficiency, with the standards for material, labour and overhead set so as to be possible of attainment. A very important part of the operation of a standard cost system is the detailed analysis of variances, the disposition of which is dependent upon the cause for the incurrence of such variances.

Before a detailed analysis can be made of the proper method of determining standards it is most important to note that there are two groups of standards—price standards and quantity standards—and for each element of expense, whether material, labour or overhead, the "variance" between standard and actual at the end of each accounting period is explained by both quantity and price differences. The present stage to which standard costing has attained, with all its shortcomings and obscurities, is by no means to be considered as the ultimate. The next stage is, possibly, just round the corner, but the exact direction to be taken is perhaps obscured. It may be towards the cost control of types of expenditure at the source, prior to distribution; or through a knowledge of marginal relationships between volume, price and profit; no one can say. It can, however, be asserted that, whatever the post-war conditions may be, cost reduction will be of the most vital importance in the rehabilitation of world trade.

The Accountant

ESTABLISHED 1874

THE RECOGNISED WEEKLY ORGAN OF CHARTERED ACCOUNTANTS AND ACCOUNTANCY THROUGHOUT THE WORLD

Vol. CIX | SATURDAY, 3rd JULY, 1943 | No. 3578

UNIFORMITY IN COSTING METHODS

THE lecture by Mr. Lawrence W. Robson, the first part of which we include in this issue, is a distinct contribution towards a re-statement of the whole costing problem. At one time there seemed a possibility that costing as expounded in the text books would become a doctrinaire theory without any very clear relation to the realities of practice; and because of that adverse tendency it has happened, as observation of numerous instances will confirm, that cost accounting has often been regarded as something separate and distinct from financial accounting, to be practised and developed by specialists, each of whom built up around a text book framework a 'system' designed to suit his particular needs and facts. Such a departmental outlook has certainly diminished the efficiency which accounting might otherwise attain and it has resulted in a failure to give to industry the accounting service that it badly needs.

The war has changed the whole face of these affairs. In many large sections of industry the Government is now almost the only customer and has rightly felt itself entitled to control the price that it is called upon to pay. Obviously, that price must be related to costs and hence, from this point of view, the question 'what has it cost?' is almost the only one that a statement of account is expected to answer. If accounts, as ordinarily drafted, are unable to give the answer, or if they give an equivocal answer, it is natural that inquiries should take another direction and that information should be taken from sources not amenable to the rigid verification that ought to be associated with the accounting idea. The evident unsatisfactoriness of such a situation has led us all back to a natural desire for standardisation of purpose, of technique and of interpretation.

Mr. Robson acutely points out that the desire so expressed is not the equivalent of a demand for Governmental planning and control; he puts the matter the other way round and reminds us that 'the future depends more on the individual than on the Government', and that it is for the individual in loyalty to the national purpose to make his active contribution to the success of national policy by so ordering his affairs as to perform his particular work in life with the greatest efficiency.

There can be no doubt that the active contribution so envisaged must concern itself with a field wider than that of the individual industrial unit. In these days units stand or fall with the fortunes of the industry of which they are a part, just as industries themselves depend for success in large degree on the conditions set up by national policy. To express the same point in another way, the utility of costing is not wholly or mainly found in the service it can render to individual undertakings, but is to be looked for in the setting up of yardsticks of comparison whereby, within given industries, efficiency can be tested and fostered.

The co-operation within industries that is thus seen to be necessary reflects itself on the oft-expressed demand for 'uniform costing methods', and the value of Mr. Robson's lecture seems to us to lie in his discussion of the real meaning of uniformity in this connection. It is certainly not a strait-jacket to be imposed on an undertaking without inquiry into or reference to its individual conditions. Every accountant knows with what astonishment he continually finds that every undertaking has some unique point, whether of organisation or of circumstances, and it would be a prime mistake to imagine that a 'system' can be invented and presented ready made for universal use. Thus the real problem is how far generalisation can go.

Mr. Robson's solution seems to be the right one. The trade association is the most effective rallying point. It is there, first, that the necessary degree of mutual confidence already exists, not to speak of the appreciation of special difficulties and problems. And it is there that technical advice can most usefully be brought into conference. Absolute uniformity can never be achieved, nor indeed is it desirable; but it is possible, as has been proved in numerous instances, to arrive at a general understanding through which expenditure can be codified under fairly narrow headings so that their aggregation can be intelligently displayed.

The benefits of common action on these lines react in two directions. Individual undertakings can assess their own efficiency first by comparison with standards and second by comparison with the performance of other units and Mr. Robson is right to insist on the importance of 'comparison' as a principle. A mere absolute cost is a barren figure unless some use be made of it. That use has been found in recent years by the development of the practice of standard costing, whereunder the emphasis is laid not on actual performance, but on performance, point by point, expressed as a ratio to a predetermined ideal or standard cost. Here management is brought into the closest relation to accounting, for the causes of variation can be sought either in shortcomings of performance or in defects of layout or plan which make good performance impossible. The setting up of the target is a matter of management, the measurement of the variation between it and performance is a matter of accounting.

Comparison between unit and unit is not so easy because differences of conditions so often vitiate comparability; but that is no criticism of the attempt to arrive at uniformity of method, for without that uniformity all comparison is indeed futile.

We return to the place to be occupied by the financial accountant in this view of the general scheme. It has been said that the function of the accountant is to gather information, to collate it and to give it out again. The definition is as helpful or unhelpful as most attempts at generalisation, but it contains a germ of truth. For the intimacy of costing and accounting is such that it is true to say that there should be no item of importance in relation to costs which should not be already included in the accounts or prepared by the accountant. The problem is to set them out in the right groups and in the right order. The co-operation which is the subject of this article should be directed to giving the financial accounts, we would almost say, a costing bias; or if that phrase may be considered too extreme we would substitute a consciousness that one of the main purposes of accounting in these days is to give *useful* information. The old use was to measure the possibility of dividend paying. The new use is to measure the probabilities of survival. That may be less exciting, but it is none the less a necessity enforced by modern circumstance. And just as unity is strength, so the joining together in a common purpose to give a common use to accounts of the several units in single industries is a contribution to co-operative progress which the community needs and expects. The key of the matter is in the hands of accountants and they must use it.

COSTING IN RELATION TO MANAGEMENT

by George Roddick, F.C.I.S., A.L.A.A., A.C.W.A.

In the leading article in this journal some weeks ago the view was expressed that costing suffered from the tendency to treat it as a separate study, a department distinct from the accounting of the business and controlled by its own experts. Such a view is open to question, and it may be contended that costing would in fact benefit by a still wider divorce from the methods and outlook of financial accounting. Admittedly costing has developed from increasingly analytical accounting, but in the complex modern factory it is a specialised study to be undertaken by experts in costing rather than accountants, and it will only be retarded by too close connection with accounting and its methods.

If it was at one time no more than the art of extracting ledger figures and distributing them among cost sections, it is now a technical study to be undertaken, after training, by men who are cost analysts in preference to cost accountants. The accounting side of their work is the simplest of their tasks. Text books display neat cost accounts in which items are debited from the financial ledgers, allocated and posted to process accounts, and the whole balanced in the orthodox double-entry style, but while this has its own place in costing, the crucial problems arise not in the accounting but in the technical aspects, and the value of costs depends on how the factory data are collected and converted into money values. The importance of technical accuracy is seldom sufficiently stressed in costing text books, yet its absence may render cost accounts worthless. By giving too much prominence to these balanced accounts the text books often place the means so much in the foreground that they have obscured the ends, the ends being the presentation to the management, in terms which the management can quickly grasp, of pictures, moving pictures, in money values, of the detailed activities of the concern.

We shall obtain a clearer idea of the aims of the cost expert if we look at costing through the eyes of the manager, instead of the eyes of the cost accountant. The latter may become so enamoured of his systems and so intoxicated with his statistics that he does not see the wood for the trees. Costs serve no useful purpose unless and until they have been communicated to the management and their implications grasped. What then does the management expect to learn from the cost department? Its questions will, broadly speaking, be five:

(*a*) What is the present cost per unit of production?
(*b*) What is the relative cost of the different lines to be sold?
(*c*) What would be the cost per unit at varying volumes of output?
(*d*) What would new and proposed lines cost?
(*e*) How are the costs made up of charges per man, machine, process or department?

In asking question (*a*) the manager aims at comparing the cost and selling price of each unit to ascertain the profit margin. In making such comparison from week to week he also gains an impression of the progress of the factory and the varying desirability of selling lines. The exact desirability, however, cannot be determined until question (*b*) is answered.

To arrive at relative costs each line must be costed under exactly similar conditions, and this will probably involve revising the routine weekly costs and calculating them on the basis of average or standard performance, eliminating factors which are not due to the lines themselves. Upon the reply to this question will depend the manager's decision to increase or to discontinue lines of manufacture and to charge extra price for special features such as finish, colour, design, &c. The answer to question (*b*) demands more technical knowledge than (*a*), and still more is required to deal with question (*c*) which involves calculation of the cost under conditions of greater or less output. In addition to the relatively simple adjustment for spreading time costs over varying production there is the more complicated calculation of efficiency at different levels of output. The divergence of each factor of production from its optimum point must be taken into the calculation and in few cases does the efficiency vary in ratio, direct or inverse, to output. At low levels of output, in addition to a heavy burden of overhead, there will be the slackness and lack of incentive which accompanies sub-normal production, while increased output may pass optimum point and, in spite of savings on overhead, involve higher costs. It has been said that 100 per cent. efficiency costs too much and the cost expert has the task of finding the cost not only of the average unit but of the marginal unit. In this, as in solving problem (*d*), he enters fields remote from accounting, and though he will have the assistance of technical departments he will require such knowledge of factory work as will enable him to understand the technical information supplied to him and, at times, to sift out facts from conflicting opinions. Clear thinking and initiative are more in evidence than the careful accuracy of the accountant.

So much for the demands upon the cost expert. Let us examine his outlook as compared with that of the accountant.

The accountant deals in records of past activities and in static surveys or balance sheets. The former are largely designed to prevent misappropriation of funds while the latter are concerned to such an extent with the liquidity of the concern as to amount to statements in preparation for winding up. The cost expert looks to the future, his most important figures are those of the weeks to come and the past is little more than a guide to what is likely to happen in the future.

Secondly, the type of knowledge to be acquired by each is of a different order, the financial man specialising increasingly in taxation and purely financial affairs, while the cost expert, mercifully exempt from the drab technicalities of taxation, must acquire at least a working knowledge of the technicalities of that fascinating and only partly explored field, factory organisation. To produce intelligent costs he must understand not only what is going on in the works but also the reason why, and this knowledge he translates into pictures in money values. His costs will be much more valuable if he builds them up from the factory side rather than waiting to carve up and allocate ledger figures. Though his information as to expense will, to a large extent, be drawn from the financial books, he should work far ahead of them and keep his costs up to date even at the sacrifice of mathematical squaring of cost and ledger accounts. His reconciliation should be such as will demonstrate that the costs and financial books are in harmony, not necessarily in agreement to the penny. If we liken the figures of both departments to the pointers on gauges then we should say that the financial gauge moves spasmodically to its new position while the cost department gauge moves day by day to record the ever changing activities of the factory.

Thirdly, the accountant spends much of his time checking that money has been spent and that the concern has prima facie received benefit. How the benefit is ultimately disposed of is beyond his vision. Stores, for example, pass from the view of the accountant after he has debited their purchase to the correct account. He does not even record their issue. It is one of the curiosities of modern accounting that the important fact of the consumpt of stores is discovered in the accounts by the indirect and somewhat backhand method of finding at the close of the period that the balance in stock is correspondingly less. Even after arriving at this figure it is not uncommon for the accountant to add to the cost of stores consumed the depreciation to market value on the stores remaining in stock, combining these dissimilar charges in a figure which defies analysis. The cost accountant assumes an interest in stores at the point where the financial accountant leaves off and his record of consumpt is immediate. The fact of purchase and even the fact of use matter less to him than how the material has been used and how the concern has derived benefit from it. The financial department checks whether the money has been spent, the onus of consideration being on the buying department, the cost department considers whether the money brings its due share of sales price and profit.

Briefly, then, the financial accountant records what has happened with emphasis on prevention of misappropriation of cash while the cost expert records how and why the happenings have taken place with emphasis on misuse of both material and labour. Each has ample scope in his own field of study, and each by specialisation can contribute in full measure to the greater efficiency of industry.

COST ACCOUNTANCY; ITS CONTRIBUTION TO MANAGEMENT AND EFFICIENCY IN THE FUTURE*

By Roland Dunkerley, F.C.W.A.

Changing times and conditions bring changing demands. This is true in all spheres of life, and in no sphere has this been more markedly exemplified than in the profession of Cost Accountancy.

Retrospect

At the time of the 1914-18 War, the profession was in its infancy. It was a recorder of history, and the use of the information which was provided was largely that of supplementing data on which estimates of prices were based.

The requirements at that time developed into a demand for information on which to fix and control prices and contracts for articles previously not made, and of war supplies generally. This demand called for a new technique in costing, and since there was little information in writing or in book form on which to draw, interchange of experience between individuals was a necessity, and out of this necessity the Institute of Cost and Works Accountants was born.

The industrial problems which arose during that war period focused attention on the essentiality of more scientific management, and the growth of small concerns into larger units made it imperative that management, to be effective, should be supplied with full information regarding every aspect of the Company's affairs.

The mere Balance Sheet and Trading Account were no longer enough, and cost information regarding jobs completed some time previously was not sufficient for its use to be effective.

This growth of the Management function brought demands on the Cost Accountancy section which had considerable influence on its technique, and prior to the present world war there had grown up systems of cost accountancy which gave information on every sphere and activity of a company.

Policies began to be shaped based on fact rather than on conjecture, and its use as a basis for prices became only one of the many uses to which cost information was being put. The necessity for the information to be up to date was imperative.

**Paper given at a series of Public Meetings recently held at Blackburn, Liverpool and Manchester, under the auspices of the local branches of the Institute of Cost and Works Accountants.*

The extension of the use of cost information in shaping the company's policies brought with it the demand for standards to be set up, against which performance could be judged. This in its turn called for the setting up of Standard Costs, and the introduction of Budgetary Control.

Budgetary Control is a system in which Management, having set its target, translates that target into all the phases of the business and then seeks information as to why deviations from the target take place.

These were roughly the stages of development which had taken place between the two wars, and which resulted in the condition which the profession of Cost Accountancy had reached when the present war came and brought with it new problems.

Immediate Past and Present

The lessons which were learnt during the last war, and the attention which had been focused on Cost Accounting in the period following that war, immediately directed official recognition by the Government of its uses and possibilities as soon as any development took place in demands for war materials to be manufactured.

Costing on scientific lines had, in the intervening period between the two wars, been introduced into the Government Ordnance Factories, and information had been accumulated which provided a basis from which contract prices for articles to be made outside could be established.

Concurrently, the development of the use of scientific costing in Municipalities and in Public Utility Companies had also made officialdom more cost-conscious and, therefore, little surprise was occasioned when, immediately the Ministry of Supply was set up, an Accountancy Section and a Cost Accountancy Section was incorporated in its organisation.

In the 1914-18 war there had been in the then Ministry of Munitions a developing Cost Accounting Section which, towards the end of that war, had played quite an effective part in dealing with war contract prices.

The introduction of the present Excess Profits Tax, with its implication that the policy to be followed was—that in the war period no business should benefit from, or improve its financial position out of the war-time demands —was succeeded by the policy that prices should be fixed which had a close relation to the cost of production, plus only a small margin, and once again the searchlight of Cost Accountancy began to be focused on the price-fixing aspect.

Under more normal and leisured conditions this would have automatically brought with it the directing of the Managements' attention to the costs of production and the possibilities of economies. Unfortunately, the times demanded action, and production was forced apace without the normal braking which would have been applied if the costs of production and prices fixed were to be the criterion of the order being placed. In order to meet demands, orders were placed and prices had to be fixed on the basis of what the cost of production actually was in the circumstances in which production was effected. Very little could be done in using the information to see that the methods and costs of production were in line with what the job was ultimately worth.

The fact that many prices had to be fixed without a solid foundation of cost information demanded that clauses be inserted in the contracts to the effect that the prices were subject to cost audit, and a good deal of discontent was caused when adjustment was necessary between the original prices and those which emerged after investigation.

The obvious answer was to fix prices based on facts, and to provide these facts presented a difficult problem.

However, once large-scale production scattered over a number of units had been established, the demand existed for a fixed price to be decided on for the various articles, and that firms should then set themselves to work within those fixed prices. Naturally, the setting up of fixed prices became an outstandingly important matter, and considerable cost investigation was necessary to see that a fair price was established.

These investigations soon proved extremely difficult from the point of view that firms in their costing and accounting methods—where these existed—did not speak the same language, and comparison between firm and firm was shown to be possible only in the totals and not in detail.

It was obvious that uniformity in the setting out of cost information was an absolute necessity if progress was to be made and comparisons made worth while, and there were efforts on all sides to deal with this drawback. Pressure was exerted on the Institute from many quarters to encourage its members towards the setting up of uniform systems of Cost Accounting by industries.

Concurrently with, and as a result of, these cost investigations (*which produced some astonishing facts*) efforts were made to introduce more up-to-date manufacturing methods and more efficient machinery, and to improve production technique generally. This has had some measure of success, and it is hoped that the lessons which have been learnt in war-time production will be translated into peace-time action and form the basis for that efficiency in production which must be the keynote of the future if national prosperity is to continue. Applied Cost Accountancy can provide the necessary information for any effort to improve efficiency and lessen the costs of production.

This necessarily brief survey of the trend of Cost Accountancy during the two wars and in the intervening period, has been made in order that we may see how the lessons and experience of the past might be applied to the future. Summarised, it can be said that the exceptional conditions pertaining during war periods call for special technique to be applied by the Cost Accountancy profession. It is not overstating the case to say that the conditions have been such that the obtaining of production was more important than the cost of production.

It might be true to say that at the present moment we are at the position of having passed through this phase, and are at a stage where much more control is being exercised by the authorities on production itself and on the cost of production, and that more regard is being paid to the fixing of contract prices.

On the other hand, the fact still remains that in a great majority of businesses any savings that are effected only add to the payments against Excess Profits Tax, and this does not encourage that close attention to the cost of production which would pertain in more normal times. It is very likely that the war will end with the outlook of carelessness towards expenses and the cost of production being the most predominant one in the minds of most of those engaged in industry.

THE FUTURE

The present stage of the war has turned the minds of the Government, of the industrialist and of the private citizen, to the question—" What of the future ? "

The word " reconstruction " has been bandied about from many angles. All anticipate a better world, but few seem to realise that this will only be a better world if it is made so, and that co-operation between capital and labour, tolerance and united efforts, and a facing up to the task before us, will be necessary if the much talked of improvement is to be attained.

The huge sums paid out during the war, the attitude towards expenditure and destruction and loss, and the demands for improvements and amenities of all kinds, not least for social security, have led to a considerable amount of loose thinking and loose talking.

So much has been, and is being, said on this matter, that it is not proposed in this paper to discuss the views of any schools of thought in this connection.

Cost Accountancy by its nature deals in facts, not theories, and from a cost accounting angle the future will bring problems for industry which will need all that is best in cost accountancy to aid Management to deal with the situation as it will undoubtedly develop, once the inertia following the war effort has been overcome.

What is this Costing : " this cost," " these costs "—expressions now being used by all sorts of people and cropping up in most unexpected places, especially used by those who would ensure the future ?

" Costs " consist of three simple elements—Material, Labour and Overhead. Wherever expenditure is incurred—that expenditure is " cost." Rightly collected, presented and used, the information provided can help to control all expenditure whether it be of material, men, minutes, machines, methods, or management, and it is universal in its application to all sections of our national life.

The nation has yet to learn what is going to be the effect of being a debtor nation instead of a creditor nation, but it is suggested that the one apparent outstanding fact will be that we shall be dependent in this country largely on our efforts to compete in the world's markets with our manufactured articles, and we must have exports if we are to prosper as a Nation. A Committee of the Federation of British Industries has recently reported that for prosperous national economy visible exports must be increased at least 40 to 50 per cent. over 1939 levels.

This country has only a limited amount of natural resources on which to draw. It will need to fall back on its manufactures, where it has a wealth of experience and craftsmen as its greatest asset, and the initiative which has been shown in the past will need to be developed in the future if we are not to suffer a decline in our position.

Uniform Costing Systems

One of the results of war conditions which has had, and will have, beneficial results, is the getting together of firms who in the past held each other off at arm's length as competitors. This co-operation has proved that the exchange of information regarding methods and processes, the discussion together of fundamental problems, the conversations on prices, etc., have made the industries and the individual firms stronger and not weaker, and the setting up of trade associations in every kind of industry is one of the features which will be carried over into the post-war world.

It is a significant fact that already upwards of 20 trade associations have established, or taken steps to establish, uniform systems of cost accounting, and the necessity for cost accounting systems is now beginning to be advocated from every side.

The Fourteenth Report of the Select Committee on National Expenditure makes special points in this connection. In paragraph 6 they deal specifically with " the necessity for the devising and applying of methods of cost measurement and price regulation," and in paragraph 65 with the benefits of uniform systems for industries.

The very powerful Conference, which met under the ægis of the Nuffield College, in their Report on " Employment, Policy and Organisation of Industry after the War," press, in paragraph 101, for " the setting up of uniform systems of cost accounting as the basis of an assurance of efficiency and of compliance with the requirements of fair and open dealing "; and the Report just issued by the Cotton Board Post-War Committee, on page 55 under the heading of " Costing," states " that a standardised costing system with its definitions generally understood and applied, is urgently needed, and that, even apart from the necessities of price management, will be to the general advantage of the industry."

Another example of this kind is contained in the recently issued post-war report prepared for the Council of Clothing Trade Associations, which advocates the preparation of a Uniform Costing System "in order that full information may be available as a basis for improving efficiency and for forward planning."

The Council of the Institute of Cost and Works Accountants, having seen the trend of these phases, some time ago directed the attention of their Research Committee to the necessity for giving assistance to their members to deal with this important development in the profession, and it is no secret that in a very short time a brochure, dealing with this matter and stating fundamental principles, will be in the hands of Members to assist them in meeting the demands.

The provision of Uniform Costing Systems and the resuscitation of detailed cost systems such as were being built up before the war phase was entered into will, however, not of themselves provide the answers to the question of what needs to be done to meet post-war demands. They are only a means to an end. Managements must apply the measures they indicate as being needed.

Problems of Management

There seems to be a general impression that the immediate post-armistice period will provide such a demand for goods that the problems arising in industry will be largely those of labour and raw material to meet them. If this is so, it will be an era which is mainly a continuation of the present-day war condition of production at any price, with its resultant dangers.

That the period will bring its own problems there can be no doubt, because the re-establishment of business, the changing over from war to peace-time productions, the re-opening of closed works, the absorption of returning personnel from the Forces, the difficulties of obtaining sources of supply for raw materials, and many other allied difficulties, will naturally bring their own specific problems for managements: but what of the period after this somewhat artificial phase is over ?

As has already been said, as an exporting country we will need to take our place as a competitor in the world's markets to meet the world's demands. Under war conditions many countries, hitherto suppliers of natural products only, have perforce had to set up their own manufacture. People have been taught to do without articles previously regarded as necessities ; they have been forced to use substitutes which may lay the foundation for complete changes of fashion, and unless there is a very great change in mental outlook there is going to be an extension of intense nationalism—especially in countries which have suffered—and a desire to be more self-contained and self-supporting than the pre-war world provided. Many are the remedies that are advocated to overcome these international problems, but fundamentally there will always be a desire to purchase goods in the best and cheapest markets, and as a manufacturing nation we must face up to this fact.

The problem facing Management, therefore, will be how we are to compete, and the only way of overcoming the disadvantage of higher wages, greater social amenities, and the maintenance of a high standard of living, against the effects of the lower wage standard countries who have now become manufacturing-minded, is by initiative and efficiency.

Capital Control

Almost every post-war reconstruction plan includes wide and varied proposals for the outlay of capital expenditure. The sums involved in the aggregate will be tremendous.

Large and small factory units will be affected, and problems arising out of the utilization of premises now used for munitions, housing estates to be within reach of industrial centres, and the provision of welfare centres, canteens and other amenities—quite apart from the expenditure within the factory itself—will be amongst the many items which will need to be dealt with. Future costs of production will have to provide for this expenditure, and all the skill and training of the Cost Accountant will need to be brought into play to assist in dealing with the many problems involved.

This question of Capital is bound to be an important one in the future, and in addition to the capital which will be locked up in fixed assets, there will remain the necessity for sufficient liquid capital being available to carry on the day-to-day business of the Company. This must be kept circulating if the necessity for uneconomic and costly overdrafts is to be avoided. Efficient cost accounting systems provide for the control of raw materials and stocks, for knowledge as to the position of jobs or material in process of manufacture, for indications of completed work awaiting delivery or accumulating finished stocks. To be forewarned is to be forearmed, and information as to approaching dangers of reduced bank balances or increasing overdrafts will avoid many crises.

Cost Accountancy will indeed need once again to concentrate its function as an aid to Management. It will perforce need to double its critical analysis of all expenses—in fact, of all forms of expenditure—and for this purpose the resuscitation of the method of setting up standards will require to be in the forefront, if the criticism is to be effective and useful in the hands of those who control. The establishment of Standard Costs is a very necessary part of modern costing systems.

Factory Efficiency Assessment

One of the post-war problems to be tackled will be that of the correct assessment of labour effort, in order that wages may be paid commensurate with the skill and effort which are required. Whilst numerous changes in manufacturing technique have taken place, and mills and workshops have been revolutionised in many ways, wages still continue to be paid on lists which are obsolete due to the changes which have been effected since they were originated. Many anomalies are apparent, and much dissatisfaction is being engendered as a result.

Management itself is also desirous of having some measuring stick which is not a changing one. "Time" and "weight" are solid bases which do not change with fashion demands, commodity prices, and sizes of articles, all of which influence the output of a factory. What is required is a unit of measurement of effort which will apply so as to give the Management a guide as to whether the output to-day is in line with what it was yesterday, even though there may be a different class of manufacture within the factory.

There is a very great field for investigation into the possibilities of some basic formula which will alike guide Management in its desire to judge its factory efficiency, and at the same time will be a foundation on which a formula for the reward of labour effort can be satisfactorily based, which will obviate a great deal of the friction which present systems generate.

Marginal Costing

It is possible that sooner or later circumstances will arise when work is desired to fill the factory and the old question will face the Management as to the price at which it will be economic to obtain it. The development of Marginal Costing was the outcome of previous questions of this type. Marginal Costing has been defined as "a development of costing which by differentiating between fixed and variable costs facilitates the true assessment of the effect on profit of changes in volume of output." In other words, what extra cost would be involved to produce this additional volume or unit over and above normal costs and expenses ? There is considerable scope in this field for perfection in the technique of Marginal Costing by Cost Accountants and for the use of the information by Management in tackling these problems.

Budgetary Costing

Years ago it used to be said that "costing concerned that which had happened": at a later period it became "that which was happening at the moment," and then just pre-war it was asked to indicate "that which was going to happen." The implementing of this last phase was being developed under a system which, as already mentioned, was termed Budgetary Control.

The profession will need to get back to the principles of Budgetary Control, where the Management policy is dissected into all the different sides of the business, and systems of cost accountancy are devised to show where the desired ends have been attained, and to trace the cause of failure where they have *not* been attained.

Management

It will be necessary, if success in a business is to be attained, to see that :—

The right and most economic material is being used, that it is of the right quality and purchased at the right price, and that it is effectively used to prevent waste ;

Effective stock control systems are inaugurated and stocks watched ;

The right class of labour is employed and is giving a fair return for the wages paid ;

The right type of machinery is used and the shop layout is correct to ensure a minimum of handling ;

Efficiency studies of the methods of production are undertaken to prevent waste in effort ;

The work is planned to ensure that time is not lost and that work in progress is not accumulating and locking up much wanted capital ;

The cost of services such as Rents, Water, Gas, Electricity—and even Bank and Insurance charges—are within reasonable bounds ;

Maintenance outlays are in line with the requirements and demands made on them ;

The expenses of selling and distribution—which include such items as Advertising and Sales Promotion—are in proportion to the services which they render; in this connection the Institute in 1940 issued a brochure on the problem of "Selling and Distribution Cost Accounting" which is commended to every Cost Accountant or executive interested in this function;

and last but not least, that the function performed by Management is efficient.

It is suggested that in the past not enough stress has been laid on the necessity for efficient management. Management to-day is an art or a profession, and not a heritage.

There has in recent years been much more attention focused on this part of the organisation of industry, and proposals have been made that one of the changes in our post-war structure shall be provision for an audit of management. There can be no better lead on this than can be obtained through the uses of efficient cost accounting systems.

Labour and Management

Another development with which the future seems to be charged is the much larger part which labour will play in the future, in control of industry than in the past. Even in the present-day organisation there is no question that a good many of the disputes, strikes and frictions with labour could, and would, be avoided, if more information was available to enable them to see whether their demands were prejudicial to the business and industry as a whole, as against their immediate personal gain. The suggestion that labour may take its place as part of the councils of the management postulates the provision of information in the form that labour understands and can readily assimilate. Trading Accounts will need to be more departmentalised and detailed than is the present practice. Managerial policies will need to be translated into detailed results, and finance will require to take its place only as one of the factors governing the business, and not as the predominant factor which has hitherto been the most general practice.

Conclusion

The future, and the problems it envisages, will undoubtedly call for a great deal of change, a great deal of initiative, a drive for efficiency within industry from the top to the bottom, and managements will be called on to make many vital decisions. No longer can these decisions be matters of opinion or conjecture. If results are to be obtained they must be based on fact; and the basis of scientific cost accounting is the provision of facts with comment giving the indications and trends which the figures portend. They must be translated into such a form and presented in such a way as to ensure the co-operation of every executive within the organisation in whatever sphere of influence he is placed, if they are to be the driving force that is envisaged.

The profession of Cost Accountancy has passed through many phases, as has been indicated. To-day it is past the stage where it needs to direct attention to its possibilities; on every hand there are indications of a growing demand for its services. It has an opportunity to render to industry a service which can be of untold benefit. It can place in the hands of Management a weapon which Management can wield for the future well-being of industry, and of the nation generally, and the Institute of Cost and Works Accountants has among its membership trained and experienced men who can, and will, play their part in the struggle that is before us.

MORE ABOUT THE INDUSTRIAL ACCOUNTANT

by Basil Smallpeice, A.C.A.

I am very glad to have the opportunity, and the privilege, of speaking to you to-day about the industrial accountant. Not that I want to inflict upon you a tedious repetition of what I said on this subject in London, and which has since appeared in print for all, who cared, to read; but I should like to try to explain why I regard it as a matter of some importance that the professional standing of the industrial accountant should be recognised both inside and outside the profession.

It will not have passed unnoticed that during the last fifteen months two of the most eminent industrial members of the Institute have been appointed to the Council of that body; and I think I speak for all of us in industry when I say that that is a matter which has given us the very greatest satisfaction. But I am anxious lest it should come to be thought, by industrial and practising accountants alike, that an organisational measure like the granting of seats on the Councils of our two bodies is all that needs to be done about the relations between the two branches of the profession. There are other things to be done; and especially in the direction of promoting a greater degree of understanding between them.

PROFESSIONAL RESPONSIBILITIES OF MEMBERS IN INDUSTRY

One particular field in which more understanding is required is this question of the professional status and responsibilities of members in industry. The industrial member, for his part, needs to understand why it is important that, whatever his own wishes in the matter, he should regard his work not merely as a commercial appointment but as having certain professional responsibilities attached to it; while on the other hand, the practising member needs to understand a little of what it means to the industrial accountant so to regard his work.

Now, why should the industrial accountant regard his job as professional in character? One answer is quite clear. Accountancy is a profession. The Institute and the Society are professional bodies. And if the industrial accountant remains a member of either of them, and some of his number are given seats on their governing bodies, he should be prepared, and indeed be able, to share the privilege of being professional and to shoulder the responsibilities that go with it.

Putting it at its lowest, the industrial accountant has to avoid doing anything that would endanger, or detract from, the professional standing of those in practice as public accountants. That is an obvious and elementary requirement. After all, it means a great deal to those in practice to be members of an honoured profession. It is not only that it is their means of livelihood. It goes very much deeper than that. It confers upon them a dignity and a prestige in society that count for much; and although the accountancy profession is no more than sixty or seventy years old, yet in that short time it has come to play an important and vital part in the economic life of the community and to be highly esteemed on all sides—a reputation which all practising members share, just as they all help to maintain and improve it by the way in which they carry out the tasks imposed upon them by society. That being so, the industrial member is in duty bound to prove that he merits professional status as well as the public accountants, and that he carries as much responsibility towards his calling as they do—a different kind of responsibility, perhaps, and exercised in a different sphere, but still a responsibility.

What, then, are these professional responsibilities that the industrial accountant carries? Those of you who are public accountants may find it difficult to imagine that there can be any at all. You can imagine, and are familiar with, standards of rectitude in your relations with your clients. But, you may wonder, how can the industrial accountant possibly carry any responsibility that is at all comparable with that which you are called upon to carry? After all, the very fact that you are in private practice means that you are liable to be sued for damages if you or your employees can be shown to be guilty of negligence in the

The greater part of an address delivered to the Liverpool Chartered and Incorporated Accountants on 23rd January, 1945.

performance of duties laid upon you by statute or otherwise. In some cases, that may mean a serious financial liability. There is nothing comparable to that, you may say, in the case of the industrial accountant. Then again, you are liable, as we are not, to sudden loss of audits, if on grounds of professional integrity you find yourselves unable to sign an audit report, or are able to sign it only with qualification. In some cases, where a major audit is involved, or where a group of minor audits are all influenced by the same client, this, too, may have severe financial repercussions on the public accountant concerned. Here, again, there is nothing comparable in the case of the industrial accountant.

I grant all that. But there is more to be said. The industrial accountant, who is a member of the Institute or the Society, is not concerned—or should not be—merely with doing a job to the satisfaction of his employers. He is also—or should be—even more concerned with doing that job in accordance with certain standards of professional integrity.

Now in many cases there may be no conflict at all between the satisfaction of his employers and those professional standards, just as in many cases there is no conflict between the wishes of the auditors and the view of the directors. If an industrial accountant, for example, were employed by an old-established company with a national or international prestige to maintain, that company could not afford—nor, indeed, would it want—to do anything contrary to the highest standards of professional practice; and the industrial accountant concerned would be in an enviable position.

Taking a Stand

There are others not so fortunate. Let me recount a few instances of conflict that have come to my knowledge in recent years. Perhaps I should mention that, in what follows, I am not drawing on my own personal experience—for I have been, and am, particularly fortunate in the companies I have worked for. But these experiences are authentic, for all that they are not my own. They may not occur every day of the week, nor to everybody; but they do occur, and one never knows when one may suddenly be confronted with a situation of the kind I am about to describe.

One case had to do with income-tax. You are all familiar with the rules governing the return of round-figure expense allowances. On this occasion the accountant concerned was required—or would have been, had he consented to it—to be party to a subterfuge which would enable payments to a director of an allowance for imaginary expenses to resemble payments for actual expenses, so as to avoid the necessity for the company secretary returning them and for the director subsequently to try to justify them to the tax authorities.

Another case arose over the presentation of costs to a Government investigating accountant. The industrial accountant concerned was instructed by his employers to load his cost figures far more than could conceivably be justified on the facts of the case, with a view to minimising the amount of the reduction in the contract price.

Another instance arose when a Chartered Accountant took over the accounts of a group of companies with international ramifications. His predecessor had been in the habit of so manipulating the charges between the various companies that the results shown by their accounts bore no direct relation to the facts of the case nor to their operating efficiency, but were in fact governed solely by considerations of tax advantage. The effectiveness of management was being judged on figures that were nothing if not grossly misleading. But when the Chartered Accountant came upon the scene, he insisted that the accounts should in the first instance show the real trading results, and that tax considerations should be relegated to the background.

Then there was a case connected with stock valuation—this case arose when an incoming Chartered Accountant superseded an unqualified accountant. The latter, with his weather eye on the tax position, had been in the habit of exercising, shall I say, an almost unlimited amount of discretion in the valuation of stock-in-trade, with the result, again, that the accounts did not reflect the true trend of results. Everybody was being misled. This practice the Chartered Accountant absolutely refused to continue, and only got his way in the end by refusing himself to sign, or to let the firm sign as long as he was employed by them, the usual Revenue certificate as to the basis of stock valuation.

Difficulties of Isolation

Now, these cases, you may think, do not amount to very much; and in three out of the four I have quoted, the industrial accountant had his way. But even where he gets his way, it is sometimes at the cost of a considerable strain on his relations with his employers. And remember that he is not in the fortunate position of an auditor who can withdraw to his practice for a year, till another audit comes round, when with any luck that little contretemps will have been forgotten. The industrial accountant has to work with his directors day in and day out, and apart from exceptional circumstances cannot escape the shadow of such a conflict. In such circumstances, there may often be no reasonable alternative for him but to resign his post. Nor should it be imagined that it is any light matter for him to do so. It is not always, or even often, a matter of just walking from one job into another. Big jobs are no easier to come by than big audits.

So, you see, the industrial accountant who takes his professional responsibilities seriously may find, if he is unlucky, that he has much to lose by his attitude. He has not the legal liabilities of the public accountant, I admit, but the decision to resign from a lucrative post, on which his whole livelihood depends, may be much more serious for him than the loss of a single audit. Yet if, in spite of that, he is ready to persist in that attitude, can it be doubted that he is as much concerned as the public accountant, though in a different way, for the honour, integrity and independence of their common profession?

The peculiar difficulty that exists in the case of the industrial accountant is that his very isolation from his parent body renders him liable to pressure, to which weaker minds may sometimes succumb. But it is precisely in such a matter as this—that is to say, in helping him to withstand this kind of pressure—that so much can be achieved through a better understanding on all sides of what is involved. For if the industrial accountant could look to his Institute, or to his Society, for moral support—if he could find there example and understanding, and perhaps advice and encouragement from other industrial accountants whose voices were heard in the government of the whole profession—then I am sure that the chances of him being weak and yielding to pressure would be considerably lessened.

Now, up to this point we have been considering the significance within the profession itself of the professional standing of the industrial accountant. I have attempted to show that many industrial accountants are in fact actuated by a very keen sense of professional responsibility for the integrity of the techniques in which they are expert.

Social Significance of Professional Loyalties

So much for that. I now want to pass on to consider the significance of that professional status outside the profession, in society as a whole. At first sight it may seem to be no more than a domestic affair, affecting only ourselves. But it has a considerable potential significance in society. For this responsibility to professional standards, which may prove on occasion to be in conflict with the supposed interests or immediate wishes of employers, introduces a new factor into the realm of business management. With that factor in operation, the employers' authority is no longer absolute; it becomes subject, in greater or less degree, to an external authority of professional standards. Thus there is introduced into the pyramid-like structure of industrial organisation, with its lines of authority and control running from the apex at the top of each unit down through various levels of the hierarchy till they reach the rank and file on its base—there is introduced into this pyramid-like structure, an invisible line of authority cutting horizontally across all these visible lines that run from top to bottom.

I do not know whether this is the kind of thing Sir Stafford Cripps had in mind when he said, a month or two back, that management ought to become a profession. But whether he had it in mind, or was only concerned with the necessity for adequate training and preparation of those committed with the task of industrial management, the fact remains that partial allegiance to an external authority is an inevitable result of the recognition of professional standards in management. And the industrial accountant, let us not forget, is part and parcel of the management structure of industry. So that, if we uphold the view I have been putting forward that the industrial accountant is a professional person with professional responsibilities, we are also encouraging the growth of an external authority of ideas and ideals, cutting across the traditional up-and-down lines of authority in industry.

But although this is something new in the realm of business management, it is not entirely without precedent or analogy. In the field of army organisation, we are quite familiar with the practice of having functional specialists, like signal officers or medical officers, subject to their brigade or battalion commanders for operational orders and for what is called 'rations and discipline', but in respect of their technical performance responsible only to their seniors in the Royal Corps of Signals or the R.A.M.C. at divisional headquarters. Moreover, that organisational feature has its counterpart in industry itself. In large or medium-sized businesses, the accountants attached to local branches or companies are subject to local management for operational orders and for 'rations and discipline', to use the army expressions once more, but are at the same time responsible directly to the chief accountant at headquarters (by whatever name he is called) for their accounting methods, technique and performance.

This kind of dual allegiance is not, therefore, unknown. But the examples I have just quoted are perhaps not strictly analogous, because they are concerned with responsibility to, and the authority of, persons; whereas what we are now considering in the case of the accounting profession is an external authority of ideas and professional standards. Even here, though, precedents may be found. Take the case of a qualified engineer employed in industry. No one would dream of assuming the right to instruct him to install a lift or a piece of machinery in such a way that it was unsafe, nor of questioning his judgment on the matter. His technical authority in that field is regarded as absolute; and the engineer himself, in asserting his technical authority, relies not merely on his own judgment, but also, and perhaps mainly, on the accumulated knowledge and combined experience of the whole engineering profession. So that we do in fact know the kind of thing that is meant when we talk of an external authority of professional standards, and have, perhaps unknowingly, had some experience of it.

Growing Centralisation of Power

Now, is it good, from the point of view of society as a whole, that there should be this interference with the right of an employer to expect the unquestioning obedience of his employees? Is it good that these new centres of power and authority should be brought into existence? I do not think that we can avoid the necessity for asking ourselves these questions; nor for finding a convincing and satisfactory answer to them. If we are a profession in the true sense of the word, we ought always to be mindful of the effect of our actions and policies on the health and structure of society; we ought not just to let things take their course, and hope for the best.

In looking for an answer, we must, I think, try to see the matter against the background of recent trends in industrial and social organisation. During the last half-century the whole trend of development has been towards more and more centralisation. This has not been due to the mere whim of man, but has been forced upon us by the achievements of science. A hundred years ago, centralisation as it exists to-day would have been technically impossible. But the invention of the telephone and wireless, the development of rapid transport by rail, sea and air—to mention only a few of man's recent accomplishments—has changed all that. And in addition we are learning the art of the scientific management of large numbers of men and women. Centralisation is now a technical possibility; and, having become possible, it has also become inevitable, because the smaller organisation is usually at a disadvantage compared with the larger.

I have no time, I am afraid, to do more than touch upon these developments, but they have been analysed in considerable detail by Dr. Karl Mannheim in his book 'Man and Society in an Age of Reconstruction'. The point is that we now find ourselves in a situation in which more and more power is being concentrated into the hands of fewer and fewer people. It is an age of large-scale organisation, brought about by technical causes. The many can be controlled by the few more effectively than ever before.

Moreover, the situation is not static. On account, again, of technical accomplishments, but also, on this occasion, to overcome social evils of industrial maladjustment, the tendency to centralised power will be carried yet further. If the recent report of the F.B.I. committee (presided over by Sir Charles Bruce-Gardner, now appointed by the Government as Chief Executive for Industrial Reconversion) can be taken as a guide, we are likely to witness an increase in the scope and authority of trade associations. Thus the pyramids of authority within firms, already large and broad based in many cases, may well come to be linked together, trade by trade, into yet larger pyramids of authority within trade groups—and so on.

However, whatever the future has in store for us, the fact that these concentrations of power already exist in modern society cannot be seriously disputed. Nor can it be denied that their presence carries with it an obvious threat to the freedom of the individual and to the area of his personal responsibility.

How are we to deal with the dangers brought to the fore by these concentrations of economic power? We cannot undo them, and go back to where we were before they came about, for they are an inevitable consequence of man's scientific accomplishments.

Need for New Checks and Balances

Now, on this question, Dr. Peter Drucker has much of interest to say in a book called 'The Future of Industrial Man'. Putting it very briefly, he argues that for freedom to survive in a highly organised industrial society—as, indeed, in any other form of society—there must never be one sole centre of power; for any centre of power will become tyrannical unless it is limited and checked by one or more competing centres of power.

History, of course, has many lessons to reinforce this point. European history in particular, as Mr. Christopher Dawson is constantly reminding us, shows that the breaking-down of power into a number of competing centres has been the source, basis, guarantee and bulwark of individual freedom in western civilisation.

It seems to me, then, that if we were to encourage the growth throughout industry of an external allegiance to professional standards, we should be helping to bring about this very tension between competing centres of power which has proved so essential an element in the growth of European culture. Confirmation of this view comes from Mr. Dawson's book, 'The Judgement of the Nations'. 'It is only,' he says, 'by strengthening the element of vocation . . . that these evils—the exploitation of the weak by the strong, and the many by the few—can be avoided. It was the strength of the English political system in the past, that in spite of its spirit of class privilege it did regard politics as a form of public service and not as an opportunity to share out the spoils of power, and that this attitude set the tone of the public services and the professions so that a high standard of personal integrity and responsibility was taken for granted.' It is therefore 'easy for the English to accept the idea of social duty and disinterested service with a sense of personal responsibility. If this spirit can be applied to the new conditions of mass society it is conceivable that a planned society might be created without the destruction of freedom'.

To conclude, then, it seems to me that the building up of professional standards and loyalties for those actually engaged within the framework of industry is not merely a matter of meddlesome interference with authority. The introduction of these new horizontal allegiances cutting across the normal vertical lines of control in industrial organisation is much more than that; it is helping to build up the organic texture of a living community.

We have always to bear in mind that the nineteenth century method of preserving freedom through a multitude of small units freely competing with one another is no longer possible in the twentieth century; technical developments have seen to that. In different circumstances we have to rely on different methods. This is an age in which, to quote Dr. Drucker, 'mass production in large units is the representative social form of our society'. And I want to suggest to you that, in such an age, the fostering of a professional consciousness in the various branches of industrial management, of which industrial accountancy is one, may well be an essential bulwark of freedom which we neglect at our peril. (Prev. Ref., p. 87.)

ECONOMICS AND COSTING

by 'Econacon'

There are numerous definitions of economic theory, but, however defined, few will disagree that it is essentially a study of efficiency, concerned with the achievement of the best results from the use of and choice between limited resources available. In scope it embraces industries, nations and the world. It becomes of special interest to the cost accountant when it deals with factories and firms.

Everybody employed in a factory is an 'economist'. The unskilled operative wishes to produce the highest output from the machine and material with which he is provided in order to obtain the best bonus. The planning department considers how to fulfil the order most efficiently from the machinery and labour that may be free at the time, from the material available or readily obtainable and from standard parts already in existence or easily adaptable. The progress chaser, concerned with the position of the orders in the shops, ready to urge any operation that may be in arrear, to suggest alternative machines or methods should difficulties arise, is, armed with his scale of preferences, which he calls precedence lists, essentially an economist. Every employee is such because, within the area of his responsibility, he is determined to get the best result that the resources at his disposition permit.

The cost accountant is also concerned with efficiency. Because his task is to mirror in figures the happenings in the works, he can occupy a vital position in any concern. Who is better qualified to advise a firm regarding the disposition of its resources than the cost accountant who is so intimately acquainted with them?

Since economics and cost accounting are both studies of efficiency, it would appear incorrect to create any chasm between them. It cannot be said, for example, that the question whether interest on capital should be included in cost relates to economics not to costing. The same theory of cost must obtain for cost accounting as for economics.

The writer hastens to say that he holds no special brief for present-day economic theory. Frequently economists, in their theorising, soar into realms which no mortal can reach. If the late Lord Stamp, in a denunciation which has become historic, condemned accountants because they had made no contribution to economic thought, economists can equally be charged with having made little contribution to accounting thought. Nevertheless, the writer believes that there are numerous concepts in economics which the cost accountant can borrow with profit, although he may desire to modify them in the light of his practical experience.

The first question that the cost accountant must answer is 'For whom is he costing?' Is he formulating principles in order to help large concerns or small concerns, huge monopolies or struggling businesses, firms making profits or firms suffering losses? From the standard text-books it seems that costing caters principally for large concerns, or at least for well-established businesses, for whose products there is a steady demand and an assured profit. This may be inferred from the figures given in examples, the types of businesses dealt with and also because many text-books end with a chapter or section showing how the principles outlined can be applied to small concerns.

What is the position in fact? Statistics issued before the war by the Chief Inspector of Factories showed that this was predominantly a country of small factories and that the small factories together employed more workpeople than the large. Any principles that the cost accountant may formulate in order to assist management should apply equally to the small concern as to the large. Such principles should be of general not local application.

In this respect economics can help the cost accountant immediately. The economist has a concept called 'the representative firm' which he uses as a basis for theories. The 'representative firm' is not small and it is not large. It is an average firm with a moderate goodwill, making profits, but, because it is perpetually subject to the rude buffets of the market, it must maintain its efficiency to continue to exist.

If we decide that the cost accountant must cost for the 'representative firm', we must next consider what methods he should employ. Job costing, unit costing, multiple costing, class costing and the like should not be regarded as different methods since the principles are the same in each case. At present there are only two methods of costing—actual costing, which deals with the money outlays which have arisen in respect of goods already produced, and standard costing, which deals with predetermined costs and gives short-cut methods of arriving at such money outlays.

The economist has carefully considered the question of method. While both inductive and deductive methods must be employed (and the two cannot finally be separated), it is believed by many that progress in economic thought can only be made by reasoning largely deductive in character. The cost accountant would, however, appear to be principally occupied with the inductive method because of his concentration on statistics of past events and his efforts to derive trends therefrom. He should consider whether deductive methods cannot help him. It is significant that all text-books stress the danger of preparing statistics which may never be used by management.

As far as the representative firm is concerned, it is very doubtful whether accumulations of statistical data can be of much assistance. For the 'representative firm' the situation is constantly changing because of the vicissitudes of the market. While it will be earning profits, it must fight to retain and increase them. It has no time to look back because it must always look ahead.

If it is agreed that statistical data will not be of much help to the 'representative firm', the concept of 'normal cost' derived from such data may also be questioned. While the economist is also concerned with normal cost (and appears indeed to have formulated the concept of the 'representative firm' to enable him to understand its long-period operation), the cost accountant will, in the light of his practical experience, consider whether figures of normal cost are of aid to management. There would not appear much that could be classed as normal in the day-to-day life of the 'representative firm'. For it, all change is normal because change is a permanent feature of business. Cost, however defined, must relate to the period and the circumstances in which it arises and that concludes the matter.

As soon as the concept of normal cost in regard to the representative firm is questioned, the cost accountant will not hurry to write off to profit and loss account items which he considers 'abnormal', including items relating to idle capacity. He can only mystify management if he presents it with figures of cost, asking it to remember diverse items which have been excluded on diverse grounds. From this point of view the dangerous divorce which has developed between cost and financial accounting breaks down. There are numerous elements in the financial accounts which influence policy, although the cost accountant ignores them in his costings. Amplify the financial accounts certainly by cost statements, but to ignore them completely can have serious repercussions.

The objection to writing off different items to profit and loss does not mean that items should never be excluded from cost. Where, however, items are excluded from the cost of a job or group of products, care should be taken to include them in the costing of another job or group. They should not be lost forever in the profit and loss account. Different considerations apply, and these are discussed later, when in a period of depression the firm's products are sold just above variable cost in order to minimise losses. Proportions of cost will then inevitably be written off to profit and loss account.

It is not proposed to enter into a detailed consideration of the economist's notion of cost. The idea that cost of production determines price has, however, been rejected. Price is not a policy, as so many cost accountants state, it is decided in the market by supply and demand. While the representative business man may influence the market in a small way, its control over him is infinitely greater.

If this is so, the cost accountant must seriously question whether his procedure can interest the business man. Although the cost accountant may admit that price is determined by supply and demand, the paramount assumption, the inarticulate premise, that underlies the argument in the text-books is that after cost has been computed, the business man has merely to add his profit and sell his goods at the figure so arrived at. This, of course, corresponds in no way with the facts of business and probably goes a long way in explaining why many business men are not interested in costing systems.

The writer asserts that the cost accountant has not dealt, in accordance with the facts of business life, with the problem that has received most thought and attention in costing, viz., that of the allocation of overheads. The method of the percentage addition has been largely rejected. Overheads are now allocated to 'production centres' on a spatial basis and then attributed to the jobs performed on a time basis. Such a procedure may be of assistance to a well-established business with an assured market, since it will have the certain knowledge that losses cannot be suffered and profits must be earned if the goods are sold. The writer doubts, however, whether such a concern will be helped to earn the highest profits by this method or whether it is of great assistance to the representative business man.

The representative business man is fighting to keep his place in an oscillating and highly competitive market. His preoccupation is to balance alternatives, and, in balancing alternatives, he will recklessly ignore items of fixed cost on some jobs, hoping to recoup these fixed costs from other jobs showing a high rate of profit. Particularly in regard to depreciation will this be the case. He will be more concerned to save money from profits to make replacements in the future than with the arithmetical depreciation of items purchased in the past. In his day-to-day policy he may largely ignore such replacements if their need is remote.

The notion that the cost of an article can be arbitrarily abstracted from the production of a factory is itself suspect. Economics teaches that costs are relative, not absolute. This is why, when dealing with seasonal industries, the cost accountant does not hesitate to telescope the bulk of the fixed costs of the year into the busy period. Only by regarding costs as relative can he cost joint products when a small quantity of one sells for the rest together. Space-time methods of overhead allocation would seem to be useless when dealing with primary and secondary products. In these circumstances cost ceases to be a fact, as so many accountants aver, and becomes very much a matter of opinion.

Economists have devoted considerable thought to the problem of marginal increments of cost. It is true, as the cost accountant says, that in a period of depression the business man can reduce his losses by selling at a price just above direct labour, direct material and variable expense, ignoring fixed expense. But if the market will not take the goods at such a reduced price, has the cost accountant paused to consider whether a still lower price can be quoted with the same object of reducing losses, although in a smaller degree?

In the writer's view the classification of cost into direct material, direct labour and fixed and variable overheads must for this purpose be abandoned. Such a classification is in any case one of convenience, since overheads contain both material and labour. The correct classification would seem to be merely that of fixed costs and variable costs. Fixed costs can include direct labour because, in a period of depression, labour will be kept on in any case for the more prosperous times. To reduce its losses the firm can quote just above its additional cost, i.e. variable cost and this might be *below* the total of direct labour, direct material and variable overheads. Naturally quotations above direct labour, direct material and variable overheads will reduce losses still further and neither policy can be pursued indefinitely.

The writer believes that cost accounting has not yet discarded the crinoline. If it is asserted that the cost accountant has been of considerable assistance to government and to industry, the former would seem to have derived greater benefit than the latter since the business man avoids contracts with costing clauses like the plague, and prefers 'fixed-price' contracts. In a democracy in which the encroachments of bureaucracy are being continually questioned, it is astonishing that the activities of the costing departments of the different Ministries remain unchallenged. No settled body of costing principles appears to have been asked for or issued. Disallowances are made entirely at the whim of the Ministries who, if they are consistent, are only so as a matter of favour not of law. There is a crying need for the substitution of law for discretion.

THE INDIVISIBILITY OF ACCOUNTANCY

By E. F. Brown, F.C.W.A.

(Being the substance of papers read recently to the Edinburgh and Manchester Branches of the Institute.)

What is " Accountancy " ?

It is symptomatic of the loose thinking which accompanies the glib use of the term that no one to whom I have put this question, has given any workable definition. It is a striking indictment that a search through authoritative works of reference and text books fails to produce any better definition of accountancy than " . . . . the art practised by an accountant."

Almost alone in attempts at definition is that to be found in the terminology published by the Institute of Cost and Works Accountants in 1937, viz., " The process of analysing, classifying and recording transactions and operations in terms of time, quantity or money " —an effort which lacks force but is not without merit.

May I then try to express what accountancy means to me.

Accountancy, I believe, *is the art of expressing in terms of value, the observable physical phenomena of a business ; it is a mirror which reflects both the movement of money or money's worth and the static situation of invested money at moments in time ; it is both dynamics and statics ; its traditional mechanism is double-entry book-keeping.*

Every facet of business is a phenomenon which is manifest in a money valuation, and only by expression in terms of money is it made recognisable and intelligible. Unfortunately, " accountancy " has come to be regarded as synonymous with the incongruities popularly called the " final accounts " of a business, a typical form of which is given below :—

MANUFACTURING ACCOUNT

To Stock	By Sales
,, Purchases	,, Stock
,, Manufacturing Wages	
,, Electric Power	
,, Rent and Rates	
,, Profit carried to P. & L. a/c.	

PROFIT AND LOSS A/C

To Office Salaries	By Profit b/d.
,, Office Expenses	
,, Advertising	
,, Carriage Outwards	
,, Directors' Fees	
,, Bad Debts	
,, Depreciation	
,, Balance carried down.	

BALANCE SHEET

Liabilities.	*Assets.*
Issued Capital	Buildings
Sundry Creditors	Plant
Reserves	Fixtures and Fittings
P. & L. a/c.	Stock
	Sundry Debtors
	Cash.

This, or something like it, is what orthodox accounts throw up. It has masqueraded as Accountancy for too long. The manufacturing account commences on the left-hand side with the addition of opening stock, material purchases, wages and *certain* expenses. When these have been set against the summation of sales and closing stock, a figure known as Gross Profit is thrown up which is subsequently transferred to the Profit and Loss Account in order that it may suffer there the deduction of further expenditures. The ultimate residue is called Net Profit.

These fictions do not represent anything which physically happens in the operation of a business. Consider the physical properties of " Opening Stock." It is raw material ; it is work-in-progress ; it is finished goods ; it is direct material ; it is direct labour ; it is indirect cost. It is all things in all places. But there is no physical combination of " purchases " with these things—not, at any rate, in toto. Are there not movements in and out of store ? " Purchases " is the sum of expenditures of different natures, some direct and some indirect.

Then again, are " manufacturing wages " conjoined in toto with " purchases ? " Are there not " direct wages " which form a union only with such purchases as are issued from store ; and are there not " indirect wages " which only unite with Direct Costs as the physical conversion of materials proceeds ?

Why then add all these things together—and, confusion added to confusion—why embellish the concoction with the addition of a few choice expenses such as " Electricity " or " Rates." How many lemons have we if we add apples to oranges ?

Strangest of all is the unnatural wedding of " Sales " with " Closing Stock," on the right-hand side.

If accountancy is to mean anything at all its job is to trace the physical movements of cost in the labyrinthine stages of manufacture and selling. Debits and credits will express motion, and balances will express the static physical situations in the manufacturing shops and warehouses of the company.

Now the techniques which, collectively, have become known as " *Cost Accountancy* " do mould themselves to all these movements of cost, and to changes in the physical nature of production. Cost Accountancy seeks at every stage to throw up figures which reflect the physical life of the business. When material is bought, for instance, it is either physically placed in a store or, alternatively, sent straight away to a producing department. The Cost Accounts, accordingly, reveal either a debit to a store account or a debit to a work-in-progress account. Wages, when paid, immediately shake off their identity as remuneration for labour and become either a debit to the direct labour content of a work-in-progress account or a debit to an account which represents the performance of some indirect function.

The so-called " Final " accounts of orthodox accountancy seem to be sadly misnamed, for they express these expenditures in their " initial " forms before industrial metamorphosis ensues. It may be claimed that the display of expenditure in its primary forms, as traditionally shown in the Trading and Profit and Loss Accounts, is valuable figuring. It is good statistics but it is not accountancy. The extraction of such data from primary accounts may provide useful control data, but as accountancy, it has no meaning.

Now if we develop our accountancy so that it reflects continuously what is really happening in the factory, we shall produce as " Final " accounts that which the Cost Accountant has grown accustomed to calling a " Sales and Cost-of-Sales Account." The statistical data which comprises the traditional Trading Account or Profit and Loss Account has not been lost ; it exists in primary control accounts and if desired, a comparative statement may be annually prepared. Certainly, a " Purchases " account will exist ; certainly a " Wages " account will exist ; likewise a " Salaries " account, and indeed, accounts for every primary classification of expense, but just as these expenditures are physically dispersed—broken up into a thousand minute bits and pieces and scattered throughout the organisation—so in our accountancy should we scatter them.

Let us try a simple analogy. Christmas has just been with us ; many of us witnessed the domestic procedure of preparing Christmas fare, much of which came from common ingredients. Let us take Christmas puddings, mince pies and cake as our examples. These were made contemporaneously whilst the currants and raisins were on the kitchen table, the various finished products for which they were used going simultaneously into production. Indicators of the prime quantities of each of the ingredients, some of which were common to all three finished products were indeed useful, but when the job was finished, with what were we presented on Christmas Day ? I doubt if many of you would have felt overjoyed had you been presented with a plate of unmixed raisins, sultanas, flour and other ingredients together with a portion of the gas oven and a phial containing the appropriate quantity of coal gas, and other kitchen sundries. All these things went into the making of Christmas fare, but what we were interested in was the pudding as a finished mixture. We were interested in the quantity of mince pies produced by those ingredients. The children were interested to see that none of the icing was wasted in the cutting of the cake.

Surely then, our final figures must throw up the results of mixing expenditure. Traditional Final Accounts do the very reverse of this. They deliberately unscramble the mixture in order to display primary forms of expenditure.

Accounts must be alive. If we buy something they must show what we bought. If we move something they must express movement. If we change the nature of something they must display conversion cost. If we scrap something accounts must disclose a loss long before " final " accounts are reached so that abnormal and excessive costs do not find their way into an inflated balance sheet asset. Such conceptions, then, reveal the mechanics of accountancy. " Movement " and " conversion " transactions are its dynamics. Stock, capital goods, and asset balances are its statics.

There is a remarkable apparition to be seen in any elementary text book on book-keeping and accounts—the Stock and Work-in-Progress Account. I called it an apparition because in its conventional form it is the merest ghost of an account containing as it does but two entries—and these merely to satisfy double entry book-keeping — during each financial period. A cash account which contained nothing but an opening and closing balance would be regarded as an absurdity, and yet the stock or work-in-progress account is but a near cousin of the cash account. On the other hand, the established forms of personal accounts and cash accounts demonstrate all that is excellent in accountancy principle. They *do* reflect the incoming and the outgoing. They *do* portray movement and they *do* throw up at any time a static position. The stock and work-in-progress accounts should be the most overworked and full-blooded accounts in the system. Everything that finally leaves the despatch department must pass by this way. The movement to be recorded is more complex than cash and the static balance at any time more critical. Considered in this light the conventional work-in-progress account is an absurdity.

I have already referred to the techniques which we call cost accountancy. Let us trace the history of this movement.

In the earlier days, there were, of course, no cost accounts—not even " costings." There were only what were known as the " Company " accounts. The ledger which held them was regarded as sacred and the venerable clerk who posted them was an object of reverence. Now what are " Company " accounts ? They are an arrangement of the sundry bric-a-brac of expenditure and income which make up both the internal and external transactions of a company. Think of these pieces of expenditure and sales as the bricks from which a more or less well designed house may be built. Given the same pile of bricks, it is obvious that different builders may well produce very different designs of house. Nevertheless, there are some traditional conventions which confine " Company " accounts to a fairly similar pattern. (*See Diagram* 1.)

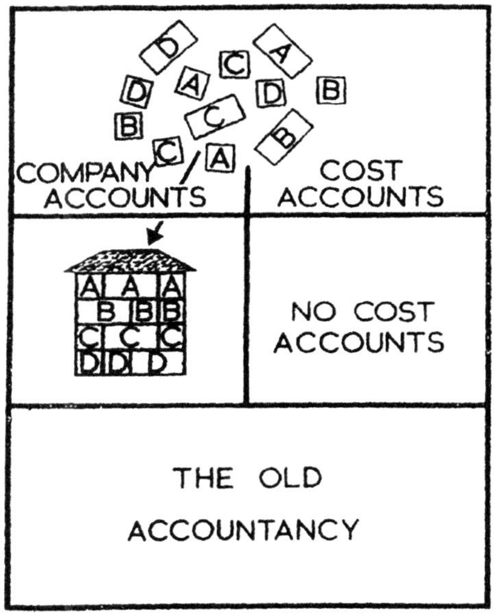

Diagram 1

It may be said that, in general, the " Profit and Loss " and " Trading " accounts consist of an arrangement of expenditures on the left-hand side collecting like kinds of expense into summated items, the whole being set against sales, by which is meant the output of goods from the factory. Profit or loss cannot be deduced from these facts alone and it is necessary to take into account those sales which do not originate from the expenditure made in the period under review but which come from the residual expenditure of a previous period —commonly called " stock." The device created to deal with this problem is the inclusion, on the left-hand side of the opening stock and the inclusion, on the right-hand side, of the closing stock, a procedure which is quite illogical upon close examination. Nevertheless, it gives the right answer, so far as final profit

---

The diagrams are to be regarded purely as symbolic of the ideas in the text. They do not purport to pictorialise the functional techniques of either accounting or cost accounting, but merely symbolise the pieces in the puzzle—" costs," " sales," " assets " and " liabilities." Their purpose is to convey the concepts of " arrangement," " rearrangement," " incomplete arrangement," " subsequently completed arrangement " and " complementary arrangements."

or loss is concerned, and the method has served its generation.

In the course of time it was realised that the operation of a business required considerably greater detailed information than that which these accounts afford, and the techniques of "costing" were born. Note that at first it was called "costing," and not "cost accounting." Costing was the vocation of a cost clerk —a man released at large to collect as many of the bricks which made up the company accounts as either he could find or were not hidden from him. He picked them up very much at random and it was remarkable indeed if he picked them all up. (*See Diagram* 2.)

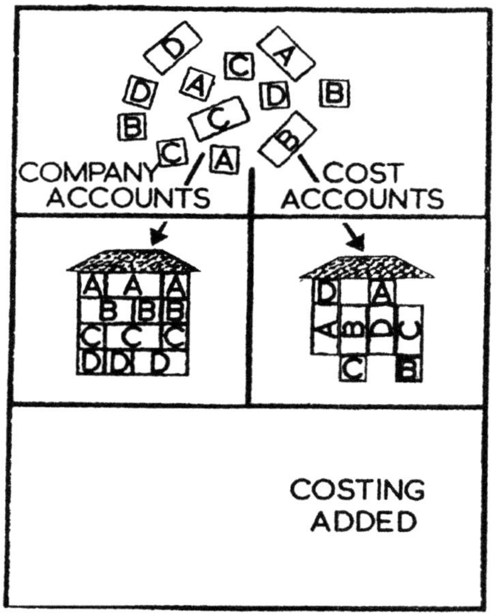

Diagram 2

However, with such bricks as he did acquire he built a house of a different pattern ; that is to say, he assembled his basic bits and pieces in a different order. What he produced was a statement of profitability favourable or adverse, attaching to individual products or to individual functions, the sum of which (if indeed he ever dared to summate them) should have equated to the profitability disclosed by the company accounts. Many of us know "to our cost" that the two answers were, almost without exception, quite different.

It was realised at last that costing as an unrelated technique was unsatisfactory. The next stage of development was—(still allowing the cost clerk to gather his information where or how he could)—to attempt to account for the differences between his figures and the company accounts at the end of the fiscal year. By statistical analysis and a good deal of cross checking it was possible to discover ultimately which of the bricks he had failed to use in building his "cost" pattern. If these bricks were then added afterwards, he said that he had reconciled his costs with the company accounts and "Reconciled Cost Accountancy" was born. (*See Diagram* 3.)

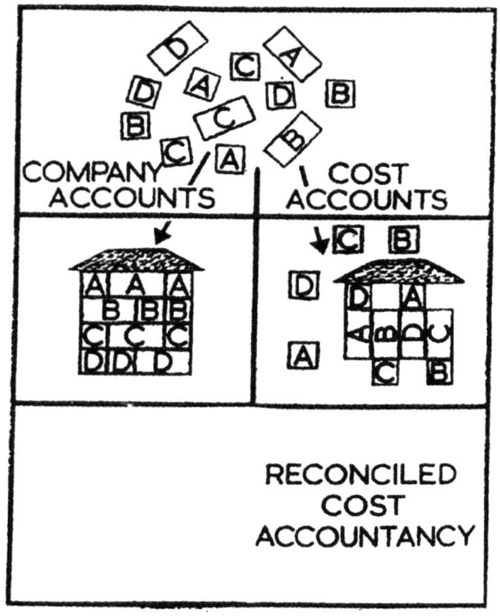

Diagram 3

This, however, was not yet good enough There was still too much hit-and-miss about it and the next stage was the introduction of a procedure which ensured that no bricks which had been used in building the pattern of the "company" accounts were omitted when building the pattern of the "cost" accounts. The method was simple enough. All that needed to be done was first to build the "company" accounts. Having then checked each brick and assigned it to its place in those accounts, it was re-used in building the "cost" accounts. So long as reasonable precautions were taken to ensure that none of the bricks were lost in the intermediary processes of analysis and synthesis, one could be sure that the total bricks used were identical in either case. This sort of thing became known as "interlocking accounts." (*See Diagram* 4.)

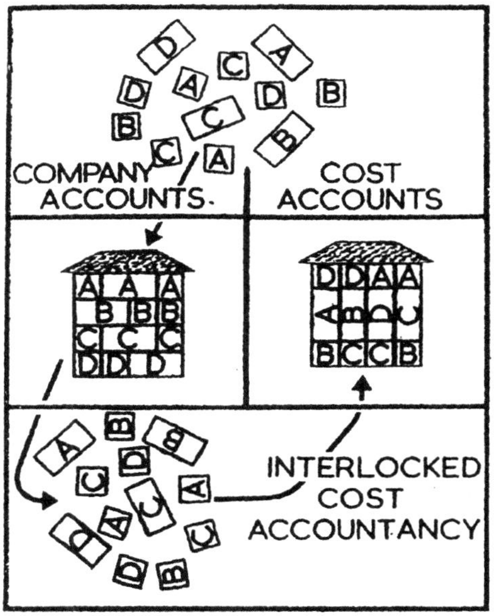

Diagram 4

Both "reconciled cost accounting" and "interlocking cost accounting" are embraced by the more modern phrase—"integrated accounts," and in their way, they have both served us well for several years, more particularly the interlocking variety, which for many businesses represents the peak of development in cost accountancy.

Development is unlikely to stop here, however, and indeed some businesses have already progressed considerably beyond this point.

To what does the future point? To this, I think; to the complete effacement of company accounting and cost accounting as separate techniques. (*See Diagram* 5.)

If the logic of interlocked cost accounts was sound, then the case for a single accountancy system must be strong indeed.

If we marry together those accountancy forms embraced by the term "cost accountancy" with the Personal Accounts and Cash Accounts of orthodox accountancy, we find that roughly we have an accountancy set-up which is virile and enlightening. Furthermore, with this homogeneity we have imposed the healthy discipline of debit and credit bookkeeping upon what once was called costing—and which hitherto should be known as industrial accountancy. We have a unified accountancy structure.

As for accountancy which fails to account—to account back for the expenditure of cash, or the movement of values—to account for all expenditure in terms of functional activity or production of goods or scrap—or any other manifestation of industrial activity—as for accountancy which does not account, it must surely give way, gradually but inevitably, to a form such as I have tried to describe.

And if industrial accountancy is the complete study of a homogeneous subject, it follows that the personality of the industrial accountant must be embraced in one man. There is no room for a so-called Financial Accountant and a so-called Cost Accountant in this economy. The late James McClure, C.A., referred to this matter in a paper read in Sheffield in 1947. I cannot improve on his comments :—

> " . . . using . . . the words 'costs' and 'finance' . . .—no clear dividing line between them is visible to me because . . . I see the balance sheet as the centre of all industrial accountancy. To me then, the cost accountant who is not a financial accountant and the

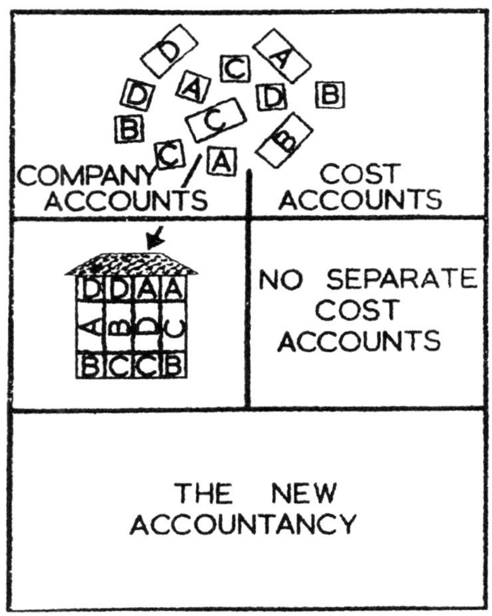

Diagram 5

financial accountant who is not a cost accountant, have the look of displaced persons. This seems to point the need for your two societies (the Institute of Chartered Accountants and the Institute of Cost and Works Accountants) to get together to reunite the divided parts of accountancy and, out of them to produce a coherent whole. Not for the sake of accountancy ; for the sake of industry. To misquote, pompously perhaps, from foreign affairs, ' accountancy is one and indivisible,' industry needs it that way."

Let me repeat McClure's words: " Not for the sake of accountancy, for the sake of industry. Industry needs it that way."

It is tragic indeed, that this crying need exists to reunite accountancy's divided parts. The error was made nearly half a century ago when " costing " began as a series of rude but promising techniques a thousand miles from the accountant's sphere. It has been coming back home ever since. Had those early pioneers but conceived cost accountancy as a projection —a development of accountancy—this article would never have been written.

Let me conclude by referring to the subject which the Council of the Institute has selected for research during the ensuing year, namely, " The Function of an Industrial Accounting Department in a Manufacturing Organisation." I do not know how this title will be generally interpreted or developed, but this is what it means to me. In the first place, I see a distinction between " industrial accounting " and what we may call " policy accounting,"—that is, relations with capital holders, banks, Inland Revenue, the customers and the suppliers of raw materials. Secondly, it seems that " industrial accounting " is a conception of accountancy which embraces all accounts, cost accounts (if we must continue to use the term) included. Thirdly, we discover we must speak of " accountancy " without the redundant adjectives " cost " or " financial." Fourthly, there is no longer any place for conceptions of reconciliation or interlocking.

And lastly, " Accountancy," without institutional caste or artificial barriers emerges— " Accountancy "—simple and realistic—one and indivisible.

THE RELATIONSHIP BETWEEN TIME AND MOTION STUDY AND COSTING

By D. L. Nicholson, A.C.G.I., B.Sc.

A paper given to the Oldham-Rochdale Group of the Institute of Cost and Works Accountants on 13th October, 1949.

The link between Time Study department records and Cost Control is a detailed subject of its own, and is closely related to other branches of modern management methods.

The basis of good management lies in selecting the most suitable policy, and steadfastly following it. This applies as much to daily decisions made by foremen and based on analyses of machine delays, as to major policy decisions made by the company directors.

In both cases the making of the decisions is relatively simple provided that all the facts are available for consideration. Herein, I believe, lies the secret of good administration. Action which is not dependent solely upon the strength and opinions of the individual (admirable though he may be), but which follows adequate information.

In the last century the industrial revolution took place, and was followed by an era of expansion.

Scientific advances followed each other closely ; bigger and better machines were developed, and gradually the economy of the whole world changed. At the beginning of the twentieth century, however, it began to be recognised that there was a field for development in industrial organisation, in addition to the developments in machine design. With increasing competition the economics of production began to be studied, and a new science was born.

This science is the scientific utilisation of labour as well as machines. Its applications are still growing.

Scientific management in all its aspects covers works costing, time and motion study, production planning, material control, market research, and almost every other management activity.

The new science is based on the same principles as every other science. The first of these principles is measurement, of which time is an outstanding fundamental. The measurement of time is vital to the organisation, work loading, and payment of labour ; to the planning of production flow, shop lay-out, and the numbers of machines required ; and to all branches of costing.

It is essential, therefore, that this measurement of time should be accurately made for all operations and processes ; that it should be preserved in proper records ; and so distributed that all concerned may make full use of it.

It is surprising to-day to note the big gaps which there are in the study of time. We should not necessarily all become time study men, but we should all become very " time conscious."

For this first principle of measurement, time study provides the units of time taken with the correct work load and with the correct rest, on piece-work or on day-work, by the average operator.

The time study man does not study the human being alone. He studies the time properties of the machine—its cutting time ; its time of traverse ; its loading time, etc., and he therefore co-operates in studying standards other than those required purely for labour performance. He reports on slow machines as well as on inefficient labour organisation. The time units must be determined in conjunction with the technical experts, and should be the best with respect to quality as well as to speed.

The second fundamental principle of a science is the careful collection and examination of readings ; the filing and grouping together of data ; and the close observation of the effects of experimentation and changing conditions.

In the same way as the laws of chemistry were discovered so were, and are, the laws of time being discovered.

The interpretation of all the information in time study records, and the submission of proposals which may lead to production economy, are duties of the time study man. These are key differences between him and the old-fashioned rate-fixer. He does not concern himself purely with studying piece rates ; he must study the work in its entirety.

Cost accountants know well the differences encountered in establishing costs over reference periods, or for comparisons between different industrial methods. Minor practical conditions may often affect the issue and make comparisons valueless.

A proper liaison between the cost accountant and the time study man, with the latter's overall survey of staffing and production conditions, can therefore have great possibilities.

The basic facts that time study can supply must be employed in a carefully designed system, with a minimum of forms and paper work, to assist all departments concerned. I do not believe that these principles are suitable only for large concerns, although modifications are necessary in small units.

The information which time study provides may be divided into two classes :—

(1) Standard data for setting budgets and production standards, and for determining the correct labour force, etc.

(2) Information on variances from standards which have been set, which can be collected and analysed periodically.

Thus, in the full development of modern management, time study links up naturally with budgetary control and standard costing. My references in this paper are mainly to these costing methods, but time study data can also be of great use in ordinary job costing. This should be evident as we proceed.

Standard Time Study Data

Cost accountants will be familiar with the difficulties experienced in practice when they draw up budgets for a machine shop or mill, and require to know some of the following facts :—

(*a*) What is the standard output from a group of machines to be ?

(*b*) In examining past output records, what delays were experienced, and how good were the operatives concerned ?

(*c*) Did any make-up in wages creep in which should not have done ?

(*d*) How many helpers or reserve tenters should be borne by the process cost ? How many operative hours per week have been borne for this reason in the past ?

(*e*) In the case of a cardroom for example, are the figures produced for machine speeds, hank slivers, waste extraction percentages, etc., accurate for each process ?

(*f*) What are the piece rates ? How accurate are they, and what allowances are paid over and above them ? What make-up has been given for delays ?

(*g*) How much should dayworkers produce ?

Obtaining this information will require a considerable amount of investigation by the cost accountant, who, as a non-factory man, may be misled. Budget numbers of operatives may well be decided by speculation, custom, or the opinions of individual foremen. Often speeds and rates of output are not available in up-to-date records and conditions are complicated by tight and loose piece rates.

Properly designed time study records can serve as a bridge between the shop foreman's pocket book of machine data, and the cost accountant's standard costs.

Work Specification

One of the most important time study documents is the work specification. It is issued when a piece rate is applied, and is in a sense, a contract between management and the operator.

It is dated and has a reference number. When it becomes out of date it is called back to the time study department and its successor is issued. It is easy to circulate a copy to the costing department as a matter of routine.

Specifications are displayed in the shop or mill and as an example, the information that would be shown in the case of the machining of a component in an engineering shop, is listed below :—

Works order No., etc., or type No.
Proper description of the part.
Sub-assembly to which it belongs.
The operation No. (to agree with the Planning Sheet).
Description of the operation.
Tools to be used, including details of the machine tool.
Speed and feed to be employed.
Material.
Duties to be performed.
Target pieces per hour for specified bonus.
Piece work price per piece.

Another example may be taken from the cardroom of a cotton mill. In this case the work specification would show the following :—

Machine speed, waste extracted, etc.
Hank fed, package size and/or weight.
Hank delivered and package details.
Breakage rate per lb. or per 100 spindles/hour.
Stopped time for cleaning.
Machine running hours available.
Target output in hanks and weight.
Machines per tenter.

Machines per helper.
Basic and target wages, piece rates and delay rates, etc.

It should be remembered that with time study all machine data are checked ; speeds are standardised where possible, and the same level of work loading is set throughout the department.

If any condition set out in the work specification changes, then adjustment is liable to be made to the piece rate. It is the boast of time study men, that every factor is considered in setting a rate, small differences are taken account of and modifications are made when necessary. Blanket piece rates to cover a range of conditions are not employed.

Therefore, any change in production conditions must be reported to the time study department at once, when the rates are reconsidered.

This rule has to be enforced and this results in work specifications being kept up to date, as well as the names of those on the distribution list, such as production planners and cost accountants.

In the same way excess payment over and above the piece rates is made for a recorded reason. This is discussed later under " Variances from Standard."

In each application the time study department is keenly interested in any saving in labour or cost that has been effected. They keep in close touch with the weekly running performance in each section ; will probably have drawn up a budgeted direct labour cost per unit themselves, and will have arranged machine output balance, etc., with the departmental supervisors.

It is important to have accurate data of the labour and machinery required for each process, so that production balance can be planned and excess costs reduced.

I revert here to the broader field of scientific management, to mention that there is an exact parallel to the use of time study records (which I have started to describe) in material control. Here properly designed drawing office specifications take the place of work specifications. These are circulated, and in the case of engineering contain the following details :—

(*a*) List of parts in each sub-assembly, etc.

(*b*) Material for each part.

(*c*) Finished parts available per unit of raw material (i.e., allowing for scrap, etc.).

Needless to say, this information would be linked up with the standard material costs through the buying office records, and to material control and the maintenance of stock levels, etc., through the production, planning or progress departments.

The information which has already been described in the standard time study data provided by work specifications, is primarily of use in setting budgets for cost and production, and indirectly for overhead expenditure. The help which time study data can give in measuring variances from these standards can now be indicated.

It is a " by-product " of piece work, and particularly of carefully organised piece work such as that based on time study, that any extra payment made over and above the standard rate is thrown up for inspection and analysis. We have thus an ideal method of measuring variances from standard as they occur weekly. Also, it is simple to total the excess payments and obtain the running efficiency of a department.

We have now arrived at the link with standard costing with which you will be more familiar than a mere engineer like myself. However, it is worth quoting the following principles of standard costing which are vitally concerned :—

(*a*) Process cost standards should be based on a reasonable level of machine and operator efficiency.

(*b*) Costs should be analysed by responsibilities, i.e., the supervisors concerned.

(*c*) Variances from standard should be analysed by both responsibilities and causes.

How better can a standard be based for a reasonable level of output than by using a time study production target calculated for the average operative working under incentive conditions, with all production factors carefully studied ?

Information on variances from standard obtained through Time Study data

We will now proceed to the second great help to costing that time study can provide.

Measurement of the weekly variances from standard or from budgets is essential for two main reasons :—

(1) In order that the budget and actual expenditure may be reconciled.

(2) So that excesses over the budget cost may be analysed for management to take control action as soon as possible.

It is an integral part of time study practice that the operating conditions shown on the work specification should be maintained, and that the operator should have every opportunity of earning the target wage.

If there is a change in conditions, or hindrance to the operator in performing the work, then the operator is entitled to compensation. It is these compensatory amounts which provide the information on variances from standard labour cost.

The following causes of excess payment are typical of a machine shop :—

(*a*) *Waiting Time*

An authorised chit must be obtained for the duration of the delay, on which is based their compensation at an agreed hourly rate. The hours delay are shown separately on the time sheets or job dockets, together with the conversion to cash by the wages department. A return is sent weekly to the foreman, analysing his operator hours time lost.

Causes of waiting are :—

No material
No tools, instructions, or plans
Waiting for the setter or overlooker or inspector
Mechanical breakdown.

It is obvious that if the foreman is having too much time lost waiting for setters, he either needs more, or he needs better setters.

(*b*) *Excess Allowances*

Rectification of faulty material, or components from the previous operation
Learning a new class of work
Use of non-standard machines or tools
Short batch allowance
Premium on hours worked overtime
Allowance for being in a higher grade of labour than budgetted, and requiring a higher price.

It now remains to collect all this information on losses and excess payments into a simple return which can be presented to management at regular intervals, and as soon as possible after the close of the week.

Labour Cost Control Returns

The control returns should cover the responsibility of the supervisor for which they are intended. For example, a carder in charge of a cardroom should receive a return which accounts for all the expenditure borne on his mill wages book, which he authorises weekly.

The returns for each section or department may be summarised on a " master return " for each section of the works or cost centre, and if necessary a " factory master return " can be prepared for the whole plant. The forms can be designed so that they are the same for all these purposes. The master forms are compiled very simply by totalling each column on the sectional returns.

A carefully designed weekly control return can become a most valuable instrument in the hands of management. It should be simple and it should show a minimum of figures. It can provide the necessary reconciliation of budgetted and actual expenditure which the accountant requires, by comparing the standard value of the output achieved and the actual expenditure, and analysing the difference or excess in detail.

It is usual to arrange that entries are made on the form for thirteen weeks in each quarter so that by looking down each column the respective trends or progress can be observed.

The labour summary or control return is prepared either from the weekly wages book or from the pay roll, time sheets or job dockets. etc., which are used for wage payments. These should be designed to enable a comptometer operator to extract the necessary analysis of expenditure, excesses and allowances, etc., in the simplest manner.

By grouping different classes of allowances in different columns in the wages books when they are filled in weekly, I have been able to get a control return prepared in under twenty minutes by a comptometer operator after the wages department have compiled the wages.

Information which may well be shown on a control return is as follows :—

(*a*) *General Pay Roll Analysis*

Direct piece-work
Direct day-work
Indirect work
Overtime work
Allowances
Total actual wages.

(*b*) *Analysis of Production Value*

Units of output produced
(It may be convenient to show this in terms of work units achieved or pounds of roving output, or some other form).
Standard value of output.

(*c*) *Analysis of Excess Wage Payment*

Change in value of work in progress
Extra indirect workers
Extra overtime work
Travelling expenses
Make-up due to day-work.

(*d*) *Allowances to Piece workers*
Training
Bad running conditions
Shortage of material
Lack of outlet
Breakdown
Cleaning
Maintenance, etc.

(*e*) Total excess wage expenditure.

Naturally the data shown varies in different works to suit the particular circumstances.

Conclusion

The manner in which the ways of compensating operators on time study piece rates enables excess labour costs to be analysed and thrown up is clear from the preceding remarks.

It is possible to employ a system of cost control returns with ordinary rate fixed piece work, but both the setting of standards and the analysis of excesses is simpler and more accurate in those cases where time study has laid the foundations.

From the point of view of costing and control it would be ideal if all labour were paid on piece work, but this is often not possible. In many cases, however, where piece work has hitherto not been introduced, time study has enabled it to be started.

This is noticeable in cotton spinning, one of the most obvious cases being on cards in the cardroom. It has also been possible to reduce the percentage of the wages paid for day work to cleaners, oilers, strippers and grinders, bobbin carriers, etc.

I have tried to deal with a large and detailed subject this evening without being drawn into figures and diagrams, because it is the *principles* which are important, every works having its own peculiarities, and the methods adopted in one might well prove unsatisfactory elsewhere.

The first question to be asked is, " What does management need to know, and how can that information be most easily obtained ? " This last statement brings me back to my opening remarks this evening.

A STUDY IN DECENTRALISATION

Being a précis of an article by E. B. Rickard, Controller, Ford Division, Ford Motor Co.

In this paper* the author tells the story of accounting decentralisation in the process of being carried out by the Ford Motor Company. It is of interest particularly in view of the projected visit of a Study Group to America to investigate the accounting methods in operation there, and as a study in appropriate practices to effect the decentralisation of our own nationalised industries, where such a process is deemed desirable.

Size of the Ford Organisation

The company is a vertical integration which provides basic raw materials, to be fabricated or processed to produce automobiles, trucks and tractors. The company owns ore properties, blast furnaces, open hearths, and a steel mill which produces 50 per cent. of its steel requirements ; it has large timber holdings, sawmills and two complete glass plants which provide a substantial amount of the glass used in its vehicles. The main River Rouge Plant generates electricity sufficient to supply a big town, the telephone installation equals that of the city of St. Louis, and the daily water consumption of 900,000,000 gallons exceeds the domestic needs of a city of almost 2,000,000 people.

Decentralisation of Management and Accounting

Up to 1946, this complex industrial machine had been operated under the direction of a highly centralised management ; after the war it became evident that operations had become so complicated that decentralisation was imperative. One of the principal considerations was the lack of adequate information by which the result of specific operations could be judged. The existing financial data was reasonably accurate as to over-all results of operations but provided no key as to the ability of any specific component to provide a profit contribution adequate in view of the capital invested in that component.

Decentralisation of management was the obvious answer. If, however, divisional management was to be equipped properly to control its affairs it was clearly necessary that it have adequate data about its operations ; decentralisation of accounting without decentralisation of managerial responsibility is feasible, but the opposite process would be unworkable ; hence decentralised management impelled decentralised accounting.

Method of Effecting Decentralisation

There were two alternatives :—

(1) Slow and cautious planning of each step well into the future ;

(2) Decentralisation in one stroke, with subsequent revisions and corrections.

The latter course was chosen and the task of setting up fifty or more accounting entities, where none existed before, was undertaken.

Divisions with Full Profit and Loss Responsibility

The organisational pattern adopted resulted in six principal divisions. The *Ford* division (responsible for Ford cars and trucks); the *Lincoln-Mercury* division (responsible for Mercury and Lincoln cars); the *International* division (in charge of all overseas operations); the *Rouge* division (responsible for the Rouge area); the *General Manufacturing* division (responsible for manufacturing activities in the Detroit area); and the *Parts and Equipment Manufacturing* division making numerous small parts of the type which the company can either make itself or buy from outside vendors.

Each division could have been treated as—

(1) *a branch*, responsible for meeting manufacturing

* Published in the N.A.C.A. Bulletin, January, 1950 (Section One).

and administrative budgets but with no responsibility for sales volume, or product design ;

(2) *a separate entity*, with full responsibility for all costs and sales and profit performance.

The latter course was chosen. Satisfactory results were produced in a reasonably short time, particularly in the Parts Equipment division, where the existence of market prices provided a yardstick for measuring the effectiveness of its operations. In other divisions, where there was no comparable product, the solution was found in having the manufacturing divisions and the end product divisions negotiate mutually satisfactory prices in the expectation that the selfish interests of each divisional management would produce realistic transfer prices.

Responsibility for Full Profit

The concept of full profit responsibility, which attaches to each division, is not extended to each plant. An individual assembly plant has little or no control over (*a*) sales volume, (*b*) engineering expenses, or (*c*) cost of purchased materials.

The responsibility at plant level was one of meeting predetermined manufacturing standards, as expressed in overhead budgets, direct labour standards and quality standards.

One of the important questions under consideration is the method to be employed to focus the attention of plant management on those elements of profit which are under their control and for which they are primarily responsible.

Accounting Control

The responsible executive is the controller. There are three levels of responsibility : (1) the central controller's office, which reports to the central management ; (2) divisional controllers, who serve divisional management ; (3) resident controllers, who serve their respective plant managers.

Several large companies have given the chief controller line responsibility for the controllers under him, on the theory that better co-ordination is thereby achieved, but in the Ford organisation the other approach has been adopted, and the divisional or resident controller is responsible to the respective managers of his division or plant. The principal service to be rendered by a divisional or plant controller is that of financial consultant or adviser ; he is regarded as an integral part of the division or plant and not merely as an arm of the central office.

The Central Controller

The central office sets basic financial and accounting policies and issues statements of uniform accounting practices to be observed by all divisions. Divisional controllers are expected to operate within the broad framework of the policies and procedures so set down but otherwise they are responsible to the divisional managers ; similarly the resident controllers answer to the plant managers with accounting functional responsibility to the divisional controllers. Unity of accounting activities is secured by this concept of accounting functional control.

Cost Control

The starting point is the determination of objectives and standards for measuring each element of cost, revenue and investment. The company does not, however, operate a standard cost system but records materials at actual cost and measures labour and overhead initially in terms of budgets or authorised amounts, and reports variances from such standards separately.

At present a survey of each location is in progress and a "best practices" standard is being fixed to provide a standard for measuring each element of cost. The performance at each location can thus be measured against the best performance at all locations, and, where possible, against standards established on a time study basis.

Importance is attached to the most important element of cost, the Ford division materials are by far the most important element. The responsibility for material cost control has been vested in the cost department in close collaboration with the manufacturing engineering, and purchasing departments. The manufacture engineering department furnishes the cost department with estimates of the most efficient method of manufacturing ; the cost department develops a reasonable cost for these processes and arrives at an estimate of the amount that should be paid to a supplier ; the purchases department, with the technical assistance of the manufacturing engineering and cost departments, sits down with the supplier and seeks to negotiate the price of each component part. As new techniques develop it is the responsibility of the purchases department to see that suppliers show the same zeal for new methods and reduced costs as would be shown by the company if the parts were made in the division itself. This implies a study of every part that goes into a Ford car or Ford truck.

Another significant element of cost consists of administrative, selling and advertising costs. A distinction is drawn between manufacturing expenses budgets and administrative and commercial budgets. In the automobile industry, the analyst of manufacturing expense must be well versed in the manufacturing phase of the job and must know the most efficient plant lay-out and process method. Analysis of administrative and commercial expense requires a different approach and a different background of knowledge such as the competitive position of the company, cost-price relationships and the expenditure necessary to ensure that the competitive position of the company is maintained.

Allocation of Central Office Expenses

Some companies allocate these expenses as a flat percentage of divisional sales. Ford's are working out a method of charging central office expenses based on the estimated benefit accruing to each division from central office services. Each division can assess the value to them of the charges made and discuss whether it would not be cheaper to perform any particular service themselves.

Similarly on engineering development charges on research work outside the control of a division ; a system must be established which will enable the division to value the service to them of a particular development. At the beginning of each year the central office plans to determine the engineering studies that will be undertaken during that year and to form cost estimates accordingly.

External Competitive Investment

The return which competitors realise on their invested capital is regarded as an all important yardstick by which tome asure the over-all effectiveness of the company's operations—the aim being to provide a better job under this inexorable standard.

THE FUNCTIONS OF THE ACCOUNTANT IN LARGE-SCALE INDUSTRY

by R. GLENDINNING, M.A., C.A., A.C.W.A.

THE functions of the accountant, no matter in what sphere of activities his duties may lie, can be considered under three broad headings, the first two of which are specific and the other general. The first two headings may be described as the purely technical and the third as the managerial.

The purely technical functions can be discussed under the two classes of:

(*a*) pure accounting; and

(*b*) control.

By *pure accounting* is meant the function of recording and presenting correctly to those to whom an account has to be given, the information relating to the financial position of a concern, or to the financial aspect of its various activities.

By *control* is meant the careful selection, presentation and interpretation of accounting, cost, and statistical information (all of which are interconnected) in order to assist management. In the exercise of the control function the accountant comes very close to managerial responsibility, for managerial decisions are based to a great extent on correct accounting information, and also on correct interpretation of that information. Although the accountant is finally only ancillary to management, the service he provides is nevertheless of the greatest importance. Even so, there are still many organisations where the value of that service is not recognised, and also, unfortunately, where the service which could be provided is not forthcoming.

Regarding his managerial functions, since the accountant is responsible for co-ordinating the efforts of the individuals comprising his staff, to that extent he himself is a manager, and has certain management problems to deal with.

The duties of the accountant in large-scale industry could be considered at length under each of the headings mentioned above. Where the field for discussion is so large, a short paper such as this can only briefly review certain aspects of the subject.

'Pure' Accounting

The purely technical function described as *pure accounting* developed much earlier than *control* in the evolution of modern industry; in fact, *pure accounting* is coeval with modern large-scale industry. This function consists of recording correctly the transactions of the organisation concerned in order to account properly for the activities of the managers to the proprietors, in the case of privately-owned industry, and to the public, in the case of nationalised undertakings. In the case of state-owned industries there is the need also to supply information assessing the efficiency of the organisation. Even in the case of privately-owned industry, particularly in America,

A paper delivered on 20th May at the twenty-first national cost conference of The Institute of Cost and Works Accountants, held in Scarborough.

there is a tendency to submit accounts which will 'meet the tests of "publicity and measurement",' by providing information to the general public as well as to employees.

The exercise of the pure accounting function calls for considerable technical skill, i.e. skill in the application of accounting techniques, which refer to the methods of recording, and of analysis, directed mainly, of course, towards the preparation of accounts and balance sheets. The precise form of accounts is not prescribed for private industry in this country, apart from the general requirements of the Companies Act. For nationalised industry, the form *is* prescribed, as was the form of accounts prior to nationalisation in the case of such industries as electricity and gas supply.

Uniformity and Consolidation

The main problems in pure accounting for large-scale industry are those of uniformity and consolidation. To present the final summary accounts, where a large unit such as I.C.I., Unilever or General Motors is involved, uniformity of treatment must be laid down. Once attained—and attainment may require settlement of various organisational and staff problems—uniformity thereafter presents no difficulty. The difficulty arises, as has happened in some of the nationalised undertakings, when the accounts, built up on differing bases, of a number of units, require consolidation. The same occurs, of course, where a privately-owned concern takes over additional units.

The other main problem is that of consolidation itself, which, although affecting temporarily some of the nationalised industries, applies more to holding companies controlling a number of operating companies, sometimes with the added complication of a minority shareholding interest.

Managerial Problems

Before dealing with the control functions, the managerial function can be mentioned.

The duties of an accountant in the general role of manager are heavier where his staff is numerous, since with large staffs, particularly where they are centralised, there is scope and need for specialisation, for standardisation of methods, and for mechanisation. Uniformity in form and substance in accounting necessitates a certain degree of standardisation of methods and approach, incorporated in manuals of procedure, &c.

Moreover, the co-ordination of the activities of large staffs requires, to a greater extent than in the small unit, the exercise of what in manufacturing industry are known as the planning and production control functions. So far as staff relations are concerned, there will inevitably be a tendency to systematise conditions of service, rates of remuneration, &c., and therefore staff matters are likely to assume greater importance in large-scale undertakings.

In the case of large staffs, special opportunities exist, too, for the adoption of training schemes to enable all, and particularly those fitted for positions of higher responsibility, to receive additional training. Moreover, the large accounting organisation provides a laboratory for the study of that branch of industrial psychology appertaining to clerical effort. This field of study so far has not received much attention, as compared with the psychology of manual or technical work, but the application of the results of such a study might have far-reaching effects.

The second main technical function, viz. *control*, presents a much more complicated problem in large-scale industries, for various reasons. Mr. J. Sandford Smith, writing recently in the *Sunday Times* of 7th May, 1950, refers to Sir Charles Renold's identification of the principal problems arising from operating on a large scale as:

> 'The remoteness of policy from the operational unit;
>
> 'The undermining of leadership;
>
> 'The conflict between the man in charge of the unit and the technical specialists.'

Mere size and geographical dispersal are largely the factors contributing to the above-mentioned problems, and to them can be added such other factors as diversity of activities. In consequence, the profit motive may, in effect, be absent to a considerable extent.

As to size, the problem is, how can top management exercise effective control over a huge industry comprised of many separate operating units, of which it is impossible to have personal knowledge in detail?

Obviously, control is possible only through the preparation and presentation of information in enough detail for the results of each operating unit to be clearly seen. Such information fulfils the dual function of assisting local management by informing them, in financial terms, of the precise effect of their actions, and also of permitting central management to see the progress made locally.

Information must be analysed to show the results of relatively small operating units, the size of which will naturally depend on the nature of the organisation. For example, where a works is concerned the unit may be the shop controlled by a particular foreman, or even the sections controlled by that foreman under different chargehands.

Aspects of Geographical Dispersal

Three special aspects of geographical dispersal may be distinguished:

(*a*) The first is one of conflicting principles in the functioning of the accounting service. On the one hand, there is the tendency towards centralisation which permits economy in clerical effort, through the application of mass production methods bringing mechanisation and also specialisation of function. On the other hand, the need for speedily available information relative to small dispersed units normally requires a measure of decentralisation. The problem is, of course, present in most organisations, and the degree of centralisation or decentralisation concerned must be settled in the light of all relative circumstances.

(*b*) Inevitably in a large organisation there is the tendency for centralisation of final responsibility. If, however, the official channel through which information and instructions normally pass is used for the raising and settling of queries arising locally, much delay may occur. This delay can, of course, occur even in a single large works, but where the industry concerned is spread geographically over the whole country, it is obvious that there must be a method for requesting and providing information on the spot, i.e. without going through headquarters.

(*c*) A third difficulty is that in submitting information, even when prepared on uniform lines, relative to units located in different parts of the country, considerable care is necessary in interpretation. Allowance must be made for differing local conditions.

The very diverse nature of activities carried on in many industrial units (e.g. I.C.I. or General Motors), both privately owned and otherwise, means that for control purposes the information presented must take the form appropriate to the activity. The analysis appropriate to a foundry, for example, is hardly suitable for a machine shop.

Weakness of Profit Motive

The profit motive is bound to be much weaker in cases where the distance between the consumer and the individuals who provide the service to the final consumer is great.

In these circumstances, there must be much greater reliance on systems of cost and statistical control than is necessary in the smaller concern where more immediate reaction can be expected when income falls relatively to expenditure. In the latter case the individuals concerned can see the need to take action more quickly and more definitely. Where such an active profit motive is absent, control information, which quickly 'spotlights' failure to reach expected standards of performance, must replace it.

This is just as true of large-scale private industry as it is of nationalised undertakings.

Reference may be made to the study by Peter F. Drucker of the organisation of General Motors in the United States—perhaps the largest independent unit in the world. In this study ('Big Business'[1]) the writer states:

> 'All divisions of General Motors, even the biggest, are judged in the final analysis by their success in a highly competitive market. Yet the individual department or unit in one of the very big divisions is too far away from the market for its performance to be related to market success. If it happens to manufacture a part or a sub-assembly which could not be sold or appraised independently, it is subject only to the yardstick of cost accounting. On the belief that this yardstick is insufficient unless supplemented by the yardstick of the market, General Motors bases its advocacy of decentralisation which relates the individual producing unit again directly to the market. The very large divisions of General Motors, however, have attained tremendous internal efficiency without decentralisation, that is, on the sole basis of cost accounting.'

Of course, General Motors, although very large, is composed of many separately functioning units. The important factor is that certain units are so far away (geographically and otherwise) from the market that their efficiency cannot be assessed by any means other than that described as 'cost accounting'.

Because of all these factors, accounting for the weaknesses of large-scale organisations described by Sir Charles Renold, there is no possible method of control other than through the regular and speedy provision of cost and statistical information.

The first requisite is cost-consciousness, no matter how achieved, and as the National Coal Board Report for 1948 says, 'This is perhaps more important than the precise form of techniques adopted'.

What is required, however, is a technique that readily shows whether or not the intentions of top management are being fulfilled and if not, where, why and by how much failure to carry out the intentions occurs. An added requirement is that the method adopted must also inculcate an attitude of cost-consciousness.

The late Lord Stamp wrote that, once when going round a provincial workshop, he was informed

> 'by a worker with a particular gadget that he was working to a budget of £2 per annum upon it. The gross figures of many millions had, through the departments, become faithfully pulverised into tiny particles of objective for thousands of remote and humbly-placed workers to a final result'.[2]

Without necessarily going the length of detailed analysis described by Lord Stamp, it seems that there is no alternative for control purposes to the setting up of standards of performance which enable both local managements and headquarters to see whether actual performance is up to reasonable expectation or otherwise. Such standards must, of course, be valid for the peculiar circumstances of each unit.

Conclusion

The fundamental problem confronting large-scale industry to-day is to decide, on the basis of the advantages compared with the clerical and technical costs involved, the manner in which and the extent to which it is desirable to control costs by means of carefully worked out and systematically set up standards. It is a question of whether to adopt a technique which positively and exactly reveals (in financial terms) deviations from the activities planned, or whether the half-instinctive assessments of the position made by already overburdened managers will serve.

[1] Heineman, London.

[2] 'Flexible Budgets.' Macdonald and Evans, London.

Physical standards (that is, standards of physical performance based on exact knowledge rather than on 'hunches') are accepted without question in the technical activities in modern industry—in fact, without these standards modern industry could not exist. 'Rule-of-thumb' methods, however, are still characteristic of much information used for purposes of cost control. If technical standards are universally accepted, is there any valid argument against the use of cost standards?

EFFICIENCY IN NATIONALISED INDUSTRIES

THE NECESSITY FOR MEASUREMENT

by W. S. RISK, B.Com., C.A., F.C.W.A.

The problems involved in maintaining and improving efficiency in nationalised industry are those of all large scale enterprises but are in a more acute form. They are accentuated, the author feels, by the monopoly inherent in nationalisation, by the absence of the necessity and desirability of showing a profit, and by merging in the public interest the conflicting interests of owners and consumers. The solution, the author suggests, lies in decentralisation and flexibility rather than in uniformity; he holds that it is possible to set standards for the measurement and promotion of efficiency and good management.

THE efficiency of nationalised industries is a subject on which much has been said, mainly of a derogatory nature, and on which many opinions have been expressed, some justified and informed and some otherwise. Whatever opinions are held and with whatever justification, it is undeniable that the absence of the incentive of the profit motive is bound to weigh heavily against efficiency; some form of measurement of, and incentive to efficiency is required to take its place.

The main industries which have been nationalised in whole or in part are coal, transport, electricity and gas.

We are concerned here not with the political but with the organisational implications, which are due to the fact that the customers have now become also the owners.

Mr. R. H. Thornton of B.O.A.C. has said that

> 'the nation as a shareholder expects a healthy trading account; as a customer it expects the moon'.[1]

Nevertheless it is suggested that the customers' viewpoint remains the stronger. We are, I think, more directly concerned with the cost of our railway fares and our coal, gas and electricity bills than we are with the profits or losses of these industries of which we, the public, are the owners.

It is obvious, however, that the greater the profit, the greater the margin which can be returned to the consumer in the form of lower charges, and this margin can be made available only through increased efficiency in the industries themselves.

Profit is the difference between the selling price to the consumer and the cost to the producer. If the producer and the consumer are one and the same person, the necessity for profit disappears but the necessity for the lowest possible cost remains.

Even if the profit incentive is denied us the cost incentive is still there. The major problem which has to be faced is how this incentive can be made to operate.

Methods of Measurement

There are two methods worthy of consideration: (1) The fixing of a standard or target cost for the industry or different costs for different sections of the industry by an independent or semi-independent body qualified and empowered to do so, or (2) allowing the industry to fix its own costs while subjecting it to periodic examination by outside authority acting on behalf of the consumers (i.e. the public).

The main difference between these two suggestions lies in the timing of the action. In the first case the action is intended to be taken in advance, the target is fixed and the onus is upon the industry to attain the target or to prove that it is unattainable.

The second case is more in the nature of a post-mortem and the onus is upon the investigators to prove that the costs are excessive.

Method (1) seems preferable, but it will be realised that both methods demand a body authorised to set standards; it is necessary to consider the composition of that body—to whom it should be responsible, what authority it should have, and how it should act. The main consideration is whether the body would be from within the industry or whether it would be completely independent and derive its authority from an outside source. It seems obvious that to obtain the necessary objectivity and impartiality of judgment that the 'standards department' (as it may be called for lack of a better name) would have to be wholly or partially independent of those responsible for production.

Mr. F. C. Hooper made the interesting suggestion[2] that an audit committee should be drawn from the industry itself, with a whole or partial change in membership each year, and that this audit committee should have represented on it all levels of management from board level down to foremen and possibly also employees. He was thinking in terms of an investigating committee.

Requirements of a Standards Department

If a standards department were to be set up in a nationalised industry it would have to meet the following conditions:

Resumé of part of a lecture delivered to the Manchester branch of the Institute of Cost and Works Accountants on 15th March, 1950.

[1] 'State-owned Enterprise: Problems of Political Control'. Study for Nuffield College, 1949.

[2] 'Nationalised Audit Service'. B.I.M.

1. It would have to derive its authority from the highest possible source within the industry itself with, possibly, outside independent representation also.

2. It would have to be composed of men of the highest standing in the industry at all levels to be represented. It would have to include the finest brains in the industry and it would have to be looked upon as an honour to be selected for service in the department. Quality not quantity, would be the watchword.

3. Its members working in the field would have to have tact as well as knowledge. There would be considerable resistance, active and passive, to their activities. It would be necessary for them to have the greatest possible authority to make decisions on the spot.

4. The standards department would be represented in all the units into which the industry is divided and would move from unit to unit, having as its main task the fixing of standards of production and cost for each unit.

5. It would have power to make suggestions to those responsible for production for whom the standards were being fixed, and, if the standing and qualifications of the standards department were high enough, it is unlikely that these suggestions would be ignored.

6. It would have absolute authority in the fixing of the standards although, naturally, it is much to be preferred that agreement should be obtained from all concerned. If this authority were not there, too much time would be wasted in discussion and more effort would be expended on arguing about the standards than in getting on with the job.

7. It would act as a clearing house for all information and methods leading to greater efficiency in production and distribution and in producing uniformity of the bases for the standards as far as possible or desirable.

8. It would act in as informal and prompt a manner as is possible with a minimum of direction from above.

9. There would be a right of appeal from the decision of the standards department only on fundamental issues and any appeal on grounds proved to be unjustified would be cause for considerable censure upon those making it.

Necessity for Decentralisation

So much for the standards or the target costs which are to take the place of profit as a measure of efficiency. Let us look now briefly at the organisational problems which have to be solved before efficiency in a large organisation can be obtained. The measurement of efficiency is, after all, only a means towards its improvement.

Apart from political implications, the justification for nationalisation is that it enables bigger decisions to be made and, if possible, carried out.

It is not necessary that *all* the decisions must, therefore, be made by those at the fountain head, although sometimes it would appear as if this was considered to be the case.

The problem of 'large scaleness' is not one which is confined to nationalised industries but it is in them that it is met with in its most extreme form.

Sir Miles Thomas has said:[1]

> 'Most businesses start small and centralised but at a certain stage of their growth there arrives a point at which they must either decentralise effectively or accept a progressive decline in all vital functions. That is the point at which a psychological decision has to be made. It is a crisis at which probably more businesses have come to wreck than any other.'

It is not easy to decentralise, but the results of not doing so are disastrous to any form of live undertaking. Sir Charles Renold describes two of the main disadvantages of too much centralisation.[2] One is the difficulty of forming at headquarters a true assessment of the situation. As he says, 'The feel of the situation cannot be passed on.' The second is that the effective leadership of the operational unit is liable to be undermined. He says, again,

> 'This is due not so much to the multitude of unending uniformities to which the unit commander is subject as to the necessity for embodying these in regulations which can hardly be other than rigid and insensitive to local circumstances.'

There must be direction and guidance from the head but it should not be such as to stultify initiative or enterprise in the operational unit.

The example of one manager who qualified his instructions thus might well be followed:

> 'If in their practical application any of these instructions appear repugnant to reason and common sense, let reason and common sense prevail.'

Operational Units

Basically, for purposes of decentralisation, the aim should be to sub-divide the industry into self-contained operational units which, while necessarily conforming with the broad policy lines, are left with a maximum of authority and responsibility within these lines. It is not enough to have a clear line of authority. It is necessary to have *sufficient* authority at each level coupled with the appropriate responsibility.

Sir Charles Renold has aptly illustrated the problem of the operational unit with a simile of fleets, squadrons and ships.[2] He defines the requirements of the operational unit as follows:

1. It must be a rational entity.

2. It cannot be sub-divided into smaller rational entities.

---

[1] 'Management in Private Enterprise and Nationalised Industry'. B.I.M.

[2] 'The Organisational Structure of Large Undertakings'. B.I.M.

3. The relations within it can be treated as domestic to itself.

4. It disposes within itself of the resources necessary to its day-to-day operations.

In the Electricity Board the sub-area is the operational unit and in the Coal Board, after much controversy, the area was chosen.

Necessary Incentives

Whatever the size of the unit, it is essential that within it there shall be allowed to operate—and there shall be encouraged—the normal incentives in industry. These can be grouped roughly in three categories.

The first is fear—fear of the consequences of slackness, laziness, inefficiency—fear of ultimately losing one's job. It is a negative incentive. The second is gain—financial gain, improvement in status and promotion. The third is ideological—pride in one's organisation, pride in one's job, pride in and affection for one's associates, seniors and juniors.

None of these incentives can operate satisfactorily unless it is within the power of the leader of the unit to punish slackness, reward efficiency and hard work and give immediate decisions on all points concerning the day-to-day or longer period operations of the unit.

Here the staff method of organisation, involving the role of the functional specialist, need not conflict as long as his services and advice are optional and not mandatory and are offered in a tactful manner.

The most serious charge which can be levelled at nationalisation, or at any large-scale organisation for that matter, is that it destroys the personal relationship and substitutes for it something impersonal and intangible. Nothing could be more soul-destroying or destructive to enterprise.

As Sir Miles Thomas has pointed out[1], there is no difference between the basic principles of management in private enterprises and in nationalised industry. A business undertaking is an organism, not a mechanism, and the humanities must be kept paramount if it is to be successful. Loyalty and pride of purpose are two of the essentials of good work. A man or a woman must have a boss or a senior who is accessible and approachable and who can in his or her wisdom give decisions, award praise and encouragement and apportion blame where necessary.

It is only by means of more or less autonomous and self-contained units that this object—this vital object—can be attained under conditions of nationalisation.

Flexibility in Preference to Uniformity

Flexibility rather than uniformity must be the watchword or aim of the organisation. Uniformity imposed from above, except as regards policy, can lead only to a levelling down. Uniformity of practice, where possible or desirable, arrived at as the result of the pooling of the practical experience of the operation units will lead to a levelling up and would be one of the objects, if not the prime object, of the standards department referred to earlier.

Uniformity for its own sake is not a good thing. Anything which stultifies or restricts the enterprise or inventiveness of the individual can lead only to disaster for industry and for our nation. Every individual is different and the better the individual the more unfavourably will he react to restrictive uniformity imposed upon him from above.

We must err on the side of giving freedom, we must allow for different personalities and if, in so doing, some anomalies are created, this need not always be a bad thing and may well be considered a small price to pay compared with the results of pursuing the policy of complete uniformity.

Competition

Major Scott of Tube Investments Ltd., deliberately misquoting Herrick, said[2]:

> 'A slight disorder in industry's dress,
> Kindling in her a liveliness,
> Does more become her than when Art,
> Is too precise in every part.'

and, as he says, the keyword is 'liveliness'.

The greatest stimulus to liveliness is competition and there seems no reason why competition within the different operational units of a nationalised undertaking should not be allowed and encouraged for the benefit of the industry and the consumer. Even if this should lead to some overlapping, no great harm would be done in the long run. Competition is simply the overlapping of one consumer by two suppliers.

Several large amalgamations in this country—and their customers—benefit greatly from allowing the original constituent firms to function as separate units and to compete one with another—a policy decision made as the result of experience of the failure of complete centralisation.

There must be competition not only between units but also within them—there must be opportunity for the best men to reach the top—a nationalised industry, like any other industry or business, is only as good as the people in it. There must obviously be no nepotism—no 'jobs for the boys'—and no political appointments.

It is easy to be critical of facts, theory and persons. It is not so easy to suggest the remedies, and still more difficult to put them into effect.

Nationalised industry, whether we like it or not, is with us to stay. Let us see to it that in time we reap the maximum benefit from it and reduce to a minimum the disadvantages inevitable and inherent in too great a centralisation of power and responsibility.

[1] 'Management in Private Enterprise and Nationalised Industry'. B.I.M.

[2] 'The Organisational Structure of Large Undertakings'. Renold. B.I.M.

COST ACCOUNTING AS AN AID TO THE MEASUREMENT OF PRODUCTIVITY

By IAN T. MORROW, C.A., F.C.W.A.

Presented at the Afternoon Session of the North-West Regional Conference of the Institute of Cost and Works Accountants at Blackpool, 21st October, 1950.

Introduction

1. A great deal of effort has been put into the study of the measurement of productivity, in the main by economists. Manufacturers and business men largely ignored this work as being of little practical use. They were much more concerned with prices, profits and costs.

2. The reasons for the current popularity of the study of productivity are not far to seek. In April, 1943, Dr. Rostas published in the *Economic Journal* an article on "Industrial Production, Productivity and Distribution in Great Britain, Germany and the United States, 1935–37." The principal source of information used by Dr. Rostas was the census of production of the three countries, and the results of this investigation seemed to indicate that productivity in America was much higher than in Great Britain. Another reason is that the stupendous war effort of the Americans was to a much greater extent than in this country paid for through an increase in the national income, i.e., an increase in output rather than by the diversion of resources from civilian consumption to military consumption.

3. After two major wars and the consequent destruction of real wealth it was found that to raise the standard of life in these islands to the level hoped for was quite impossible if the national income was to continue to expand at approximately the normal annual percentage. Possibly the last reason is the most important of all. It became clear that, if the economists' deductions were correct, an increase in British and European productivity to something approaching the American standards would solve many of the economic problems and, with them, many of the political problems which face Western Europe.

Productivity Teams

4. The various Working Parties in many instances sent missions to America, and endeavoured to compare the efficiency of industry in Britain and America. In the autumn of 1948, on the initiative of Sir Stafford Cripps and Mr. Paul Hoffman, Economic Co-operation Administration in the U.S.A. (the body responsible for the administration of Marshall Aid) set up the Anglo-American Council on Productivity. This Council is composed of representative management and labour on both sides of the Atlantic. The Anglo-American Council on Productivity has sponsored well over 20 Teams who have made studies in America of American production methods, and it is hoped by free exchange of knowledge to assist British industry to raise its level of productivity.

5. The Teams have found it difficult to furnish reliable comparisons of the productivity of industries in Britain and America, although most are prepared to state the opinion that productivity in the United States is higher than in Britain. It is perhaps summed up by the recent Grey Ironfounders' Report,[1] which says that "From the weight figures and from the Team's observations, it may be concluded with some confidence that the American industry is far more productive than the British industry, but it cannot be stated with certainty that the American industry is better by any particular percentage."

What is Productivity?

6. Why is it desirable to measure productivity? Mainly that if something can be measured, something is known about it. It is also true that if it is possible to measure accurately productivity, then it is possible to take, if necessary, remedial action.

7. In considering the assistance which costing might give to the measurement of productivity, it is as well to have some ideas as to what it is we are trying to measure. Productivity is an imprecise term, capable of many interpretations.

8. "It is often measured by the volume of output of a worker in a year, in terms of goods or services. With this definition, changes in productivity include those due to alterations in the number of hours worked, as well as in the intensity and effectiveness of the work done. For some purposes, however, output per man/hour is used as the measure of productivity, and the effect of changes in the duration of work are consequently excluded."[2]

[1] *Grey Ironfounding.* Productivity Team Report. 1950. 3*s.* 6*d.*
[2] *First Report of the Committee on Industrial Productivity.* H.M.S.O. Cmd. 7665. 1949. 6*d.*

9. The British Steel Foundry Productivity Team adopted as their definition: "Productivity is the ratio of production of wealth (goods, services and human satisfaction) to human effort expendable."[3]

10. Each of these concepts is used with good results when applied to a total industry, but is found to have serious weaknesses when applied to the output of an individual factory or department.

Yardsticks of Production

11. The output per man-hour—even if the man-hours of everyone in the undertaking are taken into account—may be misleading. A simple example will perhaps make this clear. A firm with a very heavy capital investment in automatic machinery has a much higher output per man-hour than one which is using no machinery. In fact, it is possible, by vast expenditure of money, to increase the output per man-hour, or per man-year, to quite enormous figures.

12. In considering this problem a possible solution is to compare the rate-fixed standard-hours produced.

13. The Joint Committee of our Institute and the Institution of Production Engineers gave a great deal of time to considering if this was in fact true. "It was found that even with processes the standards set varied from piece-work prices for a complete job to time standards for a single operation, these standards being arrived at from 'guesstimates,' past performances, calculations, time study observations, or element time recording. The Sub-Committee found that methods of setting standards were greatly influenced by the type of product manufactured. The heavy engineering industry lends itself more readily to rate fixing, whereas light engineering, with its short operational times and high degree of repetition, is more suited to time and motion study. Rate fixing, however, while in common use as a method of calculating payments due to labour, cannot be used for comparing efficiency and measuring productive effort, owing to the changes in the value of money from time to time and the existence of differing national monetary units. Comparisons of this nature can only be carried out in terms of time, since time is an international standard, and the unit of time—hour, minute or second—never varies over any period."[4]

[3] *Steel Founding*. Productivity Team Report. Anglo-American Council on Productivity. London. 1949. 3*s*.

[4] *Interim Report on Measurement of Productivity*. Issued by the Joint Committee of the Institution of Production Engineers and the Institute of Cost and Works Accountants. Distributors: Macdonald & Evans. London. 1949. 1*s*. 6*d*.

14. The Committee conducted an experiment with five prominent firms, and they found that the variation, for example, for fatigue allowance was from 7 per cent. to 20 per cent.; that the variation per wage payment, i.e., the addition to make sure that the men earn their expected hourly rates, was 17 per cent. The Committee therefore came to the regretful conclusion that in the present state of the art of time study, as practised in this country, it was not possible to make any valid comparisons based on standard hours.

15. The British Trade Union officials who investigated the role of Unions in increasing productivity in the United States of America, found that the American Unions have sufficient evidence to show that far from being accurate, the method has a margin of error of at least 5 per cent. In their view time studies provided nothing more than rough guides to collective bargaining.

16. In any event, time study, even if effective, would only measure the output of labour, and would not take into account the capital equipment and horse-power which assisted labour.

17. It is clear that if we are to measure productivity, we must take into account all the resources at the disposal of management. In other words, the true measure of productivity is output compared with the use of manpower, services, plant and raw materials. Sir Ewart Smith and Dr. Beeching, of the I.C.I., suggested in a paper[5] to the British Institute of Management an ingenious formula. This was:—

Volume of output per annum
divided by
Average number of men employed + manpower equivalent of capital equipment + manpower equivalent of services received + manpower equivalent of changes in raw materials.

18. Using this formula they give as an example:—

1945 Base Year.

(*a*) Capital Value of existing plant	£160,000
(*b*) National average annual income per employee in industry[6] . . .	£400
(*c*) Manpower equivalent of plant (*a*/*b*) . . .	400 man-years
(*d*) Expected remaining life of plant	10 years

[5] *Measurement of the Effectiveness of the Productive Unit*. British Institute of Management. London. 1949. 2*s*. 6*d*.

[6] Normally this need be revised only every few years.

(*e*) Manpower charge for plant (*c*/*d*) . . . 40 men
(*f*) Cost of services received . £4,840
(*g*) Manpower charge for services (*f*/*b*) . . 12·1 men
(*h*) Output . . . . 120,000 units
(*i*) Number of men employed 200

$$\text{Productivity} = \frac{120{,}000}{200 + 40 + 12{\cdot}1} = 476 \text{ units/man-year.}$$

1946.

No changes in plant.	
Manpower charge for plant .	40 men
Cost of services received .	£5,020
Manpower charge for services	12·6 men
Men saved by change in raw materials. (Correction to be included only when necessary)	3·0
Output	135,000 units
Number of men employed .	200

$$\text{Productivity} = \frac{135{,}000}{200 + 40 + 12{\cdot}6 + 3} = 528 \text{ units/man-year.}$$

1947.

Extension to plant costing .	£100,000
Manpower equivalent of new plant	250 man-years
Expected life of new plant .	10 years
Added manpower charge for plant	25 men
Total manpower charge for plant	65 men
Cost of services received .	£7,080
Manpower charge for services	17·7
Base year raw materials used .	—
Output	205,000 units
Number of men employed .	250

$$\text{Productivity} = \frac{205{,}000}{250 + 65 + 17{\cdot}7} = 616 \text{ units/man-hour.}$$

19. Thus the corresponding productivity indices for this section are:—

1945 Base Year	1946	1947
100	111	129

but even this formula involves the use of certain unknowns, such as the expected wages in an industry, and the calculation of the equivalent in man-hours of plant and services.

Use of Costing

20. If two similar articles are offered and one is pricea lower than the other, it is a reasonable assumption that the factory producing the cheaper article is either unaware of its costs of production, or is taking a smaller profit margin, or has a higher rate of productivity. It is interesting to note that this test was applied after some invidious comparisons had been made between the output of a certain commodity in this country and the output of a similar commodity in the United States, where it was stated that the United States output was six times that of the British, but when the costs of the product were compared it was found that the British article cost less than the American. Clearly allowance must be made for varying price levels and the standard of life.

21. Obviously the cost of production in Japan compared with the cost of production in Lancashire will not (unless some indices are used to adjust the costs of one country) give even an approximate idea of their productivity, but the statement that if the costs are lower then productivity is higher is fairly true within a given economy.

22. It is probably this thought that has been behind the creation of uniform costing schemes for an industry. It is, however, unlikely that firms will be prepared to allow their costs to be compared. Relatively few companies are large enough to have separate establishments producing like products, and are therefore unable to make comparisons for themselves.

23. In the paper already referred to, Sir Ewart Smith states that "It may well be asked why production costs cannot provide all the information necessary to study the effectiveness of industry. The broad answer is that the type of data at present collected for costing, and the normal mode of presentation, does not provide a reliable guide to the true effectiveness with which resources are being used in relation to the basic problem of raising the efficiency of the whole economy."

24. Sir Ewart Smith goes on to say, "On the other hand, it is possible that costing systems, supplemented by other forms of measurement, and in particular by the measurement of individual effort, may be devised to provide a satisfactory guide in future. Appropriate methods of direct or comparative measurement should be the concern and interest of all branches of management, and, properly applied, should yield far-reaching results in achieving a more rapid rate of progress than has hitherto been obtained."

25. The problem is to devise some means whereby existing records can be utilised to give management an approximately correct measure of productivity. This would involve the setting of production against the utilisation of resources, and it seems that the most likely and most fruitful source of practical results lies in the field of costing. If a product is exactly comparable, and factories which produce it are making the same products, and buying in the same proportion of finished parts and producing the same types of by-products, a product cost comparison would enable de-

ductions to be made about productivity. Unfortunately these conditions rarely exist.

26. As it is unusual to find two identical products in a manufacturing industry, consideration must be given to some other unit. Common machines or processes are much more frequent than common products. For example, in engineering, common types and sizes of machines are found in nearly every machine shop. In the different branches of textiles similar types of spinning frames and looms are met with. Products passing through a machine are, in reality, passing through a process, so that it is—within practical limits—true to say that in a given industry, even if it produces a wide variety of products, there is a series of comparable processes. The comparison of costs of similar processes or machine groups may provide worth-while data.

27. If the costs are to be of any assistance they must be very carefully defined, and it is suggested that they should be split to those directly attributable to the process, and those for which, if they are to be attributed to the process, some more or less arbitrary method must be used to apply them. Direct labour and power are obvious ones, fixed charges are others. Certain indirect charges, such as supervision, setting, cleaning labour, repairs and maintenance can be allocated without arousing a great deal of argument. It is probably simplest to calculate these costs on a monthly basis.

28. In computing some of the costs it will be necessary to take into account the probable machine or process utilisation—that is, the number of hours the machine would actually produce. The costs can be expressed either as a forecast or as an historical record; divided into the direct labour and the direct costs for the hours during which the process was actually producing and the hours the process was available (i.e., the full shift). By calculating a machine or process-hour rate it will be possible to make comparisons with similar processes either in the same factory, the same company, or even in another company. For example, the ratio of the cost per actual productive hour and per available hour is some measure of machine utilisation. A comparison of these two hourly sets of costs with others may lead to real lessons being learnt. It may be found that direct labour costs are widely different, say, through the operation of piecework. If they are making dissimilar products then it may be that the productivity in one is higher than in the other, and it will not be possible to come to any conclusion under this head. Comparison of the direct costs may show that one process is much more extravagant than another for no good reason, and economy can be established.

29. In several instances this form of comparison has led to investigation in an organisation into the cost of running a process. For example, a large group, which had machine shops in different parts of the country, instituted a study of the actual cost per actual machine-hour. This study revealed that the machine utilisation varied considerably between one factory and another, and that the cost per actual hour varied considerably. As a result, management was able to increase the machine utilisation, and at the same time to reduce their actual costs. This enabled a heavy capital programme to be cancelled, and brought about increased productivity.

30. It is quite clear that this form of measurement is not a measure of productivity, and can only be considered at best as a guide. The reduction of products to a common denominator, such as standard hours, must wait, as the Joint Committee found, on the development of time study to such an extent that the standard hours produced in the different processes can be taken as a measure of their productivity. There is at the moment a special investigation being carried out by Professor Matthew at Birmingham University, which may lead to a considerable advance in the setting up of standard techniques in time study. It is true to say that the technique of costing is sufficiently far developed to measure productivity, provided the production engineer can develop his technique of time study to a sufficient degree of accuracy to enable standard hours, or standard minutes, to be accepted as a genuine measure of output.

Conclusions

31. The problem has been sketched, and it has not been possible to offer any satisfactory solution. It seems, in the present state of knowledge, to be for practical purposes impossible to measure productivity with sufficient accuracy to enable it to be categorically stated that one factory is more productive than another, and why. This does not mean that it is not worth while attempting to measure productivity, and where this is done, even in a crude form, it nearly always stimulates an increase in productivity by focusing management's attention on possible weaknesses and inefficiency. In my opinion it is probable that costing will, one day, provide the solution, and discussions at conferences such as this may encourage and accelerate the development of a sound means of measuring productivity, based on costing.

The Accountant

ESTABLISHED 1874

18TH NOVEMBER 1950 VOL. CXXIII NO. 3961

MANAGEMENT ACCOUNTING

NEARLY fifty years ago, W. E. HENLEY was taken for a run in LORD NORTHCLIFFE's new Mercédès car. The poet, who had been sadly earthbound by lameness all his life, revelled in the fast movement through the beautiful Sussex countryside and celebrated the outing with a triumphant 'Song of Speed' in which he wrote:

> 'Speed in your daily
> Account and economy . . .
> Speed as a rapture:
> An integral element
> In the new scheme of life. . . .'

Exactly the same sentiments, though this time in measured prose, are echoed in the report, published last Wednesday, of the Management Accounting Team which was sent to the United States earlier this year by the Anglo-American Council on Productivity.

The objects of the mission were:

> 'To find out what accounting, costing and statistical information is provided for American management at different levels; by what methods it is obtained and how it is used',

and although in the time available 'only the fringe of the vast fabric of American industry could be touched', the team's investigations were nevertheless comprehensive enough to enable it to present an account of American methods which should be of considerable value to managers and accountants in industry in this country.

In the carefully considered opinion of the team, the greatest single factor in American industrial supremacy is the effectiveness of its management at all levels. This ascendancy has been achieved and maintained not by technical superiority but by a more vigorous application of known techniques, resulting in an ability to use the means of production—men and machines—to obtain the greatest output at the lowest cost. In a ruthlessly competitive market, unsheltered by price agreements or quotas, American management realises that it must continually cut unit costs or perish. This philosophy of survival is so ingrained as to be taken for granted. Productivity is concentrated on a deliberately restricted range of articles and the profit margin per unit is fixed as low as possible. By this policy, increased volume is obtained and costs reduced by means of longer runs and the better deployment of labour and machines.

The perennial problem of how to lower costs has made management in America turn to the future rather than to the past for the answer. This reorientation of outlook has had a profound effect on the status of the accountant. Most organisations have a controller at top executive level, in charge of all accounting and costing functions. He is responsible for budgeting, for comparing actual performance with approved operating plans and standards, and for reporting the results of operations to management at all levels. He is an interpreter rather than a recorder and the whole future policy of the company is largely based on his reasoned forecasts.

The team found that none of the statistical reports and returns they encountered was unknown in this country but the speed with which they were prepared was impressive. Moreover, management at all levels from top executive to foremen and chargehands, appeared expertly familiar with them whether in writing or in the form of tables or graphs, and action seemed to follow fast upon their receipt. It was noted, also, that the appearance and contents of published accounts and reports were of a high standard.

Particular attention, it seems, is paid to office organisation. Staffs are divided into highly-skilled executives and semi-skilled clerical workers. Accounting routines are broken down so that they can be done by intelligent people after a short spell of training. Most companies have internal audit departments which not only carry out accuracy checks but advise on systems and procedures. The office accommodation is well planned and physically attractive.

The methods of costing and accounting vary widely but nearly every company employs some form of budgeting, usually on a long-term basis for cost ascertainment and prices with short-term budgets set up for control purposes. Standard costs are in fairly common use but the extremes of historical and marginal costs are rarely to be found.

As a result of its investigations the team makes ten recommendations. It suggests that management should make the fullest use of budgeting and forecasting, based on accounting and costing data, in planning the future; use standards of performance (agreed with those who are to work them) and accounting control techniques so as to decentralise responsibility; consult industrial accountants in the early stages of formulating policy so that they may later report more intelligently; and take an active interest in the extension of institutions and colleges (which should give serious consideration to the American practices in this field) teaching business administration at all levels.

Industrial accountants, the team suggests, should constantly consider what information senior management (chiefly concerned with forecasting and selling targets) and other levels (dealing with day-to-day action) need; and study problems of management and technical processes to produce information which will serve as a guide to policy and action.

The four remaining recommendations are that fuller information, including sales turnover and the major elements of cost, should be given in published accounts; industry, Government departments, trade associations and other agencies producing industrial statistics should collaborate more closely and that companies should exchange more information; serious consideration should be given to the problems of redundancy which will arise if British industry advances technically and administratively as American industry has done; and an independent commission should be set up to investigate price agreements, quotas and restrictive practices and that consideration should be given to the effect of these on technical development and cost of production. Further, to consider whether such agreements and quotas should only be allowed by express parliamentary sanction. (Two members of the team, MR. BUNNETT and MR. LITTLE, were of the opinion that this recommendation was outside the team's terms of reference.)

Accepting everything that the team has so ably said about the effectiveness of American management, the question which immediately comes to mind after reading the report is: can British management attain the efficiency of the Americans simply by the more intensive application of what seems to be similar techniques? Streamlined methods need speed, precision and a certain blind obedience on the part of the large mass of the work-people, and the last of these is quite alien to the British way of thought. The working man in this country, with a long tradition of craftsmanship behind him, is more of an individualist than his American counterpart and has, understandably, a strongly developed sense of human rights. He enjoys greater security, having the backing of a highly-organised trade union and the reasonable assurance of employment. Any appeal to him must have a basis of reason.

It was quoted in this journal[1] last week that 'the proper study of management is man, common or garden man'. The immediate task, then, is to bring home to the people, at all levels, by the friendly channels of joint consultation, the compelling urgency of increasing productivity and lowering costs and they will doubtless respond. The problem of permanent prosperity, not only in this country but throughout the world, is as much one of temperament and tradition as of technique.

[1] 'Industrial management and the accountant', by A. B. Waring, A.C.A., *The Accountant*, 11th November, 1950, at page 477.

THE COST ACCOUNTANT

The Official Journal of the Institute of Cost and Works Accountants

Vol. 29—No. 7 DECEMBER, 1950

The Institute does not accept responsibility for any expression of views contained herein. All correspondence should be addressed to The Editor, 63, Portland Place, London, W.1. All matter published in this Journal is the copyright of the Institute of Cost and Works Accountants.

CONTENTS

THE MANAGEMENT ACCOUNTING REPORT

One of the British Specialist Teams sent to the U.S.A. by the Anglo-American Council on Productivity has presented its Report on Management Accounting. The subject is of cardinal importance for those pledged to the stimulation of productivity in Britain.

The Team was a blend of industrial accountants and managers. Between them all they had a wide experience in textiles, electrical engineering, steel, nationalised industry, engineering, tobacco and general administration. Members of the Ministry of Supply Technical Costs Department were also members of the Team. The leader was Ian T. Morrow, C.A., F.C.W.A., and the secretary, Stanley J. D. Berger, M.C., F.C.I.S., director of the Institute of Cost and Works Accountants.

The objects of the enquiry were "to find out what accounting, costing and statistical information is provided for American management at different levels, by what methods it is obtained, and how it is used."

Throughout the Report emphasis is laid on the significant part played in America by efficient management. In the Team's opinion "the greatest single factor in American industrial supremacy is the effectiveness of its management at all levels." This effectiveness rests not on technical superiority, but on their thorough application of techniques which are as well known in Britain as they are in the United States. Their policy is to anticipate and influence events by their decisions rather than merely to carry on as before until events force them to take new decisions.

American management has as the mainspring of all its action the well-founded belief that "unit costs must be reduced each day and every day, week in and week out, year in and year out." It makes considerable demands on industrial accountants. The speedy production of figures is insisted upon. Great efforts are made to reduce the number of routine reports; often the most valuable information passes in daily conversation.

The Report describes the American managerial structure, and perhaps the most significant feature is the versatility of the officer (usually designated "Controller") responsible for all accounting and costing functions, for budgeting, for measuring performance against approved operating plans and standards, and for reporting and interpreting the results of operations to all levels of management. He is constantly in touch with the problems that face management, and is used by his colleagues to provide information at the very earliest stages of policy formation. This has had pro-

B

found effects on the attitude of the controller to his procedures and he has developed the interpretative function of accounting and relegated the recording function to a subordinate position.

All the organisations studied emphasised that the controller belonged among top management. Both management and accountants realise that the primary purpose of accounts and costs should be to guide management in planning the future.

The Report is divided into thirteen sections, two of which—under the headings of (*a*) General Survey and (*b*) Conclusions and Recommendations—are reprinted *in toto* in this issue. The other sections deal with top management control, design and manufacture, sales, costing, financial accounting, purchasing and stock control, office management, business statistics and education for management.

No doubt the conclusions and recommendations, some of which may be regarded as controversial, will be the subject of discussion for a long time to come. It is not proposed to deal with these at this stage. It is, however, of immediate and urgent importance to underline the team's advocation that management should make the fullest use of budgeting and forecasting; should utilise standards of performance and accounting technique to enable it to decentralise responsibility, standards of performance being agreed with those who are to work them; and should bring industrial accountants into consultation in the early stages of formulating policy. Accountants on their part should constantly consider what information is required by management at different levels and should acquaint themselves with the problems of management and the technical processes involved.

Amongst the other recommendations there is a plea for the publication of fuller information by companies in their annual reports, for closer collaboration between industry, government departments, trade associations and other agencies interested in industrial statistics; for serious consideration by government and industry of the problems of redundancy likely to arise due to the anticipated advance of British industry; and for active interest on the part of management in the teaching of business administration at all levels. It is believed that the Report will be of considerable value to managers and accountants in industry in this country, and the Team are to be congratulated on the thoroughness with which they have carried out their mission.

BRITISH TEAM'S REPORT ON MANAGEMENT ACCOUNTING

Whilst the Report of the Management Accounting Team (recently returned from America and referred to elsewhere in this issue) should be read as a whole, readers will no doubt be interested in the following extracts covering the General Survey and the Conclusions and Recommendations.

GENERAL SURVEY

Introduction

1. It was inevitable, in carrying out the kind of investigation outlined, that the Team should gather information about the nature of management itself.

2. The Report is addressed to management and to accountants in industry. This section is a general and non-technical one, and should be primarily of interest to management. The sections which follow cover in more detail and more technically the various functions studied by the Team. The detailed sections are arranged so that those of interest to the "receiving end" come first—top management control, manufacturing, sales department—and those of interest to the "producing end" come last—costing, finance and accounts, purchasing, stock control and office management.

3. The terms of reference to which the Team worked were:—

"To find out what accounting, costing and statistical information is provided for American management at different levels : by what methods it is obtained and how it is used."

All the Productivity Reports already published emphasise the great lead which America has in productivity in the industries studied. Previous teams have found that output per man-hour was higher and unit costs of a product were lower than their equivalents in Britain.

4. It was clear that American industry makes little attempt to measure productivity, preferring to rely on unit costs. It was convinced, with considerable justification, that productivity must be increased if the cost of the product was to fall.

Effectiveness of Management

5. In conducting the investigation as to whether accounting, costing and statistical information assisted American management in its drive for higher output at less cost, the Team had to take into account the attitude and practices of management.

6. In the opinion of the Team, after very careful consideration, the greatest single factor in American industrial supremacy is the effectiveness of its management at all levels. It is interesting to see that this finding has been confirmed by the Trade Union Team, which said on page 51 of its report, "Trade Unions and Productivity": "Efficient management set the pace of productivity in American industry—not because of altruistic belief in social progress but from necessity." To achieve and maintain its efficiency American management makes far-reaching use of the techniques of accounting and costing.

7. One of the measures of the effectiveness of management is its ability to use the means of production at its disposal—the men and machines—without overstraining either and to produce the greatest output at the lowest cost. One of the main differences between American and British practice in management is that American management recognises this. It colours its whole approach and outlook and determines the atmosphere in which it works.

8. The effectiveness of American management and accounting rests not on technical superiority but on their thorough application of techniques which are as well known in Britain as they are in the United States. It is no excuse for the present state of affairs to say that the only way to equal the Americans in this field is to adopt their whole way of life. Given the will and the sense of urgency, there are no valid reasons why British management and accountants should not be as effective, without in any way sacrificing any of the fundamental traditions of British society.

9. In an industrial society it is expected that the general standard of life will be continually improved. This is not a natural law. It can come about only if all give of their best, but the prime responsibility rests squarely on management. Management is the only group whose

actions can be decisive in bringing about the desired increase in prosperity.

Competition

10. American management's perception of the need for high productivity at low cost is sharpened by the knowledge of the penalty of failure, possible loss of business to competitors, and ultimate bankruptcy. Not for it the soft cushion and the comfortable feather beds of price agreements and quotas, with the feathers often concealed from the public under an attractive cover of what was called in the past "rationalisation." American management has, as the mainspring of all its actions, the well-founded belief that unit costs must be reduced each day and every day, week in and week out, year in and year out. This habit of thought is so natural to American management and accountants that it is taken for granted. They are aware that, if the unit costs in real terms are not continuously reduced the standard of living will not rise, and the raising of the standard of life is a religion to Americans.

11. The effect of volume on cost is well understood, and the desire to maintain volume at the highest possible level determines many policy decisions. In price fixing the tendency is to keep the profit margin per unit low in order to get increased volume, which it is hoped will lead in turn to savings in cost due to greater machine utilisation, longer runs and more effective use of labour. Firms will intentionally restrict the range of products or varieties in order to get longer runs. This restriction in no way reduces the consumers' choice, because it obviously pays other manufacturers to produce different ranges.

12. As low cost is the main object of American industry no premium is placed on craftsmanship for its own sake. Only so much accuracy and refinement of finish are put into the article as are necessary if it is to meet the standard of the quality range for which it was originally designed. American management does not consider that quality and mass production are mutually exclusive. In its opinion it is only a question of organising machines, labour and inspection to work to the desired standard.

Fearlessness in Trying New Methods

13. The urge to reduce costs involves management in a restless search for cheaper and better methods of manufacture. Several of the companies visited had in the post-war years uprooted whole machine shops and relaid them in order to get a better flow of production. In one case a considerable investment in plant, with years of useful life still left, was entirely scrapped and new plant laid down to manufacture a different product because the management was convinced that the previous product had no future. American management does not ignore the fact that cost reduction may mean temporary difficulties for some—suppliers, employees or management—but it is recognised that in the end the national prosperity will be raised. It means fewer people producing more goods, and those who are no longer required are thrown on the labour market.

14. Changes are generally accepted as the condition of national progress and the raising of the standard of living. Labour so far has been prepared to accept them, and in many cases changes, which apparently might have led to redundancy, have reduced costs so far that the products have found a wider market and the consequent increased demand has absorbed the labour rendered surplus in the first place.

15. The team of British trade union officials in its recent Report recognises the redundancy problems and says:—

"In this new industrial role which unions are seeking to perform there is need also to develop a more positive and realistic approach to redundancy. A rising standard of living can only be achieved by increasing productivity obtained from labour-saving machinery and technical processes and working skill. Redundancy, therefore, is inevitable unless increased production enables immediate re-absorption; but redundancy is not unemployment where full employment exists. Considerable emphasis, however, is placed on the need to encourage labour mobility and flexibility, because it is becoming increasingly recognised that full employment means that there are more jobs than workers, rather than providing the redundant with jobs at the same trade and wage rates in the same locality. There are limits, in effect, to the distribution of industry based only on local social needs."

16. Possibly one of the differences in approach between the British and the Americans is that the Americans by and large are prepared to take the risk that the normal workings of the economy will take care of those who are redundant. Nevertheless, according to the Trade Union Report already mentioned, "Dismissal pay or compensation designed to break down resistance to innovation is finding favour with

many unions and companies." In Britain more positive action is required to compensate for the upheavals caused through redundancy. The attainment of flexibility in labour is worth a great effort, and with our experience of labour transfers during the late war it should be possible to evolve acceptable solutions without any infringement of personal liberty.

Price Arrangements

17. The freedom of competition which exists in the United States undoubtedly is a most important reason for the drive for lower unit costs.

18. It is important to consider whether price agreements and quotas are having an adverse effect on the British economy by restricting technological advance. At present a Commission has been set up under the Monopolies and Restrictive Practices Enquiries and Control Act, 1948. To this Commission certain cases have been referred by the Board of Trade. It will obviously take the Commission a very long time to investigate all the various restrictive practices in existence. Meanwhile, it would be a real service to British industry if an independent commission could inquire into the nature of these agreements, report on their effect on British industry, and express an opinion as to what would happen if they were removed.

19. The investigating body could also be asked to advise whether it would be in the public interest that all such arrangements should be made illegal without express Parliamentary sanction. Under present legislation price agreements and quotas are legal unless declared otherwise.

20. The constant emphasis on lower unit costs has made management in the United States look continually to the future. It has, in turn, demanded that industrial accountants should adopt the same attitude. This means that the definition of an accountant as one who "records, classifies and organises accounting data in an orderly fashion" applies only to book-keepers. Accuracy in recording the past is not enough—"the past is spilt milk anyway; the main thing is not to repeat the mistakes."

21. A new generation of managers has risen, many of whom have had training in management at the business schools attached to many of the universities, or at such institutes as the famous Massachusetts Institute of Technology. They have learned the value and utility of figure statements and what can be reasonably inferred from them. At the same time many accountants have realised that service to management is their main objective.

Organisation

22. The organisation structures which were met with during the visit were similar in many respects to those in this country. Companies made a point of publishing their organisation chart to all levels of management. The financial accounting and costing functions are strongly represented at top executive level in America. The majority of companies have a treasurer and a controller. In some large companies there is a financial vice-president as well as a treasurer and a controller. The controller often has under him a chief accountant. The distinction between the names and relative positions of the two functions are significant. The controller, as his name implies, is much more concerned with control through figures than with mere recording and he is always senior of the two.

23. The controller is normally responsible for all accounting and costing functions, for budgeting, for measuring performance against approved operating plans and standards and for reporting and interpreting the results of operations to all levels of management. He is constantly in touch with the problems that face management, and is used by his colleagues to provide information at the very earliest stages of policy formation. This has had profound effects on the attitude of the controller to his procedures, and he has developed the interpretative function of accounting and relegated the recording function to a subordinate position.

24. All the organisations studied emphasised that the controller belonged among top management. Both management and accountants realise that the primary purpose of accounts and costs should be to guide management in planning the future. This realisation springs from the desire of management to base its decisions on facts and reasoned forecasts. In spite of this acceptance, in principle, of the controllers' function, many controllers realise that they must never lose sight of the need to show how figures and statistics can contribute to effective management.

25. There is an increase in the practice of agreeing a budget of expenditure or a standard of performance with the individual at each level and then comparing the actual performance with the

agreed budget or standard. This practice is not limited to firms that have adopted systems of "standard cost control" in the form usually associated with that description. The advantage of this development is that as the individual manager, whatever his level, knows his responsibilities and the limits of his power, he feels a freedom and a confidence that let him get on with the job. This is one of the main reasons for the vigour of American management.

Provision and Use of Information

Top Management

26. The presentation of information to the board and to top executive management is fundamentally different.

27. In most instances the board receives long tabulations of figures in great detail. These reports always include a balance sheet, profit and loss account, and often the position of stocks, disposition of funds or working capital, capital expenditure, forward commitments, sales, production, and other appropriate statistics. The board lays great emphasis on keeping stocks at the right economic level, and exercises, on the whole, a tight control over capital expenditure. The board is primarily concerned with the financial results, and expects to be supplied in detail with a great deal of financial information.

28. Top executives, while naturally receiving copies of board reports and being briefed to discuss them with the board, do not regard these as their prime control statements. Forecasts and budgets are used extensively, and are revised or recast as circumstances demand. This occurs with surprising frequency. Senior management pays far more attention to forecasts than to past results. It is interested in the latter chiefly as a means of setting targets for the future and controlling subordinates. The nearer a manager is to the shop floor or to the customer, the more he is interested in current results as a guide to immediate action, and because he knows that his effectiveness will be judged by his success in reaching the target.

29. An interesting feature of several of the control statements was the variety of comparisons made. To control the execution of policy, the expenditure, sales, and profit are, in most instances, compared with at least a short-term budget and often with a long-term budget. The senior executives receive detailed profit and loss accounts for each division of the company's business. These are in many cases accompanied by schedules to show the standard cost of sales analysed by product and by territory. The profit and loss accounts and balance sheets are compared with the forecasts and in some instances with the previous month and the corresponding month of the previous year. In one or two instances it is the practice to accompany the profit and loss accounts and balance sheets with projected balance sheets and profit and loss accounts for the next three months.

30. The practices in the companies visited are as varied as in a similar group of companies in Great Britain, but the general standard of management information is higher. Advanced companies are making great efforts to reduce the routine reports given to the officers and senior executives. The most valuable information is conveyed to them in frequent discussions with the controller and his staff, and in special reports dealing with current problems and likely developments. Summaries are prepared of the detailed operating results from the production shops for top management, and are accompanied by a verbal explanation.

Government Information

31. There is much external information available to top management. Government departments in Washington collect and issue valuable statistics on productivity, production, prices, consumer income, etc. The Government statistical departments are advised by a Business Advisory Committee and a Labour Advisory Committee, consisting of representatives of business and labour. In this way the Goverment is kept fully informed of the opinions of consumers other than itself.

32. The Division of Statistical Standards was set up under the Bureau of the Budget with the task of "co-ordinating Federal reporting services, to eliminate duplication and reduce the cost of such services, and to minimise the burden of furnishing information to Federal agencies." No statistics can be collected without the approval of the Bureau of the Budget which examines the forms on which they are collected. This prevents unnecessary duplication, and improves the quality and usefulness of the statistics.

33. The Bureau of Labour Statistics collects figures of employment, earnings, man-hours, labour turnover, industrial expense, work stoppages and wage rates from about 140,000 establishments, representing 135 manufacturing industries, 20 major industrial groups and about 20

non-manufacturing industries.

34. The Department of Commerce is responsible for the census of manufacture, the census of business and the census of population. These are similar to those undertaken in Britain. It also prepares the estimates of national income and national product, consumer income, expenditure and savings. The latter estimates provide a valuable guide to trends in the level of purchasing power.

35. The Department of Commerce makes financial reports on business. It collects information on the relative position of large and small firms, the relative profitability of different industries, the rate of expansion of capital and liquid assets, the distribution of income, ratios of assets and profits to sales, and sources of borrowed funds. Comprehensive statistics of banking and related financial figures are prepared, weekly data being available on the conditions of the Federal Reserve banks. The Department also prepares statements of the U.S. balance of payments covering economic transactions between the U.S. and other countries of the world.

36. A division of the Bureau of Labor Statistics collects detailed information on productivity, both as national indices and in selected industries. As the method of measurement is known, it is possible for any firm in the industry to assess its performance against that of the whole industry.

37. The value industry places on the collection and compilation of figures is shown by the fact that on two occasions, when financial appropriations were reduced and the Department concerned had to curtail the collection of figures, certain industries, through their trade associations, paid the Government to continue the service.

Trade Associations

38. Some trade associations publish statistics of sales, orders and costs of their industry as a whole, and these can be used by individual manufacturers to check their own achievement.

Other Bodies

39. There are several private and semi-public bodies which prepare a stream of statistics, many being analyses of the Government statistics, though some are the result of original investigation. These bodies are widely supported by industry, and many executives spoke with enthusiasm of the summarised information which is provided.

Development Expenditure

40. The board of directors is often as a matter of policy prepared to spend capital more freely to enable a new product to be made or production to be increased than for the reduction of cost. It is argued that the gain or loss for not cutting costs is measurable, whereas the loss involved in missing an opportunity is immeasurable.

41. Considerable efforts are made to control expenditure on new projects. Careful assessments are made to establish the target, and the actual money spent is compared in detail with the budget as the project is developed. There is no disguising the difficulties of controlling development expenditure. Nevertheless, in the opinion of American management the efforts which are being made to do this assist in keeping expenditure down and in making development engineers cost-conscious.

Factory Management

42. The friendliness and understanding between the controller's department and the production department is remarkable. The controller's department is looked upon as an essential service to production.

43. The departmental managers or foremen and top management receive regular reports comparing actual results with the targets. Top management uses these chiefly for planning the future and setting new targets, whilst the departmental managers or foremen use them mainly as a guide to the weaknesses in the day-to-day running of the departments. It is a general rule for the departmental managers or foremen to agree standards of performance and budgets of expenditure.

44. The following are some of the subjects on which reports are most frequently given comparing actual performance with the budget:—

Operator efficiency for individual operators and summarised as departmental averages,
Numbers of personnel employed in line working against the standard number allowed,
Price variations on purchases, analysed by commodities,
Scrap,
Lost time,
Machine utilisation,
Controllable overtime,

C

Indirect shop labour expense against the standard allowed,
Factory services expense against the standard allowed,
Maintenance,
Management and clerical salaries,
Power, light, heat, etc.

45. There is a wide divergence in the amount of information given to foremen. Some companies give them as much as they ask for so long as it has some bearing on their work. Others limit it to expenditure actually under the foreman's control.

46. Labour control is mostly exercised through standard times. The standard time taken is compared with the actual time and the efficiency of each individual man shown. In many instances monthly summaries of each man's performance are kept for a permanent record to assist in assessing his qualifications for efficiency pay and promotion or, alternatively, to show possible failure to achieve standards, which may result in transfer to other work. The indirect labour hours are often compared with the budgeted indirect labour hours on a daily basis. At the end of the month the cost in terms of money is shown.

47. Allied to the control of labour is the control of machine utilisation. Every effort is made to use the machines to the utmost and idle time reports are closely studied. Scrap is controlled with equal care because it is considered a waste of valuable production time as well as a waste of material.

Prompt Use of Figures

48. None of the returns, statistics and figures described here is unknown in this country, but the promptness with which they are prepared was impressive. The daily statement, for example, is presented the following morning. Statements of figures are usually unaccompanied by written reports—again on the ground of speed. From top management to foremen and chargehands there is little fear of figures, and there is a marked ability to absorb information from tabular or graphical form as quickly as, if not quicker than, from a written text.

49. The reports are often handed out personally by the controller or a senior member of the staff, with a verbal explanation of the figures, and the controller is prepared to answer questions on the spot. Action appeared to follow fast upon receipt of the figures. Reports are expected to be used, otherwise management is ruthless in scrapping them. Formal conferences are rare, it being implicit in the whole competitive atmosphere that each man is expected to do his job and to meet his budget, or else have a very good explanation.

Published Reports and Accounts

50. Published reports are of a high order, both in appearance and contents. Owing to the joint influence of the accounting profession and the Securities and Exchange Commission the published information is amazingly full.

51. Nearly every company, for example, publishes its year's sales, in value and quantity, the amount of capital expenditure for the year, in some detail. Many publish the average number of employees, the average hours worked and the average hourly earnings. The percentage earned on share capital, on sales and on each unit of common stock is shown. The working capital and the amount of profits employed in the business are stated. An interesting feature is that in some cases a statement reconciling the opening and closing cash position is published. The figures are often enhanced by a year-by-year schedule of comparison, extending over perhaps the last 10 years. Many companies' published accounts contain a great deal of information of general interest. In some instances these are distributed to employees, and in others specially designed reports are prepared for this purpose.

Method of Obtaining Information

Office Organisation

52. Office staffs are divided broadly into highly trained executive and semi-skilled clerical It is unusual to find highly skilled clerks. Accounting routines are broken down until they can be done by intelligent people after short training. The staffs are flexible in that they are all capable of doing more than one of the simple routines. Great thought is expended on the office methods and routines, with the object of reducing costs.

Internal Auditing

53. In companies of any size there is often a separate department of internal audit. The internal audit department normally performs two functions:—

(a) Checking the books for accuracy and checking procedures to see that there are no possible leakages;

(b) Advising on systems and procedures in the accounting, administrative or production side of the organisation, and seeing that these are effective and efficient.

Office Layout and Equipment

54. The trend is towards large single offices which make for much greater flexibility. Physically the offices are attractive. Many have sound-absorbent tiles, and lighting, ventilation and decoration are of a high order. The offices are obviously considered to be as important as production shops, and the same detailed consideration is given to the planning of operations.

55. To British eyes the provision of auxiliary office equipment, such as calculating machines, addressing machines and typewriters, seemed lavish. However, much loss of time is avoided, because documents do not have to travel to and from calculating sections. The opinion was expressed that an investment of some £250 per clerk was justified. It is expected that the cost of any additional office machinery will be covered by savings in salaries within two years. By law the minimum wage in the United States is $30 per week.

56. The controller's close working with the management has made him acutely conscious of the time factor in his submission of reports. He is prepared to spend more money than would perhaps otherwise be necessary, provided this extra cost contributes to the speedy production of vital figures.

Accounts and Costs

57. A wide variety of methods of accounting and costing was seen. Nearly half the firms investigated use a system of standard cost control in the form generally associated with this title, but many more use some form of standards, forecasts, or budgets as a guide to efficiency. In general, there is no distinction between financial records and cost records. Accounting is one integrated whole.

58. Many companies have adopted accounting periods of four weeks' duration.

59. The methods of costing and the provision of control figures can be grouped into four main types:—

(1) Historical costs used for current control and for product costing;

(2) Historical costs used for current control, product costs based on standard costs;

(3) Standard costs used for the control of current operations, and the same standards used to calculate product costs;

(4) Standard costs used to control current operations based on short-term budgets, and long-term budgets used to calculate product costs.

60. It was exceptional to find a complete system of costing of type (1). Certain items, such as repairs, usually had to be spread on an estimated basis, but even in these instances a considerable amount of forecasting and budgeting was undertaken.

61. In type (2) where historical costs were used for current control and standards for product costs, the actual expenditure for the month was analysed to departments, and within the department to appropriate heads of expenditure, the current month's results being compared with the monthly average of the previous year.

62. To keep the product costs in line, actual expenditure is compared with the standard, and the differences are expressed as a percentage of standard, so that the standard cost is corrected to current conditions.

63. In type (3) where the same standards were used for current control and production costs the departments were credited with the standard value of their production and charged with the actual, and had to account for the difference. Under this scheme the differences are used not only for control but for adjusting the standard cost to current prices if required.

64. An interesting example of the control exercised by a company using this method was when the manufacturing department showed a considerable loss due to processing non-standard material. At first this loss appeared in the departmental statements, but the controller, after investigation, charged it to the purchasing department, who then claimed from the supplier. He accepted the claim but stated that, in future, he would be unable to maintain the material to the specification unless he could get a substantial increase in price. The company's research department then took up the problem and succeeded in evolving an alternative process, resulting in a much cheaper product.

65. Where type (4) is in operation the product costs are based on long-term budgets, possibly five years, both of expenditure and volume.

The practice appeared to be that in the engineering industry single-shift working, and in the textile industry double-shift working, was taken as the base. This meant, in effect, that prices were not reduced in times of boom through abnormally high volume, nor were they increased in times of depression through abnormally low volume.

66. For control purposes, fresh budgets of volume and expenditure were fixed for periods varying from a month to a year, depending on management's requirements and the nature of the company's business. The budgets also were usually set for such a period as enabled the expenditure for control purposes to be treated simply as fixed and variable, semi-variable being ignored. This often required the budgeting of manufacturing and volume variances.

67. Marginal costing, as such, appears to be comparatively little used. One company makes use of it for the calculation of product costs, but for control purposes uses a scheme of standard costs and budgetary control.

68. The differences are thrown up by the control scheme, and are written off as fixed charges in the profit and loss account. The essence of the scheme is that only directly chargeable expenses are charged to the product; all other expenses, mostly of a fixed nature, are charged direct to the profit and loss account.

69. Product costs are created by calculating the directly chargeable expenses and then adding a percentage to cover fixed charges and profits.

Comparisons

70. Many different comparisons are often used in the same company to focus attention on a particular problem. The current month's figures are compared with the same month in the previous year and with the previous month, and figures for the last three months are often given. Comparisons are also regularly made with the long-term and short-term budgets. Trends in the form of moving annual totals are sometimes found.

71. Wherever possible, comparisons are made with other companies in the industry, either through trade association returns or Government statistics.

Fixing of Budgets

72. The fixing of budgets is very closely allied to detailed forecasting based on market research. The normal method is to forecast for existing products the total demand and the company's estimated share in the potential market. In arriving at the estimate, population and income statistics and field surveys are used to supplement the company's knowledge of the market and the general economy of the country. Many outside sources of information are also used.

73. As soon as the sales forecast is complete it is passed over to the controller's department, who build up financial budgets and forecasts, balance sheets and profit and loss accounts and link these with the production budgets. Some companies assume several different sales volumes and budget a balance sheet and profit and loss account for each level.

74. In building up budgets and forecasts it is essential to have an accurate measure of expenditure and man-hours throughout the productive processes. Time-study engineers are employed in nearly every plant. In deciding on the establishment of the budget, most of the jobs in an undertaking are evaluated. The job evaluation techniques are similar to those in this country but are much more widely used.

Education for Management

75. American industrialists, like all others, are well aware that success ultimately depends on people and that the people who can contribute most to the success of the company and who can make or mar the efforts of all the others are management. At the beginning of the century there was already support for the idea that men could be trained for management by attendance at an academic institution. This led to the establishment of schools of business in a number of America's leading universities. Their success has convinced Americans that it is a practical proposition.

76. Four of these schools of business were visited. The work being done there is impressive, and must be attributed in a large measure to the quality of the staffs. These consist of practical men who are sufficiently knowledgeable to be paid fees by industry for their advice. They are not, and under this system never can be, academic in the sense that they are cut off from the day-to-day problems of an industrial society.

77. American business men support the schools of business by serving as governors, by making contributions to the funds, and by helping to place the graduates.

78. An interesting development similar to the Administrative Staff College at Henley is the Harvard Advanced Management Programme. This is intended for men selected by their own organisation as being capable of assuming greater administrative responsibilities. The course is of 12½ weeks' duration, and is devoted to the concentrated study of appropriate subjects.

CONCLUSIONS AND RECOMMENDATIONS

Conclusions

1. The most signicant factor in America leading to high production at low cost is efficient management.

2. There is no reason, inherent in the American economy or in American ability, why their management should be more efficient than British management. Some British managements have proved the truth of this conclusion.

3. The achievement in this country of an equal degree of efficiency in no way requires the sacrifice of the best characteristics of British life.

4. The principles and methods which American management applies are well known in this country, but are practised much more universally and vigorously in America.

5. The Americans are always ready to make use of technical advances to improve their efficiency, realising that only so can they raise the standard of living. This readiness is all the greater since the strict enforcement of the Anti-Trust Laws prevents the growth of price agreements, quotas and restrictive practices.

6. American managements are continually looking towards the future. Their policy is to anticipate and influence events by their decisions rather than merely to carry on as before until events force them to make new decisions.

7. They appreciate the need to base their decisions on factual information about the past and present and on reasoned forecasts of the future.

8. Their method is to set themselves targets which are as high as appear from facts and forecasts to be capable of achievement.

9. They are continually measuring their actual results against the target they have set themselves.

10. They have no hesitation in changing plans, methods, procedures or organisation if they think they can get nearer their target by doing so.

11. They have equally no hesitation in changing their target if changing circumstances make it unattainable or too easily attainable.

12. These principles and methods are applied right down the line.

13. Responsibility is decentralised to the limit.

14. The responsibility of each manager, to the level of foreman, is clearly defined in terms of the functions, results and expenditure for which he is responsible. He is set a target, which is agreed by him as reasonable, and his work is judged by his success in reaching that target, except in so far as he can show good reason for not doing so.

15. The importance of the accounting and costing function as an essential service to American management is clear from what has been said above.

16. Two main uses of accounting and costing information can be distinguished: for planning and for control.

17. For planning, forecasts are needed, both of the trend of outside events beyond the control of management and of the probable results of alternative courses of action.

18. For control, actual results must be compared from time to time with set targets to see whether plans are working out successfully or whether changes in policy are needed.

19. It is the means of control provided by the accounting and costing function which enables decentralisation of responsibility to be carried out so thoroughly and effectively.

20. Plans are translated into budgets and budgets broken down into targets for individual managers and foremen.

21. The results achieved by each manager and foreman are frequently compared with the set target. This not only enables his superiors to judge his work, but also shows him in what respects he is being successful and where are the weak points in his department.

22. There is a difference in the use made by senior and junior management of accounting information. Senior management spends much more of its time considering the future and studying forecasts and budgets for the purpose of planning and setting targets, whereas the nearer the management is to the shop floor and the customer, the more interested it is in studying recent actual results in comparison with the budgets and forecasts, as a guide to immediate action.

23. But all levels of management, from top management to foremen and chargehands, are familiar with figures and have a marked ability to absorb information in this form. The use of figures is considered an essential part of every business man's training, and courses in this subject were found in the curricula of the universities and technical colleges visited.

24. There is a difference between the type of report to boards of directors and executive officers. The boards of directors expect and receive voluminous financial information every month. Although many of the officers and senior executives also receive board reports, they do not regard them as their main source of control information.

25. The controller in many companies makes every effort to keep routine reports to the minimum. He and his staff devote more and more time to the compilation of special non-recurring reports on subjects which are occupying the attention of management.

26. All control figures are produced for the sake of guiding policy and action, and never just as a matter of interest. Every regular report is expected to be used. If it is not used it is scrapped.

27. Long elaborate written reports are avoided. Much of the most valuable information passes in personal contact between the controller's department and all levels of management. The controller's department are on the whole regarded as friendly guides rather than as blood-hounds or watch-dogs.

28. Parallel with the management's appreciation of accounting information, and contributing in large measure to this, is the controller's own understanding of management problems and technical processes. He is always kept fully informed as to what is going on in the business.

29. It is exactly because he is so identified with the attitude of the management that the controller is insistent on the greatest speed in the production of figures.

30. For the same reason, too, he has to be flexible in his approach, and may have to alter a whole system to suit the varying needs of management.

31. The actual techniques used to obtain the accounting and costing information are not new, but the application of the technical principles and the speed and service which the controller gives to the management are outstanding and impressive. Practically every company uses some form of budgeting, although it is often called by other names. Some form of standard costs is more often than not in use. Historical costing was seldom found.

32. Rather than use elaborate flexible budget techniques it is the practice to set long-term budgets for cost ascertainment and prices, and during the lifetime of this budget to set many short-term budgets which are used for control purposes. Technically this means, of course, budgeting for a variance. For example, one very large corporation always budgeted on a single shift for cost ascertainment, but in present circumstances was often running double shift, and the control budget was built accordingly. On the other hand, it was the practice throughout the textile industry to budget on two shifts for cost ascertainment, irrespective of the actual volume.

33. Industry has available to it a large quantity of external statistics prepared by government and private agencies and trade associations. Industry is prepared to support in every way the compilation of figures.

34. Managers and industrial accountants are conscious of the gap between management and accountancy, and the need to bridge this gap. On the whole they have succeeded far beyond the normal achievement in this country.

35. Management is convinced that academic training for business is well worth while, and supports in every way the graduate and undergraduate schools of business. The quality of the staff employed by the schools is high. They are, in every instance, practical men in close touch with industry, and are expected to spend a proportion of their time doing consulting work so that they shall not become too academic.

36. Office organisation is noteworthy. The office is obviously considered to be just as important as a production department, and the same care is given to organisation of staff, planning of work and physical conditions.

37. As distinct from shop labour, clerical labour is trained to do several jobs and is flexible, making for considerable economy of effort.

38. Auxiliary office machinery, such as calculating machines, is available to almost everyone in the office. This is considered an economy of both time and money.

39. There is a widespread use of internal auditors as an independent appraisal of the function of managements, policies and procedures.

40. American management encourages research work. New designs are usually developed in a separate department, and any modification work required after trials is done on the prototype. The continuous search for improved products is not allowed to disturb production, and it is a principle that once a design is approved for manufacture, modifications are not introduced. The separation of design and production is not considered to interfere with the evolution of improved types.

Recommendations

The following are the Team's recommendations:—

1. That management, in considering the future and preparing plans, should make the fullest use of budgeting and forecasting, based on accounting and costing data;

2. That top management should make use of standards of performance and of accounting control techniques to enable it to decentralise responsibility, and that all standards of performance should be agreed with those who are to work to them;

3. That top management should bring industrial accountants into consultation in the early stages of formulating policy so that they may later report more intelligently;

4. That industrial accountants should constantly consider what information is required by management at different levels, bearing in mind that senior management should be chiefly concerned with forecasting and setting targets, and other levels more with day-to-day action;

5. That industrial accountants should make great efforts to acquaint themselves with the problems of management and the technical processes in their industry, and concentrate their efforts towards producing information which will serve as a guide to policy and action;

6. That consideration should be given to the publication of fuller information by companies in their annual reports, including sales turnover and the major elements of cost;

7. That there should be closer collaboration between industry, the government departments, trade associations, and other agencies interested in industrial statistics, and that, further, there should be a greater interchange of financial and cost information between companies;

8. That an investigation be made by an independent commission into the extent of price agreements, quotas and restrictive practices, and that consideration should be given to the effect these are having on technical development and on the cost of production in the country. Further, to consider whether such agreements and quotas should only be allowed by express parliamentary sanction;

9. That serious consideration be given by government and industry to the problems of redundancy, which will arise if British industry advances technically and administratively as American industry has done;

10. That management should take an active interest in the extension of the institutes and colleges in this country to teach business administration at all levels. Further, that these organisations should give serious consideration to the American practices in this field.

Two members of the Team, Messrs. Bunnett and Little, are of the opinion that Recommendation 8 is outside the Team's terms of reference.

INTEGRATION OR RECONCILIATION?

By A. MARSHALL, A.C.W.A.

A Paper presented at the North-West Regional Cost Conference at the Adelphi Hotel, Liverpool, on Saturday, 29 September, 1951.

Introduction

1. The development of industrial accountancy has been characterised in the past by the growth of two separate but parallel techniques, viz. financial accounting and cost accounting, each with its own set of accounts, and each capable of producing a Profit and Loss Account.

2. The development of these disunited techniques was encouraged by differing requirements. Those of financial accounting were concerned primarily with the recording of all incomes and expenditures by the nature of the income or expenditure, and of arranging these transactions in such a manner as to show—

(*a*) the indebtedness of the business to its suppliers;
(*b*) the indebtedness to the business by its customers;
(*c*) the interest of its shareholders;
(*d*) a "true and fair" statement of profit or loss.

A conventional method of presenting this information has been evolved over many years by the principles and teachings of professional accountancy bodies and influenced to some extent by the requirements of a series of statutes relating to companies and partnerships.

3. The cost accounting technique, or the cost finding part of it, can be defined as a systematic recording of all financial transactions expressed in their relation to the functional factors of production, distribution and administration, properly interpreted to disclose the cost of performing a given function.

4. Cost accounting has grown up from early attempts by works managers and engineers to ascertain costs—

(*a*) out of curiosity;
(*b*) because of the compulsion of increasing competition;
(*c*) because of the impetus of Governmental insistence, in World War I, that fair and reasonable costs of production be ascertained as a basis of "cost-plus" contracts.

5. Both techniques are based on the same set of financial transactions, one classifying these transactions according to the type of expense, viz. rent, repairs, electricity, etc., and the other analysing the transactions according to the particular function necessitating the expense, costs of production of specific products being calculated on the extent to which each function was used in the manufacture of those products.

6. It seemed to the pioneers reasonable to suppose that the profit shown by the excess of income from sales over and above the summation of the costs of the goods sold should agree with the profit shown by the orthodox financial accounts. For reasons detailed below wide differences were experienced. Doubt and confusion followed, and industry was quick to realise the shortcomings of cost accounting as an unrelated technique.

7. Some of these reasons for the difference were—

(*a*) lack of proof that all expenses had been posted to the cost accounts;
(*b*) the over- or under-recovery of overhead expenses in the cost accounts arising from the following causes:—
  (i) the budgeted rate of recovery having proved too high or too low;
  (ii) the estimated activity over which the budgeted rate of recovery was calculated being either surpassed or not achieved;
  (iii) the nature of the product having changed, necessitating different expenses;
  (iv) any combination of these three;
(*c*) the method of valuation of closing stocks might, on the prudent policy of "cost or market price" in the financial accounts, have been market price, whilst in the cost accounts it was cost price;

(*d*) certain financial expenses, e.g., bank interest, might be included in the financial accounts, but not be considered items of cost in the cost accounts;
(*e*) the work-in-progress at the end of a period might contain overheads in the cost accounts but not in the financial accounts.

The sum of these differences was often great, and it was obvious that until these discrepancies were measured and arithmetical relationship between the two sets of accounts established, cost accountancy would not command the respect it sought.

8. It is interesting to note that in World War I a United States Government Bulletin was issued relating to War and Navy Department contractors, which stated that no particular accounting system was required of a contractor. The only requirements were:—

"1. That it be in accord with generally accepted and sound accounting practices.
2. That the cost calculation produce correct figures consistent with the above-mentioned principles.
3. That the cost accounts be under the control of the general accounts."

In this connection the Bulletin stated:—

"By this is meant that the accounting procedure should be such that there is a definite control, through the ledger accounts set up for the purpose, over all the detailed accounts in which the costs are distributed. Cost Accounts separately kept without such suitable proof of control are seriously open to question."

Methods of Correlation

9. Accountants in industry set about the problem of co-ordinating the two techniques and various methods were propounded—"interlocked" accounts, "reconciled" accounts, "third entry," "integrated" accounts, etc.—some of which were barely distinguishable one from the other. Basically, all these methods crystallise into two approaches.

10. The first retains the two separate sets of accounts, i.e., cost and financial accounts, whilst seeking to reconcile the results shown by each by making adjustments to the profit recorded in the cost accounts to correct any omissions of expense, over- or under-recoveries of overheads, or any difference due to the valuation of stocks. For the purpose of this paper, this approach will be called "Reconciliation."

11. The second approach was a unification of the two accountancy techniques to the exclusion of the nominal accounts for individual expenses, and the retention of the accounts for assets, liabilities, personal accounts, cash accounts, and the former "cost" accounts. This second approach is known as "Integration."

Reconciliation

12. The first stage in ensuring the similarity of any two syntheses is to ensure that what is used in one is also used in the other. In the case of cost and financial accounts this was achieved by the device of a General Ledger Adjustment Account which made certain that all original expenditures incurred (other than certain financial expenses which were considered outside the costing ambit) appearing in the financial accounts found their way to the cost accounts.

13. Each technique, having now the same original debits, treated those expenses in its own way, the one collating them by type of expense, and the other analysing and collating them by functional activity. Periodically, each technique extracted a Profit and Loss Account, and the problem of accounting for the difference arose.

14. The treatment of the expenditures by each of the two methods is indicated below.

(*a*) The Financial Ledger contained the following accounts:—

Fixed Assets	*Nominal Accounts*
Land and Buildings	Sales
Plant and Machinery	Purchases
Investments	Salaries
Goodwill	Wages
	Carriage Inwards
Current Assets	Carriage Outwards
Stocks	Rent, Rates, etc.
Debtors (total of Personal Accounts)	Repairs
	Office Expenses (telephones, postages, stationery, etc.)
Cash and Bank	
	Advertising
Liabilities	Commissions
Share Capital	Gas, Electricity, etc., etc.
Reserves	Trading and Manufacturing Account
Creditors (total of Personal Accounts)	Profit and Loss Account
Profit and Loss Appropriation Account	Cost Ledger Adjustment Account

At the end of each monthly accounting period these documents were grouped together in the conventional manner of Manufacturing and Profit and Loss Accounts.

Manufacturing Account

Sales		.....
Less Purchases (plus or minus Stock difference)	.....	
Carriage Inwards	.....	
Wages	.....	
Rent, Rates, etc.	.....	
Repairs	.....	
		.....
Gross Profit (to P. and L. Account)		.....

Profit and Loss Account

Gross Profit (from Manufacturing Account)		.....	
Less Salaries	.....		
Office Expenses	.....		
Advertising	.....		
Commissions	.....		
Carriage Outwards	.....		
		.....	
Net Profit			.....

(*b*) The Cost Ledger contained the following accounts:—

General Ledger Adjustment Account
Raw Materials Control Account
Finished Stock Account
Work-in-Progress Account (representing a summation of all the cost ledger sheets of jobs in progress)
Wages Control Account
Works Expense Control Account
Administration Expense Control Account
Selling Expense Control Account
Distribution Expense Control Account
Cost of Sales Account
Profit and Loss Account

Expenses were coded and debited to the relative expense accounts. The credits in these expense accounts, i.e. the amounts recovered by addition to the prime cost of goods as they passed through the stages of manufacture, were of necessity based on budgets of the overheads and volume of production. At the end of each monthly accounting period the profit was determined in the following manner:—

Cost of Sales Account

Factory cost of goods sold (from Finished Stock Account)	.....
Administrative Expense (amount recovered on goods sold)	....
Selling Expense (amount recovered on goods sold)	.....
Total Cost of Sales	.....

Profit and Loss Account

Sales	.....
Less Cost of Sales	.....
	.....
Add Over-recovery of Overheads	.....
Deduct Under-recovery of Overheads	.....
Profit	.....

15. The reconciliation of the two results was achieved by the use of a memorandum statement on the following lines:—

Memorandum Statement of Reconciliation

Profit as per cost accounts		.....
Add Discounts received	.....	
Sundry incomes considered outside the scope of the cost accounts	.....	
		.....
Deduct Difference between cost and market value of stocks (if latter used in financial accounts)	.....	
Sundry financial expenditures	.....	
Overhead element of work-in-progress	.....	
		.....
Net profit as per financial accounts		.....

16. Although the statement of reconciliation of itself does not appear formidable, the work involved in ascertaining the amounts to be adjusted is by no means straightforward.

17. Many firms would not consider adequate an omnibus figure of over- or under-recoveries on the overhead accounts. These over- or under-recoveries may arise from three causes:

(*a*) Increased or decreased expenditure

(b) Increase or decrease in the volume of production
(c) A change in the nature of the products made.

To dissect an omnibus figure into the amounts due to each of these causes involves a great deal of analysis and synthesis.

18. The interpretation of the phrase "cost or market value," simple as it may seem, is still a subject of discussion between accountants and tax inspectors. Does it mean an evaluation of stocks as listed at both cost price and market price, and the use of the lesser of the two aggregate stock figures? Or does it mean the calculation of individual items of stock at the lesser of the two values?

19. Whichever interpretation is used, the task of reconciliation is lengthy and troublesome. In the first case the entire stock list must be evaluated twice, the reconciliation figure being the difference between the two totals of stock. In the latter case the difference between cost and market value must be extended for each item of stock where the market value has been used, the sum total of these differences being the reconciliation figure.

20. Reconciliation as a means of relating the dual accounting technique fulfilled the requirements of arithmetical relationship of the cost accounts with the financial accounts. Its main disadvantages were that it was somewhat laborious, and that it perpetuated the duplication of accounting techniques.

Integration

21. The increasing awareness of the extravagance of two distinct accounting functions turned management's thoughts to the possibility of unifying the two functions.

22. The advent of mechanised accounting, particularly punched-card accounting, demanded that one document or one card be designed to fulfil as many purposes as possible, and the whole trend of modern thinking revolted at the continuance of any unnecessary duplication.

23. The two sets of accounts were considered together and a ruthless elimination of unnecessary accounts was carried out. The nominal accounts for individual expenses, e.g., rates, electricity, fell by the wayside and there emerged a single accounting technique, as illustrated in Fig. 1.

24. The advantages claimed by the proponents of integration are:—

(a) *Related Accounts.*—The requirements of proof of control of ledger accounts is admirably fulfilled by "Integration." This is achieved without any of the checking and counter-checking that is a feature of "Reconciliation."
(b) *Saving of Clerical Labour.*—"Integration" undoubtedly produces economies in clerical man-hours. No longer is it necessary to analyse the expenses shown in the books of original entry first for posting to financial accounts, and then re-analyse them for posting to cost accounts. The work involved in posting to the accounts now considered obsolete has been eliminated.
(c) *Saving of Expense.*—A second accountant, with his staff, books, printing and stationery, etc., has now become redundant, and the possible reductions in expenditure prove a weighty consideration in favour of integration. An additional advantage is that the professional jealousies between the two accounting staffs now disappear.
(d) *Speed.*—The cutting down of the clerical labour necessary before accounts are produced must inevitably facilitate a more speedy extraction of monthly figures.
(e) *Omissions of Expenses.*—Integration being an all-embracing accounting technique precludes the possibility of any expenses being overlooked.
(f) *Mechanisation.*—The smooth flow of accounting information in the integrated technique, and the avoidance of trying to maintain two parallel accounting routines with the same basic information, create conditions eminently suitable for the introduction of mechanised accounting.

25. The main disadvantage of integration is the need to educate some tax inspectors and also some managements to accept a form of accounts which groups expenses functionally rather than by type of expense. This is a problem which will disappear as integration becomes more widely used. For the present, most tax inspectors who will not accept functional analysis alone, will be satisfied by a detailed list of expenses which agrees in total with the amounts grouped functionally. This list can be made by sorting and tabulating expenses by code number. (Punched-card accounting, of course, would make short work of this.)

Fig. 1.

INTEGRATED ACCOUNTS.

Diagram of the Flow of Accounting Information.

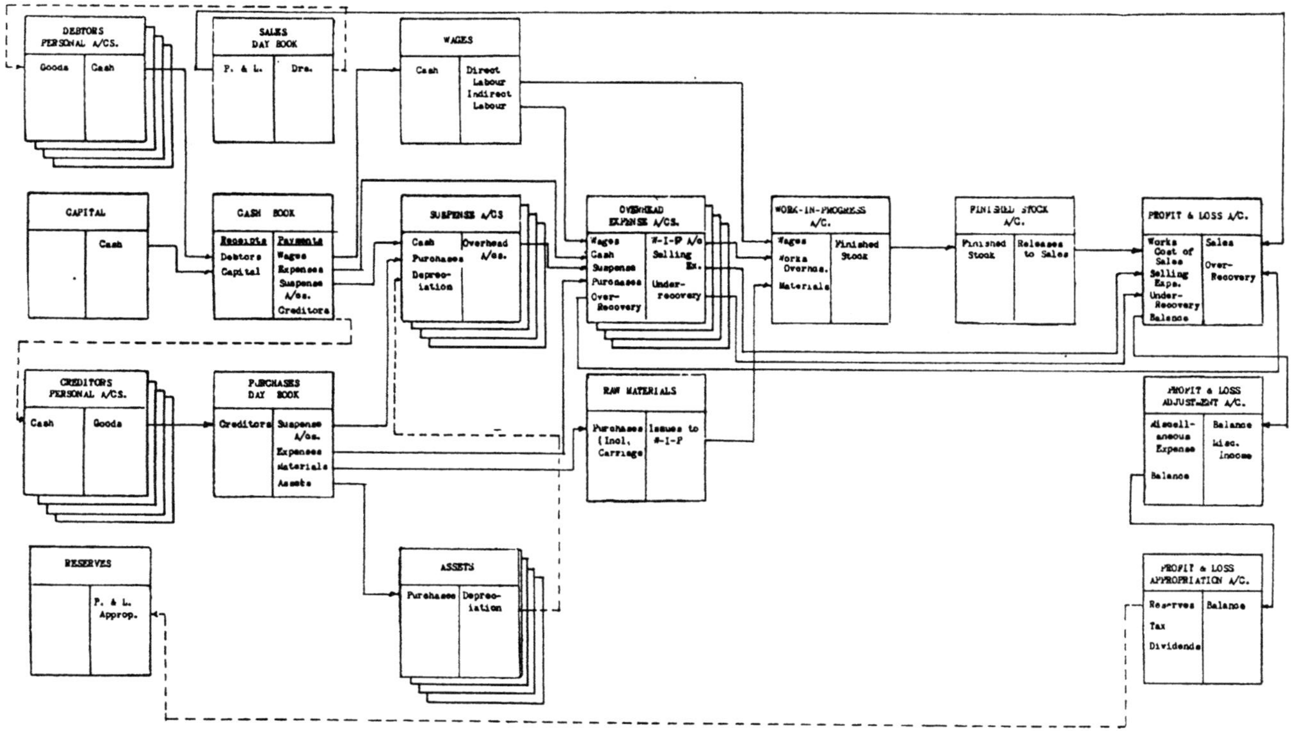

Note: *Suspense Accounts.*—These accounts are created to level out the effect of expenses incurred at less frequent intervals than the accounting period, e.g., rent payable annually would be posted to a Suspense Account, and only the proportion attributable to the particular accounting period would be debited to the Overhead Expense Accounts. Consequently, the balance shown by the Suspense Accounts at a given time represents the net figure of prepayments and amounts due but not paid. It must be realised that some recoveries must of necessity be budgeted in the absence of the actual figure during some months, and therefore the correctness of the periodic Profit and Loss Account will depend on the accuracy of the budgeting.

The real solution to the problem lies in the tax inspector's confidence in the auditors, and indeed the training of auditors to an understanding of cost accounts and the integrated technique.

Trend of Industrial Accounting

26. The evolution of accounting techniques from the early separate techniques of cost and financial accounting, first towards reconciliation and then to integration, reflects the changing view of the purpose of accounts. Previously the primary function of accounts was to measure the amount of profit relating to any particular period. Nowadays the possibility of using accounts as a virile guide to management is widely recognised and more interest is being shown in what is happening rather than in a belated measurement of what has happened.

27. In the past the tendency has been to try to adapt new accounting requirements to fit what is, as far as industrial accounting is concerned, an ageing technique. Attempts have been made to graft new shoots on the old vine without first pruning the dead wood.

28. Integration offers accounts that reflect what is physically happening in the factory. At each stage the accounts present a picture of activity, e.g., the Raw Material Account shows purchases of materials, and the carriage and freight employed to bringing them to store, whilst the Work-in-Progress Account shows materials entering the production shops, and the labour and the production facilities engaged to convert them to finished products. Each job cost ledger sheet that goes to make up the aggregate Work-in-Progress Account has a physical counterpart in the production shops. Each partly assembled product is faithfully reflected on its own job cost ledger sheet which shows to what extent that product has so far used the materials, production facilities, and other functions provided. The accounts have ceased to be the flat, dead, meaningless lists of the past, and have become more interesting and more easily understood.

29. Financial accounting presented a picture of expenses rather like a diagram of the parts that go to make a machine, whereas the new industrial accounting puts the parts together and shows how they work.

30. What of the future? Is integration the peak of accounting achievement? Prognostications are always hazardous, and prophets by their words are notorious sufferers of self-inflicted indigestion. However, it seems fairly certain that the immediate future of industrial accounting will be coloured by integral accounting, standard costs, and variable budgets. This trio represents a finely forged tool of management which will prove of great service for several years to come. Industrial accountants must constantly search for improved tcehniques, giving each careful consideration, weighing the merits or demerits in healthy argument, and must be wary of the persistent reactionaries who may be amongst their ranks.

OVERHEAD IN PERSPECTIVE

By H. Kirkham, F.C.W.A.

A paper given to the Bolton Group of the Institute of Cost and Works Accountants on 14 *January*, 1952.

Introduction

I think we must have all experienced how disarming it can be to find our most devastating arguments received without even a show of opposition—the inference being, of course, that one has overstated the obvious; or, as was said concerning certain theories put forward at the 1951 Summer School, has "succeeded in laying a ghost which no-one else has seen."

The problem which confronts me to-night is to avoid this danger of over-emphasis and the tendency to "swat a fly with a sledge hammer" whilst at the same time dealing adequately with a matter which is all too frequently misunderstood. In the case in question—the consideration of the problem of overhead—I dare to claim that the views which I shall express are not merely evidence of a swarm of bees in a rather larger than average bonnet, but are an honest attempt to point the way to the intelligent solution of problems which are encountered by all of us, and may still be awaiting clarification in some of our minds.

I appreciate that volumes have already been written about "overhead" from various points of view, by a host of interested parties who have enthusiastically pressed the claims of one or other cure-for-all-ills, ranging from the use of the all-embracing hourly rate to the marginal costing technique. You may indeed be extremely sceptical of anything new being added to the superabundance of costing views already expressed, but if that is so I hope to disillusion you and to convince you that the subject of "overhead" has not yet been universally seen in perspective, against the background of industrial conditions and in relation to the practice of cost accounting as a whole.

I realise, of course, that to some of you any great deal of attention paid to this one aspect of cost accounting may appear disproportionate to its importance in your own particular business. It may well be that your problems are much more related to direct material or direct labour costs. Much depends upon the cost ratios of direct material, direct labour and overhead. Where the cost is heaviest one can expect to find the need for the greatest amount of attention, and, if you find that overhead is of insufficient relative importance to warrant your concern you may dismiss much that I shall say as being of purely academic interest, and, to misquote Kipling, "What is more, you'll be a very lucky man, my son."

The whole conception of this evening's talk springs from a conviction born of experience that to many within and without our profession the very mention of "overhead" conjures up visions of practices akin to witchcraft, performed as a solemn ritual but without a very clear purpose. This may well be due to the fact that a long-term misconception of the nature of overhead and the problems which it creates has tended to clothe the subject in a shroud of mysticism, and the solutions which common sense might dictate have gone unnoticed in the enthusiasm for complex techniques. To parody an old rhyme:

"Eeny, Meeny, Miny, Mo,
Cost accounting techniques grow
More confounding, more prolific,
Not much use—but scientific!"

Such technique worship, and the more deplorable dogmas to which it has given birth, have insidiously tended to regiment thought, and the individual healthy application of common sense, on which progress so often depends, has to a large extent been restricted by the straight-jacket of orthodoxy.

The Nature of "Overhead"

"Overhead," or indirect cost, as it is more usefully described, is composed of ingredients contributed by any or all of the three elements of cost. It is a composite term used to describe the aggregation of indirect material, indirect labour and indirect expense, and although it may sometimes be dealt with by methods which are debatable, it is none the less a *costing reality*, with the tendency to assume increasing importance as mechanisation within industry spreads.

Having defined overhead in this way, let us not forget that there are occasions when the boundaries fixed by definition may be crossed for purposes of expediency. Cost which could with some trouble be precisely identified with a particulat cost unit at its source, and which for that reason could be strictly definable as direct cost, may nevertheless sometimes be classified as overhead, and subjected to more or less arbitrary treatment.

It is the incapacity of overhead for precise identification with any saleable commodity which creates the need for an approach which is quite different from that which is usually applied to cost of a direct nature.

For example, the incidence of direct cost can be determined at the moment when the cost is incurred. Apart from the routine recording and simple arithmetical processes involved, no great deal of effort is required to assess its ultimate point of impact or its content per unit of saleable commodity. In the matter of cost finding for such costs, the cost centre is the commodity itself.

It is in attempting to deal with the entirely different situation which is encountered in dealing with overhead that the fundamental objectives of overhead manipulation are often obscured within a maze of mathematical meanderings, and it is to be regretted that, to some, the essential purpose behind costing for overhead has become indistinguishable from the elaborate processes introduced to achieve that purpose.

The Problems Stated

Let us therefore consider afresh what treatment of overhead is called for from the cost accountant, bearing in mind that no single technique will provide the "open sesame" to the whole assortment of day-by-day cost problems, and accepting the fact that no one has a monopoly of the multifarious problems of industry. Everyone engaged in the sphere of industrial accountancy has to encounter difficulties for which there can exist no ready-made solution. Therefore the personal and commonsense approach is essential, and a "tailor-made" solution, not necessarily fashionable, is often the need.

I would suggest that, basically, the problems arising from the "fact of overhead" are associated with—

(*a*) *its control*, involving a knowledge of its cause or source of origin;

(*b*) *its incidence*, involving an assessment of its effect, totally or partially, upon unit costs.

Cost Control

Pundits in our profession are sometimes heard to state that the cost accountant does not control costs—as if that statement were needed! Cost accountants generally do not claim to be cost controllers. But I maintain that, since there can be little room for disagreement with the view that the exercise of cost control is desirable in the conducting of a business, the cost accountant should prepare such cost data as will assist the exercise of adequate control by responsible parties.

It is a generally accepted doctrine that responsibility for costs should be clearly laid down, and that, for control purposes, the collection of overheads should be by cost centres or functions readily identifiable with a responsible person. It may well be that the cost centres chosen for overhead control purposes are not ideal for use in connection with cost finding, for which an alternative display of the same total figures may be required; for example, for control purposes it may be decided to submit the total weekly cost of the toolroom to the toolroom head; for cost finding purposes an entirely different presentation, charging tool maintenance cost to production centres and new tool costs directly to product group accounts, may be necessary.

This fact should not be allowed to prejudice the decision as to the most effective method of cost presentation for control purposes. In fact, it might sometimes be inferred that, where there is complete uniformity of cost presentation for both control and cost-finding purposes, neither of these functions is being satisfactorily performed. It would appear that, under such circumstances, a compromise arrangement exists which appeals to the impractical mind.

Flexible Budgets

Obviously any presentation of overheads by functions will be of greater utility if related to a measure against which preformance can be compared. In this connection, the use of flexible budgets is worthy of adoption. If such budgets are carefully prepared, and in particular, if their reasonableness is accepted by functional heads, they will greatly facilitate the detection of extravagances, and will direct the necessary action to the appropriate quarters.

But having made this reference to the advantages which are offered in the field of cost control by the flexible budgeting technique, I would like to make it unmistakably clear that in this undoubtedly useful tool of management we might, if we are not very careful, find cause for experimentation with the technique for its own sake, rather than as a means to an end.

There is no doubt that flexible budgeting as described in the book on budgetary control issued by the Research and Technical Committee of the Institute* provides an interesting

* *An Introduction to Budgetary Control, Standard Costing, Material Control, and Production Control.* 1951. 15*s*.

study. The amount of consideration given to all aspects of the practice is a praiseworthy achievement. Unfortunately, the detailed operation of such a scheme would convey an impression of accuracy which no budgeting procedure could possibly guarantee. We find that, in this connection, a great deal of emphasis is placed on the distinction between fixed and variable overheads. In fact, semi-variable overheads are also accounted for as a separate factor in the budgeting. The result is that, having classified overheads in this way, the rather false and certainly arbitrary categorisation forms the basis for a complicated method of assessment of budgeted allowances.

In the method envisaged in the book the amounts of budgeted allowances for items of fixed semi-variable, and variable overheads require to be calculated according to formulae or read from graphs for a number of items of cost in each cost centre. The precise calculation of each item of budgeted overhead for possibly dozens of cost centres for each level of activity is a gargantuan task which, for the very reason I have already mentioned (i.e., the fact that, in spite of all this effort, accuracy will not be achieved), I do not consider worth the effort.

The same end can be served by a different, and, I would suggest, more simple approach to the same problem. In my experience it has proved quite adequate to arrive at functional overhead cost budgets synthetically, without the need to distinguish between the various degrees of fixation of cost. Functional budgets are prepared in which each item of expenditure is shown independently for chosen levels of activity. The totals thus obtained at each activity level include all local costs, be they fixed, variable, or semi-variable. From this basic information a flexible budget cost curve can be prepared for each financial year, and from it can be read the corresponding budgeted overheads for any level of activity.

Accuracy cannot be claimed for these curves, but neither is the impression of accuray created. The budget allowances becomes then a *reasonable* forecast of the cost which ought to be incurred in given circumstances. You may not agree that this alternative to the procedure described in the Institute publication is in any way an improvement upon it. I would hesitate to press my own views in face of a really determined opposition—they are, after all, only an expression of opinion. In fact I would welcome any evidence of partiality towards any other viewpoint which had been developed from a perfectly clear knowledge of particular requirements. All I hope to have achieved by describing a simple and practical method of establishing functional overhead budgets is the destruction of any idea that the Institute Research and Technical Committee, or anyone else, has any greater claim to an appreciation of your problems than you have yourself. Even in the face of the undeniable evidence of technical competence which often marks the work of others, let us never forget that in the matter of applying costing principles to industrial conditions nothing can take the place of a personal conviction that the remedy being applied is the remedy which is required *at that particular time and in those particular circumstances.*

Cost Finding

Now let us consider the special requirements of cost finding for overhead. It is by no means universally agreed that cost finding, which has as its objective the ascertainment of total cost, involving the distribution of all overheads to products, is necessary or to be desired. If we acknowledge a need for total costs in certain circumstances, as no doubt most of us do, we would do well to accept the fact that such a cost can at best be but an approximation to an intermediate ideal. This must be so, since we have seen that overhead is only overhead because it cannot be accurately or conveniently charged to a cost unit. When the cost accountant engages in the task of determining the incidence of overhead upon products, by whatever technique, he is, to some extent, encroaching upon the territory of the seer and leaving behind the realm of hard fact.

But this is only the beginning of a sad story. Not only must we swallow the truth that overhead cannot be charged accurately to a product; we must also face the complications presented by the choice between many methods of "disposing of the body."

If we are of a simple turn of mind, we may favour the use of an overall percentage on, say, direct labour cost.

But, if we really wish to justify our existence to "the boss," we shall most certainly take the trouble to calculate hourly rates. After all, being enlightened cost accountants, we know that it is "the thing" to apply overheads at the point of the tool—and, by hook, or by crook, we'll deposit them there, using an assortment of allocation bases in the process which would try the patience of Job, and which one believes (or, more truthfully, hopes) will give a fair apportionment, and result in an ultimately equitable product incidence.

However, whatever else may be said, let us bow before the inevitable—hourly rates are fashionable! They depend, of course, upon the truth of the belief that *time* is the all-important factor in the creation of overhead. But has it ever occurred to you that this belief may be a form of wishful thinking?

The passage of time—be it expressed in machine hours or man hours—is merely one of a number of factors influencing overhead.

This point of view has already been propagated on a number of occasions during the last few years, but has not yet made an appreciable impression upon current costing practices. It does not deny the usefulness of hourly rates, provided that they do not attempt to embrace all overhead. A variety of other bases for determining the incidence of remaining overhead could be used in conjunction with such rates, according to the particular product feature causing the cost to be incurred; for example, certain overheads may vary with product weight and volume, others with the complexity of design, and so on. Such careful treatment of overhead might lead us to the view that in the use of *a combination of recovery rates* lies the technique which can bring the practice of overhead recovery to perfection. But if we look closely into the matter we find that this disturbing fact remains—that, as a result of attempting to charge overhead to products proportionately to the efforts called forth on their behalf, very often the burden weighs heaviest upon those least fitted to carry it.

In seeking an explanation of this phenomenon, I have come to the conclusion that in a multi-product business certain overheads accrue to "Cinderella" products (i.e., those which cause the headaches, conferences, investigations, and red trading results) for the sole reason that they need assistance. And it may be argued in their favour that much of the overhead which is attracted towards them is incurred merely because their profitable contemporaries are in a position to finance it. In other words, such overhead belongs to the business because the business can afford it and, in its total form, requires it, irrespective of the particular product mixture. If this is true, then there appears to be a valid argument for a partial return to the ancient custom of applying arbitrary percentage rates to recover such costs.

Does the suggestion of such a primitive solution offend our inherent sense of professional prowess, and would we rather avoid the issue altogether by continuing to take refuge in the pseudo-scientific mechanisms merely because of their reputation? Or would we be prepared to jettison existing techniques, as circumstances demanded, in a constant search for something which we believe—even if we are alone in our belief—may better serve the needs of the moment?

I believe that this question suggests its own answer. Surely we must always be amenable to change if we sincerely believe that the objective of our costing is being more nearly attained thereby. This always presumes a clear knowledge of that objective, and we should do well to ask ourselves the very pertinent if ungrammatical question, "What am I costing for?" whenever a line of action is contemplated.

Marginal Costing

Having made this plea for a pioneering approach to cost problems it may seem quite illogical for me to pour cold water, if only a little, upon the seemingly new cost accounting method. I refer to Marginal Costing.

However, although the name now associated with the technique is of comparatively recent origin, the idea itself must be as old as the idea of costing by any other name. My criticism is levelled at the unimaginative and partisan controversy which has gone on for some considerable time and which may serve to underline the need for common sense in addition to technical knowledge in our approach to such matters. The advocates of this technique recommend the separation of fixed from variable overheads and would have us believe that to attempt to identify the so-called fixed overheads with products is unnecessary. The extremist opponent of this doctrine denies the very existence of fixed overhead, and has been known to go to great lengths to prove his case by drawing a series of impressive curves which prove without doubt (to himself at any rate) that all cost is variable in the long run. So-called fixed cost, he says, is a myth and liable to disappear miraculously, like the legendary bird which flew in ever-diminishing circles.

Much valuable time has been wasted in arguing the merits of these points of view, and seldom does it appear to have occurred to their advocates that neither is wholly right or wholly wrong.

Since most of us are concerned with what happens or will happen to cost within the allotted span of three score years and ten, the theory that no cost whatever is fixed should be treated no more seriously than any other game of make-belive.

Let us be realistic and accept the fact that in the short term an intelligent assessment of fixed overheads can be made, and, by deduction, the variables can also be assessed.

All this does not imply that one ought to

adopt a marginal cost technique to the exclusion of all others, but is merely in support of the belief that the acceptance of certain features *may* be advantageous *in certain circumstances*. Denial of its usefulness constitutes evidence either of reaction or egotism, or both.

However, if we accept the utility of certain features of marginal cost practice we may see equally clearly a need for total costs.

Break Even Charts

The concept of overhead as falling into the fixed cost and variable cost categories has also played a great part in the development of the well-publicised pictorial display of the cost-volume-profit relationship—the break even chart.

If one is to judge by the glut of literature dealing with the value of the break even chart in business one cannot fail to be impressed by its apparent usefulness. Unfortunately, the claims made for this device far exceed the advantages to be derived from it in practice.

There is no doubt that it is a popular method of illustrating the relationship which is claimed to exist between the three factors: cost, volume and profit, and has made a widespread impression, possibly by virtue of the fact that it gives the appearance of being somewhat in the nature of a scientific instrument. Nothing could be further from the truth, and some time spent in studying its principal characteristics may be of value, if only in stimulating new thought on the subject, and bringing into focus another factor which, equally with volume, has a bearing upon cost and profitability.

The usefulness of such a chart in business depends upon the fallacious assumption that cost is directly related to volume, and seldom is sufficient attention paid to the possibility that the cost-volume relationship is dependent upon the product mixture in the gross volume.

Quite obviously, where a single product or a number of products of similar cost proportions and selling price structures are produced, such curves could be used to some advantage, but when a varied assortment of products of different cost proportions and price structures are produced simultaneously there will be a variety of product mixtures capable of producing the same overall sales volume of output but with widely different cost and profit relationships; or alternatively there may be a variety of turnover levels derived from one activity level, according to the product incidence upon that activity. Can any chart presume to anticipate the effect upon total costs of an unknown variety of possible product volume changes, which may have some or no effect upon total company activity? In such circumstances at *each* projected level of activity the product mixture must also be forecast, and a detailed cost budget prepared, before the profitability of the project can be assessed. The graphical portrayal of such information becomes an unnecessary and worthless exercise. Unfortunately, this fact has not yet been appreciated by the vast majority of costing enthusiasts, who would appear to expect this superficially simple device to yield in an instant the answers to some of the most complex problems of industrial management.

Stock Valuation

My last example of the scope for original thought in dealing with problems associated with the existence and nature of overhead is concerned with the vital function of work-in-progress stock valuation.

We all know, of course, that the orthodox basis of valuation is "either cost or market value, whichever is the lower." It is by no means certain that we would all agree as to the interpretation of this ruling, which is neither clearly defined nor free from ambiguity. Many different shades of meaning can be attached to such a generalisation, and, accepting the existence of divergent views, let us consider some of the more contentious points.

One sometimes meets with dogmatism on the question: "To include or to exclude selling and distribution costs in a valuation of work-in-progress?" Arguments can be used to support both points of view. On the one hand, selling costs may precede manufacture, and efforts directed towards the obtaining of firm orders in advance of production may reasonably be claimed to contribute to the cost of work-in-progress (e.g., advertising, representatives, etc.).

On the other hand it may be true to argue that selling efforts are made in respect of completed products only, and should be excluded from any valuation of incompleted stocks.

In complete contrast to either of these alternatives, another school of thought propagates the belief that variable overheads only should be included in stock valuation.

The circumstances of each case should be closely studied before any choice between alternatives is made, and reiteration of the need for this discriminating approach to each and every cost problem is made for its practical rather than its rhetorical value.

Whichever basis is ultimately accepted, one thing is certain—it should be consistently used if distortion of the real trend of trading results is to be avoided.

If we were able to prolong the discussion on this topic, much time could be spent in considering the peculiar effects upon short-term (yearly) trading results, of alternative methods of dealing with cost, particularly overhead, when determining stock values.

For instance, the initial overheads applicable to the launching of the production of a new product might conceivably be treated as stock which should be written off over the life of the product. Tooling and advertising costs also might merit this form of treatment.

Alternatively, such overhead might be included in a heterogeneous mixture of overhead items, expressed in total as a "rate for a period" to be applied to, say, the labour content of work-in-progress on a time or sterling basis. The trading results would vary according to the method used, and information extracted from the cost account for any particular year might very easily lead to erroneous conclusions if the effects of the particular stock valuation practice were not fully appreciated.

In the case of unprofitable products much depends upon the cost accountant's view as to whether potential losses should be written off when incurred or only when goods are sold, and this raises the question: "Need the cost account conform to the 'cost or market value' ruling?"

Conclusions

The essence of all that has been said to-night can be concentrated into the following "Creed." These are the beliefs which I wish to propagate. You are some of the people I hope to convert. Surely the time has come when we should halt for a moment and satisfy ourselves that the road we as individuals are taking will bring us to our objective—that is, the provision of an intelligent solution to every cost problem, and of a valuable contribution towards efficient industrial direction and management.

I believe that:—

(*a*) cost accounting for overhead demands a constant awareness of the needs of the moment and a flexibility of overhead manipulation which is not inherent in any single technique;

(*b*) the cost accountant should seek to develop a precise understanding of the nature of overhead and should think and speak in unambiguous language;

(*c*) he should approach each problem in the light of existing circumstances and seek to understand, develop, and use such technique or combination of techniques as will best contribute to the solution required;

(*d*) the cost accountant who attempts to justify his overhead manipulation on the grounds of accuracy rather than utility is unpardonably dissipating energy which should be exerted in other directions.

I hope that all this will have brought you to the conclusion that there is still scope for original thought on all aspects of cost accounting; this was my original objective. Realising the limitations of available techniques, we shall be the more inclined to use them intelligently as circumstances demand, and if we accept the fact that no single technique or precise formula can supply the answer to our problems, we may bring a breath of fresh air into an atmosphere which has lulled many into a state of complacency.

For Product Safety Concerns and Information please contact our EU representative GPSR@taylorandfrancis.com Taylor & Francis Verlag GmbH, Kaufingerstraße 24, 80331 München, Germany

Batch number: 10726294

Printed by Printforce, the Netherlands